Volume 58 Number 1 January 1985

SOCIOLOGY OF EDUCATION

A Journal of the American Sociological Association

CRITICAL SOCIOLOGY OF EDUCATION: INTERNATIONAL STUDIES
Guest Editor: Philip Wexler

LIVINGSTONE
Class, Educational Ideologies, and Mass Opinion in Capitalist Crisis: A Canadian Perspective

TANGUY
Academic Studies and Technical Education: New Dimensions of an Old Struggle in the Division of Knowledge

KESSLER, ASHENDEN, CONNELL, AND DOWSETT
Gender Relations in Secondary Schooling

GASKELL
Course Enrollment in the High School: The Perspective of Working-Class Females

AGGLETON AND WHITTY
Rebels Without a Cause? Socialization and Subcultural Style Among the Children of the New Middle Class

SOCIOLOGY OF EDUCATION (ISSN 0038–0407) is published quarterly in January, April, July and October by the American Sociological Association, 1722 N Street, N.W., Washington, D.C. 20036 and is printed by Boyd Printing Company, Albany, New York. Second class postage paid at Washington, D.C. and additional mailing offices. *POSTMASTER:* Send address changes to *Sociology of Education*, 1722 N Street, N.W., Washington, D.C. 20036.

MANUSCRIPTS and communications for the Editors should be addressed to the Editor, SOCIOLOGY OF EDUCATION, Department of Sociology, University of Notre Dame, Notre Dame, IN 46556.

Concerning advertising, changes of address and subscriptions, address the Executive Office, American Sociological Association, 1722 N Street, N.W., Washington, D.C. 20036. Annual membership dues of the ASA, $40–$125 ($12 of this amount may cover a subscription to *Sociology of Education*); Associate, $40; Student Associate, $25. Subscription rate for members, $12; nonmembers, $21 U.S., $24 elsewhere; institutions, $28 U.S., $31 elsewhere; single issues, $5. New subscriptions and renewals will be entered on a calendar year basis only. *Changes of Address:* Six weeks advance notice to the Executive Office, and old address as well as new, are necessary for change of subscriber's address. Claims for undelivered copies must be made within the month following the regular month of publication. The publishers will supply missing copies when losses have been sustained in transit and when the reserve stock will permit.

SOCIOLOGY OF EDUCATION

A JOURNAL OF RESEARCH IN SOCIALIZATION AND SOCIAL STRUCTURE

PUBLISHED BY
THE AMERICAN SOCIOLOGICAL ASSOCIATION

JANUARY 1985 **VOLUME 58, NUMBER 1**

CRITICAL SOCIOLOGY OF EDUCATION: INTERNATIONAL STUDIES
Guest Editor: Philip Wexler

CONTENTS

Editor's Foreword 1

Class, Educational Ideologies, and Mass Opinion in Capitalist Crisis: A Canadian Perspective .... D. W. Livingstone 3

Academic Studies and Technical Education: New Dimensions of an Old Struggle in the Division of Knowledge .... Lucie Tanguy 20

Gender Relations in Secondary Schooling .... S. Kessler, D. J. Ashenden, R. W. Connell, and G. W. Dowsett 34

Course Enrollment in the High School: The Perspective of Working-Class Females .... Jane Gaskell 48

Rebels Without a Cause? Socialization and Subcultural Style Among the Children of the New Middle Classes ..... Peter J. Aggleton and Geoff Whitty 60

EDITORIAL POLICY

This journal exists to provide a forum for studies of the sociology of education and human social development. The aim is to publish research on how social institutions and/or individuals' experience within them impinge upon educational processes and social development. Such research could span various levels of analysis, ranging from the individual to the structure of relations among social and educational institutions. In an increasingly complex society, important educational issues arise throughout the life cycle. The content of this journal is meant to reflect this diversity by presenting a balance of papers which deal with education at the institutional and organizational levels as well as at the individual level, at all stages of schooling and with respect to all types of education. Contributions are invited from persons of any discipline whose objectives are consonant with those of this journal.

Contributors' papers are evaluated, through a peer-review process, entirely in terms of quality. *All* methodologies are welcome. The journal appears quarterly, January, April, July, and October.

A processing fee of $10 is required for each paper submitted; such fees to be waived for student members of ASA. This reflects a policy of the ASA Council and Committee on Publications affecting all ASA journals. It is a reluctant response to the rapidly accelerating costs of manuscript processing. A check or money order, made payable to the American Sociological Association should accompany each submission. The fee must be paid in order to initiate the processing of the manuscript.

SOCIOLOGY OF EDUCATION

CONTRIBUTORS

■ D. W. Livingstone received his Ph.D. from Johns Hopkins University and is Professor in the Ontario Institute for Studies in Education. His research interests include comparative political economy and education, ideologies and class consciousness, and alternative futures. He is currently engaged in several ethnographic and sample-survey studies that further trace the influences of current ideological discourse and class relations on attitudes toward education and other social policy issues.

■ Lucie Tanguy is Professor of Sociology, Centre national de la recherche scientifique, Université Paris V, where she studies the sociology of education and work. This article is part of a research project studying the evolution of workers' education in France from the end of World War II to the present.

■ Sandra Kessler received her bachelor's degree in anthropology from the University of Sydney, Australia, and is Education Officer in the Adult Literacy Information Office, NSW Department of Technical and Further Education, Australia. Her research interests include adult education, migrant education, working-class schooling, teacher unions, and socialism. This study provides a research base for her in-service work with teachers, a theoretical background for teaching working-class adults, and a methodological background for her research on migrant education. Dean J. Ashenden received his bachelor's degree in history from the University of Adelaide, Australia. He is currently a policy advisor in the Department of Education and Youth Affairs, Commonwealth Government of Australia. His research interests are the democratization of the curriculum, educational policy, teacher unions, and political economy. This study provides a research base for current policy discussions on social equity and equal access to education, and on curriculum reform in Australian schools. Robert W. Connell is Professor in the Department of Sociology, Macquarie University, Australia, where he studies gender relations, masculinity, class analysis, socialism, and the sociology of culture. This study provides an empirical foundation for his current theoretical work on the sociology of gender and a framework for his recent research on teachers. Gary W. Dowsett received his bachelor's degree from Queensland University, Australia, and is Senior Research Assistant in sociology and psychology at Macquarie University. His research interests include culture, youth employment, sexual politics, and grassroots educational innovation. This article establishes a methodology for his current research on other aspects of culture and gender and provides a research base for in-service training of teachers concerned with problems of class and sexism.

■ Jane Gaskell received her Ed.D. from Harvard University and is Associate Professor in the Department of Social and Educational Studies, University of British Columbia. Her research interests include gender, work, and education. This article is part of her ongoing research on the social organization of business education in the high school, in the community college, and on the job.

■ Peter J. Aggleton is Senior Lecturer in Sociology, Bath College of Higher Education, Avon, England. His research interests are middle-class lifestyles, the sociology of gender and sexuality, and cultural and social reproduction theory. Dr. Aggleton is currently studying the individual and social consequences of power relations within schemes of vocational and pre-vocational education in the U.K. He is also exploring the power relations implied in different approaches to the planning and delivery of nursing care. Geoff Whitty is Head of the Department of Education, Bristol Polytechnic, Avon, England, where he studies urban education, social and cultural reproduction theory, and the relation between education and the state. This article reflects his general interest in refining theories of social reproduction and transformation and his specific interest in the education of middle-class and working-class youth in public and private schools.

Notice to Contributors

(Revised September 1981)

STATEMENT OF ASA POLICY ON MULTIPLE SUBMISSION

Submission of manuscripts to a professional journal clearly implies commitment to publish in that journal. The competition for journal space requires a great deal of time and effort on the part of editorial readers whose main compensation for this service is the opportunity to read papers prior to publication and the gratification associated with discharge of professional obligations. For these reasons the ASA regards submission of a manuscript to a professional journal while that paper is under review by another journal as unacceptable.

AUTHOR'S RESPONSIBILITY: *Manuscripts which do not adhere exactly to these suggestions will be immediately returned for revision. Only articles in the form specified below will be sent out for refereeing.*

The 1974 edition of the *Publication Manual* of the American Psychological Association (available from A.P.A., 1200 17th St., N.W., Washington, D.C. 20036) is very helpful in clarifying headings, abbreviations, table preparation and the like.

Since manuscripts are evaluated as anonymous submissions, please keep identifying material out of the manuscript. Attach a cover page giving authorship, institutional affiliation, acknowledgments, and the date the article is submitted. Provide only the title as identification on the manuscript and abstract. Every effort should be made by the author to see that the manuscript itself contains no clues as to the author's identity.

Submission and Preparation of Manuscripts

1. Submit four (4) copies and retain the original for your files. Copies may be Xerox, mimeograph or multilith, but not carbons.
2. Enclose a stamped self-addressed postcard for acknowledgment of manuscript receipt. Since manuscripts will not be returned by reviewers to the editorial office, the editorial office will not return them to authors.
3. All copy must be *typed, doublespaced* (including indented material, footnotes and references) on 8½ by 11 inch white opaque paper. Line must not exceed six (6) inches. Margins must be a minimum of one inch.
4. Include four (4) copies of an abstract of no more than 150 words.
5. Type each table on a separate page. Insert a location note at the appropriate place in the text, e.g., "Table 2 about here." Send copies, retain originals.
6. Figures must be professionally prepared. Send copies, retain originals.
7. Clarify all symbols with notes in the margins of the manuscript. Circle these and all other explanatory notes not intended for printing.
8. Three kinds of footnotes are possible each serving a different purpose:

   a. Content footnotes. Content footnotes are explanations or amplifications of the text. Because they are distracting to readers and *expensive* to include in printed material, an author should include important information in the text and omit irrelevant information. *Content Footnotes Will Not Be Allowed Generally.*

   Rather than footnoting long or complicated material, such as proofs or derivations unnecessary to the text, consider (i) indicating in a *short* footnote that the material is available from the author, (ii) depositing the material in a national retrieval center and including an appropriate footnote, or (iii) adding an appendix. If an appendix is used, the reference in text should read: "(see Appendix A for complete derivation)."

   Text footnotes should be numbered consecutively throughout the article with superscript arabic numerals. If, after a footnote occurs it is later mentioned, use a parenthetical note "(see Footnote 3)," rather than the superscript number.

   b. Reference footnotes. Footnotes are used for reference purposes only to cite material of limited availability. Acceptable reference footnotes include (i) legal citations, which should follow the footnote style of *A Uniform System of Citation* (1967) published by the Harvard Law Review Association, (ii) copyright permission footnotes, (iii) unpublished works; works in progress.

   c. Table footnotes. Table footnotes are appended *only* to a specific table. Footnotes to a table should be *lettered* consecutively *within* each table with superscript lowercase letters.
9. Acknowledgments, credits and grant numbers are placed on the title page with an asterisk.

Reference Format

A. *In the Text:* All source references are to be identified at the appropriate point in the text by the last name of the author, year of publication, and pagination where needed. Identify subsequent citations of the same source in the same way as the first, *not* using "*Ibid.*," "*op. cit.*," or "*loc. cit.*" Examples follow:

1. If author's name is in the text, follow it with year in parentheses. [". . . Duncan (1959) . . ."]

2. If author's name is not in the text, insert, in parentheses, the last name and year, separated by a comma [". . . (cf. Gouldner, 1963 . . ."]

3. Pagination (without "p." or "pp.") follows year of publication after a colon. [". . . Kuhn (1970:71)."]

4. Give both last names for dual authors. Give all last names on first citation in text for more than two authors; thereafter use "et al." in the text. When two authors have the same last name, use identifying initials in the text. For institutional authorship, supply minimum identification from the beginning of the complete citation. [". . . U.S. Bureau of the Census, 1963:117) . . ."]

5. Separate a series of references with semicolons and enclose them within a single pair of parentheses. [". . . (Burgess, 1968; Marwell et al., 1971; Cohen, 1962) . . ."]

B. *In the appendix:* List all items alphabetically by author and, within author, by year of publication, in an appendix, titled "REFERENCES". The reference appendix must be complete and include all references in the text. The use of "et al." is not acceptable in the appendix; list the names of all authors. (See A.4. for text format.)

If there is more than one reference to the same author and year, distinguish them by the letters a, b, etc. added to the year. [". . . Levy (1965a:331) . . ."]

Give the publisher's name in as brief a form as is fully intelligible. For example, John A. Wiley and Sons should be "Wiley."

If the cited material is unpublished, use "forthcoming" with name of journal or publisher; otherwise use "unpublished."

Use no underlining or italics.

Examples follow:

1. *Books:*	Jud, G. J., E. W. Mills, Jr. and G. W. Burch.	
	1970	Ex-Pastors. Philadelphia: Pilgrim Press.
	U.S. Bureau of the Census	
	1960	Characteristics of Population, Volume I. Washington, D.C.: U.S. Government Printing Office.
	Bernard, C.	
	[1865] 1957	An Introduction to the Study of Experimental Medicine. Dr. Henry Copley Greene. New York: Dover.
2. *Periodicals:*	Conger, R.	
	Forth-coming	"The effects of positive feedback on direction and amount of verbalization in a social setting." Pacific Sociological Review.
	Kerckhoff, A. C. and R. T. Campbell	
	1977a	"Black-white differences in the educational attainment process." Sociology of Education 50:15–27.
	1977b	"Race and social status differences in the explanation of educational ambition." Social Forces 55:701–14.
3. *Collections:*	Davie, M.	
	1938	"The pattern of urban growth." Pp. 133–61 in G. Murdock (ed.), Studies in the Science of Society. New Haven: Yale University Press.

See recent issues for further examples.

Editor's Foreword

It is a pleasure for me to introduce these culturally, theoretically, and methodologically diverse papers as instances of a broader tradition of critical sociology of education. It is only now, more than a decade after the beginning of a renaissance in social theory that was represented in "new," "critical," or "radical" sociology of education, that this tradition has gained our collective disciplinary attention.

The social reasons for the belated interest in work of this tradition are interesting (Wexler, P., *Symbolic Movement: After the New Sociology of Education*, London: Routledge and Kegan Paul, forthcoming), but less so than its continuing vibrance, internal differences, and the multiple projections that it offers for future theory, research, and practice in the sociology of education. What began as an ideology critique and then moved toward the application of general theories of interactionism and Marxism to sociology of education has become more assertively *specific* in theorizing and in research.

The current specificity begins often as qualification of broader, though education-centered, theoretical orientations. The most noted of these were, of course, correspondence and reproduction theories. Whatever may now be our reluctance in the face of such diffuse theorizing, their perhaps overly blunt power overcame the exclusion of critical and continental theory from sociology of education. The central aspiration was simply to restore a deeply *social* understanding of education. Pursuit of a constitutively social understanding of education encouraged suspension of then prevailing interests in the individual and instrumental uses of schooling. Instead, assumed aspects of educational functions, forms, and substance were placed in social question.

The goal of rethinking the social meaning and uses of education, historicizing its organized forms, and seeing educational knowledge as fully cultural has required a long detour. The current revitalization, which I believe critical sociology of education returns to the entire discipline, flourished largely not in sociology but in educational fields like curriculum. It first appeared not in the United States but abroad, particularly in England. It did not draw sustenance from the center of American sociological discourse but was nurtured at its periphery, in European structuralist and cultural theory.

The result of a combined historic exclusion and current valuation is the danger of an apparently truncated narrative and a false impression that there is no developmental history or tradition of the work presented in this issue. Yet, each of the papers is written both from within and against quite specific aspects of the critical sociology of education. Indeed, what they most share is *revision* of the central commitments of this tradition. What is being revised are commonly held near-canonical texts and research exemplars. Especially when the authorial canon defends itself against "misinterpretation," it becomes clear that "misreading" is part of the struggle for cultural creation (Bloom, H., *Agon: Towards a Theory of Revisionism,* New York: Oxford University Press, 1982). So we should not judge to harshly the common assertion here to have gone beyond a correspondence theory of the economic production/education relation or to have surpassed nonconstructionist approaches to cultural reproduction through schooling. Rather, we should admire the courage to revise one's own formative tradition.

Livingstone, for example, in a class analysis of education from an historical materialist perspective, turns his political economy of educational restructuring toward the study of attitudes, of "subjective dispositions." Tanguy, in her post-Bourdieu political economy of curriculum, writes apologetically from within and against the theoretical, if not theoreticist, mode of French sociology of education: "To be perfectly frank, our study is basically empirical. . . ." Similarly, Kessler, Ashenden, Connell, and Dowsett study gender regimes, but against both liberal sex-role analyses and structuralist reproduction studies of gender. Gaskell shares their constructionist interest in a revision of correspondence and reproduction perspectives. But she proposes, in a field-based critique of school-tracking studies, a more fundamental, inclusionary revision: "Working-class women's knowledge of the world and the questions they ask have not been part of academic discourse."

Aggleton and Whitty also risk a deep revision of critical sociology of education. Beyond common texts, those of us who work from this tradition have shared a commitment to social progress as well as to science, a hope for a more just and rational society. The danger of that commitment surfaces when it supplants our scientific and craft criteria for knowledge and urges upon us the gauge of political efficacy. In critical sociology of education, the concept of "resistance" has opportuned that corruption. Seeing student opposition or resistance to oppressive and class-reproductive schooling as a hopeful antidote to systemic "reproduction," its proponents have conflated the criterion of optimism with another: empirical veracity. Aggleton and Whitty refuse such a political, conceptual fetish: "Any suggestion that their apparent rejection of the dominant ethos of schooling is anything more than a *contestation* needs to be viewed with serious skepticism."

These papers can be said to represent a third generation in critical sociology of education. They follow the first ideology critique and general theory phase and then the more education-centered, but still diffuse, structuralist derivations of the middle period. As a group, they stand in different relation to a broad center of heterogeneous structuralisms. Aggleton and Whitty use a language close to the British Althusserians, although their inspiration is Basil Bernstein's enduring theory of cultural processes. Kessler et al. speak in a style that is deliberately accessible to educational reform, in an anti-academicist regard for "practice." Against a structuralist background, Gaskell insists on the rationality of the participants and, with a political phenomenological sympathy, wants their voices to be heard. Tanguy, though writing with the Cartesian elegance that we have eschewed in American sociological discourse, is determined to get past the generalities of the structuralist cultural reproduction view associated with Bourdieu. In the effort to specify, she looks toward such microanalyses as time-budget studies. Livingstone also wants to show that a class analysis of education can be put on a firm empirical base. Indeed, he is one of the few to bring survey research methods to bear on the study of educational ideologies and to still retain the socially critical edge of Merle Curti's early qualitative analysis (Curti, M., *The Social Ideas of American Educators,* New York: Scribner's, 1935).

These papers only hint at international work in the tradition of critical sociology of education. There are many omissions, not least of which is "third world" sociology of education. Critical sociology of education in America has a history, and as part of an international intellectual movement, I expect that it also has a future. The fear of the unfamiliar, which delayed that future, is now subsiding. Such fear, like the criterion of political optimism, has proven itself antithetical to scholarship and to science.

Philip Wexler

CLASS, EDUCATIONAL IDEOLOGIES, AND MASS OPINION IN CAPITALIST CRISIS: A CANADIAN PERSPECTIVE

D. W. LIVINGSTONE
Ontario Institute for Studies in Education

Sociology of Education 1985, Vol. 58 (January):3–20

There is agreement among theorists of nearly all political stripes that the advanced capitalist societies are now in a period of protracted social crisis. While capital-intensive restructuring has recently permitted some industrial corporate enterprises to reverse the declining profits trend of the past decade, the private propensity to invest in new production initiatives remains generally depressed, high unemployment rates persist, especially for young people, and collective consumption capacity continues to be limited by declining real wages and high interest rates. Governments also operate under growing debt burdens and the fiscal necessity to hold down public expenditures, while both infrastructural/natural environmental requirements and established social welfare entitlements demand increases. The general public's trust in the leadership of many major institutions appears to have declined significantly since the mid-1960s (e.g., Lipset and Schneider, 1983), and numerous social indicators, such as the increasing incidence of property crimes, point to a mounting breakdown of social order.

Publicly funded educational systems have been particularly prone to criticism during this social crisis. Since World War II, increasing educational attainment levels have been associated with public perceptions of the declining general quality of schooling. More recently, declining birthrates have decreased the demand for school expansion, and growing numbers of elderly people have exerted their own social welfare priorities on government budgets. Finally, the presence of large numbers of relatively highly schooled yet unemployed youths graphically contradicts long-held assumptions about the benefits of current forms of schooling (e.g., Meyer and Rowan, 1977) and directly encourages growing questioning of the adequacy of school performance and standards. As Boyd (1983:4) puts it, "The overall effect of the context of decline is inevitably a scramble for scarce resources, intensifying special interest group activity and the politicization of education." Indeed, given the evident crucial role of schooling in shaping the next generation and the persistence of very strong popular faith in the *potential* of education to facilitate societal development (e.g., Gallup, 1982; Livingstone, Hart, and McLean, 1983), educational reform proposals have once again become a central focus in public debate about resolving the crisis (cf. Curti, [1935] 1959).

This article attempts to explain the basic impetus for educational reform initiatives in the current crisis from an historical materialist perspective and, in particular, attempts to identify major social forces influencing educational restructuring efforts.[1] More specifically, the focus is on social-class relations and the manner in which structural constraints of class location and the subjective choices of class leaders and class actors generally are related to the maintenance and change of current educational forms. The primary sources of evidence are studies that have been conducted over the past several years in Ontario—Canada's industrial heartland. These studies examine changing class structure, the educational rhetoric of leading class spokespersons, and mass opinion on educational issues. Government commissions in Ontario have recently put forward recommendations for major reorganization of both high school and higher education systems (Secondary Education Review Project, 1981; Committee on the Future Role of Universities in Ontario, 1981). This analysis considers class-based views of basic educational practices implicated in these commission reports. Different historical origins as well as different locations within the world capitalist system may be associated with

The survey data used in this article are drawn from the OISE Survey of Educational Issues, which has been conducted since 1978 under the auspices of the Ontario Institute for Studies in Education. I am grateful to Doug Hart for his assistance with the data analysis, to Kari Dehli for library research work, and to Vivian Crossman for typing. The comments of Philip Wexler and three anonymous reviewers were also appreciated. Address all correspondence to the author at the Department of Sociology of Education, O.I.S.E., 252 Bloor St. West, Toronto, Ontario M5S 1V6, Canada.

[1] The epistemological and methodological assumptions, the social vantage point, and the model of social totalities on which this interpretation is based are specified in Livingstone (1983).

some differences in patterns of educational practices among the advanced capitalist societies; and the development of public schooling in Canada and Ontario has certainly had some distinctive features (e.g., Schecter, 1977; Livingstone, 1983; and Curtis, 1984). However, most of the class tendencies referred to below are assumed to be occurring in all advanced capitalist societies currently. It is hoped that the tentative findings offered will soon be further tested by comparable studies in other advanced capitalist settings.

CLASS STRUGGLE, CRISES, AND SOCIAL RECONSTRUCTION

From an historical materialist perspective, the combination of several central dynamics has distinguished capitalism as a mode of production—namely, interfirm competition, contestation between owners and workers over surplus labor time, and continual development of society's productive forces (e.g., Castells, 1980). The owners of capital, from early merchants to current corporate executives, have encouraged the conversion of all potential products of human labor (including labor power itself) into commodities that can be bought and sold for monetary gain so that their own assets can be maintained and expand. Second, capitalist production has been sustained by the extraction of surplus labor time from workers producing saleable commodities and by owners' allocation of much of the realized profits into activities to produce more profits. At the same time, wage workers have tried to retain control of the work process and keep for their own consumption as much as possible of the value produced. Third, both interfirm competition and labor's contestation have impelled capitalists to encourage the greater development of society's productive forces while striving for control over this process; hence, private enterprises are continually trying to harness science and technological knowledge into machine-paced production systems that are more dependable than human labor-paced systems and more cost-efficient than those of competing firms.

The replacement of living labor by machinery tends to make the average rate of profit fall, which provokes countermeasures such as work speed-ups and wage reductions. The organic or structural crises of the late 1800s, the 1930s, and the current period occurred when capital tried to regain profitability by reorganizing the production process and reducing the power of the laboring classes. Increased corporate takeovers and massive layoffs combined with concerted demands for collective bargaining concessions and the rapid introduction of more automated production systems are the most obvious signs of the current capitalist attempts to restructure the economy. But as McDonnell (1978:38) has suggested,

> It should also be clear that it is wrong to see restructuring as a purely economic process consisting of the reorganization of the value composition of capital. Crises involve the totality of capitalist social relations and threaten the continuation of the process of accumulation. Therefore restructuring is a complex economic, political and ideological process to ensure the survival of capitalism and must be understood as class struggle. It involves a struggle by capital to maintain the conditions of its existence and gives rise to a continuous struggle by [the laboring classes] to resist and sometimes challenge the attempted reorganization.

The state has historically played a critical role both in mediating class struggle and in ensuring the reproduction of capitalist social relations generally (e.g., Esping-Anderson, Friedland, and Wright, 1976). During the post-World War II expansionary period, state intervention in the economy increased greatly in all advanced capitalist societies through fiscal and monetary management and through the extension of social subsistence legislation (unemployment compensation, transfer payments, health and education benefits) to the growing dependent population of unemployed people. When the average rate of profit began to fall again, the costs of legislated subsistence entitlements continued to grow. Hence, capitalists now tend to regard some of these entitlements as serious obstacles to renewed accumulation; they have increasingly lobbied for tax cuts, the reduction of total public expenditures and their reallocation to industrial infrastructure, and the reassertion of property-rights legislation. Subordinate groups have thus been forced to mobilize politically to protect their personal subsistence entitlements (Piven and Cloward, 1982; Bowles and Gintis, 1982).

To resolve this structural crisis, social movements (operating either within or against the logic of capital accumulation) must further promulgate alternative forms of economic, political, and ideological reconstruction until some combination finds sufficient popular acceptance to become a new institutional settlement (cf. O'Connor, 1981).

THE CHANGING CLASS STRUCTURE

In historical materialist theories, the primary agencies of social change have been assumed to be class groups and alliances.[2] In this analysis, classes are conceived not as categories but as relationships that are lived within historically constructed contexts. In capitalist societies, classes are partially constituted in household and community relations, but they are primarily determined by paid workplace relations. Very broadly, the current class structure of the advanced capitalist societies is composed of *capitalists,* who own the major private means of production; *proletarians,* who own only their labor power and have no real control over other workers; *intermediate workers,* who have some control over others' labor power and discretion over the use of their own labor but remain subordinate to capitalists' ownership claims or production decisions; and the *dependent population,* an array of people outside the employed workforce but containing many who are instrumental in the daily and generational reconstituting of the workforce.[3] Among capitalists, large corporate owners can be distinguished from small employers, who must continue to work alongside their employees, and from rentier capitalists, who live off investment income without direct participation in the workplace. Four broad types of intermediate workers are identifiable. Most distinct are the self-employed, or old petty bourgeoisie, who continue to work for themselves without employing other paid labor, while generally becoming less independent of corporate capitalist enterprises. Within the labor process of capitalist firms and state organizations, alike, managers or technocrats are those in charge of both disciplining the rest of the workforce and conducting technical design and planning activities. Beneath managers are supervisors, who exercise immediate disciplinary control over subordinated workers but have no assigned control over technical production design. Professional employees have no assigned supervisory control over other workers, but they do have responsibility for the detailed problem solving involved in the design and operation of production systems. Among proletarians, industrial workers engaged in the fabrication and transportation of material goods may be distinguished from nonindustrial workers involved in clerical, sales, and service activities. The dependent population is composed of homemakers, students, temporarily unemployed workers, and pensioners, many of whom live in households with either capitalists or intermediate or proletarian workers, as well as lumpen elements. Such designations within the dependent population are not very informative for class analysis without further specification of either the class positions of others in their households or the trajectories of these people themselves into or out of class positions in the production process. Indeed, lived relations of all class actors within the household, the community, and paid workplaces must be comprehended in an adequate account of class structure, class practices, and class conflict. In the following macrolevel analysis, only fairly categorical first approximations of such lived relations can be considered.

To date, very few empirical studies of the class structure of advanced capitalist societies have relied on such relations of production distinctions; most have relied on the cruder measures provided by occupational titles.[4] However, on the basis of a series of Ontario sample surveys,[5] estimates can be made of class distribution and trends in recent years. As Table 1 indicates, in 1982 the dependent population in Ontario included over 40 percent of those over age 18. Of those in the employed workforce in 1982, roughly 8 percent were self-employed and a similar proportion were large corporate or small employers. Over a third of this active workforce was comprised of professional, managerial, and supervisory employees. Their proletarian subordinates represented about half of the workforce; nonindustrial workers made up over one-quarter of the workforce, and industrial workers represented about one-fifth. The only directly comparable North American study published to date has found a quite similar class structure of the active workforce in the U.S. (Wright, Costello, Hachen, and Sprague, 1982).

Although the Ontario surveys have found no major distributional changes in class structure

[2] Some indication of the current variety of approaches to class structure analysis is provided by Carchedi (1983), Cohen (1982), Giddens and Held (1982), Resnick and Wolf (1982), and Wright (1980a).

[3] For fuller presentation of this approach to class analysis, see Livingstone (1983, Forthcoming).

[4] See Wright (1980b) for a discussion of the limitations of occupation-based class analysis.

[5] Detailed information on the research design and sample composition of the 1978 and 1982 surveys may be found in Livingstone (1979) and Livingstone et al. (1983). Results of the 1980 survey (Livingstone and Hart, 1981) have also been carefully examined in making these trend assessments. In addition to conventional sampling error, several other differences must be considered in interpreting these findings. The 1978 survey was conducted by mail questionnaire, whereas the 1982 survey involved a personal interview. More specifically, the question formats made it difficult to distinguish rentiers or "officially unemployed" from many students and the residual nonworking population in 1978; however, neither of these question differences directly affects the findings reported in the text.

Table 1. Class Structure of the Ontario 18+ Population, 1978 and 1982

General Class Location	Specific Class Position	Percent of 18+ Population		Percent of Employed Workforce		N	
		1978	1982	1978	1982	1978	1982
Capitalist	Large Employers	.7	.7	1.2	1.4	7	8
	Small Employers	5.4	2.8	9.0	5.4	55	30
	Rentiers	.5[a]	2.9	—	—	20	38
Intermediate Workers	Self-Employed	3.8	4.4	6.4	8.3	39	46
	Managers	3.3	2.8	5.5	5.2	34	29
	Supervisors	7.2	8.9	12.1 }30.0	16.8 }35.0	75	93
	Professional Employees	7.4	6.9	12.4	13.0	77	72
Proletariat	Nonindustrial Workers	18.4	15.1	30.9	28.4	190	157
	Industrial Workers	11.9	10.1	20.0 }53.4	19.0 }49.9	123	105
	Residual	1.5	1.3	2.5	2.5	16	14
Dependent Population	Homemakers	17.5	18.1	—	—	180	188
	Pensioners	9.8	12.0	—	—	101	125
	Students	2.6[a] }39.9	7.0 }43.9			27	73
	Unemployed	8.4[a]	4.5	—	—	86	47
	Residual	1.5	2.3			16	24
Total		100.0	100.0	100.0	100.0	1032	1040

[a] See footnote 5.

between 1978 and 1982, several trends suggested in Table 1 are consistent with the aforementioned central dynamics of the capitalist mode of production and with capital restructuring initiatives to restore profitability. First, a decline in the proportion of small employers, along with some reversion to self-employment, has paved the way for increased concentration and centralization of capital in the hands of large corporate firms. Second, a reduction in the hired workforce as a proportion of the population appears to have been accomplished primarily through the layoff of proletarians. Such a reduction, as well as the concomitant growth of the dependent population and the reserve labor force, is consistent with attempts by larger capitalist firms to restructure the labor process through automation and other measures to reduce the relative costs of labor most directly involved in producing and handling commodities. Third, a *relative* increase in the proportion of professional and supervisory employees may be related to capitalist firms' increased intention to design and implement more competitive technical means of production while ensuring more effective control and coordination of the labor process.[6] Although conclusions from an analysis of such limited data must remain tentative, the relative sizes of these class positions and the apparent changes in the current class structure provide the backdrop against which current associations of class with views about educational change will be considered here.

CLASS AND SCHOOLING

Schooling has become central in the reproduction of both the labor power and the class structure of advanced capitalist societies (Lazonick, 1979; Connell, Ashenden, Kessler, and Dowsett, 1982). Schools now provide many of the basic intellectual skills that all people require to work effectively and live meaningfully in a complex technological society. In addition, schools are attempting to convey more diffuse cultural orientations and more differentiated advanced skills, which may direct students to different class positions. Table 2 indicates the extent to which schooling has affected the location of individuals in the class structure of the currently employed Ontario workforce. The vast majority of corporate executives as well as most managers and professional employees have completed some form of postsecondary schooling, typically a university degree. At the other extreme, only small minorities of the industrial and nonindustrial proletariat have obtained any postsecondary schooling. Such marked class differences are consistent with the view that a major consequence of schooling has been the maintenance of a putative distinction between manual labor done by proletarians and mental

[6] For a suggestive account of this tendency, see Burris (1979).

Table 2. Level of Schooling by Class Position, Employed Ontario Workforce, 1982

Class Position	Percent Completed Postsecondary Schooling	Percent with University Degree	N
Corporate Executives	80	65	134[a]
Small Employers	47	20	34
Self-Employed	17	8	46
Managers	54	42	39
Supervisors	24	15	90
Professional Employees	68	40	90
Nonindustrial Workers	13	5	149
Industrial Workers	11	1	94
Total	27	14	559

[a] The large employer group (N=8) is replaced for detailed analyses by a special supplementary sample of corporate executives. For discussion of this special sample, see Livingstone et al. (1983).

labor performed by most of those above them in the capitalist division of labor (Sohn-Rethel, 1978; Browne, 1981). Certainly, most corporate executives, managers, and professional employees appear to have more reason to defend the established two-tier form of schooling than proletarians.[7]

In view of the centrality of schooling in the reproduction of labor power, educational restructuring initiatives should be expected in the current capital accumulation crisis. Reductions in real state expenditures on schooling, as well as on health and welfare, can lower the costs of labor power reproduction and make a greater amount of surplus value available to capitalists both directly and through state budget reallocations. However, to efficiently reproduce labor power with reduced resources, school systems in advanced capitalist societies must put greater emphasis on teaching the basic skills to all and must restrict access to more costly training in the advanced skills needed to coordinate and design the production process. In any such reorganizational efforts, the two-tier class structure of schooling becomes more evident, which serves to make its reproductive role more problematic. This general contradiction of schooling in advanced capitalism is nicely expressed by Freeland and Sharp (1979:11):

> On the one hand, the increasing organic composition of capital produces a relative surplus population which educational expansion partially absorbs but at a cost of producing a drain on surplus value which adds to the tendency of the rate of profit to fall; on the other hand, to the extent to which educational expenditure is redirected towards enhancing the productivity of productive labourers, in order to revive the rate of profit, it expands productivity, contributes to the expulsion of labour from the production process and thus creates more surplus labour to be absorbed!

This contradiction is most apparent in the current crisis.

A general correspondence of the organizational forms of school systems and paid workplaces in advanced capitalist societies has been widely noted (e.g., Bowles and Gintis, 1976; Levin, 1980). But such gross similarity of contemporary organizational forms does not indicate a simple correspondence of the constituting social relationships within schools and workplaces (e.g., Olneck and Bills, 1980; Howell and McBroom, 1982; Oakes, 1982) nor indicate that the flow of people between them can ever be taken for granted. The organizational forms of workplaces are not static; they are historically constructed, reproduced, and changed through negotiations among employers and employees. Likewise, schools are directly shaped by the social relationships between administrators, teachers, students, and parents, all with their own particular interests. Indeed, there is considerable evidence that educational organizations are particularly lacking in close internal coordination between formal management structures and teaching activities and that such loose coupling can facilitate exceptional responsiveness of the official policies of formal management structures to external pressures without seriously affecting internal social relations (e.g., Meyer and Rowan, 1978). Moreover, the flow of people between schools and workplaces is in large part mediated through individual transactions

[7] This is not to deny the role of educational attainments qualifications in facilitating substantial intergenerational class mobility, particularly during the post-1945 expansionary period (e.g., Livingstone, 1983: 72). For a relevant discussion and preliminary five-country test of the role of schooling in intergenerational class reproduction, see Robinson (1984); empirical results are vitiated, however, by data limitations that make it impossible to distinguish either corporate executives, managers, or professional employees from other class positions.

in labor markets and via state intervention. The overproduction of highly educated labor market entrants over the past decade of slow economic growth underlines both the relative autonomy of schooling and the aforementioned contradiction inherent in the schools' efforts to produce appropriately skilled labor for an advanced capitalist economy (e.g., Carnoy, 1982; Connell et al., 1982).

While any simple correspondence thesis must therefore be rejected, if class relations occur within the sphere of education as well as outside it, the development of the political economy of education to analyze educational practices per se may identify basic dimensions of educational relations that are roughly analogous to those commonly used to analyze production relations. Specifically, class relations in capitalist forms of education will be regarded here in terms of three basic dimensions: ownership of major means of cultural production and control of both political and technical aspects of relations within the schooling process itself.[8]

Ownership in education refers to the possession of major means of cultural production. As part of the tendency of capitalist enterprises to appropriate and turn into commodities all potential means of production, capitalists have appropriated many of the instruments for producing and conveying information on a wide scale. The extension and increasingly concentrated ownership of the mass media and the generalization of state-run mass systems of schooling have been the most substantial instruments of this cultural appropriation. Of course, state schooling institutions are not directly owned by capitalist enterprise; they have been established as formally separate, they are staffed out of public funds rather than private profits, and they have acquired their own internal logic of development. Nevertheless, control of the means of public schooling, most manifest in the governing bodies with power to make official policies about the form and extent of schooling provisions and the content of the curriculum, has been from the outset largely out of the hands of the proletariat, especially at postprimary levels.[9] But subordinate-class resistance to such cultural dispossession has continued in both direct and indirect ways. There have been continuing spasmodic efforts by proletarian communities to develop independent forms of education, to gain control over their local schools, and to develop and disseminate working-class curricular materials. Indeed, the pervasiveness of dominant-class cultural appropriation suggested by the general absence of working-class content in the formal curriculum, and by the reified treatment of cultural capital and ideological dominance in much of the recent research in educational sociology,[10] is belied by studies that have observed working-class language use and working-class youths' cultural practices in schools and discovered persistent sources of contrary world views (see Bisseret, 1979; Willis, 1977).

The relations within the schooling process are comparable in form to those within the labor process in capitalist enterprises in several respects. Political and technical dimensions may be analytically distinguished.[11] The *political* relations in the schooling process are interpersonal decision-making aspects of the activities involved in the everyday conduct of schooling, especially authority relations.[12] As the political relations in capitalist production have become characterized by extensive supervisory hierarchies and impersonal rules in the attempt to control wage laborers and better extract their labor, the school system has taken on a similar social organization in order to control and select students and to accomplish its own social division of labor. Schools have become more administratively centralized, and teachers' direct personal control over classroom interaction has been buttressed by the submergence of disciplinary control in detailed sets of work criteria. But, as self-motivation and self-management remain even more critical ingredients to the success of the schooling process than to the capitalist labor process, and while labor market relations remain the principal mechanism of consummating the social division of labor, even indirect coercive measures of social control and selection face greater systemic limits in schools. However, in the current economic slump and attendant fiscal crisis of the state, the capitalist-organized production system is in-

[8] Fuller development of this approach to studying educational forms appears in Livingstone (1983).

[9] For the most extensive historical examination to date, focusing on the role of subordinate groups in English educational reform, see Simon (1974).

[10] It is in the restricted sense of commodified cultural products rather than in this deeper sense of lived cultures that Bourdieu's formulation of the appropriation of cultural capital may apply. See, for example, Bourdieu (1977).

[11] For relevant recent reviews of research on the capitalist labor process, see especially Littler (1982) and Herman (1982). One of the most suggestive conceptualizations of the political and technical aspects of the schooling process appears in Levin (1976); the "macro-political" category there is comparable to the ownership dimension in the current study.

[12] On the changing forms of social control in classrooms, see, for example, Elshtain (1980). Compare Bossert (1979).

creasingly unable to utilize or sustain the post-1945 solution of increasing the accessibility of advanced schooling.

The *technical* relations in the schooling process concern the form of the actual work process of learning. Not only does the continual revolutionizing of production techniques to enhance capital accumulation require a versatile, technically knowledgeable labor force, but, more specifically, advanced capitalist machinofacture needs both a general *potential* labor force with the basic cognitive skills to follow abstract rules and perform shifting, operational detail tasks and a smaller proportion of workers who attain sufficient general scientific knowledge in specialized fields to conduct the technical adaptation, redesign, and repair of various machinofacture production systems. The overall technical form and content of school curricula and teaching methods have become increasingly standardized and segmented just as the tendential development of capitalist machinofacture has relegated a growing proportion of the potential workforce to contend for routinized, operative jobs. Holistic, critical perspectives are often proscribed even in advanced training for the most demanding specializations. Even the pace of learning is now being engineered into curriculum packages at most levels.[13] In the elite university institutions, which are preparing managerial personnel and advanced scientific researchers, teachers and students tend to have significant discretion in organizing the technical form of their learning process. But lower-level curricula must also remain flexible enough to encourage versatility as well as acceptance of routine among students and potential proletarians and to encourage development of planning and coordination skills as well as acceptance of the prospect of highly restricted specialties among many potential intellectual workers. Otherwise, the technical aptitudes of the workforce are unlikely to remain adequate to revolutionize and operate the instruments of capitalist production.

Thus, the historical relations between capitalists and proletarians have given rise to distinctly opposed general interests in the sphere of education, as elsewhere. As I have argued (Livingstone, 1983:105–6),

> With regard to cultural ownership, it is in the interest of capitalists to appropriate as much of private property as possible in the major means of cultural production, whereas it is in the interest of the proletariat to abolish private appropriation and assert communal ownership of educational resources. It is in capitalists' fundamental interest to establish hierarchical authority in the political relations of schooling, while it is in the proletariat's interest to fight for collective coordination and shared decision-making in educational work. As for the technical relations of schooling, it is in capitalists' fundamental interest to centralize advanced technical design and planning knowledge in exclusive schools as much as possible, and in the proletariat's to make all technical knowledge freely accessible.

The educational interests of intermediate workers vary markedly, primarily on the basis of the mixture of "global capitalist" and "collective worker" functions in their production relations (see Carchedi, 1977) and their respective particular relations with both capitalists and proletarians. Managers and professional employees, because of the controlling function in many of their positions and their dependence on advanced schooling to obtain such positions, often have a strong immediate interest in maintaining the established capitalist form of schooling. Those in the dependent population have similarly varied educational interests according to their location in capitalist, intermediate, or proletarian households.

How school systems respond to such contradictory class interests in the current crisis, especially at the level of formal organizational restructuring, will be influenced considerably by the subjective dispositions and concerted actions of class forces on public issues related to each of these basic dimensions of educational practice. The remainder of this article considers the recent dispositions of major class forces in Ontario on some relevant general issues.[14]

CLASS-BASED EDUCATIONAL IDEOLOGIES IN CAPITALIST CRISIS: CORPORATE BUSINESS AND ORGANIZED LABOR VIEWS

There is considerable evidence that fundamental changes in the socioeconomic structure of society entail basic transformations in the world view and levels of cognitive activities of the general population (e.g., Luria, 1976).

---

[13] See, for example, Apple (1982) and Nunan (1983).

[14] This approach is not intended to deny, for example, that subordinate classes especially have frequently engaged in educational struggles not *as a class* but rather in more limited terms as ethnic or union labor groups (see, for example, Katznelson, Gille, and Weir, 1982). Whether or not particular objective class groupings are subjectively disposed to act as a class in the current moment of educational change is precisely the question here.

While the current period of social crisis in advanced capitalist societies may not yet be one of fundamental change, it is a moment of generalized uncertainty about numerous aspects of the dominant world view of the post-War expansionary period. Ideological resettlement at such times is very much the task of the intellectuals of major social forces.

Ideologies are considered here as organized sets of conceptions that are articulated by spokespersons as ideational expressions of the interests of social groupings. As such, they are both consequences of and frames for much intellectual work, as well as most accessible instruments for the attempted reconstruction of popular cultures. When traditional intellectuals can generally treat the values and ideas of powerful groups as disembodied realities and either ignore the distinctive concerns of subordinate groups or regard them merely as deviant, we are in a condition of pronounced ideological domination or hegemony. This condition diminishes when the existence of alternative standpoints and world views is apparent and the role of human agency in creating and disseminating such views is recognized. In the current situation, spokespersons for various organized groups have been making sustained efforts to convey their perspectives and proposals for resolving the crisis to wide audiences. Only brief comment can be made here on the general character of this ideological struggle.[15] Substantial recent shifts are discernible in the relative public prominence of the three major types of ideological perspectives that have pervaded Western thought since the French Revolution: market liberalism, social democracy, and socialism.[16] In short, fundamental socialist themes of self-management and equality of condition are now scarcely visible in popular forums in most advanced capitalist countries. The social democratic emphasis on equality of opportunity and cooperation ensured by a welfare state in a mixed economy, which had prevailed throughout the latter part of the post-1945 expansionary period, is now under persistent attack in the mass media. A reconstructed market liberalism, which stresses free enterprise initiative, the individual right to property, work, and life, and the subservient role of the state (whose primary function is to guarantee private property and fair competition), is clearly on the ascent in many spheres of public discourse.[17] However, efforts to construct such a new dominant ideology have not been uncontested. Some social democratic parties have continued to manage electoral successes, and organized labor movements are becoming increasingly vocal in support of social democratic rights. Some large churches are now speaking out on behalf of their subordinate-class clientele, who bear the economic brunt of the current crisis, and are trying to encourage public discussion of alternative futures. The feminist and ecological movements have developed grassroots appeals that potentially threaten both the ideological and institutional roots of patriarchal capitalism. As Kellner (1978:58) has observed,

> Various ideological regions coexist in an often uneasy harmony, full of contradictions and reciprocal interactions. Ideologies are generated for each realm of existence and they are transmitted, refined or vulgarized, and reinforced in other realms. . . . Moreover, the relations within and among the realms of social reality, and within and among the ideological regions, are complex and shifting.

The study of educational ideologies, therefore, should not be uncoupled from consideration of material practices in the realm of education nor merely regarded as a reflection of such material practices. The approach here focuses on aspects of the current educational debate pertaining to the previously identified basic dimensions of class relations in capitalist educational practices, i.e., cultural ownership of the schools and political and technical relations in the schooling process.

There has been little critical study of changing contemporary educational ideologies in general (e.g., Center for Contemporary Cultural Studies, 1981; Johnston, 1981; Wolpe and Donald, 1983). It is reasonably clear from such general studies that in recent years, both state policy proposals and mass media editorializing about education have placed increased emphasis on themes related to market liberalism. Even less critical attention, however, has been devoted to the educational ideologies currently articulated by specific class forces (e.g., Livingstone, 1983; Shapiro, 1983). Such class-based ideologies represent vital ingredients of any new ideological settlement. Neither dominant- nor subordinate-class ideologies can be simply inferred from either

[15] Some of the most penetrating analyses of the general ideological character of this crisis with particular reference to the British case are provided by the work of Hall (1981, 1982).

[16] The historical development of these three ideological perspectives is outlined in Gamble (1981).

[17] For an insightful account of the ascendancy of the most fully articulated form of current free enterprise ideology, see Hunter (1982).

state or mass media initiatives, particularly in a period of social crisis (e.g., Dreier, 1982). Our research in Ontario has concentrated on public statements about educational issues made over the past decade by spokespersons for corporate business and organized labor. This focus is based on the assumption that these groups are still the major vehicles of class conflict in such advanced capitalist settings. As such, they provide the effective limits for state educational policy making, which is now mediated predominantly by the managerial and professional classes (Bernstein, 1977; Bourdieu and Passeron, 1979). Only brief general summaries of prevalent themes in such public statements can be cited here.[18]

Cultural Ownership of the Schools

> Education is too serious a matter to be left to educators alone. There has never been a time in history when ethics and purposes have been under greater attack by government, communities, interest groups and individuals. There has never been a time when it was so necessary for businessmen to assist the educator to turn out a product more economically, and more capable of taking a productive place in an increasingly competitive world (Temple, 1976).

> What do our children learn about the dignity of labour? What kind of attitudes are absorbed about blue-collar work? What do they learn about the significance of the labour movement—particularly its prominence in struggles for social benefits? Precious little (Fleming, 1979).

> For any society, education is the baseline on which all else stands. The value of education and training in relation to the future economic role of this province and the well-being of its people cannot be assumed, left to bureaucrats or be taken for granted in any way. . . . The vigorous participation of the entrepreneur, the businessman and the industrialist in this process is essential. In fact, it is a responsibility. The business community cannot afford to be reticent about taking a role of vocal leadership in making Canadians aware of the enormous challenges confronting us in the world economic marketplace and the implications of this for the classroom, the training centre and the university laboratory. But talking about it, or shouting from the rooftops about it, will not be enough. In the future, the business community will have to involve itself in the learning places of the nation to a much larger degree than in the past (Stephenson, 1983).

The most basic assertion in most corporate statements is an identity of genuine public interest in education with the self-interest of businessmen. Currently, renewed economic growth is the overriding common goal, and assertions are made that priority must be given to harmonizing educational outputs with business needs. Essentially, corporate spokespersons are now demanding the curtailment of competition with business interests in the sphere of educational policy making. There is an insistent emphasis on reshaping student attitudes toward business, typically conveyed as a need for greater "economic literacy." Such claims are rooted in the belief that the school system must act as a service industry for corporate business and that the products of that system must find places within a labor market largely constituted by private employers. Corporate spokespersons are increasingly explicit in regarding the schools as central instruments for reinvigorating the popular legitimacy of corporate business and particularly for encouraging more active student commitment to the business system but with lower expectations.

Labor spokespersons tend to see the current content of school programs as a threat to working-class identity and solidarity and to the legitimacy and renewal of working-class organizations. The schools are broadly criticized for transmitting a version of the current social order and its history that favors business interests. Labor leaders typically demand balanced treatment of different interests in curricular content and distributive justice for individuals of subordinate-class origins in the allocation of symbolic and material rewards of schooling. Labor interests are virtually never equated universalistically with the public interest but are frequently presented as the interests of the majority of citizens. When the issue of control of schooling is explicitly raised, it is typically in terms of a fuller consultative role for trade unions alongside business representatives in designing and evaluating new programs (e.g., work experience and other school-work linkage programs) or more generally in terms of support for greater local community control of schools.

Political Relations in the School

> For some, the "reality" of the workplace, and the accompanying work-oriented discipline, means a harsh adjustment from

[18] More subtle accounts and descriptions of the data bases, as well as comparisons with earlier class-based educational discourses, may be found in Livingstone (1983).

> the "anything goes" atmosphere of high school. . . . In some classrooms these home-spawned attitudes are reinforced by a lack of discipline and a feeling that quite a number of these students are unmanageable. The end result, in some cases, is student indifference. Again let me pose the question: has the pendulum moved too far? Are we allowing too much freedom in the classroom (Wyatt, 1980).

> We feel that the return to a rigid compulsory curriculum is neither desirable nor justifiable. . . . The slogan "back to the basics" implies a serious restriction in subject choices available to students, as well as a return to row-seating, drills, memory-work and regurgitation tests, and teacher-centred learning. . . . We cannot agree with the regressive and misleading calls for a return to what was in the past (Metro New Democrats-Labour Council of Metropolitan Toronto, 1980).

For corporate leaders, political relations in the schooling process are now most critically a matter of better controlling the patterns of everyday conduct within the schools. At the center of their critique of educational practices are issues of student discipline. An equation of school discipline with labor discipline is typically espoused. Proper school discipline is stressed as essential to students' subsequent acceptance of labor discipline, and the fundamentals of labor discipline are presented as the attitudinal and behavioral requirements of the learning process. In both instances, the emphasis is upon acceptance of external constraint and externally defined standards. Most obviously, this means regular attendance and consistent compliance with management rules and directions in both school and work settings. The goal, however, is more ambitious—namely, to shape a personality more appropriate to the social responsibilities of work and citizenship. Corporate spokespersons over the past decade have consistently expressed concern that the indulgence and permissiveness of the schools have seriously undermined acceptance of work discipline. However, they are also critical of a passivity among students, which they feel is incompatible with the internalized self-discipline and self-direction required in some degree of most workers in modern industry. The demand is essentially that the schools instill a toleration of externally directed, routinized work while developing capacities for independent judgement and initiative. A frequently implied and increasingly stated resolution of this dilemma is the imposition of tougher testing standards to help identify students' inherent capacities.

While labor spokespersons have understandably refrained from supporting the use of the schools to instill work discipline, they are much farther from elaborating a model of political relations within the school congruent with their own class interests than spokespersons for corporate business. Labor leaders have generally supported liberalized authority relations within the classroom. Such support, however, is not predicated upon a perceived congruence between child-centered education and labor interests. Class-based streaming and middle-class bias in the curriculum are seen to have continued in spite of liberal reforms. Liberal authority relations are supported because the back-to-basics and discipline-oriented movements are identified with desires to narrow the scope of the curriculum and limit the resources available for education of disadvantaged groups. What is notably absent in the education statements of most union spokespersons is any reference to the relationship between relatively liberal authority relations in the school and the authority relations in the workplace or the union hall. There is little or no discernible counterpart to the kind of correspondence argument developed by spokespersons for corporate business, wherein school discipline parallels work discipline.

Technical Relations in the Learning Process

> There appear to be three major areas where young graduates entering the workforce are deficient: One is basic skills. The second is an inability to communicate adequately, and the third area is an apparent lack of personal philosophy of work ethic. . . . Obviously we have missed a vital area. To my mind we must readjust the value system of our society, including the parents, the pupils, and the educators. We must gear more of our thinking toward encouraging skills training (Wyatt, 1980).

> We're graduating hundreds of thousands of students from our high schools, colleges and universities, with little or no job skills. . . . Canada has an international reputation of having the best educated unemployed labour force in the world. We must have a national manpower planning policy before we can have a workable national manpower training program. We need to know where the shortages are now and where they will be five and even ten years down the road (Carr, 1980).

Corporate interest in the technical relations of the learning process is now focused on "rationalization" and increasing productivity, primarily through simplification and standardization of the tasks for both students and teachers at lower levels of the school system. Corporate spokespersons believe the curriculum should be reoriented to reduce frills and promote general preparatory skills for work. Within this are included not only basics but the economic literacy that is seen as a key element in rejuvenating the work ethic. Teachers are still granted the central role in this reduced and concentrated curriculum, but that role is to be increasingly augmented by educational technology. The growing corporate demand that the "education coat be cut" according to the "job market cloth" does not mean a tight matching of primary- and secondary-level program content to job content. Rather, it entails instruction in general preparatory skills that are open-ended and can be built upon or refined in a range of different work settings. In other words, it means the creation of labor market entrants who will be increasingly technically adaptable and capable of mobility among work settings in response to rapidly changing workplace technologies.

Labor spokespersons have become increasingly preoccupied with the skill content of the learning process as unemployment has mounted, and they now quite clearly oppose corporate statements at several key points. There is labor resistance to any rationalization attempts that would reduce the range of the curriculum and develop a standardized basic skills program. They believe basic skills should be taught in a way that reflects the total needs and interests of individuals. Second, labor spokespersons express great interest in an organization of skills training that could provide continuity of employment and a cushioning of shocks due to changing economic conditions. This view is stated most clearly in support for preservation and extension of the licensed trades model for comprehensive technical skill training and allocation of work, as well as in demands that the educational system encompass job-related skill training. The emphasis is increasingly placed on training for employment rather than for employability. Thus, labor spokespersons are generally opposed to the kind of rationalization of the learning process proposed by corporate leaders and to the implication that greater productivity is achievable with reduced educational resources. Labor leaders regularly support alternate demands for *added* curricular content and *extensions* of school services. Any decline in productivity as measured by performance in basic-skill subjects is ascribed by union spokespersons primarily to inadequate educational resources, which cannot meet the special needs of a diverse and disadvantaged school population. Opposition to corporate interests regarding the technical relations in schooling is, however, limited insofar as labor demands for schools to train well-rounded workers do not explicitly confront and counterpose alternatives to currently highly segmented labor markets and increasingly specialized technical work processes.

The foregoing is a highly selective and partial sketch of the prevalent surface logics of educational ideologies recently expressed by corporate business and organized labor in Ontario. Very little of the actual texture of these class-based educational ideologies or of variations within them has been conveyed, to say nothing of the dynamic relations of such conceptions with lived class experience of the central contradictions of capitalist production and education. All that can be concluded here with any confidence is that with regard to cultural ownership, labor ideologues do not systematically question general capitalist appropriation of schooling at this point and are only expressly concerned to infuse more working-class curricular content and consultation within this dominant form of schooling. With regard to the schooling process itself, as in the labor process generally within advanced capitalism, the contradictions between capitalist and proletarian interests remain more direct. The immediate interests of the capitalist and working classes are now frequently expressed as real oppositions on specific schooling process issues, especially such technical aspects as skill-training requirements and provisions. It is on these dimensions of the schooling process that ideological struggle among capitalist and proletarian leaders appears to have increased most in the current crisis.

CURRENT MASS OPINION ON EDUCATIONAL ISSUES: A CLASS ANALYSIS

However clearly articulated and widely disseminated such class-based educational ideologies may be, it is their resonance with and incorporation into ordinary people's efforts to make sense of their own experience that is likely to be most decisive for whatever new educational settlement emerges from the current crisis. The interactions in such processes between recognized and potential class leaders on the one hand and different mass publics on the other are still very poorly understood.[19] On the basis of the several On-

[19] The insights of Gramsci (1971:5–23, and passim) regarding such mutual interactions in pre-1930s advanced capitalist settings remain highly suggestive for such contemporary analyses. Empirical research on audience perceptions of contending sources of public ideological discourse has barely begun. See, for example, Hartman (1979).

Table 3. Support for Greater Emphasis on Business Rights and Workers' Rights in the Schools by Class Position, 1980

	More Emphasis on Business Rights			More Emphasis on Workers' Rights			
Class Position	Agree (%)	Dis-agree (%)	Not Stated (%)	Agree (%)	Dis-agree (%)	Not Stated (%)	N
Corporate Executives	77	10	13	24	52	24	138[a]
Small Employers	91	1	8	30	47	23	47
Self-Employed	73	12	15	39	45	16	54
Managers	62	16	22	37	30	33	28
Supervisors	80	6	14	41	42	17	97
Professional Employees	79	8	13	48	21	31	70
Nonindustrial Workers	78	10	12	54	21	25	162
Industrial Workers	75	10	15	53	29	18	136
Homemakers	72	10	17	42	30	28	229
Pensioners	68	6	26	46	28	27	151
Students	74	9	17	49	25	27	67
Unemployed	79	3	19	62	23	15	35
Total	74	9	17	46	30	24	1121

[a] Special supplementary sample of corporate executives. See Livingstone and Hart (1981).

tario mass-opinion surveys referred to earlier (Livingstone, 1979; Livingstone and Hart, 1981; Livingstone et al., 1983), this section will discuss the recent subjective dispositions of those in different class positions regarding some alternative educational provisions related to the aspects of cultural ownership of the schools and political and technical relations in the schooling process that have been emphasized in the public statements of corporate and labor leaders.[20]

Attitudes About Cultural Ownership

These surveys have consistently found strong *individual* appreciation of the cultural capital thesis (i.e., the restricted capability of lower-class modes of learning to appropriate useful knowledge from the standard school curriculum). That is, corporate executives, managers, and professional employees assess the usefulness of their own formal schooling much more highly than do proletarians and most others (Livingstone, 1983:81). However, the sense of differential *class* appropriation of education is much less acute. For example, despite considerable research evidence and organized labor's critiques to the contrary, it is widely believed that there is pluralistic class control of community colleges and that students from all classes have equal opportunities to obtain a higher education in Ontario (Livingstone, 1983:156–58). On the issue of whether or not there should be greater community control of the schools, the population in general and proletarians in particular have expressed quite divided views; most notably, corporate executives have persistently and almost unanimously opposed any move to greater community control (Livingstone, 1983:162).

With regard to curriculum content per se, survey respondents were asked in 1980 whether schools should give more emphasis to teaching students about (a) business and property rights in the free enterprise system, and (b) the labor movement and workers' rights. As Table 3 indicates, a small majority of both industrial and nonindustrial workers, as well as most unemployed workers, supported more emphasis on workers' rights in the curriculum. A small majority of corporate executives expressed opposition, and those in most other class positions exhibited quite mixed views. However, proletarians were even more strongly in favor of increasing curricular emphasis on business rights, as were strong majorities in all other class locations. Thus, corporate executives displayed relatively consistent views of their class interests, whereas all sections of the proletariat displayed more inconsistent views and a largely unquestioned support for business rights even at this specific content level of cultural appropriation. Established forms of capitalist cultural appropriation of the schools appear to remain ideologically quite secure.

[20] There has been some survey-based research on the association of various occupation-based measures of social class with educational attitudes (e.g., Shaw, 1979) but none to my knowledge relying on relations of production distinctions.

Attitudes About Political Relations in Schooling

Mass perceptions and preferences concerning the internal decision-making process in schools have been assessed on a variety of issues in these surveys but with prime attention to the degrees of freedom and authority exercised by teachers and students in high schools. With regard to the diffuse issue of student discipline in general, corporate leaders' stated views are clearly widely shared. Majorities in all class positions have expressed the sentiment that the schools are now too permissive, and many believe that lack of discipline is the school's biggest problem (Livingstone and Hart, 1981; cf. Gallup, 1982). Popular views on desirable systems of discipline and student freedom of choice have been somewhat more diverse. In the early 1970s, the Ontario population and intermediate workers in particular were very much in favor of greater student freedom in the classroom (e.g., Livingstone, 1976; Livingstone, 1983). But mass opinion subsequently appears to have moved more into line with corporate rhetoric about restoring teacher authority. In 1978, survey respondents were asked for their preferences among three basic models of teacher-student authority relations within high school classrooms: (1) teachers have a great deal of authority, students have at most an occasional voice in classroom affairs; (2) teachers have primary authority, but students can negotiate for major changes from teachers' directions; and (3) students have at least equal authority to teachers and co-manage classroom affairs. As Table 4 summarizes, the most teacher-centered model was chosen by at least a plurality in all class positions. Corporate executives and small employers strongly supported this model. Later surveys have found that the views of those in most other class positions have moved closer to capitalist views on related discipline issues (Livingstone, 1983).

Compared with the growing popularity of this antipermissiveness ethos, more divided views have persisted concerning the locus of administrative control of schooling. Regarding the responsibility for testing high school students' academic progress, for example, the public as a whole and nearly all class positions are quite evenly split between preferences for local teacher responsibility and preferences for centralized testing. The notable exception is again corporate executives, the vast majority of whom favor reliance on central testing authority over local control (Livingstone, 1983; Livingstone et al., 1983).

Attitudes About Technical Relations in Schooling

As the central practical activity of educational institutions that is most directly and fully experienced by most people, the learning process and its objectives might well be expected to be the prime focus of distinct educational views related to different groups' material conditions. The rare historical studies of class-based educational ideologies have centered on the aims and objectives of the learning process per se (e.g., Williams, 1961). The Ontario surveys have probed mass opinions on several aspects of the learning process generally related to skill requirements, a major preoccupation in much recent public discourse about learning objectives. The summary issue of curricular priorities will be considered here.

Survey respondents have been asked to express their preferences among a wide variety of possible curricular objectives at each level of schooling. In general, growing priority has

Table 4. Desired Form of Decision Making in High School Classrooms, by Class Position, 1978

Class Position	Teacher with Great Deal of Authority (%)	Decisions Negotiated with Students (%)	Students with At Least Equal Authority (%)	Other/ Don't Know (%)
Corporate Executives	80	14	3	3
Small Employers	64	15	2	19
Self-Employed	50	35	7	8
Managers	48	33	9	10
Supervisors	59	25	4	12
Professional Employees	52	32	13	3
Nonindustrial Workers	41	33	10	16
Industrial Workers	51	18	12	19
Homemakers	47	23	6	24
Pensioners	44	24	4	28
Students	37	16	29	18
Unemployed	36	19	19	26
Total	47	25	9	19

been expressed through the past decade for job training and more recently for basic reading, writing, and number skills. The development of creativity and critical-thinking skills has also retained a relatively high priority. But most of the possible objectives that are less evidently connected to the sphere of production (e.g., moral education, physical fitness, Canadian history, political education, art, and cultural studies) have been considered unimportant (Livingstone et al., 1983). Substantial class differences have consistently been found, especially at the high school level. Table 5 indicates the basic patterns of high school curricular priorities expressed in the most recent survey. Corporate executives and industrial workers are quite opposed on the issues, as they have been in prior surveys since 1978. The majority of corporate executives give top priority to basic skills or creativity and critical-thinking skills and very little importance to job training in high school; industrial workers and the unemployed display quite the reverse tendencies and show majority support for job training. Professional employees are also more likely to favor basic or generic skills over job training in high schools, but those in most other class positions express at least plurality support for job training as the top high school curricular priority.

Finally, mass receptivity to corporate leaders' proposals to rationalize the instructional process may be gauged by looking at opinions concerning what should be done with the major organizational resource implicated in such a restructuring initiative—namely, teaching staffs. The Ontario surveys have asked whether teachers should be laid off in the current situation or retained and redeployed to either reduce class size or provide more programs for disadvantaged children. Table 6 summarizes the findings of the most recent survey. A strong majority of corporate executives and rentier capitalists have consistently expressed the desire to lay off teachers. Strong majorities in virtually all other class positions have expressed the desire to retain teachers. These clearly opposed sentiments between the corporate executive core of the capitalist class and the proletariat, with its organized labor core, could animate serious conflicts over the specific alternative forms of educational restructuring proposals now emerging. It should be noted, however, that corporate leaders have been sufficiently sensitive to the widespread support for retaining teachers to couch their specific proposals in more indirect and curriculum-centered terms.

CONCLUSION

The foregoing juxtaposition of prevalent elements of class spokespersons' public discourse on education with class-specific expressions of mass opinion about education represents at best a modest step toward understanding social-class effects on educational policy making. Even the most consistent of the schematic patterns reported here need to be confirmed by careful ethnographic study before there can be much confidence in their operative validity for actual class groupings. Nevertheless, several preliminary conclusions may be ventured on the current educational crisis:

1. Compared to all other class groupings, corporate executive spokespersons and members exhibit an impressive degree of coherence and consistency in their views

Table 5. Most Important Curricular Priority for High Schools, by Class Position, 1982

	Highest Priority			
Class Position	Job Skills (%)	Basic Skills (%)	Creativity/ Critical Thinking (%)	Other/ Don't Know (%)
Corporate Executives	18	40	29	13
Small Employers	47	21	23	9
Rentiers	41	20	14	25
Self-Employed	58	19	14	9
Managers	40	18	20	22
Supervisors	42	24	18	16
Professional Employees	22	21	35	22
Nonindustrial Workers	45	16	12	26
Industrial Workers	53	14	6	27
Homemakers	41	26	7	26
Pensioners	38	24	2	36
Students	51	18	12	20
Unemployed	54	16	6	25
Total	44	20	12	25

Table 6. Preferred Treatment of Surplus Teachers, by Class Position, 1982

Class Position	Retain Teachers (%)	Lay-Off Teachers (%)	Not Stated (%)
Corporate Executives	26	69	5
Small Employers	54	34	12
Rentiers	40	57	3
Self-Employed	53	43	4
Managers	58	37	5
Supervisors	65	33	2
Professional Employees	72	22	6
Nonindustrial Workers	78	22	0
Industrial Workers	65	29	6
Homemakers	75	18	7
Pensioners	65	29	6
Students	80	14	6
Unemployed	71	25	4
Total	69	26	5

about basic aspects of educational provisions. But other capitalists express more mixed views rather than forming a solidary force with the corporate core to lead a new educational settlement.

2. The greatest source of opposition to any corporate-led settlement of the current crisis is the proletariat. Much of this opposition is focused on the most concrete level of the learning process. To tailor training programs to the capitalist job market cloth today is to stress the basic technical skills (i.e., literacy and numeracy) and the basic social skills (e.g., responsibility, and flexibility) required for rapid changes of technical competence in accumulation-driven machinofacture. Conversely, to address many workers' aspirations, job training programs must focus on more specific jobs and include a sufficiently comprehensive array of advanced technical skills to ensure some economic security. The irresolvability of this contradiction in advanced capitalist market economies and its deepening in periods of economic slump are quite clearly reflected, for example, in the consistently opposed opinions on high school learning objectives offered by corporate executives and industrial workers, as well as in continual dispute about the adequacy of virtually all employment training programs.
3. The active support of some intermediate class groupings, because of their relatively large and growing size in the employed workforce, is likely to be decisive for efforts of either capitalist or proletarian forces to resolve the current crisis in their own favor. Unless many of their numbers can be convinced that the corporate-proposed rationalization of schooling will benefit them, they are quite unlikely to willingly support substantial resource cutbacks or the reversal of social democratic access entitlements.
4. Overall, the findings suggest the continuation of education policy crisis. Both general and class-specific opinion exhibit dissensus and division on a number of basic organizational issues implicated in any restructuring (e.g., centralized versus local control issues). Perhaps more to the point, only the corporate executive class position displays sufficient collective subjective coherence to nurture a sustained educational change movement, and a number of corporate views currently tend to be held in isolation rather than resonating into larger class alliances.

Of course, public discourse and mass-opinion surveys are relatively ephemeral aspects of social reality. At best, they can point to sentiments that can serve as one of the bases of social practice. The specific social consciousness expressed within different class positions is constantly vulnerable to renewed ideological struggle by organized agencies of different class forces. The potential significance of our findings for anticipating political practice is difficult to assess, particularly because mass-opinion surveys are largely a post-World War II phenomenon. We have no such surveys in earlier protracted capitalist crises to tell us about comparative levels of expressed mass opinion or their relations with the practical actions of major class forces. Indeed, very few other current-opinion surveys of educational or social issues that permit a class analysis of their results are available in any of the advanced capitalist societies;[21] there are a great

[21] For a valuable reference source dealing with mass opinion on various aspects of social welfare in eight "rich nations" when social democratic ideology was still prevalent, see Coughlin (1980).

many that ignore or serve to obscure the existence of class-based attitude differences. Gender, ethnicity, and age-based relations, as well as educational attainment and various other particular social locational factors, have their own influences on social consciousness and can also serve to specify some of the patterns of attitudes toward school reforms presented here. But the class-based relationships reported in this article remain statistically significant when controls are made for such factors.[22] Only empirical studies centrally concerned with classes as lived relationships rather than as one of many scalar or categorical variables can provide the information needed to further reveal the underlying dynamics of the current educational policy crisis in advanced capitalist societies.

REFERENCES

Apple, M.
1982 "Curricular form and the logic of technical control: Building the possessive individual." Pp. 247–74 in M. Apple (ed.), Cultural and Economic Reproduction in Education. Boston: Routledge and Kegan Paul.

Bernstein, B.
1977 "Classes and pedagogies: Visible and invisible." Pp. 511–34 in J. Karabel and A. H. Halsey (eds.), Power and Ideology in Education. New York: Oxford University Press.

Bisseret, N.
1979 Education, Class Language and Ideology. London: Routledge and Kegan Paul.

Bossert, S.
1979 Tasks and Social Relationships in Classrooms. Cambridge: Cambridge University Press.

Bourdieu, P.
1977 "Cultural reproduction and social reproduction." Pp. 487–511 in J. Karabel and A. H. Halsey (eds.), Power and Ideology in Education. New York: Oxford University Press.

Bourdieu, P. and J. C. Passeron
1979 The Inheritors. Chicago: University of Chicago Press.

Bowles, S. and H. Gintis
1976 Schooling in Capitalist America. New York: Basic.
1982 "The crisis of liberal democratic capitalism: The case of the United States." Politics and Society 11:51–93.

Boyd, W. L.
1983 "Rethinking educational policy and management: Political science and educational administration in the 1980s." American Journal of Education 92:1–29.

Browne, K.
1981 "Schooling, capitalism and the mental/manual division of labour." Sociological Review 29:445–73.

Burris, V.
1979 "Capital accumulation and the rise of the new middle class." Review of Radical Political Economics 10:1–31.

Carchedi, G.
1977 On the Economic Identification of Social Classes. London: Routledge and Kegan Paul.
1983 Problems in Class Analysis. London: Routledge and Kegan Paul.

Carnoy, M.
1982 "Education, economy and the state." Pp. 79–126 in M. W. Apple (ed.), Cultural and Economic Reproduction in Education. Boston: Routledge and Kegan Paul.

Carr, S.
1980 Speech quoted in E. Finn, "The million jobless lack needed skills," Toronto Star, September 8, 1980.

Castells, M.
1980 The Economic Crisis and American Society. Princeton: Princeton University Press.

Centre for Contemporary Cultural Studies
1981 Unpopular Education: Schooling and Social Democracy in England Since 1944. London: Hutchinson.

Cohen, J.
1982 Class and Civil Society: The Limits of Marxian Critical Theory. Amherst: University of Massachusetts Press.

Committee on the Future Role of Universities in Ontario
1981 Preliminary Report. Toronto: Ontario Ministry of Education.

Connell, R. W., D. J. Ashenden, S. Kessler, and G. W. Dowsett
1982 Making the Difference: Schools, Families and Social Division. Sydney: George Allen and Unwin.

Coughlin, R.
1980 Ideology, Public Opinion and Welfare Policy. Berkeley: University of California Press.

Curti, M.
[1935] The Social Ideas of American Educators.
1959 Paterson, NJ: Littlefield, Adams and Company.

Curtis, B.
1984 "Capitalist development and educational reform: Comparative material from England, Ireland and Upper Canada to 1850." Theory and Society 13:41–68.

Dreier, P.
1982 "Capitalists vs. the media: An analysis of an ideological mobilization among business leaders." Media, Culture and Society 4:111–32.

Elshtain, J.
1980 "The social relations of the classroom: A moral and political perspective." Telos 27:97–110.

[22] While false precision has been an endemic problem in research quantifying expressed social attitudes, it should be noted that only class differences that are statistically significant at the .05 confidence level with each of these other factors singly controlled have been cited in the text.

Esping-Anderson, G., R. Friedland, and E. O. Wright
1976 "Modes of class struggle and the capitalist state." Kapitalistate 4/5:186–220.

Fleming, B.
1979 "The child as learner and worker." Canadian Labour (September 7):14.

Freeland, J. and R. Sharp
1979 "Education, the state and the reproduction of labour power: Some background considerations to the Williams Report." Paper presented at the Weekend Seminar, Understanding the Current Crisis in Education, Macquarrie University, September 22–23.

Gallup, G. H.
1982 "The 14th annual Gallup Poll of the public's attitudes towards the public schools." Phi Delta Kappan 64:37–51.

Gamble, A.
1981 An Introduction to Modern Social and Political Thought. London: Macmillan.

Giddens, A. and D. Held (eds.)
1982 Classes, Power and Conflict: Classical and Contemporary Debates. Berkeley: University of California Press.

Gramsci, A.
1971 Selections from the Prison Notebooks. New York: International.

Hall, S.
1981 "Moving right." Socialist Review 11: 113–37.
1982 "A long haul." Marxism Today:16–21.

Hartman, P.
1979 "News and public perceptions of industrial relations." Media, Culture and Society 1:255–70.

Herman, A.
1982 "Conceptualizing control: Domination and hegemony in the capitalist labour process." Insurgent Sociologist 11:7–22.

Howell, F. and L. McBroom
1982 "Social relations at home and school: An analysis of the correspondence principle." Sociology of Education 55:40–52.

Hunter, A.
1982 "The ideology of the new right." Pp. 309–32 in K. Fox, M. Hetzel, T. Riddell, N. Rose, and J. Sazama (eds.), Crisis in the Public Sector. New York: Monthly Review Press.

Johnston, K.
1981 "The production of conservative educational ideologies." Discourse 2:9–21.

Katznelson, I., K. Gille, and M. Weir
1982 "Public schooling and working-class formation: The case of the United States." American Journal of Education 90:111–43.

Kellner, D.
1978 "Ideology, Marxism, advanced capitalism." Socialist Review 42:37–65.

Lazonick, W.
1979 "The subjection of labour to capital." Review of Radical Political Economics 10:1–31.

Levin, H.
1976 "A taxonomy of educational reforms for changes in the nature of work." Pp. 83–114 in M. Carnoy and H. Levin (eds.), The Limits of Educational Reform. London: Longman.
1980 "Workplace democracy and educational planning." Pp. 123–216 in M. Carnoy, H. Levin, and K. King (eds.), Education, Work and Employment. Vol. 2. Paris: UNESCO.

Lipset, S. M. and D. Schneider
1983 The Confidence Gap: Business, Labor, and Government in the Public Mind. New York: Free Press.

Littler, C.
1982 The Development of the Labour Process in Capitalist Societies. London: Heinemann.

Livingstone, D. W.
1976 "Images of the educational future in advanced industrial society: An Ontario inquiry." Canadian Journal of Education 1:13–30.
1979 Public Attitudes Toward Education in Ontario 1978. Toronto: OISE Press.
1983 Class, Ideologies and Educational Futures. Philadelphia: Falmer.
Forthcoming Class and Class Consciousness in Advanced Capitalism.

Livingstone, D. W. and D. J. Hart
1981 Public Attitudes Toward Education in Ontario 1980. Toronto: OISE Press.

Livingstone, D. W., D. J. Hart, and L. McLean
1983 Public Attitudes Toward Education in Ontario 1982. Toronto: OISE Press.

Luria, A. R.
1976 Cognitive Development: Its Cultural and Social Foundations. Cambridge, MA: Harvard University Press.

McDonnell, K.
1978 "Ideology, crisis and the cuts." Capital and Class 4:34–69.

Metro New Democrats-Labour Council of Metropolitan Toronto
1980 Municipal and Education Program. Toronto: New Democratic Party of Ontario.

Meyer, J. W. and B. Rowan
1977 "Institutionalized organizations: Formal structure as myth and ceremony." American Journal of Sociology 83:340–63.
1978 "The structure of educational organizations." Pp. 78–109 in M. Meyer and associates (eds.), Environments and Organizations. San Francisco: Jossey-Bass.

Nunan, T.
1983 Countering Educational Design. London: Croom Helm.

Oakes, J.
1982 "Classroom social relations: Exploring the Bowles and Gintis hypothesis." Sociology of Education 55:197–212.

O'Connor, J.
1981 "The meaning of crisis." International Journal of Urban and Regional Research 6:301–29.

Olneck, M. and D. Bills
1980 "What makes Sammy run? An empirical assessment of the Bowles-Gintis correspondence theory." American Journal of Education 89:27–61.

Piven, F. and R. Cloward
1982 The New Class War. New York: Pantheon.
Resnick, S. and R. Wolff
1982 "Classes in Marxian theory." Review of Radical Political Economics 13:1–18.
Robinson, R. V.
1984 "Reproducing class relations in industrial capitalism." American Sociological Review 49:182–96.
Schecter, S.
1977 "Capitalism, class and educational reforms in Canada." Pp. 373–416 in L. Panitch (ed.), The Canadian State. Toronto: University of Toronto Press.
Secondary Education Review Project
1981 Final Report. Toronto: Ontario Ministry of Education.
Shapiro, H. V.
1983 "Class, ideology and the basic skills movement." Interchange 14:14–24.
Shaw, P.
1979 "Social class and citizens' opinions of their local public schools." Unpublished Ph.D. dissertation, Columbia University.
Simon, B.
1974 Studies in the History of Education. 3 volumes. London: Lawrence and Wishart.
Sohn-Rethel, A.
1978 Intellectual and Manual Labour. London: Macmillan.
Stephenson, B.
1983 "Notes for an address to the Board of Trade of Metropolitan Toronto." Pp. 12–13 in Ministry of Education and Ministry of Colleges and Universities, January 17.
Temple, G.
1976 "What business can do about education." Canadian Business 49:44–48.
Williams, R.
1961 The Long Revolution. London: Chatto and Windus.
Willis, P.
1977 Learning to Labour. Westmead: Saxon House.
Wolpe, A. M. and J. Donald (eds.)
1983 Is There Anyone Here from Education? Education after Thatcher. London: Pluto.
Wright, E. O.
1980a "Varieties of Marxist conceptions of class structure." Politics and Society 3:323–69.
1980b "Class and occupation." Theory and Society 9:177–214.
Wright, E. O., C. Costello, D. Hachen, and J. Sprague
1982 "The American class structure." American Sociological Review 47:709–26.
Wyatt, H. E.
1980 "Walking the education tightrope." Speech presented to the Third Congress of the Canadian School Trustee's Association, June.

ACADEMIC STUDIES AND TECHNICAL EDUCATION: NEW DIMENSIONS OF AN OLD STRUGGLE IN THE DIVISION OF KNOWLEDGE

LUCIE TANGUY
Centre national de la recherche scientifique,
Université Paris V

Sociology of Education 1985, Vol. 58 (January):20–33

INTRODUCTION

The studies emanating from the sociology of education over the past decade, in France at least, have attempted to demonstrate that the school is essentially an instrument participating in the reproduction of relationships between social groups and classes (Baudelot and Establet, 1971; Bourdieu and Passeron, 1970). Most of these studies have therefore taken a macrosociological approach. They have attached scant importance to identifying the processes that produce these societal structures or to exposing the underlying mediations, notably at the microsociological level. More particularly, since the 1960s sociology has been less interested in what goes on inside the black box—school—than in what comes out of it. Yet several decades ago, Durkheim (1938), in his book *L'Evolution pédagogique en France*, attempted to unify an analysis of the relationship between social structure and the process of educational transmission. Until quite recently, then, curriculum analysis was left to pedagogues, with the exception of Bourdieu, who has studied curricula in terms of cultural

I want to thank Gwenneth Galilee and Joyce Schonfield for translating this paper into English.
Address all correspondence to the author at C.N.R.S. Paris V, U.E.R. sciences de l'éducation, 28 rue Serpente, 75006 Paris, FRANCE.

legitimation, and Isambert-Jamati (1970), who has traced the evolution of French secondary-school disciplines over the last century. During this same period, a group of English sociologists close to Young (1971) and influenced by the work of Bernstein (1971, 1973, 1975) stated that the sociology of education should affirm its autonomy with respect to other branches of sociology and lay claim to the field of curriculum as its own specific object of study.

These new sociological approaches have been evolving in a decade marked by the crisis in the ideologies of education and social progress, a critique of the hegemony of science, a recognition of the diversity of knowledge, and the wider realization that the realm of knowledge is itself structured by relations of dominance. Concurrently, we have seen attempts at new educational practices, which have sought to transform pedagogical relations (mainly the teacher-student relationship) and have emphasized the affective rather than the cognitive dimension of education, personal fulfillment rather than the acquisition of knowledge (Karabel and Halsey, 1977; Bernbaum, 1977).

The very latest trend to emerge in sociological analysis questions the basic function of education—the transmission of knowledge. This critical discourse on education has been formulated by different social groups, who use it to express their own particular aspirations and expectations. Among these groups are the organizations of parents, notably working-class parents (speaking through the labor unions), whose children leave school at the end of the compulsory period without a single diploma or occupational qualification and, at times, with a level of education that is lower than what is considered necessary today.[1] The employers' professional organizations have also been criticizing the educational system for teaching knowledge that is abstract, for being out of touch with the economic and technical realities of the day, and even for discouraging young people from going into manual and industrial work. Political experts and leaders believe that in the present period, marked as it is by technological mutations and an intensification of international economic competition, the French educational system should be directed more towards the production of technical skills.

All of this indicates a return to the debate over general and technical education and the place and role of each. It can be recalled that in the mid-1960s, the economic planners had already taken up the subject when they planned a modification of the flow of students to secondary education, which would have favored technical instruction. As has been shown above, many of the social attacks on education today center on its role in producing specific skills or on the knowledge figuring in the different educational sections.

Thus, the field of knowledge, which some may have thought was relatively untouched by social relations, is in reality both the stage and the object of struggles between groups and social classes. These struggles take place at different levels and revolve around two essential issues: the inclusion of particular knowledge in the various sections and the appropriation of this knowledge. The debates over the first issue are virtually invisible, totally concealed behind the veil of science and specialization; they are pursued for the most part by experts and specialists, who intervene to decide what knowledge should figure in the curriculum in the event of the reform of a particular discipline (or to contest such decisions). Occasional criticisms of the curriculum or of the place of a particular section in the total educational system, such as those mentioned above, are the only visible signs of this debate. Struggles over the second issue appear more frequently in the public arena. They underpin the main movements for the democratization of education. This is conceived most frequently as an extension of compulsory schooling and as the opening of the sections hitherto reserved for the elite to the mass of the population, but it seldom goes hand in hand with a social critique of the knowledge figuring in the curricula. In fact, for several years, the controversy surrounding the *collège unique*[2] in France focused more on the structures of secondary education than on its internal organization or curricula. It is only in the last few years, as a result of the failure of large numbers of students in the collège, that the school has become the object of new expectations: equal opportunity for all and equal success for all. Of course, it does not follow that all social groups are able to pass from the stage of criticism to a formulation of systematic opinions on education and curricula. This is hardly surprising, since domination implies a withholding of the conditions that would give access to this state of awareness and statement of overall purpose.

To avoid a unilateral approach focusing on

[1] In 1981, following a number of earlier experiments, the French government set up a scheme for training this particular category of young people 16 to 18 years old. The training period lasts about 1,200 hours; half of this time is spent in a training center, the other half in a real job setting in commerce or in industry.

[2] The *collège* is the first level of secondary education and enrolls students aged 12 to 16 years.

one aspect or moment in this struggle waged around knowledge and how it is appropriated, one needs to reconstitute the whole process encompassing the production, distribution, and use of knowledge; that is, one needs to create a political economy of knowledge. We shall confine ourselves here to a single phase in this process: distribution (or at least one of its aspects), a function assigned to the school system in all advanced societies. More specifically, we will address a few crucial yet neglected issues: Does the school system program the same type of knowledge in all sections, apportioning it unequally, or does it assign different types of knowledge relating to different spheres of social activity?

In so doing, we will analyze the institutional divisions within secondary education in France: divisions between the academic sections, which procure greater chances of entering higher education, the long technical sections, which prepare the future technicians, and the short technical sections, which prepare future manual and office workers for industry, business, and commerce. In the process, we will show the kinds of relationships that exist between the hierarchy of the different sections and the hierarchy of different types of knowledge, and the shifts and reorientations these hierarchies have undergone in response to pressures from certain social groups. We will also give a brief account of the development of vocational training in France.

Our investigation draws primarily on French sociological literature, but it also takes into account Anglo-Saxon writings available in France. It is based on a number of assumptions that need to be explained. First, curricula are taken as knowledge. Rather than seeking to separate knowledge from the ideology in which it is wrapped—a vain and naïve endeavor—we take what the school counts as knowledge to be just that. We also take the view that the appropriation of scientific knowledge is today a key issue in the advanced industrial societies for every class or social group aspiring to wield power—not necessarily the power of domination, but the power of understanding, of giving a meaning, the power of interpreting or of acting on the environment.

METHOD

All societies institute ways of testing the knowledge acquired in educational establishments. In France, this is done by examination, which, by its very prevalence, reflects the centralized educational system that followed in the wake of the centralization of the political institutions. In this analysis, we will take as our starting point the examinations sanctioning secondary studies: the *baccalauréats*, the *Brevet d'études professionnelles* (BEP, vocational certificate), and the *Certificat d'aptitude professionnelle* (CAP, certificate of vocational proficiency).

The baccalauréat is an institution that is still very much with us. Though it is no longer a passport to the ranks of the bourgeoisie (Goblot, [1925] 1967), it remains, despite all, the first university diploma. The examinations sanctioning the short technical cycle—the CAP or BEP—confer no such symbolic title, though they play an active role in promoting recognition of the value of labor (both its use-value and its exchange-value), a recognition that in production relations is realized, for example, through the various occupational categories. The number of subjects figuring in these examinations, the status attached to each through the assignment of a coefficient, the breakdown between compulsory and optional papers and between written and oral tests can be seen as so many indications of the logic of the instruction that the examinations claim to measure.

But this approach has its limits. If examinations do in fact condition pedagogy, they also allow for considerable variations in the pedagogical practices, which we cannot measure. Examinations and pedagogy are two levels of the same reality: the educative act, whose complexity cannot be apprehended by a single approach. If the focus is put on the examinations, the main themes and major characteristics of the educative act will be made clear. But what is really taught in the classroom and, even more, what the students actually learn will remain obscure.

Furthermore, if this approach makes it possible to grasp the knowledge included in or excluded from technical education as objectivized facts in examinations, it does not lend itself to analyzing this distribution as a product of conflicts or struggles between social groups. The objective force assumed by the social distribution of knowledge within the school at a given time appears independently of its genesis. Once these origins are forgotten, it becomes difficult to reconstitute the tensions and confrontations that accompanied them.

As the latter are thus no longer amenable to our investigation, and as we are in no position to say who decides to maintain or change curricula and who opposes these decisions, we will attempt to reveal the principles that regulate their selection and organization in the different school sections. The distribution of knowledge within the school may be analyzed on the basis of the general criteria that govern the organization of any educational process: time, the number of school subjects and how they are examined, and the leading orientation of the knowledge constituting each section.

THE ROLE OF TIME IN DIFFERENTIATING THE VARIOUS SCHOOL SECTIONS

In France the distinction between academic and technical studies goes hand in hand with another organizational distinction based on the use of time: some sections are long (academic and technical), others are short (technical only) (Tanguy, 1983a). But there is a question whether or not this use of time is a decisive factor in differentiating between the academic and technical sections, and if so, what does it mean? Apparently there is nothing surprising in this: The short technical cycles cover two school years following the common first cycle, and the long cycles cover three. The school year is hence the unit of measurement[3] and rightly so, because the school is organized along the same pattern for all schoolchildren in France, whether they attend an academic or vocational institution or primary school: namely, 32 weeks of schooling and 20 weeks of vacation. But the similarity ends there. The school week for a lycée student preparing a literary or scientific baccalauréat varies from 23 to 26 hours according to the section chosen, whereas for a student preparing a technical baccalauréat or vocational certificate it lasts from 36 to 40 hours. Thus, the school year is about 1.4 times longer in the technical sections than in the academic sections. This means that the distinctions made between the long and short cycles are legitimate, since the long cycles involve three years of study and the short cycles only two, and mystifying, since the annual number of hours devoted to compulsory courses is greater in the so-called short technical cycle than in the long academic cycle. The data in the following table illustrate this point.

	Short Technical Cycle	Long Technical Cycle	Long Academic Cycle (Literary or Scientific Baccalauréat)
Number of hours in school week	36	36	26
Number of weeks in school year	32	32	32
Number of hours in school year	1,152	1,152	832
Number of school years	2	3	3
Number of hours of compulsory schooling	2,304	3,456	2,496

In reality, students will spend a varying number of years on the school benches, and this has particular repercussions for working-class families, who bear the brunt of the cost implied. The prime concern of the state, which finances and operates the school system, is to shorten and condense schooling in the light of a rationale that applies, as we shall see, in the work process.

But the abstraction of time inherent in the use of the school year as a yardstick underpins a linear and unidimensional representation that substitutes physical measurement for a social approach to time. The quantitative relationships so established conceal relationships characteristic of different uses of time in technical education and academic studies. *Length* (number of school years) and *density* (number of hours per school week) tend to be combined in inverse relationships within these two types of education.

The short dense period of technical education is thus set against the long, more diluted period of academic studies. It must be said, however, that here we are talking about time in the classroom and not about study time outside the classroom, which may not be the same as that prescribed by the school. Although it cannot be reckoned with any accuracy, it is well known that students in the academic sections tend to do more homework than those in the technical sections. Thus, the organization of time in academic studies is based on the displacement of part of the learning process outside the school, a displacement that is of considerable significance.

This organization of time facilitates the acquisition of social skills outside school and prepares the student for leisure. Even if this time is not fully devoted to the acquisition of lifestyles and types of social consumption specific to certain social classes, such as artistic consumption in all its forms, this potential use of time is an implicit part of the learning process in academic studies, but not in technical education. Without knowing the respective time budgets of students in technical and academic education, it is impossible to proceed further in analyzing and interpreting the way time is divided between homework and social and cultural out-of-school activities. However, it must be recognized that the use of time in

[3] In 1978, technical-school pupils attending short courses tended to complete them at roughly the same age as students pursuing academic studies: 72 percent of the former and 71 percent of the latter were born in 1959 and 1960 (French Ministry of Education, 1979).

school is related to the use made of time by the various social groups and classes according to their position in the division of labor. The period of school instruction, dense or loosely knit, condensed or diluted, is also a time of acquiring different kinds of attitudes towards knowledge.

Differences in the ratio of schoolwork to homework are constitutive factors in the functioning of the school system: Fewer school hours imply more hours required for homework. This mode of organizing schooling facilitates the acquisition of relatively dynamic and critical attitudes towards knowledge and fosters certain qualities and behavior patterns, such as the ability to manage one's own time. It postulates, as we have seen, an active approach on the part of the individual to his/her studies.

By contrast, in technical education—and especially in the short technical sections—virtually all the teaching is directed towards the students as a group in the classroom. The time pattern of technical studies does not demand the same degree of individual commitment; such commitment is of course a *sine qua non* for the successful completion of studies, but less personal effort is demanded.

A high time-density in technical education may appear a necessary attribute, inherent in the very nature of the studies, which require the use of machinery and apparatus and a concentration of workbench facilities (at both the school and the workplace), more or less precluding the displacement of the learning process outside the school. But this attribute is bound up with the duration of studies: The longer the course, the lower its density. It should be noted, moreover, that the acquisition of technical skills is far more intensive in secondary education (both long and short) than in the common primary school and collège, and this category of knowledge does not figure alongside the so-called core subjects (languages, mathematics, natural sciences, and literature). The inclusion of technical subjects in the general curriculum has been a highly controversial topic for several years. Certain social groups, notably the employers' and workers' unions, and certain political leaders have been urging that technology be included among the compulsory subjects at the collège level. But the teachers and the intellectual petty bourgeoisie (who run the school parents' organizations) protest energetically against such projects.

This breakdown of study time between school and home—its natural complement—implicitly assumes certain relationships between school and the family. The time pattern of so-called academic studies (sciences or the arts) takes for granted the family's cooperation: The transfer of part of the learning process away from the school implies an investment on the part of the family and a tacit acceptance of the intellectual and cultural models proposed by the school. The time patterns of technical education, on the other hand, seem to stem from a recognition of the separation of school and family; far from assuming family cooperation, they seem to take for granted the absence of material and cultural conditions that would back up the pedagogical activities of the school. They reflect the dichotomy noted in other respects between school and the working-class family (the main "clients" for technical education, particularly in the short sections). The same cannot be said for the academic streams, which are extensively patronized by the various strata of the middle classes, who work closely with the school in transmitting the academic and cultural capital.

Instructional methods vary widely between technical education and academic studies and may even be diametrically opposed. As we shall see, whereas technical and particularly short technical education consists for the most part of work-oriented knowledge and know-how, academic studies impart knowledge that is devoid of any immediate utility. The former is guided by the needs of production, whereas the latter operates under no such constraints.

In conclusion, the condensed period of technical education—with some nuances depending on whether the courses are long or short—represents the basic minimum required for the acquisition of skills essential to the worker, whereas the longer and looser-knit pattern of academic studies represents the period needed for the acquisition of knowledge and practices divested of any vocational content.

Of course, there are also differences within technical education in the length of the school week: Future factory workers spend approximately 36 hours per week in school and future office workers spend approximately 33 hours. These differences reflect those existing between blue- and white-collar workers. Although the number of hours they work may be the same, these hours are less intense for the latter than for the former; and the school system, which has the task of training the future labor force, inculcates these differences in habits, work rhythms, and the exercise of brawn and brain. In the long run, the gap could narrow both at work and at school. For example, the length of instruction for clerical and industrial jobs is the same (36 hours weekly), and their work patterns are becoming increasingly similar.

Short technical education, preparing students for employment in industry or business, assigns scant importance to skills that require a long familiarization process or to skills whose social applications are doubtful, if not remote. Technical education focuses on the present; science and humanities straddle the past and the future. In the former, the constraints of social time rule out the acquisition of knowledge that is not immediately exploitable. Thus, the school replaces the teaching of a formal and universal language such as mathematics with instruction in computing methods, formulae, and results. An acquaintance with the laws of matter through experiment is subordinated to a knowledge of operational outlines.

The analysis we are proposing cannot be applied universally; because it is confined to secondary education, its findings cannot, for example, be extended to higher education, whose time attributes must be interpreted in different terms. (We are talking not about culture-oriented academic studies but about specialized studies; the time density in the elite university-type institutions [Grandes Ecoles] clearly conforms to imperatives different from those governing secondary technical education.)

Last, we point out the paradoxical nature of this use of time, which assigns short dense periods of schooling to students considered "slow" by scholastic norms, inevitably making the learning process more difficult.

ACADEMIC STUDIES AND TECHNICAL EDUCATION: AN ORGANIZATION OF KNOWLEDGE GEARED TO LEGITIMATE CULTURE OR TO THE PRODUCTION AND DISTRIBUTION OF MATERIAL WEALTH

The distinction between academic studies and technical education does not derive solely from the length of time dictated by society for the completion of specific courses; it stems far more from the categories of knowledge figuring in the curricula. For some, this distinction is primarily reflected in the range and diversity of fields covered, which may be gauged by the number of subjects taught. From this standpoint, academic studies may be qualified as broad, and technical education as narrow. This interpretation assumes a one-dimensional ranking of knowledge in an unambiguous hierarchy. But, and this goes without saying, technical education proceeds from another conception of the ordering and transmission of knowledge: It includes scientific knowledge, instruction in its material manifestations (techniques, machines, and tools), and practical applications.

In this study, we grouped school subjects included in the various sections of secondary education by discipline, identifying them by their object of study: man, society, communication, nature, action on matter or objects. We then conducted an "economic" analysis of the values assigned to each of these groups in the examinations measuring attainment in the different branches of secondary education.

The disciplines taught were tentatively broken down into six broad groups:

1. Knowledge focused on man as an individual and as a producer and generator of ideas, thought, and art—e.g., literature and philosophy
2. Knowledge focused on an understanding of society and social, political, and military history, etc.—the social sciences, history, and geography
3. Knowledge and skills geared to communication with other peoples—namely, foreign languages (their separation from the first two classes of knowledge may be contested but is warranted on the grounds that they are valuable instruments in fostering international exchanges of both goods and ideas)
4. Knowledge of nature—the various branches of the physical and natural sciences
5. Mathematics, inasmuch as it is a formal, abstract, and universal language necessary to the understanding of certain natural sciences (e.g., physics), though it must not be confused with them
6. Knowledge and know-how geared to material or economic activities (administration or management)—industrial and accounting technologies as well as factory skills

Armed with these admittedly imprecise and fragile tools, we will attempt to describe the main orientations of the knowledge in the curricula of the various sections, and in the process, we will question, at least in broad terms, the types and patterns of thinking that are thereby inferred.

Before doing so, we point out one very fundamental difference in the organization of examinations between academic studies and technical studies. The academic baccalauréat comprises a series of tests with differing ratings; success or failure is determined by a weighted average of the marks obtained on the tests. The technical baccalauréats and vocational examinations consist of two complementary sets of papers, both of which are compulsory, covering academic and vocational subjects. It is necessary to achieve an average in both sets of papers, which tends to show that there is not a single, one-dimensional ranking of knowledge but two: theoretical knowledge and the operational skills required for its application. The one cannot compensate for the other, since both are equally necessary.

Apart from this similarity in the organization of examinations in the technical and vocational sections, the way in which these two orders of knowledge are combined, as well as the nature of the technical knowledge itself, differs widely between the industrial section and the commercial and administrative sections; the former is geared to production, the latter are geared to the distribution and management of material wealth (including money). Leaving aside these differences inherent in technical knowledge, we will address the two salient features revealed in Table 1.

The Preponderance of Production-Oriented Knowledge

The classification of the subject matters making up the technical baccalauréat follows the institutional discourse that separates scientific and technical studies. But is this division legitimate, and if so, what is its rationale?

Gille (1978) draws a clear distinction between technical knowledge (*connaissance technique*) and science in the institutional sense and as a realm of knowledge dissociated from any practical application. Nonetheless, he maintains that "while the epistemological approach of science emerges quite clearly, the same cannot be said by a long chalk for technology. Mathematical logic is a unity while technological logic is multiform" (Gille, 1979:15).

The category of technical knowledge produced by the institutional division of knowledge is also multiform, since it combines subjects (such as applied mechanics and technology), industrial organization and methods (the manufacturing process, tooling), and workshop practice. This combination is largely arbitrary, and its justification resides only in the division between science and technology, a division rooted in the social order. As Lévy-Leblond (1977:148) very aptly points out, "We have thus reached a paradoxical situation in which the more a science is involved in production or—simply—in social life, the more it is divested of its 'scientific' character." How many people would think of including in a discussion of contemporary physics not only the electromechanics of household equipment and the telephone, or automobile mechanics, but also basic radio and television electronics, fluid dynamics in plumbing, or physical chemistry for the amateur photographer? Yet if scientific teaching and training were to be based on these everyday phenomena, the pedagogical and ideological implications would be immense. What actually takes place is a veritable reification of knowledge, which, once out of the hands of the specialists, is divested of its scientific content; i.e., all theoretical and hence critical appropriations are excluded to leave room only for empirical manipulations (Lévy-Leblond, 1977).

The school follows this double movement in which (1) academic science advances by displacement and exclusion, rejecting the knowledge that enters into the production process, and (2) theoretical knowledge, which is assimilated into the production system, is sepa-

Table 1. Distribution of Coefficients Assigned to the Subjects Compulsorily Tested in Secondary Examinations

	Academic Studies								Technical Education			
	Philosophy/ Humanities (A)		Economics and Social Sciences (B)		Math and Physical Sciences (C)		Math and Natural Sciences (D)		Technical Baccalauréat (Mechanics)		BEP (Mechanics)	
Discipline	Coefficient	Percent of Baccalauréat	Coefficient	Percent of Baccalauréat	Coefficient	Percent of Baccalauréat	Coefficient	Percent of Baccalauréat	Coefficient	Percent of Baccalauréat	Coefficient	Percent of Certificate
Literature and philosophy	8	40	5	25	4	20	4	20	4	10	2	9.1
Social sciences, history, geography	3	15	7	35	2	10	2	10	0	—	1	4.5
Foreign languages	7	35	5	25	2	10	2	10	2	5	0	—
Physical and natural sciences	0	—	0	—	7	35	8	40	4	10	3	13.6
Mathematics	2	10	3	15	5	25	4	20	5	12.5		
Technology and workshop practice	0	—	0	—	0	—	0	—	25	62.5	16	72.7
Total	20	100	20	100	20	100	20	100	40	100	22	100

NOTE: A measure of the value accorded to the various categories of knowledge can be obtained by setting the coefficient assigned them against the total of coefficients. Thus, the genuinely literary disciplines represent 40 percent of baccalauréat A, 20 percent of baccalauréat C, 10 percent of a technical baccalauréat, and 9.1 percent of a vocational certificate.

rated from practical knowledge, which is left for the workers who have to run the machines.[4]

This tendency to separate theory from empirical knowledge and know-how is far more prevalent in the short technical courses than in the long ones. This is borne out by the value attached to the accomplishment of a material task in the workshop, which represents 44 percent of the tests in a vocational certificate (BEP) and 16 percent in a technical baccalauréat. Despite the very considerable difference between these percentages, both of these forms of technical education are characterized by the primacy accorded to manipulative skills and know-how; these account for 62.5 percent of the technical baccalauréat and 72.7 percent of the industrial vocational certificate (BEP).

A Schooling that Alienates Man as a Social Being

The inclusion of different knowledge in the various sections confirms a dual process of appropriation and deprivation of knowledge: i.e., appropriation of the knowledge that is geared towards understanding matter and deprivation of the knowledge essential for the political subject. This process marks the organization of technical education, particularly the industrial courses, in two ways: (1) through a denial of any instruction in philosophy, whose questioning of man and systems of thought are thereby excluded from the training of a whole category of young people, who have every chance of finding themselves somewhere in the production and distribution system, and (2) through the slight place accorded to history, geography, and the social sciences, which, though included in the earlier school curriculum, are not tested by examination, implying that they are not considered very vital to technicians.

While our analysis of the knowledge prescribed and excluded in technical education does not necessarily imply that technical education creates alienated individuals, we stress that the elimination of the social sphere from an essentially production-oriented pedagogy constitutes both a paradox and a demonstration of ideological force, for the organization of production serves as a backdrop against which the techniques used in production are presented as neutral and natural facts. This exclusion of societal concerns from technical curricula leads to a neutralization of techniques and a reification of social production.[5] Industrial-technical education seems totally rooted in the present without reference to the past; man[6] is perceived as an object rather than as a subject. The process fosters and "makes absolute certain capacities but ignores others because they appear fortuitous and of no utility within the economic system" (Kosik, 1970:67). Its function is to inculcate the aptitudes, proficiencies, and interests required for the accomplishment of specific tasks in industry and administration. Other aptitudes or talents are relegated to the sphere of private life. While it is true that individuals learn through life experience some of the things that school has denied them—for example, an awareness of social contradictions—one cannot discount the hypothesis that this mode of prescribing knowledge could serve to promote a unilateral and fetishistic vision of reality.

Last, we believe that academic studies, geared to the mastery of the fundamentals of institutionally constituted scientific knowledge, tend to neglect the question of their application and remain rooted in legitimate culture. Technical education, oriented towards production and distribution, accords primacy in differing degrees to the practical applications of knowledge.

SHIFTS IN THE STATUS OF KNOWLEDGE, DIFFERENTIATION OF INTELLECTUAL WORK, AND CHANGES IN THE REPRESENTATIONS OF KNOWLEDGE

So far, we have focused on the different categories of knowledge included in academic and technical studies. We now turn to recent changes within the hierarchy of these sections and discuss how these changes have affected

[4] The renowned French physicist Paul Langevin explained one day how the notion of electrical potential introduced in secondary education during his last years at the lycée represented at the time a peak of theoretical abstraction and difficulty. This concept is now given material expression in the everyday use of 110– and 220-volt electric lamps and household appliances. But this knowledge remains empirical and partial. The separation between theory and practice reaches its apogee here.

[5] This process clearly takes on very different forms in the so-called economic and social sections, where the techniques taught apply to information, business organization, management, and commerce. The relationships between these technical skills applied to the social sphere and the knowledge produced by the corresponding disciplines—the economic and social sciences—are still to be explored.

[6] This notion refers less to "man in general" than to a Gramscian conception of man as "a complex of social relationships." Man evolves and changes continually as his social relationships change (Gramsci, 1975).

the separation between academic and technical education and their respective statuses.

Academic studies appear to be broken down into two broad groups—the sciences and the humanities—whose interrelationship has radically altered over the last twenty years. In the first place, the established hierarchy has been reversed. Today the maths and physics baccalauréat (C) is a passport to all branches of higher education (not only to the physical and economic sciences but to the humanities and medicine), regardless of the family of disciplines to which they belong (Cherkaoui, 1982). Curiously, the medical milieu was for a long time opposed to a scientific baccalauréat that obliged candidates to take some literary courses.[7] This changing relationship has taken a long time, but the process has accelerated considerably in the last decade. In 1959, about 45 percent of those passing the baccalauréat were in the literary sections; in 1970, the proportion dropped to 38.6 percent; and in 1979 to 18.5 percent.

This reversal of the hierarchical relationship between the sciences and the humanities—which is also a reversal of the associated hierarchies of knowledge and ideologies—has gone hand in hand with a strong drift away from the literary sections (64,502 students enrolled in 1970, and only 39,828 enrolled in 1979), a trend that is certainly correlated with the distribution of scientific and literary knowledge.

If we dissect the literary baccalauréat, its monolithic character is exposed. When we apply the distribution of coefficients in Table 1 to the breakdown of knowledge according to its object—humanity and its history versus nature—we find that the humanities represent 90 percent of this baccalauréat, and mathematics the remainder. (The natural sciences are not represented in the literary baccalauréat.)

By contrast, baccalauréat C gives preponderance to the natural sciences (40 percent), which outrank mathematics and the humanities, to which roughly equal weights are attached. The split between the natural sciences and the humanities is thus better balanced: 40 percent versus 60 percent. This balance is a result of the much broader curricula in the so-called scientific sections (C and D). These sections cover the whole range of learning except the applied sciences, which belong exclusively to the technical sections. With this exception—and it is an important one—holders of the scientific baccalauréat today have the broadest education; in particular, it is those preparing for baccalauréat C who tend to study the most diverse subjects, all of which are geared, albeit in different ways (ancient and modern languages, artistic studies, etc.), towards a knowledge of man.

Far from being monolithic, the so-called scientific sections combine in relatively balanced proportions the two main categories of knowledge constituting all education inasmuch as they are the products of human history. Associated with a slight preponderance of the natural sciences, this configuration of knowledge presents the requisite properties for the education of an elite: a broad initiation into the main branches of knowledge as they exist today and a deeper insight into the dominant branches of this knowledge.[8]

These observations lead one to wonder whether academic studies do not confer that property considered an attribute of the bourgeoisie—namely, the ability to perceive oneself as a whole and the world as a whole, the ability to relate the specific to the general. Shils (1972), among others (Gouldner, 1979; Bernstein, 1971, 1973, 1975), has described a set of qualities that characterizes the culture of the intellectuals. These qualities allow them to dissociate themselves from what is tangible, concrete, and particular in order to approach theory, formalization, and general principles; in brief, they allow them to detach themselves from reality and strive towards an abstract thought embracing both the past and the future. But this abstract thought will be oriented differently depending on whether the language acquired is one that, though general, respects diversity and is critical in approach, like the language of philosophy or literature, or is universal and standardized, like the languages of mathematics and the natural sciences.

Can one, then, following Rose and Rose (1977), maintain that in teaching these lan-

[7] Isambert-Jamati (1972:134) reminds us of the social status of the scientific baccalauréat at the turn of the century: "Those who, coming from the lower strata of society, opted for the sciences, are well advised to do so and for two reasons: they will render a service to the economy while ensuring themselves an excellent career, while at the same time they allow the literary sections to be purer, since students in the humanities must be considered as an elite destined to maintain among us the taste for things of the spirit."

[8] This trend towards a separation between the literary and scientific sections, between man and nature, reflects other divisions: namely, divisions between values and feelings (which are the domain of literature and philosophy) and facts (which are the domain of the sciences) and between ethics and logic. This separation is all the more significant because it is reflected in a sexual differentiation. Though narrowing, the gap is still real: Among 100 boys preparing an academic baccalauréat, 28 presented a literary baccalauréat and 72 a scientific baccalauréat; among girls the percentages were 58.5 and 41.5 (French Ministry of Education, 1981).

guages separately, in instituting them as legitimate modes of learning, the school not only contributes to the training of various groups of the middle classes but tends concurrently to construct two dominant modes of thought and philosophy: idealism and mechanistic materialism? The former allows the individual to evolve in the realm of ideas, representations, and values but leaves him totally helpless in the realm of material objects and techniques; the latter gives him an awareness of the material world but tends to depoliticize the social sphere, treating it in purely technical terms. We shall leave these issues open, because they cannot find a response in this study.

Is the Separation Between Academic and Technical Education Changing?

The trend observed in secondary education over the last fifteen to twenty years seems to point in this direction and may be briefly described as follows:

1. The percentage of those passing the baccalauréat has risen in one generation from 11.5 (in 1965) to 25.3 (in 1979) (French Ministry of Education, 1981).[9]
2. The relative proportion of baccalauréats A, C, and D, which were the first to be organized and which constitute the surest path to higher education, has fallen: In 1970, these baccalauréats accounted for 72.9 percent of all baccalauréat diplomas; in 1979, they accounted for only 54.8 percent (French Ministry of Education, 1981).
3. The new baccalauréats in the economic and social sciences and the technical baccalauréats have rapidly gained a foothold: These now account for 14.2 percent and 28.3 percent of all baccalauréat diplomas (French Ministry of Education, 1981).

The rapid expansion of technical education and, in particular, economic-technical education, which is related to the increase in secondary-school enrollment, points to a change in the relation between academic and technical education but not to a reversal in the academic hierarchy governing this relation. Opposing trends seem to be at work today; some tend to maintain or reinforce this hierarchical relationship (between the scientific and industrial-technical sections, for example), while others seem to blur it, as in the case of the economic and social-science sections and the economic and social-technical sections. The boundary established between scientific academic studies and industrial-technical education, in terms of their constitutive categories of knowledge, remains very distinct, as has been shown. However, the boundary between the economic and social-science baccalauréat and the economic-technical baccalauréat is much hazier. It is true that the latter reserves a smaller place for literature, philosophy, and foreign languages and places a premium on the instrumental aspect of knowledge; but the split between science and techniques in their social applications is not as clear-cut as the split between science and techniques applied to nature. Because our analysis has been limited to stating the categories of prescribed knowledge and their place in the different sections, it cannot go any further. The next step would involve questioning the curricula from within.

However, the social composition of the different educational sections clearly shows the absence of a distinct split between academic studies in general and technical education. Of course, the students in the scientific C section (which has the greatest prestige) and in some of the literary sections belong in their great majority to the middle class; and the short technical sections attract a majority of working-class students. But between these two extremes, other sections of academic studies exist—namely, the humanities and the economic and social sciences (B), whose social composition is akin to that found in the long technical sections, thereby demonstrating that the boundary between academic and technical education is not definitive.

Even if we cannot describe and explain in precise terms how and why these changes are coming about, we can at least say that they are borne by movements that emerge here and there to advocate a higher status for technical knowledge and its assimilation, along with its associated representations and values, into legitimate culture. It would be necessary to give a more complete definition of the social groups behind these movements;[10] but they do seem to share one particular characteristic—they all possess technical knowledge. They tend to assume the role of spokesman for the common good when they urge that the school adapt to the social mutations engendered by the introduction of new technologies.

The fact remains that these changes in the status of knowledge do not seem to challenge the rules governing its distribution, even though this distribution has led to the con-

[9] The rate was 0.62 in 1851, 1.05 in 1906, and 4.4 in 1946 (French Ministry of Education, 1981).

[10] In France, two periodicals provide a forum for these movements: *Culture et technique*, published by the Center for Research on Technical Culture, and *Milieux*, published by the Center for Research on Industrial Civilization.

Table 2. Socioeconomic Background of Male and Female Students in French Public Schools, 1981

	Educational Section[a]						
Father's Occupation	CAP	BEP	2eT	2eAB	2eA	2eC	2eA1A2
Agricultural workers	1.51	1.31	0.72	0.82	0.66	0.48	0.49
Clerical, sales workers	7.46	9.52	10.46	10.60	10.47	8.55	9.66
Workers	52.27	44.14	34.58	32.02	26.47	18.82	19.48
Service personnel	6.81	5.19	3.25	3.68	2.99	1.77	2.06
Artisans	3.86	4.35	4.67	4.72	4.82	3.43	3.88
Small merchants, shopkeepers	2.61	3.56	3.71	4.65	4.65	3.97	3.86
Farmers	3.77	5.83	4.84	5.44	3.67	4.24	2.83
Subtotal	78.29	73.90	62.23	61.93	53.73	41.26	42.26
Employers (commerce and industry)	0.54	0.93	1.55	1.79	2.21	2.37	2.10
Top management professions	1.35	3.21	10.77	10.72	16.20	29.90	26.88
Middle management	5.28	9.20	16.35	15.58	17.98	20.16	20.41
Others	14.54	12.76	9.10	9.98	9.88	6.31	8.35
Total	100	100	100	100	100	100	100

Source: French Ministry of Education (1982).

[a] CAP and BEP are the short technical sections; 2eT is the long technical section. Academic sections are 2eAB (economic and social sciences), 2eA and 2eA1A2 (literary sections), and 2eC (scientific section).

struction of monolithic sections, which, as Durkheim affirmed, "could not train minds," i.e., "inculcate the habits and attitudes indispensable to a valid approach to the different aspects of reality" (1938:383).

CHANGES IN VOCATIONAL TRAINING IN FRANCE

The first part of our analysis has dealt with the specific kinds of knowledge characterizing the academic and technical sections of French secondary education. We next described changes at work in the hierarchy of these sections and shifts in their respective statuses. We will now apply the same approach to short technical education, which assumes responsibility for the vocational training of future workers in industry, business, and commerce. In this respect, it is important to show what type of knowledge is prescribed for these future workers and to compare its organization with the organization governing the other sections, notably the long technical program (which theoretically trains future technicians). In the process, we will give a rough outline of the changes taking place within this field, changes that are giving rise to lively debates and reform projects.

Short technical education is the most recent member of the family of technical education, which in France starts at the top (*écoles d'ingénieurs*), works down to the middle (technicians), and focuses last on those who operate the production process. It began as part of the production process (with the Astier Law of 1919), but at the end of World War II it was detached from production and taken over by the school under the tutelage of a state body.[11] Though it is no longer directly controlled by the production system, it is nevertheless still dependent on this system for its organization, form, and content.

This vocational education is a juxtaposition of two distinct components—academic studies and vocational training—which together constitute the basis on which school and industry vie for the right to dispense such instruction, each claiming an extension of its prerogatives.

On studying vocational examinations and how they have developed, we found that (1) knowledge that is directly and immediately exploitable—namely, technology and practical studies—predominates, and (2) this preponderance has been on the wane since the late 1960s, when new training modes began to be introduced.

Since technical education is mainly the study of the production processes, it is essential to know how schools approach the issue and, in particular, how the science of production processes—i.e., technology—is taught to future workers. To address this issue, we reviewed the questions asked in practical and theoretical technology examinations over the last twenty-five years. The specific characteristics we have brought to light do not all reflect a homogeneous classification principle but express in diverse ways the social relationship that underpins technical teaching to future workers. These investigations are reported in

[11] Seven hundred and fifty thousand students are currently enrolled in this branch of education and will form the factory and office workers of tomorrow; 220,000 young people are receiving instruction in the form of alternance training.

detail elsewhere (Tanguy, 1983b); we will summarize our main conclusions here.

In eliminating the social and economic factors—such as the specificities of the production process, large- or small-scale manufacturing, type of product, quality, and cost—that determine how problems are resolved, the school system plays a part in the reification of technique. Hence, the need for or relativity of such techniques in a given situation totally escapes the control or understanding of those who perform them: Instead of learning to master them, the future worker, unaware of the why and wherefore, learns only to use them.

Furthermore, from the nature and form of the questions recurring invariably in technology examinations, it can be seen that the knowledge taught to future workers consists for the most part of (1) facts, such as operating instructions (materials and tools to be used, sequences of operations, and other standards); (2) findings or formulae established through mathematics, physics, or practical experiment; and (3) processes detached from their principles. The way in which the questions are formulated seems to signify that it is less important for the future worker to acquire an understanding of matter (the requisite properties and hence composition of a given component in the light of its function in a particular mechanism) than to be able to read instructions.

The study of the technical tests comprised in vocational examinations since the mid-1960s also shows that this discipline is tending more and more to be taught in an abstract and formal way. This has entailed the substitution of a unified, homogeneous, and standardized language—that of technology—for the varied, heterogeneous languages of the different trades. Though it pushes back the limits of the particular languages of the individual trades, this universal language does not yield its full powers to tomorrow's workers, since it is presented in a truncated manner and is simply confined to instruction in reading formulae, tables, and codes. But this familiarity with formulae and codes, this proficiency in reading and using a standardized technical language, is essential for the worker if s/he is to operate within today's industrial system.

For the same reason, it seems that the technical knowledge taught to future workers in school no longer consists of the practical knowledge handed down from worker to worker (and in part developed by them); it is formalized technical knowledge of the same type as that taught to future technicians. However, knowledge of production processes transmitted by this vocational section is fragmented and reduced to knowledge in the form of results. It does not imply an understanding of the production process itself, since this is necessarily a social phenomenon, and the social sphere has been eliminated from technical education. Our analysis thus reveals that the mode of distribution of technical knowledge to future workers is significantly different from that used in the long technical section. It relies on processes of exclusion, separation, and reification, following the rationale of the social hierarchy.

Yet, while the school draws on the social division of labor in transmitting knowledge, it never totally adjusts to this division and tends even to extend its limits. The school teaches future workers a type of knowledge that, while not strictly necessary for the execution of manual tasks, however skilled, is necessary for the organization of production. Thus, in today's schools, the future worker will acquire skills that are needed and applied by technicians in time and method study services—skills such as drafting and operating instructions for transforming and assembling materials.

We thus arrive at an interpretation that runs counter to the one proposed a few years ago (Lautier and Tortajada, 1978; Grignon, 1971): The school not only provides better instruction in production processes than in the conditions of production, but it also tends to stamp its own logic on the training process. This had led some observers to speak of the "scholarization" of vocational training. From this perspective, it appears as a particular mode of scholarization, which recruits its students at the end of the compulsory schooling period from those who have failed to learn adequately the academic disciplines, such as mathematics and French. This scholarization of vocational training, and the concomitant transformation affecting the recruitment of teachers,[12] is marked by the reduction of practical knowledge and the absence of instruction in the social norms of production. As such, it provides the background for a search for new modes of training based on the alternating school/company principle (Tanguy and Kieffer, 1982). This displacement of part of the training process to the company is legitimated less by the need for practical instruction in the workings of the production process at a particular moment in time—which cannot be transferred to the school—than by the need to become familiar

---

[12] Until the early 1970s, the majority of technology and trade teachers were skilled workers in the production sphere. Since then, they have been recruited from above, from those who possess a higher technical diploma but lack experience in production.

with the social conditions of production: i.e., knowing how to work at a given place according to the imperatives of the production line, learning the knowledge held by workers (which goes under the name of experience, for want of a better word, but which is crucial to the smooth running of the production process), and acquiring certain social and physical qualities. In brief, the enterprise, which is organized and functions on the (enforced) cooperation principle of a collective, appears as a necessary complement to school, which recognizes only the individual.

Moreover, while in some respects vocational training is moving towards a technical education that cuts across vocational compartmentalization and responds to the exigencies of new forms of work organization, in other respects it is moving away. What is at stake today is the definition of a form of vocational training that at the same time prepares the individual for life in the working world.

CONCLUSIONS

An analysis such as ours, dealing with the formal organization of curricula, is necessarily limited and will be open to the criticisms that certain English sociologists address to proponents of an objectivist conception of curriculum (Esland, 1971). Even though we have dealt with objectivized facts, we do not support this theory; nor are we, for that matter, close to the interactionist current of Anglo-Saxon sociology, which emphasizes the interactive and intersubjective characteristics of social life. To be perfectly frank, our study is basically empirical and is part of a larger questioning of the political economy of knowledge, a project that remains to be constructed.[13] In France this type of investigation has attracted little interest in the sociological community; this explains why it has been relatively difficult for English sociological literature of the last decade to get a foothold here, thus creating an obstacle for the elaboration and confrontation of scientific problematics and propositions.

Having said this, we recall that our objective has been an analysis of the division between academic and technical education—one of the most pronounced institutional divisions in the French school system and the target of current political and ideological debates. This division is revealed, as has been shown, both in the use of time governing the organization of studies and in the combination of different categories of knowledge constituting the various sections. This study highlights some of the salient features of the modes of knowledge distribution in school: appropriation/alienation of different categories of knowledge, which in our opinion is one of the mechanisms by which the relations of dominance are achieved. While the school organizes for future workers and technicians the conditions for the appropriation of a knowledge of matter, it deprives them of the knowledge that is necessary for them as social beings and political subjects (i.e., to the extent that production processes are taught without reference to the social and economic factors that surround their realization). This appropriation/alienation of knowledge is shown to be the product of market relations in education. It is one of the prerequisites for the presence in the market of a labor force dispossessed of general social skills but equipped with the particular qualities necessary for production: familiarity with machines, familiarity with the technical jargon, acceptance of the idea that techniques are natural phenomena, and, thereby, acceptance of the necessity of the established productive order. This process is particularly evident in the short technical section, which teaches future workers.

The division between academic and technical education is still real, but it is evolving away from a clear-cut and sharp cleavage. In particular, the hierarchical relationship between these two types of education may well be losing strength. In France, academic education still has the highest status, but there has been a reversal of the hierarchical relations within it. Whereas in the 1950s the literary sections were most in demand, now it is the scientific sections that provide a passport to all branches of higher education, including the most highly esteemed of all—the Grandes Ecoles. This hierarchical reversal within the academic section is accompanied by the development of technical education, which tends simultaneously to acquire a higher status.

These movements are developing in a period of crisis, in which all political discourse stresses the importance of the social mutations engendered by the introduction of new technologies, and the school is the target for a growing number of expectations relating to job prospects. Nonetheless, it must be admitted that a cleavage does exist between the school, which still excludes technique from the culture it transmits, and the social movements, which try to integrate technique and its associated values into legitimate culture. That this cleavage is perpetuated, even in a subdued form, makes one wonder if this inferiorization of technical education is not at least partly the product of power relationships within the school system, in which the most influential

---

[13] In this sense, it is close to works like Apple's (1979).

social forces—the intellectual petty bourgeoisie, to which the teachers belong—cultivate a negative and alienating vision of technique. While the teachers agree in theory that technical knowledge has the right to a higher status, in their practice they continue to assign it the second-rate status of a nonacademic education meant for the poor achievers in mathematics and French. This mode of negative selection for technical education is particularly pronounced at the short technical level.

The state of power relationships within the school cannot adequately account for the reproduction, shifts, or reversals in the hierarchy of knowledge, since this phenomenon has its roots outside the walls of the educational institution. Our analysis thus leads to a set of questions concerning the place and role of technical knowledge in the emergence of new social and occupational hierarchies.

REFERENCES

Apple, M. W.
1979 Ideology and Curriculum. London: Routledge and Kegan Paul.

Baudelot, C. and R. Establet
1971 L'Ecole capitaliste en France. Paris: Editions Maspéro.

Bernbaum, G.
1977 Knowledge and Ideology in the Sociology of Education. London: Macmillan.

Bernstein, B.
1971 Class, Codes and Control. Vol. 1. Theoretical Studies Towards a Sociology of Language. London: Routledge and Kegan Paul.
1973 Class, Codes and Control. Vol. 2. Applied Studies Towards a Sociology of Language. London: Routledge and Kegan Paul.
1975 Class, Codes and Control. Vol. 3. Towards a Theory of Educational Transmission. London: Routledge and Kegan Paul.

Bourdieu, P. and J. C. Passeron
1970 La Reproduction. Paris: Editions de Minuit.

Cherkaoui, M.
1982 Les Changements du système éducatif en France, 1950–1980. Paris: Presses Universitaires de France.

Durkheim, E.
1938 L'Evolution pédagogique en France. Paris: Presses Universitaires de France.

Esland, G.
1971 "Teaching and learning as the organisation of knowledge." Pp. 70–115 in M.F.D. Young (ed.), Knowledge and Control: New Directions for the Sociology of Education. London: Collier-MacMillan.

French Ministry of Education, SEIS
1979 Tableaux Statistiques No. 4853. Paris: French Ministry of Education.
1981 "L'Evolution du nombre de bacheliers (1851–1979)." Etudes et documents 2:9–18.
1982 "Origine socio-professionnelle des élèves, filles et garçons, enseignement public." Tableaux Statistiques No. 5132. Paris: French Ministry of Education.

Gille, B.
1978 Histoire des techniques. Paris: Editions Gallimard.
1979 "La Notion de système technique." Technique et culture 1:8–18.

Goblot, E.
[1925] 1967 La Barrière et le niveau. Paris: Presses Universitaires de France.

Gouldner, A.
1979 The Future of Intellectuals and the Rise of the New Class. London: Macmillan.

Gramsci, A.
1975 "Qu'est-ce que l'homme?" Pp. 175–85 in F. Ricci (ed.), Gramsci dans le texte. Paris: Editions Sociales.

Grignon, C.
1971 L'Ordre des choses. Paris: Editions de Minuit.

Isambert-Jamati, V.
1970 Crises de la société, crises de l'enseignement. Paris: Presses Universitaires de France.
1972 "La Notion d'orientation dans l'enseignement secondaire. Analyse historique des critères proposés dans les textes officiels." L'Orientation scolaire et professionnelle 2: 129–41.

Karabel, J. and A. M. Halsey
1977 Power and Ideology in Education. New York: Oxford University Press.

Kosik, K.
1970 La Dialectique du concret. Paris: Editions Maspéro.

Lautier, B. and R. Tortajada
1978 Ecole, Force de travail et salariat. Paris: Editions Maspéro.

Lévy-Leblond, J. M.
1977 "Mais ta physique?" Pp. 112–65 in H. Rose et al. (eds.), L'Idéologie de/dans la science. Paris: Editions Le Seuil.

Rose, H. and S. Rose
1977 L'Héritage problématique: Marx, Engels et les sciences de la nature." Pp. 19–36 in H. Rose et al. (eds.), L'Idéologie de/dans la science. Paris: Editions Le Seuil.

Shils, E.
1972 The Intellectual and the Powers and Other Essays. Chicago: University of Chicago Press.

Tanguy, L.
1983a "Savoirs et rapports sociaux dans l'enseignement secondaire en France." Revue française de sociologie 24:227–54.
1983b "Les Savoirs enseignés aux futurs ouvriers." Sociologie du travail 3:336–52.

Tanguy, L. and A. Kieffer
1982 L'Ecole et l'entreprise, l'expérience des deux Allemagnes. Paris: La Documentation Française.

Young, M.F.D. (ed.)
1971 Knowledge and Control: New Directions for the Sociology of Education. London: Collier-MacMillan.

GENDER RELATIONS IN SECONDARY SCHOOLING

S. Kessler, D. J. Ashenden, R. W. Connell and G. W. Dowsett
Macquarie University

Sociology of Education 1985, Vol. 58 (January):34–48

PROBLEM AND APPROACH

Sex Inequality and Education

There is abundant evidence that inequality between women and men is a very general feature of Western education systems. Differential treatment and differential outcomes for both staff and students have been extensively documented by research over the past decade.[1] In the same period, considerable energy has been spent trying to change it. A stock of nonsexist curriculum materials and teaching aids have been produced, and centers have been set up to disseminate them. In Australia, as in other advanced capitalist countries, there is a campaign to end gender stereotypes in career counselling and subject choice, to get more girls into mathematics, science, and traditionally masculine trades and professions. Sexual harassment is being made an issue in schools and colleges. There are equal-opportunity policies in force in some states, and antidiscrimination laws apply, if unevenly, to education.

Yet the effect of this activity so far has been slight. The resources devoted to it are, at best, painfully small in comparison to the scale of the problem. In New South Wales, for instance, although the funds for the Non-Sexist Education Unit have been maintained in the last year, only a fraction of one teaching consultant's time per region in the public school system has been allocated for nonsexist curriculum development. Moreover, such slender resources are often under threat, both from ideological attacks by the political Right and from cost-cutting campaigns within the bureaucracy.

Furthermore, this work is not always certain of its directions. There is a continuing dilemma about the value of sex-segregated schools or classes. Almost all the educational debate has been about heterosexuals; there is very little serious work on discrimination against homosexuals in the education system. There are problems concerning the mainstream curriculum that are just beginning to emerge; and there are massive, though so far almost undiscussed, problems about how specialists should work with classroom teachers to change sexism in schools.

At this point there is a need not only to renew the campaign for resources for countersexist educational work but also to rethink basic ideas. This article is intended as a contribution to that task. It reports research on gender relations in Australian secondary schools and proposes a line of theoretical analysis that bears on some of the dilemmas of current practice.

The Problems of Sex-Role Analysis

By and large, the discussion of gender and education has been guided by the concept of sex roles. The idea that boys and girls are socialized into different but complementary roles, which then shape their expectations of life and other people's expectations of them, is an appealing one. It fits much common-sense knowledge of how children are treated and provides a language for describing the pressures exerted by parents, peers, mass media, and schools. Perhaps most important, it provides a strategy for change: "One must break down the stereotyped expectations and redefine the accepted boundaries of women's and men's respective roles." This, broadly, is the strategy pursued by liberal feminism. It can also be made to work for men, as shown by men's liberation publicists such as Nichols (1975) and Farrell (1974).

There is no doubt that this line of thought has been useful in opening up educational issues. It has provoked a reexamination of the hidden curriculum and the many ways in which schools and teaching materials have reinforced

---

This article is based on *Ockers and Disco-Maniacs,* a booklet for teachers published in 1982 by the Inner City Education Centre, Sydney, Australia. The material has been extensively revised for publication in this journal. We want to thank the Inner City Education Centre; the now-defunct Education Research and Development Committee, which mainly funded the research; the teenagers, their parents, and their teachers who took part in it; Heather Williams, who did most of the typing; and Pam Benton, who got it all together. Address all correspondence to the authors c/o R. W. Connell, Department of Sociology, School of Behavioral Sciences, Macquarie University, North Ryde, NSW 2113, Australia.

[1] Notable examples are the Australian Schools Commission's 1975 report, *Girls, School and Society,* and the 1979–80 special issues of the *Harvard Educational Review* on "Women and Education."

passivity, dependence, and restricted ambition among girls. Thinking about conventional masculinity and femininity in terms of roles points clearly to the social character of behavior and can suggest useful classroom activities, such as role-playing exercises and discussion of the social expectations felt by the students.

Yet there are problems. The sex-role concept is not as commonsensical as it often seems. It was introduced into mainstream social science in the 1930s and 1940s, and it displaced other concepts of gender relations, which had focused more sharply on questions of power and marginality.[2] Talking about gender relations in terms of roles, internalized expectations, attitudes, and traits directs attention away from larger structures and focuses explanations of inequality on what is going on inside the heads of the subordinated group. It is a classic case of blaming the victim. As Franzway and Lowe (1978) point out in an excellent, brief critique, the idea of sex roles exaggerates the importance of individual attitudes and minimizes the importance of the economic and social forces to which those attitudes are a response. For instance, when a working-class family tries to ensure that the husband rather than the wife stays in full-time work, it is a question of rational judgment in the face of economic necessity rather than a matter of role expectations. Given a highly discriminatory labor market, men can generally get higher-paying jobs. If reformers focus just on attitudes and expectations in such situations, attempts at reform will misfire.

Furthermore, schools, operating in their traditional fashion, do not simply reproduce sex stereotypes or confirm girls in subordinate positions. Certainly they do that much of the time. But they have also long been a vehicle for women who reject conventional expectations and wish to construct their own intellectual lives and careers. There is, therefore, a need for a more sophisticated understanding of gender in its relations with education.

The Theory of Gender Relations

Such an account has begun to appear in recent years from two main directions. First, authors such as Game and Pringle (1983) and O'Donnell (1984) have closely analyzed social relations in the workplace and the segregation of the labor market. It has become clear that the sexual division of labor is not a superficial pattern of discrimination that might be cured by employers' change of heart. It is a fundamental structure that is constitutive of industrial and social authority, intricately interwoven with the design and application of technology, and crucial to profitability. Schooling not only reflects this but also helps constitute it. As O'Donnell argues, the development of the schooling system is part of the process that produces a sex-discriminatory labor market.

The second important development has been the attempt to combine the analysis of gender, as a psychological and interpersonal matter, with an understanding of how a social order as a whole reproduces itself. As Burton (1985) argues, this has been one of the key lines of development of feminist social theory in the last decade. Interesting examples of this work are Chodorow's (1978) psychoanalytic sociology of gender, which discusses how the sexual division of labor gets entrenched in the unconscious, and Willis's (1977) account of masculinity among British working-class youth. Arnot (1981, 1982) develops the line of thought in what is now the most sophisticated theoretical analysis of gender and education available.

This work has been important in bringing structures of power and large-scale social dynamics onto center stage. It is clear that role theory underestimated what it was up against. The schools are an arena in which a complex, often contradictory, emotionally and sometimes physically violent politics of gender is worked out. The strength of the reaction against well-meaning minor reforms is understandable.

Yet there are problems with this theoretical framework too. There is a strong tendency towards functionalism in reproduction theory.[3] It is difficult to incorporate the dynamics of historical change into social-reproduction analyses. There is a tendency to treat "male" and "female" as simple categories and to ignore their complexities and internal structuring. Homosexuality, once again, tends to get written out of the discussion of gender.

We argue, then, that the theoretical framework needs to be shifted further. First, we must find ways of talking about large-scale structures without reifying them and about personal practices without losing their large-scale contexts. To some extent this is a general problem of theoretical social science, which requires the development of an adequate theory of practice (cf. Giddens, 1979; Sartre, 1976; Connell, 1983). Second, we must find the right research techniques so that the issue can be worked out in relation to a particular problem. The research reported in this article uses tech-

---

[2] The history of sex-role theory is reviewed in Carrigan, Connell, and Lee (1983), where these other perspectives are described.

[3] This is documented, for the reproduction theory in Althusser, Bourdieu, and Lefebvre, in Connell (1983:Ch. 8).

niques that we hope will allow these connections to be made. We shall return to the theory of gender after considering some of the empirical evidence.

Method

The project reported here was conducted in 1977–78 in twelve Australian secondary schools; the examples to be discussed in this article are drawn from four of them. A sample of one hundred 14- and 15-year-old students was drawn from two contrasting social-class milieux. Fifty came from working-class families, whose children were enrolled in large suburban coeducational comprehensive schools, which in the Australian education systems are provided by the state governments. Fifty came from ruling-class families, who sent their children to high-fee private colleges, mostly single-sex institutions loosely connected with the major churches. Half came from the city of Adelaide, half from Sydney; regional differences turned out to be negligible. Half were girls and half were boys; sex differences were not negligible.

Each student became the starting point for a cluster of interviews. We conducted relatively long, tape-recorded, focused interviews separately with the student, both parents, as many of the student's classroom teachers as possible, and the school principal. All interviews were done by one or other of the four authors. The main topics covered were pupils' current school performance and relationships with teachers; pupils' school history; pupils' occupational plans and ideas about school leaving; pupils' family and peer relationships and influences on the above; parents' working lives and the social relations of work; the families' educational and economic histories; teachers' views and expectations of the pupils; teachers' relations with the families; teachers' practices and views of teaching; teachers' personal and professional backgrounds and views of the schools they had worked in, including the current one; and relations among teachers in the school.

A cluster of interviews then became the basis for a detailed case study of a particular pupil, in which the authors made a collective attempt to understand the person in terms of the whole network of social relations and socioeconomic circumstances in which the relevant family and school found themselves. This is a very time-consuming and labor-intensive process; but we argue that some such step is necessary if researchers are to understand the relation between individual practice and social structure in more than summary or schematic ways. As the file of completed case studies built up (two years of work produced 43 case studies, at which point funds and time were exhausted), analyses of issues and themes across cases became possible. It also became possible to analyze particular schools as institutions and, finally, to analyze the dynamics of class and sex groupings on the larger scale. In a second round of analysis, the procedure was repeated with case studies of teachers (a total of 37 were produced in three years). Material from the other interviews has also been used but in a less intensive way.

We stress that the case-study method was used here to analyze social relations rather than individual psychology, though questions of personal style, emotion, and motivation certainly do come through. Similarly, the sampling was designed to approach certain kinds of relationships, not to define *a priori* categories. Both class and gender are systems of social relations, not systems of categories. These relations have histories on both the large and the small scale; they interweave to form characteristic situations. When we refer to ruling-class families or to working-class schools, we are referring to a particular kind of situation, in which people develop the practices that are the focus of the following discussion.

It is extremely difficult to make a summary report of evidence that has been analyzed in case-study form. Even Freud complained of the problem. We are conscious that the following accounts of teachers, pupils, and families are drastically simplified. There is no way around this in the context of a journal article. All we can do is ask readers to bear in mind that the details given are not isolated anecdotes but extracts from a very much larger body of evidence and analysis. Those interested will find further details of method, field findings, and analysis of results in *Making the Difference* (Connell, Ashenden, Kessler, and Dowsett, 1982) and in *Teachers' Work* (Connell, 1985). The theoretical argument on gender relations is developed in the context of social theory and class analysis in Connell (1983); in relation to masculinity and sex-role theory in Carrigan et al. (1983); and in relation to psychoanalysis in Carrigan and Connell (1984).

EXTRACTS FROM FIELDWORK

The material available is very extensive. For this article we thought it more important to illustrate major dynamics than to present either representative cases or especially striking individuals. The first section illustrates an important pattern of interaction between activist teachers and nonacademic kids in a working-class school. Next, we describe gender dynamics operating at the school level in the contrasting examples of two ruling-class schools. We then look at gender dynamics in families—first those in which the authority of men has been contested or eroded and then those in which it has been successfully asserted. Finally, we return to the schools and discuss the ideas and practices of two teachers who are grappling with the problems created by these dynamics in another working-class school.

Interactions in a Working-Class School: Resistance and Promotion

Arlette Anderson is a young teacher at Rockwell High School, a state comprehensive school in a relatively new, working-class suburb. It was her first appointment after she finished teacher training. When she arrived, she was shocked by the hostility of her pupils. Within a day or two, one of the boys offered her a direct sexual insult: "Why haven't you got a boyfriend? Is there something wrong with you?" This was but one instance of massive resistance by the kids; and in response, she formed an unflattering picture of them. She described the boys as "ocker deluxes"[4] and the girls as "loud-mouthed disco-maniacs."

Arlette is nobody's doormat, and she bounced back, confronting the kids with their sexism. She tells them what she thinks the boys will be like in ten years: beer-bellied, boozing at the RSL club, totally lacking respect for women. They laugh. In a Year 8 class she organized a debate about the role of women; universal opinion among the boys was that women should stay home and have babies. The boys shy away from classes like Domestic Science: "I'm not doing that; my Dad says sewing's sissy." The girls, meanwhile, learn by the end of their first year in high school that having a boyfriend is a matter of status, and they jeer at those who have missed out. "They don't seem to have any idea of sisterhood at all," Arlette concludes, depressed. The girls agree with the boys that the proper business of a woman is to be a mother. Arlette has pleaded with them. Aren't they interested in even a small career? "Oh no, I want to be a mother."

Bill Poulos, at first sight, might be thought of as a classic example of the "ocker deluxes." He has a contemptuous attitude towards women. He has begun to establish sexual relations with girls in the neighborhood and treats his girlfriend in a decidedly exploitative way. He is in with the "smoking crowd," as a teacher notes, and turned up drunk at a school dance. He is a tough proposition for his teachers—hard to control and very difficult to teach.

Bill is not just bored with school; he is actively angry with it. He feels that he was unjustly put in a bottom class when he came up to the high school, that he has been stigmatized as a result, and that most of the teachers do not give him credit when he does try with his work. However, he has a good relationship with one teacher, who gives him extra attention. He is resentful of the arbitrary authority and petty injustices of school life and has a rich fund of examples: a teacher who screamed at him—he walked out of the class and did not come back; inexplicable decisions by the school authorities, such as stopping competitive football; undeserved canings and detentions; and so forth. He wants to leave school and start an apprenticeship, against his father's advice.

There are some painful experiences, strong emotions, and more than a touch of self-doubt behind Bill's stroppiness towards his teachers. Yet there is also a logic to the combination of aggressive masculinity and resistance to school. Bill's claim to masculinity is reinforced by a tough, don't-push-me-around stance toward school authorities and by petty delinquencies like smoking and drinking. Conversely, his resistance to the school is stiffened by a need to protect a bruised sense of self and to assert his masculine claims to authority and personal space.

The situation is different for girls. Heather Arlott seems to be one of the "disco-maniacs." Though from a different ethnic group, she comes from an economic background similar to Bill Poulos's: Her father is a contract laborer and her mother is a packer in a factory. Most of the time her teachers find her as difficult as Bill; maybe more difficult. When a teacher yelled at Bill, he walked out; when teachers yell at Heather, she yells right back. She will not do what she is told unless she wants to. She laughs out loud, stirs the class and, like Bill, has a fund of stories about teachers' injustices. "Hell to teach" is the staffroom consensus about her. The exception is on the sports field. Heather is an excellent athlete and appreciates the coaching she gets from her teachers.

Heather's resistance to school is quite like the boys', but the situation in which she does it, and therefore its effect, is very different. While resistance among boys confirms and even exaggerates their masculinity, the same behavior among girls violates conventional femininity. The convention is that proper girls

---

[4] *Ocker* is an untranslatable term with overtones of macho masculinity, working-class slovenliness, aggressive Australian nationalism, and expertise in the national sport—beer drinking. The RSL (veterans' club), mentioned in the next paragraph, is by general repute the epitomy of ockerdom.

should be controlled, polite, and biddable; swearing, smoking, yelling at teachers, and truanting are more like protests against femininity than confirmations of it. Heather is a strong person, not just in the physical sense. She is not going to be put down by the Arlette Andersons of this world, nor by the Bill Pouloses. The school resistance of young women like this is a genuine challenge to their subordination as women.

Yet Heather is by no means masculine in style or outlook. She is a keen dancer and often goes with her friends to the local disco. Though she has not thought much about getting married, she has no particular objection to the idea. Indeed it is very likely that she will have to. Working-class girls leaving school early because of conflict with the school are thrown into the least secure part of the labor market. Youth unemployment currently runs up to 35 percent in areas like Rockwell. Within a few years, Heather's best chance of economic security will probably be to attach herself to a husband. Even then, given the decline in real wages, she will have to hold a job to keep a family much above the poverty line.

Much of this is not known very clearly in the Rockwell High staffrooms. The conditions of teachers' work make it difficult for most of them to learn much about their pupils' personal backgrounds; and Heather's own responses inevitably antagonize the teachers, because she makes their work more difficult. Though Heather really needs help from teachers like Arlette Anderson in understanding this difficult and contradictory aspect of her life, and though Arlette really has something to give students like Heather by way of a new understanding, in practice they stand off from each other across a barrier of mistrust and incomprehension.

The girls who are different, in Arlette's eyes, are the "bright" ones in the upper streams, those selected for academic success and headed—some of them at least—for matriculation. It is these girls who are finding something useful in Arlette's feminist ideas. We interviewed a number of girls in the "A stream" at Rockwell High. While they express a good deal of tension and uncertainty about their futures, it is clear that they are contemplating patterns of work and marriage that are very different from those open to girls like Heather Arlott. For many of them, the sympathetic support of teachers like Arlette Anderson is the key to their project of constructing a career.

In Two Ruling-Class Schools: Change and Reaction

What is an uncertain prospect to the A stream at Rockwell High is a vivid reality to their counterparts at Auburn College, a prestigious and expensive private school for young ladies. While less than 30 percent of Rockwell High's pupils go through to the Year 12 Matriculation exams, about 90 percent of Auburn College's pupils do; and they do to some purpose. Auburn's pupils are consistently carrying off high honors in the hard sciences (math, physics, and chemistry) and winning entry to the professional faculties at universities.

This school has, in fact, recently undergone a renovation of staff and curriculum, caused partly by changed ideas about careers for women among its clientele, augmented by feminist ideas among its staff.[5] Formerly, the school's main concern was to produce young women properly fitted out for marriage, motherhood, and ruling-class social networks. Its main concern now is to equip the girls for academic competition and entry into the professions. The social set among the girls has lost its place in the sun to the academic high-flyers; and the consequences for relationships with the men of their class are already being registered, a little apprehensively, by their parents. Fathers contemplate their daughters' possible impact on the business world; mothers wonder if they will reject the traditional model of femininity-in-marriage.

We see here a shift towards a model of femininity in which marriage is expected to be integrated with professional careers, and the simple subordination of women's work to husbands' careers is challenged. No corresponding change has occurred in the ruling-class boys' schools.

Nevertheless, in boys' schools too, the school is an active maker of gender, in this case masculinity. A major focus is sport and the emotions surrounding it. This is very clear at Milton College, a boys' private school whose clientele is similar to Auburn's—i.e., mainly business and professional families. Every Saturday in the season, the boys play football against age-grade teams from similar schools under the eyes of their teachers (the coaches) and their parents, who come to shout encouragement, praise, and criticism. Winning the match matters to all three groups. Demotion to a lesser team can be deeply distressing to the boys. One boy we interviewed, small for his age, actually suffered concussion more than once before a teacher could persuade him and his father that he should play in a lighter grade.

Is this a cult of healthy bodies and school spirit slightly overdone? No, there is something much more systematic here. Football at

[5] We have discussed the transformation of this school in detail in another article (Connell et al., 1981).

Milton College is, above all, a medium for the construction of a particular kind of masculinity. It celebrates toughness and endurance, relentlessly promotes competitiveness and fear of losing, and connects a sense of maleness with a taste for violence and confrontation. Moreover, because the game has an honored place in this school, the kind of masculinity it promotes, the tough and macho kind, subordinates other kinds of masculinity. The boys who for reasons of physique, capacity, or preference have been relegated to study, nonviolent games, debating, and the like are condemned by the football heroes to be known as "the Cyrils," a term indicating effeminacy.

Three Families: Patriarchy Eroded

At the top end of the labor market, formal education has plainly been important as a route leading women into the professions. But this has not always worked smoothly, as is shown in the life of Dr. Somerset, the mother of one of the girls at Auburn College. Sally Somerset, who is working very hard at school and doing well, is headed for the university and one of the professions; she is still undecided which. Dr. Somerset went to a private girls' school herself and was its first graduate to become a doctor. But her promising career was cut short when its demands conflicted with her husband's. She was forced to give up the job and has not practiced for nearly twenty years. That was a bitter experience, and it shaped her view of women's place in the world in ways that have influenced her daughter's schooling. It is one important pressure behind Sally's trajectory towards the professions and a new model of marriage.

Of course theirs is a very privileged situation. But there is pressure for change in working-class families too; married women in these families have taken jobs as office cleaners, chicken packers, checkout operators, sandwich makers, label stickers, and so on. It was clear in many of our interviews with parents that wives who earned a wage did have an important resource in the internal politics of the marriage. Heather Arlott's mother, for example, works in a boring and low-paying job, but she is an equal partner in the family and vigorously resists any attempt to impose authority on her from any quarter, including the school.

In some cases the independence goes further. Mrs. McArthur, who works as a clerk in a small firm, has no particular belief in solidarity among women. In fact she finds most women at her office small-minded and irritating and prefers dealing with men. Yet men's pretensions infuriate her. She is sharply conscious of managers' prejudice against women and of the limits therefore set to her own prospects; she is one of those women who run a business from behind the scenes while the men take most of the profits and all the prestige. She walked out of a first marriage, which she found unsatisfying. She is now without question the dominant partner in her second marriage, and the authority figure in her family as well as its main earner.

In situations like this, there is a real and conscious shift from earlier models of womanhood. This is often conveyed to daughters, just as Dr. Somerset's views on independent womanhood have been. In Sally Somerset's case this led to an embrace of the academic curriculum, an enthusiastic endorsement of the educational goals of her school; but in working-class life it is very likely to lead to conflict with the school. That is true, for instance, of Mrs. McArthur's daughter Kate. We have mentioned the state of war between Heather Arlott and Rockwell High. With Kate McArthur it is, if anything, worse. She is stubborn, opinionated, and regarded as a troublemaker. Like Bill Poulos, she is angry at the school for having shoved her into a low stream. She is fighting every authority in sight, her mother and the teachers equally. The teachers' picture of Kate is almost wholly negative. She is demanding to leave school so she can go on the dole—an ambition her mother is scathing about.

It is easy to see here that a strong and unconventional mother has conveyed some of those qualities to her eldest daughter. It is also understandable that the teachers, confronted with angry resistance, fail to see Kate's vulnerability and need. The education that working-class mothers got in their own childhood gave them no resources for understanding and working through the complex changes that are occurring in gender relations. It seems that the schools are proving no more useful to many of their daughters.

Yet conflict with the school is not the inevitable outcome of these changes. Elaine Markham is a member of the A stream at Rockwell High, in fact one of the school's academic stars. Her mother is a person quite like Mrs. McArthur—equally the source of strength in the family and conscious of prejudice against women. Mrs. Markham had wanted to become a journalist but was bitterly disappointed when forced to leave school early because *her* mother could see no point in education for women. Having fought free of a dominating mother, she is determined that her girls will not repeat her frustration and has pushed them hard at school. Elaine has taken over this project, internalized it, and become competitive at school. Like her mother, she is contemptuous of "the little housewife" and of her schoolmates who are growing up in that image. Though she will not go as far as "Women's Libbists," burning bras and demonstrating in the street, she firmly supports the overall idea of women being equal. But all this has not come easily. She sometimes comes home from school in tears, caused by tension and frustration. She talks of the school as a "dead" place. She is thinking about leaving early despite her academic success.

The corollary of Mrs. Markham's strength is Mr. Markham's marginality. Elaine's father is a storeman and earns below average wages, which is why his wife had to take a job. He came from a very poor family, left school at age 15, and has held a range of jobs. He gets pushed around a good deal at work, and while he is antagonistic toward unions, he is angry at his bosses for not giving him recognition and a better wage. He finds that their pressure for profit erodes the service his unit can give and offends his pride in workmanship. The work situation, in short, constantly erodes his self-esteem. He tried to assert patriarchal rights in the family; for example, he refused to take on a share of the housework when his wife took a job. But the main consequence has been that he has become increasingly marginal in the household. The women have concluded that he has failed as a husband and father; and he too, rather wistfully, now accepts that opinion of himself.

Two Families: Patriarchy Affirmed

Such situations of contested or eroded patriarchy are not found in the majority of families. The pressures experienced by Mr. Markham are common, but the outcome is often different.

For example, Mr. Poulos, Bill's father, has faced pressures at work possibly more severe than Mr. Markham's, including a serious industrial accident, loss of his job, and a permanent loss of earning power. But he has successfully asserted patriarchal authority at home; his wife has accepted a subordinate place. Mr. Poulos's male-supremacist attitudes—"Thank heaven I haven't got a daughter," "I'm boss here"—go unchallenged. Bill's masculinity has been formed against this background, and it is plain that he has absorbed much of his father's outlook. Some hypermasculine interests, notably boxing, have been passed on. More importantly, Bill is beginning to reproduce the same pattern of relationships with women, treating his girlfriends the way he has seen his father treat his mother.

Because it is frequently assumed that the successful reproduction of such patterns in the younger generation is a smooth and easy process, it is worth dwelling for a moment on the difficulty and pain that is really involved. The economic and personal stresses on Mr. Poulos have been severe. His masculinity, especially the way his sense of self is bound up with being a head of family and a good provider, has been sustained only at the cost of harsh struggle, which has left its mark in his attitudes toward women. Bill's relationship with his father is tense. He was severely beaten in childhood; after all, being beaten "made a man of me," says Mr. Poulos. Bill is resentful of his father now, especially over the issue of school leaving.

Bill's self-esteem is also under attack, not only from most of the teachers, who would be glad to see the back of him, but also from many of the other kids, who insult him because he is Greek. His family derides his enthusiasm for surfing. Another enthusiasm, music-making, is pursued entirely outside the school, since the music curriculum there is exotic and academic by turns. Bill is frustrated at the point where he really does want to make contact with the school. It is clear that his masculinity is being constructed in the context of a great deal of conflict, anxiety, and frustration. That he is in no sense an isolate—he has plenty of friends of both sexes and gets on well with his mother—perhaps makes this point even more significant.

The amount of effort that goes into apparently straightforward role modelling or social reproduction can also be seen in the Prince family. Here, things are a good deal more comfortable. The family revolves around the work and leisure of Mr. Prince, who holds a steady job as a maintenance worker for a public authority and is a leading figure in the local junior football league. Mrs. Prince is a nearly full-time secretary and a full-time mother. They have a comfortable and well-equipped home, which they built themselves in one of the older and more secluded streets of Rockwell.

Delia, their 15-year-old, is everyone's picture of a nice girl. She is quiet and pleasant, a shade diffident, and cooperative with her teachers. She would like to be a veterinarian, but if she does not get the necessary grades, she will take a clerical job, as her mother and older sister have. She then expects to marry at age 20 and have her children.

It all looks effortless. Not so. The central place that Mr. Prince's work and interests hold in the family was achieved at the cost of Mrs. Prince's ambition to become a nurse. He did not like the hours, so she gave it up. She got a job in a bank but, in accordance with its policy, was sacked when she married.

Mrs. Prince did not stay at home when the kids were little, because she was working to pay off the block of land they built their house on. She now feels guilty about having neglected them and is running herself into the ground trying to be the perfect mother as well as a wage earner. Delia's peer relations are very carefully supervised; her parents even introduced her boyfriend to her! Her mother made her abandon a peer group who smoked and got drunk on weekends. In short, the production of Delia's conventional femininity has involved a lot of work and anxiety on all sides.

Two Teachers: Working on Gender

In gender relations in the school, as in so much else, teachers are central. The teachers do the main work of maintaining the conservative gender regimes of ruling-class schools like Milton College; and teachers were central to the remaking of the gender regime at Auburn College.

The teachers in state schools with working-class clientele face more complicated gender issues, and their responses are varied. In the course of our interviews we met a wide spectrum of attitudes. Some are antifeminist. Some are complacent. Some are grappling with the issues but more or less in the dark; for example, some are struggling with working-class kids' resistance to school without seeing the gender dynamics involved, usually because of lack of knowledge of the families. Others like Arlette Anderson are consciously addressing issues of sexism.

What this last group are doing is itself very diverse. We have described Arlette's attempt to attach at least some of her charges to a project of academic advancement. Let us briefly introduce two other teachers, who are working in another school with a similar catchment, which we call Greenway High.

Margaret Atwill, in her fifties when we interviewed her, is one of the few women in her generation who approached teaching as a full-scale career from the start. She has risen through the ranks, has done her country service,[6] has been a department head and a subject consultant, and is currently deputy principal in a large working-class school. Women of her generation characteristically faced a conflict between conventional femininity and a career. Margaret has not married; but she has not abandoned what she values in femininity. Kindness, gentleness, and nurturance have remained leading features of her personal style and have specially flavored her relations with girls.

Yet she is not a home science teacher or even a humanities teacher. On the contrary; she is a science teacher and has made a career as a specialist and curriculum consultant in what is regarded as an exceptionally hard-edged and rigorous subject. It is possible that this made the career/femininity issue even harder for her. At all events, she is determined not to become a bluestocking, not to become tough, and she does not regard herself as a feminist.

Nevertheless, what she is doing has a great deal to do with the problems created by sexism. She is the only woman among the senior staff of her school. Consequently, she has been made the school's de facto expert in "problems that involve girls": truancies, family traumas, emotional crises, pregnancies, conflicts with male staff, and so on. Her position is somewhere between the old post "Mistress in Charge of Girls" and an informal trouble-shooter for the rest of the administration—the men hand over these problems to her with an almost audible sigh of relief. Because her position is informally defined, her responsibilities are open-ended and endless. Lately, for instance, there has been increasing harassment of the girls at bus stops after school. Margaret has instituted a patrol to try and stop it, and she has had to do it herself.

By contrast, Mary Coleman's classroom career has just begun. She is a humanities teacher and is now in her second school, just a few years out from an honors Arts degree and a very frustrating teacher-training course. Unlike Arlette Anderson, she is teaching in a mainstream academic area. She labors to convince her somewhat skeptical students of the importance of general ideas.

Like Margaret Atwill, she does not see herself as a feminist. But she is very much aware of sexism in the school. She notes that the principal, a man, does not like women and has "as little to do with them as he possibly can." She notes the underrepresentation of women in the upper levels of the school and the extra burden of work that falls on those who are there, notably Margaret.

Like Arlette Anderson, she is conscious of sexism among the boys. Of a particular ethnic group she remarks, "They're treated like little gods; they're brought up to think they're definitely superior to women," and notes how that carries over into their relationships with women teachers. But she attributes the origin of this to the family, not to the school.

She is content if the school treats boys and

[6] Teachers in the Australian state systems, especially those seeking promotion, are normally required to spend some time teaching in small rural schools. This is a key means by which women have been disadvantaged in the promotion structure.

girls with formal equality; and she cannot see any overt discrimination in what her school is currently doing: "I haven't seen in this school any evidence that girls are treated worse than boys or that girls are told they're girls and therefore they're going to be bad at maths and science or whatever." The boys can do home economics, the girls can do metalwork; but it does not bother Mary that very few do. Her critique of sexism is directed to staff meetings, not to the classroom.

INTERPRETATION

Rethinking Gender and Schooling

Most discussions of sexism in education have assumed that the school produces sex-role conformity in one way or another. Thus, the important 1975 Australian Schools Commission report summarized its argument by saying that "throughout its curriculum and organisation the school differentiates between male and female students in ways which reinforce sex-stereotyped expectations" (Australian Schools Commission, 1975:78).

It is true that there are many ways in which schools mark out conventional gender differences. Girls' uniforms are skirts and dresses, boys' are slacks and suits. On sports days, girls are put in netball teams, boys in football. Timetables force choices between metalwork and cookery; because it is assumed that girls will become secretaries and boys draughtsmen, it is difficult for either to be the reverse.

The argument about stereotyped expectations is correct up to a point but does not catch the full force of this. The school is actively engaged in constructing gender. In this light we can see the cult of football at Milton College as a powerful masculinizing practice, quite consciously designed to that end. At Auburn College, the school is actively engaged in *re*constructing gender. Rockwell High, whose progressive headmaster has just abolished competitive sport, is trying, in a less systematic way, to do the same.

The stereotype argument is more seriously wrong in assuming that the school tends to impose just one sex-role pattern on its boys and one pattern on its girls. This is plainly not the case in either ruling-class or working-class schools. Even Milton College produces both the football heroes *and* "the Cyrils." Rockwell High produces Bill Poulos *and* the A-stream boys. Auburn College produces both the new professionals *and* the socialites, who have lost their preeminent position.

What the school is mainly doing here is arbitrating among different kinds of masculinity and femininity. Perhaps we should say that since much of this occurs outside the scope of any conscious policy, the school provides a setting in which one kind or another becomes hegemonic. The cult of football, for instance, does not and cannot obliterate all other kinds of masculinity. Indeed, Milton College needs boys whose character allows them to focus on academic work, because their high results in public examinations sustain the school's leading position in the marketplace. Therefore, it produces other masculinities but marginalizes them, while giving most honor and admiration to a tough and dominant virility.

We may summarize these observations by saying that the school as an institution is characterized at any given time by a particular *gender regime*. This may be defined as the pattern of practices that constructs various kinds of masculinity and femininity among staff and students, orders them in terms of prestige and power, and constructs a sexual division of labor within the institution. The gender regime is a state of play rather than a permanent condition. It can be changed, deliberately or otherwise, but it is no less powerful in its effects on the pupils for that. It confronts them as a social fact, which they have to come to terms with somehow.

A great deal of what happens in schools is outside the immediate view of the school authorities. There is an unofficial school, constructed by the kids themselves, that exists in the gaps and crannies of the official institution. It is in this informal peer-group life that much of the politics of gender is worked out. It is here, for instance, that pressure to compete in sexual attractiveness to boys becomes a reality for the girls, a major source of the divisiveness that Arlette Anderson observed. The gender regime of the school includes the relationship between these processes and the policies of the authorities. Some teachers deliberately try to intervene in the kids' peer relationships. Arlette is one; Margaret Atwill is another. Other teachers do not intervene; and the contradictions between different teachers' strategies are fruitful sources of difficulty for the school.

A major reason the gender regimes of schools have proved difficult to analyze is that some of the most important effects are indirect, involving mechanisms that do not at first glance appear to be related to sex and gender. One such mechanism is the process of academic selection. In working-class high schools, selection in the form of "streaming" or "setting" and differential drop-out after the legal leaving age split off a relatively small group of boys and girls and define them as winners: the A stream at Rockwell High, for example. The process encourages in this group a kind of masculinity oriented to competitive achievement and a kind of femininity directed towards careers. The difficulties encountered have already been discussed in the case of Elaine Markham. More efficiently, the system of academic competition constructs a group of losers, such as Bill Poulos and Kate McArthur, and shapes sexual identities for them, as these cases suggest and as the research by Samuel (1983) and others on school resisters confirms.

At a deeper level, the academic curriculum itself, the core of the knowledge that the secondary school offers, is connected to the power relations of gender in the larger society. This issue is as yet poorly understood, but we can glimpse some of its main dimensions. First, the academic curriculum is constructed on a principle of authority: What is taught in schools is guaranteed by the authority of university disciplines. This authority is overwhelmingly in the hands of men, notably senior academics. Thus, the academic curriculum is based on knowledge that reflects practices and institutions controlled by men.

Second, the academic curriculum depends on clear-cut distinctions between right and wrong and between relevant and irrelevant. It has little room for ambiguity, for multiple layerings of truth and meaning, or for open-ended explorations. Some recent feminist research suggests that such a perspective on knowledge and such forms of expression are characteristic of masculine thinking. We qualify this and suggest that it is associated with a particular kind of masculinity that is currently hegemonic. Subordinated groups have a more decentered ego and a less single perspective on the world. Thus, the academic curriculum expresses the perspective of the dominant group in the dominant sex.

Third, the curriculum is divided into compartments, or subjects, that reflect the priorities of the dominant group. This organization of knowledge does not correspond to the needs of subordinate groups. For example, unemployed inner-city youth need survival science, not geography and chemistry. There have been some attempts to respond to these needs—for example, in "transition education" programs for working-class youth in Australia, and in women's self-education resources, such as *Our Bodies, Our Selves* (Boston Women's Health Collective, 1975). But such efforts remain marginalized in the schools.

Finally, the singleness of knowledge in each subject area finds expression in a technical language. "Learning the subject" means mastering its technical terms and adopting its special style. A good deal of feminist research suggests that femininity does not find expression this way (Eisenstein and Jardine, 1980; Marks and de Courtivron, 1981). Rather, its expression is likely to be oblique and discontinuous—such as the kind of expression stigmatized by men as "women's gossip"—and may even occur in the silences, rather than in what is explicitly said. Gay consciousness, too, has often found oblique and muted expression. The academic curriculum expresses a relation between knowledge and language that arises mainly from hegemonic masculinity.

The character of the curriculum in turn raises questions about the people who teach it. It is curious that much progressive writing on education has ignored teachers—their aspirations and ideas about what they are doing, their personal histories and emotional make-up, their work histories, industrial situations, and unions. The same is true of discussions of sexism in education, with some notable exceptions (e.g., Sexton, 1969). It is important to note that sexism in schools affects teachers as well as pupils. This is not just a matter of discrimination against women teachers, though that is real enough. Arlette Anderson is not joking when she calls her principal a male chauvinist; and Mary Coleman is sincere in her sympathy for Margaret Atwill, the only woman in a heavily masculine school executive.

It is also important to examine the teachers' relations with their pupils. The whole system of gender relations is a major source of the tensions and difficulties teachers face in working-class schools. These range from drastic problems of discipline with rebellious kids like Heather Arlott and Bill Poulos, to the more subtle problems of student motivation or the hidden injuries of gender suffered by Elaine Markham and Delia Prince.

Teaching inevitably involves emotional relationships. How these issues are handled thus depends on the construction of masculinity and femininity in the teachers' own lives. The families sketched in this article produced the current generation of kids; families very much like them produced most of their teachers. The teachers have also been through a specific kind of training; many of the younger teachers in the schools encountered feminism in the universities and colleges and have reinterpreted their own lives in its light. Finally, as career teachers, their masculinities and femininities are worked out further as they deal with problems of authority and discipline, the curriculum, their own careers, and the complex emotions involved in caring for kids. To understand the gender regime of a school, one must understand the way gender relations impinge on different groups of teachers, the responses they make, and the strategies they try to follow.

It is clear that a patriarchal gender regime is embedded, at a number of levels, in virtually every recess of the Australian education system. There is every reason to think the same is true in other, comparable countries. This may appear to be a pessimistic conclusion, and in relation to the high hopes of liberal feminists and sex-role theorists it probably is. But if this conclusion forces us to see the whole structure as much more massive and intricate, that is not all on the debit side of the ledger. We can also see more of the tensions and incoherencies of the structure and hence the possibilities of structural change. It is the task of theory to try to make those clear.

Implications for Theory

The biological basis of gender has been one of the most difficult issues to grasp in discussions of sexism. In some way, the social relations of gender are built on the physical differences between males and females and on their different ways of participating in the reproduction of the species. But how is that to be recognized without falling back on the discredited doctrine that gender is the social expression of male and female biology? The evidence on schooling suggests a very different relationship. In the process of growing up—and this is very clearly shown in the experience of puberty—the bodily process becomes an object of social practice. The social relations of gender become embodied, quite literally, in the construction of masculinity and femininity. The gender regime of a high school is not an expression of sexual biology so much as a social means of dealing with it. In many respects it contradicts, rather than expresses, the biological statute. The result is a dialectic of biosocial development rather than an expressive relationship.

The evidence from education also points to some fundamental features of the social relations involved in gender. The literature on sexual equality often takes "men" and "women" as unproblematic, fixed categories. This is reasonable for first-approximation statistical studies, but it is disastrous if taken as a basis of theoretical analysis. Gender is a complex social structure, not a simple one. It involves a range of institutions, from the family to the state, together with their interactions. It involves different levels of personality, a very wide range of types of social interaction, and it produces a complex differentiation of people around the axes of masculinity and femininity. Even apparently very simple examples of conventional masculinity and femininity prove to be underpinned by a complicated network of social practices. Delia Prince is worth recalling—one of the "great gray mass in the middle" (as they often appear to teachers), who never attract much attention or do anything very surprising. It is easy to think, therefore, that there is no stress, drama, or contradiction in their lives. That would be a serious mistake.

One aspect of the complexity of gender that is very clear in the material already presented is the diversity within masculinity and femininity. The biological processes producing male and female bodies interact with a whole range of different family patterns, courses of growth, institutional pressures, and personal choices. The dialectic issues in many kinds of emotional attachment, different personality traits, and different ways of participating in social life. Delia Prince, Elaine Markham and Heather Arlott illustrate the diversity within the one milieu; they all live within a few blocks of each other.

Yet this variation is not random. Particular kinds of behavior, particular ways of being, are culturally dominant. These are the ones that come to be seen as the pattern of masculinity or femininity in general and are often assumed to be the natural characteristics of each sex. Other kinds of behavior and character are defined as deviant or inferior and attract derision, hostility, and sometimes violence. We have come to refer to the dominant patterns as "hegemonic masculinity" and "emphasized femininity." Their hegemony within particular institutions is defined by the gender regimes discussed above in relation to schools. It is clear that the pattern that is hegemonic in one institution is not automatically so in another.

To call them "hegemonic" and "emphasized" is to stress that they are not necessarily the *most common* patterns—the mistaken assumption made by most sex-role theorists. Not many men or boys really are the strong, cool, fit, competent, macho types who populate cigarette ads and other such daydreams, though most men's lives are still affected by the presence and potency of that image. What is hegemonic at any given time depends on how the relations among different kinds of masculinity and femininity have been worked out. That negotiation is one of the key roles of the school.

Negotiation is perhaps too mild a word for a process that involves unequal resources and a considerable amount of coercion. Part of this is a matter of direct control and force. We have referred to the bullying of "the Cyrils" by the football heroes at Milton College, the muted violence that the school permits. Girls at ruling-class schools are mostly protected from such treatment, but working-class girls are much more exposed to it. Physical intimidation of women by young men in the streets of Rockwell was mentioned by several of the mothers we spoke to and is one of the reasons they place more restrictions on the movements of their daughters after dark than on their sons. The sexual harassment of girls by boys is one of the issues Margaret Atwill has to deal with at Greenway High. Force is also a component of patriarchal authority within many families, as the case of Bill Poulos illustrates. Studies of domestic violence (Johnson, 1981; Craney and O'Donnell, 1982) demonstrate that this is far from an isolated case.

In other families, such as the Markhams, an internal struggle for power occurs and is resolved by other means. Who wins out in such circumstances largely depends on the resources that can be mobilized. A number of forces have caused women as a group to have less economic resources than men, often a great deal less. These include the way the labor market has generally assigned women to low-paying or part-time jobs; the way the education system has excluded women from most trade and professional training; and the way the relationship between jobs and families has made women rather than men leave jobs (like Mrs. Prince) to take on child care, thus losing seniority, skills, experience, and confidence.

To generalize, one of the key dimensions of gender relations is power. Analysis shows that the power dimension of gender regimes exists inside families as well as schools. The schools, in turn, connect to the larger structure of the state and are part of the sense in which we must understand the state as a patriarchal institution, constituted by sexual politics as well as by class dynamics.

In none of these cases is the pattern of power or the sexual division of labor completely fixed, as we have seen in working-class mothers' return to the labor market. The gender regimes of schools are capable of being changed, as Auburn College illustrates. The consciousness of groups of participants alters, as the emergence of feminism among teachers shows. The character of sexuality itself changes. The pattern of sexual relationships found among the kids in contemporary high schools has altered from what it was a generation ago; the students now are sexual beings in a much more open and obvious way, a change especially important for girls.

Gender relations, then, are historical. The pattern they assume in any society is produced by its particular history and is always in a process of transformation. Even when change is slow to the point of being invisible, the principle should be kept in mind, because it directs attention to the ways in which the patterns of gender are constantly being produced in everyday life. An awareness of the tensions and contradictions of that production process, the difficulties it encounters, and the resistance it arouses, is vital in understanding the way the structure changes as a whole.

It is a safe generalization that power is never exerted without arousing some kind of resistance. Women's liberation and gay liberation are the most organized and visible forms of resistance to patriarchal power at present, but they are not the only forms. Mrs. McArthur, Mrs. Markham, their daughters, and Heather Arlott embody a working-class feminism connected with the very large changes in women's employment and the power balance inside families. It is a feminism without banners, with a flavor and set of concerns different from those of the intellectuals' feminism, but nonetheless involving a real challenge to men's power and to the restriction of women's lives. The same is true among teachers. There are many who, like Margaret Atwill and Mary Coleman, would not call themselves feminists but who are nevertheless confronting the same issues and trying, in a variety of ways, to do something constructive about them. There are others, like Arlette Anderson, who have a well-developed conception of the issues.

Countersexist programs in the schools, then, do not face a scene of total desolation. There is a widespread, though inchoate, concern with sexuality, sexism, and discrimination; and there is reason to think this grows out of some structural changes and can be mobilized to produce more. If the resources and ideas were widely available, a lot of people would use them. It is time to consider who and how.

Implications for Practice

The main current approach to the reform of sex inequalities in education is the equal-opportunity strategy. Its central idea is the elimination of all obstacles to advancement by talent—i.e., the prejudices, self-doubts, and extra burdens that hold women back from advancement through education. The forms it takes are campaigns to get girls into new areas such as trades and mathematics; elimination of sexist stereotypes from teaching materials; struggles for equal promotion rights for women teachers; and so on.

Given that the resources already committed to reforming sexism are slender, one is reluctant to be critical of anyone who is seriously trying. Yet our evidence argues strongly that there are serious weaknesses in this approach. First, the equal-opportunity strategy assumes that the institutions in which advancement is sought are more or less neutral. That is far from the truth: Not only is the education system mainly controlled by men, but it actively constructs gender and actively produces women's subordination. Second, the knowledge that is sought is not neutral. When the culture makes an equation between masculinity and technical expertise, not only do competence and expertise become part of the definition of masculinity, but masculinity also comes to define valued expertise. Women pursuing expertise may find it being redefined as they reach for it. Third, equal-opportunity programs have almost nothing to say to boys that might affect their part in the construction of gender relations. Fourth, by taking the categories "men" and "women" for granted and by focusing on the goal of access, such strategies deemphasize the question of gender construction and hence tend to ignore the oppression of homosexuals in the educational system. Finally, equal-opportunity strategies are usually deliberately class-blind in a way that makes them liable to be class-biased. A program that encourages girls to enter professional or semiprofessional careers by stressing academic advancement has an entirely different effect in a working-class school like Rockwell High than it has in a ruling-class school like Auburn College. In the former, such a program can only reach a minority. It separates them from the bulk of girls, who are defined as failures and frequently pushed into opposition to the school's program. In such circumstances equal-opportunity strategies are likely to defeat themselves.

We argue, then, that what is good in equal-opportunity programs has to be placed in a new context and in various ways given new aims. In broad terms, it is a question of directly addressing the issues that equal-opportunity strategies take for granted. The aims should be to empower subordinated groups, rather than give selective access to existing hierarchies; to democratize the curriculum by reorganizing knowledge to advantage the disadvantaged; and to mobilize support for democratization of the schools in relation to gender, as much as other structures of power.

In this kind of program the curriculum is strategic, and it is important that there are already movements and resources for democratic curriculum change in the schools. The academic curriculum may be hegemonic, but it is not the only one available. Craft teaching, for instance, embodies a different organization of knowledge and often involves very different teacher-pupil relations. The academic curriculum also contains contradictions. The claim to universality that it makes—the attempt to embody the best in human culture is one of the admirable things about it—is plainly at odds with the way it functions to exclude the majority of students from full participation in the culture. That kind of contradiction gives teachers room to move.

Reform means reconstructing the relationships among the four main groups who are immediate actors in the sexual politics of schools: the teachers, girls, boys, and parents. In helping girls change their situation in gender relations, it is necessary to develop their personal strength and confidence. There is a risk, when this is converted into schemes of assertiveness training and the like, of substituting issues of personal style for issues of substance. Girls like Heather Arlott and Kate McArthur are already angry and aggressive enough; that is part of their strife with the school. Girls like Delia Prince, however, might benefit from programs to develop girls' self-confidence.

What all of these girls mainly need are real sources of power: marketable skills, much more knowledge of what is happening to them, solidarity with others in their situation,and the chance to get decent jobs. Any program that is a point of entry to those questions is worthwhile. The key thing is the substance of competence and control over their own lives.

In winning that, the relationships girls are able to form with their teachers are important. We have already seen how much they vary. Arlette Anderson had reached a stand-off with the nonacademic girls but was getting on famously in classes with the A stream. Margaret Atwill was succeeding with the nonacademic girls but mainly outside the classroom. The teachers at Auburn College were practically being swept along by the pressures for academic achievement and professional training among their elite clientele. But none of them seem to have made much progress with the issue of resistance to school among girls. This is a crucial problem for countersexist strategy, for it is both a point of opportunity—as we noted with Heather Arlott, resistance to school often involves resistance to subordination as women—and a point of peculiar difficulty, because the girls are in conflict with the institution through which most educational programs have to operate. There are models for teachers working with school resisters (see Hawkins, 1982); we have documented one remarkable case from this study, a teacher working mainly with boys, in another article (Connell et al., 1984). Changes must be made in teachers' working conditions and in the labor process before they can work effectively with girls who are resisting school.

Given that gender relations are constantly being produced afresh in everyday life, boys must also be considered important clients for countersexist education. They tend to stay out at present, partly because they are not addressed and partly because they are easily made antagonistic. If, as they are told, women's liberation means women on top, what can it mean for them except the loss of masculinity, which is something they have been strenuously taught to fear?

Yet there is something more positive to build on. We talked to a good many boys who were not threatened by the *idea* of equality for women; some of them firmly supported it. Their difficulty was in seeing how it related to them in practice. Adolescent boys' desire to understand the changes going on in their own lives, as well as the changes in the world around, provide strong motives for exploration and learning, which teachers can employ. Men teachers have a particular responsibility and opportunity here, because what they say and do influences what kind of masculinity is hegemonic in the school. Countersexist programs can speak directly to boys about forms of masculinity that do not involve aggression and dominance over women.

Finally, the relationship between teachers and parents demands attention. Parents are often seen as the villains of the piece, full of reactionary attitudes and suspicion of teachers. There have certainly been some hair-raising episodes when the political Right has mobilized, claiming to speak for parents, to block new curricula and sex-education programs, such as the occasion in 1978 when new social science curricula were banned in Queensland (Smith and Knight, 1981). But our strong impression is that in such cases, the Right speaks mainly for itself. The parents we interviewed were concerned not so much that the school should keep out of this area, but that what it did should be done responsively and well.

More than this, the schools can find significant resources among parents for work on these questions. Mothers like Dr. Somerset are strongly behind the program of schools like Auburn College. The experience, outlook, and energy that we have spoken of as "working-class feminism" could likewise be an important resource for schools like Rockwell High. The difficulty is in tapping it, for it is also characteristic of working-class schools that there is a great gulf between the teachers and most of the parents, a product of the class relations that operate in mass education. Yet it can be crossed, even on issues of sex and gender. Many parents will be receptive to well-thought-out initiatives from the schools, because they are very much aware that things have been altering in this area of life. They sense the historical changes, and they sense their importance for the kids, though they often do not know what to make of them or what to do about them. There is space here for work by teachers. One of the most constructive moves for the sexual politics of education would be to make it possible for teachers in general to use it.

There is no guarantee that these uncertainties and possibilities will be resolved in a progressive direction, that is, one that actually diminishes sex inequality and gender-related oppression. There is a formidable resistance, some dimensions of which this article has suggested. Change is not always for the good; new forms of sex discrimination and exploitation have emerged in recent years along with moves towards equality. Yet the central fact, perhaps the most important point our interviews have demonstrated, is that the complex of gender inequality and patriarchal ideology is not a smoothly functioning machine. It is a mass of tensions, contradictions, and complexities that always have the potential for change. While there is that potential, there is also the possibility of constructive educational work.

REFERENCES

Arnot, M.
1981 Class, Gender and Education. U.K.: Open University Press.
1982 "Male hegemony, social class and women's education." Boston University Journal of Education 164:64–89.

Australian Schools Commission
1975 Girls, School and Society. Canberra: Australian Schools Commission.

Boston Women's Health Collective
1975 Our Bodies, Our Selves. 2nd ed. New York: Simon and Schuster.

Burton, C.
1985 Feminism and Social Theory. Sydney: Allen and Unwin.

Carrigan, T. and R. W. Connell
1984 "Freud and masculinity." Forthcoming.

Carrigan T., R. W. Connell, and J. Lee
1983 Hard and Heavy Phenomena: The Development and Underdevelopment of the Sociology of Masculinity, 1900–1980. Sydney: School of Behavioural Sciences, Macquarie University.

Chodorow, N.
1978 The Reproduction of Mothering. Berkeley: University of California Press.

Connell, R. W.
1983 Which Way Is Up? Essays on Sex, Class and Culture. Sydney: Allen and Unwin.
1985 Teachers' Work. Sydney: Allen and Unwin.

Connell, R. W., D. J. Ashenden, S. Kessler, and G. W. Dowsett
1981 "Class and gender dynamics in a ruling-class school." Interchange 6:102–17.
1982 Making the Difference: Schools, Families

and Social Division. Sydney: Allen and Unwin.
1984 "Teaching for survival: Joe Riley and the working class." Social Alternatives 4:11–14.

Craney, J. and C. O'Donnell
1982 Family Violence in Australia. Melbourne: Longman Cheshire.

Eisenstein, H. and A. Jardine (eds.)
1980 The Future of Difference. Boston: Barnard College Women's Center and G. K. Hall.

Farrell, W.
1974 The Liberated Man. New York: Random House.

Franzway, S. and J. Lowe
1978 "Sex-role theory: Political cul-de-sac?" Refractory Girl 16:14–16.

Game, A. and R. Pringle
1983 Gender at Work. Sydney: Allen and Unwin.

Giddens, A.
1979 Central Problems in Social Theory. London: Macmillan.

Harvard Educational Review
1979-80 Women and Education. Special Issues 49.4 and 50.1.

Hawkins, G.
1982 Resistances to School. Sydney: Inner City Education Centre.

Johnson, V.
1981 The Last Resort. Melbourne: Penguin.

Marks, E. and I. de Courtivron (eds.)
1981 New French Feminisms. Brighton: Harvester.

Nichols, J.
1975 Men's Liberation. New York: Penguin.

O'Donnell, C.
1984 The Basis of the Bargain. Sydney: Allen and Unwin.

Samuel, L.
1983 "The making of a school resister: A case study of Australian working-class secondary schoolgirls." In R.K. Brown and L.E. Foster (eds.), Sociology of Education. 3rd ed. Melbourne: Macmillan.

Sartre, J. P.
1976 Critique of Dialectical Reason. London: New Left Books.

Sexton, P.
1969 The Feminized Male. New York: Random House.

Smith, R. and J. Knight
1981 "Political censorship in the teaching of social sciences." Australian Journal of Education 25:3–19.

Willis, P.
1977 Learning to Labour. Farnborough: Saxon.

COURSE ENROLLMENT IN THE HIGH SCHOOL: THE PERSPECTIVE OF WORKING-CLASS FEMALES

JANE GASKELL
University of British Columbia

Sociology of Education 1985, Vol. 58 (January):48–59

This article argues for a new approach to the study of tracking in the high school, an approach that emphasizes the active and knowledgeable role students play. In addition to the more frequently studied issue of class segregation in school tracking, the article examines the often overlooked phenomenon of gender segregation. Interviews with girls who selected business courses are used to illustrate how students' knowledge of the school and of the society produces course choices that in turn tend to reproduce class and gender categories.

One way that schools create differences among students is by enrolling them in different courses. This process of differentiation sets students on different paths towards adulthood. Academic courses prepare students for the university and for professional and managerial jobs. Industrial arts courses orient students towards blue-collar work. Math and science courses allow them to enter technological fields. Business courses teach them what is involved in secretarial or sales jobs. Home economics courses prepare them for domestic tasks. In a very concrete organizational form, one can see the genesis of the divisions that shape adult life.

There is a good deal of evidence that class, ethnicity, race, and gender are related to the courses students take (Breton, 1970; Heyns, 1974; Porter, Porter, and Blishen, 1982). Working-class students and students from minority ethnic and racial groups are less likely to take academic courses. Girls are more likely to take home economics courses and courses that prepare them for clerical and secretarial jobs. Boys are more likely to take industrial arts courses. Course enrollment is thus one

Address all correspondence to the author at the University of British Columbia, Vancouver, British Columbia, CANADA V6T 1Z5.

way the categories of gender, class, and race are reproduced in the school and are linked to adult social position. Despite its key place in the production of the existing social order, course enrollment has been neglected by educational theorists interested in reproduction; instead, they stress ideology and socialization in the school (e.g., Apple, 1982).

The question of how differential course enrollment comes about needs much more careful empirical and theoretical attention. In the academic literature, terms such as "placed in," "selected," "decided on," "chose," "channelled into," "assigned to," and the noncommittal "end up in" can all be found and are usually assumed, not explored. Ability grouping, which is done solely by the teacher, has been equated with curriculum differentiation (Persell, 1977). In general, the sociological literature assumes that course enrollment patterns are produced by the school, not by the students. It explores the criteria the school uses to sort students (Heyns, 1974; Davis and Haller, 1981) and the role school records and counsellors play in placing students in different tracks (Clark, 1960; Cicourel and Kitsuse, 1963; Rosenbaum, 1976). There is, however, a psychological literature that uses models emphasizing students' choices and the importance of students' attitudes, perceptions, self-concepts, and psychological traits (Meece et al., 1982).

The issue is partly empirical and should be studied more carefully. There are important variations between schools and over time in the number and kind of options offered to students and in the relative importance of student choice and school assignment in determining course enrollment. Historically, high schools have moved from a single course of study to a relatively fixed hierarchy of curriculum tracks to a more open system of curriculum options (Boyer, 1983; Porter et al., 1982; Laxer, Traub, and Wayne, 1974). The causes and consequences of these variations need to be explored. It is important to specify the particular arrangements in any school that is being studied. A regression equation that describes the relationships prevailing at one point in time cannot be generalized unless the kinds of institutional arrangements it is describing are known.

There are also variations within schools among different kinds of courses, so it is important to specify which course is being discussed. Bernstein's notions of framing and classification are useful in analyzing these differences (Bernstein, 1975). Enrollment in a tightly framed and classified subject like English is strongly influenced by the school's assessment of ability. Enrollment in art or music classes is more open to student choice. The two may be linked, as in the school Rosenbaum (1976) studied, where ability grouping in core subjects in the junior high school was translated into a wide variety of curriculum options in the senior high.

The question of choice versus placement involves more than empirically sorting out which model applies in any particular case. It involves theoretical issues of the relationship between individual agency and structure. In every case, both the student's orientation and the school's organization are involved. Even in a relatively open system, school staff limit the available choices, shape the way students see themselves and their options, and offer advice, veiled threats, encouragement, and strongly worded suggestions. In a relatively closed system, students must still comply, but preferably, they are made to see that the courses they are taking are in their best interests. The problem, then, is to reconceptualize the issue in a way that incorporates both the orientation of the student, i.e., individual consciousness, and the organization of the school, i.e., social structure. This takes us to the heart of a major problem in social theory. Structural theories and correspondence theories have for too long regarded individual action as an unproblematic reflection of social structure. They have misrepresented the consciousness of the relatively powerless by assuming it can be constituted as an internalization of the dominant ideological messages. Such claims are empirically incorrect. As Giddens (1979:72) points out,

> A good case can be made that only dominant class groups have ever been strongly committed to dominant ideologies . . . all social actors, no matter how lowly, have some degree of penetration of the social forms which oppress them.

Structural theories also misrepresent power as an entity residing in powerful people or positions rather than in interactions. This underplays the political importance of relatively powerless groups. In Giddens's words, "Power relationships are always two way; that is to say, however subordinate an actor may be in a relationship, the very fact of involvement in that relationship gives him or her a certain amount of power over the other. Those in subordinate positions in social systems are frequently adept at converting whatever resources they possess into some degree of control over the conditions of reproduction of those social systems" (Giddens, 1979:6). Teachers are quite aware of this dialectic in the schools. Students must be actively persuaded of the logic of the educational enterprise, and some are never persuaded.

In emphasizing students' choices, it is important to avoid a model that reifies and decontextualizes their attitudes and traits. As Laws (1976) points out in her discussion of women's work aspirations, motivation is dynamic and responsive to the social context, rather than static and individually "owned." For example, an individual may be hardworking in one setting but lazy in another if the one setting provides more incentives and a more congenial atmosphere than the other.

Willis's work (1977, 1981) is an attempt to deal with these complexities. He explains how a group of working-class lads "chose" working-class jobs, and he incorporates a careful structural analysis of the school and the society in which the choices emerged. He concentrates on the lads' choices: "The difficult thing to explain about how working-class kids get working-class jobs is why they let themselves . . . . It is much too facile simply to say that they have no choice. There is no obvious physical coercion and a degree of self-direction" (Willis, 1977:1). He emphasizes their "sense of activity and practice and what feel like (and are to the participants) circumstances creatively met" (Willis, 1977:3).

In this article, I will explore how course enrollment differences arise by adopting this theoretical orientation and by emphasizing students' belief that they choose, while embedding their orientations in a specific institutional context. This approach avoids some of the problems in earlier research on course tracking and points to the need for more case studies of specific tracking practices in specific courses and schools.

METHOD

The data in this study are drawn from a series of interviews with young people in Vancouver, Canada. One hundred male and female students were interviewed in 1976 during their last year of high school. This article is based only on the responses of the 47 girls.

The students interviewed came from three high schools, all of which were in neighborhoods that were below the average attainment levels in the 1971 census. Parents' occupations could not be systematically surveyed, because the school put restrictions on the questions that I could ask. However, none of the students who volunteered this information had professional parents.

I explained to the students that I was interested in the relationship between school and work, and I asked those who were planning to go to work next year to volunteer for an interview. The guidance counsellors supported the study and urged students to participate. They also tried to ensure that a wide variety of students (from their point of view, of course) were included in the resulting sample. This method of selecting students was dictated by the school; therefore, I cannot guarantee that the sample is representative. However, as the schools themselves are not representative of any known population, other selection procedures would not have increased the confidence with which the results can be generalized. As the social and educational context in which these girls' perceptions were generated is specific, I can make no claims that their perceptions are shared widely by high school females. This research must be treated as a particular case study in a particular setting, not as a report on a representative group of female adolescents. More research on other populations is necessary to explore the issues raised in this study.

The interviews covered the courses a student was taking, her reasons for taking the courses, her response to the courses, her work experience, her work plans, and her views of femininity and of gender divisions at school, at work, and in the family. I use terms like "a few" and "most" to describe their responses, because using the exact numbers would suggest a quantitative certainty that is not warranted by the research design. A second interview was carried out a year later, but information from that interview is not included in this article.

The interview format allowed a fairly extensive discussion of school, work, and gender. It was loose enough to allow the students' own categories and assumptions to emerge. The young people were encouraged to describe how their world was structured and what they liked and disliked about it. They were pushed to explain what they took for granted and to consider what was wrong with alternate routes. Their explanations and common sense emerged in the interviews in a way that a questionnaire would not allow. However, the accounts of motivation elicited in the interviews must be regarded as those the students deemed appropriate in an interview with a university researcher. Different accounts might well have been elicited with different audiences in different settings. When discussing schooling with one's children, when reminiscing with one's schoolmates, or when talking to a university-based interviewer, different rules apply and different accounts are appropriate. I have no way of checking how the accounts students gave me differ from or are similar to other accounts. Can we make any statements about what students know or what they believe without specifying the context in which the account is given? Some would say no (Mishler,

1979). However, the value of the interview is in eliciting a public account. These accounts are important because they challenge some of the interpretations of course choice that have been provided in the academic literature. They are also politically important, because they constitute public discourse.

The process of coding and analyzing the interview comments was complex. The interviews were transcribed and read several times. They were then analyzed by sorting comments into categories such as division of labor in the home, bringing up children, and the importance of work for women. Profiles of individual students were also developed in order to understand the interrelationships among attitudes. The original transcripts were often reread by more than one research assistant in order to check for accuracy and relevant additional information.

The Vancouver schools have little ability grouping before grade 10, and curriculum options open up, subject to a complex set of distribution requirements, in grade 11. The options are defined not as ability tracks but as a series of choices in different departments—music, history, business education, French, home economics, and so on. Relatively speaking, the process seems fairly open to student and parent input. The official school-board policy is that enrollment decisions are ultimately the responsibility of the family, although the school has some input. The student handbook states that course decisions are "a joint responsibility shared by students, parents, and staff, to ensure a suitable program is undertaken, but final responsibility rests with the parents." This is different from the school policies described by Cicourel and Kitsuse (1963) and Rosenbaum (1976).

Instead of focusing on all course choices, which I assume are handled in the same way, this article focuses on the choice of business courses. There are two reasons this particular choice is important. First, choosing business courses means opting out of the academic, i.e., high-status, stream. This is an important step towards reproducing one's position in the working class. Academic courses prepare students for postsecondary schooling. Professional and managerial jobs are likely to require postsecondary schooling; working-class jobs are not. Much of the concern about curriculum differentiation has arisen from its functions in segregating and channeling working-class children (Bowles and Gintis, 1976; Lazerson and Grubb, 1974).

Second, the enrollment in business courses is overwhelmingly female. This gender division in course enrollment corresponds to the sexual segregation of the labor force. Secretarial and sales jobs have all the characteristics of quintessentially female work—little responsibility and power, low pay, and little room for advancement. Thus, the girls in this study chose courses that were likely to reproduce not only their class position but also their subservient gender position.

THE ISSUE OF CHOICE

There is a good deal of evidence that students believe they choose their curriculum track, whatever the coercive practices of the school actually are. Jencks et al. (1972) note that 84 percent of all students surveyed in the Coleman report said they were in the track they chose. Rosenbaum (1976) reports that 87 percent of his noncollege students stated that they chose the track they were in. Davis and Haller (1981) also found a strong relationship between what students chose and where they ended up. They note that two-thirds of those whose choices are discrepant with their placement are in a higher track than the one they chose, which reinforces the importance of understanding what makes nonacademic curricula attractive to students.

The girls interviewed in this study were no different. It was striking that they saw themselves as completely responsible for their curriculum choices: "I did what I wanted. It made sense to me." They provided a variety of reasons for taking the courses they did and rarely mentioned pressure from their parents or the school.

Only a couple of girls directly attributed their course enrollment to the guidance counsellor or the school:

> The counsellors look at your grades. So I took commercial . . . basically because my counsellor told me. She seemed to think I would be better fitted to those courses.

> I wanted to take academics, but they wouldn't let me.

These comments suggest a number of things that have been pointed out in the literature. Grades are important, and curriculum tracks have many features similar to ability tracks. Moreover, counsellors can take an active role that goes beyond formal school policy. But the Vancouver counsellors appeared to have neither the authority, resources, nor respect to play a critical role in course selection.

> The counsellors we've got here are just completely terrible. They don't know what they're doing . . . to tell you the truth, I think [names the school] counsellors just don't get enough training or whatever it takes to become a counsellor.

> There is not enough counsellors. They're having to take care of a whole grade of people. They're spending most of their time running through the papers and there's not much time for them to sit around and rap.

> Counsellors are no good. [They are] just phys. ed. teachers who have been moved to guidance.

Many of the students felt that counsellors could be ignored, and they exercised their power to disregard them.

> The counsellors suggested daycare, but that means one or two more years at Langara [a community college]. I don't want more school.

> The counsellor kept saying you'll never get a job unless you can type. But I just picked what I'd enjoy.

Like guidance counsellors, parents infrequently had a direct influence on course selection. Although they were given the official and legal responsibility for course choices, they were not part of the everyday processes of the school and thus were least likely to be well informed. Few students reported a direct intervention by their parents. Most of the students said that their parents let them do whatever they wanted: "They let me make up my own mind." If advice was offered, it was to include academic courses and to keep open the options for postsecondary education.

> My parents encouraged me to take arts and sciences to go to university and be a teacher.

> My dad advised science. I didn't like science, but I figured he knew better. But now I wish I had taken more business courses. They were what I really liked. I thought they were fun.

These students saw themselves making choices, often creative ones, designed to resolve the dilemmas that arose out of the structure of schooling, femininity, and work. Understanding why they took certain courses thus involves understanding their reasoning, rather than simply understanding the power and interests of parents, teachers, and guidance counsellors. Their assumption of responsibility for course choice was important because it led them to accept the consequences of their choices and to blame themselves for the restricted options they faced later. It affected the organization and morale of the school, because students tended not to blame or feel beholden to the teachers or counsellors on issues of course enrollment. In these ways, the students' consciousness both drew on the existing structures and served as part of the process of recreating those structures.

WHY CHOOSE NONACADEMIC COURSES? THE REPRODUCTION OF CLASS

One of the major divisions among courses is between academic courses, which fulfill the prerequisite for university entrance, and other courses, which do not. Most of the literature on tracking has conceived of a single vertical axis of differentiation with academic courses at the top. The use of this axis arises from and clearly displays the class hierarchy involved in course selection.

The student handbook highlights the importance of the postsecondary/no postsecondary divide by printing the entrance requirements for universities and community colleges. Course descriptions clearly indicate those courses that are designed for postsecondary students:

> This is a valuable course for students in preparation for further English courses at the university.

> This course is required for most universities and technical institutions.

> Feedback from BCIT, Langara and university students indicate this course is of tremendous advantage to biology related courses in their area.

The handbook also indicates the academic ability required for entrance:

> A better than average achievement in English is necessary for success in this course.

> An average or better mark in mathematics correlates well with success.

In emphasizing the relationship between a student's achievement and her choice of academic courses, schools construe class differences as achievement and ability differences. Those who are less bright take vocational courses and get working-class jobs. Such is the IQ ideology (Bowles and Gintis, 1976) or the masking of cultural privilege through an ideology of unequal giftedness (Bourdieu and Passeron, 1979).

Was this the perspective of these girls? A few girls did describe their choice of courses in light of some fairly stable notions of their abilities and their personalities, which suggest a hierarchical world in which brains and hard work are rewarded:

> I'm not university material. I don't have that much brains.

> I'm lazy. I wouldn't work unless I have to.

But most of these girls believed that their choices arose not out of their unequal giftedness but out of a quite sensible inability to tolerate the pointlessness and childishness of school. They did not like school, especially the academic courses, and they did not think that what they could learn there was useful. They suggested that in such an environment, any reasonable person would opt out:

> It was ridiculous. . . . Maybe ten minutes of it you can learn.
>
> School is boring. You can't change it.
>
> I don't like the rigid system—hour after hour—or demanding notes if you are sick or late. I miss classes because I won't be missing anything.
>
> I stared out the window and at my hands, like everyone else.

These girls questioned the justificatory ideology of the school rather than being socialized into it. They located difficulties in the educational environment that confronted them and in the lack of decent opportunities that existed there, instead of in their own abilities and attitudes. But this unmasking of the school's ideological rationale did not lead them to challenge the organization of the school. It led them to find ways around it, to try to pick the best set of courses they could out of a bad lot.

They tried to come up with personal solutions that would minimize the discomfort school caused them. They took courses that were easy (i.e., courses that did not intrude too much into other, more important aspects of life), fun (i.e., courses that involved less time sitting at a desk, more work experience, and more interaction), and useful (i.e., courses that transmitted skills that had some direct utility in the labor market or in leisure activities). These criteria led them far away from an academic program.

Bowles and Gintis (1976) suggest different motives for the selection of vocational courses—motives deduced from structural differences in the schooling and work experiences of working-class and middle-class families. Working-class jobs and vocational courses are more likely to be characterized by alienation, a clear hierarchy of control, and punitiveness (see also Oakes, 1982). Therefore, working-class families prefer stricter, more routinized educational practices. Similarly, "that professional and self-employed parents prefer a more open atmosphere and a greater emphasis on motivational control is a reflection of their position in the division of labour" (Bowles and Gintis, 1976:133). Track assignment, they conclude, springs from working-class students' self-concepts and preferences, which are appropriate to their future position at work.

Such a straightforward correspondence does not characterize the consciousness of the girls in this study. They saw course differences in more substantive terms. They rejected academic schooling not because it was too open but because they believed it was irrelevant. Vocational courses were perceived as less regimented and less confining than academic courses. Other studies suggest that this explains a good deal of the appeal of work/study and career awareness courses (Farrar, De Sanctis, and Cowden, 1980; Watts, 1980).

Willis explains that his lads chose working-class jobs because they valued manual labor over mental labor, they resisted authority, and they wanted diversion and enjoyment. Though these girls were more diverse in their cultural traditions and expressions of disenchantment with mental labor than Willis's lads, there were some common themes in their responses. They were quite able to question the educational paradigm that asserts the fair exchange of cooperation and work for knowledge and moral superiority. They wanted a break from regular schooling and saw practical job skills as more worthwhile than irrelevant academic information.

The girls' accounts construe course divisions as horizontal rather than vertical: Some people like some things, others like different things. However, they live in a world where higher marks and academic pursuits are associated with higher status, more economic opportunities, and more money. In schools, marks are the official currency, and as the course descriptions make clear, high marks go with academic courses. It is hard for an aware participant in the school or the society to ignore completely the vertical nature of the divisions.

These young women produced accounts of course differences that indicate an awareness of the hierarchical nature of school programs. According to these girls, students in academic courses "think they're better." "University is necessary to really get ahead these days." These comments were not offered as easily or as often as other accounts, but the contradictions and diversity they indicate must not be ignored. To some extent, different students produced different emphases in their accounts. A few were more likely to say, in effect, "I am dumb and the bright kids go on to university." Other students were more likely to indicate that school is boring and that anyone sensible would have as little to do with it as possible. But sometimes, one individual gave contradictory accounts. These contradictions suggest, as Sennett and Cobb (1972) have indicated, that there are hidden injuries associated with nonparticipation in academic success, even when cultural forms and an understanding of oppressive relations make alternative meanings available. These injuries are hidden in that they are not easily elicited in interviews with higher-status persons. They may be produced more often in the kind of in-depth and personal discussions used by Sennett and Cobb.

Does this mean the girls really believed that they were inferior or that the system was unjust? The question is unanswerable in these terms. Both kinds of accounts are real. Different methodologies will reveal more of one than of the other. What is at issue in this study are public, everyday, easily and frequently elicited responses. These have both political and practical significance in the school and in the labor market. The girls discussed the choice of vocational courses as a choice to avoid the worst stresses and irrelevancies of school. The structure and organization of school was critical for them. They suggested that if school work had been more involving or more useful, they might have chosen otherwise. Their acquiescence in the process of selecting themselves out rested on their understanding of the school experience. Their critique of school did not go very far. It focused on individual teachers, counsellors, and specific course content rather than on the organization of the entire venture. It did not lead these girls to suggest much in the way of alternatives except better teachers and more work experience (Gaskell and Lazerson, 1981). They overwhelmingly rejected the value of school and the school's equation of academic performance with merit and deserved power, but they accepted the school's power to create links between academic performance and success in the labor market.

WHY TAKE BUSINESS COURSES? THE REPRODUCTION OF GENDER DIVISIONS

In the high schools I studied, not a single girl took industrial education at the grade 12 level, but almost all the girls who were not planning to continue their schooling took at least one business course. The gender segregation of courses is very large, but its existence has been ignored in the literature on tracking because a single vertical axis has been used to describe the differences among courses: "The use of the terms high, average and low track classes seemed to cut through the terminology differences at the different schools and levels, and identify classes according to their essential characteristics in terms of student classification" (Oakes, 1982:201). Although a unidimensional vertical ranking of courses displays class divisions, it makes gender divisions disappear. Girls are just as likely to be in the high-track, academic courses. Gender divisions appear as horizontal divisions within each track—for example, as language versus science options in the academic track, or as business versus industrial options in the vocational track.

Gender divisions in the school curriculum correspond to divisions in the labor force, just as class divisions do. The correspondence between school tracks and gender divisions must be taken as seriously as the correspondence between school tracks and class divisions. Occupational segregation by gender has influenced the way curriculum options are defined at school, and the organization of this school training has affected the shape of occupational segregation by providing a generous supply of skilled female workers trained at the public's expense for a narrow range of jobs.

Why did the girls choose the business courses and not the industrial courses? There were four factors that were mentioned in their accounts: the advantages of clerical work, the availability of specific skill training in business courses, the lack of opportunities in industrial work, and the impact of domestic labor.

The girls overwhelmingly chose clerical courses in order to prepare themselves for clerical jobs. The course descriptions make clear that this is the purpose of the courses. In the school calendar, the business course descriptions stress usefulness in the labor market, specifically in secretarial work: "as many types of written language projects as are relevant to office work will be included"; "should be capable of handling books in a small business firm"; "qualifies a student for a high standard secretarial position." These are the courses that were most attractive to the girls. Other, more general courses attracted a greater mixture of males and females. These include courses in general business ("investing your money, conditions of employment, home-ownership and mortgages, etc."); accounting, marketing, and distributive education ("to develop in the student personality and skills which will enable him to become an intelligent consumer and achieve success in the field of marketing"); career exploration ("to overcome the tendency of students to drift into careers with the result that they find their jobs largely unfulfilling"); and personal finance ("to enable students to make the best possible use of their income through sound money management").

Why is clerical work attractive? Most importantly, the jobs that are available to women in a competitive labor market are clerical jobs.

> I don't like typing, but it is the easiest way to get a job. It's boring and tedious just sitting there. But if you can get a job you might as well take it.

> The only jobs are for secretaries these days. You might as well get trained.

> [I took commercial courses] because I wanted to be someone's secretary. You know, there is a big demand for secretaries.

This perception, many would argue, is a misguided one. Clerical jobs are disappearing with the introduction of new technology. There are more opportunities for women in other areas of work (Menzies, 1981). But one-third of all employed Canadian women and over half of all employed female high school graduates work in clerical jobs (Statistics Canada, 1980). The girls accurately perceived that there are a large number of clerical jobs of many different types in many different locations. The women they knew who had jobs had clerical jobs. It is difficult for a counsellor or a new economic survey to discount the students' overwhelming experience of where the jobs are.

Moreover, the literature on youth employment shows that youth are twice as likely to be unemployed as adults are and that they tend to take the first job that comes along (Osterman, 1980; Blackburn and Mann, 1979). In a period of economic crisis, this is even more pronounced. Instead of choosing a job, the job chooses them. As one girl put it, "If you can get a job, you might as well take it."

Clerical work has other attractions besides its relative availability. It has higher status than blue-collar work and provides more security and better working conditions. When asked why she took commercial courses, one student responded,

> To fall back on commerce. My mother forced me to. She is a janitoress and she said I could do better than her. She sees all these women working in an office and she said you're going to do better than that.

It provides a setting that is comfortable to work in, where there are likely to be other young working-class women to socialize with. It is attractive because it is a women's occupation.

> Girls together can be funny and dirty. I can be more open with women around.

The organization of training for clerical work also provides an incentive to take commercial courses. The girls pointed out that these courses were directly relevant to finding a job, unlike other courses in the high school. The courses in industrial education prepare students not to enter a trade but to embark on trades training after graduation ("recommended for students going on in engineering or architecture"; "designed to fulfill the requirements for admission to vocational school") or to develop avocational skills ("the skills necessary to repair and maintain his own vehicle"; "constructing a stereo") and sometimes intellectual skills ("to illustrate the fundamental principles of science"). They do not provide the edge in the labor market that commercial skills do. If anything, they have such low status that employers and community colleges prefer academic students. Carpentry courses do not make one a carpenter. One still has to go through an apprenticeship. The same is true for other industrial arts courses and for the home economics courses.

Only commercial courses provide skills that give an immediate advantage in the labor market. If they did not learn to type and understand office work, the girls were running the risk of getting no job at all. In a competitive labor market, taking clerical courses was the best way these young women could prepare themselves for the jobs that they saw as available to them.

This view that business courses are the only sensible option for nonacademic girls was shared even by young women who could provide extremely negative accounts of clerical work and business courses. They regarded these as boring or, at best, "not so bad": "It's always inside and just sitting down at the desk and doing nothing." These girls felt pressed to take the business courses "to fall back on" in case they couldn't find another job. The courses were a safety net, the wisest choice because they were directly relevant to finding a job.

If the advantages of office work and training were not enough to attract a girl, the disadvantages of the male alternative, industrial work, were likely to repel her. Many of the girls felt that the industrial courses and industrial work were difficult, dirty, and uninteresting. The most common response to the question "Why didn't you take industrial education?" was "I'm not interested."

> It's o.k. for girls to do what they want—be carpenters or whatever. But it's not for me. I just don't like it.

They described how socialization had shaped their responses:

> Maybe it's the way I've been brought up.

> We've always been taught to be the soft touch, like the cute sex, just sitting there.

> I was pushed away from it as a little girl—dolls, not hockey and trucks.

They even had plans to change it:

> I think [girls] should be encouraged into other jobs, but not just from our age. I think from elementary school, because you get

> dolls and the little guys get trucks. So you're always influenced on that kind of a path.

> You've got to be trained from the beginning to make things equal. I'd like to start a camp. I wouldn't tell the kids who were boys and who were girls. No girls' and boys' bathroom. Everyone would be exposed to everything—trucks and dolls.

But given their current interests and achievements, it did not make sense to do industrial work.

Some girls, despite their socialization, were interested in industrial work:

> I like to do the jobs men do. I think they are more interesting.

> I wish I had taken woodwork. I like working with wood.

> It would be exciting to be a truckdriver. But I wouldn't know how to go about it.

> Men's jobs pay more.

Thus, the status, activity, money, and even unfamiliarity of male work gave it a certain appeal.

However, their perception of barriers inside and outside the school came into play. Peer and teacher pressure, which often amounted to sexual harassment, made industrial courses a very difficult choice.

> When I was going into grade 10, I tried it [auto] but it was a mistake. There were all guys in the class and I felt too stupid.

> The second year I was the only girl in the class, and I felt really stupid, so I didn't want to go back.

> This year I got into Auto Mechanics 12. It was all guys and when I walked in they thought I was really stupid. You know, "Oh, we got a girl," and they were irate, so I transferred out.

> Because I am a girl, and there are only boys taking the courses, I'd get a name in the school. Girls are rowdy who take it.

> The teacher is a male and he doesn't encourage females. He gives us mostly written work. We used to complain, and he would say, "Well, the boys can do it for you." He probably thought it [auto class] was dangerous for us.

Barriers in the labor market also seemed to make industrial courses a waste of time:

> They wouldn't hire a female. It distracts everyone.

> I was thinking of going for an electrician, and then someone said something: "What? You're a girl!"

Furthermore, they felt that the working conditions would be difficult:

> Truck drivers are weird people and they would harass her.

> You couldn't talk about the same things if men were around—what you did last night, and all that.

Thus, socialization and the perception of opportunities combined to make industrial education a much less favored option. Socialization did not "take" with all the girls; but the perception of opportunities ensured that even those who were not traditional in their interests still chose the traditional options.

A final factor in course selection was the issue of domestic labor. Most of the girls assumed that they would have primary responsibility for the domestic labor in their families (Gaskell, 1983). This by no means arose from a wholesale endorsement of the domestic ideology. Although about a quarter of the girls said domestic work was what they were particularly suited for and wanted to do, most said they would feel trapped at home, wanted the independence provided by a paying job, and said housework was a chore that should be shared. But they wanted husbands and they wanted children, so they felt they would have to do the domestic work for a variety of reasons based in their perception of the world and the opportunities available to them. Men, they said, would not or could not do it.

> Sharing the housework would be wonderful. But it is not going to happen. He'd [boyfriend] never help with the floors or the dishes. I know him too well.

Alternate forms of childcare, which could free them for a paying job, were perceived to be inadequate. No man could or would stay home with the kids.

> Men aren't used to it and don't want to do it.

> Daycares and babysitters are not good for children.

> You'll be a better mother if you stay home with the kids and not throw them out with the babysitter . . . because they learn bad habits.

Moreover, as women, they were likely to be contributing less to the family income than their husbands; so they felt they should be the ones to pick up the extra domestic work and, when necessary, give up their paying jobs.

> The most practical approach would be the one with the most money would work.

As a result of all these calculations, even those girls who had no particular desire to do domestic labor expected to drop out of the labor force or work part-time when they had small children. Even though many assumed that they would return to work after their children had grown up, their views of this later period were very hazy. What they planned for was largely the next five to ten years. They wanted to get their training over with quickly so that they could get a job and have some independence for a few years. They were less likely than boys to feel that they had years to explore the labor market. This added to the attractiveness of business courses and clerical jobs. They could do their training quickly in high school, and the training would develop a skill that would always be useful and flexible. Furthermore, clerical jobs were relatively available and could be pursued part-time.

What these young women knew about their world produced the obvious choice of business courses. They saw a world in which business courses had many advantages and industrial courses had few. Their knowledge was based in some very tangible structural conditions—the opportunity structure in the labor market, the vocational role of business courses, the existence of sexual harassment in male occupations, and the assumption of family responsibilities by women. These are "penetrations" of the structure, seeing it as it is. The girls sometimes objected to this structure. They did not like sexual harassment in class. They felt that employers should hire women in nontraditional jobs. They did not want to do all the domestic chores in the home. But for all these perceptions of different conditions for men and women and their professed commitment to equality of opportunity, their conscious, rational, self-preserving calculations helped to reproduce gender segregation for themselves and others. They did not see this as a predetermined or imposed fact but as one they actively chose as best for themselves.

There were different routes to the same decisions. Some girls incorporated domestic ideology more fully than others. Some resisted secretarial work more strongly than others.Some found the option of work in male areas more tempting than others. While their choices may not have been made with the sense of elation and confidence that Willis's lads expressed, they were regarded as reasonable, even good solutions to the problems the social structure confronted them with. What is striking is not that some girls resisted, but that despite their resistance, so many of them continued to choose very traditional paths through school, paths that reproduced both class and gender categories.

DISCUSSION

Why is it important to examine the girls' perceptions of the world? It scarcely needs to be pointed out that these girls did not produce adequate analytic accounts of the process of course selection in high schools. Their representations are interpretations, as all accounts are, involving selecting, highlighting, cutting and editing. In their stories, they underplayed some of the things they knew in order to maintain their own dignity. They used the same factors that others used to justify different choices. Their information on labor markets, men, teachers, and so on, was based on specific experiences and particular ideological assumptions.

However, these accounts highlight some aspects of school and work and gender relations that are concealed by other investigations. As Smith (1977:16) points out in a brief history of the development of the women's movement, "Shifts in the women's movement came about in part as women from other spaces than those originating the movement began to be heard and listened to—housewives, for example, who refused to be despised, women who had children or wanted children and could not accept the derogation of motherhood that was important in the early stages. . . . Issues and analyses had to shift and deepen accordingly."

A political process is different from an academic one, but the conception of how new knowledge is developed is useful. Working-class women's knowledge of the world and the questions they ask have not been part of academic discourse. Awareness of their views challenges the silence of social science on some issues and points to the biases inherent in the formulation of others.

These young, white, working-class women stressed their self-direction in selecting courses, challenging academic work that construes them as simply assigned to places by the school. They highlighted the importance of job opportunities and sexual harassment in course choice, issues that have often been overlooked in school-based research. They pointed out the unique role high school business courses play in providing saleable skills, which raises structural and historical questions about why business education was incorporated into the school curriculum in a form that so closely reproduces work relations and skills, while industrial and home economics courses take a form that is much less closely linked to work. Certifiable training for industrial jobs remains outside the high school.

These girls stressed the role of domestic labor in career planning and course choice. They challenged the view that the important differences between courses can be represented by one vertical axis of academic respectability and that vocational courses are more attractive because they are more closely supervised. These are all perspectives that need to be added to the literature on curriculum differentiation in the high school.

Second, an understanding of the perspectives of these girls gives us a more adequate understanding of how class and gender categories are reproduced in the school. Research on education has tended to assume that reproduction occurs when the relatively powerless internalize the views of the powerful. Studies of schooling have emphasized a process of socialization to the hidden curriculum, which ensures acquiescence and explains students' consciousness. Analyses of what the school's message is—the IQ ideology, the traditional gender code—have substituted for analyses of the students' understanding of these messages. This approach produces theories of reproduction in which subordinate groups appear as "cultural dopes," so oversocialized into dominant ideologies that they cheerfully behave in ways that counter their own experience of the world, as well as their own interests. Its factual claims are wrong: People do not so completely believe dominant ideologies. Its political and policy implications are also profoundly undemocratic. Such an approach treats subordinate groups as misguided, backwards, and conservative rather than as aware and self-directed actors in a world that is stacked against them. It thus suggests that they will have little that is useful to say about what changes should take place.

The limits of socialization and the more problematic nature of consent have been increasingly recognized in studies of the labor process, and some of the parallels to schooling are worth noting. From Braverman's (1974) assumption of management's power to control the conditions of production, we have moved to studies of "contested terrain" (Edwards, 1979), "manufacturing consent" (Burawoy, 1979), and working-class culture (Palmer, 1979). There is also a tradition in feminist scholarship that has emphasized that women's consciousness is not simply an internalization of male forms but contains its own alternate interpretations, commitments, and connections (Rowbotham, 1973; Olsen, 1978; Rubin, 1976; Janeway, 1980; Bernard, 1981; Gilligan, 1982; Finn and Miles, 1982). The relation between women's consciousness and man's world is complex and involves accommodation, resistance, and self-imposed and externally imposed silences. Correspondence does not account for their relationship.

This brings the issue of structural change back into an intimate, but dialectical rather than mechanical, relation with consciousness. For these girls, change would have involved a far-reaching shift in their perception of reality. It would have meant new notions of where job opportunities lie, what men are like, and what skills are valued by employers. These beliefs were forged in their daily experiences, and new accounts that contradicted their experience were likely to be found wanting, to be reinterpreted, or to lead to distrust of the source of the new account. They knew, for their own good reasons, what the world was like, and their experience acted as a filter through which any new message was tested, confirmed, rejected, challenged, and reinterpreted. Changing their minds would have meant changing the world they experienced, not simply convincing them of a new set of ideals around equality of opportunity and the desirability of a different world.

REFERENCES

Apple, M.
1982 Cultural and Economic Reproduction in Education. London: Routledge and Kegan Paul.

Bernard, J.
1981 The Female World. Chicago: Aldine.

Bernstein, B.
1975 Class, Codes and Control. Vol. 3. Towards a Theory of Educational Transmission. London: Routledge and Kegan Paul.

Blackburn, R. M. and M. Mann
1979 The Working Class in the Labour Market. London: Macmillan.

Bourdieu, P. and J. C. Passeron
1979 The Inheritors. Chicago: University of Chicago Press.

Bowles, G. and H. Gintis
1976 Schooling in Capitalist America. New York: Basic.

Boyer, J. L.
1983 High School: A Report on Secondary Education in America. New York: Harper and Row.

Braverman, H.
1974 Labor and Monopoly Capitalism. New York: Monthly Review Press.

Breton, R.
1970 "Academic stratification in secondary schools and the educational plans of students." Canadian Review of Sociology and Anthropology 7:1

Burawoy, M.
1979 Manufacturing Consent: Changes in the Labor Process under Monopoly Capitalism. Chicago: University of Chicago Press.

Cicourel, A. and J. Kitsuse
1963 The Educational Decision Makers. New York: Bobbs-Merrill.

Clark, B.
1960 "The cooling out function in higher education." American Journal of Sociology 45:569–76.

Davis, S. and E. Haller
1981 "Tracking ability and SES: Further evidence on the revisionist-meritocratic debate." American Journal of Education 89:283–304.

Edwards, R.
1979 Contested Terrain: The Transformation of the Workplace in the Twentieth Century. New York: Basic.

Farrar, E., J. De Sanctis, and P. Cowden
1980 The Walls Within: Work Experience and School Reform. Cambridge, MA: Huron Institute.

Finn, G. and A. Miles
1982 Feminism in Canada. Montreal: Black Rose.

Gaskell, J.
1983 "The reproduction of family life: Perspectives of male and female adolescents." British Journal of Sociology of Education 4: 19–38.

Gaskell, J. and M. Lazerson
1981 "Between school and work: Perspectives of working class youth." Interchange 11: 80–96.

Giddens, A.
1979 Central Problems in Social Theory. London: Macmillan.

Gilligan, C.
1982 In a Different Voice. Cambridge, MA: Harvard University Press.

Heyns, B.
1974 "Selection and stratification in schools." American Journal of Sociology 79:1434–51.

Janeway, E.
1980 Powers of the Work. New York: Knopf.

Jencks, C. et al.
1972 Inequality. New York: Basic.

Laws, J. L.
1976 "Work aspiration of women: False leads and new starts." Signs 1:33–50.

Laxer, G., R. Traub, and K. Wayne
1974 Student Social and Achievement Patterns as Related to Secondary School Organizational Structures: The Individualized System. Toronto: OISE.

Lazerson, M. and N. Grubb
1974 American Education and Vocationalism. New York: Teachers College Press.

Meece, J. L., J. Eccles Parson, C. M. Kackala, S. B. Goff, and R. Futterman
1982 "Sex differences in math achievement: Toward a model of academic choice." Psychological Bulletin 91:324–48.

Menzies, H.
1981 Women and the Chip. Montreal: Institute for Research on Public Policy.

Mishler, E.
1979 "Meaning in context: Is there any other kind?" Harvard Educational Review 49: 1–19.

Oakes, J.
1982 "Classroom social relationships: Exploring the Bowles and Gintis hypothesis." Sociology of Education 55:197–212.

Olsen, T.
1978 Silences. New York: Delacorte.

Osterman, P.
1980 Getting Started: The Youth Labor Market. Cambridge, MA: MIT Press.

Palmer, B.
1979 A Culture in Conflict: Skilled Workers and Industrial Capitalism in Hamilton, Ontario, 1860–1914. Montreal: McGill University-Montreal Queen's University Press.

Persell, C.
1977 Education and Inequality. New York: Free Press.

Porter, J., M. Porter, and B. Blishen
1982 Stations and Callings: Making it Through the School System. Toronto: Methuen.

Rosenbaum, J.
1976 Making Inequality: The Hidden Curriculum of High School Tracking. New York: Wiley.

Rowbotham, S.
1973 Women's Consciousness, Man's World. Harmondsworth, Middlesex: Penguin.

Rubin, L.
1976 Worlds of Pain. New York: Basic.

Sennett, R. and J. Cobb
1972 The Hidden Injuries of Class. New York: Knopf.

Smith, D.
1977 Feminism and Marxism. Vancouver: New Star.

Statistics Canada
1980 Women in the Labour Force: 1978–1979. Ottawa: Ministry of Labour.

Watts, A. G.
1980 Work Experience Programmes—The Views of British Youth. Paris: OECD.

Willis, P.
1977 Learning to Labour. Farnborough, England: Saxon House.
1981 "Cultural production is different from cultural reproduction is different from social reproduction is different from reproduction." Interchange 12:48–67.

REBELS WITHOUT A CAUSE? SOCIALIZATION AND SUBCULTURAL STYLE AMONG THE CHILDREN OF THE NEW MIDDLE CLASSES

PETER J. AGGLETON
Bath College of Higher Education

GEOFF WHITTY
Bristol Polytechnic

Sociology of Education 1985, Vol. 58 (January):60–72

This article presents the results of an ethnographic investigation into the subcultural practices of a group of new-middle-class students undertaking academic study in an English college of further education. It seeks to contribute to debates stimulated by neo-Marxist writing in the sociology of education concerning the radical significance, or otherwise, of student "resistance" to schooling. Sets of responses to aspects of the schooling process are identified, and continuities between these responses and those within family and subcultural sites, together with those across generations, are explored in the constitution of a grammar of modes of cultural affirmation and challenge. The analysis suggests that there is little evidence that challenges directed against principles of control within sites or carried across sites constitute effective resistances to prevailing patterns of class or gender relations in English society. In the light of this, the article concludes that the role of members of the new middle class in processes of social transformation remains to be demonstrated.

INTRODUCTION

In recent years, sociologists of education have shown increasing interest in student responses to the process of schooling. Early studies by Werthman (1963), D.H. Hargreaves (1967), and Lacey (1970), investigating student perspectives and strategies of negotiation within secondary schools both in America and in Britain, provided a starting point for more broadly based interpretative inquiries throughout the 1970s and 1980s.

Working within symbolic interactionist and social phenomenological frameworks, studies by Woods (1979), Ball (1981), and Turner (1983) have done much to explore the nature of student subjectivity and practice in educational settings and have helped constitute a number of typologies of student responses to schooling. Concurrent with such research, however, have been explorations seeking to forge links between processes within schools and those concerned with the cultural and social reproduction of class and gender relations. In seeking to move beyond the early social reproduction theories of Althusser (1971) and Bowles and Gintis (1976), researchers such as Willis (1977), McRobbie (1978), Connell, Ashenden, Kessler, and Dowsett (1982), and Anyon (1983) have explored the ways in which student responses may contribute to the cultural production/reproduction of forms of practice that serve as a basis for the social reproduction and transformation of class and gender relations. In particular, such studies have seen radical potential in the challenging and "resistant" behaviors of pupils while acknowledging that, all too often, such challenges serve to further consolidate existing class and gender relations.

This article arises from a number of concerns that have emerged from such investigations. In particular, it arises from the debate stimulated by neo-Marxist writing in the sociology of education about the radical significance, or otherwise, of student "resistance"[1] to schooling. Much of this work takes as its starting point the now classic study of "resistance" among a group of working-class "lads" in an English secondary school, *Learning to Labour* (Willis, 1977). Though sometimes regarded as a celebration of working-class "resistance" to capitalist schooling from a socialist standpoint,

We are grateful to the Social Science Research Council (UK), subsequently renamed the Economic and Social Research Council, for their support for the study upon which this article is based. We would like to thank Basil Bernstein, of the University of London Institute of Education, and Leslie Rothaus, of the University of Wisconsin-Madison, for many hours of illuminating discussion. Those familiar with their work will appreciate the extent to which this article has been influenced by their insights. We would also like to thank John Fitz, Michael Olneck, Marilyn Toft, and Philip Wexler for their useful comments on a earlier draft of this article, and Helen Thomas, who typed it. Address all correspondence to the authors at Bath College of Higher Education, Newton Park, Bath, BA2 9BN, ENGLAND.

[1] Later in this article we shall elaborate on what we take *resistance* to be, but for the present we intend the use of this term to include, somewhat eclectically, all forms of behavior that apparently challenge the routine and structuring of the schooling process.

it has also been seen as a deeply pessimistic work in that, as its subtitle implies,[2] it shows that this "resistance" is ultimately reproductive of existing patterns of social relations rather than transformative of them. Willis (1981) has subsequently argued that neither view is entirely in line with his theoretical argument, which suggests that the significance of "resistances" to schooling is not given, but is dependent upon how they are worked with and how they articulate with other practices within the social formation. A similar view emerges from Anyon's work in American elementary schools (Anyon, 1981a, 1981b), though she has been criticized by A. Hargreaves (1982) for regarding almost any negative response to schooling as a potential challenge to capitalist social relations, thus devaluing any utility that the concept of "resistance" might otherwise have. Hargreaves implies that the development of a typology of student responses to schooling might overcome this problem, though if the significance of responses is dependent upon their articulation with other practices within the same site and elsewhere, a more dynamic and empirical analysis of particular cases would clearly be necessary.

Because it concentrates upon a group of working-class students, Willis's work is unable to throw any light on the significance of negative responses to schooling among middle-class students, responses that are also sometimes characterized as "resistances." The question therefore arises whether these are properly described as *resistances* in the sense that, if they become articulated with other practices in appropriate ways, they have the potential to become transformative rather than reproductive in their effects. The extent to which the potential to transform society lies not merely (or even mainly) with the traditional working class but rather with (among others) disaffected professional and middle-class groups within educational settings has, of course, been a matter of considerable debate among social theorists ever since the emergence of the countercultures of the 1960s (Roszak, 1968; Marcuse, 1969; Gintis, 1972). In addition, some writers on the political right and the political left have identified teachers and social workers as potential vanguards of revolutionary activity. Such views are implicit in Anyon's analysis of student responses in her five schools, two of which she regarded as working-class schools and the other three as middle-class, affluent professional, and executive elite schools respectively. Within all these settings, she found nonreproductive aspects that could be worked upon by teachers to produce potentially transformative effects (Anyon, 1981a, 1981b). In particular, she has suggested ways in which a program using the *penetrative consciousness* of students,[3] politicizing their cultural resistance and developing counter-ideologies, might be undertaken by teachers not only in working-class schools but also in her affluent professional school (Anyon, 1981b). Most recently (Anyon, 1983), she has considered how far pupil responses to schooling may be considered potentially transformative, rather than merely reproductive, of gender relations as well as class relations.

THE STUDY

In this article, we will explore some of these issues by analyzing the data from an empirical study carried out by one of the authors among a group of "new middle class" students attending a college of further education in a small English city, which, with a certain lack of originality, we shall call Middletown (Aggleton, 1984). Middletown is a city with relatively little traditional industry, and many of its residents are employed in administrative, educational, and other professional occupations. It is also a tourist center and a city with longstanding associations with the arts. It has therefore attracted as residents many members of the new middle class and, in particular, that fraction of the class that Bernstein (1977) terms *agents of symbolic control.*[4] The students in the study were aged 16 to 20, and the majority of their parents were engaged in teaching, lec-

---

[2] Willis's (1977) book is subtitled *How Working Class Kids Get Working Class Jobs*.

[3] By the term *penetrative consciousness*, Anyon (1981b) seems to be seeking to develop Gramsci's (1978) distinction between practical and theoretical consciousness. Practical, or everyday, consciousness is an amalgam of class perceptions, dominant and dominating ideologies, and a "kernel of penetrative practical understanding," which includes "cultural modes of resistance to oppressions and exploitations at school, at home, at work and by institutions of the media" (Anyon, 1981b:126–29). Such understandings may be practically worked with by teachers to facilitate collective and coherent insight into contradictory social experience.

[4] By the term *agents of symbolic control*, Bernstein (1977) is referring to that fraction of the new middle class concerned with the dissemination of new forms of social control. Agents of symbolic control appear to have come into existence with the development of forms of corporate capitalism, and their origins appear to be intimately connected with a shift in modality of social control from forms that were relatively explicit in their operation to those that were relatively implicit. Such agents play important roles in the cultural reproduction of dominating forms of practice.

Table 1. Class Location of Respondents' Families by Theorist (Total of Twenty Families Investigated)

Theorist	Class	Number of Families
Ehrenreich and Ehrenreich (1979)	Professional and Managerial Class (PMC)	18
	Petit Bourgeoisie	2
Bernstein (1977)	Agents of Symbolic Control (New Middle Class)	19
	Working Class/Indeterminate	1
Poulantzas (1975)	New Petit Bourgeoisie (Fraction 2)	17
	Traditional Petit Bourgeoisie	3
Carchedi (1977)	Old Middle Class	3
	New Middle Class	5
	Working Class	12
Wright (1980)	Semi-autonomous Employees	16
	Managers and Supervisors	1
	Petit Bourgeoisie	1
	Self-employed	2

turing, social work, or various artistic or creative pursuits. There is not complete agreement among contemporary class theorists about where this group should be located within the class structure. The classification of the respondents' families depends upon the type of class analysis adopted (see Table 1).

The particular group of students was selected because their tutors at the college regarded them as anomalous in that, despite coming from homes high in *cultural capital*[5] (Bourdieu and Passeron, 1977), they lacked motivation towards academic study and seemed likely to attain and be content with relatively low grades in their final examinations. From an initial core of respondents thus identified, a final group of thirteen male and fourteen female students was selected by the creation of a snowballed sample based on mutual association and friendship. Because of sibling relationships within the group, the respondents came from a total of twenty families.

In analyzing the data from this study, we were interested in exploring how far the responses of this group to schooling could be regarded as potentially transformative in their effects. However, as it was clear to us from the studies mentioned earlier that determinate effects were likely to be the result of the articulation between students' responses to schooling and other social practices across different sites of experience, we felt it necessary to study the practices of the group not only at the educational site but also in what we shall term the family site and the subcultural site. The latter also encompassed the part-time paid employment of many of the respondents. Before reporting on the detailed findings of the study in these different sites of experience, it may prove useful to outline briefly how we have come to conceptualize the ways in which practices within and across sites articulate with each other to produce hegemonic and counter-hegemonic effects.

The Concept of "Resistance"

With regard to the variety of practices referred to within the literature as "resistance," it is clearly necessary to make distinctions between a number of features of practice. First, we need to distinguish between "resistant" *intentions* and "resistant" *effects*. The former may, in some instances, lead to the latter, but all too often they become turned back upon themselves to produce essentially hegemonic outcomes. There are clear examples of this in the work of Willis (1977), McRobbie (1978), and Anyon (1981a, 1983). Second, we should take care to specify the *targets* of acts of "resistance." In particular, we should distinguish between acts of challenge directed against power relations operating widely and pervasively throughout the social formation and those directed against localized principles of control (Bernstein, 1977, 1982). We intend to call the former acts *resistances* (no quotation marks), the latter *contestations*. Third, we need to remain sensitive to the possibility that there may exist a tension between "resistant" subjectivity and

[5] By the term *cultural capital*, Bourdieu and Passeron (1977) are referring to cultural goods transmitted by pedagogic action within families. Such goods include particular social and linguistic competences, cultural style and behavior, and particular self-perceptions and aspirations.

"resistant" behavior (Giroux, 1983); and within the former of these two stages in the working up of oppositional practice, there are likely to exist two separate moments. The first of these may take the form of transitory, sporadic, and personal insights into the nature of power and control relations. The second is a moment likely to be more socially and collectively shared, in which insights become more systematically organized so as to prefigure counter-hegemonic practice.[6] Fourth, there exists the possibility that "resistant" behaviors witnessed at one site of practice (say the home) may be the result of "resistant" intentions *displaced* from another site of experience (say the school). Such displacements may take place when modes of challenge, taking their origins in contexts where the effects of power and control are felt most strongly, are transported to other sites (Gintis and Bowles, 1980).

Finally, we should remember that it is the net effect of articulations between practices across sites of experience and within different, but interrelated, sets of power and control relations that establishes the overall balance between hegemonic and counter-hegemonic tendencies. A necessary, though not sufficient, basis for the analysis of the origins and effects of "resistances" must therefore involve an ethnographic interrogation of the *articulation* between hegemonic and counter-hegemonic practices *across* different sites of experience. (Appendix A provides a provisional description of such a grammar of affirmatory and challenging practice, which attempts to remain faithful to the above considerations.)

In this article we shall attempt to work with these distinctions in a discussion of the data generated from the empirical study of the practices of our particular group of students in their various sites of experience.

The Family Site of Experience

Gaining access to the families of these students was a relatively easy matter because of some of the cultural features of their homes. Compared with traditional working-class or managerial middle-class homes, there was little sense that these homes were an essentially private domain to be protected from the gaze of outsiders. It therefore proved possible to visit each respondent's home on at least three occasions during the fieldwork so that the nature of social practice within these settings could be observed. It will be clear in what follows that our analysis of the cultural practices within these homes draws much of its inspiration from the pioneering work of Bernstein (1971, 1977).

One of the most prominent features of these homes was, in fact, a *selective blurring of classificatory relationships*[7] (Bernstein, 1977) both within the home and between the home and the outside world. Most of the activities in these homes centered upon a large living area on the ground floor, a kitchen or breakfast room, perhaps, into which were introduced (in an apparently chaotic fashion) objects and practices conventionally associated with other settings. Through these common living areas would pass a stream of visitors, dropping in and stopping for short periods to talk over coffee. The blurring of categories in such settings was found to be informed by underlying principles of selection. Thus, it was only certain sorts of objects and practices that came to be imported into the home from outside it. Artefacts indicating acquaintance with the worlds of fine and creative art were particularly in evidence in the form of art posters or theater or gallery programs. Similarly, postcards, apparently carelessly left lying about or pinned to cork boards, the backs of doors, or sides of shelves, all seemed to originate from overseas. The most frequent visitors to these homes also revealed a concern with the arts and the media and with the foreign and the exotic. Authors, artists, and film directors were particularly in evidence. Members of Middletown's artistic and literary communities, especially men who were openly gay, were frequently present. Conversation seemed to be used to reveal acquaintance with the latest forms of literary or artistic practice or to display personal commitments to socialism,

[6] The necessity for a consideration of two "moments" in the working up of counterhegemonic strategy and practice has been suggested by Anyon (1981b) and Giroux (1983) in their attempts to identify, and work with, radical pedagogy using the penetrative consciousness of American school attenders. We are grateful to Leslie Rothaus of the University of Wisconsin–Madison for suggesting the theoretical and practical utility of such a distinction within the present analysis.

[7] For Bernstein (1977), the term *classification* refers to the strength of the boundary existing between different types of contents within a communicative relationship. In a strongly classified communicative relationship, contents are clearly demarcated. In a less strongly classified relationship, such clear boundaries between contents in a message system are less apparent. The appendix to "Class and Pedagogies: Visible and Invisible" (in Bernstein, 1977) provides an excellent illustration of how such a mode of analysis might be applied to concrete situations. Bernstein has also suggested that the boundaries between contents are themselves the expression of power relations, an argument developed in a more recent paper (Bernstein, 1982).

feminism, peace, or ecology. Stickers indicating the families' commitments to such causes were also displayed on outside windows.

There was also a blurring of distinctions between work and leisure, in particular, between paid employment outside the home and family-oriented pursuits within it. The nature of parental occupations meant that work associated with paid employment was often carried out in the home, and time was not neatly divided between a nine-to-five working day and home-centered evening and weekend activity. Some parents held tutorials for their students in their homes, others held academic soirees or undertook their counselling responsibilities at home. Involvement in drama and other artistic pursuits was often organized from home or spilled over into it. Thus, the more conventional distinctions that exist in modern industrial societies between employment, the home, and leisure pursuits were less easy to discern in these particular families.

This selective blurring of public and private modes of practice had important implications for those socialized within such contexts. As we shall see, interactions with particular notions of cultural acceptability and worth were to have profound consequences for the ways in which our respondents came to negotiate their educational and subcultural sites of experience. But the cultural features of the home also meant that respondents and their friends and acquaintances could be monitored and invisibly screened within the family site. For example, the open living spaces through which visitors passed, and in which the members of the family spent much of their time talking, arguing, and reading, afforded those present the opportunity to observe the behavior of others with some intensity. Parents were thus able to share considerable insight into the motives, projects, and subjectivities of their offspring—insight further consolidated by the process of elaborate verbal justification required when absence from the household was being sought. Freedom to visit friends and stay out late was granted to the respondents from a relatively early age, provided the parents were given access to details of what this involved. Similarly, many had been encouraged to drink alcohol or smoke marijuana within the home, thus keeping such practices under parental scrutiny and supervision. Permission to sleep with a friend of the opposite sex was also granted in many cases but subject to parents receiving relatively detailed information about the intentions of those involved, their degree of commitment, and the extent to which it would contribute to the personal development of their offspring. Successful negotiation of such encounters thus involved respondents in the use of strategies of communication in which personalized control over meaning was both displayed and reasonably accepted. This, in turn, had important implications for the way in which the respondents negotiated their educational sites of practice.

However, parental surveillance strategies of this type did seem to have differential effects for female and male respondents. Parents' concern with the development of industrious, committed, and personalizing heterosexual involvements led them to encourage different modalities of practice among their male and female offspring. There appeared, for instance, to be differential limits to the degree of liberalism involved in the encouragement of sexual liaisons. Female respondents were more insistently interrogated about the nature of their present and proposed heterosexual involvements, while males were more readily granted permission, and even encouraged, to absent themselves overnight for liaisons, which were perceived to be important for their personal development but did not seem to involve the degree of commitment required of female respondents. Parents also displayed a deep ambivalence about homosexual practices; while they openly welcomed gay men into their homes as friends, they viewed with considerable alarm the possibility of homosexual activity among their offspring. In one case, this went as far as a threat to invoke therapeutic counselling. These limitations to the liberalism of the parental generation had profound implications for the cultural practices of the respondents and for the extent to which they were reproductive or transformative in their effects.

The Educational Site of Experience

The parents of students in the present study showed considerable interest in the education that their daughters and sons obtained. Many of them had taken deliberate steps to ensure that respondents attended either primary schools in Middletown with integrated day and child-centered curricula or private "free schools" close by. For many respondents, transfer to secondary school had been a further occasion for parental intervention. At the time of the fieldwork, secondary education in Middletown was organized on the basis of single-sex provision in all but one school. It was therefore significant that less than one-third of the respondents attended such single-sex schools.

However, once at secondary school, respondents showed considerable antipathy towards certain aspects of the schooling process. These included compulsory attendance at religious assemblies, the need to wear a school uniform, the need to attend school between certain hours, and teachers' nonacceptance of the strategies of verbal self-justification that respondents used to negotiate contexts and possibilities. Reactions towards these elements of perceived oppression varied in intensity from minor arguments with teachers and the refusal to wear a school uniform to persistent absence from school and confrontations with head teachers and senior staff. In a number of instances, had it not been for parental intervention, respondents would have been required to transfer out of the school because of these strategies of response.

Challenges against aspects of the process of secondary schooling concerned with the management of spatial and temporal arrangements and challenges against teachers' use of positional control techniques (Bernstein, 1977) affirm the importance of personalized control over the use of time and space (a prevalent practice in respondents' homes) at the same time that they pose a threat to the dominant order of the school. The refusal to accept the imposed timetable by arriving late for class, the use of self-justification as a tactic in arguments with teachers, and the adoption of styles of self-presentation articulating with personal ideological and political commitments may therefore be seen as effects arising from the *transportation of practices* (Gintis and Bowles, 1980) from the family site to the school.

However, since such challenges were directed primarily against principles of *control* within the localized context of the school (and not, in Bernstein's [1982] terms, against relations of power), and since such strategies of challenge help consolidate forms of *habitus*[8] associated with personalized control over systems of meaning, we should be less than optimistic about the outcomes of such struggles for processes of social transformation. Indeed, while such challenges resulted in respondents leaving school at age 16 to attend a college of further education, their continued presence after transition was to have further consequences for the manner in which students negotiated their educational experience in this latter context.

Two such effects are worthy of special attention. The first of these relates to curricular choices made at Middletown College of Further Education (MCFE). Table 2 clearly demonstrates the way in which students selectively responded to the subjects available in the curriculum of MCFE. Those most likely to fall

Table 2. Respondents' Curricular Choices at Middletown College of Further Education (MCFE)

Subject	Number of Respondents Enrolled in Classes Connected with This Subject at Some Point Throughout the Fieldwork[a]
Fine Art	15
History of Art	16
English Literature	19
Communication Studies	10
Theater Studies	7
History	3
Sociology	12
Psychology	2
Geography	1
Science Subjects	2
Mathematics	0
Languages	4

[a] Students at MCFE enrolled in either two or three classes for post-sixteen nonvocational study.

within spheres of cultural acceptability, as it was defined within the home, were the ones most likely to be studied. Hence, history of art, fine art, English literature, theater, and communication studies were by far the most commonly preferred options. The pure sciences and mathematics were much less frequently studied. Furthermore, students' attendance at classes tended to be sporadic, and their preparation of essays and assignments was similarly uncommitted. When questioned about this, they frequently made reference to the limited possibilities for personal expression existing even within chosen curricular options. As a result, they selectively appropriated elements from the curriculum, involving themselves particularly with those allowing the greatest amount of personal expressivity. Hence, visits to art galleries and theaters were well attended, as were film and theater production classes. On the other hand, classes requiring the committed production of written work or an acquaintance with the opinions and writings of others were not popular. As they had done at secondary school, respondents also showed an unwillingness to attend classes at predefined times and places.

It is therefore possible to find elements of both affirmation and challenge in respondents' behavior at this site as practices transported from the family articulate with those in educational settings. It is important to note, however, that students' opposition to aspects of the schooling process was *noncollective* in form. Indeed, many of them actively eschewed involvement in collective struggle organized concurrently by student councils and student unions, preferring to challenge *personally* the

[8] By the term *habitus*, Bourdieu and Passeron (1977) are referring to social perceptions, habits of thought, and modes of practice common to a class or class fraction.

principles of control within educational contexts. In view of this, such challenges should be seen as contestations whose specificity affirms the significance of *personal* control over the management of space, time, and systems of meaning. As such, they may well contribute towards hegemonic tendencies within processes of cultural reproduction. At the same time, however, they may also have consequences for the individuals concerned, since irregular class attendance and limited involvement in academic study are modes of practice likely to militate against success in examinations.

The Subcultural Site of Experience

Outside home and college contexts, preferred sites for student activity included the Wheel Inn, a large bar in the center of Middletown; the Tube Club, a discotheque popular with Middletown's gay community; and the Dugout Club, a late-night bar. During the day, popular meeting places included an open-plan coffee area in the local arts center and respondents' own homes. Nonpreferred contexts included discotheques owned by commercial chains and bars where "straights" (those of comparable age to respondents, but in full-time paid employment) were to be found. Towards the end of the fieldwork, many respondents had obtained casual work in restaurants and fast-food outlets, which also became preferred sites for subcultural activity.

When asked about the significance of these contexts, students frequently replied that in such situations, they might meet interesting people with interesting ideas—that is, people knowledgeable about fine art, literature, cinema, and radical politics. A number of female respondents also commented that being in these contexts had enabled them to develop understandings about sexual politics and feminism. In part, such explorations seem to have been triggered by males' dominate use of physical space in these settings. They frequently monopolized space by spreading their clothes over several adjacent seats and by throwing beer, peanuts, and crisp packets at each other, causing females on many occasions to separate themselves physically from them, thereafter developing an incipient critique of patriarchal practice. Males also used strategies of conversational control, telling denigratory jokes about others present, talking and laughing at high volume, and making comments with sexist implications.

Talk about others was a dominant practice in this and other subcultural settings, and a great deal of time was spent "taking the piss" out of those around. Such social strategies conformed to a pattern and involved a critique of another person's apparent identity, followed by the substitution of a more authentic understanding. For example, someone's stance might be analyzed as "posey" or "pretentious," and the individual exhibiting it might thereafter be interpreted as someone behaving that way out of an inherent "insecurity" or "snobbishness." Another's hair or preferred clothing might be seen as "trendy" (a term of denigration)—a sure sign of the person's real "need to be accepted." Such tendencies, involving the deconstruction and reconstruction of personal identity in a process of *personal authentication,* were part of a more general concern to observe others in an attempt to understand their motives. However, in addition to demonstrating respondents' attempts to gain personal control over systems of meanings relating to individuals, such strategies created conditions in which a *problematization of interpersonal intimacy* occurred.[9] In particular, since status among respondents seemed to be intimately connected with the ability to successfully authenticate the identity of others, there existed both a desire for involvement in such a process (in order to achieve status) and a more general apprehension that this might lay the self open to being authenticated by others as a "bitch" (a term applied to both female and male respondents) or a "gossip." This concern for insight into the motives of others shows once again the effects of practices transported from the family site to the subcultural site.

Respondents wore second-hand clothes bought from charity shops or found in family wardrobes. Among males, cricket flannels, cotton jackets, and collarless shirts were popular early in the fieldwork. Later, these were replaced by foreign items—Italian shirts and trousers, African print shirts, and American sports clothing from the 1950s, purchased from second-hand stores in London. Among females, there were two prevailing styles of dress: Androgynous, sloppy sweatshirts (inside out) and loose-fitting dark cotton trousers were worn on some occasions, and exotic cocktail dresses or 1960s-style polyvinylchloride miniskirts and lurex tops were worn on others. On one occasion, a student visiting the social security office arrived by taxi wearing a veil, court shoes, and a 1950s-style satin sun dress.

[9] By suggesting that there existed a relative *problematization of interpersonal intimacy* for respondents in the present study, we are highlighting the tension created by strategies in which personal identities and projects were subjected to systematic interrogation and critique. Such practices militate against the development of mutuality, trust, and significant levels of socialness.

Hairstyles, too, for both sexes, tended to include elements of the foreign and exotic, in addition to elements from more commercially available subcultural styles of the time (punk, new romanticism, affluent chic). For males, very short (almost skinhead) styles were subsequently replaced by those involving the slicking back of newly grown hair with oil. Highlighted and dyed hair was common among both females and males. For females, elaborate backcombing and the selective use of henna and color gave way, on some occasions, to unwashed and unkempt looks—styles that many associated with conscious challenges against dominating modes of feminine practice.

It is possible to see in this selective appropriation of elements of dress an exploration of both class and ethnic location. Rarely, if ever, were "received" or mediated modes of dress or hairstyling witnessed among respondents. Indeed, "High Street" and magazine fashion were universally denigrated. Instead, in yet further attempts to exert personal control over meaning, respondents symbolically plundered a variety of cultural possibilities falling within criteria of cultural worth similar, once again, to those operating within their homes.

A further aspect of subcultural practice related to the type of work students undertook. Two fast-food restaurants, specializing in the sale of beefburgers, kebabs, and chili dishes, were well frequented by respondents, both as staff and as consumers. In both of these settings, personal acquaintance with management enabled employees to negotiate the occasions and manner in which they worked. Standards of appearance, timekeeping, and style of service were some of the more obvious aspects of employment amenable to personal control. Moreover, it also proved possible to engage in sustained conversations with visiting friends while working in these locations. We can therefore see that such contexts afforded a weakening of distinctions between work and leisure, allowing opportunities for personal control similar to those witnessed in respondents' homes and striven for within educational settings.

Finally, we need to comment about dominant modes of sexual practice. Here, significant differences in the nature of sexual involvements were found between females and males. The latter operated with clear distinctions between heterosexual relationships that were perceived as offering opportunities for long-term personal development and those that were not. Both types of relationship were engaged in, often simultaneously. Females, on the other hand, perceived as inappropriate any heterosexual involvements other than those implying degrees of commitment and personal development. Indeed, a number of them criticized girls outside college with whom males were casually involved, seeing them (and not the males concerned) as cheap or common. For females, therefore, heterosexual involvements had to be perceived as offering opportunities for personal development before they were entered into. Differences also existed in the extent to which homosexual relationships took place. For males, these tended to be relatively rare, taking place only on the occasional drunken evening during holiday. For females, personal commitments towards modes of feminist practice impelled a number of them to deliberately participate in homosexual relationships in addition to committed heterosexual relationships.

Continuity, Transformation, and the Reproduction of Class Relations

By looking at the nature of students' responses at these three sites of experience, it is possible to identify a number of areas of continuity between their responses and their parents' responses.

For both of these groups, there existed conspicuous tendencies associated with the attempted control of systems of meaning. For parents, such concerns were witnessed both in their paid employment as agents of symbolic control and in their preferred practices within the home. Their selective importation of elements of experience connoting degrees of cultural acceptability and worth and their attempts to carefully monitor the social practices of their children are related to such general tendencies. For students, these were to be witnessed in their acquisition and use of specific sets of communicative strategies by which to negotiate personal freedoms over the use of space and time inside and outside the home and in their responses to formal educational contexts. Their desire to explore to the limit personalizing possibilities within the secondary-school curriculum created confrontations with teachers and administrators, which, in many cases, were instrumental in securing their eventual transition to a college of further education at the age of 16. This desire was also responsible for their selective response to the range of curricular options available at college and for their partial commitment to the pursuit of academic study once there.

These responses to formal educational provision are discontinuous with those of their parents. For the latter, postschool education was a desirable goal. Twenty-two out of forty parents had attended institutions of further or higher education immediately after leaving school. Others had undertaken similar study subsequently, and thirty-two of them had first degrees or teaching diplomas at the time of the fieldwork. Thus, in a clear majority of cases, parents placed high value upon further and higher education. This did not seem to be mirrored among the students: On the whole, their academic grades were poor, and four years after fieldwork commenced, only three had become involved in committed academic higher education.

Such generational discontinuities call for explanation, and we suggest that the beginnings of this may be found in parents' encouragement of acquaintance with artefacts and experiences ensuring familiarity with the creators of the fine arts, theater, and mediated art forms. For students, these aspects of artistic production thereby come to be taken for granted and accepted as everyday elements of experience (which was not the case for parents). Thus, they no longer exist within a realm of distant and unfamiliar practice. However, the specificity of the manner by which these modes of acquaintance were encouraged was such that respondents came to perceive these artefacts and practices as intimately associated with the intrinsic qualities of *individual* creators and not with more general processes of cultural production, of which individual creators are but a part. Such *authorial ideologies* (Eagleton, 1978), emphasizing the immanent talents of individuals as creators of fine art, militate against others emphasizing the importance of training, diligence, and industrious commitment in the pursuit of creative and expressive goals. Hence, we can begin to better understand why respondents displayed antipathy towards elements of self-denial, ritualized training, and prior effort in the attainment of qualifications in these same areas of practice. Instead, they acted as if their own innate talents and cultural capital would, *of themselves,* provide sufficient basis for entry into, and success within, fields of practice associated with creative art forms.

The pursuit of personalizing possibilities within education has, as we have seen, additional consequences for academic attainment. Fifteen out of twenty-seven students in the present study left college of further education with no qualifications other than those they possessed upon entering college. However, some four years later, such underachievements were found to have had relatively insignificant consequences for employment possibilities at a time of high national youth unemployment. All the students involved in the present study were in paid employment at this time—working as theater staff, video and film technicians, staff in cocktail bars and chic restaurants, or as personal assistants to those in the worlds of fine and mediated arts.

Such trajectories seem to suggest that the challenges directed against aspects of the schooling process within secondary education and at college of further education are far from structural in their effects. Rather, they are concerned with the winning of *personal* autonomy within social relations. Respondents' affirmation of *communicative strategies* attempting personal control over systems of meaning in these contexts may thereby serve to consolidate a mode of *habitus* by which students are later able to secure paid employment in spheres of practice intimately associated with institutionalized processes of symbolic control. Their challenges, which should be referred to as within-modality reproductive contestations (see Appendix A), thereby serve what are essentially hegemonic moments in processes of cultural and social reproduction. They provide an important focus for the generational reproduction of a cultural basis for class divisions.

Continuity, Transformation, and the Reproduction of Gender Relations

Parental surveillance of respondents' practice was one of a number of factors contributing to a problematization of interpersonal intimacy for students in the present study. Other factors included those associated with tendencies towards the *personal authentication of others*—practices very much in evidence subculturally. Such processes, serving to deprivatize and publicize the desires of others, demonstrate clearly some of the tensions existing between personalization and socialization as cultural possibilities. As Wexler has recently argued,

> Intimacy is at once less than full socialness, because it privatizes desires—and more than commodified personalism because the realization of desire requires the valuation of another human being. Intimacy [is therefore] at the moving center of the over-riding structural contradictions between personalization and socialization (Wexler, 1983:150).

Indeed, insistent surveillance, the deconstruction of other people's projects, and the trading of commodified identities of others are all practices that serve to fragment and commodify our experience of other persons.

Yet such degrees of problematization were to have different effects for female and male students. We earlier suggested that patriarchally constituted messages within families ensured that females acquired degrees of competence within heterosexual relationships and a respect for the value of personalizing monogamous commitment. Such tendencies, we argue, relate at least in part to parental concern for personal development through industrious and committed heterosexual practice. However, their existence also betrays a concern that female respondents acquire a competent heterosexualized femininity. As such, they may be motivated by particular ideologies towards what Brunt (1982) has called a *hidden essentialism* informing middle-class female heterosexual practice. In writing of recent tendencies encouraging middle-class women to become experts in sensuality and heterosexual practice, she has argued that

> constructed as models of feminine conduct, both the "new" sensuous woman and the heroines of romance have a vocational attitude to their sexuality. Their aim is to build a sexual career with the ultimate purpose of trapping those men whose superior economic status and resources go with a barely controllable sexual appetite. In pursuit of the best lifestyle on offer, the sensual woman must display a wide repertoire of sexual technique as her best exchange commodity (Brunt, 1982:158).

In such ways, we can begin to understand why potential boyfriends were carefully screened by parents of female students and why their friendship with openly homosexual men was encouraged (since they were perceived by parents as likely to pose little threat to the attainment of such competences).

Yet such strategies can also have unintended consequences. For some females at least, their interest in establishing personally developing sexual relationships encouraged them to participate in homosexual relationships. Such motivations may take their origins, at least in part, from the influence of new feminist ideologies within respondents' homes: ideologies emphasizing the expansion of boundaries relating to permissable sexual relations and challenging the patriarchal nature of sexual commitment as practiced within the nuclear family. As such, these practices may be seen as affirmations of the political and ideological commitments of both generations of females in the present study.

However, it would be equally important to view such explorations as cultural challenges, winning ideological space from modes of patriarchal surveillance practiced subculturally by males. As intentioned resistances sharing some degree of systematic insight into the nature of heterosexual gender oppression, these could be forms of practice potentially prefigurative of emancipatory struggle. Nevertheless, we argue that there also exist factors militating against the development of such modes of critical insight and practice into effective resistances. Some of these may relate to the influence of patriarchal stigmatization tendencies relating to homosexual involvement; others, to the extent to which females themselves remained concurrently committed to the value of personalizing monogamous heterosexual relationships. Thus, for example, when questioned, a majority of female students continued to articulate a belief in the value of such relationships in addition to their commitment to feminist struggle. We therefore suggest that there exist a number of disorienting factors militating against the development of effective resistances from such forms of cultural challenge.[10]

If articulations between affirmatory and challenging tendencies within the gendered practice of female students held some possibility for transformative effects, this was not so obviously true for males. They, it will be recalled, drew clear distinctions between heterosexual liaisons that were perceived as offering opportunities for personal development and those that were not. Involvement in the latter took a serial form; relationships varied in their intensity and degree but nevertheless provided a basis for commodification tendencies, since involvement other than that minimally necessary to establish and consummate sexual relations must, of necessity, result in an objectification of the partner. Involvement in the former type of relationship seemed to be far rarer. Indeed, male students professed to finding it difficult to meet female partners offering possibilities for personal development. Given the prevalence of minimal self-investment within relationships and the tendencies towards objectification described above, this seems to us to be unsurprising.

Yet such patterns of practice share some similarity with those displayed by their fathers. They too publicly avowed a firm belief in the importance of committed, industriously pursued, and perceptibly personalizing heterosexual involvements while they participated in more casual serial heterosexual liaisons. At the same time, both generations of males showed little sign of personal involvement in homosexual practice. Furthermore, they showed little

---

[10] We are grateful to Leslie Rothaus for having suggested the basis of the preceding interpretations. Similar themes are now being explored in her own fieldwork, "Punk Femininity In and Out of School."

willingness to critically analyze their sexual involvements. While females used both public and private opportunities to develop modes of critical appreciation and practice, males showed little interest in questioning the basis around which their own sexual practices and involvements came to be constituted. We therefore suggest that the gendered practice of males in the present study displayed even fewer tendencies towards processes with potentially transformative effects than that of the females.

CONCLUSIONS

It seems, then, that the practices of this particular group of new-middle-class students are essentially hegemonic and thus reproductive in their effects. Therefore, any suggestion that their apparent rejection of the dominant ethos of schooling is anything more than a *contestation* needs to be viewed with considerable skepticism. There is little evidence in this study that such challenges directed against the principles of control operative in particular sites, or carried across from one site to another, are actually effective resistances to the prevailing patterns of power relations in English society.Even the limited examples of discontinuity between this group's practices and their parents' culture seem ultimately to be reproductive in their effects. At most, they are attempts to win a limited degree of personal autonomy within a broader acceptance of existing sets of relations. Any concern that their teachers may have that their response to schooling poses a threat either to their personal futures or to the fabric of Western society seems to be premature, to say the least.

Of course, this does not, of itself, imply that the practices of this group lack the potential to become effective resistances in any circumstances. The possibility that they could become articulated with other practices to produce such effects always remains open. However, there are important elements of their practice, especially those that seem to have developed out of their parents' culture, that militate against this. In particular, the emphasis on the personalized and personalizing nature of authentic commitment makes it difficult for these students to develop their critique of prevailing power and control relations into more collectively and systematically organized counter-hegemonic practices. In this, the *form* of parental culture seems to have been more powerful in the socialization process than its *content*, for the students seem more suspicious of displaying commitment to causes as represented by unions or political parties than did their parents. This poses considerable problems for any program of radical pedagogy designed to work with the contestations of such students to produce a sense of solidarity with broader oppositional struggles in society (Anyon, 1981b; Giroux, 1983).

There is certainly little in this study to suggest that the *contestations* of this group towards localized principles of control can be easily developed into *resistance* to broader patterns of class relations. With regard to gender relations, the position is somewhat less clear. Though the critique of patriarchal relations offered by the female respondents showed some signs of developing into an alternative mode of collective practice within the group, it did not become actively oppositional to the continuance of patriarchal relations in general. Nevertheless, it might have developed differently in different circumstances, and it certainly displayed more potential for becoming an effective resistance than did any of the other contestations identified in this study. On the other hand, it seems the emphasis on personalized modes of practice elsewhere within the culture of the group gives even this challenge a form that isolates it from other transformative movements in society at large, so that the practices of this relatively privileged group may not be as readily won to the broader feminist movement as it might at first sight appear. Thus, in reflecting upon the significance of the study as a whole, we can only conclude that the role of this group in social transformation remains to be demonstrated, though it is central to our argument that ultimately, the issue can only be resolved through pedagogical and political practice. On the evidence of this study, however, there may be even more difficulties confronting those who wish to politicize the contestations of this group than those who wish to do so with the equivalent of Willis's "lads."

Appendix A. A Partially Constituted Grammar of Modes of Challenge (Contestation and Resistance)

Target of acts of challenge	Power relations		Principles of control operative at the same experiential site			Principles of control operative at other experiential sites		
Subjectivity of agents concerned	Conscious challenge directed against power relations		Conscious challenge directed against principles of control at present site			Challenge directed against principles of control at other experiential sites displaced to present experiential site		
Objective behavior of agents concerned	Individualized INTENTIONED RESISTANCE		None of challenge ACQUIESCENCE	Against principles of control at present site CONTESTATION		None of challenge DISGRUNTLEMENT	Against principles of control at present site CONTESTATION	
	Collective SYSTEMATIC INTENTIONED RESISTANCE							
Effects	Counter-hegemonic	Hegemonic		Counter-hegemonic	Hegemonic		Counter-hegemonic	Hegemonic
(a) for the same set of power relations	WITHIN MODALITY EFFECTIVE RESISTANCE	WITHIN MODALITY REPRODUCTIVE RESISTANCE	MODES OF ACQUIESCENCE	WITHIN MODALITY EFFECTIVE RESISTANCE	WITHIN MODALITY REPRODUCTIVE CONTESTATION	MODES OF DISGRUNTLEMENT	WITHIN MODALITY EFFECTIVE RESISTANCE	WITHIN MODALITY DISPLACED REPRODUCTIVE CONTESTATION
(b) for other sets of power relations	ACROSS MODALITY EFFECTIVE RESISTANCE	ACROSS MODALITY REPRODUCTIVE RESISTANCE		ACROSS MODALITY EFFECTIVE RESISTANCE	ACROSS MODALITY REPRODUCTIVE CONTESTATION		ACROSS MODALITY EFFECTIVE RESISTANCE	ACROSS MODALITY DISPLACED REPRODUCTIVE CONTESTATION

NOTE: Such a grammar takes as its starting point the existence of subjective challenges on the part of agents. It should be possible to construct a similar grammar of affirmations and boredoms, which would take as its starting point the absence of such subjectivities. It is probably best to conceive of hegemonic and counter-hegemonic tendencies as dialectally related to one another. Reproductive resistances contain at lease the seeds of effective ones.

REFERENCES

Aggleton, P. J.
1984 "Reproductive 'resistance': A study of the origins and effects of youth subcultural style amongst a group of new middle class students in a college of further education." Unpublished Ph.D. thesis, University of London.

Althusser, L.
1971 "Ideology and ideological state apparatuses." Pp. 123–73 in L. Althusser (ed.), Lenin and Philosophy and Other Essays. London: New Left Books.

Anyon, J.
1981a "Social class and school knowledge." Curriculum Inquiry 11:3–42.
1981b "Elementary schooling and distinctions of social class." Interchange 12:118–32.
1983 "Intersections of gender and class: Accommodation and resistance by working-class and affluent females to contradictory sex-role ideologies." Pp. 19–38 in S. Walker and L. Barton (eds.), Gender, Class and Education. Lewes: Falmer.

Ball, S. J.
1981 Beachside Comprehensive. Cambridge: Cambridge University Press.

Bernstein, B.
1971 Class, Codes and Control. Vol. 1. Revised ed. London: Routledge and Kegan Paul.
1977 Class, Codes and Control. Vol. 3. Revised ed. London: Routledge and Kegan Paul.
1982 "Class, modalities and the process of cultural reproduction: A model." Pp. 304–55 in M. Apple (ed.), Cultural and Economic Reproduction in Education. London: Routledge and Kegan Paul.

Bourdieu, P. and J. C. Passeron
1977 Reproduction in Education, Society and Culture. Beverly Hills: Sage.

Bowles, S. and H. Gintis
1976 Schooling in Capitalist America. London: Routledge and Kegan Paul.

Brunt, R.
1982 "An immense verbosity: Permissive sexual advice in the 1970s." Pp. 143–70 in R. Brunt and C. Rowan (eds.), Feminism, Culture and Politics. London: Lawrence and Wishart.

Carchedi, G.
1977 On the Economic Identification of Social Classes. London: Routledge and Kegan Paul.

Connell, R. W., D. J. Ashenden, S. Kessler, and G. W. Dowsett
1982 Making the Difference. Sydney: George Allen and Unwin.

Eagleton, T.
1978 Criticism and Ideology: A Study in Marxist Literary Theory. London: New Left Books.

Ehrenreich, B. and J. Ehrenreich
1979 "The professional-managerial class." In P. Walker (ed.), Between Labour and Capital. Hassocks: Harvester.

Gintis, H.
1972 "Activism and counter-culture: The dialectics of consciousness in the corporate state." Telos 12:42–62.

Gintis, H. and S. Bowles
1980 "Contradiction and reproduction in educational theory." Pp. 51–66 in L. Barton, R. Meighan, and S. Walker (eds.), Schooling, Ideology and the Curriculum. Lewes: Falmer.

Giroux, H. A.
1983 Theory and Resistance in Education. London: Heinemann.

Gramsci, A.
1978 Selections from the Prison Notebooks of Antonio Gramsci. London: Lawrence and Wishart.

Hargreaves, A.
1982 "Resistance and relative autonomy theories: Problems of distortion and incoherence in recent Marxist analyses of education." British Journal of Sociology of Education 3:107–26.

Hargreaves, D. H.
1967 Social Relations in a Secondary School. London: Routledge and Kegan Paul.

Lacey, C.
1970 Hightown Grammar. Manchester: Manchester University Press.

Marcuse, H.
1969 An Essay on Liberation. Harmondsworth: Penguin.

McRobbie, A.
1978 "Working class girls and the culture of femininity." Pp. 96–108 in Women's Studies Group, Centre for Contemporary Cultural Studies, Women Take Issue. London: Hutchinson.

Poulantzas, N.
1975 Classes in Contemporary Capitalism. London: New Left Books.

Roszak, T.
1968 The Making of a Counter-Culture. London: Faber and Faber.

Turner, G.
1983 The Social World of the Comprehensive School. London: Croom Helm.

Werthman, C.
1963 "Delinquents in school: A test for the legitimacy of authority." Berkeley Journal of Sociology 8:39–60.

Wexler, P.
1983 Critical Social Psychology. London: Routledge and Kegan Paul.

Willis, P.
1977 Learning to Labour. Farnborough: Saxon House.
1981 "Cultural production is different from cultural reproduction is different from social reproduction is different from reproduction." Interchange 12:48–67.

Woods, P.
1979 The Divided School. London: Routledge and Kegan Paul.

Wright, E. O.
1980 "Varieties of Marxist conceptions of the class structure." Politics and Society 9:323–58.

U.S. Postal Service

STATEMENT OF OWNERSHIP, MANAGEMENT AND CIRCULATION

Required by 39 U.S.C. 3685)

1A. TITLE OF PUBLICATION	1B. PUBLICATION NO.	2. DATE OF FILING
SOCIOLOGY OF EDUCATION	0 0 3 8 0 4 0 7	9/20/84

3. FREQUENCY OF ISSUE	3A. NO. OF ISSUES PUBLISHED ANNUALLY	3B. ANNUAL SUBSCRIPTION PRICE
Quarterly	4	$21.00

4. COMPLETE MAILING ADDRESS OF KNOWN OFFICE OF PUBLICATION *(Street, City, County, State and ZIP+4 Code) (Not printers)*

1722 N Street, N.W., Washington, D.C. 20036

5. COMPLETE MAILING ADDRESS OF THE HEADQUARTERS OF GENERAL BUSINESS OFFICES OF THE PUBLISHER *(Not printer)*

1722 N Street, N.W., Washington, D.C. 20036

6. FULL NAMES AND COMPLETE MAILING ADDRESS OF PUBLISHER, EDITOR, AND MANAGING EDITOR *(This item MUST NOT be blank)*

PUBLISHER *(Name and Complete Mailing Address)*

American Sociological Association, 1722 N Street, N.W., Washington, D.C. 20036

EDITOR *(Name and Complete Mailing Address)*

Maureen Hallinan, Department of Sociology, University of Wisconsin, Madison, WI 53706

MANAGING EDITOR *(Name and Complete Mailing Address)*

7. OWNER *(If owned by a corporation, its name and address must be stated and also immediately thereunder the names and addresses of stockholders owning or holding 1 percent or more of total amount of stock. If not owned by a corporation, the names and addresses of the individual owners must be given. If owned by a partnership or other unincorporated firm, its name and address, as well as that of each individual must be given. If the publication is published by a nonprofit organization, its name and address must be stated.) (Item must be completed.)*

FULL NAME	COMPLETE MAILING ADDRESS
American Sociological Association	1722 N Street, N.W., Washington, D.C. 20036

8. KNOWN BONDHOLDERS, MORTGAGEES, AND OTHER SECURITY HOLDERS OWNING OR HOLDING 1 PERCENT OR MORE OF TOTAL AMOUNT OF BONDS, MORTGAGES OR OTHER SECURITIES *(If there are none, so state)*

FULL NAME	COMPLETE MAILING ADDRESS
none	

9. FOR COMPLETION BY NONPROFIT ORGANIZATIONS AUTHORIZED TO MAIL AT SPECIAL RATES *(Section 423.12 DMM only)*
The purpose, function, and nonprofit status of this organization and the exempt status for Federal income tax purposes *(Check one)*

- [X] (1) HAS NOT CHANGED DURING PRECEDING 12 MONTHS
- [ ] (2) HAS CHANGED DURING PRECEDING 12 MONTHS

(If changed, publisher must submit explanation of change with this statement.)

10. EXTENT AND NATURE OF CIRCULATION *(See instructions on reverse side)*	AVERAGE NO. COPIES EACH ISSUE DURING PRECEDING 12 MONTHS	ACTUAL NO. COPIES OF SINGLE ISSUE PUBLISHED NEAREST TO FILING DATE
A. TOTAL NO. COPIES *(Net Press Run)*	3,688	3,500
B. PAID AND/OR REQUESTED CIRCULATION 1. Sales through dealers and carriers, street vendors and counter sales	none	none
2. Mail Subscription *(Paid and/or requested)*	2,470	2,580
C. TOTAL PAID AND/OR REQUESTED CIRCULATION *(Sum of 10B1 and 10B2)*	2,470	2,580
D. FREE DISTRIBUTION BY MAIL, CARRIER OR OTHER MEANS SAMPLES, COMPLIMENTARY, AND OTHER FREE COPIES	none	none
E. TOTAL DISTRIBUTION *(Sum of C and D)*	2,470	2,580
F. COPIES NOT DISTRIBUTED 1. Office use, left over, unaccounted, spoiled after printing	1,218	920
2. Return from News Agents	none	none
G. TOTAL *(Sum of E, F1 and 2–should equal net press run shown in A)*	3,688	3,500

11. **I certify that the statements made by me above are correct and complete**

SIGNATURE AND TITLE OF EDITOR, PUBLISHER, BUSINESS MANAGER, OR OWNER

William V. D'Antonio

PS Form 3526, July 1984

(See instruction on reverse)

ASA ROSE MONOGRAPH SERIES

published by Cambridge University Press
***Ernest Q. Campbell*, Editor**

The Editorial Board of the *Rose Monograph Series* welcomes manuscripts dealing with the full range of sociological topics. Published by Cambridge University Press and officially sponsored by the American Sociological Association, the *Series* provides an outlet for distinguished contributions to the discipline.

The *Rose Monograph Series* was established in 1968 by Arnold and Caroline Rose to publish sociological monographs that may be either theoretical or empirical in nature. All ASA members can submit manuscripts of 100 to 300 pages in length for evaluation by the editors. Any systematic, focused work on a sociological topic is eligible for consideration, be it qualitative or quantitative, theoretical or empirical, pure or applied, comparative or case, topically traditional or emergent. Unrevised dissertations cannot be considered.

Members of the Editorial Board welcome the opportunity to discuss projects with authors in advance of submission, though in no sense is this a requirement.

Monographs published in the *Rose Monograph Series* include:

Black Students in Protest: A Study of the Origins of the Black Student Movement, by Anthony M. Orum
Class, Race and Worker Insurgency: The League of Revolutionary Black Workers, by James A. Geschwender
Education, Employment and Migration: Israel in Comparative Perspective, by Paul Ritterband
Interorganizational Activation in Urban Communities: Deductions from the Concept of System, by Herman Turk
Opening and Closing: Strategies of Information Adaptation in Sociology, by Orrin E. Klapp
Patterns of Scientific Research: A Comparative Analysis of Research in Three Scientific Fields, by Lowell L. Hargens
Protest and Participation: The New Working Class in Italy, by John R. Low-Beer
Religion and Fertility, by Joseph Chamie
Sociological Explanation as Translation, by Steven Turner
Tasks and Social Relationships in Classrooms: A Study of Instructional Organization and Its Consequences, by Steven T. Bossert
The Study of Political Comment, by John DeLamater
Working Daughters of Hong Kong, by Janet Salaff

Submit 3 copies of a manuscript for consideration to:

Ernest Q. Campbell, *Series* Editor
Department of Sociology
Vanderbilt University
Nashville, TN 37235

Volume 58 Number 2 April 1985

SOCIOLOGY OF EDUCATION

A Journal of the American Sociological Association

HOFFER, GREELEY, AND COLEMAN
Achievement Growth in Public and Catholic Schools

WILLMS
Catholic-School Effects on Academic Achievement: New Evidence from the High School and Beyond Follow-Up Study

ALEXANDER AND PALLAS
School Sector and Cognitive Performance: When is a Little a Little?

JENCKS
How Much Do High School Students Learn?

SOCIOLOGY OF EDUCATION (ISSN 0038–0407) is published quarterly in January, April, July and October by the American Sociological Association, 1722 N Street, N.W., Washington, D.C. 20036 and is printed by Boyd Printing Company, Albany, New York. Second class postage paid at Washington, D.C. and additional mailing offices. *POSTMASTER:* Send address changes to *Sociology of Education*, 1722 N Street, N.W., Washington, D.C. 20036.

MANUSCRIPTS and communications for the Editors should be addressed to the Editor, SOCIOLOGY OF EDUCATION, Department of Sociology, University of Notre Dame, Notre Dame, IN 46556.

Concerning advertising, changes of address and subscriptions, address the Executive Office, American Sociological Association, 1722 N Street, N.W., Washington, D.C. 20036. Annual membership dues of the ASA, $40–$125 ($12 of this amount may cover a subscription to *Sociology of Education*); Associate, $40; Student Associate, $25. Subscription rate for members, $12; non-members, $21 U.S., $24 elsewhere; institutions, $28 U.S., $31 elsewhere; single issues, $5. New subscriptions and renewals will be entered on a calendar year basis only. *Changes of Address:* Six weeks advance notice to the Executive Office, and old address as well as new, are necessary for change of subscriber's address. Claims for undelivered copies must be made within the month following the regular month of publication. The publishers will supply missing copies when losses have been sustained in transit and when the reserve stock will permit.

SOCIOLOGY OF EDUCATION

A JOURNAL OF RESEARCH IN SOCIALIZATION AND SOCIAL STRUCTURE

PUBLISHED BY
THE AMERICAN SOCIOLOGICAL ASSOCIATION

APRIL 1985 **VOLUME 58, NUMBER 2**

CONTENTS

Foreword .... The Editors 73

Achievement Growth in Public and Catholic Schools ....
.... Thomas Hoffer, Andrew M. Greeley, and James S. Coleman 74

Catholic-School Effects on Academic Achievement: New Evidence from the High School and Beyond Follow-Up Study .... J. Douglas Willms 98

School Sector and Cognitive Performance: When is a Little a Little? ....
.... Karl L. Alexander and Aaron M. Pallas 115

How Much Do High School Students Learn? .... Christopher Jencks 128

EDITORIAL POLICY

This journal exists to provide a forum for studies of the sociology of education and human social development. The aim is to publish research on how social institutions and/or individuals' experience within them impinge upon educational processes and social development. Such research could span various levels of analysis, ranging from the individual to the structure of relations among social and educational institutions. In an increasingly complex society, important educational issues arise throughout the life cycle. The content of this journal is meant to reflect this diversity by presenting a balance of papers which deal with education at the institutional and organizational levels as well as at the individual level, at all stages of schooling and with respect to all types of education. Contributions are invited from persons of any discipline whose objectives are consonant with those of this journal.

Contributors' papers are evaluated, through a peer-review process, entirely in terms of quality. *All* methodologies are welcome. The journal appears quarterly, January, April, July, and October.

A processing fee of $10 is required for each paper submitted; such fees to be waived for student members of ASA. This reflects a policy of the ASA Council and Committee on Publications affecting all ASA journals. It is a reluctant response to the rapidly accelerating costs of manuscript processing. A check or money order, made payable to the American Sociological Association should accompany each submission. The fee must be paid in order to initiate the processing of the manuscript.

SOCIOLOGY OF EDUCATION

CONTRIBUTORS

■ Thomas Hoffer is Research Analyst at the National Opinion Research Center. He is currently working toward his Ph.D. in sociology at the University of Chicago. This article is part of his dissertation research on the comparison of public and private high school students' academic achievements, high school dropouts, and postsecondary goals and attainments. Andrew M. Greeley is Professor in the Department of Sociology, University of Arizona, and Research Associate at the National Opinion Research Center. He specializes in the sociology of religion. James S. Coleman is Professor in the Department of Sociology, University of Chicago, and Research Associate at the National Opinion Research Center. He specializes in the sociology of education.

■ J. Douglas Willms is Assistant Professor at the University of British Columbia and Research Fellow at the Centre for Educational Sociology, University of Edinburgh. His research interests include program evaluation, school effectiveness, and special education. He is currently studying American and British educational policies that affect the selection and allocation of pupils to different forms of secondary education.

■ Karl L. Alexander is Professor in the Department of Sociology, The Johns Hopkins University. His research interests include the sociology of education and social stratification. This article is part of his ongoing research on school organization and the effect of organizational variations on the educational process and educational outcomes. Aaron M. Pallas is Associate Research Scientist in the Department of Sociology, The Johns Hopkins University. This article reflects his interest in the proper specification of school-effects models and in organizational and curricular effects on educational achievements.

■ Christopher Jencks is Professor of Sociology and Urban Affairs at Northwestern University. His research interests include stratification, work, and social policy.

Notice to Contributors

(Revised September 1981)

STATEMENT OF ASA POLICY ON MULTIPLE SUBMISSION

Submission of manuscripts to a professional journal clearly implies commitment to publish in that journal. The competition for journal space requires a great deal of time and effort on the part of editorial readers whose main compensation for this service is the opportunity to read papers prior to publication and the gratification associated with discharge of professional obligations. For these reasons the ASA regards submission of a manuscript to a professional journal while that paper is under review by another journal as unacceptable.

AUTHOR'S RESPONSIBILITY: *Manuscripts which do not adhere exactly to these suggestions will be immediately returned for revision. Only articles in the form specified below will be sent out for refereeing.*

The 1974 edition of the *Publication Manual* of the American Psychological Association (available from A.P.A., 1200 17th St., N.W., Washington, D.C. 20036) is very helpful in clarifying headings, abbreviations, table preparation and the like.

Since manuscripts are evaluated as anonymous submissions, please keep identifying material out of the manuscript. Attach a cover page giving authorship, institutional affiliation, acknowledgments, and the date the article is submitted. Provide only the title as identification on the manuscript and abstract. Every effort should be made by the author to see that the manuscript itself contains no clues as to the author's identity.

Submission and Preparation of Manuscripts

1. Submit four (4) copies and retain the original for your files. Copies may be Xerox, mimeograph or multilith, but not carbons.

2. Enclose a stamped self-addressed postcard for acknowledgment of manuscript receipt. Since manuscripts will not be returned by reviewers to the editorial office, the editorial office will not return them to authors.

3. All copy must be *typed, doublespaced* (including indented material, footnotes and references) on 8½ by 11 inch white opaque paper. Line must not exceed six (6) inches. Margins must be a minimum of one inch.

4. Include four (4) copies of an abstract of no more than 150 words.

5. Type each table on a separate page. Insert a location note at the appropriate place in the text, e.g., "Table 2 about here." Send copies, retain originals.

6. Figures must be professionally prepared. Send copies, retain originals.

7. Clarify all symbols with notes in the margins of the manuscript. Circle these and all other explanatory notes not intended for printing.

8. Three kinds of footnotes are possible each serving a different purpose:

   a. Content footnotes. Content footnotes are explanations or amplifications of the text. Because they are distracting to readers and *expensive* to include in printed material, an author should include important information in the text and omit irrelevant information. *Content Footnotes Will Not Be Allowed Generally.*

   Rather than footnoting long or complicated material, such as proofs or derivations unnecessary to the text, consider (i) indicating in a *short* footnote that the material is available from the author, (ii) depositing the material in a national retrieval center and including an appropriate footnote, or (iii) adding an appendix. If an appendix is used, the reference in text should read: "(see Appendix A for complete derivation)."

   Text footnotes should be numbered consecutively throughout the article with superscript arabic numerals. If, after a footnote occurs it is later mentioned, use a parenthetical note "(see Footnote 3)," rather than the superscript number.

   b. Reference footnotes. Footnotes are used for reference purposes only to cite material of limited availability. Acceptable reference footnotes include (i) legal citations, which should follow the footnote style of *A Uniform System of Citation* (1967) published by the Harvard Law Review Association, (ii) copyright permission footnotes, (iii) unpublished works; works in progress.

   c. Table footnotes. Table footnotes are appended *only* to a specific table. Footnotes to a table should be *lettered* consecutively *within* each table with superscript lowercase letters.

9. Acknowledgments, credits and grant numbers are placed on the title page with an asterisk.

Reference Format

A. *In the Text:* All source references are to be identified at the appropriate point in the text by the last name of the author, year of publication, and pagination where needed. Identify subsequent citations of the same source in the same way as the first, *not* using "*Ibid.*," "*op. cit.*," or "*loc. cit.*" Examples follow:

1. If author's name is in the text, follow it with year in parentheses. [". . . Duncan (1959) . . ."]

2. If author's name is not in the text, insert, in parentheses, the last name and year, separated by a comma [". . . (cf. Gouldner, 1963 . . ."]

3. Pagination (without "p." or "pp.") follows year of publication after a colon. [". . . Kuhn (1970:71)."]
4. Give both last names for dual authors. Give all last names on first citation in text for more than two authors; thereafter use "et al." in the text. When two authors have the same last name, use identifying initials in the text. For institutional authorship, supply minimum identification from the beginning of the complete citation. [". . . U.S. Bureau of the Census, 1963:117) . . ."]
5. Separate a series of references with semicolons and enclose them within a single pair of parentheses. [". . . (Burgess, 1968; Marwell et al., 1971; Cohen, 1962) . . ."]

B. *In the appendix:* List all items alphabetically by author and, within author, by year of publication, in an appendix, titled "REFERENCES". The reference appendix must be complete and include all references in the text. The use of "et al." is not acceptable in the appendix; list the names of all authors. (See A.4. for text format.)

If there is more than one reference to the same author and year, distinguish them by the letters a, b, etc. added to the year. [". . . Levy (1965a:331) . . ."]

Give the publisher's name in as brief a form as is fully intelligible. For example, John A. Wiley and Sons should be "Wiley."

If the cited material is unpublished, use "forthcoming" with name of journal or publisher; otherwise use "unpublished."

Use no underlining or italics.

Examples follow:

1. *Books:*

Jud, G. J., E. W. Mills, Jr. and G. W. Burch.
1970 Ex-Pastors. Philadelphia: Pilgrim Press.

U.S. Bureau of the Census
1960 Characteristics of Population, Volume I. Washington, D.C.: U.S. Government Printing Office.

Bernard, C.
[1865] An Introduction to the Study of Experimental Medicine. Dr.
1957 Henry Copley Greene. New York: Dover.

2. *Periodicals:*

Conger, R.
Forthcoming "The effects of positive feedback on direction and amount of verbalization in a social setting." Pacific Sociological Review.

Kerckhoff, A. C. and R. T. Campbell
1977a "Black-white differences in the educational attainment process." Sociology of Education 50:15–27.
1977b "Race and social status differences in the explanation of educational ambition." Social Forces 55:701–14.

3. *Collections:*

Davie, M.
1938 "The pattern of urban growth." Pp. 133–61 in G. Murdock (ed.), Studies in the Science of Society. New Haven: Yale University Press.

See recent issues for further examples.

Editors' Foreword

In April 1982, we published a special issue of *Sociology of Education* on the debate surrounding Coleman, Hoffer, and Kilgore's 1981 report, *Public and Private Schools*. The articles in the special issue discussed the substantive issues contained in the report as well as methodological problems and interpretation of findings. In the report, Coleman, Hoffer, and Kilgore concluded that private schools were superior to public schools in promoting academic achievement and were closer to the common-school ideal of equalizing educational opportunities for students with different racial and ethnic backgrounds. Their critics refused to concede that a significant portion of the differences between private- and public-school achievement levels could be attributed to school-sector differences. The articles in the special issue, like the report itself, were all based on cross-sectional analyses of the first wave (1980) of the High School and Beyond (HSB) survey of high school sophomores and seniors. Consequently, while methodologically rigorous, the analyses left unanswered questions that could only be addressed with longitudinal data.

This issue of *Sociology of Education* returns to the private-school *versus* public-school debate, using analyses of the first two waves of the HSB data. These longitudinal data not only permit a reexamination of the findings obtained in the cross-sectional analyses but also shed light on the causal processes that relate school sector to student achievement.

In the first article, Hoffer, Greeley, and Coleman present two sets of analyses. The first set is a longitudinal extension of Greeley's cross-sectional analysis of the effects of public and Catholic schooling on the achievement of black and Hispanic students. The second is a longitudinal extension of the Coleman, Hoffer, and Kilgore cross-sectional analysis. Both sets of results are consistent with the researchers' earlier findings, and the authors again conclude that Catholic schools are more effective than public schools in fostering academic achievement.

Willms, in the second article, offers another interpretation of the HSB data. Using a model different than Hoffer, Greeley, and Coleman's, he finds considerably smaller differences between Catholic- and public-school students and thus concludes that there is no appreciable Catholic-school effect.

In the third article, Alexander and Pallas report that the longitudinal data reveal greater achievement growth among Catholic-school students than among public-school students. However, they argue that these differences in achievement are quite small. Using statistical techniques different from those used by Hoffer, Greeley, and Coleman, they find no special advantage in Catholic-school attendance for minority students. Moreover, contrary to Hoffer, Greeley, and Coleman, they find no common-school effect of Catholic schools.

Jencks, in the final article, provides a clear and useful overview of these three studies. He outlines the differences in their methods, models, and interpretation of results. In addition, he underscores the remaining areas of debate and provides requisites for the kinds of data needed to bring the debate to a more satisfactory conclusion.

These articles exemplify the growing body of research on the effects of private and public schooling on student achievement. They extend the extant literature on school effects by attempting to identify the processes that link type of school to student outcomes. In so doing, they are part of a new emphasis that is evident in much recent research on schooling—namely, a concern with the factors that mediate organizational effects on academic achievement. This research is richer, by far, than the input-output models of schooling that were prevalent in the sixties and early seventies because it explains *how* schools influence student learning. We are pleased that *Sociology of Education* has been able to present this body of research to its readers in a systematic way. Though our deliberate focus on the private-school *versus* public-school debate ends with this issue, we remain open to receiving additional papers that will further our understanding of the schooling process.

Maureen T. Hallinan
Editor
Michael R. Olneck
Deputy Editor

ACHIEVEMENT GROWTH IN PUBLIC AND CATHOLIC SCHOOLS

THOMAS HOFFER
ANDREW M. GREELEY
JAMES S. COLEMAN
National Opinion Research Center

Sociology of Education 1985, Vol. 58 (April):74–97

This article brings together independent longitudinal extensions of Greeley's (1982) and Coleman, Hoffer, and Kilgore's (1982b) analyses of public-school and Catholic-school student achievement differences. Drawing on a variety of analytic techniques, we find that Catholic schools have a positive effect on verbal and mathematics achievement growth from the sophomore to senior year of high school. The magnitude of the Catholic-school effects ranges from about one-half to one grade equivalent for students of average background. The Catholic-school effects are larger for black, Hispanic, and lower-SES students, and somewhat smaller for white and higher-SES students. We find that Catholic schools produce higher-achieving students because they place more students in academic programs, require more semesters of academic coursework, and assign more homework.

INTRODUCTION

After the first data collection of the High School and Beyond (HSB) study of sophomores and seniors in American high schools in 1980, we reported the results of studies that compared the effects of public and private schools on achievement. Two of us (Coleman and Hoffer) examined the differential effects of Catholic schools, other private schools, and public schools on the student population as a whole (Coleman, Hoffer, and Kilgore [CHK], 1982b); and one (Greeley) focused upon the differential effects of Catholic and public schools on black and Hispanic students (Greeley, 1982).

These analyses not only examined somewhat different questions but also used somewhat different methods and measures. The conclusions, however, were consistent: Both analyses found that Catholic high schools are more effective than public high schools. The Greeley analysis found that the advantage of Catholic-school attendance is especially pronounced for black and Hispanic students. The CHK analysis found that the average effect of Catholic schools is about one grade level in mathematics, vocabulary, and reading comprehension. Consistent with the Greeley analysis, CHK also found that the Catholic-school effect is somewhat larger for minority and lower-SES students.

These results were strongly challenged. Apart from the spontaneous reaction of persons concerned with protecting the public schools, a number of social scientists came to the public schools' defense. Critiques of the CHK analysis can be found (together with replies by CHK to these critiques) in the *Harvard Educational Review* (November 1981) and in two issues of *Sociology of Education* (April/July 1982 and October 1983). These critiques of the CHK analysis also implicitly (and in some cases explicitly) criticized the Greeley analysis, for the results of our two analyses were consistent, though carried out independently.

Data from a second time point, the spring of 1982, are now available, thus allowing us to examine changes among the 1980 sophomores over a two-year period. These data are especially interesting, because they include scores on achievement tests that were given to sophomores in 1980 and again to seniors in 1982, making it possible to examine achievement growth over the junior and senior years of high school.

The new data make possible an unusual event in social science: They allow us to test a set of quantitative inferences about institutions with data generated by those institutions after the initial inferences have been made. To what degree are the original inferences correct? To what degree are certain of the critics correct in arguing that there is little or no differential effect of Catholic and public schools on achievement?

In pursuing these questions jointly, we confront a serious problem: The Greeley analysis and the CHK analysis used somewhat different methods, treated the sample somewhat differently, and asked related but not identical questions. These variations in technique were useful in the cross-sectional analysis, because the consistency of the results across variations

---

Order of authorship is random. Please direct inquiries and requests for supporting documentation to Thomas Hoffer, NORC, 6030 South Ellis Avenue, Chicago, IL 60637.

in method indicated some robustness of the inferences. However, for testing the inferences with longitudinal data, these variations can become problematic. Definitions and procedures necessitate some arbitrary decisions, ways of approaching a problem differ, and styles of reporting results and pursuing a sequence of findings differ. To resolve each of these differences by compromise would be to lose many of the virtues of the two approaches. Therefore, to compare the longitudinal and cross-sectional results of both analyses, it appears most sensible to carry forward both techniques.

The next section is a longitudinal extension of the Greeley (1982) analysis, and the section following that is a longitudinal extension of the CHK (1982b) analysis. There are two modifications: (1) Although the Greeley cross-sectional analysis used unweighted data, the longitudinal extension uses data weighted to represent the U.S. student population; and (2) although the CHK cross-sectional analysis compared both Catholic schools and other private schools to public schools, the longitudinal analysis is limited to Catholic schools because of the small size and heterogeneity of the sample of non-Catholic private schools.

The final section of the article examines the consistencies and inconsistencies between the two analytical sections and draws together the results from both approaches. It also examines studies by Alexander and Pallas (1985) and Willms (1985) and discusses the points of convergence and divergence between their results and those presented here.

1. LONGITUDINAL EXTENSION OF THE GREELEY ANALYSIS

In this section, we extend the analysis begun in Greeley (1982). The methodological skepticism of that study is retained: We assume the presence of a school effect only after we have attributed as many school-related differences as possible to differences in individual and family input and only when we can link the residual difference to actual school programs and policies. We therefore attribute to student-input variables, as opposed to school-effect variables, such influences on academic performance as the students' college plans, which might themselves be the result of their school experience.

The objections to our earlier reports can be summarized as follows:

1. Any apparent effects are merely the result of a higher learning curve for Catholic-school students, due to selection.
2. The effect of Catholic schools is confined to the most able students and to those from homes where there is strong motivation and support for academic achievement.
3. Catholic schools seem to have an effect because they eliminate their disciplinary problems by expelling them from the school.
4. The effect of Catholic schools is confined to the students whose parents have made repeated decisions to send them to Catholic schools.
5. The apparent effect of Catholic schools disappears when track assignment is controlled, because most Catholic-school students are assigned to an academic track.
6. The differences between Catholic- and public-school outcomes cannot be linked to specific institutional policies and programs.

The first objection is addressed in section 2, the extension of the CHK analysis. In that analysis, it is shown that when senior test scores are regressed upon sophomore test scores and background variables, two areas of achievement, science and civics, show *no* significant Catholic-school effect. The other five tests, however, show highly significant effects (see Tables 2.2 and 2.3). If the apparent Catholic-school effect were due to selection, it would be uniform over all areas of achievement. But as the tables show, it is not.

In this section, we will bring evidence to bear on objections 2 through 6. First we will determine the indices of the presence or absence of an effect.

In the 1982 HSB follow-up study, seniors were given the same achievement tests that they were given as sophomores in 1980. Thus, one can measure an individual student's improvement (or lack of improvement) on the same test two years later. In principle, three different findings regarding the Catholic-school advantage in test scores between the sophomore and senior years are possible:

a. The difference in test scores between Catholic- and public-school students may diminish. Perhaps the public schools work more effectively with their students once the problem students have dropped out.
b. The difference between Catholic- and public-school students may not change. In the sophomore year, Catholic-school students had almost seven more correct answers on the achievement test (a summary of reading, vocabulary, math, and writing test scores). A continuation of that difference, indicating no relative in-

Table 1.1. Average Sophomore and Senior Test Scores for Public- and Catholic-School Students

	Public			Catholic			
Test	Sophomore 1	Senior 2	Difference 3	Sophomore 4	Senior 5	Difference 6	Catholic Advantage (col. 6–col. 3)
Reading	6.97	8.21	1.24	8.67	10.34	1.67	0.43
Vocabulary	8.74	10.88	2.14	11.24	13.82	2.58	0.44
Math1	10.39	11.90	1.51	13.54	16.06	2.52	1.01
Math2	2.61	3.01	0.40	3.44	4.06	0.62	0.22
Writing	8.51	10.22	1.71	10.62	12.50	1.88	0.17
Total	37.22	44.22	7.00	47.51	56.78	9.27	2.27
Science	9.13	10.09	0.96	10.14	11.30	1.16	0.20
Civics	4.62	5.73	1.11	5.53	6.61	1.08	−0.03
Total	13.75	15.82	2.07	15.67	17.91	2.24	0.17

crease or decrease in the Catholic-school advantage, would suggest that there was no sector effect between the sophomore and senior years and that the difference measured in the sophomore year may have been an ability difference rather than a sector difference.

c. The difference in test scores between Catholic- and public-school students may increase, indicating the presence of a sector effect beyond family and individual input influences.

To measure the *change* in school effects between the sophomore and senior years, we use the sophomore test score as a surrogate for ability, motivation, knowledge, industry, and other related variables. That part of the sophomore achievement difference that is due to prior school effects rather than to student input is taken as given.

Alexander, Pallas, and Cook (1981:619) discuss the use of endogenous measures of ability and find that they "behave much like pre-determined measures." While they prefer temporally prior ability measurement, they are willing to settle for cross-sectional ability measurements to investigate school-process effects. They take it for granted that temporally prior ability measurement is a highly effective technique for controlling input variables in order to measure a possible school-process effect.

To simplify the analysis in this section, we constructed a composite achievement variable by summing the scores from five of the tests.[1] Science and civics were excluded, because we found that the Catholic-school effect was confined to the other five tests (see Tables 2.2 and 2.3). As Table 1.1 shows, the third possibility discussed above—a relative increase in the Catholic-school advantage between the sophomore and senior years—is confirmed. The combined test score of the public-school students increased from 37.22 to 44.22, while the test score of the Catholic-school students increased from 47.51 to 56.78. Thus, between the sophomore and senior years, the Catholic-school advantage in vocabulary, reading, math, and writing increased from 10.29 correct answers to 12.56—an increase of 2.27 items. Note that this is not a repetition of the sophomore finding. For the purposes of this analysis, the sophomore standing is taken as the starting point. Thus, we find not a sustained Catholic-school advantage—the second of the three possibilities outlined above—but an increased Catholic-school advantage. This 2.27-item increase in the Catholic-school advantage over public school is the principal dependent variable for the rest of this analysis.

Objection 2: The effect of Catholic schools is confined to the most able students and to those from homes where there is strong motivation and support for academic achievement.

The notion that it is only the advantaged or especially the advantaged who benefit from attending Catholic secondary schools is widespread. Even Catholic-school teachers and administrators frequently lament that they are not really helping the poor. But as Table 1.2 shows, they really are helping the poor. The evidence directly contradicts the conventional wisdom about the differential effectiveness of Catholic schools: It is the most disadvantaged Catholic-school students who are the most likely to profit from attending Catholic secondary schools—i.e., those from low socioeconomic backgrounds, members of the black or Hispanic communities, those with low sophomore test scores, and those who start off their high school careers with disciplinary problems.

[1] As in Greeley (1982), the achievement-test scores analyzed in this section are formula scores. However, direct comparison with cross-sectional analysis is not possible, because the current analysis is based on weighted data.

Table 1.2. Catholic-School Advantage in Test-Score Increase between the Sophomore and Senior Years, by Background Status

	Catholic Advantage	Sample Size	
		Public	Catholic
By SES			
Lower quartile	2.37	4,096	311
Middle quartile	1.68	7,736	992
Upper quartile	1.86	3,390	736
By minority status			
Minority	3.94	4,108	664
White	1.76	11,269	1,394
By sophomore test scores			
Lower quartile	2.65	3,410	215
Middle quartile	3.47	7,762	1,095
Upper quartile	1.16	4,205	748
By sophomore year suspension			
Was not suspended	2.04	13,316	1,820
Was suspended	2.97	1,302	162

Note that one of the results of this concentration of the sophomore-to-senior Catholic-school advantage among the disadvantaged is what CHK have called the common-school effect. The philosophy of American public education has always been that it is the role of the common or public school to produce greater social equality, to minimize the differences that exist among population groups. However, we found that the difference between minority and nonminority students in public schools was not only larger than it was in Catholic schools, it *grew* between the sophomore and senior years by 1.3 items for the five tests. In the Catholic schools it *declined* by 0.9 items for the five tests. Thus, it is the Catholic schools that are more likely to have a common-school effect.

Objection 3: Catholic schools seem to have an effect because they eliminate their disciplinary problems by expelling them from the school.

This objection is often heard from public-school administrators, but it has also been made by academic critics of our earlier analyses, who sometimes regard it as self-evident. However, the evidence from the HSB data, although indirect, does not support this objection. Among students who reported that they had been suspended during their sophomore year, those in the Catholic sector were more likely to be in the same school as seniors than those in the public sector (63 percent to 56 percent). (Retention rates for students without disciplinary problems were 78 percent in the public schools and 87 percent in the Catholic schools.) Moreover, as Table 1.2 shows, Catholic-school students who had disciplinary problems as sophomores showed greater sophomore-to-senior advantage in test-score improvement over their public-school counterparts than those who did not have sophomore disciplinary problems. Thus, students who are disadvantaged by discipline problems, like students with other disadvantages, benefit even more from the last two years of a Catholic school than students who do not have discipline problems.

The Catholic school's ability to retain its disciplinary problems is not a private-school phenomenon. The other private schools in the HSB sample retained only 38 percent of their sophomore disciplinary problems (and 66 percent of their students without disciplinary problems).

Objection 4: The effect of Catholic school is confined to the students whose parents have made repeated decisions to send them to Catholic schools.

It is possible to measure, at least in some fashion, parents' decisions to send a young person to Catholic school. One can determine how many years of Catholic education a student has had and hypothesize that each year's decision to pay the substantial extra cost of a Catholic-school education is some measure of parents' seriousness about educational outcome. Of course, such a determination excludes all effects of previous Catholic-school attendance on sophomore scores.

As Table 1.3 shows, there is a Catholic-school advantage in sophomore-to-senior gains for all students, regardless of minority status and previous Catholic schooling. There is a slightly lower estimated Catholic-school advantage for white students who had no Catholic elementary school, and there is a significantly lower advantage for minority students who had no Catholic elementary school; but for both groups, the Catholic-school advantage is present.

Table 1.3. Catholic-School Advantage in Test-Score Increase between the Sophomore and Senior Years, by Minority Status and Number of Years in Catholic Grammar School

	Catholic Advantage	Sample Size	
		Public	Catholic
White			
0	0.90	10,162	173
1–7	1.13	703	415
8	1.16	404	806
Minority			
0	2.53	3,805	117
1–7	4.79	243	262
8	4.02	60	285

Objection 5: The effect of Catholic schools disappears when track assignment is controlled.

Some of the critics of the previous NORC research have assumed that academic-track assignment is a surrogate measure of ability (see Peng and Fetters, 1981; Goldberger and Cain, 1982). They note that Catholic-school students are much more likely to be in the academic track than in general or vocational tracks and thus are likely to have higher ambitions and greater ability than public-school students. These critics argue that track assignment is independent of sector and that taking track assignment into account explains the differences between Catholic-school and public-school outcomes.

In fact, a control for track assignment does reduce the difference in achievement growth between Catholic- and public-school students by about half: The overall Catholic growth advantage of 2.3 is reduced to 1.1 among academic-track students and to 1.5 among nonacademic-track students. These figures indicate, however, that the Catholic-school advantage is *not* eliminated and that it is *not* confined to the academic track. Indeed, even though Catholic-school students in the nonacademic track are a much smaller part of the Catholic educational enterprise, they have a greater sophomore-to-senior advantage over their public-school counterparts than do the students in the academic track.

Equating the Catholic growth advantages that remain after controlling for track assignment with the extent of the Catholic effect is tantamount to assuming that track is determined prior to enrollment—i.e., that track has the same explanatory status as family background. It is certainly reasonable to hypothesize, however, that school sector influences track assignment independently of family background. Table 1.4 indicates that such a sector influence is in fact very substantial: Controlling for SES and sophomore achievement, we find that Catholic-school students, on the average, are 22 percent more likely to be assigned to an academic track (averaging all nine differences in Table 1.4). These results show that there is a strong effect of Catholic-school attendance on curriculum assignment.

Table 1.4. Percent Assigned to Academic Track in Public and Catholic Schools, by Parents' SES and Sophomore Achievement (Sample Sizes in Parentheses)

Type of School and Parents' SES[b]	Sophomore Achievement[a] Low	Middle	High
Public			
Low	12 (2,221)	22 (2,493)	49 (498)
Middle	15 (1,925)	29 (5,136)	62 (2,358)
High	19 (308)	45 (1,804)	80 (2,039)
Catholic			
Low	18 (82)	47 (211)	74 (75)
Middle	36 (146)	59 (651)	80 (353)
High	39 (36)	81 (394)	91 (395)

[a] The measure of sophomore achievement is a standardized composite of the six achievement-test scores collapsed into the lower, the middle two, and the upper quartiles (HSB codebook variable BYTESTQ).

[b] The measure of parents' SES is the HSB codebook composite (FUSESQ) collapsed into the lower, the middle two, and the upper quartiles.

Objection 6: The differences between Catholic- and public-school outcomes cannot be linked to specific institutional policies and programs.

This objection is based on the assumption that for comparable students, the demands of public and Catholic schools are the same or, if not the same, are unrelated to achievement. But as Table 1.5 shows, Catholic-school students are much more likely than public-school students to study five or more hours a week; and this propensity to study is true for both white and minority students in both the academic and the nonacademic tracks.

Moreover, Catholic-school students in both tracks are much more likely than public-school students to take advanced courses in mathematics, though not in science (see Table 1.5). The differences in mathematics are especially great among minority students in the nonacademic track: Minority Catholic-school students in a nonacademic track are nearly twice as likely to take second-year algebra and almost three times as likely to take geometry. This advantage, however, largely vanishes in science courses. The experience of being in a nonacademic track is obviously very different in Catholic and in public schools, especially for minority students. The payoff in Catholic-school attendance in mathematics is greater for minorities than for nonminorities, greater for those in the nonacademic track than for those in the academic track. In other words, the common-school effect is especially strong for the multiply disadvantaged.

It is now possible to sort out the influences that might account for the apparent Catholic-school effect in the sophomore-to-senior test-score change. In general, there are three different sets of variables that could enter into the

Table 1.5. Percent of Students in Public and Catholic Schools Completing Homework and Advanced Coursework, by Track and Race-Ethnicity

	Nonacademic Track		Academic Track	
	White	Minority	White	Minority
Public				
Homework[a]	17	18	44	39
Advanced courses				
Algebra I	71	57	97	86
Algebra II	30	25	80	63
Geometry	38	25	88	66
Trigonometry	10	6	56	32
Physics	9	14	40	25
Chemistry	19	16	71	50
Sample size (average)	7,890	3,790	5,240	1,410
Catholic				
Homework[a]	31	24	51	54
Advanced courses				
Algebra I	94	76	98	96
Algebra II	57	45	83	80
Geometry	73	65	94	93
Trigonometry	25	15	63	53
Physics	11	11	35	26
Chemistry	30	21	69	60
Sample size (average)	405	212	1,065	503

[a] Five or more hours per week.

Catholic-school outcome: (1) measured background variables, to which we attribute family and student characteristics, which are independent of the school; (2) measured school variables; and (3) residual variables, which are unmeasured background or school variables. We use multiple-regression analysis, in which variables are entered into an equation in a specific causal order. By using this technique, we are able to account for portions of the Catholic-public difference in test-score gain, showing for each new variable the amount of explanation it adds to that provided by the prior variables. In the analysis, the measured background variables are used to account for whatever variance they can; then, the measured school variables are added to account for some part of the remaining variance. The remaining unexplained difference between Catholic and public schools in the sophomore-to-senior test-score change is attributed to the unmeasured residual variables. Note that in the logic of this approach, no effect that can be explained by a background variable is attributed to a school variable, and any effect that cannot be explained by either the school variables or the background variables is considered unexplained and is *not* regarded as a school effect.

Table 1.6 is a verbal specification of the model. It describes each variable in the regression equation and how that variable is measured. Eight different background variables are included in the model: (1) the sophomore test score, which is used to measure ability, motivation, knowledge, and previous education; (2) parents' education, occupation, and income, which is specified by a composite SES scale; (3) student's race; (4) student's Hispanic ethnicity; (5) parents' decisions to send the student to Catholic school, which is specified by the number of years of Catholic grammar school the student attended; (6) parents' plans for student's further education (specified by father's plans; if mother's plans are entered into the equation, there is no change in the variance explained); (7) parents' participation in school activities; and (8) the student's own college plans, specified by whether s/he plans to attend a four-year college after graduation.

Four different school variables are included in the model: (1) the student's track assignment; (2) the number of advanced courses the student has taken; (3) the extent of discipline problems in the school (based on the student's report); and (4) the number of hours the student spends on homework each week.

In Tables 1.7 and 1.8, we apply the model stated in Table 1.6 to the sophomore-to-senior test-score difference between Catholic- and public-school students to see what part of the Catholic-school advantage may be assigned successively to background, school, and residual components. Thus, the model in Table 1.7 represents eleven different regression equations. When sophomore-to-senior gain is regressed on Catholic-school enrollment, the Catholic-school advantage is 2.19 correct answers. When sophomore achievement is added to the equation to control for students' initial

Table 1.6. Theoretical Model to Explain Catholic-School Advantage in Test-Score Increase between the Sophomore and Senior Years

A. Background variables
  1. Ability, motivation, knowledge, and previous education (sophomore test score)
  2. Parents' education, occupation, and income (SES scale)
  3. Student's race (0–1)
  4. Students' Hispanic ethnicity (0–1)
  5. Parents' decisions to send student to Catholic school (number of years of Catholic grammar school student attended)
  6. Parents' plans for student's further education (father's plans)
  7. Parents' participation in school activities (Is parent a school volunteer?)
  8. Student's college plans (Does student plan to attend a four-year college after graduation?)

B. School variables
  1. Track assignment
  2. Number of advanced courses student has taken (three variables: semesters of English courses taken between 10th and 12th grade; sum of [0–1] responses to whether advanced mathematics courses taken; and sum of [0–1] responses to whether advanced science courses taken [see Table 1.5 for list of advanced math and science courses])
  3. Extent of discipline problems in the school (sum of responses to five variables measuring the extent of the following problems: students not attending school, cutting classes, talking back to teachers, not obeying instructions, and fighting with one another)
  4. Amount of time spent on homework (hours per week)

C. Residual variables

Statistically significant unexplained variance that cannot be attributed to school or background as we are able to measure them

levels of achievement, the Catholic-school advantage increases to 2.67.[2] Then, when socioeconomic status, race, and Hispanic ethnicity are added, the difference diminishes to 2.17 correct answers. When the number of years in Catholic grammar school is added to this set, the difference diminishes to 1.57 correct answers, and so on.

In brief, of the 2.19-item Catholic-school advantage in test-score increase, approximately 50 percent (or one correct answer) can be explained by Catholic students' higher levels of individual and family background, and 1.08 remain unexplained. When track and advanced coursework are taken into account, the difference is diminished to 0.04; and when discipline and homework are added, the difference falls below zero. In other words, about one half of the sophomore-to-senior Catholic-school advantage can be explained by background; the other half is related to things that occur in the school, measured here by curriculum assignment policies, advanced coursework, homework, and discipline climate.

In Table 1.8, the same explanatory model is applied to minority students, to students who were in the lower two quartiles in sophomore test scores, and to low-SES students. For all these students except the minorities, the residual differences are statistically insignificant, and half or more of the explained Catholic advantage can be accounted for by the set of school-experience variables.

We have no explanation for the substantial unexplained advantage of minority students in Catholic schools ($b = 2.16$, $t = 2.4$), and further analysis of the issue is beyond the scope of this article. For now, it is sufficient to

[2] This increase in the Catholic-public difference results from the ceiling effect—i.e., the expected gain is less when initial achievement is high. Thus, the Catholic gain was depressed more than the public gain because sophomore achievement was higher.

Table 1.7. A Model to Explain Catholic-School Advantage in Test-Score Increase between the Sophomore and Senior Years

	Catholic Advantage
Catholic advantage in sophomore-to-senior gain	2.19
A. Net of sophomore achievement	2.67
+ Socioeconomic status, race, ethnicity	2.17
+ Years in Catholic school	1.57
+ Father's college plans for respondent	1.39
+ Parents' participation in school	1.33
+ Respondent's own college plans	1.08
B. Track	0.41
+ Advanced coursework	0.04
+ Disciplinary climate	−0.42
+ Time spent on homework	−0.49
Sample Sizes	
Public 15,377	
Catholic 2,058	

Table 1.8. Model to Explain Catholic-School Advantage in Test-Score Increase between the Sophomore and Senior Years, by Minority Status, Sophomore Test Score, and Parents' SES

	Minority Respondents[a]	Low-Score Respondents[b]	Low-SES Respondents[b]
Catholic advantage in sophomore-to-senior gain	3.94	3.58	1.90
A. Net of sophomore achievement	4.82	3.91	2.43
+ Socioeconomic status, race, ethnicity	4.26	3.01	2.27
+ Years in Catholic school	4.42	2.48	1.75
+ Father's college plans for respondent	4.32	2.24	1.48
+ Parents' participation in school	4.31	2.18	1.47
+ Respondent's own college plans	3.87	1.87	1.27
B. Track	2.90	0.91	0.64
+ Advanced coursework	2.34	0.01	−0.02
+ Disciplinary climate	2.26	−0.10	−0.36
+ Time spent on homework	2.16	−0.25	−0.47
Sample sizes			
Public	4,108	7,181	8,043
Catholic	664	686	729

[a] Blacks and Hispanics.
[b] Lower two quartiles on HSB composite variables.

note that the much higher probability of academic-track assignment, the more rigorous coursework demands, and the greater number of hours spent on homework explain a large share (1.7 items) of the background-adjusted difference.

Critics argue that the amount of time spent on homework and the number of advanced courses taken are not school-effect variables. They contend that even after all the background variables specified in the model have been controlled, homework and advanced coursework are the result of the student's personality and unmeasured background variables, not school demands. But since homework and advanced coursework account for the sophomore-to-senior Catholic-school advantage net of all the prior background variables, we can at least presume that they are school-effect variables.

We can examine indirectly whether greater academic effort in the Catholic school can be attributed to the demands of the school or to the demands of the student's personality. If the difference in effort were due to personality differences, then we would expect the Catholic-public difference to be small when track and college plans are taken into account, especially because Catholic schools put into an academic track students who in public schools would be in a general or vocational track. Yet the differences remain, and the greatest difference between Catholic- and public-school students in the number of advanced courses taken is found precisely among those students who have the least motivation for taking such courses—namely, students in the nonacademic track (see Table 1.9). Moreover, the greatest difference between Catholic- and public-school students in the number of hours spent on

Table 1.9. Number of Advanced Courses Taken and Hours Spent on Homework, by Track and College Plans

	Nonacademic Track		Academic Track	
	Does Not Plan to Attend College	Plans to Attend College	Does Not Plan to Attend College	Plans to Attend College
Public				
Number of advanced courses taken	1.6	2.7	3.5	4.6
Hours spent on homework per week	2.9	4.0	4.6	6.1
Catholic				
Number of advanced courses taken	2.6	3.7	3.8	4.7
Hours spent on homework per week	3.7	5.4	5.1	6.8

homework is not among those in the academic track but among those in the nonacademic track. It seems reasonable to conclude from Table 1.9 that the differences between Catholic- and public-school students in these two variables, particularly in the amount of time spent on homework in the nonacademic track, are the result not of differences in students' ambitions but of differences in the demands of public and Catholic schools.

This inference is strengthened when we examine out-of-school behavior. As Table 1.10 indicates, Catholic-school students do not seem to be any more serious outside school than their public-school counterparts, even when we do *not* take into account student's track assignment, background, and college plans. There are no important differences between the students in T.V. watching, dating, talking to friends, or driving around in automobiles. These results, taken together with those somewhat lower correlations of Table 1.9, suggest that Catholic-school students take more demanding courses not because they are more serious about school but because their schools require them to do so.

The results reported in Tables 1.7 through 1.10 strongly support the proposition that the test-score advantage of Catholic-school students arises from a specific school effect over and above any family or student-input effect, and that the school effect can be attributed to school policies and programs—i.e., placement of students into an academic track, demands for more homework, requirements for more advanced courses, and (less importantly) greater disciplinary stability.

2. LONGITUDINAL EXTENSION OF THE CHK ANALYSIS

It is difficult to draw inferences about differential effects of different institutions on achievement using nonexperimental data, because selection into an institution is not random; it is determined by factors that may affect achievement. Thus, elimination of apparent institutional effects that are spurious—i.e., a result of selection—is the most important task. In our earlier analysis, we were forced to use family-background characteristics as statistical controls; but additional information is available in the 1982 data, and it is now possible to use the 1980 sophomore scores as statistical controls. Thus, we can examine growth in achievement in the public and private sectors over the two-year period. In such analyses, the student's sophomore score is a statistical control on the senior score; therefore, the hypothesis that differences (in either direction) are due to selection is more difficult to maintain.

The most straightforward inference is that differential change is due to differences in the two school environments to which students are exposed. This is expressed in equation (1), which gives predicted senior achievement as a function of sophomore achievement and school sector:

$$\hat{y}_2 = a + b_1 y_1 + b_2 x, \quad (1)$$

where $\hat{y}_2$ is predicted senior achievement score, y_1 is sophomore achievement score, x is school sector (0 = public, 1 = Catholic), b_1 is the effect of sophomore score on senior score, and b_2 is a preliminary measure of the effect of Catholic school on senior score. This same equation can be rewritten to show the predicted growth in achievement from sophomore to senior year:

$$\hat{y}_2 - y_1 = a + (b_1 - 1)y_1 + b_2 x. \quad (2)$$

Equation (2) makes clear that the effect of the Catholic school expressed by b_2 is an effect on *growth* in achievement over the two-year period. Table 2.1 reports the Catholic-school increments in growth for the six tests that were given to students in their sophomore and senior years. These increments are values of the coefficients b_2 in equation (1) or (2). The table shows estimates of substantial Catholic-school effects. Column 5 shows that on average, Catholic-school students gained 0.8 to 1.7 grade equivalents more than public-school students in the two-year period.

Table 1.10. Recreational Patterns of Students in Public and Catholic Schools, and Correlations of Recreational Variables with Advanced Coursework Factor

	Public	Correlation with Advanced Coursework Factor	Catholic	Correlation with Advanced Coursework Factor
Percent watching T.V. three or more hours per day	36	−.16	31	−.15
Percent dating weekly	61	.07	60	.01
Percent talking to friends daily	76	−.07	83	−.08
Percent driving around daily	25	−.07	24	−.10

Table 2.1. Estimates of Catholic-School Effect on Achievement Growth in Six Tests (Standard Errors[a] in Parentheses)

	1	2	3	4	5
Test	Number of Items	Average Number Correct in Public School at Sophomore Level	Average Growth in Public School	Catholic Increment in Growth	Catholic Increment as Grade Equivalent (col. 4)/ [.5(col. 3)]
Reading	19	9.3	1.00	0.66 (.121)	1.3
Vocabulary	21	11.0	1.75	0.72 (.119)	0.8
Mathematics	38	19.1	1.46	1.24 (.192)	1.7
Writing	17	10.5	1.31	0.64 (.114)	1.0
Science	20	11.2	0.79	0.37 (.109)	0.9
Civics	10	5.9	0.84	0.33 (.079)	0.8

NOTE: The test scores reported here and in the remaining tables of section 2 are the numbers of items correctly answered. As in section 1, all analyses use the sample weights (HSB codebook variable PNLTSTWT).

[a] Standard errors are adjusted for an assumed design effect of 1.5. This adjustment is carried out throughout section 2.

A better understanding of achievement growth for low- and high-achieving students can be obtained by examining the average senior achievement levels for students with given sophomore achievement levels. Figures 1 and 2 show the average senior scores on the vocabulary and mathematics tests for students classified according to their sophomore scores. For example, public-school students who got 12 vocabulary items correct as sophomores got an average of 13.8 correct as seniors; Catholic-school students who got 12 correct as

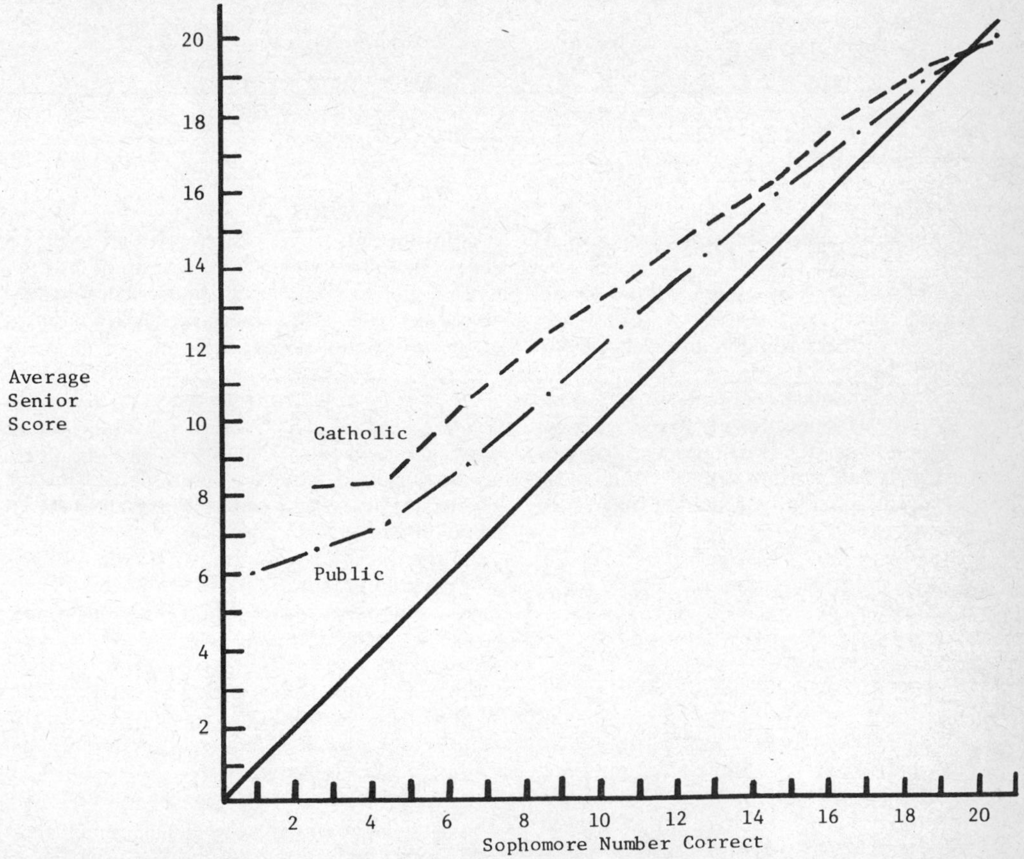

Figure 1. Average Senior Score by Sophomore Number Correct: Vocabulary

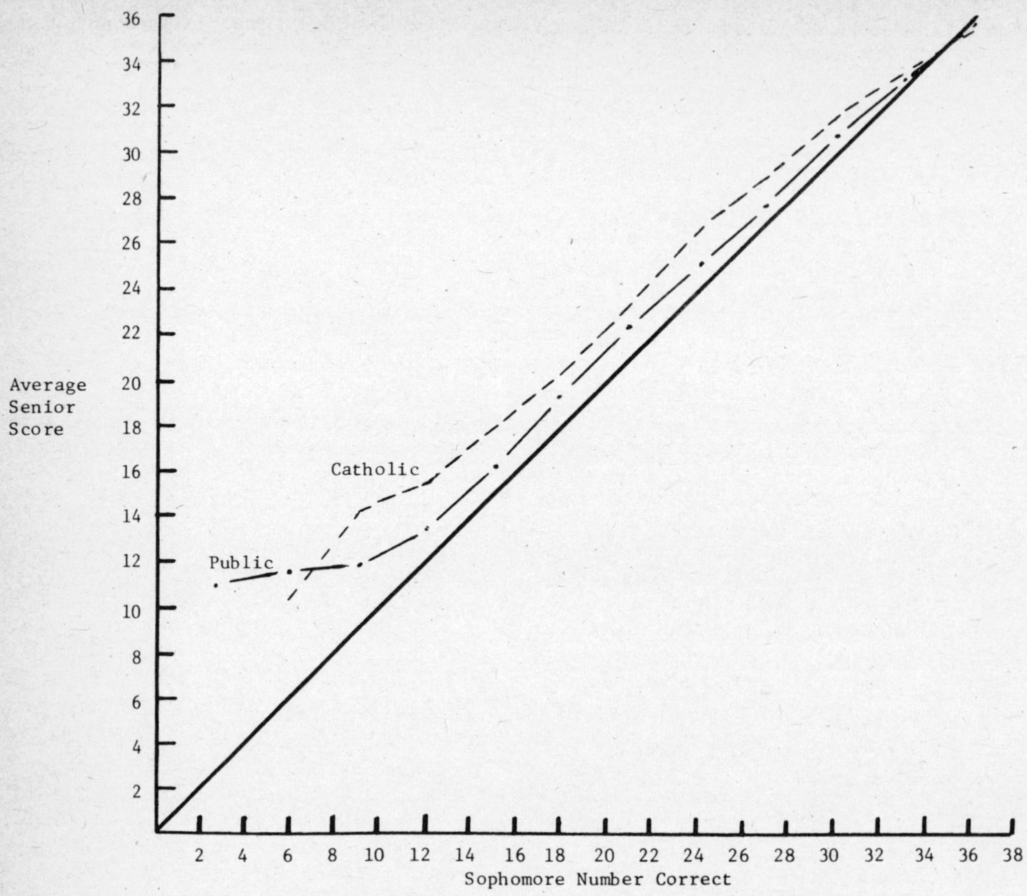

Figure 2. Average Senior Score by Sophomore Number Correct: Mathematics

sophomores got an average of 14.6 correct as seniors.

Figures 1 and 2 show that Catholic-school students at almost all levels of sophomore achievement outperformed public-school students when they were seniors. The sector differences in mathematics are about the same magnitude as the sophomore-to-senior gain for public-school students (i.e., the vertical distance from the public line to the main diagonal), and about two-thirds that magnitude in vocabulary.

This analysis controls for initial achievement and thus controls for the effect of selection on achievement at grade 10; but it is possible that it does not also control for an effect of selection on *growth* in achievement. Put another way, public-school and Catholic-school students not only experienced different school environments over the two-year period, they also experienced different home environments. Two students who had different home environments over this period, like students who had different school environments, can be expected to show differential gains.

Consequently, we augment the analysis shown in equation (1), Table 2.1, and Figures 1 and 2 by incorporating family-background characteristics. Expressed as an extension of equation (2), the equation is

$$\hat{y}_2 - y_1 = a + (b_1 - 1)y_1 + b_2 x + b_3 z, \quad (3)$$

where z is a vector of family-background characteristics, and b_3 is a vector of coefficients expressing the effect of family background on achievement growth over the two years.

In the base-year study, we found considerably greater family-background effects in public schools than in Catholic schools. Thus, in the analysis reported here, we have again allowed for the interaction of family background and school sector by regressing senior achievement on sophomore achievement and family background separately for public- and Catholic-school students.[3]

[3] We do not understand why Goldberger and Cain (1982) vehemently object to our allowance for interaction effects.

Table 2.2. Estimates of Catholic-School Effect on Achievement Growth of Average Public-School Student in Six Tests, Controlling for Family Background (Standard Errors in Parentheses)

Test	Average Number Correct in Public School at Sophomore Level	Average Growth in Public School	Catholic Increment in Growth	Catholic Increment as Grade Equivalent
Reading	9.3	1.00	.53 (.15)	1.1
Vocabulary	11.0	1.75	.70 (.14)	0.8
Mathematics	19.1	1.46	.78 (.24)	1.1
Writing	10.5	1.31	.73 (.13)	1.1
Science	11.2	0.79	.10 (.14)	0.3
Civics	5.9	0.84	.14 (.09)	0.3

NOTE: See note to Table 2.1.

The present analysis includes five more measures of individual background than the base-year analysis. These additional measures are (1) region of the country, (2) respondent's sex, (3) whether or not the respondent had college plans in the 9th grade, (4) whether or not the respondent was handicapped (according to self-description), and (5) urban/rural residence. These measures of individual background are included in addition to the background variables used in the base-year analysis. The individual measures of income, parents' education, and household possessions we used in our base-year analysis are replaced here by a single SES composite variable, which also includes some additional variables that our base-year models excluded: father's occupational status and four additional household possessions. The composite, which is included in the public-use data sets, was constructed by standardizing each of the individual component variables and averaging the sum of the components. Ten measures of background, which we used in the base-year analysis, but which we did not include in the SES composite, are also used in the present analysis.[4]

Results of the analysis are presented in Table 2.2. This table shows that when family background is controlled, the Catholic increment is somewhat reduced (compare Table 2.1) but remains substantial for four of the six tests. For science and civics, the estimated increments are much smaller and not statistically significant. The lack of a substantial Catholic-school effect in science, which was also found in the earlier analysis of sophomore test data, provides an indirect confirmation of a Catholic-school effect in the other areas, operating through the greater academic demands placed on Catholic-school students. As we showed with the sophomore data (Coleman and Hoffer, 1983:226), Catholic-school students in both academic and general tracks take considerably more specialized mathematics courses (second-year algebra, trigonometry, geometry, calculus) than public-school students, though this is not true for chemistry and physics.

The estimated Catholic-school increments shown in Table 2.2 are for students with initial achievement and family background comparable to that of the average public-school student. Because this analysis included interactions between sector and family background and between sector and initial achievement, the increments may differ for other students. Table 2.3 presents the estimated Catholic-school effect for students with initial achievement and background comparable to that of the average Catholic-school student. As the table shows, the increments for the average Catholic-school student are smaller, because this student is closer to the ceiling on the achievement tests (see Figures 1 and 2). Equivalently, the Catholic-school effects are more pronounced for students from lower socioeconomic backgrounds or with lower initial

[4] The ten additional background measures are (1) number of siblings, (2) rooms in household, (3) whether both parents or guardians are present in household, (4) whether mother worked before respondent was in elementary school, (5) whether mother worked while respondent was in elementary school, (6) extent to which respondent talks to parents about personal experiences, (7) whether father expected respondent to go to college when respondent was a sophomore, (8) whether mother expected the same, (9) Hispanic ethnicity, and (10) race. The HSB codebook names for the full set of background variables we used are as follows: RACE (respondent's race and Hispanic ethnicity), BYSES (parents' SES), FY106 (number of siblings), BB103 (rooms in household), BB036b—e (presence or absence of both parents), BB037b&c (mother working or not working when respondent was young), BB047g (extent respondent talks to parents), BB050a&b (parents' educational expectations for respondent), SCHREGN (region of the country [3 dummy variables]), FY100 (rural/small town/suburb/city residence [3 dummy variables]), SEX (respondent's sex), FY103a—g (whether or not respondent is handicapped), BB068b (whether or not respondent planned to go to college in 9th grade).

Table 2.3. Estimates of Catholic-School Effect on Achievement Growth of Average Catholic-School Student in Six Tests, Controlling for Family Background (Standard Errors in Parentheses)

Test	Average Number Correct in Catholic School at Sophomore Level	Predicted Growth in Public School	Catholic Increment in Growth	Catholic-School Effect as Predicted Public-School Grade Equivalent
Reading	10.7	0.93	.42 (.10)	.9
Vocabulary	13.1	1.66	.44 (.09)	.5
Mathematics	22.1	1.72	.68 (.15)	.8
Writing	12.1	1.22	.35 (.08)	.6
Science	12.0	0.83	.10 (.09)	.2
Civics	6.6	0.73	.10 (.06)	.3

NOTE: See note to Table 2.1.

achievement than they are for students from higher socioeconomic backgrounds or with higher initial achievement. This phenomenon is analyzed in some detail below; for the present, it is sufficient to note that the general results shown in Tables 2.1 and 2.2 hold: There are strong positive Catholic-school effects in reading, vocabulary, mathematics, and writing (at least four standard error differences) and weak and statistically insignificant effects in science and civics.

Differential Effects of Background between Sectors: The Common-School Effect

An important subsidiary issue to the assessment of overall sector effects is how the relationship of student background to achievement varies between sectors. In the base-year analysis, we found that socioeconomic background, race, and ethnicity tended to be more weakly related to achievement in the Catholic schools than in the public schools. This finding led us to conclude that the Catholic high schools more closely approximate the common-school ideal than do the public schools. Critics attacked this conclusion, arguing that low-SES and minority students in Catholic schools exceed their public-school counterparts in initial achievement more than high-SES and white students do.[5] For example, if only the most able lower-SES students enrolled in Catholic school, then the apparent effect of SES would be lower in the Catholic sector. This assumption can now be tested. With test performance measured at two points in time, we can statistically control for sophomore achievement (i.e., initial achievement) when examining senior achievement.

The method used here to test for the presence of a common-school effect differs somewhat from that used in the original analysis. The present analysis constitutes a more stringent test: It examines the relative effects of race, ethnicity, and SES *within* school in the two sectors. Thus, differences in achievement growth due to enrollment in schools with different average SES, racial, or ethnic compositions are statistically controlled. Though the effects of these variables on between-school differences in growth represent an important issue (addressed at a later point in this article), the effect examined here is only the within-school component of the overall effect.

To estimate the within-school differentiating effects of race, ethnicity, and SES on achievement growth, senior achievement in each of the six areas is regressed on individual and school mean[6] measures of race and ethnicity, the codebook SES composite, and sophomore achievement, separately by sector. Table 2.4 presents the sector differences in the within-school regression coefficients for these variables. The table indicates that the effects of race, ethnicity, and SES are generally lower in the Catholic schools. The coefficients for race in the Catholic schools are much lower than those in the public schools, except in science. The average difference over all six tests is about one half of the average public-school coefficient. Hispanics are even more advantaged in the Catholic schools than blacks. The average difference over the six tests is over 60 percent of the average public-school coefficient. The effects of SES are also smaller, on average, in the Catholic schools, though the average difference is not as large and there is a reversal in science.

[5] This criticism could not, however, explain why the effect occurred only in the Catholic schools, not in the other private schools, where socioeconomic background is as highly related to achievement as it is in the public schools. It is logically possible for the public sector to show lower effects of school-average SES, race, and ethnicity, and thus to compensate for the within-school common-school effects found in the Catholic schools. However, we have carried out those analyses and do not find such effects.

[6] Individual students' values for the independent variables are removed from the computation of their respective school means. The mean values thus represent averages for each individual's schoolmates.

Table 2.4. Sector Differences in Estimated Effects of Background and Sophomore Achievement Variables on Senior Achievement (Standard Errors of Differences in Parentheses)

Test	Black	Hispanic	SES	Sophomore Achievement
Reading	−.57	−.38	.32	−.020
	(.47)	(.34)	(.15)	(.026)
Vocabulary	−.52	−.67	.22	.061
	(.44)	(.32)	(.15)	(.023)
Mathematics	−.25	−1.02	.03	0
	(.76)	(.56)	(.25)	(.024)
Writing	−.49	−.72	.12	.083
	(.28)	(.29)	(.13)	(.024)
Science	.16	−.14	−.07	.050
	(.43)	(.32)	(.14)	(.028)
Civics	−.29	−.04	.12	.032
	(.28)	(.20)	(.10)	(.031)

NOTE: Sector differences are obtained by subtracting the Catholic regression coefficients from the public coefficients. The regressions include the school-level means of the four individual-level variables shown in this table.

The existence of a common-school effect can be seen in another way as well: Just how much, in the two sectors, does senior achievement depend on sophomore achievement? The greater this dependence, the more a student whose achievement is low as a sophomore is "locked into" low performance. This may occur through tracking into different programs or through grouping into homogeneous sections, or it may occur because few demands are placed on low-performing students, and they are simply passed through the system. The fourth column of Table 2.4 shows the sector differences in the within-school regression coefficients for sophomore achievement-test scores. For four of the six dependent variables, the regression coefficients show that senior achievement is less dependent on sophomore achievement in the Catholic schools than in the public schools. In reading, the senior test score is more dependent on the sophomore score in the Catholic sector, and in mathematics the dependency is equally strong in both sectors.

However, a second question arises when we compare the dependence of senior achievement on sophomore achievement in each sector. Does the relative advantage of some portions of the student body occur at the expense of the other portions? That is, in this case, do the higher-achieving students in Catholic schools gain *less* than their counterparts in public schools?

The dependence of senior performance on sophomore performance can be seen graphically in Figures 1 and 2, which show average senior achievement as a function of number of items correct on the sophomore test. These graphs show that the greater sophomore-to-senior growth among Catholic-school students holds for students at all levels of sophomore achievement. (The other four tests, not presented in graphs, show the same result.) This suggests that the pronounced advantages of lower-achieving Catholic-school students do not result in higher-achieving students learning less than they would in the more differentiated public schools.

In summary, these results generally support our original common-school hypothesis: The differentiating effects of race and ethnicity are consistently less in the Catholic schools than in the public schools. The effect of SES on achievement growth is also lower in Catholic schools, though the Catholic-school superiority is somewhat less pronounced. We have also addressed the common-school hypothesis by asking whether senior achievement is more or less dependent on sophomore achievement in the Catholic schools, and we have shown that the differentiating effects of Catholic-school attendance tend to be lower in this respect as well. While the statistical significance of the sector differences is low for most of the comparisons shown in Table 2.4, the consistency of the Catholic-school advantage is strong support for the common-school hypothesis.

Comparing Students with Equal Propensities for Catholic-School Enrollment

Rosenbaum and Rubin (1983) have proposed a stronger test for elimination of selectivity bias than the linear-regression methods used above. They point out that fewer assumptions are made (for example, the assumption of linearity in effects of background variables) if comparisons are limited to those persons who are comparable in their propensity to be selected into the treatment. The method entails a two-step process. First, each student's propensity to be enrolled in a Catholic school is estimated. Second, the achievement of public- and Catholic-school students who have the same propensity to be in a Catholic school is compared.[7] In practice, the sample is divided into propensity-score quintiles, and comparisons are made within each quintile. If the sector differences are similar in each quintile, then we can infer that the overall sector effects are in fact applicable for students from all backgrounds. If these differences are approximately the same as the Catholic-school effect mea-

[7] See Rosenbaum and Rubin (1983) for details. If certain variables within a quintile remain related to achievement, a within-quintile regression may be carried out to control for their effects.

Table 2.5. Catholic-School Effect on Senior Achievement, by Propensity Quintile

	Quintile				
Test	1	2	3	4	5
Reading	.318	.631	.444	.134	.358
	(.469)	(.343)	(.266)	(.241)	(.189)
Vocabulary	.402	.613	.555	.045	.410
	(.508)	(.338)	(.255)	(.216)	(.164)
Mathematics	.634	.751	.642	.765	.665
	(.736)	(.566)	(.425)	(.371)	(.296)
Writing	.856	.490	.557	−.091	.335
	(.496)	(.339)	(.243)	(.201)	(.155)
Science	−.714	.292	−.172	−.027	.085
	(.439)	(.314)	(.235)	(.208)	(.194)
Civics	.182	.247	.124	−.020	.015
	(.317)	(.230)	(.165)	(.142)	(.108)
Approximate sample size[a]					
Public	3,323	3,052	3,087	2,964	3,061
Catholic	119	223	328	417	845

NOTE: Catholic-school effects are estimated from pooled regressions of senior achievement on sophomore achievement, race, Hispanic ethnicity, composite SES, number of rooms in the home, number of siblings, and the sector dummy.

[a] Cases with missing values on one or more of the variables used in the logistic regression were deleted from the analysis. The sample sizes shown here are averages across the six tests of the numbers of cases with no missing values.

sured with a linear-regression model, the assumptions implicit in that analysis are confirmed.

Our analysis includes such a test. First, we determined each student's propensity for or probability of Catholic-school enrollment, based on a logistic regression.[8] Then, following the recommendation of Rosenbaum and Rubin (1983), we stratified the sample into quintiles of the propensity score and estimated Catholic-school effects within each of these homogeneous groups.[9]

The results of this analysis are shown in Table 2.5. Reading across the rows of the table from the lowest propensity quintile (i.e., those students who are least likely to enroll in Catholic school) to the highest propensity quintile, there does not appear to be any strong pattern of increase or decrease in the estimated Catholic-school effects. The estimates of the Catholic-school advantage in mathematics are the most stable, fluctuating little between the first and fifth quintiles. In reading, vocabulary, and writing—the other three areas in which the overall estimates indicated substantial sector effects—the estimates tend to be quite stable and in the expected direction in the first, second, third, and fifth quintiles, but they are sharply lower in the fourth quintile. The reasons for this estimated drop in verbal achievement gains—a drop that is not at all present in mathematics—are not clear; but the quintiles on both sides of this quintile give confidence that the effects are not confined to those students with especially high or low likelihoods of enrolling in a Catholic school.

Table 2.5 indicates that the overall sector effects on achievement estimated in earlier tables are found within homogeneous subsamples defined in terms of propensity for Catholic-school enrollment. Moreover, in the two areas of achievement in which we found no overall sector effects—science and civics—the absence of effects holds across the stratified

[8] Students' propensities for Catholic-school enrollment are estimated by a logistic regression of sector (Catholic = 1, public = 0) on the set of background measures used in the base-year analysis (substituting the composite SES measure for parents' education and income and household possessions) plus a composite measure of sophomore achievement. Because our analysis of sector entry in the base year found that the relationships of background to entry varied for white, black, and Hispanic students (CHK, 1982b: Ch. 3), the logistic regression was fit on a stratified basis. Propensity scores (in the form of probabilities of Catholic enrollment) were then obtained for each student.

[9] As indicated in footnote 7, relations of background to achievement remaining within quintiles can be controlled by within-quintile regression analysis. To determine which variables required further adjustment, we carried out a sector-by-quintile analysis of variance for each of the twelve predictor variables. We found that significant main and interaction effects of sector within quintiles remained for sophomore achievement, SES, rooms in household, number of siblings, race, and Hispanic ethnicity. Consequently, we controlled for these variables in within-quintile regressions of senior achievement, which we used to obtain estimates of the Catholic-sector effects.

sample. (The sole exception to this latter generalization is found in the large, but insignificant, negative effect of Catholic-school attendance on science achievement among those students who are least likely to attend Catholic school—the first propensity quintile.)

Rates of Learning and Forgetting

Figures 1 and 2 show that in both sectors, the absolute gains differed for students at different levels of initial achievement, and it is useful to understand why the higher-achieving students gained less. It is possible to understand the process if we conceive of each item separately and if we think of the student in either of two states for each item: knowing the answer or not knowing it. The principal process over the period of two years is a learning process; but there is also a forgetting process for those items that have been learned. For example, a sophomore who correctly answered 35 out of 38 items in mathematics could forget 35 items and learn only 3 by the time s/he was a senior, while another sophomore who correctly answered only 1 item could forget only 1 item and learn 37. Thus, the overall process of change can be represented as follows:

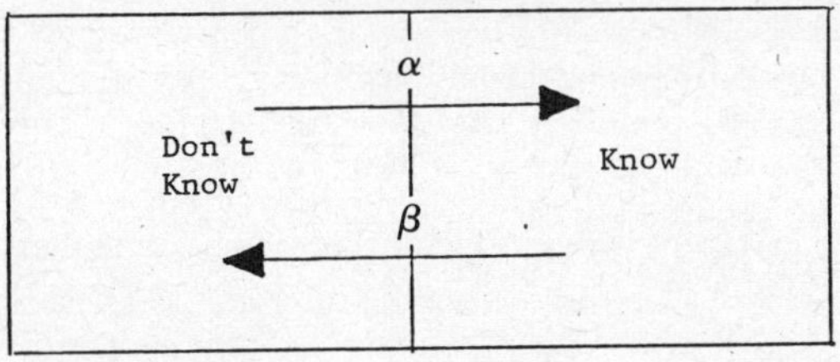

For each item, there is a learning rate, α, from not knowing to knowing, and a forgetting rate, β, from knowing to not knowing. If, for simplicity, we assume that all items are alike, that the learning and forgetting rates are constant over time, and that these rates are the same for all students in a given sector, then it is possible to estimate the values of α and β in the public and Catholic schools. If $p_i(0)$ is the proportion of items that student i knows at the sophomore year, and if $p_i(t)$ is the proportion student i knows at the senior year, then with the above assumptions, $p_i(t)$ is related to $p_i(0)$ by an especially simple relation:

$$p_i(t) = a + bp_i(0), \tag{4}$$

where a and b are functions of α, β, and t.[10].

We derived the learning and forgetting rates reported in Table 2.6 by estimating a and b for Catholic and public schools through linear regression and then by estimating α and β from these (see footnote 10). Of course, these estimates depend on the model used and on the assumptions underlying it. One particularly strong assumption is that all students have the same learning and forgetting rates. Since they do not, the model may not fit the data, as is shown for Catholic-school students in mathematics, where the forgetting rate is negative, an impossibility under the assumptions of the model.

Despite the assumptions on which they are based, these estimates give some further insight into the differences between the two sets of schools, because they are based on changes in individuals, not merely on changes in each sector. The results show that although Catholic-school students had higher forgetting rates on three of the six tests, they had consistently higher learning rates than public-school students—roughly one and one-half times higher. This means that those who did not know an item were much more likely to learn it in Catholic schools than in public schools, although the retention was no greater, in general, in Catholic schools than in public schools.

By abandoning the assumption that rates are alike for all students in each sector, we can calculate more precise learning and forgetting rates for particular subsets of students. If rates differ for different students, and if the differences depend on family background, then a portion of the public-Catholic difference in

---

10 The process is described by the equation $dp/dt = \alpha(1-p) - \beta p$. Solving this for $p(t)$ gives

$$p(t) = p(0)e^{-(\alpha+\beta)t} + \frac{\alpha}{\alpha+\beta}\left[1-e^{-(\alpha+\beta)t}\right].$$

This equation has the same form as equation (4), where

$$b = e^{-(\alpha+\beta)t}$$

and

$$a = \frac{\alpha}{\alpha+\beta}\left[1-e^{-(\alpha+\beta)t}\right].$$

If we take $t=2$ years, then

$$\alpha = \frac{-a \log b}{2(l-b)}$$

and

$$\beta = -\alpha - \tfrac{1}{2}\log b.$$

See Coleman (1968, 1981:Ch. 3) for further discussion.

Table 2.6. Estimated Learning and Forgetting Rates in Public and Catholic Schools

Test	Learning Rates		Forgetting Rates	
	Public	Catholic	Public	Catholic
Reading	.088	.121	.035	.022
Vocabulary	.093	.165	0	.047
Mathematics	.041	.070	.004	−.008
Writing	.141	.230	.019	.017
Science	.101	.154	.043	.055
Civics	.251	.352	.080	.099

NOTE: The rates are calculated using estimates of a and b derived from bivariate regressions of senior achievement on sophomore achievement run separately for each sector.

learning rates is due to differences in average family backgrounds in public and Catholic schools. It turns out (see Coleman, 1981: Ch. 3) that if family-background characteristics contribute additively to the learning rate (and correspondingly subtract from the forgetting rate), an appropriate way to estimate the differences in learning and forgetting rates between public and Catholic schools net of family-background differences is simply to extend equation (4) to multiple regression. This was carried out earlier in the analysis leading to Tables 2.2 and 2.3.[11] Although we will not carry out those calculations here, the regression coefficients on which Tables 2.2 and 2.3 are based could be used to estimate these rates.[12]

[11] Because forgetting rates are quite small relative to learning rates, the assumption that background factors subtract an amount from the forgetting rate equal to the amount they add to the learning rate is probably a poor one. A multiplicative model, as well as other variations, is discussed in Coleman (1981:Ch. 3).

[12] The transformations necessary to obtain α and β in Catholic schools for students with backgrounds comparable to some standard background, such as the average public-school student's background, are as follows:

$$\alpha = \frac{(a_c + \sum_{k=2}^{m} b_{kc}\overline{X}_{kp}) \log b_{lc}}{2n(b_{lc}-1)}$$

and

$$\beta = ½\log(b_1 - \alpha),$$

where b_{kc} is the kth regression coefficient in the Catholic-school equation, n is the number of items in the test, b_{lc} is the regression coefficient for the sophomore test, and $\overline{X}_{kp}$ is the average value for background characteristics k for public-school students.

Growth Rates Compared to Pseudogrowth Estimated in the Base Year

None of the effects estimated in this analysis until this point can be directly compared with those obtained in the cross-sectional analysis, since that analysis estimated effects on the *level* of achievement obtained, and the analysis reported here estimates effects on *growth* in achievement. However, in the cross-sectional analysis, sophomore-to-senior learning rates were estimated by comparing sophomores' and seniors' scores on three subtests, in reading, vocabulary, and mathematics. The actual learning rates of the 1980 sophomores between their sophomore and senior years can be compared to these imputed learning rates. This provides the closest approximation to a direct test of the estimates in the cross-sectional analysis using the longitudinal data.

Because of noncomparability of the cohorts in the cross-sectional analysis, it was not possible to estimate true learning rates. Therefore, we estimated three rates under different assumptions in an attempt to bracket the true rates. The rates may be expressed as the rate in a learning equation:

$$\frac{dp}{dt} = q\ (1-p), \tag{5}$$

where p is the probability that the item is answered correctly, dp/dt is the change in this probability, and q is the learning rate, expressed as the probability that an item will be learned in a year, given that it is not already known. This is a simplification of the process described in the preceding section; it ignores the forgetting process, which cannot be estimated by comparison of cohorts, as was necessary with the cross-sectional data.

The rates estimated from raw and background-adjusted scores are favorable to the public sector and are probably overestimates of the true rates. Those estimated from the dropout-adjusted scores are favorable to the Catholic sector and are probably underestimates of the true rates. From these estimates, it was inferred that in vocabulary and mathematics, Catholic-school students showed unambiguously higher learning rates than public-school students. In reading, however, there was ambiguity, since the public-sector rates were higher according to one set of estimates, and the Catholic-sector rates were higher according to another. It is these imputed learning rates to which the actual gains in achievement of the 1980 sophomores in public and Catholic schools can be compared.

Using the results presented in Table 2.2, it is

possible to estimate the learning rate q, net of family background, for students with a family background like that of the average public-school student, now based on actual changes in achievement rather than on the cohort comparisons estimated with the cross-sectional data. Furthermore, although the learning model estimated here is simpler than that of the preceding section because it assumes a zero forgetting rate, it does control for family-background differences that affect the learning rate. The estimated rates are shown in Table 2.7, along with the earlier estimates.[13]

The learning rates estimated from the longitudinal data correspond very well to those estimated from the cross-sectional data. The cross-sectional estimates for vocabulary and for the Catholic-public difference in reading appear to be too low; otherwise, the correspondence appears quite good. Thus, the longitudinal data confirm this aspect of the cross-sectional analysis, though they indicate that the Catholic-school effects may have been underestimated.

Table 2.7. Estimated Learning Rates from 1980 Cross-Sectional Data Using Sophomore and Senior Scores on Subtests and from Longitudinal Data Using Full Tests

Test	Public	Catholic
Reading		
Cross-sectional		
Raw scores	.11	.10
Background-adjusted	.09	.09
Dropout-adjusted	.06	.07
Longitudinal	.05	.09
Vocabulary		
Cross-sectional		
Raw scores	.10	.13
Background-adjusted	.08	.12
Dropout-adjusted	.05	.10
Longitudinal	.10	.14
Mathematics		
Cross-sectional		
Raw scores	.08	.08
Background-adjusted	.05	.06
Dropout-adjusted	.02	.05
Longitudinal	.04	.06

Sector Effects on School Experiences Related to Achievement

Up to this point, we have identified sector effects on achievement only residually, as the differences in achievement growth that remain after controlling for influences external to the schools. The argument for positive effects of Catholic-school attendance can, of course, be strengthened if we identify the ways in which Catholic schools generate the estimated advantages. This longitudinal extension of the CHK analysis corresponds to the examination carried out in section 1 under objection 6.

In the base-year analysis, we identified, on theoretical grounds, two analytically independent mechanisms through which Catholic schools may realize their students' estimated gains: academic demands and disciplinary standards. After controlling for family background and other extrascholastic influences, we found that Catholic-school students took more mathematics and foreign language courses and spent more time on homework than public-school students. We also found that Catholic schools had lower rates of absenteeism and class cutting and that Catholic-school students had more favorable perceptions of their school's disciplinary climate (CHK, 1982b:Table 6–20). To test the hypothesis that the sector differences remaining after controlling out-of-school influences can be explained by these sector differences in academic demands and disciplinary standards, we regressed achievement on both the background and the school-experience measures and standardized the regression equations to obtain predicted achievement levels. The standardization procedure was designed to estimate how much the average student in one sector would achieve if s/he attended a school with the same academic demands and disciplinary standards that the average student in the other sector experienced. The results of this procedure indicated that public-school students would generally achieve at levels comparable to their Catholic-school peers if public schools maintained the same academic demands and disciplinary standards as Catholic schools (CHK, 1982b: Table 6–21).

The models estimated here differ in two respects from those estimated in the base-year analysis. Critics of our earlier work argued that if Catholic schools increase individual students' achievement, they do so not because of school policies but because of the higher initial achievement and social backgrounds of the other students in the school (McPartland and McDill, 1982). To test for this possibility, we estimated the sector effects on school aggre-

[13] The estimate is made by integrating equation (5) to give

$$q = -\tfrac{1}{2}\log\left[\frac{1-p(t)}{1-p(0)}\right].$$

Given the numbers of items in each of the tests (column 1 of Table 2.1), $p(t)$ for public- and Catholic-school students are obtained from the figures displayed in Table 2.2.

gate student achievement and background and the effects of these compositional variables on senior achievement. A second criticism of our original work concerned our exclusion of students' curriculum program from the analysis. Therefore, we included a measure of program enrollment, which we treated as endogenous to sector as well as to student background and sophomore achievement.

The estimation procedure employed here consists—as in the base-year analysis—of two steps. In the first step, we estimated the effects of school sector on the school-experience variables for students with the same background and sophomore achievement as the average public-school student. In the second step, we regressed senior achievement on the full set of background and prior-achievement variables and the school characteristics and experience variables. We then standardized these regression results to the background of the average student in the public sector and to the predicted levels on the school-experience variables for the same type of student in the Catholic sector.

The results of the first step of this procedure are presented in Table 2.8. The figures in the "public" and "Catholic" columns are the predicted levels of each of the school-experience variables for a student with background and sophomore achievement equal to that of the average public-school student. The figures in the "Catholic advantage" column are simply the differences between the sectors' predicted levels of the school-experience variables. These results indicate that Catholic-school students generally have substantial advantages compared to their public-school counterparts on these measures of school characteristics and experiences that are presumed to contrib-

Table 2.8. Predicted Levels of School-Experience Variables, Standardizing to Average Public-School Sophomore Achievement and Background (Standard Errors of Differences in Parentheses)

	Public	Catholic	Catholic Advantage
Average sophomore achievement			
Reading	9.25	10.27	1.02
Vocabulary	11.01	12.47	1.46
Mathematics	19.08	21.33	2.24
Writing	10.48	11.63	1.15
Science	11.15	11.83	0.68
Civics	5.91	6.47	0.56
Average SES (composite)	−0.04	0.27	0.31
Proportion Hispanic	0.12	0.12	0
Proportion black	0.12	0.07	−0.05
Proportion with 8th-grade college plans	0.59	0.76	0.17
Probability of being in academic program	0.37	0.61	0.23 (.023)
Hours of homework per week	4.00	5.01	1.01 (.220)
Semesters of coursework since sophomore year			
English literature	3.64	3.85	0.21 (.056)
Foreign languages	1.10	1.43	0.33 (.100)
Mathematics	2.37	2.67	0.30 (.076)
Science	2.03	2.13	0.10 (.085)
History/social studies	3.10	3.29	0.19 (.086)
Advanced coursework			
Honors English (0–1)	0.27	0.22	−0.04 (.025)
Number of advanced math courses[a]	2.08	2.74	0.66 (.054)
Number of advanced science courses[b]	1.34	1.54	0.19 (.042)
Attendance			
Absenteeism[c]	2.45	2.18	−0.27 (.063)
Cut class sometimes (0–1)	0.40	0.23	−0.17 (.023)
Perceived student behavior[d]			
Absenteeism	1.61	2.25	0.64 (.012)
Cutting class	1.55	2.30	0.75 (.024)
Students fighting	2.09	2.54	0.46 (.012)
Students threatening teachers	2.84	2.94	0.10 (.004)

[a] Sum of responses to five dichotomous items asking student whether or not s/he has taken Algebra I, Algebra II, geometry, trigonometry, and calculus.

[b] Sum of responses to three dichotomous items asking student whether or not s/he has taken biology, chemistry, and physics.

[c] Ordinal variable ranging from 1 (never absent) to 7 (21 or more days absent); refers to the first semester of the 1981–82 school year.

[d] These items ask students to rate the seriousness of the problems in their schools. Responses range from 1 (often happens) to 3 (rarely or never happens). School-level averages of the items are used in this analysis.

ute to achievement. The Catholic-school effects on other student characteristics are treated here as evidence of sector selectivity plus, in the case of school-aggregate sophomore test scores, the effect of sector prior to the sophomore year. Selectivity is a much less likely explanation for the remaining advantages displayed in the table. When background and sophomore achievement are controlled, we find that Catholic-school students complete more homework and coursework in academic subjects, show lower rates of absenteeism and class cutting, report that various discipline problems are less serious in their schools, and are about 23 percent more likely to be enrolled in an academic program.

To determine the extent to which these Catholic-school advantages account for sector effects on achievement, it is necessary to estimate the effects of the school-experience variables on achievement. This was done by regressing each of the six achievement tests on the full set of individual and school-aggregate measures of background and sophomore achievement and the school-experience variables shown in Table 2.8. The figures in the "Catholic advantage" column were then multiplied by these regression coefficients. The results of these multiplications using the public-school regressions are displayed in Table 2.9. The figures in each row of the table indicate the amount of improvement (or decline, when the comparative sign is negative) that public-school students could be expected to realize on each achievement test if they were at the same level on the row variable or sets of variables as their Catholic-school counterparts. For each test, then, the sum of the row components provides an estimate of the total amount of improvement that public-school students would realize if they had the same school experiences as Catholic-school students. This total can be compared with the estimated sector effects from Table 2.2 in order to obtain an idea of how adequate our explanatory effort has been.

The results shown in Table 2.9 indicate that the explanatory success is in fact limited. Of the four areas of achievement that show substantial sector effects—reading, vocabulary, mathematics and writing—only in mathematics is there a sector difference on these explanatory variables that can fully account for the observed sector effect. The reason for the model's success with mathematics is the exceptionally large effect of advanced mathematics coursework coupled with the substantial positive effect of Catholic-school enrollment on the numbers of these courses that students take. In contrast to this pattern, the effects of English and foreign language coursework on verbal achievement are much smaller, and Catholic-school effects on courses completed in these areas are relatively slight and even negative in advanced English studies.

Despite the limited success of the explanatory effort, certain points are worth noting. Table 2.9 indicates that the less-restrictive academic-program entry criteria in Catholic schools promote higher achievement. The greater amount of time spent on homework and lower rates of absenteeism in the Catholic schools also improve achievement in each of the six areas. Limitations notwithstanding, then, these findings suggest avenues through which student achievement can be improved in the public schools.

3. COMPARISON OF THE ANALYSES

In sections 1 and 2 of this article, we extended the Greeley (1982) and CHK (1982b) cross-sectional analyses of the 1980 HSB data using the achievement-test results from the 1982 follow-up study. We used the same methods in these longitudinal extensions that we used in the earlier cross-sectional analyses. This results, of course, in some differences in presentation, and it is useful to discuss the differences in the methods and the consistency of the results.

Differences in Method

The extension of the Greeley analysis in section 1 is largely based on a combined test

Table 2.9. Achievement Differences between Public and Catholic Schools due to Differences in School Functioning, for Students Similar to the Average Public-School Student

	Reading	Vocabulary	Mathematics	Writing	Science	Civics
Background and sophomore achievement composition of school	.022	.076	.131	.033	−.025	.073
Academic program	.185	.179	.201	.127	.113	.134
Hours of homework per week	.037	.039	.065	.039	.025	.034
Academic coursework	−.023	−.018	.927	−.022	.282	.010
Discipline	.011	.007	.056	.042	.019	.015
Perceived student behavior	−.018	.131	.084	.038	−.017	.024
Total accounted for	.21	.41	1.46	.26	.40	.29
Total to explain (from Table 2.2)	.53	.70	.78	.73	.10	.14

score, which includes reading, vocabulary, mathematics (both parts), and writing and excludes science and civics, which were found to be little affected by Catholic-school enrollment. The combined score is based on formula scores for individual tests. The extension of the CHK analysis in section 2 treats each of the six tests separately. The score on each test is simply the number of items correct.

The regression analysis reported in section 1 (Tables 1.7 and 1.8) is based on pooled samples of public- and Catholic-school students, and the analysis reported in section 2 is stratified by sector. The stratification procedure allows the effects of the independent variables to vary by sector, while pooling without including explicit interaction terms constrains the effects to be equal. Since the advantages of Catholic-school attendance are greatest for students from lower socioeconomic backgrounds, the section 1 estimates are probably somewhat low for these students and somewhat high for students from higher socioeconomic backgrounds.[14] There are various other methodological differences between the sections, but these are apparent in the presentations and need not be mentioned here.

Consistency of Results

Both analyses found the same relative Catholic-school advantage on the achievement tests, and Table 1.1 and nearly all the tables in section 2 show that Catholic-school effects in science and civics are negligible. This same absence of effects was found at the sophomore level in an earlier study (Coleman and Hoffer, 1983:226).

However, when we compare Tables 1.7 and 2.2, we find an apparent inconsistency in the results of the two analyses. In Table 2.2, the total Catholic increment in growth for the four tests (excluding science and civics) after family background is controlled is 2.74 (the sum of the four increments in the penultimate column of the table). The corresponding figure from Table 1.7 is 1.08, before track is included. This inconsistency, however, is at least partly due to the allowance in section 2 for interaction with family background, which shows that the Catholic-school effect differs for students with different backgrounds. (For the average Catholic-school student, the effect, from Table 2.3, is 1.89.)

We can also compare Table 1.2 and Table 2.4. In Table 1.2 the Catholic-school advantage is shown for several groups, including those differing in socioeconomic status and minority status. Table 2.4 shows the different effects of race, ethnicity, and SES on achievement in public and Catholic schools. If the differences between public and Catholic schools are added for the four tests, we see that the *differential* advantage of Catholic-school attendance is 1.83 for blacks and 2.79 for Hispanics. In Table 1.2, the differential advantage for minority students is 2.18. The correspondence is rather good. On the other hand, Table 1.2 shows a reasonably strong differential effect for students of low socioeconomic status, while Table 2.4 shows a weaker SES effect. Table 2.4 shows a consistent differential effect for students with low sophomore test scores, which is consistent with Table 1.2, although quantitative comparisons are not possible.

The analysis in section 1 is somewhat more successful in the search for characteristics that differentiate public and Catholic schools and that might account for the Catholic-sector effect (see Tables 1.7, 1.8, 2.8, and 2.9). This appears in part to be due to the explanatory power of the advanced coursework variables and to the lack of sector interactions with background and schooling variables in the section 1 analysis. There are, of course, a number of additional aspects of the analyses that treat different questions and thus cannot be compared. The above comparisons indicate reasonable consistency despite the different methodological tools used and thus indicate the robustness of the results.

Comparison with Alexander and Pallas

Alexander and Pallas (1983, 1985) also analyzed the data from the 1980 HSB study and the 1982 follow-up but found small or negligible Catholic-school effects on achievement.

There is a fundamental methodological difference between Alexander and Pallas's (1985) analysis and the analyses presented here: They adjusted the test-score correlations—but no other correlations—using reliabilities that were estimated by other investigators who analyzed the same data. The adjustment is not trivial: It increases the correlation between sophomore and senior tests, which is already high, to a very high level.

Given this difference, what do Alexander and Pallas find? Their principal result is expressed in their Table 2, which presents Catholic-school effects as fractions of a year's growth. A comparison with our analysis in

[14] A major contention of some critics of the CHK analysis (see Goldberger and Cain, 1982) is that pooled regressions rather than separate public and private regressions are warranted. We have demonstrated the weakness of that contention elsewhere (CHK, 1982a). In the analyses reported here, we use both techniques and show that the effects occur with either.

section 2 is possible, using fractions of a year's growth from Table 2.2. The comparisons are given in Table 3.1.

Some of Alexander and Pallas's results are very close to ours, although their estimates for reading and writing are considerably below our estimates. They summarize the differences they find, excluding civics, as "about two thirds of a year's growth." Our estimate, excluding science and civics, is about a year's growth.

The issue, however, is not two thirds of a year's growth versus a year's growth. Alexander and Pallas argue that either difference is quite small—less than 0.1 standard deviation. What they neglect to recognize is that this extra year's (or two thirds of a year's) growth occurs over the two-year period. Thus, according to our estimates in section 2, the average public-school student is only learning at about two thirds of the rate at which his counterpart in a Catholic school is learning. In other words, the public-school student is learning two grade equivalents in two years, while the Catholic-school student is learning three grade equivalents.

To be sure, the average growth in either school is small relative to individual differences in performance. But we do not abandon schooling for that reason. If it is to be argued, as Alexander and Pallas do, that the extra benefit of Catholic school as measured by these tests is small, then it can be said that the extra benefit of the last two years of high school is small. It should be noted that part of the reason Alexander and Pallas find the Catholic-school effect particularly small is that they fail to recognize that it is a differential growth between grades 10 and 12, not the *total* Catholic-school effect. They compare it to the effect found in the cross-sectional analyses at grades 10 and 12 as if it were a measurement of the same effect. But it is clearly not that; it is an additional effect *beyond* the 10th grade. The cross-sectional estimates were estimates of the cumulative effect up to grade 10 or grade 12.

Table 3.1. Catholic-School Effect for Average Public-School Student, from Table 2.2 and Alexander and Pallas (1985:Table 2)

Test	From Table 2.2	From Alexander and Pallas, Table 2
Reading	1.1	0.5
Vocabulary	0.8	0.7
Mathematics	1.1	0.8
Writing	1.1	0.6
Science	0.3	0.3
Civics	0.3	−0.1

Alexander and Pallas also fail to find a general common-school effect. Both sections 1 and 2 of this article show the strength of that effect, and the analyses in section 1 document it in great detail. The very simplest of analyses (see Figures 1 and 2) show that the extra gains in Catholic schools are especially great among the students who are low achievers in their sophomore years. Other simple comparisons show it as well. For example, the variance in achievement within Catholic schools went *down*, rather than up, for three of the tests (vocabulary, writing, civics), while it went up for all six tests in the public schools. Of the eighteen correlations of race, Hispanic ethnicity, and socioeconomic status with the six achievement tests, nine went down in Catholic schools, while only three went down in the public schools.

In the face of all this evidence, Alexander and Pallas's analysis shows no consistently higher relation of race, Hispanic ethnicity, or socioeconomic status to achievement in the public sector than in the Catholic sector. Indeed, their regression coefficients (Alexander and Pallas, 1985: Table 4) show a *lower* relation of achievement growth to these three background characteristics. How can this be? The answer appears to lie in the "correction" of correlations for reliability, which they carried out before any regressions were done. This operation raised the sophomore-senior test correlations in the public sector to extremely high levels, leaving very little variance to be explained by any other variable. This correction has a major effect on the results: In four of Alexander and Pallas's regression analyses, the multiple R^2 in the public schools, when only three additional variables were used, was greater than .9; in our analyses (and in Willms's [1985]), the multiple R^2 ranged from around .4 to around .7. Thus, it is no wonder that Alexander and Pallas's regression coefficients for race, Hispanic ethnicity, and socioeconomic status are especially small in the public sector and highly variable in both sectors. This correction also presumably accounts for the deviation of their estimates of a Catholic-school effect from ours in Table 3.1.

Comparison with Willms

Willms (1982, 1985) also examined the effects of schooling on achievement using the 1980 and 1982 HSB data and, like Alexander and Pallas, concludes that no substantial Catholic-school effects are present. His analysis is similar to our analysis in section 2, but it differs in certain methodological and interpretive points. The principal interpretive difference lies in Willms's use of the posttest variance as a standard of comparison for Catholic-school effects. Our criticisms of Alexander and Pallas's reliance on this standard are applicable to Willms's study as well.

The principal methodological differences are twofold. First, Willms uses sophomore test scores in reading, vocabulary, and basic mathematics (28 of the 38 items) as ability controls in all regressions, along with the sophomore score for the test being examined and background characteristics. This may capture sophomore achievements that affect growth on the other three tests.

Second, Willms relies on estimates from single regressions for all students, rather than separate regression equations for public- and Catholic-school students. This forces the relation of all other statistical controls to be alike for Catholic and public schools. In one analysis, he introduces interactions between the Catholic sector and the other statistical controls but dismisses his results because the interaction terms appear to add little explanatory power to the model.

The effect of each of these differences is to lower the estimated Catholic-school effects. The inclusion of the additional sophomore tests as controls is a defensible strategy; however, as we have noted, the only possible drawback of our strategy of allowing for sector-by-background interactions is that it can reduce the efficiency of the estimates.

To assess the consequences of additional controls for sophomore achievement for our results, we added them to the analysis that generated the estimates in Table 2.2. The results are presented in Table 3.2. Inclusion of the additional controls used by Willms does reduce the estimated sector effects, but not by much. All four of the tests for which statistically significant differences were found continue to show significant differences. The conclusions of our analysis are not affected by the inclusion of these additional controls.

Table 3.2. Comparison of Sector Effects in Equations With and Without Additional Statistical Controls for Reading, Vocabulary, and Mathematics (Standard Errors in Parentheses)

	Without Added Controls (from Table 2.2)		With Added Controls	
Test	Items	Grade Equivalent	Items	Grade Equivalent
Reading	.53	1.1	.35 (.14)	0.7
Vocabulary	.70	0.8	.66 (.14)	0.8
Mathematics	.78	1.1	.70 (.24)	1.0
Writing	.73	1.1	.62 (.12)	0.9
Science	.10	0.3	−.10 (.13)	−0.3
Civics	.14	0.3	.04 (.09)	0.1

NOTE: Values of R^2 in the public sector in each of these equations range from .40 (for civics) to .72 (for mathematics) and exceed those reported in Willms (1985:Table 7), where comparisons are possible, so our estimates of effects are not due to less-effective statistical controls.

CONCLUSION

The results we have shown make it difficult to believe that the impact of Catholic school on sophomore-to-senior achievement growth is no greater or only trivially greater than that of the average public school. As we stated above, if one concludes that these differences in growth are trivial, one must also conclude that the growth in achievement in the last two years of high school is trivial.

American educators and educational researchers typically assume that Catholic schools are academically inferior to public schools. They attribute this inferiority to larger classes, less-professional teacher training, more limited resources, smaller per-pupil costs, and religious narrowness, which they believe restricts thought and imagination. To show that Catholic schools, for all their apparent weaknesses, are not worse than public schools may not be too unsettling. But to suggest, as we have, that in terms of academic outcome they might be somewhat better is such a reversal of the conventional wisdom that one might well expect intense debate. How could schools that have always been thought to be somewhat less effective be more effective, and how could schools thought to undermine the American ideal of the common school somehow be closer to that ideal than the public schools?

Because Catholic schools compete with free public schools for their students, some see our earlier results as divisive and harmful to the public schools. Two points should be made in response to this. First, the greater effectiveness of the Catholic schools, which must compete, against strong economic odds, for students, suggests that a little competition might not be harmful for American public schools. The special success Catholic schools have had with the disadvantaged provides added confirmation, because it is the public schools these students attend that come closest to having a captive audience.

Second, our results provide some basis for

policies that might benefit achievement, whether in the public or private sector. Despite the somewhat different approaches of our two investigations, there is convergence in the explanation for the differential effectiveness of Catholic and public schools. Although the analyses do not fully account for the differential effects, there is consistency in the results. Catholic schools place in an academic track many students whose sophomore achievement would relegate them to a general or vocational track in public schools. Catholic schools demand more homework and advanced coursework, especially from those who are disadvantaged in one way or another and especially from those who are not in the academic track. These differences are also consistent with the common-school findings of both analyses: Catholic schools are especially beneficial to the least-advantaged students—the minorities, the poor, and those whose initial achievement is low. For these students, the lack of structure, lower demands, and lower expectations found in many public schools are especially harmful.

Our analyses show that those public schools that make the same demands as the average Catholic school produce comparable achievement. This point has frequently been overlooked in the present controversy. The difference in average scores between Catholic- and public-school students reflects the lower demands of many public schools. In the one area in which Catholic schools do not make coursework demands greater than the average public school—i.e., science—there is no Catholic-school effect.

There is, of course, a remaining question: Why are Catholic schools able to make more demands on their students? But we can just as well ask, Why are some public schools unable to make such demands? International studies, which show that greater demands are made in nearly all developed countries, make the question even more pointed (see Husén, 1967). Indeed, the difference between Japanese and American public schools makes the Catholic-public sector differences pale by comparison. The question of how American public schools can modify their policies in this direction, though it is beyond the scope of this article, is quite pertinent to both educational research and educational policy.[15]

---

[15] One possible explanation advanced by Greeley is that Catholic schools did not abandon stringent academic demands in the late 1960s and early 1970s in the name of social relevance, as did some public schools, because they were not so well connected into the network of professional educational fashions and because they lacked the resources and the flexibility to search for relevance.

REFERENCES

Alexander, K. L. and A. M. Pallas
1983 "Private schools and public policy: New evidence on cognitive achievement in public and private schools." Sociology of Education 56:170–82.
1985 "School sector and cognitive performance: When is a little a little?" Sociology of Education 58:115–28.

Alexander, K. L., A. M. Pallas, and M. A. Cook
1981 "Measure for measure: Ability data in school process research." American Sociological Review 46:619–32.

Coleman, J. S.
1968 "The mathematical study of change." In H. M. Blalock and A. B. Blalock (eds.), Methodology in Social Research. New York: McGraw-Hill.
1981 Longitudinal Data Analysis. New York: Basic.

Coleman, J. S. and T. Hoffer
1983 "Response to Taeuber-James, Cain-Goldberger and Morgan." Sociology of Education 56:219–34.

Coleman, J. S., T. Hoffer, and S. Kilgore
1982a "Achievement and segregation in secondary schools: A further look at public and private school differences." Sociology of Education 55:162–82.
1982b High School Achievement. New York: Basic.

Goldberger, A. S. and G. G. Cain
1982 "The causal analysis of cognitive outcomes in the Coleman, Hoffer and Kilgore report." Sociology of Education 55:103–22.

Greeley, A.
1982 Catholic High Schools and Minority Students. New Brunswick, NJ: Transaction.

Húsen, T. (ed.)
1967 International Study of Achievement in Mathematics: A Comparison of Twelve Countries. New York: Wiley.

McPartland, J. M. and E. L. McDill
1982 "Control and differentiation in the structure of American education." Sociology of Education 55:77–88.

Peng, S. and W. Fetters
1981 Review of Draft Report of Minority Students in Catholic Secondary Schools by Andrew Greeley. Washington, D.C.: National Center for Education Statistics.

Rosenbaum, P. and D. Rubin
1983 "The central role of the propensity score in observational studies for causal effects." Biometrika 70:41–55.

Willms, J. D.
1982 "Achievement outcomes in public and private schools: A closer look at the 'High School and Beyond' data." Stanford Institute for Research on Educational Finance and Governance.
1985 "Catholic-school effects on academic achievement: New evidence from the High School and Beyond follow-up study." Sociology of Education 58:98–114.

CATHOLIC-SCHOOL EFFECTS ON ACADEMIC ACHIEVEMENT: NEW EVIDENCE FROM THE HIGH SCHOOL AND BEYOND FOLLOW-UP STUDY

J. DOUGLAS WILLMS

University of Edinburgh and University of British Columbia

Sociology of Education 1985, Vol. 58 (April):98–114

This study compares the growth in academic achievement of public- and Catholic-school students during their last two years of high school. The study uses the High School and Beyond data on over 20,000 students who participated in the 1980 base-year study and the 1982 follow-up study. Previous studies of public- and private-school effectiveness, including the controversial Coleman, Hoffer, and Kilgore (1981) study, have been limited to the 1980 cross-sectional data, which do not include information on student ability prior to entering high school. The follow-up data enable a comparison of the growth in achievement on outcome measures that were specifically designed for that purpose. I estimated Catholic-school effects with four different statistical models. Each model regresses senior test scores on sophomore pretest scores; sophomore test scores in reading, vocabulary, and general mathematics; and a set of background variables describing student characteristics and family background. Three of the models include background measures from previously published studies; the fourth model is a parsimonious model including only the most important control variables. I conducted several subsidiary analyses to ensure that the results were not substantially biased due to such factors as the method of handling missing data, the differential dropout rate between the two sectors, and the ceiling effects on the outcome measures. I also examined the extent to which the achievement tests were valid indicators of student growth in academic achievement. The results suggest that there are no pervasive Catholic-school effects. Public schools had a small advantage in science and civics; Catholic schools had an advantage in reading, vocabulary, mathematics, and writing. All of the effects were very small: On average, the Catholic-school advantage was only about 5 percent of a standard deviation. However, the analyses also suggest that the tests are relatively poor measures of academic growth during the junior and senior years of high school. Therefore, we cannot be certain that the tests are sensitive enough to detect differences that might exist between public and Catholic schools in their effects on student achievement.

Coleman, Hoffer, and Kilgore (CHK) report that sophomores in Catholic high schools score about 15 to 20 percent of a standard deviation higher in reading, vocabulary, and general mathematics than their public-school counterparts, after controlling for differences in family background (CHK, 1981, 1982a, 1982b, 1982c). They attribute the better performance of Catholic-school students to the disciplinary climate and the quality of instruction in Catholic schools. Coleman (1981) used these findings to suggest that an expanded role for private education in the U.S. should be encouraged through a variety of public-policy mechanisms.

CHK (1981) used data from the first wave of the High School and Beyond (HSB) study of over 58,000 students in over 1,000 U.S. secondary schools. They attempted to adjust for differences in student intake between public and private schools by using several control variables describing student characteristics and family background. The study was limited, however, in that the most important control variable—scholastic aptitude prior to entering high school—was not available in the 1980 data. The certainty of their estimates, therefore, depends on the adequacy of their statistical model to control for selection differences; and many subsequent analyses of the data (Noell, 1981, 1982; Alexander and Pallas, 1983;

This article is a revised version of "Public and Private School Outcomes: Results from the High School and Beyond Follow-up Study," which was presented at the Annual Meeting of the American Educational Research Association in New Orleans, April 23–27, 1984, and is available from the Stanford Institute for Research on Educational Finance and Governance. The research for this report was supported by the Centre for Educational Sociology, University of Edinburgh. The analysis and conclusions do not necessarily reflect the views or policies of this or any other organization. I would like to thank Peter Burnhill, Peter Cuttance, and other colleagues at the Centre for Educational Sociology for their useful comments on this article. Sally Kilgore, Michael Olneck, and one anonymous reviewer also provided many useful comments, particularly concerning the standardization of effect sizes and model specification. I am grateful for their contributions.
Address all correspondence to the author at the Centre for Educational Sociology, University of Edinburgh, 7 Buccleuch Place, Edinburgh, SCOTLAND EH8 9LN.

Willms, 1983, 1984b) attempted to address the problem. CHK (1982c:123) acknowledged the problem of selection bias, stating that "the existence of measures at two points in time will help remove some of the uncertainty; but even then, uncertainty will remain."

Measures at two points in time are now available.[1] In the spring of 1982, the National Center for Education Statistics (NCES) collected the second wave of data for the HSB study. The high school seniors in the 1982 wave are a subset of the students who participated as sophomores in the 1980 study. The new wave of data enables us to compare the achievement-test scores of seniors in public and private schools while controlling for their sophomore test scores.

The purpose of this study is to present more accurate estimates of Catholic-school effects than was possible with only the 1980 cross-sectional data. The estimates are based on the test scores of all students who participated in both the 1980 and 1982 studies. The "intervention period," for which Catholic-school effects are estimated, includes the last two years of high school. The analysis uses scores on four achievement tests that were specifically designed to assess the impact of schooling during that period. If Catholic schools perform better than public schools in promoting academic achievement during the final two years of high school, then the test scores of Catholic-school seniors should be substantially higher than the test scores of public-school seniors, even after controlling for their sophomore test scores. It is possible that either the public or Catholic schools have their greatest impact during the first two years of secondary schooling; however, to address that question accurately, we require data on student achievement prior to entering secondary school. In this study, I assume that, on the average and within each sector, the relative effectiveness of schools during the last two years of high school is comparable to the relative effectiveness during the first two years.

To estimate Catholic-school effects on senior test scores, I use the same sets of control variables used in three previously published studies (CHK, 1981; Noell, 1982; Willms, 1984b). In each case, I extend the model to include statistical controls for sophomore achievement. These models provide estimates of the expected gain in achievement for a student who attended a Catholic school, rather than a public school, during his or her junior and senior years. The use of three separate models should not be considered a fishing expedition for the best results; I use these different specifications to produce a range of estimates of a Catholic-school effect, which provides more certainty about the true size of the effect. Also, I use the results from the three models to develop a parsimonious model, which I use to demonstrate the robustness of the results across different statistical methods. I conclude with a discussion of the possible sources of bias in these estimates and other limitations of the study.

DATA BASE AND VARIABLES

The HSB sample is a two-stage stratified cluster sample. In the first stage of the base-year (1980) survey, 1,022 schools were sampled from a total frame of 26,095 schools. The sample included oversampled strata of public alternative schools, private schools, and schools that were over 30 percent black and Hispanic. In the second stage, approximately 36 sophomores in each school were asked to complete an identification booklet and questionnaire and to take a battery of timed cognitive-achievement tests. The first follow-up (1982) study included all 1980 sophomores who were still enrolled in their base-year schools and a stratified subsample of school leavers, including those who dropped out, transferred, or graduated early. These students were asked to complete a questionnaire and to retake the 1980 test battery. Jones et al. (1983) provide further details of the sample design and the questionnaires.

This study uses data for 21,772 public- and Catholic-school students who completed the test batteries in both years. I exclude dropouts from the sample for most analyses; however, I repeat the major analyses with dropouts to ensure that their exclusion does not substantially bias the estimates of Catholic-school effects in either direction.[2] The analyses use a design weight to account for the stratified structure of the sample. Appendix A shows the weighted and unweighted sample sizes, with and without dropouts, for the various public and Catholic substrata. I do not use data for students in non-Catholic private schools because this sub-

[1] The HSB data are available from the National Center for Education Statistics, 400 Maryland Ave. SW, Presidential Building, Washington, D.C. 20202.

[2] I did not attempt different analyses with the transfer students. Out of 28,116 students who participated in the follow-up study, only 4.2 percent transferred to other schools. Eighty-nine percent of the transfer students finished in public schools; 11 percent finished in religious or other private schools. I am assuming that the small number of students who transferred from a public school to a private school, or vice versa, will not bias the results.

sample is small—only 27 schools—and its randomness is compromised by nonparticipation (Goldberger and Cain, 1982).

The HSB test battery was developed by the Educational Testing Service of Princeton, New Jersey. It includes seven tests: Three of the tests—reading, vocabulary, and general mathematics—measure basic academic skills; the other four tests—advanced mathematics, writing, science, and civics—were designed specifically to measure skills that are taught during the junior and senior years of high school. Table 1 shows the means and standard deviations of the test scores for the total sample and for each sector. Dropouts were excluded from the sample in these calculations. Heyns and Hilton (1982) provide a comprehensive review of both the general achievement and the curriculum-specific tests.

Senior scores on the four curriculum-specific tests are the main dependent measures in this study. The advanced mathematics test measures skills in algebra, geometry, and trigonometry—skills that were not measured on the general mathematics test. The writing test measures writing ability and knowledge of basic grammar. The science test is composed predominantly of items from tests used by the National Assessment of Educational Progress (NAEP). Tests constructed by NAEP are based on domains of content that represent the academic goals of a representative sample of U.S. high schools. The civics test measures knowledge of various principles of law, government, and social behavior.

I also include scores on the three tests of basic academic skills to enable comparisons with earlier work and as a means to judge the sensitivity of the curriculum-specific tests. In an earlier draft of this article (Willms, 1984a), I did not include scores on these tests, because it was difficult to infer that they were affected by school instruction during the junior and senior years of high school. CHK (1982c: 130) previously felt the same way about these tests:

> It might be argued that the lack of growth from the sophomore to the senior year can be explained by the fact that these tests do not cover subject matter that is an explicit part of the curriculum in the later years of high school. The mathematics items are all rather elementary, involving basic arithmetic operations, fractions, and only a few hints of algebra and geometry. Explicit attention to reading comprehension and to vocabulary expansion is not part of standard curricula in the 10th through 12th grades. We would, thus, not expect the variation in intensity and scope of the academic courses taken during these years. . . . to have a direct impact on the variations in the sophomore to senior test score gains. Two or three of the tests given to sophomores (science, civics, writing composition skills) should reflect such curriculum variations when they are administered again in 1982 to these same students as seniors.

The main analyses include statistical controls for both prior academic achievement and family background. The controls for prior academic achievement include the sophomore scores on the tests used as the outcome measures (i.e., the pretest) and the sophomore scores on the three tests of basic academic skills. I include the latter three tests to adjust for differences in some of the general academic skills that affect the rate of progress in other academic subjects. There is some danger of overadjustment, but without these additional

Table 1. High School and Beyond Achievement-Test Scores

	1980 Sophomores						1982 Seniors					
	U.S. Total		Public		Catholic		U.S. Total		Public		Catholic	
Test	Mean	SD	Mean	SD	Mean	SD	Mean	SD	Mean	SD	Mean	SD
General achievement tests												
Reading (19 items)	9.305	3.856	9.207	3.859	10.586	3.584	10.293	4.129	10.175	4.313	11.833	3.783
Vocabulary (21 items)	11.124	4.277	10.982	4.274	12.982	3.863	12.866	4.510	12.699	4.521	15.058	3.724
General math (28 items)	14.746	5.784	14.585	5.803	16.850	5.094	15.872	6.326	15.663	6.330	18.576	5.615
Curriculum-specific tests												
Advanced math (10 items)	4.419	2.076	4.380	2.073	4.931	2.040	4.706	2.228	4.651	2.220	5.411	2.216
Writing (17 items)	10.535	3.867	10.421	3.874	11.991	3.462	11.808	3.880	11.686	3.909	13.367	3.096
Science (20 items)	11.186	3.704	11.127	3.731	11.949	3.241	11.950	3.751	11.878	3.776	12.878	3.271
Civics (10 items)	5.943	2.011	5.894	2.015	6.567	1.850	6.784	2.086	6.738	2.095	7.365	1.876

NOTE: Means and standard deviations are based on the weighted sample, excluding dropouts.

controls, the likelihood of underadjustment due to measurement error in the pretest is probably greater. Assuming that scores on these three tests are related to posttest performance, their inclusion increases the power of the analysis and reduces the bias due to underadjustment (see Reichardt, 1979). In a later section, I discuss the possibility of overadjustment and repeat the main analyses without these additional controls.

The measures describing student characteristics and family background are the same as those used by CHK (1982c), Noell (1982), and Willms (1984b), with some exceptions. Most of the questions on student characteristics and family background were repeated in the follow-up questionnaire. I assumed that seniors' responses to these questions were better indicators of student and family characteristics during the intervention period than sophomores' responses and therefore used data from the follow-up questionnaire. I used the composite sex and race variables that were constructed by NCES following their extensive review of missing data and contradictory information in the two surveys. I also used NCES's SES variable, which is a composite of father's occupational prestige score, father's and mother's education, family income, and a scale of eight household items.[3] The variables denoting the percentage of students in the school who were black or Hispanic were derived from questionnaires distributed among the school administrators. Table 2 shows the means and standard deviations for the measures of student characteristics and family background used in the various models.

ESTIMATES OF CATHOLIC-SCHOOL EFFECTS

To estimate Catholic-school effects, I use ordinary-least-squares regression[4] and an additive model: Senior test scores are regressed on a dummy variable denoting public- or Catholic-school attendance; the sophomore scores on the corresponding pretest; the sophomore scores on the reading, vocabulary, and general mathematics tests; and a set of variables describing student characteristics and family background. In the first three models, the variables describing student characteristics and family background are from models previously used to adjust for differences that existed between public- and Catholic-school students prior to their entry into high school. The fourth model, which I refer to as the reduced model, contains a shorter list of variables describing student characteristics and family background. In all analyses I use pairwise deletion of missing data and the HSB design weights. I express the size of the Catholic-school effect as a fraction of the pooled within-group standard deviation of the senior tests. After presenting the results, I discuss the rationale for this standardization and examine several of the assumptions underlying my choice of statistical techniques.

Results from the Four Models

Model 1: ANCOVA Model with CHK Covariates. The first model includes statistical controls for the sophomore pretest, the three tests of basic academic skills, and the set of 17 covariates used by CHK (1981) in their cross-sectional analyses: family income; mother's education; father's education; race and ethnicity; number of siblings; number of rooms in the home; presence of both parents; whether the mother worked while the student was in elementary school; whether the mother worked before the student was in elementary school; the presence of encyclopedias, a typewriter, more than 50 books, and a calculator in the home; whether the student talks with his or her parents; and the mother's and father's aspirations for the student to attend college.

The estimates of Catholic-school effects for a student with average U.S. characteristics, for each of the seven tests, are shown in column 1 of Table 3. The estimates for the science and civics tests are both negative (−.028 and −.007, respectively), indicating a small public-school advantage; whereas the estimates for the advanced mathematics and writing tests are positive (.027 and .067, respectively), indicating a small Catholic-school advantage. On the three general achievement tests, the estimates also favor Catholic schools and are slightly larger than those observed on the curriculum-specific tests. The vocabulary test shows the largest effect—10.9 percent of a standard deviation. In the next section, I will discuss the statistical and substantive significance of these effects.

---

[3] Willms's (1983, 1984b) SES composite was derived from a principal components analysis of fathers' and mothers' education and occupational prestige. That variable has a correlation of 0.81 with the 1980 NCES composite.

[4] OLS regression assumes that the model is correctly specified and that the residuals are not correlated with the lagged variables. The latter assumption would likely be invalid if there were only a short interval between test administrations; however, in the present study the posttests were administered two years after the pretests. Therefore, unless there were some quirks of administration at the school level, such as an extension of the allotted test time on both occasions, it is unlikely that there will be a strong correlation between residuals and the lagged variables.

Table 2. Means and Standard Deviations for Variables Used as Statistical Controls for Student Characteristics and Family Background, for the Total Sample and by Sector

	U.S. Total		Public		Catholic	
Control Variable	Mean	SD	Mean	SD	Mean	SD
Sector (0 = public, 1 = Catholic)	.071	.256	0	0	1.000	0
Annual family income (8 categories)	4.454	2.047	4.393	2.043	5.283	1.920
Mother's level of education	3.214	2.195	3.163	2.174	3.861	2.353
Father's level of education	3.636	2.565	3.558	2.540	4.622	2.669
Race (1 = black, 0 = other)	.120	.324	.124	.330	.058	.235
Ethnicity (1 = Hispanic, 0 = other)	.124	.329	.126	.332	.091	.288
Number of siblings (plus 1)	3.840	1.707	3.835	1.702	3.898	1.764
Number of rooms in home	6.867	1.852	6.825	1.848	7.417	1.819
Both parents present (1 = yes)	.762	.426	.755	.430	.848	.359
Mother worked when child in elementary school	.589	.492	.590	.492	.574	.495
Mother worked before child in elementary school	.391	.488	.395	.489	.334	.472
Encyclopedia in home	.882	.322	.878	.328	.940	.238
Typewriter in home	.757	.429	.748	.434	.877	.328
More than 50 books in home	.846	.361	.841	.366	.914	.280
Pocket calculator in home	.883	.321	.880	.325	.929	.257
Talks with parents (4 categories)	2.248	1.136	2.246	1.136	2.262	1.138
Mother thinks student should go to college (1 = yes)	.645	.478	.632	.482	.818	.386
Father thinks student should go to college (1 = yes)	.568	.495	.553	.497	.764	.425
Sex (1 = female, 0 = male)	.506	.500	.503	.500	.548	.498
Handicapping condition (1 = yes)	.075	.263	.076	.265	.055	.228
School region (1 = Northeast)	.220	.414	.209	.407	.358	.479
School region (1 = North Central)	.300	.458	.298	.455	.392	.488
School region (1 = South)	.228	.420	.241	.428	.058	.234
8th-grade college expectations	.542	.498	.529	.499	.708	.455
Student's SES	−.041	.717	−.067	.715	.308	.646
Within-school mean SES	−.041	.384	−.069	.374	.317	.326
Percent of students black	13.333	22.420	13.927	22.927	5.754	12.151
Percent of students Hispanic	4.877	12.739	4.730	12.749	6.752	12.467
Student has taken geometry or trigonometry (1 = yes)	.559	.497	.535	.499	.862	.345
Student has taken 2 or more years of science (1 = yes)	.533	.499	.522	.500	.681	.466
Student has taken 3 or more years of English (1 = yes)	.795	.404	.787	.409	.896	.306
Student has taken 2nd-year algebra (1 = yes)	.488	.500	.470	.499	.724	.447

NOTE: Means and standard deviations are based on the weighted sample, excluding dropouts.

Model 2: ANCOVA Model with Noell's (1982) Covariates. The second model includes the same controls for prior academic achievement but uses Noell's (1982) controls for student characteristics and family background. His background measures include the full CHK list above plus controls for gender, handicapped status, region of the country, and the student's retrospective report of college expectations in the eighth grade. Estimates for Model 2 are shown in column 2 of Table 3. The additional control measures reduce the effects by about 1 percent of a standard deviation across all seven tests. Most of this change arises from the additional controls for gender, handicapped status, and college expectations; the region variables are not statistically significant predictors of senior test scores across the seven tests.[5]

Model 3: ANCOVA Model with Willms' Covariates. In previous studies (Willms, 1983, 1984b) I examined the effects of student-body composition on academic achievement and the range of school effectiveness within the public and private sectors. I conjectured that schools serving students with higher average levels of socioeconomic status might show greater gains in academic achievement for several reasons, such as higher-quality peer interactions, more

[5] Some of the region variables were statistically significant for certain tests because of the large sample sizes; however, in all cases they were weak predictors (standardized betas <0.022).

Table 3. Estimates of Catholic-School Effects on Growth in Academic Achievement on the Seven HSB Achievement Tests, Controlling for Student Characteristics, Family Background, and Prior Academic Achievement, with Four Sets of Covariates (Dropouts are Excluded from the Sample)

	Model			
Test	1	2	3	4
General achievement tests				
Reading	.037	.038	.064*	.046
Vocabulary	.109*	.099*	.090*	.112*
General math	.067*	.055*	.077*	.092*
Curriculum-specific tests				
Advanced math	.027	.019	.030	.048
Writing	.067*	.056	.068*	.069*
Science	−.028	−.035	−.012	−.018
Civics	−.007	−.019	−.014	.000

NOTE: Estimates of Catholic-school effects are expressed as fractions of the pooled within-group standard deviation of the posttest. Controls for prior academic achievement in all four models include scores on the corresponding pretest plus the sophomore scores in reading, vocabulary, and general math. (The analyses for reading, vocabulary, and general math include only two tests as additional controls, rather than three.) The controls for family background and student characteristics for each model are as follows:

Model 1: family income; mother's education; father's education; race and ethnicity; number of siblings; number of rooms in the home; presence of both parents; whether or not mother worked while student was in elementary school; whether or not mother worked before student was in elementary school; presence of encyclopedias, typewriter, books, and calculator in the home; whether or not child talks with parents; mother's and father's aspirations for student to attend college.

Model 2: same as Model 1 plus sex, handicapped status, region, and student's college expectations in the eighth grade.

Model 3: socioeconomic status, race, ethnicity, sex, school mean socioeconomic status, and percent of blacks and Hispanics in the school.

Model 4: socioeconomic status, race, ethnicity, sex, presence of both parents, handicapped status.

* Estimates are statistically significant using the ± 3-sigma rule suggested by Goldberger and Cain (1982).

enriched curricula, higher teachers' expectations, or better teaching and disciplinary climates. I attempted to control for these contextual influences in the model by including the within-school means of the background measures as proxies for all the factors associated with school context.

Contextual effects are a part of what we usually call school effects, and one could argue that a comparison of public- and Catholic-school performance should not include statistical controls for student-body composition. However, the distinction between school effects arising from the demographic concentration of students and school effects arising from other school factors is important for assessing the impact of certain educational policies. My comparison of schools serving similar student populations showed that the range of school effectiveness within each sector far outweighed any differences between them. I concluded that a policy that induced a migration of students from public to Catholic schools would probably be counter-productive: It would change the character of the student population in Catholic schools in such a way that their average achievement levels would be lowered.

Therefore, in addition to the individual-level controls for student characteristics, family background, and prior academic achievement, Model 3 includes three measures to capture the effects of student-body composition: the average socioeconomic status of students in the school and the percentage of blacks and Hispanics in the school. The percentage of females in the school was not related to academic achievement in my previous work; therefore, it is not included in this analysis.

The results from this model are shown in column 3 of Table 3. The effect sizes are almost identical to the effect sizes found in Model 1. The most important predictors of senior test performance are the pretest scores, the tests of prior academic achievement, socioeconomic status, sex, race, and ethnicity. The contextual variables show weak effects across all seven tests.

Model 4: The Reduced Model. The estimates of the regression slopes for many of the variables describing student characteristics and family background in the above three models were not statistically significant across all seven tests, and some were significant for only one or two of the seven tests. In particular, in Models 1 and 2, parameter estimates for many of the SES variables, such as the possession of certain household items, were not statistically significant. The parameter estimates for the contextual-effects variables in Model 3 were also very small (standardized betas < 0.026) across all seven tests, and in most cases they were not statistically significant. In order to isolate the effects of the most important variables and provide a simpler description of the processes affecting senior achievement-test scores, I estimated the parameters with a re-

Table 4. Regression Equations Estimating Catholic-School Effects on Seven Achievement-Test Scores for Average U.S. Student, Controlling for Student Characteristics, Family Background, and Prior Academic Achievement

	Reading		Vocabulary		General Math		Advanced Math		Writing		Science		Civics	
	b	SE	*b*	SE	*b*	SE	*b*	SE	*b*	SE	*b*	SE	*b*	SE
Intercept	1.549*	.086	3.321*	.086	2.545*	.117	.559*	.053	3.042*	.085	3.958*	.085	2.652*	.058
PRIVATE	.189	.076	.502*	.076	.581*	.104	.106	.047	.267*	.074	−.068	.070	0	.048
Sophomore test	.439*	.008	.549*	.007	.704*	.007	.262*	.008	.390*	.008	.414*	.007	.199*	.008
READING 10	—	—	.216*	.008	.175*	.011	.047*	.005	.108*	.008	.113*	.007	.099*	.005
VOCAB 10	.221*	.007	—	—	.132*	.009	.022*	.004	.109*	.007	.111*	.006	.091*	.004
GEN MATH 10	.045*	.005	.095*	.005	—	—	.156*	.003	.119*	.005	.100*	.004	.058*	.003
SES	.130*	.031	.419*	.031	.543*	.042	.149*	.019	.127*	.030	.152*	.028	.047	.020
BLACK	−.211*	.065	−.620*	.065	−.187	.089	.074	.040	−.372*	.063	−.905*	.060	.017	.042
HISP	−.303*	.063	−.614*	.062	−.566*	.085	−.063	.038	−.444*	.061	−.652*	.057	−.184*	.040
FEMALE	.045	.039	.144*	.039	−.482*	.053	−.179*	.024	1.250*	.041	−.552*	.036	.219*	.025
BOTHPAR	.161*	.047	.134	.047	.247*	.065	.109*	.029	.236*	.046	.132*	.043	.113*	.030
HANDICAP	−.318*	.074	−.339*	.074	−.376*	.101	.096	.045	−.605*	.072	−.259*	.067	−.262*	.047
R^2	.60338		.66899		.68747		.50453		.59085		.60903		.39632	

NOTE: Regressions are based on the weighted sample, excluding dropouts. Standard errors are based on a nominal sample size (see footnote 8).
* Estimates are statistically significant using the ± 3-sigma rule suggested by Goldberger and Cain (1982).

duced model that included only the following controls for student characteristics and family background: socioeconomic status, race, ethnicity, gender, handicapped status, and presence of both parents in the home.

I did not include the variable describing eighth-grade college expectations, even though it was statistically significant across all four tests in Model 2, because I felt that students' retrospective accounts of their earlier college plans were probably unreliable and might be affected by present aspirations. Variables describing students' present aspirations might be endogenous to the schooling process and therefore should be excluded from the model.

Table 4 shows the parameter estimates for all variables included in the reduced model. Most of the background covariates are statistically significant[6] across all seven regressions. The estimates of Catholic-school effects found in Model 4 (column 4 of Table 3) are 0.8 to 3.7 percent of a standard deviation larger than those found in Model 2, which has the longest list of control variables. Although some precision may have been gained by reducing the model, Model 4 seems to slightly underadjust for differences in student intake between the two sectors. This underadjustment is not serious: In the next section I will show that estimates vary by up to 5 percent of a standard deviation in either direction, depending on the model considered and the statistical techniques used. The results of the reduced model lie approximately in the middle of a range of possible estimates.

TECHNICAL CONSIDERATIONS

Several statisticians have criticized the statistical techniques used by CHK (1981). The chief criticism concerns the adequacy of CHK's model to control for differences in student intake between the two sectors. The present analysis, which uses longitudinal data instead of cross-sectional data, attempts to address the problem of selection bias by examining the *growth* in academic achievement during the last two years of high school. However, because achievement tests are never perfectly reliable, it is difficult to assess growth accurately with only two waves of data; three or four waves are preferable (Rogosa, Brandt, and Zimowski, 1982; Willett, 1985). I use what is perhaps the most conventional method for comparing two groups with pretest-posttest data; however, this approach may produce biased estimates of Catholic-school effects because of the limitations of two-wave data. This section explains the chief problem with two-wave data and describes how the present analysis attempts to address it.

This section also addresses several other criticisms of the CHK analysis (see Goldberger and Cain, 1982; Cain and Goldberger, 1983; Heyns and Hilton, 1982; Noell, 1982; National Academy of Sciences, 1981). These criticisms concern the statistical significance of the estimated Catholic-school effects, the method of handling missing data, the use of a single-equation (ANCOVA) model rather than a two-equation model, differential student attrition, and the sensitivity of the achievement

[6] Standard errors were determined using a nominal sample size, which was based on the number of students who entered the analysis, not on the number of schools. The HSB design weights (PNLTSTWT) were multiplied by the ratio of the unweighted sample size to the weighted sample size for all students who took the test battery in both years. Estimates greater than three standard errors were considered statistically significant. The 3-sigma criterion was used, rather than the conventional 2-sigma criterion, to account for the clustered nature of the sample (see Goldberger and Cain, 1982).

Table 5. Estimates of Catholic-School Effects on Growth in Academic Achievement, Based on Gain Scores and Three ANCOVA Models with Varying Levels of Statistical Control

Test	Gain Scores	ANCOVA with Control for: Pretest	Pretest and Students' Background[a]	Pretest, Students' Background, and Prior Achievement
General achievement tests				
Reading	.068	.144	.095	.046
Vocabulary	.080	.160	.119	.112
General math	.103	.148	.111	.092
Curriculum-specific tests				
Advanced math	.094	.186	.113	.048
Writing	.029	.147	.101	.069
Science	.048	.107	.052	−.018
Civics	−.022	.138	.059	.000

NOTE: Estimates of Catholic-school effects are expressed as fractions of the pooled within-group standard deviation of the posttest.
[a] Background characteristics include socioeconomic status, race, ethnicity, sex, presence of both parents, and handicapped status.

tests to the effects of schooling during the intervention period. I will discuss each of these issues below.

Measurement Error and Unequal Growth Rates for Different Subpopulations

The simplest, most straightforward estimate of Catholic-school effects is a simple gain or difference score. Following Bryk's (1980) notation, the treatment effect, or Catholic-school effect, is given by

$$\alpha = \overline{Y}_{CATH}(t_2) - \overline{Y}_{PUB}(t_2) - \beta[\overline{Y}_{CATH}(t_1) - \overline{Y}_{PUB}(t_1)] \quad (1)$$

where $\overline{Y}_{PUB}(t_1)$, $\overline{Y}_{PUB}(t_2)$, $\overline{Y}_{CATH}(t_1)$, and $\overline{Y}_{CATH}(t_2)$ are the public- and Catholic-school mean scores, respectively, at times 1 (1980) and 2 (1982). Gain scores set β equal to 1.

The chief objection to a gain-score analysis is that "it does not provide a test for the presence of an interaction of the treatment with the pretest" (Reichardt, 1979: 183; see also Linn and Slinde, 1977; O'Connor, 1972). A negative correlation of gain scores with initial status is common; indeed, the change scores for all seven tests used in this analysis are negatively correlated with the sophomore scores.[7] One might argue, therefore, that using a simple gain-score analysis gives the public schools an unfair advantage, because they have a larger proportion of students with low pretest scores, and low scorers on the pretest stand to make the greatest pretest-to-posttest gains.

The problem, however, is that we cannot determine the extent to which the *observed* relationship between growth and initial status is a true difference in the growth patterns of students with varying initial ability levels or an artifact of measurement error, such as regression to the mean or a ceiling effect. If we had perfectly precise measures at both time 1 and time 2, then we might expect a *positive* relationship between growth and initial status; that is, we might expect the initially more-able students to grow at a faster rate than the less-able students. Indeed, the present data show that high-SES students with the same pretest score as low-SES students show greater pretest-to-posttest gains. Thus, two countervailing forces contribute to the observed relationship between growth and initial status: measurement error and differential growth rates for different types of students. Data on students' test scores for at least three points in time are necessary to accurately assess differential growth rates.

With two-wave data, ANCOVA is probably the most frequently used technique to take account of initial differences between two groups. The estimates of Catholic-school effects for the ANCOVA model are given by equation (1), where β is equal to the pooled within-group regression coefficient of the posttest on the pretest. Columns 1 and 2 of Table 5 show the estimates of Catholic-school effects based on gain scores and ANCOVA for each of the seven achievement tests. Both sets of estimates include statistical controls for only the pretest scores.

One major source of bias in the ANCOVA

[7] The correlations between growth scores (i.e., senior score minus sophomore score) and sophomore scores for each test are as follows: reading, −0.27; vocabulary, −0.24; general mathematics, −0.16; writing, −0.35; science, −0.39; civics, −0.47.

model is measurement error in the pretest, which always leads to underadjustment (Reichardt, 1979). The reliabilities of the pretests range from 0.53 to 0.85 (Heyns and Hilton, 1982), so there is a strong likelihood that the ANCOVA model with only the pretest as a covariate underadjusts for selection differences between the two sectors. Unequal growth patterns for different subpopulations are also a potential source of bias in ANCOVA estimates. For example, we expect that students from disadvantaged backgrounds, given the same pretest score, would grow less than students from privileged backgrounds. Therefore, the single covariate model would underadjust for differences in growth rates between the two sectors. A third source of bias, which can lead to either overadjustment or underadjustment, is related to a possible changing structure of behavior (Cronbach et al., 1977). For example, test performance in science may be more strongly related to reading ability than to science ability at the time of the pretest, but that relationship could change during the junior and senior years, Reichardt (1979) describes this source of bias in greater detail. Overall, given the reliabilities of the pretests and our knowledge about differences between the types of students who enroll in public and Catholic schools, it is safe to say that the ANCOVA model, with only the pretest as a covariate, underadjusts for differences between the two sectors. Therefore, the estimates in column 2 of Table 5 overstate the size of the Catholic-school effects. What is required is a more complete model that adjusts for differences between the two sectors in student characteristics, family background, and other achievement variables measured before the intervention period.

Column 3 of Table 5 shows the estimates of Catholic-school effects with controls for both the pretest and the six measures of student characteristics and family background that were included in the reduced model. The background measures are added to account for initial differences in relative growth rates between different types of students. These estimates, however, may still overstate Catholic-school effects because of measurement error in the pretest.

Finally, column 4 of Table 5 shows the estimates of Catholic-school effects when the three tests of basic skills are added to the model. The model is now identical to the reduced model in Table 3 (column 4). The addition of the three premeasures reduces the effects by a small amount—on the average about 4.3 percent of a standard deviation across the seven tests. Therefore, if there is a bias due to overadjustment, it is relatively small. Furthermore, because of the unreliability of the pretests, it is more likely that the estimates in column 3 are biased upward due to an underadjustment associated with measurement error, in which case the estimates in column 4 are more accurate.

Another potential source of bias, which is part of the measurement error problem, is ceiling effects. Students scoring a high mark on the sophomore test are limited in the number of additional correct answers they can obtain on the senior test two years later. The Catholic sector, which enrolls a larger proportion of students from advantaged backgrounds, has a larger proportion of students scoring at the ceiling or close to the ceiling on all sophomore tests (see Table 6). The problem is particularly acute for the writing and civics tests: 16.1 and 15.7 percent of the Catholic-school students scored at the ceiling or one item below the ceiling on the sophomore writing and civics tests, respectively, compared with only 9.6 and 10.0 percent of the public-school students. The bias arising from ceiling effects is somewhat ameliorated by the ANCOVA adjustment used in this study, but the Catholic-school effect may still be understated.

CHK (1981, 1982b, 1982c) used a growth-rate measure that is "unaffected by the existence of a ceiling" (1982c:147) to analyze differences between the separate samples of sophomores and seniors in 1980. Goldberger and Cain (1982) showed that the CHK formula favored the Catholic sector, compared with a more conventional formula. Neither formula is appropriate for estimating Catholic-school effects that can be compared with those presented in Table 3 above, because the estimates in this article are based on longitudinal (two-wave) data that include adjustment for several other factors.

If we assume that Catholic-school effects are constant over all levels of the pretest, then we can check whether a serious bias arises from ceiling effects by repeating the regression analyses in Model 4 with a subsample that excludes those who scored at or close to the ceiling on the sophomore test.[8] The results differ from those based on the entire sample by less than 0.75 percent of a standard deviation. We can assume, therefore, that the bias arising from ceiling effects on any of the seven tests is negligible.

---

[8] The estimates of Catholic-school effects for the full sample, except those who scored at the ceiling or one item below the ceiling, based on the reduced model, are as follows: reading, 0.047; vocabulary, 0.114; general mathematics, 0.085; advanced mathematics, 0.052; writing, 0.073; science, −0.016; civics, −0.007.

Table 6. Percentage of Public- and Catholic-School Students Scoring at the Ceiling or One Point Below the Ceiling on the Sophomore and Senior Achievement Tests

	Public		Catholic	
Test	Sophomore Test	Senior Test	Sophomore Test	Senior Test
General achievement tests				
Reading				
Percent at ceiling −1	1.2	2.5	1.4	4.5
Percent at ceiling	.4	1.1	.6	2.0
Vocabulary				
Percent at ceiling −1	.9	2.3	2.6	8.1
Percent at ceiling	.3	1.6	1.0	3.6
General mathematics				
Percent at ceiling −1	.9	3.4	1.3	3.1
Percent at ceiling	.6	1.9	.3	2.3
Curriculum-specific tests				
Advanced mathematics				
Percent at ceiling −1	2.6	4.1	3.3	6.8
Percent at ceiling	1.0	2.1	1.5	2.5
Writing				
Percent at ceiling −1	6.3	11.2	10.5	17.8
Percent at ceiling	3.3	7.5	5.6	11.9
Science				
Percent at ceiling −1	.8	1.6	1.0	1.8
Percent at ceiling	.2	.3	.1	.4
Civics				
Percent at ceiling −1	7.5	15.2	12.1	20.0
Percent at ceiling	2.5	7.6	3.6	10.9

NOTE: Estimates are based on the weighted sample, excluding dropouts.

Statistical Significance of Estimated Catholic-School Effects

Students are the unit of analysis in the ANCOVA models presented above, and the degrees of freedom used to calculate the standard errors are based on the number of students, not the number of schools. However, the HSB study was based on a two-stage sample: Schools were sampled first, then students were sampled within schools. Standard errors based on the assumption of simple random sampling do not take account of the dependencies that exist among students within the same school. Therefore, the nominal standard errors reported here are understated and need to be adjusted upward. Goldberger and Cain (1982:107) expressed the same concern about the CHK results and recommended "that readers use a ± 3-sigma (or ± 4-sigma) rule, rather than the usual ± 2-sigma rule, in assessing statistical significance." In their final report, CHK (1982c) provided empirically estimated standard errors, which ranged from 1.04 to 2.12 times the nominal standard errors reported in their earlier report (CHK, 1981; see also Cain and Goldberger, 1983). Therefore, Goldberger and Cain's recommendation is appropriate for most estimates.

When the more liberal ± 3-sigma rule is used, the estimates of Catholic-school effects for the advanced mathematics, science, and civics tests are not statistically significant. The estimated effect for the writing test, which ranges from 5.6 (Noell model) to 6.9 (reduced model) percent of a standard deviation is statistically significant in three of the models when the ± 3-sigma rule is used; but it is not statistically significant when the ± 4-sigma rule is applied. Therefore, for the four curriculum-specific tests, there are no consistently statistically significant effects across the four models. All the effects are less than 7 percent of a standard deviation.

The Catholic-school effects for the three tests of basic skills range from 4 to 11 percent of a standard deviation. When the ± 3-sigma rule is used, the estimates for the reading test are not statistically significant, except in the Willms model. The effects for the vocabulary and general mathematics tests are statistically significant, even under the more conservative ± 4-sigma criterion. These effects are only about half the size of those found by CHK with the 1980 cross-sectional data; however, they raise two important questions. First, why are there statistically significant Catholic-school effects for two of the three tests of basic skills but no consistently significant effects across the four tests that were specifically designed to measure the effects of schooling during the last two years of high school? One would be less surprised if the pattern were reversed—i.e., if there were substantial Catholic-school effects for the curriculum-specific tests but no effects for the tests of basic skills. Second, how important is a 10 percent effect? I will address both of these questions in the discussion of test validity below and in the final summary.

Method of Handling Missing Data

I used pairwise deletion of missing data in all the regression analyses presented above. Because the sample used in this study includes only those students who completed the test battery in both the sophomore and senior years and excludes students who left school in their junior or senior year, the amount of missing data is fairly small: Less than 4 percent of the data for any specific follow-up test are missing, and less than 2.5 percent of the data for any of the base-year tests or any background variables used in the reduced model are missing. Noell (1982) and Willms (1983) compared estimates of private-school effects using pairwise deletion and listwise deletion in cross-sectional analyses of the HSB data, and both found that the estimates based on listwise deletion were 1 to 3 percent of a standard deviation less than the estimates based on pairwise deletion.

I repeated the regression analyses in the reduced model using listwise deletion. The listwise estimates of Catholic-school effects are smaller for every test than the pairwise estimates, but the difference is less than 2 percent of a standard deviation.[9] When listwise deletion is used, none of the effects for the curriculum-specific tests are statistically significant, even when the more liberal ± 3-sigma rule is applied.

All the analyses in this study have used an additive model, which includes a dummy variable denoting sector and constrains the regression slopes within each sector to be parallel. The nonadditive model, which was used by CHK, fits separate regressions of test scores on background variables within each sector. There has been considerable discussion about which model is most appropriate. Goldberger and Cain (1982) suggested that the conventional single-equation approach (i.e., additive model) was adequate to fit the data. Later they provided evidence (Cain and Goldberger, 1983) from unpublished analyses by Peter Mueser (Graduate School of Business, University of Chicago) that after some moderate adjustments are made for clustering and missing-value imputations, the test of homogeneous regression slopes could not be rejected. Noell (1983) also defended the use of the additive model; he showed that when interaction terms, which allow for different regression slopes within the two sectors, are added to the model, the increment to R^2 is less than 0.5 percent. McPartland and McDill (1982) also showed that the nonadditive model was unnecessary.

Coleman and Hoffer (1983) responded to these criticisms by pointing out that the use of a nonadditive model does not result in biased estimates when the additive model is correct; it only reduces its efficiency. They also added that the use of the increment to R^2 is inappropriate because of the unequal sample sizes in the public and Catholic sectors.

Table 7 presents the parameter estimates for the reduced model with sector-by-background interaction terms added. This is equivalent to fitting separate regressions within each sector (i.e., the nonadditive model). First, when we compare the R^2 values in the nonadditive model (Table 7) with those in the additive model (Table 4), we see that the increase in R^2 arising from the addition of the interaction terms is less than 0.1 percent across all seven regressions. Second, when we examine the parameter estimates for the interaction terms using the ± 3-sigma rule, we see that none of the terms are statistically significant in six of the seven regressions. For the writing regression there is a statistically significant interaction for "both parents present" with sector status; however, the parameter estimate is very small (standardized beta = −0.038).

On the basis of these results, we can conclude that the additive model is more appropriate than the nonadditive model for estimating Catholic-school effects. Compared with estimates based on the additive model, estimates based on the nonadditive model are about 2 percent of a standard deviation smaller for the advanced mathematics and science tests and about 4.5 percent of a standard deviation larger for the vocabulary and writing tests. Estimates for the other three tests are virtually identical in the additive and nonadditive models.[10]

Dropouts have been excluded from all the analyses up to this point. Approximately 14.5 percent of the public-school students and 2.3 percent of the Catholic-school students left school between their sophomore and senior

[9] The estimates of Catholic-school effects for the reduced model, based on listwise deletion of missing data, are as follows: reading, 0.037; vocabulary, 0.111; general mathematics, 0.083; advanced mathematics, 0.042; writing, 0.053; science, −0.021; civics, −0.002.

[10] The estimates of Catholic-school effects, based on the nonadditive model, are as follows: reading, 0.052; vocabulary, 0.157; general mathematics, 0.094; advanced mathematics, 0.027; writing, 0.116; science, −0.034; civics, 0.002.

Table 7. Regression Equations Estimating Catholic-School Effects on Seven Achievement-Test Scores, Controlling for Student Characteristics, Family Background, Prior Academic Achievement, and All Sector-by-Background-Factor Interactions

	Reading		Vocabulary		General Math		Advanced Math		Writing		Science		Civics	
	b	SE	*b*	SE	*b*	SE	*b*	SE	*b*	SE	*b*	SE	*b*	SE
Intercept	1.559*	.089	3.254*	.089	2.518*	.122	.589*	.055	2.957*	.087	3.927*	.088	2.639*	.060
PRIVATE	.225	.371	1.904*	.370	.996	.507	−.351	.226	1.898*	.365	.363	.361	.223	.253
Sophomore test	.436*	.008	.552*	.007	.705*	.007	.261*	.008	.390*	.008	.417*	.008	.198*	.008
READING 10	—	—	.218*	.008	.175*	.011	.045*	.005	.110*	.008	.112*	.008	.099*	.005
VOCAB 10	.221*	.007	—	—	.132*	.010	.024*	.004	.109*	.007	.111*	.007	.092*	.005
GEN MATH 10	.146*	.005	.095*	.005	—	—	.154*	.003	.121*	.005	.100*	.005	.060*	.003
SES	.127*	.032	.415*	.032	.534*	.044	.154*	.020	.116*	.031	.134*	.029	.039	.020
BLACK	−.224*	.067	−.620*	.067	−.184	.091	.077	.041	−.371*	.065	−.900*	.062	.010	.042
HISP	−.318*	.065	−.638*	.064	−.593*	.088	−.078	.039	−.457*	.063	−.663*	.059	−.181*	.041
FEMALE	.029	.040	.160*	.040	−.466*	.055	−.172*	.025	1.262*	.042	−.564*	.037	.212*	.026
BOTHPAR	.180*	.049	.164*	.049	.245*	.067	.120*	.030	.268*	.047	.143*	.044	.116*	.031
HANDICAP	−.329*	.076	−.368*	.076	−.350*	.104	.104	.046	−.614*	.074	−.258*	.069	−.265*	.048
PRIVATE by sophomore test	.039	.031	−.040	.027	−.016	.026	.010	.030	.001	.031	−.045	.030	.010	.031
PRIVATE by READING 10	—	—	−.013	.031	−.013	.042	.032	.019	−.031	.031	.011	.029	.003	.020
PRIVATE by VOCAB 10	−.008	.027	—	—	.003	.038	−.019	.017	−.016	.027	.003	.026	−.010	.018
PRIVATE by GEN MATH 10	−.011	.019	−.013	.019	—	—	.034	.014	−.034	.020	−.002	.018	−.015	.013
PRIVATE by SES	.032	.124	.007	.124	.098	.170	−.035	.076	.079	.120	.262	.113	.098	.079
PRIVATE by BLACK	.271	.327	.176	.326	−.127	.446	−.219	.199	.195	.316	−.113	.298	.214	.208
PRIVATE by HISP	.217	.267	.553	.266	.552	.365	.249	.163	.367	.259	.220	.243	−.074	.170
PRIVATE by FEMALE	.217	.153	−.251	.152	−.256	.209	−.079	.093	−.202	.160	.147	.141	.099	.098
PRIVATE by BOTHPAR	−.399	.214	−.593	.213	.040	.292	−.223	.131	−.623*	.207	−.224	.195	−.055	.137
PRIVATE by HANDICAP	.196	.332	.617	.331	−.471	.453	−.214	.202	.238	.321	.001	.302	.081	.211
R^2	.60359		.66961		.68758		.50541		.59164		.60927		.39657	

NOTE: Regressions are based on the weighted sample, excluding dropouts.
* Estimates are statistically significant using the ± 3-sigma rule suggested by Goldberger and Cain (1982).

years (Peng, 1983).[11] Differential attrition presents the same problem as differential selection, but the potential bias to the estimates is in the opposite direction.

To illustrate, suppose the Catholic sector encouraged students of low ability to remain in school until graduation, even though they were showing small gains in academic achievement. Also suppose that comparable students in the public sector left school before graduation. If this were the case, then a comparison of public- and Catholic-school test scores for only those students who remained in school would be unfair: The Catholic-school effect would be understated. More precisely, if the statistical adjustments do not account for factors that are associated with low achievement gains *and* with dropping out, then the estimates of Catholic-school effects will be biased downward. If the model that adjusts for differences in students' ability and background characteristics is well specified, then the extent of bias due to differential dropout rates will be negligible.

On the other hand, one can argue that dropouts should not be included in the analysis because these students received different amounts of schooling during the intervention period. Many students drop out of school for reasons other than poor scholastic performance—e.g., marriage, pregnancy, illness, or employment (Peng, Takai, and Fetters, 1983). If these students had remained in school, they probably would have performed as well as the other students in the school, other factors being equal. However, because they left school and did not receive instruction throughout the intervention period, one expects their scores to be lower than the scores of comparable students who did not drop out. Therefore, because proportionately more students dropped out of public schools than Catholic schools, the estimates of Catholic-school effects would be biased upwards if dropouts were included in the analyses.

Table 8 presents the estimates of Catholic-school effects in the four models previously presented. The estimates are based on the entire sample of students who took the test battery in both years, including dropouts. Com-

[11] The weighted estimates calculated from Appendix A are slightly different from Peng's estimates: 14.5 percent for public schools and 4.2 percent for Catholic schools. My figures differ from Peng's because my sample includes only those students who completed the test battery in both the sophomore and senior years.

Table 8. Estimates of Catholic-School Effects on Growth in Academic Achievement, Controlling for Student Characteristics, Family Background, and Prior Academic Achievement (Dropouts are Included in the Sample)

Test	Model 1	2	3	4
General achievement tests				
Reading	.038	.036	.053	.046
Vocabulary	.116*	.104*	.097*	.119*
General math	.082*	.066*	.087*	.105*
Curriculum-specific tests				
Advanced math	.037	.028	.042	.057
Writing	.091*	.080*	.079*	.092*
Science	−.013	−.024	−.001	−.005
Civics	.031	.000	−.003	.019

NOTE: See note to Table 3.
* Estimates are statistically significant using the ± 3-sigma rule suggested by Goldberger and Cain (1982).

paring these estimates with those in Table 3, which do not include dropouts, we observe that the increase in Catholic-school effects ranges from 0.010 to 0.024 across the seven tests. This increase is very small and meaningless in an analysis of the differential effects of public and private schools. The increase is probably due to the amount of coursework completed by those who remained in school for the full two years. The lower dropout rate in Catholic schools may, in itself, be an important Catholic-school effect; however, the differences between public- and Catholic-school dropout rates do not present a serious threat to the validity of the results presented in Table 3.

Validity of the Achievement Tests

I performed a simple check to determine whether the scores on the curriculum-specific achievement tests used as dependent variables in this study were sensitive to the amount of coursework completed during the intervention period. I added a dummy variable to the reduced model to test whether students who had taken two or more years of science since the beginning of their sophomore year scored higher on the senior science test, with all other factors in the model held constant. Their scores are significantly higher (using the conservative ± 4-sigma rule) than the scores of students who had less than two years of science instruction, but the difference is small—approximately 8.5 percent of a standard deviation.

Similarly, I estimated the effect on the advanced mathematics test scores of taking either geometry or trigonometry. Those who had taken at least one course in either of these two subjects, on the average, scored 25 percent of a standard deviation higher than those with the same initial ability who had not taken either subject. The effect of taking second-year algebra is also about 25 percent of a standard deviation. Both of these effects were statistically significant using the conservative ± 4-sigma rule.

To check the validity of the writing test, I estimated the effect of taking three or more years of English courses, compared with less than three years. The effect is relatively small—only 5.2 percent of a standard deviation. This finding is not surprising, because writing instruction is only a small part of many high school English courses, particularly at the upper level. A variable that directly measured the time spent on writing instruction would probably show stronger effects.

Although it is somewhat reassuring that the tests are at least sensitive to these crude measures of the amount of coursework completed, the average gains on all the tests are very small. On most achievement tests, students gain about one full standard deviation per year during elementary school (Glass, McGaw, and Smith, 1981:103), but smaller gains are typical during secondary school, depending on the nature of the test and the skills examined. Table 9 shows the average amount of growth per year during the two-year period on each of the HSB tests for three separate subsamples of students. The first subsample includes all students who completed the twelfth grade; the second subsample includes all students who completed the twelfth grade and who scored above the mean on each of the respective pretests; the third subsample includes only those students who dropped out of school prior to the intervention period. The average growth per year is expressed in numbers of items correct and as a fraction of the pooled within-group standard deviation of the posttest.

The average gains on the general achievement tests are not extraordinary. We expect students to make only minor gains, if any, on these tests during their last two years of high school. However, the gains on the curriculum-specific tests are also small. This finding is disappointing. One hopes that students would have gained at least one half of a standard deviation per year on these tests if the tests were at all sensitive to the effects of instruction. For example, one expects that on the science test, which has 20 items, the average student would have scored 3 or 4 items higher on the posttest after two years of instruction. They did not: The average growth was only three quarters of one item for the two-year period. On the four curriculum-specific tests, the average growth ranges from

Table 9. Average Growth Per Year on the Seven HSB Achievement Tests, for Students who Completed Grade 12, for Students who Scored Above the Mean on the Pretest and Completed Grade 12, and for Students who Dropped Out of School Before Starting Grade 11

Test	Students Completing Grade 12: All Students	Students Completing Grade 12: Students Scoring Above the Mean on the Pretest	Students Dropping Out Before Grade 11
General achievement tests			
Reading (19 items)	.49 (.12)	.10 (.02)	.17 (.04)
Vocabulary (21 items)	.87 (.20)	.54 (.12)	.53 (.12)
General math (28 items)	.56 (.09)	.29 (.05)	−.01 (−.00)
Curriculum-specific tests			
Advanced math (10 items)	.14 (.06)	−.23 (−.10)	.00 (.00)
Writing (17 items)	.64 (.17)	.18 (.05)	.33 (.09)
Science (20 items)	.38 (.10)	−.04 (−.01)	.28 (.08)
Civics (10 items)	.42 (.20)	.05 (.03)	.20 (.10)

NOTE: Estimates are expressed as the number of additional items correct and as fractions of the pooled within-group standard deviation of the posttest.

6 to 20 percent of a standard deviation per year (column 1 of Table 9).

The small amount of growth on each of the HSB tests is even smaller for students with high pretest scores (see note 7). The average growth per year for students who scored above the mean on the pretest is less than zero for two of the tests (advanced mathematics and science) and ranges from 0.05 to 0.54 on the other five tests (column 2 of Table 9). Those who scored below the mean on the pretest have somewhat larger growth scores; however, gains for students who did not attend school during the intervention period were about half as large as gains for those who did attend (column 3). Therefore, we have been estimating sector differences with tests that show virtually zero growth for half of the population and a very small amount of growth for the other half of the population, much of which is achieved by students who did not attend school during the intervention period.

Standardization of the Effects

Throughout this article I have expressed the size of the Catholic-school effect as a fraction of the pooled within-group standard deviation of the senior test scores. I chose this metric for three reasons. First, it facilitates comparisons of estimates of Catholic-school effects found in this study with those observed in earlier studies; for example, see CHK's (1982a) summary of different estimates of Catholic-school effects. Second, it is the "most informative and straightforward measure of an experimental *effect size*" (Glass et al., 1981:162) and "can take on added meaning [when referred] to the effects of well-known interventions" (p. 103). Third, the standardization makes no assumption about the amount of growth that is due to school factors, as opposed to nonschool factors.

It is also possible to express the size of the Catholic-school effect as a fraction of the standard deviation of the gain scores. This metric is somewhat appealing because it attempts to determine how much a student gains by attending a Catholic school, relative to the amount of gain to be had. However, the observed variance in gain scores depends on the variation in the true growth rates among different types of students (e.g., students with low, average, and high SES) and on measurement error in the pretest and the posttest. If the true growth rates in a particular academic subject were relatively uniform among students with different backgrounds, and if we could measure their growth with a highly reliable test, then even a small Catholic-school effect would appear large if expressed as a fraction of the standard deviation of gain scores. On the other hand, if there were wide variation in the true growth rates among pupils with different backgrounds, and if our test were not very reliable, then even a large Catholic-school effect would appear small if expressed as a fraction of the observed standard deviation of gain scores. For this reason, I prefer the conventional metric for expressing the size of the Catholic-school effect.[12]

[12] The effects reported in this article can be converted to fractions of the standard deviation of the gain scores by multiplying them by the ratio of the pooled standard deviation of the posttest to the standard deviation of the gain scores. They are as follows:

Test	Pooled SD of Posttest	SD of Gain Scores
Reading	4.11	2.96
Vocabulary	4.47	2.89
General math	6.28	3.76
Advanced math	2.22	1.94
Writing	3.86	2.91
Science	3.74	2.73
Civics	2.08	2.06

It might also be tempting to calculate the average growth per month for each test and express the Catholic-school effect in months of schooling. This standardization, however, is misleading. It assumes that *all* the observed growth on these tests is the direct result of schooling and that there is no growth in the absence of schooling. This assumption might be valid if we were measuring progress in Latin, because nonschool factors could be presumed minimal, assuming we could construct a test that reflected growth in Latin achievement across a variety of Latin curricula. But some of the growth on the outcome measures, especially on the three tests of basic skills, is not the result of school factors. This is evident in the growth achieved by students who dropped out of school before the intervention period. Furthermore, because the growth on these tests is so small, a months-of-schooling standardization dramatically overstates any observed Catholic-school effects. For example, on the 17-item writing test, *0.06 item* represents one month of schooling. With a months-of-schooling metric, the very small observed Catholic-school effect in writing—0.25 item for the two-year period—would be expressed as four months of schooling. For another example, girls showed pretest-to-posttest gains on the writing test of 1.25 items more than boys with similar backgrounds. This is an effect of 0.32. A researcher reporting this finding in months of schooling would conclude that during a two-year period, girls gained 20 more months of growth than their male counterparts.

SUMMARY AND CONCLUSIONS

I have conducted several analyses to address the question of Catholic-school superiority. The analyses used the HSB data on over 20,000 students who completed a questionnaire and test battery in 1980 and 1982. Previous analyses have been limited to the 1980 cross-sectional data, which do not include information on student ability or academic achievement prior to entering high school. This study examines the growth in academic achievement from the sophomore to senior years. Estimates are based on three tests of basic academic skills and four tests that were specifically designed to measure the effects of schooling during the last two years of high school. For each test, I estimated a Catholic-school effect, which is the expected gain in achievement for a student who attends a Catholic school, rather than a public school, during the last two years of high school. The estimates include statistical adjustment for student characteristics, family background, and prior academic achievement.

Analyses of the 1980 cross-sectional data have shown that the estimates of Catholic-school effects are very sensitive to the statistical models used and to the outcome measures considered. Therefore, I estimated Catholic-school effects for each of the seven achievement tests with four different models. Three of the models include background measures from previously published studies (CHK, 1981; Noell, 1982; Willms, 1984b). The fourth model was constructed after an examination of the first three models and includes only the most important control variables. I conducted several subsidiary analyses to ensure that the results were not substantially biased due to such factors as the method of handling missing data, the differential dropout rate between the two sectors, and ceiling effects on the outcome measures.

Overall, on the basis of the results for the curriculum-specific tests, the study suggests that there is no pervasive Catholic-school effect on academic achievement. The estimates for the science and civics tests show a public-school advantage: They range from 1.2 to 3.5 percent of a standard deviation for the science test and from 0 to 1.9 percent of a standard deviation for the civics test. These effects, however, are not statistically significant. The estimates for the advanced mathematics and writing tests show a Catholic-school advantage: They range from 1.9 to 4.7 percent of a standard deviation for the advanced mathematics test and from 5.6 to 6.9 percent of a standard deviation for the writing test. After moderate adjustments are made to account for the clustered sample design (Goldberger and Cain, 1982), these effects are not statistically significant for the advanced mathematics test, but in three of the four models, the effects are significant for the writing test.

The results for two of the three tests of basic skills (vocabulary and general mathematics) indicate a small, statistically significant Catholic-school advantage of about 7 to 10 percent of a standard deviation. Irrespective of statistical significance, these effects are also very small. An effect of 10 percent of a standard deviation is enough to change a student's rank in his or her class from the 50th to the 54th percentile. An advantage of this size would have little relevance to a student's future college opportunities: The Scholastic Aptitude Test (SAT) scores of freshmen in the most selective universities are about two full standard deviations higher than the scores of freshmen in mediocre state colleges (Willms, 1984b).

The chief limitation of this study is the adequacy of the achievement tests to measure gains in achievement during the last two years of high school. This analysis suggests that they are not adequate measures of academic growth for at least half of the students in the HSB sample. Therefore, although the findings indicate that there is no pervasive Catholic-school effect, we cannot be certain that the tests were sensitive enough to detect differences between public and Catholic schools in their effects on students' achievement. If the tests had measured more advanced skills in biology, physics, chemistry, mathematics, and English, then we might have observed significant Catholic-school effects. At present, this must remain an open question.

In conclusion, policy decisions should not be based on the assumption that either public or private schools produce better achievement outcomes. One of the principal findings of the CHK (1981) study—that growth in achievement is greater in the private sector—has been invoked to suggest that the role of private schooling in American education should be increased. However, this study, which is based on a longitudinal analysis of growth in student achievement, finds no substantial differences between comparable students in the public and private sectors.

Appendix A. Unweighted and Weighted Sample Sizes for Students with Test Scores in Both Sophomore and Senior Years

	Unweighted *n*		Weighted *n*	
Sample Strata	Including Dropouts	Excluding Dropouts	Including Dropouts	Excluding Dropouts
Public				
Regular	16,576	15,356	3,279,637	2,813,120
Alternative	574	474	24,846	17,138
Cuban Hispanic	199	176	13,639	11,275
Other Hispanic	2,064	1,867	104,353	86,179
Total	19,413	17,873	3,422,475	2,927,712
Catholic				
Regular	1,301	1,287	214,847	206,454
Black	808	785	15,479	14,272
Cuban Hispanic	250	239	2,065	1,880
Total	2,359	2,311	232,391	222,606

REFERENCES

Alexander, K. L. and A. M. Pallas
1983 "Private schools and public policy: New evidence on cognitive achievement in public and private schools." Sociology of Education 56:170–82.

Bryk, A.
1980 "Analyzing data from premeasure/postmeasure designs." Pp. 235–60 in S. Anderson et al. (eds.), Statistical Methods for Comparative Studies. New York: Wiley.

Cain, G. G. and A. S. Goldberger
1983 "Public and private schools revisited." Sociology of Education 56:208–18.

Coleman, J. S.
1981 "Private schools, public schools, and the public interest." The Public Interest 64:19–31.

Coleman, J. S. and T. Hoffer
1983 "Response to Taeuber-James, Cain-Goldberger and Morgan." Sociology of Education 56:219–34.

Coleman, J. S., T. Hoffer, and S. Kilgore
1981 Public and Private Schools. Report to the National Center for Education Statistics. Chicago: National Opinion Research Center.
1982a "Achievement and segregation in secondary schools: A further look at public and private school differences." Sociology of Education 55:162–82.
1982b "Cognitive outcomes in public and private schools." Sociology of Education 55:65–76.
1982c High School Achievement. New York: Basic.

Cronbach, L. J., D. R. Rogosa, R. E. Floden, and G. G. Price
1977 Analysis of Covariance in Nonrandomized Experiments: Parameters Affecting Bias. Stanford: Stanford Evaluation Consortium.

Glass, G. V., B. McGaw, and M. L. Smith
1981 Meta-Analysis in Social Research. Beverly Hills, CA: Sage.

Goldberger, A. S. and G. G. Cain
1982 "The causal analysis of cognitive outcomes in the Coleman, Hoffer and Kilgore report." Sociology of Education 55:103–22.

Heyns, B. and T. L. Hilton
1982 "The cognitive tests for High School and Beyond: An assessment." Sociology of Education 55:89–102.

Jones, C., M. Clarke, G. Mooney, H. McWilliams, I. Crawford, B. Stephenson, and R. Tourangeau
1983 High School and Beyond 1980 Sophomore Cohort First Follow-Up (1982) Data File User's Manual. Washington, D.C.: National Center for Education Statistics.

Linn, R. L. and J. A. Slinde
1977 "The determination of the significance of change between pre- and posttesting periods." Review of Educational Research 47:121–50.

McPartland, J. M. and E. L. McDill
1982 "Control and differentiation in the structure of American education." Sociology of Education 55:77–88.
National Academy of Sciences
1981 Report of the Meeting of a Panel to Review the Statistical Methodology of the Report, "Public and Private Schools". Washington, D.C.: National Academy of Sciences.
Noell, J.
1981 "The impact of private schools when self-selection is controlled: A critique of Coleman's 'Public and Private Schools'." Washington, D.C.: Department of Education.
1982 "Public and Catholic schools: A reanalysis of 'Public and Private Schools'." Sociology of Education 55:123–32.
1983 "A response to Coleman, Hoffer and Kilgore." Sociology of Education 56:203.
O'Connor, E. F.
1972 "Extending classical test theory to the measurement of change." Review of Educational Research 42:73–98.
Peng, S.S.
1983 "High school dropouts." Report No. 83–221b. Washington, D.C.: National Center for Education Statistics.
Peng, S. S., R. T. Takai, and W. B. Fetters
1983 "High school dropouts: Preliminary results from the High School and Beyond survey." Paper presented at the Annual Meetings of the American Educational Research Association, Montreal.
Reichardt, C. S.
1979 "The statistical analysis of data from nonequivalent group designs." Pp. 147–205 in T.D. Cook and D.T. Campbell (eds), Quasi-experimentation: Design and Analysis Issues for Field Settings. Chicago: Rand-McNally.
Rogosa, D., D. Brandt, and M. Zimowski
1982 "A growth curve approach to the measurement of change." Psychological Bulletin 92:726–48.
Willett, J. B.
1985 "Investigating systematic individual differences in academic achievement." Unpublished PhD. dissertation, Stanford University.
Willms, J. D.
1983 "Do private schools produce higher levels of academic achievement? New evidence for the tution tax credit debate." Pp. 223–31 in T. James and H.M. Levin (eds.), Public Dollars for Private Schools: The Case of Tuition Tax Credits. Philadelphia: Temple University Press.
1984a "Public and private school outcomes: Results from the High School and Beyond follow-up study." Paper presented at the Annual Meetings of the American Educational Research Association, New Orleans.
1984b "School effectiveness within the public and private sectors: An evaluation." Evaluation Review 8:113–35.

SCHOOL SECTOR AND COGNITIVE PERFORMANCE: WHEN IS A LITTLE A LITTLE?

KARL L. ALEXANDER
AARON M. PALLAS
The Johns Hopkins University

Sociology of Education 1985, Vol. 58 (April):115–128

Coleman, Hoffer, and Kilgore's claims regarding the effects of Catholic schools on cognitive achievement have evoked much controversy. Critics have argued that Catholic schools enroll students of superior academic competency, and that Coleman et al., using cross-sectional testing data, could not distinguish differential sector effectiveness from this selection effect. The first follow-up (1982) of the High School and Beyond base-year sophomore cohort allows a stronger design for studying this issue. We use sophomore test performance to control for input-level differences in competency while predicting senior test performance in several cognitive domains. The omission of such input controls leads to a substantial upward bias in the estimate of Catholic-school effects on achievement. We also show that the so-called common-school effect found by Coleman and his colleagues disappears when appropriate input-level test controls are applied. Our best estimate of the Catholic-school effect on cognitive growth from the sophomore to senior year, using aggregate sophomore-to-senior change in performance as a yardstick, is about two thirds of a year's growth. We judge differences of this magnitude to be substantively trivial because they correspond to less than 0.1 standard deviation in test performance. We conclude that sector differences in test performance are too small to warrant the attention they have received.

Are private high schools more effective than public high schools? As is well known, Coleman, Hoffer, and Kilgore (1981a) claimed they were and, in so doing, set off a vigorous and heated debate that has yet to be put to rest. Despite numerous analyses, reanalyses, critical exchanges, and strongly held convictions, we are little closer to reaching agreement on the matter than when the issue was first joined. How can it be that so much effort has shed so little light?

The problem, we believe, is that no one—neither Coleman and his colleagues nor their many critics—has had access to the kind of data needed for a proper consideration of the question. Coleman, Hoffer, and Kilgore (hereafter, CHK) compared the effectiveness of public and private schools using cross-sectional data from the High School and Beyond (HSB) project. The data set included scores for high school sophomores and seniors on a battery of tests developed for the project by the Educational Testing Service (Heyns and Hilton, 1982). CHK estimated differences in educational effectiveness by comparing the test scores of public- and private-school students after adjusting for social background characteristics. Since measures of test performance before high school were not available in the HSB data set, CHK were not able to adjust also for ability differences that might have predated high school.

Because of this design limitation, the superior performance of private-school students on the HSB tests is equivocal as evidence of differential effectiveness. Does this pattern occur because private schools are better at promoting cognitive development, as CHK conclude, or simply because such schools enroll better students in the first place? Since neither their data, their design, nor their analysis precludes the latter possibility, many have deemed CHK's evidence suspect and their conclusions unwarranted. From the critics' point of view, the effectiveness hypothesis has yet to be put to a proper test.

And so the debate is joined. In their defense, CHK have made many efforts to work around the selection problem: They have used extensive socioeconomic controls as proxies for test performance; they have studied patterns of cognitive growth using something akin to a synthetic cohort analysis; and they have experimented with econometric methods that might adjust for selection biases. The critics, in turn, have questioned the adequacy of these

---

This research was funded by grant no. NIE-G-83-0002 to The Johns Hopkins University Center for the Social Organization of Schools. The opinions expressed in this article do not necessarily reflect the position or policy of the National Institute of Education, and no official endorsement by the Institute should be inferred. We gratefully acknowledge the helpful comments of Christopher Jencks and Doug Willms on an earlier version of this article. Address all correspondence to the authors at the Department of Sociology, The Johns Hopkins University, Baltimore, MD 21218.

efforts and have proposed additional controls and bases of comparison (e.g., controls for track membership), which they think would improve upon those used by CHK. Indeed, these strategies have been used in several recent analyses, and their use does tend to attenuate sector differences (Noell, 1982; Willms, 1983; Alexander and Pallas, 1983; Morgan, 1983).

CHK, in turn, have argued that high school track is not a proper proxy for differences in student competency. Likewise, they have rejected other published attempts to deal analytically with the selection issue using cross-sectional data, such as Page and Keith's (1981) attempt to distinguish ability components in the HSB test battery from achievement components. With but few concessions to their protagonists, CHK have held to their original claims.

This is where the debate stands at present. Neither side has produced the proverbial smoking gun, and neither side seems much impressed with the arguments advanced by the opposition. The reason for this stalemate, we believe, is that all the contending parties have had to argue around, and work within, the constraints of cross-sectional data. Fortunately, new data are now available, which should move the debate off stage center.

The HSB design made provision for the retesting of its original (1980) sophomore sample two years later. This phase of the HSB fieldwork is now complete, and the data have recently entered into the public domain. These data hold great promise for clarifying the question that was first posed, but never satisfactorily addressed, by CHK. We can now examine how individual patterns of test performance change between the sophomore and senior years and determine whether such change is more pronounced among private-school students than among public-school students. These data, then, allow us to control for input-level test performance and directly test the hypothesis that private schools are more effective than public schools in promoting cognitive development.

The conceptualization that guides our analysis is depicted in Figure 1. It is very similar to that proposed by Kilgore (1983) in response to our earlier criticism of her work with Coleman and Hoffer. We indicated then that we had no particular objection to this framework but felt strongly that neither she nor we were able to do justice to it. With the HSB follow-up data, though, its implications can be evaluated properly.

As in our earlier analysis, sector effects are estimated net of differences in various student characteristics (i.e., SES, race, and gender)

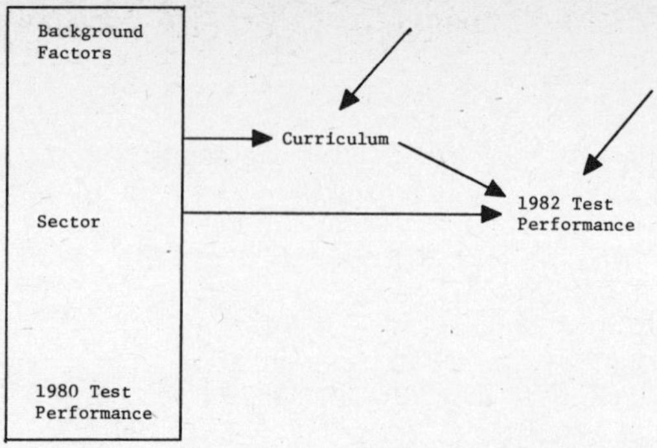

Figure 1. A Model of Cognitive Achievement

and in measures that tap regional variation. Here, though, we add sophomore test performance as another input control. One difference between this specification and our previous one is that now high school track membership (academic or general) intervenes between sector and the several domains of senior test performance. In our earlier analysis, we used high school track as a proxy for unmeasured cognitive differences; but this is no longer necessary, since direct controls are available. Rather, we can now evaluate the importance of track membership as an aspect of school organization. CHK argued this in response to our earlier analysis and to other analyses that used the track variable as we had (e.g., Morgan, 1983). They contended that channeling a large percentage of students into the college track was one of the ways private schools realized their superior performance.

The proper interpretation of the curriculum variable in these analyses is a matter of considerable importance, for sector differences within tracks are generally much smaller than those observed overall (Peng and Fetters, 1981; Willms, 1983; Alexander and Pallas, 1983). If one thinks of the track variable as a proxy for unmeasured student differences, then the available evidence offers little indication of differential sector effectiveness. If, on the other hand, one thinks of tracking as an important mechanism of school policy, then the differential effectiveness hypothesis receives stronger support (although still in the absence of proper controls for student competency differences). Now that a baseline assessment of test performance is available, we can grant CHK their preference on the track membership issue.[1] This framework, then,

[1] We should note, though, that even with entry-level test performance controlled, sector differences in patterns of curriculum placement may be due to student choice factors rather than organizational factors. That is, the choice of both sector and cur-

allows us to estimate the effects of sector on patterns of cognitive growth and to determine how these effects are mediated through patterns of curriculum placement.

As in our earlier study, we limit our comparison to public and Catholic schools, because the HSB project included too few non-Catholic private schools to allow secure generalizations—a point conceded by CHK (1981b, 1982a). We also exclude vocational-track students because of their sparse numbers in Catholic schools. Though it is not reflected in Figure 1, all analyses are performed separately for public and Catholic schools so that interactions involving the sector distinction will not be obscured. CHK have placed great importance on such interactions and have been especially critical of studies (e.g., Noell, 1982) that fail to make provision for them (CHK, 1982a; Coleman and Hoffer, 1983). Since one of our purposes is to evaluate the resilience of their conclusions from the HSB cross-sectional data, we thought it best to defer to their preference here as well, although we do not believe the matter is as important as they do.

There is, however, another reason for proceeding in this way. Doing so allows us to reevaluate CHK's claim that Catholic schools better approximate the common-school ideal than do public schools. The basis for their conclusion is that differences in test performance associated with race, ethnicity, and socioeconomic origins are less pronounced in the Catholic schools. We, along with others (Bryk, 1981; Goldberger and Cain, 1982; Cain and Goldberger, 1983), have expressed the concern that this pattern too might simply reflect selection differences (i.e., Catholic schools have a disproportionate enrollment of highly capable minority and disadvantaged youngsters). Hence, we will be interested to see how the inclusion of a suitable input control for test scores affects this detail of the results, as well as the more general matter of overall sector effects.

In the next section, we review sample-selection considerations, measurement procedures, and techniques of analysis.

METHODS

This analysis uses data from the HSB base-year (1980) and first follow-up (1982) surveys. Our strategy is to use 1980 sophomore test scores as input controls in equations predicting 1982 senior test performance. A particularly important consideration in attempting to model sophomore-to-senior growth is how dropouts are handled. For instance, if the dropout rate is higher in public schools, and if dropping out is associated with poor test performance, then the public-Catholic difference in test performance would likely be attenuated were dropouts lost from the sample. CHK (1982b, 1982c) attempted to estimate sophomore-to-senior learning rates using a synthetic cohort-like approach with adjustments for student background differences and dropout differences, but those efforts have been received quite critically (Goldberger and Cain, 1982).

Fortunately, this problem is averted in the HSB panel, because dropouts were included in the first follow-up survey along with several other classes of students (e.g., transfers). Hence, we are able to model sector differences in patterns of cognitive growth while retaining dropouts in the analysis.[2] The HSB base-year sample consisted of roughly 30,000 sophomores in more than 1,000 high schools. Students still enrolled in their base-year schools at the time of the first follow-up were sampled with a probability of 1.0. Students who were no longer attending their base-year schools at the time of the first follow-up (i.e., dropouts, early graduates, and transfers) were sampled at lower rates. The sample allocation consisted of 25,150 still-in-school seniors, 2,601 dropouts, 1,290 transfers to non-HSB schools, and 696 early high school graduates. Properly weighted, this sample projects to the population of roughly 3,800,000 high school sophomores in 1980. The HSB weighting factor for cases having both base-year and follow-up

riculum may be dictated by family and student preferences, which are not well accounted for in our framework. If this is the case, then some portion of the relationship between sector and curriculum would be spurious, and our estimations would still overstate the contribution of organizational processes to the quite different patterns of curriculum placement observed in public and Catholic schools.

[2] Although we think it quite important that the HSB went to such lengths to retain dropouts in the first follow-up, a case could also be made for excluding them from consideration. Since we are interested in the impact of school sector on cognitive development between the sophomore and senior years, it is reasonable to consider only youngsters who were susceptible to such influence throughout the interval, or at least to adjust somehow for the abbreviated exposure of dropouts. Moreover, since most dropouts are low achievers from public schools, and since they have not fully realized whatever cognitive benefits derive from staying in school, retaining them in the analysis might depress the estimates of growth in the public schools. Despite such concerns, it turns out that the pattern of sector differences is virtually identical whether dropouts are included or excluded. As a practical matter, then, the decision concerning the treatment of dropouts is of little consequence, and we perform all analyses with dropouts retained, as had been our original inclination.

testing data is used throughout our analyses. Further details on the sample and data collection may be found in Jones et al. (1983).

Questionnaire and testing data were collected as part of the first follow-up. The response rate for completed tests ranged from 78 percent, for the dropout sample, to 90 percent, for the still-in-school sample. These figures compare favorably to the response rates for the base-year sophomores (77 percent) and the base-year seniors (72 percent). In light of these figures, it appears that the HSB retesting program was highly successful, which simplifies our analysis plan considerably.

The HSB project administered the same battery of tests to the 1980 sophomore cohort in the spring of the base-year (1980) and first follow-up (1982) phases of data collection. The tests covered reading, vocabulary, mathematics, writing, science, and civics education. The mathematics score is the sum of the scores on two mathematics subtests. Additionally, a composite score was constructed by summing the scores on the first three tests (reading, vocabulary, and mathematics). The writing, science, and civics tests were designed to measure curriculum-specific achievement. For all tests, we use what are referred to as formula scores. These are raw scores (i.e., number of items correct) adjusted for guessing. Reliabilities for the sophomore tests, reported by Heyns and Hilton (1982), range from .53, for civics, to .85, for the Mathematics I test. From these figures, the estimated reliability for the composite is .92. As an expedient, we apply these reliabilities from the sophomore tests to the senior tests as well. Independent reliabilities for the follow-up battery will probably be available shortly, and we expect them to be somewhat higher than those for the sophomore instruments. However, we would be very much surprised if they were appreciably different from the sophomore values, and as will be discussed below, we have also performed all our analyses without any such corrections, implicitly assuming perfect reliabilities for the tests. Since these latter results are not much different from the adjusted estimations, and since the true senior reliabilities are probably closer to the sophomore reliabilities than to unity, we are not much concerned by this procedural compromise. Further information on the HSB tests can be found in Heyns and Hilton (1982).

The other variables used in the analysis are taken either from the sophomore questionnaire or, in the case of our school location measures, from the stratifying information used in drawing the HSB sample of schools. We include measures of family SES, students' race/ethnicity, and students' sex as background controls. The sources and coding of these data are summarized in Table 1.

RESULTS

To determine whether Catholic schools produce superior test performance, we performed several within-sector regression analyses. These differed from one another in the mix of control variables they included. The sample size, using listwise deletion of missing data, varies across dependent variables and ranges from 13,587 to 14,333 in the public-school equations and from 2,074 to 2,114 in the Catholic-school equations.

All our estimations use a "standard" set of controls, which includes selected student

Table 1. Independent Variables Used in Regression Analyses

Variable Description	Variable Name	Codes and Sources
School sector	PUBPRIV	Coded 1 if Catholic; 0 if public (HSB Question FLAG17)
Region	NEAST NC SOUTH	Coded 1 if Northeast; 0 otherwise Coded 1 if North Central; 0 otherwise Coded 1 if South; 0 otherwise (West is omitted category) (HSB Question FLAG19)
SES	SES	An equally weighted linear composite of standardized measures of father's education, mother's education, father's occupation, family income, and household items (HSB Question FLAG25)
Race/ethnicity	BLACK HISPANIC	Coded 1 if black; 0 otherwise Coded 1 if Hispanic; 0 otherwise (HSB Question FLAG22)
Sex	SEX	Coded 1 if female; 0 if male (HSB Question FLAG21)

background characteristics (race, gender, and family SES) and variables that capture regional differences in the distribution of schools. These are the same input controls used in our earlier analysis of the senior-year cross-sectional data (Alexander and Pallas, 1983), and they reasonably reflect the control strategies generally used in this literature.

For our major substantive analysis, which we report first, sophomore test scores are added to this set of background controls. Since the HSB project administered parallel test batteries in the sophomore and senior years, we are in the fortunate position of being able to adjust for prior levels of performance in the same cognitive domain before judging sector differences. Sector differences in senior test performance net of sophomore patterns reflect the impact of sector on cognitive growth between the two administrations and, in that sense, reveal how much of the "added value" is attributable to school sector. Despite our many other differences, the parties to this debate have at least agreed that this is the preferred way to study school effects on cognitive outcomes (Alexander and Pallas, 1982; Coleman, 1982).

Although this is probably the strongest nonexperimental design for investigating patterns of cognitive development between the sophomore and senior years of high school, one potential problem is that it neglects sector differences in patterns of performance through the spring of the sophomore year. More will be said of this later, but for now, we wish simply to emphasize that our analysis looks forward from the sophomore year. Of course, it would be a peculiar sort of effective school that exhausted its impact in the first year or two. Because of this consideration, as well as others to be discussed below, we are not especially troubled by this design limitation. Neither, we gather, are CHK, since they went to great lengths to approximate such a change analysis when neither design nor data were especially suited to the task.

In the analyses that follow, all regression results have been corrected for attenuation (cf. Nunnally, 1977) due to random errors of measurement in the cognitive performance measures. Both the sophomore input test controls and the senior criterion measures have been corrected using the reliability estimates discussed above.

Table 2 presents our best estimates of how school sector conditions cognitive development between the sophomore and senior years. Because these sector differences are derived with the sophomore-year counterparts of the outcome measures controlled, the results indicate whether cognitive growth (i.e., improved test performance) is actually greater among Catholic-school students. Our ability to take account of input-level performance differences in this way should allay most concerns regarding selection biases.

To generate the estimates in Table 2, we evaluated the paired public and Catholic equations for each outcome by means of a regression standardization (Althauser and Wigler, 1972; Iams and Thornton, 1975). Actually, we performed two such standardizations. The first calculated predicted outcome levels by applying public-school predictor means to the separate sector parameter estimates. It is from these calculations that we derived the estimates in Table 2. This approach provides the levels of test performance that would be expected if Catholic and public schools enrolled students similar to those presently attending public schools and if both sets of schools had the same regional distribution as the present mix of public schools.

We also performed a second set of calculations, which was parallel to the first but which used Catholic-school means throughout. These

Table 2. Estimates of Sector Differences in Sophomore-to-Senior Patterns of Test-Score Change from the HSB Panel

Test	Estimated Formula-Score Difference	As Fractions of a Year's Growth	As Fractions of the Test Standard Deviation
Composite	1.649	.66	.08
Reading	.311	.53	.06
Vocabulary	.707	.69	.12
Mathematics	.665	.76	.06
Writing	.509	.64	.10
Science	.125	.29	.03
Civics	−.029	−.05	−.01

NOTE: Estimates are derived from parallel regressions, which have been evaluated at the public-school means. The predictors used are three dummy variables for region of the country, a dummy variable distinguishing blacks from whites, a dummy variable distinguishing Hispanics fron non-Hispanics, a sex code, an SES composite, and the sophomore-year counterpart of the outcome test. All correlations involving tests have been corrected for random error using reliability estimates reported in Heyns and Hilton (1982).

calculations estimate how large the differences would be if Catholic and public schools enrolled students similar to those now attending Catholic schools and if both sets of schools had the same regional distribution as the present mix of Catholic schools. These results (along with those highlighted in Table 2) are presented in Table 3. For now, though, we focus on the differences that are observed at the public-school means, because these correspond most closely to the sort of policy change contemplated by CHK—that is, broadened access to private schools for the kinds of students who presently attend public schools. Although the pattern of results is not very different under the two assessments, sector differences are consistently smaller when the Catholic-school means are used. CHK observed a similar pattern in their original analyses.

The first column in Table 2 presents the results of these computations at the public-school means as simple formula-score differences. The entries are obtained by subtracting the mean level of test performance for public-school students from the value predicted for similar students who attend Catholic schools. Although it is difficult to judge the significance of these figures without a more tangible frame of reference, we suppose it is of some interest that all the differences, except that for the composite, are well below a single item. More informative, though, are the representations of these differences in the second and third columns.

The second column expresses these differences as fractions of a year's growth. A similar standard was used by CHK in much of their work and is the basis for their summary generalization that Catholic-school students perform about a year above public-school students. Their estimate of a year's growth was computed as half the background-adjusted

Table 3. Adjusted Sector Differences in Test Outcomes, with Tests Corrected for Attenuation

Test and Control	Evaluated at Public Means	Evaluated at Catholic Means
Composite		
(1) Background and input test	.08	.06
(2) Background	.30	.18
(3) Background, input test, and curriculum	.08	.06
(4) Background and curriculum	.22	.09
Reading		
(1) Background and input test	.06	.04
(2) Background	.22	.12
(3) Background, input test, and curriculum	.04	.03
(4) Background and curriculum	.13	.05
Vocabulary		
(1) Background and input test	.12	.05
(2) Background	.32	.19
(3) Background, input test, and curriculum	.12	.05
(4) Background and curriculum	.25	.12
Mathematics		
(1) Background and input test	.06	.07
(2) Background	.27	.15
(3) Background, input test, and curriculum	.05	.06
(4) Background and curriculum	.19	.06
Writing		
(1) Background and input test	.10	.04
(2) Background	.27	.17
(3) Background, input test, and curriculum	.09	.03
(4) Background and curriculum	.21	.10
Science		
(1) Background and input test	.03	.04
(2) Background	.09	−.01
(3) Background, input test, and curriculum	.03	.03
(4) Background and curriculum	.02	−.08
Civics		
(1) Background and input test	−.01	−.03
(2) Background	.16	.04
(3) Background, input test, and curriculum	−.02	−.04
(4) Background and curriculum	.08	−.04

NOTE: The adjustment involves a regression standardization in which the following background controls are used: NEAST, NC, BLACK, HISPANIC, SEX, SES. Regressions are corrected for unreliability in test-score predictors and outcomes.

difference in average performance levels between their public-school sophomore sample and their public-school senior sample. Their estimates, then, are derived from a cross-sectional comparison of the average performance levels of two different student cohorts. Our estimates, on the other hand, reflect patterns of individual change over the two-year interval covered by our panel. They are simply half the difference between the 1980 and 1982 test means.

Because of these and other procedural differences, our standard of a year's growth is not directly comparable to CHK's. We should also mention that CHK mainly used short versions of the HSB tests (these were identical for the sophomore and senior cohorts and hence allowed for more precise internal comparisons) and measured performance as the number of correct responses without adjustment for guessing. Hence, many considerations preclude straightforward comparison of our results with theirs. Nevertheless, it is possible to judge the approximate correspondence of our respective estimates of a year's difference by expressing them as fractions of each project's test-score standard deviation. To derive their estimates, we use the sophomore public-school standard deviation; to derive our estimates, we use the pooled sophomore standard deviation. For reading, vocabulary, and math, our estimates are 0.13, 0.20, and 0.09 standard deviation, respectively. The corresponding estimates from CHK's data are 0.18, 0.17, and 0.11 (computed from CHK [1982c:Tables 6–3 and 6–7]), which are quite close to ours. This should probably be of some comfort to CHK, since their procedures were unavoidably quite indirect.

In the second column of Table 2, each adjusted formula-score difference is expressed as a fraction of a year's average growth in that cognitive domain. The sector difference does not reach CHK's standard of one year in any of the seven tests. The largest difference is in math, where Catholic-school students have an advantage of about three fourths of a year. For the other two tests that tap more generic competencies, the sector difference is a bit smaller—about two thirds of a year in vocabulary and merely half a year in reading.

The last three tests are subject-specific assessments. These cover writing, science, and civics. Several critics (Heyns and Hilton, 1982; Goldberger and Cain, 1982) have argued that such curriculum-linked tests would be a more appropriate basis for judging school effectiveness, since they tap knowledge that is presumably acquired largely in school. Although these tests were available for the HSB sophomores in the base year of the project, CHK (1982a) declined to consider them because companion tests were not available for the base-year senior cohort. The tests were readministered during the first follow-up, however, and we are able to include them in the present analysis.

Sector differences for these three subject-specific tests are generally smaller than those estimated for the more generic competencies. The difference on the writing test—0.64 year—is the largest of the three, and it is about as large as the difference on the vocabulary test. For the other two tests, sector differences are much smaller, and the difference for civics actually favors the public schools. These figures, then, do not indicate that Catholic-school students do especially well on curriculum-linked tests. In fact, their advantage is actually smaller on these assessments, a pattern that is contrary to expectation if organizational efficacy is what really is at issue.

These differences all fall short of CHK's standard of a year's difference, but it is still difficult to know whether they are large or small in any absolute sense. CHK present their finding of about a year's difference as though it were a sizeable gap, but they do not tell us the basis for this judgement. In fact, their book discusses the *two-year* sophomore-to-senior public-school difference (which is the basis of the year benchmark) as though it were rather small (cf. CHK, 1982c:140–41). Is half a small difference large enough to be deemed important? They seem to believe so but fail to say why.

Setting aside the civics results, a reasonable summary for our data would probably be closer to two thirds of a year, which would correspond to about one third of a small difference. Again, is this large enough to justify the conclusion that Catholic-school students have an important advantage? The standard of a year's growth is not very helpful here, and it is for this reason that we prefer the base of comparison built into the third mode of presentation.

The last column of Table 2 expresses the estimated sector differences as fractions of the test battery standard deviation. These comparisons allow us to judge the average test-score difference across sectors against the variability in the trait. This seems to us to be the best of the less-than-ideal options that are available, and by this standard the sector differences quite clearly are small. Only two differences—for the vocabulary and writing tests—are even as large as 0.1 standard deviation, itself a very modest threshold. For the other two domains studied by CHK—reading and math—the differences are but 0.06 standard deviation. As before, the figures for the subject-specific tests are even smaller.

A technical concern not attended to in these

estimations, however, involves potential ceiling constraints on performance levels in the Catholic sector. If a disproportionately large fraction of Catholic-school students performed extremely well on the sophomore tests, then their prospects for improvement on the second assessment might be artificially limited, and so too their progress relative to poorer performing public-school students. We examined this possibility in several ways. First, as Heyns and Hilton (1982) suggest, ceiling effects for a group are a problem if the group's mean performance level is within one standard deviation of the maximum possible score on the test. We calculated this value for each follow-up test, including the composite. The Catholic mean fell below this standard only on the writing test. On the other tests, the Catholic means ranged from 1.2 standard deviations (for the civics test) to 1.9 standard deviations (for the science test) below the maximum.

As a further check on whether the disproportionate number of high base-year performers in the Catholic sector might attenuate our estimates of sector differences, we reestimated our equations for students whose base-year score was at least one standard deviation above the pooled sample composite mean and for students whose score was at least 1.5 standard deviations above the pooled sample mean. For the first group, the adjusted public-Catholic difference on the follow-up composite was virtually identical to that estimated for the entire sample. But for the extremely high-performing group (i.e., those scoring 1.5 or more standard deviations above the base-year mean), the estimated sector difference is considerably smaller than the sector difference for the total sample. If we take this as evidence of a ceiling effect (rather than, say, differential effectiveness), and if Catholic-school students were substantially overrepresented above this threshold, then the average sector difference might well be attenuated as a consequence. However, there is no evidence of such disproportionality: 14 percent of all Catholic-school students scored in this range, compared with 11 percent of all public-school students. This excess of 3 percent in the Catholic sector could hardly introduce sufficient *differential* bias to our results. Together, then, these two checks suggest that ceiling effects are not a problem in these data.

Thus, the estimates in Table 2 pass several important tests of technical adequacy, and they are, we believe, the best evidence on the issue presently available.[3] There is little reason to think that the cognitive performance of public-school students would be much improved by exposing them to the sort of educational environment available in Catholic schools. For example, if we assume that these competencies are normally distributed[4] and that the present public-school average is the 50th percentile, then the massive restructuring of schooling entertained in these calculations would boost the public-school mean on the test-battery composite to only the 53rd percentile. On the separate tests, the improvements would be two percentile points in reading and math and five points in vocabulary, and gains on the subject-specific tests would be even more modest. What then of CHK's claim that Catholic schools are educationally superior to public schools? If trivial advantage is what they meant by such a claim, then we suppose we would have to agree. But judged against reasonable benchmarks, there is little basis for such a conclusion.

Incidentally, when CHK's corresponding cross-sectional results are considered as fractions of the test standard deviations, the differences range from 0.144 to 0.189 standard deviation for the sophomore cohort and from 0.114 to 0.284 standard deviation in the senior analysis (computed from information provided in CHK [1982c:Tables 6.7 and 6.21]). In fact, in two of the three possible comparisons, their estimates are substantially larger than even our uncorrected figures. The smallest difference is in vocabulary, for which our estimate is 0.17 standard deviation, compared to their sophomore estimate of 0.189. (Their senior cohort estimate, however, is 0.284.) For reading and math, their sophomore estimates are about one-third larger than ours.

Clearly, then, our panel analysis indicates a

[3] An *SOE* referee also questioned the implications of correcting test-score correlations for attenuation, fearing that this would leave so little independent variability in the senior-year outcomes that the effects of other predictors would be unstable. Notwithstanding such concerns, we believe there is good justification for taking account of available information regarding measurement error in the tests. If these traits are highly stable over time, as they seem to be, then such constraints ought to be reflected in our analysis, just as they presumably limit organizational intervention in the real world. Nevertheless, the picture is not very different in the absence of such adjustments. The uncorrected sector estimates, analogous to those reported in column 3 of Table 2, are as follows: composite, .12; reading, .10; vocabulary, .17; math, .10; writing, .14; science, .05; civics, .09. Although these are sizeable proportionate increases over the corrected estimates, they are still quite small overall, and of course, we know them to be overly generous.

[4] They are actually positively skewed, but for our illustrative purposes, the distributional complexities are not especially important.

considerably smaller Catholic-school advantage, when judged either as fractions of a year's growth or as fractions of the test standard deviation. This pattern of differences seems to substantiate the concern expressed by many that CHK's design and analysis overstate the public-Catholic performance difference that is attributable to organizational factors. Our own evaluation of the sector effects in Table 2 is that differences below 0.1 standard deviation are too small to be considered of practical importance.

These, then, are our major substantive results and conclusions. Several subsidiary issues that arose repeatedly in the exchanges between CHK and their critics are considered in Table 3. In this table, comparisons are reported at both the public-school means and the Catholic-school means, and the estimates from Table 2 are included (row 1) to serve as a base of comparison. To simplify matters, we only report sector differences as fractions of the test standard deviation. This corresponds to the third column of results in Table 2.

The first issue considered in Table 3 is the adequacy of background measures as proxies for test-score controls. It will be recalled that CHK had to rely upon such surrogates. Despite the reservations voiced by many, they have held to the position that these served their purposes adequately. We are able to evaluate this by estimating sector differences using only background controls (the second row of results) and then by comparing these against the estimates obtained when test controls are added to the analysis (our substantive results, reported in the first row).

If CHK are correct in their opinion that background controls adjust adequately for selection differences, then the two sets of results should line up rather closely. Clearly, though, they do not. In fact, the differences are generally quite substantial: The estimates obtained with background controls alone are from two to four times greater than the estimates obtained when test controls are added. These comparisons demonstrate again (e.g., Alexander, McPartland, and Cook, 1980) that background proxies are simply inadequate when attempting to assess the impact of school organization on cognitive outcomes.

The second issue considered in Table 3 is whether curriculum placement plays an important role in mediating the (small) Catholic-school advantage obtained in our substantive analysis. It will be recalled that CHK argued, in response to those who proposed using the curriculum variable as a proxy for unmeasured student factors, that sector differences in curriculum placement are a result of school policy differences and, hence, that curriculum is an important organizational variable. We are now in a position to evaluate how much of the sector effect is actually mediated through curriculum placement.

This is accomplished by adding curriculum to the analysis and by comparing the sector differences that are obtained when curriculum is not controlled (row 1) with those obtained when curriculum is controlled (row 3). The difference between these two estimations would reflect the anticipated mediation. Most of the estimates, however, are unaffected by the addition of curriculum, and changes that do occur are extremely slight. Hence, we find little support for CHK's argument that sector differences in tracking policy are an important organizational means by which Catholic schools promote high levels of test performance. (Of course, the adjusted sector differences themselves were so slight that there wasn't much for the curriculum variable to mediate in the first place.)

The last issue considered in Table 3 is how well the curriculum variable served the interests of CHK's critics, who argued that its use in the absence of test-score controls would reduce selection biases. This can be judged by comparing row 4, the results when curriculum is added and test controls are dropped, with row 1, the results when test controls, but not curriculum, are used (the preferred approach), and with row 2, the results when only background controls are used. Here again, the pattern is rather clear. Although the estimated sector differences when curriculum is used as a proxy for test scores are generally a good bit larger than those obtained when test scores are controlled directly, they are at least a notable improvement over the estimates derived when background controls alone are used. It thus seems clear that the curriculum-controlled estimates are preferable to the background-adjusted estimates, but we do not take much solace in having been so vindicated. What we had not realized when urging the merits of the curriculum proxy was how far off the mark its use still left us.

The last issue we consider is whether achievement processes in Catholic schools better approximate the common-school ideal than do those in public schools, as CHK claim. They have found that test scores are less strongly related to student background characteristics in the Catholic sector. But since these results were derived without proper controls for prior test performance, they should also be deemed provisional.

The detailed regression results behind the comparisons in rows 1 and 2 of Table 3 speak to this issue. It will be recalled that the first of these estimations had test controls, and the

Table 4. Within-Sector Background Effects on Test Performance With and Without Input Test Controls

Test and Background Controls	(1) Public Background Controls Only	(2) Catholic Background Controls Only	(col. 1–col. 2)	(3) Public Background and Input Test	(4) Catholic Background and Input Test	(col. 3–col. 4)[a]
1982 composite						
Black	−10.287	−9.636	−.651	.352	− .312	0
Hispanic	−11.202	−9.624	−1.578	−.733	−1.108	0
SES	10.141	5.995	4.146	.844	1.245	0
R^2	.282	.154		.916	.875	
Reading						
Black	−2.540	−1.724	−.816	−.238	−.227	−.011
Hispanic	−2.764	−2.219	−.545	−.137	−.518	0
SES	2.365	1.468	.897	.212	.265	0
R^2	.212	.104		.871	.829	
Vocabulary						
Black	−3.428	−2.680	−.748	−.187	−.049	−.138
Hispanic	−3.296	−2.736	−.560	−.293	−.674	0
SES	2.934	1.675	1.259	.264	.109	.155
R^2	.290	.157		.937	.867	
Mathematics						
Black	−5.187	−5.776	0	.366	−.097	0
Hispanic	−5.733	−5.233	−.500	−.502	−.194	−.306
SES	5.311	3.160	2.151	.536	1.107	0
R^2	.253	.141		.921	.862	
Writing						
Black	−2.823	−2.115	−.708	−.226	−.279	0
Hispanic	−2.795	−2.447	−.348	−.268	−.678	0
SES	2.051	1.106	.945	.248	.339	0
R^2	.264	.178		.801	.717	
Science						
Black	−3.509	−3.371	−.138	.004	−1.288	0
Hispanic	−3.102	−2.185	−.917	−.197	−.565	0
SES	1.958	1.400	.558	.067	.459	0
R^2	.297	.180		.933	.817	
Civics						
Black	−.992	−1.035	0	−.273	−.595	0
Hispanic	−1.389	−1.602	0	−.328	−1.006	0
SES	1.249	.699	.550	.136	.318	0
R^2	.206	.127		.861	.715	

[a] Entries for which the Catholic-school coefficients are larger in absolute value than the public-school coefficients have been set to zero.

second did not. Hence, differences in the background coefficients between the second and the first will reveal whatever distortion might be due to the omitted test control.

Table 4 presents these background coefficients. The first two columns are from the public and Catholic equations when sophomore test performance is not controlled. The third column is the simple difference between them. The last three columns are the corresponding estimates from the equations that include test scores. To highlight the issue, comparisons in which the Catholic-school coefficients are larger in absolute value than their public-school counterparts have been set to zero.

It is apparent from these estimates that support for the common-school hypothesis evaporates under the second specification. In 18 of the 21 comparisons from the first analysis, the differences are in line with CHK's expectations. That is, the effects are smaller in the Catholic equations. But when sophomore test scores are controlled, the pattern changes dramatically: 17 of the 21 differences actually favor the public schools, and the remaining differences have shrunk considerably from their original values.

We conclude that the relationship of student background characteristics to patterns of cognitive development between the sophomore and senior years is very similar in public and Catholic schools.[5] It is not the case, then, that

[5] The *SOE* referee who questioned the propriety of our attenuation adjustments argued that this pattern results from instability of the parameter estimates for the SES and race/ethnicity variables. In fact, a similar pattern is obtained when the unad-

minority students and students from low-SES households are more successful in Catholic schools than in public schools. Here, too, CHK's conclusions are not sustained.

DISCUSSION

To recapitulate, our reading of the results in Tables 2, 3, and 4 suggests two main conclusions. First, and most important, there is little support for the notion that cognitive development in Catholic schools significantly outpaces that in public schools between the sophomore and senior years. Our second conclusion is that background characteristics relate to test performance in similar fashion in the public and Catholic schools. We thus find no support for CHK's common-school hypothesis that minority and disadvantaged students are especially well served by Catholic schooling. Our remaining comments elaborate upon the first of these two conclusions.

Our analysis does indicate a small Catholic-school advantage for most outcomes when assessed for the kinds of students who presently attend public schools. The advantage is somewhat larger for more generic competencies than for subject-specific assessments, but even in the former areas, most differences are less than 0.1 standard deviation. These correspond to about two thirds of a year's growth, on average, and some are a good bit smaller. When sector differences are evaluated for the kinds of students who attend Catholic schools, the Catholic-school edge is generally even smaller yet.

In our opinion, this average difference of 0.67 grade level between public and Catholic schools is quite modest (less than 0.1 test-score standard deviation) and certainly far too small to warrant CHK's contention that public schooling is inferior to Catholic schooling. Hence, the variability in test performance that can be attributed to sector differences is minute relative to the overall variability in cognitive skills. These sector effects simply do not matter much, and talking about them as though they do is both poor science and a poor basis for informing public policy. These were our earlier conclusions, and further analysis seems to sustain them.

We believe this judgment is well grounded in the best available evidence, yet one might well ask how we can so cavalierly dismiss a Catholic-school advantage on the order of two thirds of a year of cognitive growth. Surely this is no small difference. Or is it? This question, we think, is actually the crux of the issue. Two thirds of a year's growth might well turn out to be substantively trivial—a potentially quite important, and entirely serendipitous, revelation.

CHK's conclusion that Catholic schools promote about a year's cognitive growth beyond that realized in public schools is now known to overstate the Catholic-school advantage by about one third, on average. But their interpretation, we believe, was even more generous, for it overstated the practical implications of this year's difference. We grant that one year's growth seems like an awful lot when the upper bound is two (the fraction here would be 0.5), but what if the total change over this period doesn't amount to much? This, in fact, seems to be what we are seeing in the HSB data.

The average (two-year) increment in senior test scores over sophomore scores in our data is 0.286 standard deviation. The absolute change ranges from 0.40 standard deviation, on the civics test, to 0.18 standard deviation, in math. (These figures represent an average improvement of 1 item on the 10-item civics test and 1.7 items on the 38-item math test.) These estimates of average growth over the two-year interval are certainly far more substantial than the fluctuations around that average that are attributable to sector differences (excluding civics, for which the comparison favors public schools, the average public-Catholic difference across the other six tests is 0.075 standard deviation), but they hardly signify dramatic improvement. For example, if we again assume these traits to be normally distributed and the sophomore mean to be the 50th percentile, the senior follow-up mean, averaged across all tests, would fall just above the 61st percentile on the sophomore distribution. The civics mean would fall at the 66th percentile and the math mean would fall at the 57th percentile, which illustrates the range of improvement implied by these figures. Thus, about 40 percent of the seniors still scored below the sophomore average across a rather wide range of cognitive criteria after two additional years of schooling!

Jencks (1985) perceived these implications of our analyses and suggested two possibilities: Either the HSB tests are not sufficiently sensitive to what is taught in school, or there is not much cognitive growth altogether during the last two years of high school. If the latter were the case, then not only would it not matter

---

justed sophomore test scores are used as input controls. When input controls are not used, 18 of the 21 coefficients favor the common-school hypothesis. But when input controls are used, this drops to 10 of 21, and the margin of advantage for 9 of these 10 coefficients is substantially reduced. Hence, neither the adjusted nor the unadjusted estimates provide evidence that minority and lower-SES youngsters would be better off in Catholic schools.

which sector one attended, it seemingly would not matter much whether one stayed in school at all!

Although we can do little more at present than acknowledge such provocative possibilities,[6] we certainly take them seriously. In fact, we would not be much surprised if both proved true: Schools might have their greatest impact on subject-specific achievements, and the sorts of general competencies tapped by the HSB battery might not change much, on average, beyond midadolescence. This second possibility is consistent with results we have seen on other data sets (Alexander et al., 1980), but we want to be cautious not to overstate its implications. Cognitive outcomes are only one consideration among many that should enter into an evaluation of what schools and schooling do to youngsters; and even in the cognitive domain, we know woefully little regarding the mastery of subject-specific skills and knowledge. Moreover, even though there is not much average growth over the high school years, for particular students and even for particular kinds of students, educational interventions can make a considerable difference. Our recent studies of the effectiveness of the so-called new-basics curriculum (Alexander and Pallas, 1984) and the contribution of differential math and science coursetaking to the shortfall of girls relative to boys on the SAT-M (Pallas and Alexander, 1983) certainly underscore the practical importance of curricular content. All this suggests that the differential experiences that do have an important positive impact must be relatively infrequent or available to relatively few students. An authoritative accounting of what sorts of interventions matter most and for what sorts of students their payoffs are greatest comprise an important agenda for future research, but we do not expect that it will have much at all to do with the differential effectiveness of public and Catholic schools.

Finally, in the introduction to the present analysis, we acknowledged a lingering uncertainty. Our results do not address the possibility of sector effects on test scores through the tenth grade. CHK studied sophomore patterns of test performance and interpreted them as reflections of differential sector effectiveness; their critics, ourselves included, felt they were more likely due to selection differences. However, neither they nor their critics could muster conclusive evidence on the issue, and this remains the case still. Lacking a proper evaluation, we must therefore continue to rely on circumstantial indications and reasoned judgment.

Consider the data reported in Table 5. These are zero-order correlations relating background characteristics to each other and to the test-battery composite. Results for the other tests would be quite similar. We focus first on the zero-order associations between background and sophomore test performance across the two sectors. These are smaller in the Catholic schools than in the public schools. CHK interpret the lower Catholic-school correlations between background characteristics (SES and race/ethnicity) and test scores as evidence for their common-school hypothesis. Of course, they focused on how these correlations expressed themselves in a regression analysis, but this is incidental to our point. Others suspected that these differences simply reflected that low-SES and minority students who attended Catholic schools were somewhat exceptional in the first place. The correlations in Table 5 relating background and test performance in the two sectors do not distinguish between these two interpretations. They could have been generated either by differential selection processes or by differential sector effectiveness.

Other correlations in Table 5, though, are unambiguously the result of selection processes. In particular, the correlations between minority-group status and SES necessarily reflect selection differences. Table 5 shows a sizeable negative association between race/ethnicity and SES in the public schools, which is consistent with our knowledge about the relative ranking of minorities in American society generally. In the Catholic schools, however, the black/nonblack dichotomy is virtually uncorrelated with SES. This is a peculiar pattern to be sure.

While it is at least conceivable that private-school organization could attenuate the link

Table 5. Zero-Order Correlations of Race/Ethnicity and SES with Sophomore Test Performance, by Sector

	1980 Composite	SES
Public		
Black	−.247	−.193
Hispanic	−.231	−.165
SES	.453	—
Catholic		
Black	−.138	−.052
Hispanic	−.190	−.142
SES	.254	—

NOTE: Test correlations are corrected for attenuation.

[6] In fact, we are presently using the HSB data in a study that compares the test scores of dropouts with the test scores of those who persist through graduation (Alexander, Natriello, and Pallas, 1985). These results should inform the question of whether staying in school does accrue cognitive benefits.

between background and test performance, it is highly dubious that any sort of organizational intervention could alter the connection between minority status and socioeconomic disadvantage. It is striking, therefore, that SES and minority status should be so loosely coupled among Catholic-school youth. What we see, then, are selection differences of the same magnitude as the test-score correlation differences. Clearly, selection differences *could be* large enough to account for both the sophomore common-school pattern and the superior performance of Catholic-school students on the sophomore tests. This is hardly conclusive, but to us it is at least suggestive. The burden of proof continues to rest upon those who favor the effectiveness hypothesis, and it seems to us a considerable burden indeed.

Rather than persist in the elusive quest for substantial Catholic-school effects on cognitive performance, a more constructive agenda for the future might be to ponder why Catholic schools do not outpace public schools by the sort of margin that their many advantages seem to anticipate. This pattern of results from public-Catholic comparisons does indeed strike us as provocative (and potentially important) but not at all for the reasons given by CHK.

REFERENCES

Alexander, K. L., J. M. McPartland, and M. A. Cook
1980 "Using standardized test performance in school effects research." Pp. 1–33 in R. Corwin (ed.), Research in Sociology of Education and Socialization. Vol. 2. Greenwich, CT: JAI Press.

Alexander, K. L., G. Natriello, and A. M. Pallas
1985 "For whom the school bell tolls: The impact of dropping out on cognitive performance." Paper to be presented at the Annual Meetings of the American Sociological Association, Washington, D.C.

Alexander, K. L. and A. M. Pallas
1982 "Reply to Coleman." American Sociological Review 47:822–24.
1983 "Private schools and public policy: New evidence on cognitive achievement in public and private schools." Sociology of Education 56:170–82.
1984 "Curriculum reform and school performance: An evaluation of the 'New Basics'." American Journal of Education 92:391–420.

Althauser, R. P. and M. Wigler
1972 "Standardization and component analysis." Sociological Methods and Research 1:97–135.

Bryk, A. S.
1981 "Disciplined inquiry or policy argument." Harvard Educational Review 51:497–509.

Cain, G. G. and A. S. Goldberger
1983 "Public and private schools revisited." Sociology of Education 56:208–18.

Coleman, J. S.
1982 "The use of 'ability' measures as controls for concurrent or subsequent achievement." American Sociological Review 57:819–21.

Coleman, J. S. and T. Hoffer
1983 "Response to Taeuber-James, Cain-Goldberger and Morgan." Sociology of Education 56:219–34.

Coleman, J. S., T. Hoffer, and S. Kilgore
1981a Public and Private Schools. Report to the National Center for Education Statistics. Chicago: National Opinion Research Center.
1981b "Questions and answers: Our response." Harvard Educational Review 51:526–45.
1982a "Achievement and segregation in secondary schools: A further look at public and private school differences." Sociology of Education 55:162–82.
1982b "Cognitive outcomes in public and private schools." Sociology of Education 55:65–76.
1982c High School Achievement. New York: Basic.

Goldberger, A. S. and G. G. Cain
1982 "The causal analysis of cognitive outcomes in the Coleman, Hoffer and Kilgore report." Sociology of Education 55:103–22.

Heyns, B. and T. L. Hilton
1982 "The cognitive tests for High School and Beyond: An assessment." Sociology of Education 55:89–102.

Iams, H. and A. Thornton
1975 "Decomposition of differences: A cautionary note." Sociological Methods and Research 3:341–52.

Jencks, C.
1985 "How much do high school students learn?" Sociology of Education 58:128–35.

Jones, C., M. Clarke, G. Mooney, H. McWilliams, I. Crawford, B. Stephenson, and R. Tourangeau
1983 High School and Beyond 1980 Sophomore Cohort First Follow-Up (1982) Data File User's Manual. Washington, D.C.: National Center for Education Statistics.

Kilgore, S.
1983 "Statistical evidence, selectivity effects and program placement: Response to Alexander and Pallas." Sociology of Education 56:182–86.

Morgan, W. R.
1983 "Learning and student life quality of public and private school youth." Sociology of Education 56:187–202.

Noell, J.
1982 "Public and Catholic schools: A reanalysis of 'Public and Private Schools'." Sociology of Education 55:123–32.

Nunnally, J. C.
1977 Psychometric Theory. New York: McGraw-Hill.

Page, E. and T. Keith
1981 "Effects of U.S. private schools: A techni-

cal analysis of two recent claims." Educational Researcher 10:7–17.
Pallas, A. M. and K. L. Alexander
1983 "Sex differences in quantitative SAT performance: New evidence on the differential coursework hypothesis." American Educational Research Journal 20:165–82.
Peng, S. and W. Fetters
1981 Review of Draft Report of Minority Students in Catholic Secondary Schools by Andrew Greeley. Washington, D.C.: National Center for Education Statistics.
Willms, J. D.
1983 "Do private schools produce higher levels of academic achievement? New evidence for the tuition tax credit debate." Pp. 223–31 in T. James and H. M. Levin (eds.), Public Dollars for Private Schools: The Case of Tuition Tax Credits. Philadelphia: Temple University Press.

HOW MUCH DO HIGH SCHOOL STUDENTS LEARN?

CHRISTOPHER JENCKS
Northwestern University

Sociology of Education 1985, Vol. 58 (April):128–135

One major purpose of the High School and Beyond (HSB) study was to assess the impact of different kinds of schooling on how much students learned in the last two years of high school. The test battery administered to sophomores in the spring of 1980 therefore included measures of achievement in six areas: reading, vocabulary, math, writing, science, and civics. HSB readministered identical tests to the same individuals in the spring of 1982, when most of them were seniors.

Even before the 1982 follow-up data became available, Coleman, Hoffer, and Kilgore (1982a, 1982b) had concluded on the basis of the 1980 data on sophomores and seniors that Catholic-school students learned substantially more than public-school students during their last two years in high school. This conclusion evoked a storm of protest. A number of critics, including Alexander and Pallas (1983) and Willms (1983), reanalyzed the 1980 data. They argued that the alleged benefits of Catholic schooling were either far smaller than Coleman et al. had claimed, statistically insignificant, a byproduct of specification error, or all three. All parties to this debate agreed, however, that the 1980 data were not ideal for estimating the effect of Catholic schooling, since there was no completely satisfactory way of knowing what seniors in 1980 were like when they were sophomores in 1978, or what sophomores in 1980 would be like when they became seniors in 1982.

Hoffer, Greeley, and Coleman (1985), Willms (1985), and Alexander and Pallas (1985) have now used the 1982 follow-up data for the 1980 sophomores to check their earlier claims. All three sets of authors read the new data as supporting their earlier claims. Since these claims were contradictory, the reader is likely to be confused. The remainder of this article tries to reduce the confusion. The first section examines the reasons these three articles end up with different estimates of the sector effect. The second section asks whether we should regard the estimated effects as large or small.

WHY THE SECTOR EFFECT VARIES

All three articles agree on the following points:

1. Sophomores scored higher in Catholic schools than in public schools on all the tests administered in 1980.
2. Between their sophomore and senior years, Catholic-school students' raw scores on all tests except civics increased more than public-school students' raw scores. On the civics test, both groups gained the same amount.
3. When other measured sophomore characteristics are controlled, Catholic-school students still show a larger gain than public-school students on the reading, vocabulary, math, and writing tests. On the science and civics tests the results are less clearcut, varying with the exact estimation procedure.

Nonetheless, the three articles produce varying estimates of the sector effect. This variation has three main sources: (1) variation in the authors' choice of sophomore control vari-

---

I am indebted to Thomas Hoffer for supplying a variety of useful numbers on very short notice. Address all correspondence to the author at the Center for Urban Affairs and Policy Research, Northwestern University, 2040 Sheridan Road, Evanston, IL 60201.

ables, (2) variation in the kinds of students for whom the authors estimate the sector effect, and (3) variation in the tests the authors emphasize.

All three articles control ethnicity and SES. But Hoffer et al. generally control only one sophomore test score, namely, the score on the sophomore test for which they are analyzing subsequent gains. When predicting senior reading scores, for example, they usually control only sophomore reading scores, and when predicting senior math scores, they usually control only sophomore math scores. Alexander and Pallas do the same thing, but they adjust the observed correlation matrix for attenuation due to unreliability in the relevant tests. This adjustment lowers the estimated effect of Catholic schooling. Willms does not adjust for attenuation, but he controls three or four sophomore scores, depending on which senior score is the dependent variable. Controlling more sophomore scores lowers the estimated effect of Catholic schooling.

The magnitude of the sector effect also varies according to whether or not one assumes that the effect of sophomore characteristics varies by sector. Hoffer et al. and Alexander and Pallas use a two-equation model, in which the effects of sophomore characteristics can vary by sector. This yields two equally valid estimates of the sector effect. To estimate the mean benefits of Catholic schooling for Catholic-school students, they use the public-school equation to predict how much the average Catholic-school student would have learned in a public school and then compare this predicted value to Catholic-school students' actual scores. To estimate the mean cost of public schooling to public-school students, they use the Catholic-school equation to predict how much the average public-school student would have learned in a Catholic school and then compare these predicted means to public-school students' actual means. Since public-school students are less advantaged than Catholic-school students, and since sectoral differences have more effect on initially disadvantaged students in the HSB sample, the cost of public schooling to public-school students is generally greater than the benefit of Catholic schooling to Catholic-school students.

Willms argues that this two-equation model is unnecessary. He uses a single-equation model to estimate the average effect of sophomore characteristics on senior achievement in both sectors. He then estimates the effect of Catholic schooling by adding a dummy variable that distinguishes students in the Catholic sector. This approach assumes that the sector effect is the same for all sorts of students. If the analyses were identical on other grounds, Willms's approach would estimate the effect of Catholic schooling on students somewhat more advantaged than the average public-school student and somewhat less advantaged than the average Catholic-school student (Rogosa, 1980).

Table 1 shows how these methodological differences affect the estimated sector effect. To make the numerical results comparable, I have expressed all three articles' estimates of the sector effect as percentages of the relevant public-school students' predicted gain between the sophomore and senior years. The top row of the first column, for example, shows that Catholic-school students gained 45 percent more on the HSB reading test between their sophomore and senior years than public-school students with the same initial characteristics.[1] To see how methodological changes alter the apparent size of the sector effect, the reader should look at the bottom row of the table, which shows the average sector effect for all six HSB tests.

To assess the impact of alternative sophomore controls, the reader should first compare Hoffer et al.'s estimates of sector effects when they control only one sophomore test to their estimates when they control three or four tests (compare columns 1 and 2 or 6 and 7). Controlling more sophomore tests lowers the estimated sector effect by 11 or 12 percent. Since sophomore performance on a single test is clearly a fallible proxy for initial ability and motivation, and since controlling more tests improves our estimates of initial ability and motivation, columns 2 and 7 are surely preferable to columns 1 and 6. Thus, all Hoffer et al.'s estimated sector effects, except those in their Table 3.2, are upwardly biased.

Alexander and Pallas's adjustment for attenuation yields essentially the same average sector effect as a model that controls three or four sophomore tests (compare columns 2 and 3 or columns 7 and 8). Nonetheless, for both

---

[1] In Table 1, as in all the articles under discussion, the HSB test scores are assumed to be interval scales. This is probably not exactly true. Hoffer et al. and Willms analyze raw scores. Alexander and Pallas analyze formula scores, which are adjusted for guessing. These are not generally a linear transformation of each other, so they cannot both be interval scales. If guessing leads to floor effects, or if there are ceiling effects, as Hoffer et al. suggest, raw scores will not constitute an interval scale. If the items vary in difficulty, and if difficulty does not increase in linear fashion, scores will again not constitute an interval scale. None of the articles under discussion explores these issues in detail. One simple preliminary test would be to look for nonlinear relationships between sophomore and senior scores on the same test.

Table 1. Incremental Effect of Catholic Schooling as a Percent of Public-School Gain between the Sophomore and Senior Years, with Various Controls

	For Students at Catholic-School Mean in Sophomore Year					For Students at Public-School Mean in Sophomore Year			
	Hoffer et al. Controlling for:		Alexander and Pallas Controlling for		Willms Controlling for	Hoffer et al. Controlling for:		Alexander and Pallas Controlling for	
Test	One Test (1)	3 or 4 Tests (2)	"True" Score (3)	SE (4)	3 or 4 Tests (5)	One Test (6)	3 or 4 Tests (7)	"True" Score (8)	SE (9)
Reading	45	31	18	10	16	53	35	27	14
Vocabulary	27	26	14	5	28	40	38	35	8
Mathematics	40	32	44	9	36	53	48	38	16
Writing	29	23	13	7	20	56	47	32	11
Science	12	−10	19	10	−14	13	−13	15	17
Civics	14	2	−7	8	−2	17	5	−4	10
Average	28	17	17	—	13	39	27	24	—

Sources (by column):
1. Hoffer et al. [(Table 2.3, col. 3)/(Table 2.3, col. 2)].
2. Hoffer, personal communication. The equations are identical to those that Hoffer et al. used in constructing their Table 3.2, but the sector effect is evaluated at the Catholic-school means.
3. Alexander and Pallas ([(Table 2, col. 2)/2][(Table 3, Model 1, col. 2)/(Table 3, Model 1, col. 1)]).
4. Standard errors for the point estimates in column 2, supplied by Hoffer, personal communication.
5. Willms [(Table 3, Model 1) (Footnote 12, col. 1)/(Table 1, col. 9 − Table 1, col. 3)].
6. Hoffer et al. [(Table 2.2, col. 3)/(Table 2.2, col. 2)].
7. Hoffer et al. [(Table 3.2, col. 3)/(Table 2.2, col. 2)].
8. Alexander and Pallas [(Table 2, col. 2)/2].
9. Standard errors for the point estimates in column 7, supplied by Hoffer, personal communication.

theoretical and practical reasons, estimates from a model that controls a wide range of sophomore tests are preferable to estimates from a model that controls a single "true" score. The theoretical argument is that sophomore scores measure several different things: initial knowledge, aptitude, motivation, etc. An infinitely long test covering a single domain is an ideal measure of a student's initial knowledge of that domain, but it is not an ideal measure of aptitude or motivation. A composite that covers many different domains is likely to measure aptitude and motivation more accurately. Suppose, to take an extreme example, that the advanced math test covered only differential calculus. Suppose, in addition, that the test required students to fill in correct answers, so that guessing was not a problem, and that students who had studied differential calculus always got all the questions right, while students who had not studied differential calculus always got all the questions wrong. Finally, suppose that only 0.01 percent of sophomores had studied calculus, compared to 5 percent of seniors. The KR-20 reliability of such a test would be 1.00. But sophomore scores on the test would not predict senior scores at all accurately. Sophomore scores on other tests (e.g. general math) might, however, predict senior scores quite accurately, because they might predict whether students would take calculus.

The practical reason for skepticism about efforts to control a single "true" sophomore score is that we do not have the reliabilities we need to correct the HSB correlations for attenuation. Alexander and Pallas use KR-20 reliabilities. The KR-20 reliability depends on the length of the test and the correlation between items. It estimates the average correlation between alternate forms of the test administered at a single point in time. A KR-20 reliability implicitly defines all item-specific sources of variation in performance as error. This means it can only be used to correct correlations between alternate forms of a test, not between repeated administrations of the same test. Since HSB administered exactly the same tests to sophomores in 1980 and seniors in 1982, the item-specific "errors" measured by the KR-20 reliabilities can be expected to persist over time, making the KR-20 correction inappropriate. The item-specific sources of variance measured by the KR-20 reliability may be either larger or smaller than the time-specific sources of variance. The only way to find out is to compare the KR-20 reliabilities to test-retest reliabilities, but the latter do not exist for the HSB tests.

Nonetheless, while Alexander and Pallas's correction for attenuation is problematic in principle, it does not seem to distort their findings about the sector effect in any important way. When Hoffer et al. control three or four sophomore tests instead of only one, their estimates of the sector effect agree quite closely with Alexander and Pallas's estimates (compare columns 2 and 3 or 7 and 8). Willms's single-equation model also yields estimates quite close to Alexander and Pallas's estimates and to Hoffer et al.'s corrected estimates for students currently enrolled in Catholic schools (compare column 5 to columns 2 and 3).

The second major source of disagreement over the estimates derives from the fact that both Hoffer et al. and Alexander and Pallas emphasize the likely effects of Catholic schooling on the average public-school student, whereas Willms estimates the effect of Catholic schooling on the assumption that it is the same for all students. In choosing between these approaches, both Hoffer et al. and Willms emphasize conventional tests of statistical significance. Hoffer et al. test for sector differences in the effects of initial advantages by regressing each senior test score on its sophomore counterpart, along with SES, a dummy for being black, and a dummy for being Hispanic. They run separate regressions for the public- and Catholic-school samples and then compare coefficients. In 20 of 24 possible comparisons, initial advantages have more impact on senior achievement in public schools than in Catholic schools. Assuming a design effect of 1.5, only 6 of the 24 comparisons yield a sector difference more than twice its standard error, but all 6 of these differences are in the same direction, so we can hardly attribute the overall pattern to chance.

Since Willms distinguishes between advanced and general math, he has seven senior scores rather than six. He regresses these seven scores on nine or ten sophomore characteristics, depending on the test, and ends up with 53 coefficients measuring the effect of ethnicity, SES, a two-parent family, and sophomore test scores. He then adds interaction terms to see if these coefficients vary systematically by sector. Of the 53 interaction terms, 32 indicate that initially disadvantaged students gain more in Catholic schools, while 21 indicate that initially disadvantaged students gain more in public schools. Assuming a design effect of 1.5, only one of these interactions is twice its standard error.

Neither analysis is ideal for identifying interactions. Some of the apparent interactions in Hoffer et al.'s Table 2.4 might have disappeared had they controlled the additive effects of more sophomore tests. Some of the apparent "noise" in Willms's Table 7 might have disappeared had he collapsed different sophomore tests into a single composite. But the fundamental problem here is sample size. Because the Catholic-school sample is relatively small, all these interactions have large sampling errors. This does not necessarily mean we can afford to ignore them, as Willms argues. His Table 7 shows, for example, that between their sophomore and senior years, black students in public schools gain 0.224 point less on the HSB reading test than comparable white students. It also shows that the coefficient of the interaction between race and Catholic-school attendance is +0.271. The average effect of race on senior scores in the Catholic sector is thus positive, if trivial (0.271 − 0.224 = 0.047). The average student gains only 1.0 point on this test between the sophomore and senior years. If black skin reduces a student's expected gain by one quarter in the public sector while it exerts no negative effect in the Catholic sector, that is an important difference. But the 95 percent confidence interval for this interaction runs from −0.37 to +0.86 point. Therefore, Catholic schools may actually be far worse for blacks than public schools, or they may be enormously better. We just can't say without a much larger sample.

The same difficulty arises when we try to assess the likely effect of Catholic schooling on the average public-school student. We must use the relatively small Catholic-school sample to predict how well the average public-school student would have done in a Catholic school. The resulting estimates have quite large sampling errors. According to column 7, for example, between the sophomore and senior years, the typical public-school student's math score would have risen 48 percent more in a Catholic school than in a public school. But the sampling error of this estimate is ±16 percent (see column 9). The 95 percent confidence interval therefore ranges from 17 to 79 percent. This range does not include zero, so the point estimate is statistically significant by conventional standards. But talking about statistical significance in this context (or almost any other) is a form of magical thinking intended to create a feeling of certainty when none is justified. The confidence interval includes values so low as to be relatively trivial and so high as to be staggering. It also includes the point estimate for the effect of Catholic schooling on the typical Catholic-school student (32 percent). Given this range of uncertainty, there can be no "right" resolution to the argument. All we can say is that although there is some evidence that Catholic schooling is especially effective for initially disadvantaged students, this evidence should not be taken too seriously unless it is corroborated in other samples. The fact that Coleman, Hoffer, and Kilgore (1982a, 1982b) found the same pattern among seniors in these schools in 1980 does, however, support their general argument.

Table 2. Predicted Annual Gain in Achievement, as a Fraction of the Sophomore Public-School Standard Deviation, by Sector

	For Students at Catholic-School Mean in Sophomore Year			For Students at Public-School Mean in Sophomore Year			Sustained Annual Sector Effect Over 9.5 Years	
Test	Public School (1)	Catholic School (2)	Difference (3)	Public School (4)	Catholic School (5)	Difference (6)	For Average Catholic-School Student (7)	For Average Public-School Student (8)
Reading	.13	.17	.04	.13	.17	.04	.013	.023
Vocabulary	.19	.24	.05	.20	.27	.07	.020	.034
Mathematics	.12	.16	.04	.10	.15	.05	.016	.028
Writing	.16	.20	.04	.17	.25	.08	.018	.028
Science	.13	.12	−.01	.11	.09	−.02	−.001	.009
Civics	.20	.20	.00	.21	.22	.01	.004	.017
Average	.15	.18	.03	.15	.19	.04	.012	.023

Sources (by column):
1. col. 2–col. 3.
2. Hoffer et al. [(Table 2.3, col. 2) + (Table 2.3, col. 3)].
3. Hoffer, personal communication.
4. Hoffer et al. [(Table 2.2, col. 2) + (Table 2.2, col. 3)].
5. col. 4 + col. 6.
6. Hoffer et al. (Table 3.2, col. 3).
7. Alexander and Pallas [(Table 3, Model 2, col. 2)/9.5].
8. Alexander and Pallas [(Table 3, Model 2, col. 1)/9.5].

NOTE: All raw scores for computations in columns 1 through 6 are standardized using sophomore public-school standard deviations provided by Hoffer.

The third major source of variation in estimates of the sector effect is variation between tests. The effects for the "three R's" (reading, vocabulary, math, and writing) are much greater than for "nontraditional" subjects (science and civics). Hoffer et al. suggest that this is because Catholic schools deemphasize science. They do not try to explain the results for civics. Are we to assume that if Catholic schools tried, they could boost science and civics achievement as much as they now boost reading, vocabulary, math, and writing achievement? If so, the gains in reading, vocabulary, math, and writing, which Hoffer et al. stress in their first section, are our best estimate of the potential sector effect. Or should we assume that if the Catholic schools devoted more attention to science and civics they would have less time for the three R's, and their advantage in those areas would decline? If so, the average gain for all six tests is the best estimate of the potential sector effect. None of the three articles seems to me to address the implications of these differences between tests with much care.

The foregoing comparisons suggest that the apparent discrepancies between the three articles' empirical results have three sources:

1. Hoffer et al. do not control enough sophomore tests.
2. Both Hoffer et al. and Alexander and Pallas estimate the effect of Catholic schooling on students with sophomore characteristics at the public-school means, whereas Willms estimates the effect of Catholic schooling on the assumption that it is the same for all students.
3. The first section of Hoffer et al.'s article focusses exclusively on tests that show Catholic schools to be unusually effective.

ARE THE EFFECTS OF CATHOLIC SCHOOLS LARGE OR SMALL?

Even if the authors of these three articles could agree about the numerical magnitude of the sector effect, they would disagree about whether it was large or small. So will many readers. Table 1 suggests that the effects are relatively large, because it focusses on the *ratio* of Catholic- to public-school gains.[2] Table

[2] Public-school students gain about one grade equivalent per year by definition. The average Catholic-school advantage, reported in column 2 of Table 1, thus translates into a grade-equivalent advantage of 2(.17) = 0.34 year from the sophomore to the senior year. For students who start out at the public-school mean, the point estimate is 27 percent rather than 17 percent (see column 7 of Table 1), which translates into an average advantage of about 0.54 grade equivalent in Hoffer et al.'s Table 3.2. These estimates are lower than those reported in most of Hoffer et al.'s tables because they are derived from a model that controls more sophomore tests.

2 shows why both Willms and Alexander and Pallas regard the effect as small. It shows the absolute difference between the two sectors, expressed as a proportion of the sophomore standard deviation in public schools. The estimates are from Hoffer et al.'s basic model with two or three more sophomore test scores controlled. I have converted all values to annual equivalents by dividing the change from 1980 to 1982 by two.

Public-school students' scores on the HSB tests rise by an average of 0.15 standard deviation per year. Catholic-school students' scores rise by an average of 0.18 standard deviation per year if they start out at the Catholic-school mean and by 0.19 standard deviation per year if they start out at the public-school mean. The annual increment attributable to Catholic schooling thus averages 0.03 or 0.04 standard deviation per year. By conventional standards this is a tiny effect, hardly worth serious study. But conventional standards may be misleading in this case.

The 27-percent increase in the learning rate shown in column 7 of Table 1 leads to an absolute advantage of only 0.04 standard deviation per year, because the annual increase in test performance in the public schools is itself very small by conventional standards—only 0.15 standard deviation per year. As Willms notes, studies of elementary schools typically report much larger gains. In the early years of elementary school, students typically gain a full standard deviation each year. Willms suggests that the small standardized gains indicate deficiencies in the HSB tests. He may be right, but other tests have produced much the same results. Project Talent, for example, administered a wide range of cognitive tests to a national sample of 9th graders in 1960 and then readministered the same tests to 12th graders in 1963. The Talent sample gained 0.23 standard deviation per year in vocabulary, 0.20 in reading, 0.19 in social studies, and 0.19 in arithmetic reasoning (Jencks and Brown, 1975). The 1965 Equality of Educational Opportunity survey found similar differences between 9th and 12th graders (Coleman et al., 1966).

A more plausible reason for the small standardized gains in the junior and senior years is that the sophomore standard deviation is very large in absolute terms. If students have not been exposed to a subject, their performance on the "pretest" will be uniformly low. This makes it easy to raise their mean scores by one standard deviation. If we start with a group of students who hardly read, for example, it should come as no surprise that a few months of instruction enable the average student to read better than any one student was able to read at the start—a gain of several standard deviations. By the sophomore year, however, almost all students have had considerable opportunity to master the material covered by most of the HSB tests. As a result, their performance is extraordinarily variable. On the 19-item reading test, for example, there were five alternatives per item, so a student could get 4 items right by chance alone. Ten percent of all sophomores did no better than chance. Two percent got 18 or 19 items right, which is probably more than the average college graduate would get right. Small wonder, then, that another year of instruction, on top of the ten preceding years, produces a relatively small standardized gain. Expecting large annual gains in reading comprehension among juniors and seniors is like expecting large annual gains in swimming performance among juniors and seniors who have been training since childhood.

Whether or not an annual increment in test performance of 0.03 or 0.04 standard deviation per year in the Catholic schools is important depends on whether it is confined to the last two years of high school or whether it also occurs in earlier grades. If the effect is confined to the last two years of high school, Catholic-school students will end up only 0.06 to 0.08 standard deviation ahead of their public-school counterparts, which is not of much practical importance. If the effect is found at all grade levels, *and if it is cumulative,* then students who spend twelve years in a Catholic school will end up 0.36 to 0.48 standard deviation ahead of their public-school counterparts, which is of great practical importance. For those who prefer to think in terms of grade equivalents, as Hoffer et al. do, we can say that if the 17-percent advantage observed in grades 11 and 12 is found in grades 1 through 10 as well, the advantage by 12th grade will be 2 years. If the advantage is 27 percent, the cumulative advantage over 12 years will be 3.2 years.

One way to decide whether the sector effect in grades 11 and 12 is similar to that in grades 1 through 10 is to look at the cumulative impact of Catholic-school attendance on senior scores. It seems safe to assume that almost all Catholic-school seniors had attended a Catholic high school since the beginning of 9th grade. Hoffer et al.'s Table 1.3 suggests that the typical Catholic high school student had also had about 5.5 years of Catholic elementary schooling. This implies that the typical Catholic-school senior had had a total of 9.5 years of Catholic schooling.

Alexander and Pallas's Table 3 reports test-score differences between Catholic- and public-school seniors, controlling only for

SES, region, ethnicity, and sex. Averaging across all six HSB tests, students with the background of the average Catholic-school senior score 0.11 standard deviation higher in Catholic than in public schools, and students with the background of the average public-school senior score 0.22 standard deviation higher in Catholic than in public schools. This suggests that each additional year of Catholic schooling raises the typical Catholic-school student's achievement by 0.11/9.5 = 0.01 standard deviation per year, and that each year of public schooling depresses the typical public-school student's achievement by about 0.02 standard deviation. The figures are a bit higher for the reading, vocabulary, math, and writing tests and lower for science and civics.

These estimates of the cumulative impact of Catholic schooling are clearly smaller than Hoffer et al.'s, Willms's, and Alexander and Pallas's estimates for the last two years of high school. There are at least three possible explanations for this. First, and most obvious, the HSB sample may have yielded an inflated point estimate of the sector effect simply by chance. The confidence intervals for the sector effects do, after all, include annual effects of 0.01 or 0.02 standard deviation per year. Second, the sector effect may really be larger in high school than in elementary school. There is good reason to believe, for example, that Catholic and public elementary schools have more similar curricula than Catholic and public high schools. This could easily make the difference in student achievement smaller.

Third, sector effects may decay over time. Many other academic programs, such as compensatory education, lead to fairly large short-term increases in achievement but to much smaller long-term increases. There is no reason this pattern should not recur for Catholic schools. Suppose, for example, that the effect of a year of Catholic schooling was to raise performance at the end of the year by 0.05 standard deviation, but that if everything was equal the following year the advantage decayed to 0.01 standard deviation. We would then observe a two-year effect of 0.06 standard deviation, just as HSB implies, and a twelve-year effect of 0.16 standard deviation, which is also consistent with HSB. Unfortunately, the HSB study measured achievement at only two points in time, so we cannot compare short-term and long-term effects using the HSB data.

CONCLUSIONS

Four substantive conclusions can be drawn from the first three articles in this issue:

1. Juniors and seniors learn slightly more in Catholic high schools than in public high schools.
2. The magnitude of this advantage is uncertain. The point estimates average 0.03 or 0.04 standard deviation per year in HSB, depending on whether we focus on the typical Catholic-school sophomore or the typical public-school sophomore. But the confidence interval for the population value is very broad (see Table 2) and the effect varies by test.
3. The evidence that Catholic schools are especially helpful for initially disadvantaged students is quite suggestive, but not conclusive.
4. The cumulative effect of twelve years of Catholic schooling is only about three times the apparent effect of the last two years of Catholic high school, either because Catholic elementary schools are less distinctive than Catholic high schools, or because the short-term benefits of Catholic schooling mostly dissipate over the long run.

Two methodological conclusions also seem justified:

1. In comparing different educational practices, we need data on the cumulative effect of many years of exposure to the practice in question. Studies based on one or two years of exposure seldom tell us much. First, they typically yield point estimates of the annual effect with such large sampling errors as to be almost useless. Second, without information on the cumulative impact of a practice over many years, we cannot tell whether short-term benefits persist over time.
2. When a "treatment" lasts only a few years, evaluations must follow up alumni several years after the program is over in order to determine whether the effect persists over time. Conclusions based entirely on short-term effects should never be taken very seriously, since experience has repeatedly shown that long-term effects are far smaller than short-term ones.

REFERENCES

Alexander, K. L. and A. M. Pallas
1983 "Private schools and public policy: New evidence on cognitive achievement in public and private schools." Sociology of Education 56:170–82.
1985 "School sector and cognitive performance." Sociology of Education 58:115–28.

Coleman, J. S., E. Q. Campbell, J. McPartland, A. M. Mood, F. D. Weinfeld, and R. L. York
1966 Equality of Educational Opportunity. Washington, D.C.: U.S. Government Printing Office.

Coleman, J. S., T. Hoffer, and S. Kilgore
1982a "Cognitive outcomes in public and private schools." Sociology of Education 55:65–76.
1982b High School Achievement. New York: Basic.

Hoffer, T., A. M. Greeley, and J. S. Coleman
1985 "Achievement growth in public and Catholic schools." Sociology of Education 58:74–97.

Jencks, C. and M. Brown
1975 "The effects of high schools on their students." Harvard Educational Review 45:273–324.

Rogosa, D.
1980 "Comparing nonparallel regression lines." Psychological Bulletin 88:307–21.

Willms, J. D.
1983 "Do private schools produce higher levels of academic achievement? New evidence for the tuition tax credit debate." Pp. 223–31 in T. James and H.M. Levin (eds.), Public Dollars for Private Schools: The Case of Tuition Tax Credits. Philadelphia: Temple University Press.
1985 "Catholic-school effects on academic achievement: New evidence from the High School and Beyond follow-up study." Sociology of Education 58:98–114.

Volume 58 Number 3 July 1985

SOCIOLOGY OF EDUCATION

A Journal of the American Sociological Association

WILSON
The Impact of School Desegregation Programs on White Public-School Enrollment, 1968–1976

EDER
The Cycle of Popularity: Interpersonal Relations Among Female Adolescents

LEITER AND BROWN
Determinants of Elementary School Grading

BROWN AND SAKS
The Revealed Influence of Class, Race, and Ethnicity on Local Public-School Expenditures

VELEZ
Finishing College: The Effects of College Type

SOCIOLOGY OF EDUCATION (ISSN 0038–0407) is published quarterly in January, April, July and October by the American Sociological Association, 1722 N Street, N.W., Washington, D.C. 20036 and is printed by Boyd Printing Company, Albany, New York. Second class postage paid at Washington, D.C. and additional mailing offices. *POSTMASTER:* Send address changes to *Sociology of Education*, 1722 N Street, N.W., Washington, D.C. 20036.

MANUSCRIPTS and communications for the Editors should be addressed to the Editor, SOCIOLOGY OF EDUCATION, Department of Sociology, University of Notre Dame, Notre Dame, IN 46556.

Concerning advertising, changes of address and subscriptions, address the Executive Office, American Sociological Association, 1722 N Street, N.W., Washington, D.C. 20036. Annual membership dues of the ASA, $40–$125 ($12 of this amount may cover a subscription to *Sociology of Education*); Associate, $40; Student Associate, $25. Subscription rate for members, $12; non-members, $21 U.S., $24 elsewhere; institutions, $28 U.S., $31 elsewhere; single issues, $5. New subscriptions and renewals will be entered on a calendar year basis only. *Changes of Address:* Six weeks advance notice to the Executive Office, and old address as well as new, are necessary for change of subscriber's address. Claims for undelivered copies must be made within the month following the regular month of publication. The publishers will supply missing copies when losses have been sustained in transit and when the reserve stock will permit.

SOCIOLOGY OF EDUCATION

A JOURNAL OF RESEARCH IN SOCIALIZATION AND SOCIAL STRUCTURE

PUBLISHED BY
THE AMERICAN SOCIOLOGICAL ASSOCIATION

JULY 1985 **VOLUME 58, NUMBER 3**

CONTENTS

The Impact of School Desegregation Programs on White Public-School Enrollment, 1968–1976 . . . . *Franklin D. Wilson* 137

The Cycle of Popularity: Interpersonal Relations Among Female Adolescents . . . . *Donna Eder* 154

Determinants of Elementary School Grading . . . . *Jeffrey Leiter and James S. Brown* 166

The Revealed Influence of Class, Race, and Ethnicity on Local Public-School Expenditures . . . . *Byron W. Brown and Daniel H. Saks* 181

Finishing College: The Effects of College Type . . . . *William Velez* 191

EDITORIAL POLICY

This journal exists to provide a forum for studies of the sociology of education and human social development. The aim is to publish research on how social institutions and/or individuals' experience within them impinge upon educational processes and social development. Such research could span various levels of analysis, ranging from the individual to the structure of relations among social and educational institutions. In an increasingly complex society, important educational issues arise throughout the life cycle. The content of this journal is meant to reflect this diversity by presenting a balance of papers which deal with education at the institutional and organizational levels as well as at the individual level, at all stages of schooling and with respect to all types of education. Contributions are invited from persons of any discipline whose objectives are consonant with those of this journal.

Contributors' papers are evaluated, through a peer-review process, entirely in terms of quality. *All* methodologies are welcome. The journal appears quarterly, January, April, July, and October.

A processing fee of $10 is required for each paper submitted; such fees to be waived for student members of ASA. This reflects a policy of the ASA Council and Committee on Publications affecting all ASA journals. It is a reluctant response to the rapidly accelerating costs of manuscript processing. A check or money order, made payable to the American Sociological Association should accompany each submission. The fee must be paid in order to initiate the processing of the manuscript.

SOCIOLOGY OF EDUCATION

CONTRIBUTORS

■ Franklin D. Wilson is professor of sociology and chair of the Department of Afro-American Studies at the University of Wisconsin—Madison. His primary research interests are migration and labor markets.

■ Donna Eder is associate professor of sociology at Indiana University. Her research interests include the sociology of education and social interaction. This article is part of a larger study examining adolescent peer relations and culture.

■ Jeffrey Leiter is associate professor of sociology at North Carolina State University, where he studies organizations, industry, and education. This article reflects his interest in organizational and stratification processes in schools. James S. Brown is assistant professor of social work at North Carolina State University. His research interests include family decision making, sibling coalitions and family power structures, and contextual factors in teaching and learning situations. This article reflects his interest in patterns of interaction between students and teachers and the consequences of these patterns for educational outcomes.

■ Byron Brown is professor of economics at Michigan State University, where he studies microeconomics and the economics of education. Daniel H. Saks is professor of economics and education policy at Vanderbilt University. His research interests include labor economics, microeconomics, and the economics of education. Professors Brown and Saks are currently studying the problem of production of learning in schools and the allocation of teachers' and students' time.

■ William Velez is assistant professor of sociology at the University of Wisconsin—Milwaukee. His research interests include stratification, labor force behavior, and the sociology of education. This article is part of his ongoing research on the college attainment process. He is currently studying the process of transfer from two-year to four-year colleges. He also plans to study access to higher education to determine the relative strengths of the predictors of access for white, black, and Hispanic students.

Notice to Contributors

(Revised September 1981)

STATEMENT OF ASA POLICY ON MULTIPLE SUBMISSION

Submission of manuscripts to a professional journal clearly implies commitment to publish in that journal. The competition for journal space requires a great deal of time and effort on the part of editorial readers whose main compensation for this service is the opportunity to read papers prior to publication and the gratification associated with discharge of professional obligations. For these reasons the ASA regards submission of a manuscript to a professional journal while that paper is under review by another journal as unacceptable.

AUTHOR'S RESPONSIBILITY: *Manuscripts which do not adhere exactly to these suggestions will be immediately returned for revision. Only articles in the form specified below will be sent out for refereeing.*

The 1974 edition of the *Publication Manual* of the American Psychological Association (available from A.P.A., 1200 17th St., N.W., Washington, D.C. 20036) is very helpful in clarifying headings, abbreviations, table preparation and the like.

Since manuscripts are evaluated as anonymous submissions, please keep identifying material out of the manuscript. Attach a cover page giving authorship, institutional affiliation, acknowledgments, and the date the article is submitted. Provide only the title as identification on the manuscript and abstract. Every effort should be made by the author to see that the manuscript itself contains no clues as to the author's identity.

Submission and Preparation of Manuscripts

1. Submit four (4) copies and retain the original for your files. Copies may be Xerox, mimeograph or multilith, but not carbons.
2. Enclose a stamped self-addressed postcard for acknowledgment of manuscript receipt. Since manuscripts will not be returned by reviewers to the editorial office, the editorial office will not return them to authors.
3. All copy must be *typed, doublespaced* (including indented material, footnotes and references) on 8½ by 11 inch white opaque paper. Line must not exceed six (6) inches. Margins must be a minimum of one inch.
4. Include four (4) copies of an abstract of no more than 150 words.
5. Type each table on a separate page. Insert a location note at the appropriate place in the text, e.g., "Table 2 about here." Send copies, retain originals.
6. Figures must be professionally prepared. Send copies, retain originals.
7. Clarify all symbols with notes in the margins of the manuscript. Circle these and all other explanatory notes not intended for printing.
8. Three kinds of footnotes are possible each serving a different purpose:

   a. Content footnotes. Content footnotes are explanations or amplifications of the text. Because they are distracting to readers and *expensive* to include in printed material, an author should include important information in the text and omit irrelevant information. *Content Footnotes Will Not Be Allowed Generally.*

   Rather than footnoting long or complicated material, such as proofs or derivations unnecessary to the text, consider (i) indicating in a *short* footnote that the material is available from the author, (ii) depositing the material in a national retrieval center and including an appropriate footnote, or (iii) adding an appendix. If an appendix is used, the reference in text should read: "(see Appendix A for complete derivation)."

   Text footnotes should be numbered consecutively throughout the article with superscript arabic numerals. If, after a footnote occurs it is later mentioned, use a parenthetical note "(see Footnote 3)," rather than the superscript number.

   b. Reference footnotes. Footnotes are used for reference purposes only to cite material of limited availability. Acceptable reference footnotes include (i) legal citations, which should follow the footnote style of *A Uniform System of Citation* (1967) published by the Harvard Law Review Association, (ii) copyright permission footnotes, (iii) unpublished works; works in progress.

   c. Table footnotes. Table footnotes are appended *only* to a specific table. Footnotes to a table should be *lettered* consecutively *within* each table with superscript lowercase letters.
9. Acknowledgments, credits and grant numbers are placed on the title page with an asterisk.

Reference Format

A. *In the Text:* All source references are to be identified at the appropriate point in the text by the last name of the author, year of publication, and pagination where needed. Identify subsequent citations of the same source in the same way as the first, *not* using "*Ibid.,*" "*op. cit.,*" or "*loc. cit.*" Examples follow:

1. If author's name is in the text, follow it with year in parentheses. [". . . Duncan (1959) . . ."]

2. If author's name is not in the text, insert, in parentheses, the last name and year, separated by a comma [". . . (cf. Gouldner, 1963 . . ."]

3. Pagination (without "p." or "pp.") follows year of publication after a colon. [". . . Kuhn (1970:71)."]
4. Give both last names for dual authors. Give all last names on first citation in text for more than two authors; thereafter use "et al." in the text. When two authors have the same last name, use identifying initials in the text. For institutional authorship, supply minimum identification from the beginning of the complete citation. [". . . U.S. Bureau of the Census, 1963:117) . . ."]
5. Separate a series of references with semicolons and enclose them within a single pair of parentheses. [". . . (Burgess, 1968; Marwell et al., 1971; Cohen, 1962) . . ."]

B. *In the appendix:* List all items alphabetically by author and, within author, by year of publication, in an appendix, titled "REFERENCES". The reference appendix must be complete and include all references in the text. The use of "et al." is not acceptable in the appendix; list the names of all authors. (See A.4. for text format.)

If there is more than one reference to the same author and year, distinguish them by the letters a, b, etc. added to the year. [". . . Levy (1965a:331) . . ."]

Give the publisher's name in as brief a form as is fully intelligible. For example, John A. Wiley and Sons should be "Wiley."

If the cited material is unpublished, use "forthcoming" with name of journal or publisher; otherwise use "unpublished."

Use no underlining or italics.

Examples follow:

1. *Books:*	Jud, G. J., E. W. Mills, Jr. and G. W. Burch.	
	1970	Ex-Pastors. Philadelphia: Pilgrim Press.
	U.S. Bureau of the Census	
	1960	Characteristics of Population, Volume I. Washington, D.C.: U.S. Government Printing Office.
	Bernard, C.	
	[1865] 1957	An Introduction to the Study of Experimental Medicine. Dr. Henry Copley Greene. New York: Dover.
2. *Periodicals:*	Conger, R.	
	Forthcoming	"The effects of positive feedback on direction and amount of verbalization in a social setting." Pacific Sociological Review.
	Kerckhoff, A. C. and R. T. Campbell	
	1977a	"Black-white differences in the educational attainment process." Sociology of Education 50:15–27.
	1977b	"Race and social status differences in the explanation of educational ambition." Social Forces 55:701–14.
3. *Collections:*	Davie, M.	
	1938	"The pattern of urban growth." Pp. 133–61 in G. Murdock (ed.), Studies in the Science of Society. New Haven: Yale University Press.

See recent issues for further examples.

THE IMPACT OF SCHOOL DESEGREGATION PROGRAMS ON WHITE PUBLIC-SCHOOL ENROLLMENT, 1968–1976

FRANKLIN D. WILSON

University of Wisconsin—Madison

Sociology of Education 1985, Vol. 58 (July):137–153

This article examines the findings of a national study of the impact of school desegregation programs on white public-school enrollment trends in school districts grouped according to region, metropolitan status, and source of pressure to desegregate. The analysis is based on a larger and more diverse sample of districts than was used in previous studies. It shows that the increased exposure of white pupils to black pupils (or interracial contact) substantially affects the demography of school systems and leads to reductions in white enrollment. Moreover, the adverse effect of increased interracial contact is not limited to school districts that have implemented desegregation programs, although these districts experience an accelerated rate of white enrollment decline. White enrollment losses appear to be short term, limited primarily to the year a desegregation program is implemented. An important implication of these findings is that white enrollment trends are sensitive not to the programmatic components of desegregation strategies but rather to the amount of change in interracial contact that such strategies bring about.

INTRODUCTION

The primary objective of this study is to determine whether school desegregation leads to a reduction in the representation of whites in public school systems, and particular attention is given to whites' responses over time. In addition, this study assesses the impact of program characteristics and the involvement of particular implementing agents in the desegregation process. An assumption implicit in public-policy discussion of effective desegregation strategies is that a great deal of the enrollment loss associated with the implementation of a desegregation program can be avoided if greater care is taken in selecting the components of the program. The plausibility of this assumption is evaluated empirically in this article.

The reported acceptance of the equality of minorities by whites in various sectors of American society has increased substantially since the early 1960s (see Taylor, Sheatsley, and Greeley, 1978; Pettigrew, 1979, 1980; Taylor, 1979). Not surprisingly, however, while white America generally accepts racial equality as an ideal, considerable resistance has accompanied efforts to translate these ideals into reality. At issue are the methods and timing of integration and whites' perceptions of the effects of integration on their lives (Bobo, 1983).

Whites have generally supported the notion of racial integration in public schools, but they have consistently resisted desegregation induced by external pressure. Some writers (e.g., Coleman, Kelly, and Moore, 1975) maintain that court-ordered, systemwide plans to redistribute pupils are self-defeating, because they undermine the viability of school systems by either causing or accelerating the loss of white students. Their conclusions gave rise to considerable controversy, but the findings of recent studies tend to support them.

In recent years, the controversy surrounding the adverse effects of school desegregation has subsided considerably. Indeed, many of the most frequently cited antagonists in the debate appear to have reached consensus, agreeing that school desegregation leads to substantial white enrollment declines (Farley, Richards,

---

An earlier version of this article was issued as a project report in the series "Studies in Racial Segregation," supported by funds granted under contract HEW-100-76-0196 and by funds granted to the Institute for Research on Poverty, University of Wisconsin—Madison, pursuant to the provisions of the Economic Opportunity Act of 1964. Data acquisition and processing were supported in part by Population Research Center Grant 5P01-HD-0-58776, awarded to the Center for Demography and Ecology of the University of Wisconsin—Madison by the Center for Population Research of the National Institute of Child Health and Human Development. Special thanks are extended to Halliman H. Winsborough, Michael Olneck, and anonymous reviewers, whose comments were very helpful in revising an earlier version of this article. The assistance of Barbara Weston in the preparation of this article is also gratefully acknowledged. Conclusions and interpretations are the sole responsibility of the author. Address all correspondence to the author at the Center for Demography and Ecology, University of Wisconsin, 4412 Social Science Building, 1180 Observatory Drive, Madison, WI 53706.

and Wurdock, 1980; Ravitch, 1978; Rossell, 1978; Armor, 1978; Rossell et al., 1981). This apparent consensus has led some researchers (Rossell, Ravitch, and Armor) to conclude that the basic issue has been settled. However, a review of the most recent studies of the effect of school desegregation on changes in white enrollment indicates that issues related to conceptualization, methodological approach, and geographic context still need to be resolved. For example, although many researchers agree that changes in white enrollment are responsive to the implementation of desegregation programs, they do not agree on the timing nor the magnitude of the response. In addition, virtually all the relevant studies to date have focused on the largest central-city school districts, which have substantial black enrollments. Few researchers have ventured beyond the boundaries of central cities to ascertain whether desegregation in other geographic contexts is accompanied by declines in white enrollment. Although this focus on large central-city districts can be defended on the grounds that these districts enroll the majority of black public-school pupils (approximately 58 percent, based on 1976 estimates by the U.S. Office of Civil Rights [1968–76]), they represent only 8 percent of the 1,748 districts that enroll one hundred or more black students (see Wilson, 1982). It is also worthwhile to note that, proportionately, a greater number of noncentral-city districts have implemented more extensive desegregation programs than central-city districts. Hence, public debate on the efficacy of school desegregation programs would be greatly enhanced by broadening both the investigation of the issues in question and the empirical universe for which the issues are relevant. This article addresses these concerns in the hope that subsequent discussions can proceed from a broader base than that offered by previous studies.

PREVIOUS STUDIES

With the possible exception of studies by Coleman et al. (1975) and Mumford (1973), most of the earlier studies (e.g., Bosco and Robin, 1974; Farley, 1975; Rossell, 1975; Jackson, 1975; Pettigrew and Green, 1976) report that school desegregation has no effect on changes in white enrollment in central-city districts. Since 1976, however, studies reporting no effect during the year of implementation are clearly in the minority. Most researchers agree that desegregation effects are discernible during the year of implementation, and results reported thus far are impressive; but because of problems and omissions that will be discussed below, these studies should not be considered definitive.

The most important issues that surfaced during the earlier discussions of Coleman et al.'s (1975) findings are still central to the debate. For example, among studies that report implementation-year effects, there is considerable variability in the magnitude of the estimated effects. Coleman et al. reported that under certain conditions, desegregation could result in twice the normal loss of white pupils. Armor (1978), on the other hand, estimates that the loss rate during the implementation year is four times higher than the normal rate, and Rossell (1978) found that the loss of white pupils can be as high as 14 percent above the normal rate. Finally, Farley et al. (1980) estimate that desegregation is associated with a 6 percent decline in white enrollment in large central-city districts and a 2 percent decline in smaller districts.

Part of the variability among these estimates of implementation-year effects no doubt reflects differences in analytical approaches. Farley et al. reported that the three analytic models they evaluated yielded three different estimates of desegregation effects. Another part of the variation observed among these studies, however, is probably due to differences in the operationalization of dependent and independent variables. For example, Rossell used percentage of reassigned white pupils as a measure of desegregation impact, and Coleman et al. and Farley et al. used changes in school segregation as their measure. In both instances, whether or not a desegregation program is implemented is confused with the program's effect on reducing racial isolation.

The policy implications of the impact of school desegregation can best be addressed by focusing on the long-term effects rather than on any implementation-year effects that may be compensated for later. Most studies that have analyzed annual enrollment data report little or no long-term effects of school desegregation (Rossell, 1978; Coleman et al., 1975; McConahay and Hawley, 1977; Sly and Pol, 1978; Farley et al., 1980; U.S. Commission on Civil Rights, 1977; Fitzgerald and Morgan, 1977).[1] However, Snyder and Kelly (1977) found significant long-term effects of desegregation programs on white enrollment changes in non-South central-city districts. Armor (1978), in his study of 22 central-city districts, reports that in 15 and 6 of these districts, over 50 and 30 percent, respectively, of the white enrollment losses over periods of at least seven

[1] The U.S. Commission on Civil Rights (1977) has conducted the only study of both central-city and noncentral-city school districts.

years could be directly attributed to school desegregation. In sum, though the balance of the evidence indicates that school desegregation has no long-term effects, this issue should be investigated further using a larger number of districts and a somewhat different analytic approach.

Desegregated school districts vary considerably in the character and extensiveness of their programs and in the source of pressure to desegregate (i.e., federal or state court, federal or state agency, school district; see Wilson [1982]). Yet we know little of how these features of desegregation programs (particularly in combination) affect the retention capacity of a school district. Katzman's (1978) review of a few case studies suggests that the form or instrument of desegregation does not affect the outcome; but Armor's (1978) study suggests that these factors are of fundamental import. Other studies have attempted to identify specific aspects of desegregation plans that may lead to increased white withdrawal. These include white pupil reassignment (Rossell, 1978; Lord, 1975; Pride and Woodward, 1978; Giles, 1977); the phasing in of plans (Rossell, 1978); the focus on elementary schools or high schools (Coleman et al., 1975); the relationship between the percentage of black students and reduction in segregation (Rossell, 1978; Coleman et al., 1975; Giles, Cataldo, and Gatlin, 1975; Giles, 1977); the geographic scope of the plan (Farley et al., 1980; Amor, 1978); and whites' access to surrounding suburban schools with very low minority enrollments (Rossell, 1978; Farley et al., 1980; Coleman et al., 1975; Armor, 1978).[2]

CURRENT INVESTIGATION

The previous section has pointed out some of the major conceptual and methodological problems associated with other investigations. This study addresses several of the unresolved issues in a much broader analytic and geographic context than has previously been possible. It focuses on four interrelated sets of issues. First, it examines whether school desegregation leads to a reduction in the representation of whites in public school systems, giving particular attention to whites' response over time. Second, it examines whether the alleged adverse effects of school desegregation programs are due to the involvement of particular implementing agencies—i.e., the courts, the Department of Health and Human Services (DHHS, formerly HEW), and school districts. Court-directed school desegregation programs involving busing have been repeatedly identified as the major cause of white enrollment declines. Surprisingly, there have been no studies to determine, in a comparative context, whether the implementing agent or the character of the desegregation program affects outcomes. An analysis of this issue is important, since it will allow us to determine whether agent, program characteristics, or other concerns are more important in shaping responses to desegregation.

A related issue to be explored below is whether white enrollment changes are responsive to both the implementation of a desegregation program—i.e., the event—and the magnitude of change in interracial contact that occurs as a result of the implementation. Most previous analyses have focused on the effects of the magnitude of change in interracial contact, measured by a segregation index. But the actual implementation of a desegregation program may have a significant effect on white enrollment, even when there is little change in interracial contact (see Taeuber et al., 1981).

Desegregation programs potentially limit

---

[2] Virtually all the studies have used an index of metropolitan school segregation to estimate the responsiveness of whites to central-city/suburban differentials in school segregation when districts serving the former are desegregated. It is often argued that whites will withdraw to suburban districts if central-city districts are desegregated and if suburban districts have low concentrations of minority students. A negative coefficient for the effect of metropolitan school segregation on white enrollment change indicates the sensitivity of whites to between-district variation in school segregation: the higher the level of between-district segregation, the greater the withdrawal of whites to suburban districts with low concentrations of minority students. Researchers have not been sensitive to two issues associated with the use of this index and the interpretation of its effect on white enrollment change. First, the selection of the sample of metropolitan school districts included in the Office of Civil Rights (OCR) survey is a possible source of bias in the estimated effects of the index, the extent of which is not known at this time (see discussion of the sample below). Only in 1974 and 1976 is it possible to derive reasonable estimates of the number of suburban districts and their respective student populations. Second, the use of an index of metropolitan school segregation involves the interpretation of the effect of the index on white enrollment change in districts serving central cities. A statistically significant negative coefficient for the effect of metropolitan school segregation on white enrollment change implies that implementation of a desegregation program has long-term effects, since whites who relocate to suburban areas are not likely to return, and subsequent enrollment increases will probably not be sufficient to compensate for this loss. Although this is the most appropriate interpretation of the effect of metropolitan desegregation on white enrollment change, it is not the interpretation emphasized in the literature.

parents' selection of the school environments they feel are best for their children. The considerable resistance and controversy that accompany court-mandated programs, for example, may in part reflect parents' concerns about the loss of autonomy in the school-selection process (see Bobo, 1983). Hence, the uncertainty that some parents feel may cause them to withdraw their children from an affected school system even if the initial amount of change in interracial contact mandated by the program is small.

Finally, the assessment of desegregation effects is incorporated into a more general analytical model, in which it is possible to determine whether whites' response to changes in interracial contact caused by a desegregation action is a magnification of their expected response to changes due to the general process of residential selection and differentiation. Previous studies clearly indicate that the residential decisions of whites are affected by the racial composition of residential areas and the institutional structures serving these areas (Molotch, 1972; Wegmann, 1975; Orfield, 1978; Katzman, 1978; Farley, Bianchi, and Colasanto, 1979; Wilson, 1979; Bradbury, Downs, and Small, 1982; Downs, 1981). Wilson (1979) found that in 43 of 63 central-city school districts, the increased presence of blacks of elementary-school age in residential areas led to increased utilization of private (and parochial) schools and out-migration among whites, even after controlling for the general ecological characteristics of school-attendance zones. These results (as well as those from other studies) indicate that substantial numbers of whites will seek to avoid attending schools with blacks regardless of the form or instrument of interracial contact. Within this context, then, it is appropriate to determine whether the total number of whites who withdraw from public schools reflects the *amount of change* in interracial contact mandated by a desegregation action, an acceleration of the *rate* at which whites withdraw their children from public schools under the general process of residential selection, or both. Findings indicate that the magnitude of change in white enrollment is a function of the extent of change in interracial contact regardless of whether the latter is due to a desegregation program or to residential selection and differentiation.

Data Sources

Data for the analyses reported below were obtained from a variety of sources, including the Office of Civil Rights' annual school surveys, the U.S. Commission on Civil Rights' survey of school superintendents, and a DHHS-funded study of school desegregation activities. Specific features of each of these data sets will be discussed as they are incorporated into particular analyses.

Since 1968, the Office of Civil Rights (OCR) of the U.S. Department of Health and Human Services (DHHS) has produced annually (except 1975) a data file containing school enrollment figures by race for a sample of the nation's school districts (U.S. Office of Civil Rights, 1968–76). This investigation of enrollment trends begins with the statistical manipulation of these data. The extent of coverage of the nation's school districts varies substantially in the annual school files released by OCR. In 1968, 1970, and 1972, the fall survey covered approximately 8,000 school systems enrolling approximately 92 percent of all public-school students and 98 percent of minority public-school students. The 1969, 1971, and 1973 surveys covered smaller samples of school districts selected from the previous year's larger samples. The selection of districts in the odd-numbered years reflected OCR's interest in compliance activity in districts with high concentrations of minority students. The 1974 and 1976 surveys covered approximately 3,000 districts, but the districts were chosen to permit statistical estimation of enrollment trends in all school districts. (Unfortunately, no survey was conducted in 1975.)

The districts included in the analyses presented below are a subset of those surveyed by OCR. The selection of districts for analysis reflected two major considerations. First, the analysis of enrollment trends requires construction of a longitudinal profile of a district's enrollment level and racial composition. Second, it was considered appropriate to focus only on those districts containing sufficient numbers of blacks to make the analysis of changing enrollment levels meaningful. Hence, the analyses include only those school districts that were surveyed in every year, that had at least two schools, and that met the following enrollment criteria: (a) less than 1,000 students and average annual black enrollment between 10 and 90 percent; (b) 1,000 to 3,499 students and average annual black enrollment between 5 and 95 percent; and (c) 3,500 or more students and average annual black enrollment between 3 and 97 percent.

In addition to the annual enrollment data, this study also utilizes limited information on the implementation of school desegregation programs by individual school districts. This information was obtained from two national surveys—one sponsored by the office of the Assistant Secretary for Planning and Evaluation of DHHS and conducted by the Rand Corporation (Cox, 1979) and one sponsored by the

Table 1. Percentage of Public School Districts Included in the Analysis, by Geographic Area and Source of Pressure to Desegregate, 1968–1976

Desegregation Status and Source of Pressure to Desegregate	South: Central Cities ($N=103$)	South: Suburbs ($N=165$)	South: Nonmetropolitan ($N=831$)	Non-South: Central Cities ($N=96$)	Non-South: Suburbs/ Nonmetropolitan ($N=78$)
Desegregated					
State agency or school district	8.74	18.18	12.39	39.58	33.33
Federal or state court	68.93	27.27	24.91	17.71	6.41
DHHS	7.77	13.94	11.55	1.04	2.56
Unknown[a]	2.91	21.82	34.66	0.00	6.41
Total	88.35	81.21	83.51	58.33	48.71
Not desegregated	11.65	18.79	16.49	41.67	51.29
Total	100	100	100	100	100

NOTE: See text for description of data sources.

[a] Districts included in this category experienced at least a twenty-point decline in school segregation during one year between 1968 and 1976.

U.S. Commission on Civil Rights (1977). In both surveys, districts were asked to provide information on school desegregation programs they implemented during the 1960s and 1970s. The DHHS-sponsored survey is the primary source of information on the characteristics of desegregation programs implemented by school districts; it covered a large number of districts and the information is more recent and more extensive.

It is impossible to judge the overall quality of the data gathered from these surveys. One indicator of possible bias is the disagreement between the surveys, in approximately 15 percent of the cases, over the year of desegregation or the agent involved. These discrepancies were resolved by relying on the OCR data and on information provided by other analyses. Of somewhat greater concern is that a substantial number of districts refused to provide relevant information to the DHHS-funded study. Where possible, information from the U.S. Commission on Civil Rights was used. Unfortunately, there still remained a considerable number of desegregated districts for which no specific program information was available. This deficiency will seriously compromise efforts to distinguish between effects due to the implementation of a desegregation program and those due to the impact of that program on reducing racial isolation.

RESULTS

Summary Statistics

Previous discussions of desegregation impact have focused almost exclusively on central-city school districts and have given little attention to the effects of implementing agents and program characteristics in different contexts. The districts included in this study represent a variety of geographic areas. Table 1 provides a percentage breakdown of these districts by desegregation status and source of pressure to desegregate. Most of the districts included in the sample had implemented some type of desegregation program by 1976, although the percentages vary substantially by region. The four principal implementing agents were involved in each geographic area; but state agencies and school districts were the major initiators in the non-South, and federal and state courts were the major initiators in the South.

The classification of districts presented in Table 1 provides the principal analytic context for this study. As the table indicates, quite a few of the desegregated districts did not provide information on source of pressure to desegregate. These districts are classified as desegregated because each experienced at least a twenty-point decline (on a scale of 0 to 100)[3] in school segregation in a single year between 1968 and 1976.

---

[3] The index of dissimilarity is used to measure school segregation (see Taeuber and Taeuber, 1965; Taeuber and Wilson, 1981). It is defined as follows:

$$D = \left[\frac{\sum_{i=1}^{n} T_i |P_i - P|}{2TP(1-P)} \right] \times 100,$$

where D is the index of dissimilarity; T_i and T are the numbers of pupils in a school and district, respectively; P_i and P are the proportions of blacks in a school and school district, respectively; and the summation is over schools. The value of the index will be zero if the difference between each P_i and P is zero, and it will attain its maximum value in uniracial schools.

The exposure index was first suggested by Cole-

Table 2 provides summary information on levels of school segregation, interracial contact, and white public-school enrollment by geographic area and source of pressure to desegregate. Between 1968 and 1976 the level of segregation of black and white pupils declined, and the percentage of black pupils in the school of the average white child (exposure of whites to blacks, or interracial contact) increased substantially (see footnote 3). Although the average school district in each geographic area experienced declines in school segregation,the implementation of a desegregation program was probably the most important factor in reducing the extent of racial isolation among black and white pupils in 1968. Not surprisingly, reductions in racial isolation were greater in the South and in school districts subject to court pressure to desegregate.

Results presented elsewhere (Wilson, 1982) provide some insight into the results reported here. First, courts have been most active and more effective in districts with higher levels of school segregation and high concentrations of black students. Except in the South, DHHS's efforts to reduce segregation levels have been only slightly more successful than the efforts of state agencies and school districts. The kinds of districts different desegregation agents have targeted for program implementation also vary by size and geographic location. For example, desegregation programs are more likely to be initiated outside the South in small to moderate-size districts with low concentrations of minorities, where the amount of effort necessary to achieve racial balance in schools is minimal.

While southern school districts experienced greater reductions in racial isolation, non-South school districts experienced greater declines in white enrollment levels. Declining birth rates and net out-migration from the North and East probably contributed significantly to these regional differences; even non-South school districts that did not implement desegregation programs between 1968 and 1976 experienced significant declines in white enrollment (see Taeuber and Wilson, 1978; Long, 1981; Long and Frey, 1982). White enrollment declines were greater in school districts subject to court pressure to desegregate, except in suburban school districts located in the South.

A Model of Net Change in Public-School Enrollment

The remainder of this article examines whether school desegregation activities contributed to the white enrollment declines evident in Table 2. The point of departure for manipulating white enrollment trends is a matrix of dimension n by k. The rows of this matrix are school districts ($i = 1, \ldots, n$), the columns are time periods ($j = 1, \ldots, k$), and the cells are white enrollment figures for the ith district and the jth time period. (Since OCR did not survey districts in 1975, enrollment figures for this year were obtained by interpolation from the 1974 and 1976 data.) Virtually all studies of white enrollment changes, using different statistical models, have manipulated some combination of the information contained within this matrix. The current investigation uses a lagged endogenous variable regression model to estimate the impact of desegregation programs on white enrollment. This specification avoids some of the statistical problems associated with the use of difference scores or percentage-change measures as dependent variables (see Heise, 1970; Kessler and Greenberg, 1981). The log of the initial value of the dependent variable is included in the equation, so the partial-regression coefficients can be interpreted in percentage-change terms—namely, annual percentage increase or decrease in white enrollment associated with a unit change in the independent variables. In addition, the use of the log transformation minimizes the effects of outliers and reduces the extent of heteroscedasticity in the error term. The estimation equation is of the following form:

$$\log(WHITE_T) = \beta_0 + \beta_1 \log(WHITE_{T-1}) + \beta_2 BLACK_{T-1} + \beta_3 \Delta EWM_{T-1,\,T} + \beta_4 BLK{<}35\% + \beta_5 \%BLK * \Delta EWM + \beta_6 PRE\text{-}BEFORE + \beta_7 BEFORE + \beta_8 DURING + \beta_9 AFTER$$

man et al. (1975) as a useful measure of interracial contact in public schools. It is an unstandardized version of their "S" index (see also Zoloth, 1976; Taeuber and Wilson, 1981) and is defined as follows:

$$EWM = \left[\frac{\sum_{i=1}^{n} W_i \left(\frac{B_i}{T_i} \right)}{\sum_{i=1}^{n} W_i} \right] \times 100,$$

where B_i and W_i are the numbers of black and white students in the school, and T_i is the total number of students ($T_i = B_i + W_i$). EWM varies from zero to Q, where Q is the percentage of the total district enrollment that is black ($B_i/T_i \times 100$). The value of Q is the upper limit of EWM, because the percentage of blacks in the school of the average white pupil is determined by the relative number of blacks in the school system.

Table 2. Summary Statistics on Racial Isolation and White Public-School Enrollment Levels, by Geographic Area and Source of Pressure to Desegregate, 1968–1976

Source of Pressure to Desegregate, by Geographic Area	Average School Segregation[a]		Average Exposure of Whites to Blacks[a]		Average White Enrollment	
	1968	Percent Change 1968–76	1968	Percent Change 1968–76	1968	Percent Change 1968–76
South central cities	77.83	−37.05	8.09	19.52	28,640	−20.45
State agency or school district	68.46	−34.91	6.64	17.80	32,212	−18.34
Federal or state court	83.19	−43.72	9.65	23.17	17,654	−20.14
DHHS	65.96	−22.91	7.51	9.42	32,494	−18.58
Unknown	77.24	−45.13	11.18	23.75	10,277	−8.00
Not desegregated	61.13	−6.59	15.15	4.90	17,770	−28.27
Non-South central cities	61.44	−14.66	13.06	8.01	39,888	−29.22
State agency or school district	56.60	−14.12	13.00	6.77	24,338	−26.93
Federal or state court	64.58	−31.11	11.29	15.80	69,014	−35.11
DHHS	63.46	−4.22	18.84	11.74	28,645	−40.33
Unknown	—	—	—	—	—	—
Not desegregated	64.65	−8.43	13.72	5.80	42,562	−28.62
South suburbs	57.70	−32.39	12.08	11.40	8,982	20.65
State agency or school district	43.65	−21.01	13.99	11.31	5,880	23.76
Federal or state court	76.00	−39.83	5.71	14.85	15,375	17.84
DHHS	68.59	−39.33	9.03	13.32	8,878	16.74
Unknown	64.37	−49.70	15.69	17.50	3,992	17.80
Not desegregated	28.91	−7.36	17.53	−2.03	8,574	27.91
Non-South suburbs and nonmetropolitan areas	47.96	−15.21	17.14	11.83	8,059	−27.70
State agency or school district	39.57	−15.26	20.52	10.73	7,576	−34.45
Federal or state court	58.82	−39.44	14.89	33.91	10,992	−50.67
DHHS	51.81	−42.00	9.32	15.09	6,861	−22.93
Unknown	48.29	−19.35	13.27	10.44	10,399	−14.52
Not desegregated	51.82	−10.29	16.09	9.79	7,782	−22.32
South nonmetropolitan areas	67.54	−49.36	12.13	24.56	2,871	19.64
State agency or school district	63.71	−46.57	12.12	19.98	3,533	3.29
Federal or state court	85.57	−62.52	7.60	36.19	3,982	−13.39
DHHS	63.89	−46.68	11.79	18.51	3,655	2.83
Unknown	77.87	−62.96	11.38	31.29	1,796	52.21
Not desegregated	23.99	−4.84	20.83	0.53	2,410	25.16

[a] See footnote 3 for a description of these measures.

$$+ \beta_{10} YEAR + \beta_{11} COUNTY + \sum_{i=12}^{23} \beta_i AREA*AGENT + \sum_{j=24}^{27} \beta_j STATUS*\Delta EWM + e, \quad (1)$$

where log($WHITE_T$) and log ($WHITE_{T\text{-}1}$) are the natural logs of white enrollment for the current year (T) and previous year (T-1); $\Delta EWM_{T\text{-}1,T}$ is the change in the proportion of black children in the school of the average white child (exposure of white pupils to black pupils, or interracial contact; see footnote 3 for definition of this measure); $\%BLACK_{T\text{-}1}$ is the percentage of enrollment that was black in the previous year; $BLK < 35\% = 1$ for annual observations in which black enrollment is less than 35 percent; $\%BLK*\Delta EWM$ is the product of percentage black and change in exposure if the former is greater than 34 percent; $PRE\text{-}BEFORE = 1$ for all annual observations of desegregated districts up to four years prior to the implementation of a desegregation program (T-n to T-4); $BEFORE = 1$ for all annual observations of desegregated districts up to and including one year prior to implementation (T-n to T-1); $DURING = 1$ for all annual observations of desegregated districts up to and including the year of implementation (T-n to T); $AFTER = 1$ for all annual observations of desegregated districts up to and including the years after implementation (T-n to T+n); $YEAR$ is calendar year rescaled (e.g., 1968 = 0 and 1976=8);

COUNTY = 1 if a district is countywide and serves a central city; *AREA*AGENT* = 1 for annual observations of desegregated districts stratified by source of pressure to desegregate (i.e., courts, DHHS, district, or state agency) and geographic location (i.e., region/metropolitan status/central-city status); and the *STATUS**ΔEWM terms are cross-products formed by multiplying each of the desegregation-status variables (i.e., *PRE-BEFORE, BEFORE, DURING,* and *AFTER*) by a change-in-exposure index (i.e., ΔEWM) that corresponds to the time period referenced by the former variables.

Some of the terms included in equation (1) require further explanation. The desegregation-status variables—*PRE-BEFORE, BEFORE, DURING, AND AFTER*—are included to determine whether white enrollment trends exhibit a particular pattern before, during, and after the implementation of a major desegregation program. Districts that did not desegregate are coded zero on all these variables. Previous research indicates that enrollment declines first appear during the years prior to implementation, reach a peak during the year of implementation, and return to predesegregation levels during the years $T+n$.

Also at issue is whether the enrollment patterns of desegregated districts differ from the patterns of districts that did not desegregate. Most previous studies assume that enrollment changes in desegregated districts up to T-3 to T-2 years prior to the implementation year are similar to changes that occurred in districts that did not desegregate. Thus, enrollment changes in desegregated districts reflected in the variable *PRE-BEFORE* should be similar to changes in districts that did not desegregate, since one can assume that enrollment changes occurring up to year T-4 would not have been affected by the implementation of a desegregation program. This assumption is tested empirically in this study.

The coefficients for the desegregation-status variables are the net differences in intercepts between observations of desegregated and nondesegregated districts and between observations of desegregated districts before, during, and after implementation of a desegregation program. For example, the coefficient for *PRE-BEFORE* is the net difference in intercept between the observations of desegregated and nondesegregated districts prior to implementation (T-n to T-4); and the coefficient for *AFTER* is the net difference in intercept between annual observations of desegregated districts after implementation ($T+1$ to $T+n$) and observations representing the year of implementation (T).

Finally, the desegregation-status variables allow us to distinguish between effects associated with the implementation event and those associated with the magnitude of change in interracial contact that occurs as a result of the implementation of a major desegregation program. Desegregated districts included in the "Unknown" category in Tables 1 and 2 are excluded from this and subsequent analyses because of the ambiguous way in which the desegregation status for these districts was determined. In these districts it is not possible to distinguish between event effects and effects attributed to the magnitude of change in interracial contact, since the latter are used to define the former.

It is appropriate at this point to ascertain (1) whether the effect of changes in interracial contact on white enrollment trends is a function of whether or not such change is deliberate and (2) whether the effect varies according to the timing of the change. An important assumption implicit in previous research is that declines in white enrollment occur primarily when a district deliberately alters the racial composition of its schools. That is, white avoidance response to desegregation is assumed to be more a symbol of defiance than a manifestation of concerns about lowered educational standards, the breakdown of discipline, physical and verbal abuse, and racially prejudiced attitudes. But whites' avoidance of residential areas with high concentrations of blacks or in racial transition indicates that the implementation of a desegregation program is not the only condition under which whites withdraw their children from public school systems.

Table 3 indicates that increased interracial contact is not limited to any particular desegregation interval. In desegregated districts ("Pre-before" to "After" subgroups), the amount of annual change in interracial contact is due not only to desegregation programs, which deliberately alter the racial composition of schools, but also to changes in population composition. Four of the five subgroups of districts that did not desegregate also experienced average annual increases in interracial contact. We can assume that most of this change reflects changes in the racial composition of school-attendance zones.

The amount of change in interracial contact in desegregated districts is generally greater than that experienced in districts that did not desegregate, but there is substantial variation between the subgroups of desegregated districts. Declines in the level of school segregation may not occur all in one year, because a district may implement several desegregation plans or phase in a single plan over several

Table 3. Average Annual Change in the Indices of Exposure of White Pupils to Black Pupils (Interracial Contact) by Desegregation Status, Source of Pressure to Desegregate, Metropolitan Status, and Region, 1968–1976

Source of Pressure to Desegregate and Desegregation Status	South: Central Cities	South: Suburbs	South: Nonmetropolitan	Non-South: Central Cities	Non-South: Suburbs/ Nonmetropolitan
Pressure from courts					
Not desegregated	.6529	−.2252	.0594	.6967	1.0880
Pre-before	.6047	.2605	8.8271	.6800	.6754
Before	1.5001	1.6957	2.7659	2.2463	1.2216
During	11.2959	11.0057	30.0733	6.0863	11.2842
After	1.6790	.2830	3.4272	1.3131	3.4272
Pressure from district, state, and DHHS					
Not desegregated	.6529	−.2252	.0594	.6967	1.0880
Pre-before	.3466	.8215	.5500	.3614	.2095
Before	.6319	.9632	1.4769	.5330	1.5671
During	5.2429	12.7206	16.8696	1.9383	2.6366
After	.9100	.2132	.4821	.7869	1.0938

NOTE: See footnote 3 for definition of change in exposure.

years. The response of parents in these instances may vary depending on the amount of change that occurs, the degree of controversy surrounding the plan, and whether or not their children are directly affected by the plan. In previous studies, the effect of a desegregation program on white enrollment during the implementation year is confused with changes that occur in previous or subsequent years. As is evident in Table 3, the largest amount of change in interracial contact occurs during the implementation year, but changes also occur in the years immediately before and after this year. At issue, then, is whether white enrollment changes are more responsive to changes in interracial contact at particular stages of the desegregation process.

To determine whether white enrollment is more responsive to administratively induced change in interracial contact and whether it is responsive to the timing of such change, a test for subgroup differences in the effects of changes in interracial contact is used. The cross-product terms, $STATUS^{*}\Delta EWM$, are included in equation (1) for this purpose. The coefficients for the cross-product terms are the net differences in slopes between the effects of change in exposure on white enrollment change at different intervals. For example, the partial-regression coefficient for $PRE\text{-}BEFORE^{*}\Delta EWM$ represents the difference between the effect of change in exposure in desegregated districts during the years $T\text{-}n$ to $T\text{-}4$ and the effect in districts that did not desegregate (where the latter is the omitted category). Similarly, the coefficient for $AFTER^{*}\Delta EWM$ is the net difference in slope between the effect of change in exposure on white enrollment change in desegregated districts during the years $T+1$ to $T+n$ and the effect in the year of implementation (T).

The coefficient for $PRE\text{-}BEFORE^{*}\Delta EWM$ indicates whether the effect of change in exposure on white enrollment change in desegregated districts is similar to the effect in districts that did not desegregate, when it can be assumed that the effects of a desegregation controversy would not have been present. This approach is more reasonable than assuming that the experience of districts that did not desegregate is the same as the experience of desegregated districts when they were not affected by the controversy.

The decision to use change in the exposure of white pupils to black pupils as a measure of the impact of a desegregation action is based on the assumption that it is changes in the actual racial mix of schools that white parents use as a basis for deciding whether to withdraw their children from a school system. The index of dissimilarity, Coleman's "S" index, and Rossell's index of pupils reassigned under desegregation ignore the influence of population composition and hence do not take into account the actual amount of change in interracial contact resulting from a particular desegregation action (see Coleman et al., 1975; Clotfelter, 1978; Lieberson, 1981; Lieberson and Carter, 1982). Several authors have proposed adjusting the exposure indices to remove the influence of changes in the numbers of black and white pupils presently in the system and to minimize simultaneity bias (see Coleman et al., 1975:95–96; and Clotfelter, 1978).[4]

---

[4] The use of the unadjusted exposure index results in simultaneity bias, because school racial composition is affected by changes in the number of whites in

In the analysis presented below, the unadjusted indices are used, since all the proposed adjustment procedures require making strong assumptions about what the racial composition of individual schools would have been if this factor were affected only by the implementation of a desegregation program. Actually, changes in population composition, which affect the racial composition of school-attendance zones, can, like the implementation of a desegregation program, affect the value of an exposure index. Thus, its influence should not be eliminated, particularly if one wishes, as in this analysis, to assess whether whites respond to changes in the racial mix of schools even in the absence of desegregation.

The student population used to compute percentage black and measures of interracial contact consists only of white and black pupils. Estimates of the Hispanic and the Native and Asian American student populations are not included in the data file used in this analysis. This is unfortunate, because the presence of members of these groups in significant numbers could affect whites' responses to the increased presence of blacks in their schools.[5]

Finally, because of declines in the birth rate since 1969, fewer children have been entering elementary schools. Although declines have not been uniformly felt by all districts because of interdistrict net migration trends, it is important to control for this source of enrollment change. The variable *YEAR* is included in equation (1) for this purpose.

Our expectations about the effect of each of the independent variables on white enrollment are based on previous research findings (see Rossell et al., 1981). Accordingly, we expect that percentage black, calendar year of observation, changes in exposure of whites to blacks, and the interaction of percentage black with changes in exposure will each have negative effects on white enrollment; whereas previous white enrollment and county district will have positive effects.

Table 4 reports results of the analysis to determine annual white enrollment level based on the estimation of equation (1). Each district included in the analysis is represented by nine annual observations between 1968 and 1976. The desegregated districts included in the "Unknown" category in Tables 1 and 2 are excluded. In Table 4, districts that desegregated on their own initiative or because of pressure from DHHS or a state administrative agency are grouped into the category labeled

Table 4. Determinants of Annual White Public-School Enrollment Levels, 1968–1976

Variable	Partial Coefficient	
Desegregation impact[a]		
Desegregation status		
Pre-before (T-n to T-4)	.0252	(.0252)[b]
Before (T-3 to T-1)	.0444*	(.0696)
During (T)	−.0369*	(.0328)
After (T+1 to T+n)	−.0025	(.0303)
Change in exposure, T-1 to T		
Not desegregated	−.0053*	
Pre-before	.0014	(−.0040)
Before	.0031*	(−.0009)
During	−.0127*	(−.0135)
After	.0246*	(.0111)
Change in exposure × percent black	−.0002*	
Black enrollment < 35 percent	−.0272*	
Location and agent		
South		
Metropolitan		
Central cities		
Court	.0277	
Agency	.0141	
Suburbs		
Court	.0209	
Agency	.0161	
Non-South		
Central cities		
Court	.0234	
Agency	.0343	
Suburbs/nonmetropolitan		
Court	−.0827*	
Agency	−.0155	
Other variables		
White enrollment, T-1 (log)	.9561*	
Percent black	−.0021*	
Calendar year	−.0003	
County	.0702*	
Intercept	.4177	
Mean white enrollment (log)	8.2383	
R^2 (corrected)	.9683	
Number of observations	8,469	
Number of districts	941	

[a] Districts that did not desegregate between 1968 and 1976 are the omitted category. Districts included in the "Unknown" category in Tables 1 and 2 are excluded from this analysis.

[b] These coefficients represent the net difference in enrollment change between districts that did not desegregate and districts that did desegregate. They were obtained by adding the coefficient for a particular category to the sum of the values for all preceding categories.

* The regression coefficient is twice the size of its standard error.

the system. However, this source of bias does not pose a serious problem here because of the use of a semilog lagged regression model.

[5] It is important to note here that reduction in the level of school segregation of blacks and whites has been the principal goal of most desegregation programs. Between 1968 and 1976, little change occurred in the extent of school segregation of whites and the other minority groups (see Wilson, 1982).

"Agency" because of the small number of districts in each of these categories.

The explanatory power of the analytical model under review is very high, due principally to the inclusion of previous-year enrollment as an independent variable.[6] Other versions of this model were estimated, but none exceeded the current model in explanatory power.[7] The independent variables related to annual white enrollment are grouped into three categories in Table 4 to facilitate discussion of their effects. Primary attention is given to the effects of those variables that measure the impact of a desegregation action—namely, the desegregation-status variables, change in exposure, and the interaction of percent black and change in exposure.

The desegregation-status variables are included in the model to determine whether white enrollment responds to the desegregation controversy independently of changes in interracial contact. The distinction, although somewhat arbitrary, is necessary, because the intent is to isolate the influence of factors during a particular interval. The partial coefficient for *PRE-BEFORE* captures the net difference in enrollment trend between districts that did not desegregate and districts that eventually did desegregate, when it can be assumed that the effects of a desegregation action would not have been present. This coefficient is not statistically significant, which indicates that prior to the introduction of the desegregation controversy, white enrollment trends in districts that eventually desegregated were similar to those prevailing in districts that did not desegregate. This is an important finding, since it indicates that no selectivity was involved in the targeting of districts for the implementation of a desegregation program. More importantly, the absence of significant differences provides a reference point from which to evaluate subsequent enrollment trends.

The relative sizes and statistical significance of the coefficients for *BEFORE* and *DURING* indicate substantial net changes in the white enrollment patterns of desegregated districts immediately prior to and during the implementation year. The values in parentheses indicate, however, that these changes represent net enrollment gains above those experienced by districts that did not desegregate. These results do not support the earlier-stated expectation that some of the enrollment declines other researchers have associated with changes in interracial contact might be due to other factors.

Virtually all previous investigations have used an index of change in the racial distribution of pupils in schools as a measure of the impact of desegregation on white public-school enrollment. The amount of decline in white enrollment is believed to be highly responsive to per-unit increases in interracial contact brought on by a desegregation action. That convention is followed here as well, except that an effort is made to determine whether the *rate* of change in white enrollment to increased interracial contact changes during particular stages of the desegregation process. It was suggested earlier that assessment of the impact of a desegregation action should be incorporated into a more general analytical model, in which it is possible to determine whether whites' response to changes in interracial contact due to a desegregation action is a magnification of their expected response to changes due to the general process of residential selectivity and differentiation. Findings reported in the literature of urban ecology indicate that whites tend to withdraw from residential areas, or institutional structures serving these areas, when the representation of blacks increases. Thus, it is important to ascertain the *rate of decline* in white enrollment that is associated with increased interracial contact in districts that have not desegregated and to compare this rate with that observed in desegregated districts during particular stages of the desegregation process.

To address the above issues, partial coefficients for each of the desegregation-status variables were estimated. These coefficients are reported in Table 4. In districts that did not desegregate, increased interracial contact led to statistically significant declines in white enrollment. For every 1 percent increase in interracial contact, white enrollment declined by approximately 0.5 percent. This finding lends

[6] An alternative way to define the dependent variable is to take the difference between the log of enrollment in year T and the log of enrollment in year T-1. In this case, the multiple R^2 values would be less, but the regression coefficient for each independent variable, except white enrollment at time T-1, would be identical.

[7] In one version, the addition of the *STATUS*ΔEWM* terms resulted in a statistically significant increase in explained variance over a model in which the effect of change in exposure on annual white enrollment is assumed to be constant across all years. In another version, the estimation of separate equations for each of the *AREA*AGENT* subgroups did not result in a statistically significant increase in explained variance over that obtained from estimating a single equation. In other words, the effects of variables such as change in exposure and percentage black did not vary across central cities, suburbs, and nonmetropolitan areas, whether desegregated by the courts, DHHS, a state agency, or under the district's own initiative.

support to the argument that it is not the form or medium through which interracial contact changes that leads to declines in white enrollment but rather the fact of change itself that is important. It is entirely possible, however, that enrollment changes even in the nondesegregated districts bear the imprint of the desegregation controversy, given the attention it has received in the media and the likelihood that many of these districts, because they are highly segregated, are candidates for some form of action.

The above findings indicate that white enrollment decreases when the potential for interracial contact increases. An additional issue that these findings can help resolve is whether the rate of change in white enrollment to increased interracial contact changes under desegregation. In other words, does the *rate of decline* in white enrollment accelerate, remain constant, or decline under desegregation? An answer to this question can be obtained by comparing the partial coefficients for districts that did and did not desegregate and by comparing the coefficients for the subgroups of desegregated districts ("Pre-before" to "After" groups).

The partial coefficient for the "Pre-before" subgroup is the net difference in the rate of response of white enrollment to changes in interracial contact between districts that desegregated and districts that did not desegregate, measured at least four years prior to the implementation of a desegregation program. This coefficient is not statistically significant, which indicates that the response of whites to increased interracial contact at least four years prior to implementation was the same in districts that did and did not desegregate. Apparently, the process of racial selection leading to declining white enrollment in desegregated districts prior to the introduction of the desegregation controversy was similar to that which occurred in districts that did not desegregate. Moreover, if we extend the comparison to include periods reflecting the desegregation interval (e.g., "Before" to "After" subgroups), we see that the implementation of a desegregation program did change the *rate of response* of white enrollment to increased interracial contact. This is indicated by the coefficients in parentheses; the original net-difference coefficients have been transformed to reflect the actual rate of change in white enrollment associated with unit increases in interracial contact. The rate of change in white enrollment associated with a 1 percent change in interracial contact declines between the intervals T-n to T-4 and T-3 to T-1, accelerates substantially during the year of implementation, and completely reverses its direction in the postdesegregation period. The positive coefficient for the postdesegregation period is an artifact of the coalescence of two unrelated events. This association is consistent with the existence of a short-term response to the implementation of a program, in which districts recover some of their enrollment losses in the postdesegregation years, even though during these years they may continue to experience increases in interracial contact. Hence, the increase in enrollment is not a response to increased interracial contact. Districts that phase in their desegregation programs are likely to experience this pattern.

The partial-regression coefficient for the product of previous-year (T-1) percentage black and change in interracial contact between T-1 and T is another indicator of the effect of demographic desegregation on white public-school enrollment. The value for this variable indicates that white enrollment declines accelerate if percentage black exceeds one third of total enrollment. This result is consistent with previous research, and it is expected, because the absolute number of blacks that a white pupil encounters in his/her school environment is greater in a district with large black enrollments, even if the amount of change in interracial contact is identical to that occurring in a district with small black enrollments.

The effects of some of the other variables included in Table 4 are also of interest. First, contrary to previous arguments, districts that desegregated under court order did not experience greater net enrollment declines (except in non-South suburban/nonmetropolitan areas). The considerable attention given the role of the courts in promoting white flight, via the mandatory assignment of pupils to other schools, appears unwarranted. Court involvement per se does not lead to enrollment decline. Rather, the kinds of districts targeted by the courts —i.e., those districts that are less susceptible to corrective actions initiated by other agents—are more likely to experience declines in white enrollment.

Second, central cities did not experience greater net declines in white enrollment than suburban and nonmetropolitan districts. This finding also appears to be counter to conventional wisdom, because central-city residents are believed to have greater access to alternatives to public schools. Third, previous-year percentage black had negative effects on white enrollment changes. These results are expected, since percentage black represents the maximum potential contact whites will have with blacks if the goal of desegregation is to completely eliminate racial isolation (see footnote 3). Fourth, central cities that are part of county districts did not experience net enrollment losses when they desegregated—a finding that was also expected (see Rossell et al., 1981). Finally, the statistically insignificant coefficient for the effect of calendar year indicates the absence of a secular trend in enrollment changes.

Program Characteristics

Desegregated school districts exhibit considerable variability in the character and extensiveness of their programs and in the source of pressure to desegregate. Unfortunately, little is known of how these features of desegregation plans (particularly in combination) affect the retention capacity of a school district. The DHHS-sponsored survey (Cox, 1979) contains information on the character of desegregation programs implemented by some school districts. This information is used here to assess the effects of program characteristics on white enrollment changes. With this objective in mind, equation (1) is augmented with additional variables as follows:

$$\begin{aligned}\log(WHITE_T) = \sum_{k=1}^{l} \beta_k \chi_k \\ + \beta_{11} MAN + \beta_{12} PLAN \\ + \beta_{13} SCHOOL + \beta_{14} GRADE \\ + \beta_{15} AREA + \beta_{16} TRAVEL \\ + \beta_{17} ABSENT, \qquad (2)\end{aligned}$$

where log ($WHITE_T$) and $\Sigma_{k=1}^{l} \beta_k \chi_k$ are defined as in equation (1); *MAN* = 1 if a district's major desegregation program included the mandatory assignment of white pupils; *PLAN* = 1 if a district implemented more than one desegregation plan; *SCHOOL* is the percent of schools involved in the most extensive desegregation plan; *GRADE* = 1 if a district phased in its major desegregation program by grade level; *AREA* = 1 if the major desegregation plan was phased in by geographic area; *TRAVEL* is the percentage of minority students transported under the major desegregation program; and *ABSENT* = 1 if no information was available on the above variables in the DHHS-sponsored survey. Annual observations reflecting the years prior to the implementation of a desegregation program are coded zero on all the above variables. School districts that did not desegregate are excluded from this analysis, since the focus is on the relative effects of program characteristics.

We expect that mandatory assignment of white pupils, percentage of schools involved in desegregation, and the phasing in of a program by year, grade, or geographic area will each have a negative effect on white enrollment (see Rossell et al. [1981] and previous discussion), whereas percent of minority students bused will have a positive effect. Rossell et al. note that phased-in desegregation plans tend to promote white withdrawal, because they allow parents more time to identify alternative schooling for their children. On the other hand, the percent of minority students bused tends to have a positive effect on white enrollment changes, because if more minority students are bused, fewer whites will have to be bused. This is not the most appropriate measure, because it does not take into account the actual number of whites bused under a desegregation plan.

Table 5 reports partial-regression coeffi-

Table 5. Effects of Agent and Program Characteristics on Annual White Public-School Enrollment, 1968–1976

	Partial Coefficient	
Variable	Model 1	Model 2
Location and agent		
South		
Metropolitan		
Central cities		
Court	.0768*	.0874*
Agency	.0475	.0484
Suburbs		
Court	.0642*	.0696*
Agency	.4550*	.0444*
Nonmetropolitan		
Court	.0084	.0149
Agency	.0006	.0082
Non-South		
Central cities		
Court	.0842*	.0887*
Agency	.0797*	.0814*
Suburbs/nonmetropolitan		
Court	−.0615	−.0274
Agency	−.0203	−.0122
Program characteristics		
Mandatory assignment	−.0002	.0042
Percent of schools involved	−.0001	−.0001
Plan phased in by grade	−.0194	−.0158
Plan phased in by area	.0098	.0057
Plan phased in by year	.0046	.0067
Percent of minorities bused	.0001	.0001
Feature of plan not indicated	−.0445*	−.0407
Number of observations	6,129	
Number of districts	681	

NOTE: School districts included in this analysis are known to have desegregated between 1968 and 1976, based on responses to two surveys. Models 1 and 2 include controls for previous-year white enrollment, previous-year black enrollment, calendar year, district, and whether observation reflected periods before (T-3 to T-1), during (T), and after ($T+1$ to $T+n$) the year of implementation. Model 1 also includes controls for change in exposure and the product of change in exposure and percent black. The omitted category in the regression consists of annual observations reflecting the period T-n to T-4 years before the year of implementation (pre-before).

* The regression coefficient is twice the size of its standard error.

cients for two models of the effects of agent or source of pressure to desegregate and program characteristics on white public-school enrollment trends. Model 1 includes all the variables specified in equation (1); Model 2 excludes the change-in-exposure indices and the product of change in exposure and percentage black. The involvement of courts in promoting desegregation appears not to have adversely affected white public-school enrollment trends: The coefficients for courts, even when they are statistically significant, are of the same sign and approximate size as the coefficients for administrative agencies (i.e., "Agency"). Also, net of other features of desegregation programs, changes in white enrollment are not associated with the characteristics of desegregation programs, even if allowance is made for the possibility that the influence of these characteristics is transmitted through changes in interracial contact (compare coefficients for Models 1 and 2). These results support the conclusion that change in interracial contact is the primary source of the influence of desegregation programs.

Assessment of the Total Effect of Desegregation

The effort to assess the effect of desegregation on changes in white public-school enrollment thus far has focused on the separate influences of three factors—namely, desegregation status, change in exposure, and the interaction of change in exposure and percentage black. In this section, the effects of these factors are combined to derive an estimate of the overall impact of desegregation actions on white public-school enrollment. Table 6 reports observed and predicted average annual percentage changes in white public-school enrollment. The observed values represent the actual change in white public-school enrollment experienced by the districts included in the analysis. The total predicted values were obtained by applying the coefficients derived from the estimation of equation (1) to the observed data for individual districts. Finally, the values reported in the last column represent the impact on white public-school enrollment of desegregation status, change in exposure, and the product of change in exposure and percentage black. These values were obtained by summing the predicted values reported in the last column of Table 7 and multiplying by 100.

The total predicted values correspond rather closely to the observed values, indicating that the specifications included in equation (1) capture practically all the variations in annual white enrollment. The variations among the values reported in the last column of Table 6 are of greater interest. The relative sizes and signs of these values clearly indicate that the impact of desegregation actions was limited to the year of implementation. The positive values for the years after implementation indicate that the average school district recovered some if not all of the enrollment loss that occurred during the implementation year, and that the small declines in the values for the total are not due to the continuing adverse effect of desegregation. One can also note that the implementation of a

Table 6. Predicted and Observed Average Annual Change in White Public-School Enrollment, by Desegregation Status and Percent Black

Percent Black and Desegregation Status	Observed Total[a]	Predicted: Total[b]	Predicted: Desegregation Impact[c]
Less than 35 percent			
Not desegregated	0.17	0.38	9.92
Pre-before (*T-n* to *T*-4)	−0.27	−0.49	−1.17
Before (*T*-3 to *T*-1)	−0.67	−0.77	5.02
During (*T*)	−1.75	−0.70	−19.62
After (*T*+1 to *T*+*n*)	0.22	0.18	23.80
Greater than 35 percent			
Not desegregated	−1.26	−3.87	11.74
Pre-before (*T-n* to *T*-4)	−2.76	−5.29	0.44
Before (*T*-3 to *T*-1)	−1.64	−1.35	4.72
During (*T*)	−14.06	−16.66	−35.26
After (*T*+1 to *T*+*n*)	−0.58	−0.19	24.87

[a] Actual average annual percent change in white public-school enrollment.

[b] Predicted average annual percent change in white public-school enrollment, based on coefficients derived from estimation of equation (1).

[c] Predicted average annual percent change in white public-school enrollment, based on the impact of desegregation status, change in exposure, and change in exposure × percent black, estimated from coefficients derived from equation (1). These values were obtained by summing the appropriate values in Table 7 and multiplying by 100.

Table 7. Predicted Average Annual Percent Change in White Public-School Enrollment, Based on the Effects of Desegregation Status, Change in Exposure, and Change in Exposure × Percent Black

Variable/Subgroup	Partial Coefficient[a] (β)	Mean of Variable ($\overline{X}$)	$(1-e^{\beta\overline{X}})$[b]
Desegregation status			
Not desegregated	.4177	.2763	.1223
Pre-before	.4430	.0289	.0128
Before	.4873	.1312	.0660
During	.4505	.0719	.0329
After	.4480	.4917	.2464
Change in exposure			
Not desegregated	−.0053	.2960	−.0016
Pre-before	−.0040	.7667	−.0031
Before	−.0009	1.8456	−.0017
During	−.0135	17.9298	−.2149
After	.0111	.5712	.0064
Black enrollment < 35 percent			
Not desegregated[b]	−.0272	.7962	−.0215
Pre-before	−.0272	.7918	−.0214
Before	−.0272	.5203	−.0141
During	−.0272	.5255	−.0142
After	−.0272	.5463	−.0148
Change in exposure × percent black			
Not desegregated[b]	−.0002	14.1713	−.0033
Pre-before	−.0002	23.3006	−.0053
Before	−.0002	75.1273	−.0171
During	−.0002	813.0228	−.1706
After	−.0002	17.8851	−.0041

[a] Partial-regression coefficients were taken from Table 4. A single estimate of the effect of these variables was obtained, under the assumption that their effects do not vary by desegregation status.

[b] An estimate of predicted change.

desegregation action in districts in which black enrollment exceeded one third of total enrollment resulted in almost a doubling of white enrollment loss. Although the rate of white enrollment decline accelerated during the year of implementation, a substantial increase in interracial contact during this year was primarily responsible for the overall decline in white enrollment. Since the postdesegregation interval covered here ranges from one to eight years, we can conclude that desegregation had no long-term effect.

Finally, one can also note that these estimates of white enrollment declines in the year of implementation are higher than those reported in previous studies, probably because these estimates are interval-specific, and distortions due to the combination of all time periods are therefore reduced.

SUMMARY

The principal issue addressed in this article is whether school desegregation programs lead to a reduction in the representation of whites in public school systems. In addition, an effort was made to determine whether program characteristics or the involvement of a particular implementing agent affected the amount of enrollment change that occurred. The analysis of these issues involved two sets of comparisons. First, enrollment trends in districts that desegregated and districts that did not desegregate were compared. Second, enrollment trends in desegregated districts before, during, and after the implementation of a desegregation program were compared.

The results support the following conclusions: First, enrollment trends among white public-school pupils in desegregated districts four years prior to the implementation of a desegregation program were essentially the same as those prevailing in districts that did not desegregate. Thus, increased interracial contact led to similar declines in white enrollment in districts that did not desegregate and in districts that eventually desegregated, when the former districts were somewhat removed from the desegregation controversy. It appears that substantial numbers of whites seek to avoid attending schools with blacks regardless of the form or instrument of social contact. Patterns of withdrawal and nonentrance can be induced by broader ecological processes of residential differentiation and selection.

Second, during the desegregation interval, a

period extending roughly from three years prior to implementation to the postdesegregation years, the implementation of a desegregation program did change the rate of response of white enrollment change to increased interracial contact. The rate of decline, estimated by partial-regression coefficients, decreased up to the year of implementation, increased substantially during that year, but decreased again in the implementation years. This reversal in the later years is probably due to the recovery of some of the enrollment loss from the previous year.

Third, the absolute number of whites lost to a public school system was due primarily to the amount of increase in interracial contact. The greatest declines in white enrollment occurred during the year in which the largest increase in interracial contact occurred—the year of implementation. Also, districts in which black enrollment exceeded one third of total enrollment experienced almost twice the enrollment loss experienced by other districts. The associations appear to be invariant with respect to geographical location of districts—i.e., region, metropolitan status, or central-city status.

Finally, program characteristics, net of other relevant factors, did not affect white enrollment. Moreover, contrary to expectation, involvement of the courts did not lead to greater white enrollment declines than involvement of other implementing agents. These findings, in light of others stated previously, clearly indicate that altering the features of desegregation programs will have little effect on white enrollment trends if the programs substantially change the racial composition of affected schools.

REFERENCES

Armor, D.J.
1978 "White flight, demographic transition, and the future of school desegregation." Paper presented at the Annual Meetings of the American Sociological Association, San Francisco.

Bobo, L. D.
1983 "Whites' opposition to busing: Symbolic racism or realistic group conflict?" Journal of Personality and Social Psychology 45:1196–1210.

Bosco, J. and S. Robin
1974 "White flight from court-ordered busing." Urban Education 9:87–98.

Bradbury, K. L., A. Downs, and K. A. Small
1982 Urban Decline and the Future of American Cities. Washington, D.C.: Brookings Institution.

Clotfelter, C. T.
1978 "Alternative measures of school desegregation: A methodological note." Land Economics 54:373–80.

Coleman, J. S., S. D. Kelly, and J. A. Moore
1975 "Trends in school segregation, 1968–73." Working Paper 722-03-01. Washington, D.C.: Urban Institute.

Cox, M.
1979 A Description of School Segregation Since 1965. Rand WN-10436-HEW. Santa Monica, CA: Rand.

Downs, A.
1981 Neighborhoods and Urban Development. Washington, D.C.: Brookings Institution.

Farley, R.
1975 "Racial integration in the public schools, 1967 to 1972: Assessing the effects of governmental policies." Sociological Focus 8:3–26.

Farley, R., S. Bianchi, and D. Colasanto
1979 "Barriers to the racial integration of neighborhoods: The Detroit case." Annals of the American Academy of Political and Social Science 441:97–113.

Farley, R., T. Richards, and C. Wurdock
1980 "Social desegregation and white flight: An investigation of competing models and their discrepant findings." Sociology of Education 53:123–39.

Fitzgerald, M. R. and D. R. Morgan
1977 "Assessing the consequences of public policy: School desegregation and white flight in urban America." Paper presented at the Annual Meetings of the Midwest Political Science Association, Chicago.

Giles, M. W.
1977 "Racial stability and urban school desegregation." Urban Affairs Quarterly 12:499–510.

Giles, M. W., E. F. Cataldo, and D. S. Gatlin
1975 "White flight and percent black: The tipping point re-examined." Social Science Quarterly 58:85–92.

Heise, D.R.
1970 "Causal inferences from panel data." Pp. 3–27 in E. F. Borgatta and G. W. Bohrnstedt (eds.), Sociological Methodology 1970. San Francisco: Jossey-Bass.

Jackson, G.
1975 "Reanalysis of Coleman's 'Recent trends in school integration'." Educational Researcher 4:21–25.

Katzman, M. T.
1978 "The quality of municipal services, central city decline, and middle-class flight." Research Report R78-1. Cambridge, MA: Department of City and Regional Planning, Harvard University.

Kessler, R. C. and D. F. Greenberg
1981 Linear Panel Analysis: Models of Quantitative Change. New York: Academic Press.

Lieberson, S.
1981 "An asymmetrical approach to segregation." Pp. 61–82 in C. Peach, V. Robinson, and S. Smith (eds.), Ethnic Segregation in Cities. London: Croom Helm.

Lieberson, S. and D. K. Carter
1982 "Temporal changes and urban differences in residential segregation: A reconsideration." American Journal of Sociology 88: 296–310.

Long, J.
1981 "Population deconcentration in the United States." Current Population Reports CPS 81-1, Special Demographic Analysis. Washington, D.C.: U.S. Government Printing Office.

Long, L. and W. Frey
1982 Migrational Settlement 14. United States. Laxenburg, Austria: International Institute for Applied Systems Analysis.

Lord, J. D.
1975 "School busing and white abandonment of public schools." Southeastern Geographer 15:81–92.

McConahay, J. J. and W. D. Hawley
1977 "Attitudes of Louisville and Jefferson County citizens toward busing for public school desegregation: Results from the second year." Unpublished manuscript, Duke University.

Molotch, H.
1972 Managed Integration: Dilemmas of Doing Good in the City. Berkeley, CA: University of California Press.

Mumford, L.
1973 "White flight from desegregation in Mississippi." Integrated Education 11:12–26.

Orfield, G.
1978 Must We Bus? Washington, D.C.: Brookings Institution.

Pettigrew, T. F.
1979 "Racial change and social policy." The Annals of the American Academy of Political and Social Science 441:114–31.
1980 "Racial change and the intrametropolitan distribution of black Americans." Pp. 52–79 in A. P. Solaman (ed.), The Prospective City. Cambridge, MA: MIT Press.

Pettigrew, T. F. and R. L. Green
1976 "School desegregation in large cities: A critique of the Coleman 'white flight thesis'." Harvard Educational Review 46:1–53.

Pride, R. A. and J. D. Woodward
1978 "Busing plans, media agenda, and white flight: Nashville and Louisville." Paper presented at the Annual Meetings of the Southwestern Political Science Association, Houston.

Ravitch, D.
1978 "The white flight controversy." The Public Interest 51:135–49.

Rossell, C. H.
1975 "School desegregation and white flight." Political Science Quarterly 90:675–95.
1978 Assessing the Unintended Impacts of Public Policy: School Desegregation and Resegregation. Washington, D.C.: National Institute of Education.

Rossell, C. H., J. Schofield, R. Cronin, R. Mahard, J. Egler, V. Cook, R. Tompkins, W. Trent, and L. Ward
1981 A Review of the Empirical Research on Desegregation: Community Response, Race Relations, Academic Achievement, and Resegregation. Nashville, TN: Institute for Public Policy Studies, Vanderbilt University.

Sly, D. F. and L. G. Pol
1978 "The demographic context of school segregation and desegregation." Social Forces 56:1072–86.

Snyder, D. and W. R. Kelly
1977 "School desegregation and decline in white enrollment: Structural sources of north-south differences." Unpublished manuscript, Department of Sociology, Indiana University.

Taeuber, K. E. and A. F. Taeuber
1965 Negroes in Cities. Chicago: Aldine.

Taeuber, K. E. and F. D. Wilson
1978 "The demographic impact of school desegregation policy." Pp. 135–52 in M. E. Kraft and M. Schneider (eds.), Population Policy Analysis. Lexington, MA: Lexington Books.
1981 "Measures of school racial segregation: An evaluation." Draft Report 1A to the Department of Health, Education, and Welfare. Madison, WI: Institute for Research on Poverty, University of Wisconsin.

Taueber, K. E., F. D. Wilson, D. R. James, and A. F. Taeuber
1981 "A demographic perspective on school desegregation in the U.S.A." Pp. 83–105 in C. Peach, V. Robinson, and S. Smith (eds.), Ethnic Segregation in Cities. London: Croom Helm.

Taylor, D.G.
1979 "Housing, neighborhoods, and race relations: Recent survey evidence." The Annals of the American Academy of Political and Social Science 441:26–40.

Taylor, D. G., P. Sheatsley, and A. Greeley
1978 "Periods of change: American racial attitudes." Scientific American 238:42–49.

U.S. Commission on Civil Rights
1977 Reviewing a Decade of School Desegregation, 1966–1975. Washington, D.C.: U.S. Government Printing Office.

U.S. Office of Civil Rights
1968–76 Directory of Public Elementary and Secondary Schools in Selected Districts: Enrollment and Staff by Racial/Ethnic Group. Washington, D.C.: U.S. Government Printing Office.

Wegmann, R. G.
1975 "Neighborhoods and schools in racial transition." Growth and Change 6:3–4.

Wilson, F. D.
1979 "Patterns of white avoidance." The Annals of the American Academy of Political and Social Science 441:132–41.
1982 "Trends in school segregation: 1968–1976." Discussion Paper No. 699. Madison, WI: Institute for Research on Poverty, University of Wisconsin.

Zoloth, B.
1976 "Alternative measures of school segregation." Land Economics 52:278–98.

THE CYCLE OF POPULARITY: INTERPERSONAL RELATIONS AMONG FEMALE ADOLESCENTS

DONNA EDER
Indiana University

Sociology of Education 1985, Vol. 58 (July):154–165

Despite evidence that friends are extremely important to adolescents, there has been little research on early adolescent peer relations, especially on peer relations among girls. The research that exists suggests that girls and boys have very different relationships with peers and that entry into middle school is often a difficult transition for adolescent girls. This article examines peer relations among girls in a middle school setting using data from a larger ethnographic study. We found that a system of social stratification developed during the middle school years, resulting in a clear, stable hierarchy of cliques by eighth grade. Friendships with popular girls became an important avenue for peer status. At the same time, however, many popular girls tended to avoid interactions with students of lower status, leading to strong feelings of resentment and dislike. Thus, there developed a cycle of popularity, in which feelings toward popular girls moved from positive to negative, eventually making them some of the least liked individuals in the school. Implications of this cycle of popularity for peer relations, self-esteem, and adult friendships are discussed.

INTRODUCTION

One consistent and somewhat troublesome finding in research on adolescent females is that they are more concerned with popularity than with achievement or success (Rosenberg, 1965; Douvan and Adelson, 1966; Coleman, 1966; Rosenberg and Simmons, 1975). While boys' self-esteem is tied to achievement, girls' self-esteem is tied to their interpersonal relationships (Douvan and Adelson, 1966).

Rosenberg and Simmons (1975) found that girls' concern with being well liked and their lack of interest in success develop during early adolescence. Prior to that, girls and boys are equally concerned with achievement in school and have similar aspirations for success in future jobs. However, between late childhood (ages 8 to 11) and early adolescence (ages 12 to 14), girls' desire to achieve decreases, and their desire to be well liked increases. During this same period, girls also become more concerned with others' opinions of them and show a marked increase in self-consciousness. In general, during early adolescence, girls' concerns become increasingly differentiated from boys' and become more focused on interpersonal relations than on achievement.

I am grateful to Stephanie Sanford, Cathy Evans, and Steve Parker for their assistance in data collection and for their helpful comments. I would also like to thank Barbara Reskin, Sue Fisher, and two anonymous reviewers for their helpful suggestions on an earlier draft. This research was supported by NIMH Grant No. 36680-01 and Spencer Grant No. 44-329-02. Address all correspondence to the author at the Department of Sociology, Indiana University, Ballantine Hall, Bloomington, IN 47405.

There is evidence suggesting that this shift in concerns is accompanied by lower self-esteem. Simmons, Rosenberg, and Rosenberg (1973) found that girls experience a significant decrease in self-esteem during early adolescence. A later study found that this drop in self-esteem was associated with entrance into junior high school and with other social and developmental factors (Simmons et al., 1979). This suggests that there may be something about the transition to a junior high or middle school setting that is particularly difficult for girls.

Despite these findings, few studies have focused on female peer relations during this important developmental period. Most sociometric studies of children's friendships have been conducted in elementary school, and the few ethnographic studies of children's friendships that have been done have focused mainly on preadolescent and adolescent boys (Thrasher, 1927; Sherif et al., 1961; Cusick, 1973; Fine, 1981).

Two studies that examined peer relations during adolescence identified different bases of peer status for boys and girls. Coleman (1966) and Schofield (1981), in their studies of high school and middle school students, found that males obtained status primarily through athletic achievement and that females, who were not given the same opportunity to excel in athletics, obtained status from social success. For girls, social success was the closest thing to athletic achievement.

What is most lacking in the literature on adolescents are studies that focus on girls' relationships with other girls. It is often assumed that girls are most concerned with their social success or popularity among boys. But adolescent girls may be equally concerned with their popularity among other girls. Likewise, though it is assumed that girls' avoidance of success stems mainly from a concern with being liked by boys, it may in fact have other motivations as well.

Girls' friendships undergo considerable change with the transition to a middle school setting. First, students in middle school have a larger population from which to choose friends, which encourages the development of more distinct friendship groups or cliques. In one sociometric study that included older students, Hallinan (1979) found that the number of cliques increased steadily between fourth and eighth grade. Second, middle school students can participate in more extracurricular activities, which provide new sources of peer status. Specifically, athletic activities provide males with a clear avenue for status, and cheerleading provides an elite group of females with high status.

There are at least two differences between athletics and cheerleading as sources of status. One concerns the extent to which selection is based on objective, achievement-related criteria. Achievement is obviously important in athletics, but it is generally less important in cheerleading. Selection of cheerleaders is usually based on a number of criteria, including poise, personality, and appearance. Many of these criteria are influenced by a girl's current status in school and her family background. In schools where cheerleaders are selected by the student body, prior popularity becomes even more important.

A second difference concerns the number of people involved in each of these activities. A large number of boys are involved in athletic activities, but only six to eight girls per grade are selected as cheerleaders. Consequently, athletics provides more than enough candidates for membership in a top group; cheerleading does not. It is likely, therefore, that some girls will gain entrance into the top group through other means, which may have nothing to do with achievement and are likely to be more subjective.

This article explains why girls become increasingly concerned with interpersonal relationships during the transition to middle school. In particular, it examines how changes in girls' relationships with other girls contribute to an increased concern with popularity and a decreased concern with achievement. It also provides a better understanding of why girls become increasingly other-directed and insecure during early adolescence.

First, differences in the overall structure of friendship groups and changes in group membership between the sixth and eighth grades are examined. Then, the dynamics of interaction between members of different groups, particularly groups with different statuses, are explored.

Much of the article focuses on the importance, for girls, of social avenues for peer status, especially friendships with popular girls. The dynamics of this particular status process are explored in detail, showing how popular girls come to be viewed as snobbish or stuck-up when they fail to respond to friendly initiations from less popular girls. This leads to the surprising finding that popular girls are not always well liked. The implications of the negative stereotypes of popular groups for peer interaction, female socialization, and status processes among adults will also be considered.

AN ETHNOGRAPHIC STUDY OF EARLY ADOLESCENT PEER RELATIONS

The findings reported in this article are part of a larger study of adolescent peer relations and socialization, which involved in-depth observations of informal and organized peer activities in a middle school setting.[1] There were a number of reasons for making ethnographic observations a central aspect of this study. First, there is an increasing awareness that children's friendships are influenced by the context in which they occur. Dyadic friendships are influenced not only by larger friendship groups such as cliques but also by the status structure of these cliques, by school activities, and by the school environment. Thus, to understand the processes of friendship formation and change, we must examine peer relations within their social context.

Second, because many aspects of peer relations are closely related, it is necessary to collect data on several aspects simultaneously. This article focuses on the close relationship between peer friendships and peer status. Had we looked at peer status alone, we may have failed to understand its important implications for students' friendships and social well-being.

An ethnographic approach also enables us to see peer relations from the students' point of view. This is particularly important for understanding the meaning of terms such as *popularity*. We found that popularity had different meanings to different students and that these meanings changed over time. Had we assumed that popular students were well liked,

[1] For a discussion of peer socialization see Sanford and Eder (1984) and Eder and Sanford (forthcoming).

we would have failed to understand the meaning of popularity for many students in the school.

For the ethnographic stage of the study, we selected a school that enrolled students from a range of socioeconomic backgrounds, including students from working-class and lower-class families. The school was located in a medium-size midwestern community and enrolled approximately 250 students per grade. Some of the students came from surrounding rural areas. Most of the students were white, but a small number of black students were also enrolled. The school's extracurricular program, which emphasized athletic activities, was typical among middle schools. Vocal and instrumental music programs were also available in the school curriculum.

During the first year of the study, two researchers observed extracurricular and informal activities twice a week. (A female research assistant observed for a five-month period and I observed for the entire year.) We spent much of this time observing interactions during the lunch period, since this was the most opportune time for students to meet informally. In addition, we observed informal interaction before and after school, during special events such as school picnics and dances, and during and between classes. For two months during the second year, a second research assistant and I made follow-up observations of the same girls and observed some new girls in similar activities.

The ethnographic stage of this study had several goals. The first goal was to collect data on adolescents of different ages and social backgrounds. Thus, both researchers attended lunch periods for each of the three grades (sixth, seventh, and eighth). One observer usually sat on the side of the cafeteria occupied by predominantly middle- to lower-middle-class students; the other sat on the side occupied largely by working-class and lower-class students.[2] The students we studied came from a range of social-class backgrounds—from lower class to upper-middle class—but the majority came from middle- and working-class families. We also observed groups that represented the full range of social statuses within the school, including one of the lowest-status groups and one of the highest-status groups. Most of the groups we observed were all female, but we did observe a few mixed-sex groups. A male observer is currently collecting similar data on adolescent boys in the same setting.

The second goal was to avoid association with adults and adult roles and to enter the adolescents' world as peers rather than as authority figures. Thus, we introduced ourselves to students, rather than be introduced by teachers or principals, and we tried to enter the lunchroom environment much as new students would. Many of our initial contacts were made through students we met at extracurricular activities and social activities outside of school.[3] Once we met some students and were accepted by them, it was relatively easy to get to know many of their friends.

The third goal was to follow peer relations over a relatively long period of time. Since we were interested in how these relations changed, it was essential that we stay in the same setting and follow certain groups for long periods. This limited the number of groups we could observe, but because we had several observers and attended all three lunch periods, we were able to study many different groups. Altogether, we collected data on approximately 190 students in fourteen groups, which represents over one third of the girls in the school at the time of the study.

The fourth goal was to collect data using a variety of methods. During the ethnographic stage, we observed the informal and organized activities of most of the groups and conducted in-depth interviews with group members.[4] The interviews were used to corroborate interpretations from our observations and to collect additional information on attitudes and perceptions.

One advantage of observing during the lunch period was that we could share an activity with students, namely eating lunch, and thus establish rapport fairly quickly. Because of this rapport and because we were in the setting on a regular basis for an extended period of time, we are quite confident that our data represent typical patterns of peer relations at this school. Although we informed students that we were studying adolescent interaction and friendship, we did not take notes openly while observing informal activities. Between lunch periods we wrote brief notes, and immediately after leav-

[2] The development of this stratified seating arrangement is discussed in the following section.

[3] The research assistant's previous observations at a local girls' club provided some initial contacts.

[4] The interviews were conducted with small groups of girls to keep the situations as natural as possible and because previous research has found that children are often more at ease and more verbal when interviewed with their peers (Labov, 1972). In a few cases, interviews were also conducted individually. While group members openly disagreed on several occasions, it is possible that all viewpoints were not represented. However, we are confident that the comments expressed in interviews reflected students' real attitudes, because they corresponded to both their actual behavior and their informal comments to us and to their friends.

ing the setting, we recorded detailed notes with a tape recorder. We also tape recorded the interviews and some of the lunch conversations.[5] Our field notes include the seating patterns of the groups we observed and information about the content of their conversations. These notes were coded on a variety of dimensions, including peer relations.[6] We also recorded field notes of girls' athletic practices, since these practices included examples of peer interaction between members of different groups. These notes were coded and analyzed in a similar manner.

Groups were defined according to lunchtime seating arrangements. Any student who sat with a group two or more times was considered a group member. Comments such as "This isn't your group" or "Your group's outside" indicated that these seating patterns reflected meaningful group boundaries. Also, comparisons with questionnaire data (i.e., responses to the question, "Who do you hang around with at school?") indicated that these seating patterns corresponded to reported interaction patterns.[7] Though most of the students selected their best friends from their group, not all group members chose each other as best friends. Thus, the groups represented students who spent time together at school, not necessarily students who were close friends.

THE DEVELOPMENT OF A SOCIAL STRATIFICATION SYSTEM

We found considerable differences in peer relations across the three grades. In the sixth grade, there were few stable cliques and no cliques that appeared to have more status than others. In the seventh grade, the cliques were more stable and a hierarchy was beginning to emerge. By eighth grade, there was a clearly defined hierarchical system of stable cliques.

This stratified social system developed from a number of sorting processes. As mentioned above, one way students defined group boundaries was through seating arrangements at lunch. During the first year of the study, the three grades had separate lunch periods. Students could sit wherever they wanted during their lunch period, and they expended considerable effort to ensure that they sat with the people they liked. This was accomplished mainly by saving seats for friends. But, this strategy was also used to prevent certain girls from sitting with a group. If one of these girls approached an empty seat at the table, she was often told that the seat was being saved for someone else.

Sixth graders had the most flexible seating patterns during lunch. Few groups sat together regularly throughout the year, and most girls sat with different groups on different days. Because seating arrangements were continually negotiated, we saw open attempts to include and exclude certain girls. In the following example from our field notes, Penny was excluded from a group that she had previously sat with:[8]

> Some visitors were sitting at their table, so they were trying to save the remaining seats for their friends. The main conflict arose when Penny sat in one of those seats and they told her all of them were saved. She looked a little dejected that they weren't going to let her sit with them. Then she looked around and said "Well, where's Pam's group" and went over and talked to them.
>
> (Field notes, March 10, grade 6)

Seating patterns among seventh graders were more stable; many students sat with the same group for months at a time. Also, a hierarchy of groups, which did not exist among the sixth graders, had developed. The highest-status group included seven of the eight cheerleaders and six student council members, including the class president. This was the most stable group in the seventh grade: Twelve of the seventeen girls who sat with this group were permanent members.

Another seventh-grade group included four student council members. This group also had relatively high status, and it was clear that certain girls preferred it over other groups. Betty, for example, showed a clear preference, as indicated in the following field notes:

> Much later on, Betty joined in and sat next to Darlene, and again, the two girls who always come with her didn't get involved in the main group. Betty seemed more interested in being with this group of girls than with her other two friends, who are always getting left out.
>
> (Field notes, September 24, grade 7)

---

[5] These recordings of lunch conversations are currently being transcribed for use in future analyses.

[6] The codes were then entered into a computer along with information on the activity, observer, grade level, month of observation, and page number of field notes. Using UNIX, a word processing program, we were able to quickly identify all field notes for a particular code. This greatly facilitated the analysis of our extensive field notes.

[7] Questionnaires, which included a number of sociometric questions regarding interaction, friendship, and status choices, as well as questions about family background, were given to all sixth-grade students in both years. We then collected additional questionnaire data on the same students in subsequent grades.

[8] All names of people and places are fictitious.

Betty continued to sit with this group for most of the year, but her two friends joined a different group.

Another status division in seating arrangements developed during the seventh grade. All the higher-status groups described above, along with several other groups, sat on one side of the cafeteria. These students often wore name-brand clothes, and many of them appeared to be from middle-class backgrounds. The students on the other side of the cafeteria appeared, from their dress, to be primarily from lower- and working-class backgrounds. It was clear that students were also aware of this difference. One day, a seventh grader asked me if I always sat on this side of the cafeteria. I said "yes" and asked her if she did. She said that she always did, because it was the side where the "good people" sat.

By eighth grade, the seating arrangements were very stable; most students sat with the same group for the entire year. The two top groups merged to form one large mixed-sex group, which included all eight cheerleaders, many of the male athletes, and eleven student council members. The social-class division in seating patterns was also more apparent in eighth grade. Only a few students from middle-class backgrounds sat on the side of the cafeteria with the less popular students.

Changes in group membership during the year provided additional information on the sources of peer-group status among adolescent girls. There were two main avenues for mobility into the elite group—being a cheerleader or being a friend of a cheerleader. For example, during the entire year, only four girls joined the top eighth-grade group. One was a cheerleader and another was her best friend. Both of these girls were welcomed into this very exclusive group. Similarly, one of the cheerleaders who was not already a member of the top seventh-grade group joined it shortly after the year began.

There was no clear top group in sixth grade during most of the year, but after cheerleading tryouts, a large group, which included four of the new cheerleaders, began to sit together quite regularly. Also, after the new cheerleaders did some routines at a pep session in the spring, they made conscious attempts to sit together at lunch:

> I noticed that Jane had saved a place on either side of her. Some girls were asking if they could sit there, and she was telling them that they were reserved for the cheerleaders. However, Betty's two friends were sitting with the group even though they weren't cheerleaders. Judy noticed this and told Doreen that she and Peggy had asked to sit with them and they said no, it was just the cheerleaders, but that now they had let Betty's friends sit there.
>
> (Field notes, April 16, grade 6)

On this day, the attempt to exclude all non-cheerleaders was not successful, since Betty wanted to include her two best friends. Other girls, like Judy and Peggy, were not successful in joining the group, even though they were very interested in being part of the group and did sit with them on other days. In general, once cheerleaders were chosen, many girls wanted to sit with them at lunch.

During the second year, one of the lunch periods was dropped, so students from different grades ate lunch together.[9] Two sixth-grade girls (the class president and her best friend) sat with the popular seventh and eighth graders. After cheerleading tryouts, five of the seven new cheerleaders joined this group.

Near the end of the year, we asked the students in the groups we had been observing if some students in their grade were more popular than others and why. Being a cheerleader and being a friend of a cheerleader, along with having money and being attractive, were considered important avenues for popularity among girls. The following response from two eighth graders was typical:

> R—I wonder how somebody like her gets to be popular in the first place.
> D—They hang around with the cheerleaders.
> K—Yeah, you hang around popular kids and you usually become popular.
>
> (Interview, May 20, grade 8)[10]

Sixth graders could not participate in cheerleading, but being friends with seventh- and eighth-grade cheerleaders and with popular girls in the sixth grade was important.

> H—She's real popular. She's nice. She's pretty. That's why she's popular.
> R—Think so?
> H—Then all of *her* friends are popular and all of *their* friends are popular.
> R—Why are all her friends popular?
> H—Because they're all friends I suppose.
>
> (Interview, April 7, grade 6)

Thus, friendships with other girls are important avenues for status, and this has important implications for the meaning of popularity, for peer relations between groups, and for adolescent girls' growing concern with being well liked.

---

[9] The groups were less stable in all grades during the second year, partly because students did not always eat during the same lunch period. Whether or not this change also affected friendship groups will be examined through sociometric analyses.

[10] R stands for researcher.

THE MEANING OF POPULARITY

From our interviews and informal talks with girls, we found that popularity had a number of different meanings. On the one hand, popular girls were the most *visible* in the school; they were the girls most people knew by name. This was clearly seen as one of the advantages of being popular. According to girls who were not popular, the nice part about being popular is that "everybody knows you." Also, popular girls received the most attention from others. According to one of the popular girls, "the good part [about popularity] is that you get a lot of attention." In contrast, girls who were not popular felt that their achievements were often ignored:

> N—Now if I was popular, when I won that contest everybody would have been jumping around and sayin', "Oh! Natalie won! Natalie won!" But it wasn't like that. Since I wasn't popular, everybody just kind of thought, you know, like "Big deal!"
>
> (Interview, April 20, grade 8)

Visibility both preceded and followed membership in the elite group. Among sixth-grade girls, one of the main determinants of visibility was attractiveness. Even popular girls admitted that this was an important factor in popularity. The other factor that affected visibility was cheerleading. The cheerleaders were clearly the most visible group of girls in the school. The two athletic events they cheered for—boys' basketball and football—were the main social events in the school.

Becoming a member of the elite group also added to one's visibility, because the entire group was often the focus of the attention of others, particularly those who sat on the same side of the cafeteria. During lunch, the behavior of top-group members was often the topic of conversation among those in other groups, but the top group seldom paid attention to students who were not in their group.

Most of the girls agreed that popular students were more visible, but not all felt that popular students were more well liked. Some girls described popular girls as nice and friendly and considered being well liked another advantage of popularity. But other girls described popular girls as stuck-up and unfriendly and clearly stated their dislike for them. Still others expressed some ambivalence on this point:

> R—You say that everybody likes popular people, but actually you say you don't like them.
>
> O—It depends, actually, on what kind of mood you're in, whether you like them or whether you—
>
> N—Or whether you're in the mood to put up with them!
>
> (Interview, April 20, grade 8)

To the extent that popular girls are well liked, one might ask whether being well liked precedes or follows popularity. Girls who were friendly and outgoing experienced an increase in popularity, but girls who became identified as members of the top group also experienced an initial increase in positive sentiment. This was most obvious among the newly elected cheerleaders. Many of the girls wanted to sit with the cheerleaders at lunch and made special attempts to be friendly toward them. For example, when it looked as though cheerleading might be eliminated from the school budget, Sylvia made a point of telling Carrie, one of the new cheerleaders, that she had written a letter to President Reagan telling him how important cheerleading was for school spirit and how hard some of her friends had worked to become cheerleaders. Also, if one of the new cheerleaders was upset about something, there were usually many girls around to comfort her.

Cheerleaders and other popular girls experience an increase in positive sentiments because their friendship is an important avenue for social status. When certain girls are first identified as candidates for popularity, many girls want to become their friends. Girls who are outgoing and responsive to others are especially well liked, since their friendship is so highly valued.

However, there is a second stage in this *cycle of popularity*, during which popular girls face increasingly negative sentiment. This stage is also influenced by the importance of social avenues for peer status among adolescent girls and by the nature of social interaction in middle school settings. To better understand this second stage, we will next look at peer relations between groups.

PEER RELATIONS AND SOCIAL INTERACTION

One of the important facts about school life is that students have little opportunity to physically separate themselves from other students. Most unstructured activities take place in relatively crowded environments such as the lunch room. Consequently, students develop symbolic ways to distinguish their group from the many other students who are always present.

The students we observed used many of the strategies people use to avoid interaction with others in a public setting, such as avoiding body contact and eye contact (Goffman, 1963; Lofland, 1973). For example, students who were in the same class would walk by each other without any acknowledgment. In fact, acknowledgement by someone outside of one's peer group was an important and reportable event.

We also found that students in high-status groups often ignored friendly initiations from students in other groups, giving the impression that they were rude or snobbish. Some of these instances involved members of the same athletic team, as shown in the following notes from gymnastics practice:

> Allison said "Hi" to Patty, who said nothing to her. Allison then made some comment about her being stuck-up. Then she again said "Hi" and again got no response from Patty. She told Marsha, "She's in a bad mood. She's not saying 'Hi' to me." But later she said, "She's stuck-up."
>
> (Field notes, November 6, grade 7)

Allison offered two different explanations for Patty's failure to acknowledge her. First she explained that Patty was in a bad mood and may not have felt like talking to anyone that day. Then she concluded that Patty was stuck-up. Of these two attributions, the second was more common for this type of behavior. In fact, many of the popular girls in the school were considered snobbish. This was due in part to their failure at times to engage in interaction with other girls:

> What the sixth graders talked about today was that people try to be nice to a popular girl but that she's very snotty and does not talk to anyone. Apparently, when most people go up to somebody who is snotty and popular, they will not get a response from her and can't even engage in a conversation with her. She just ignores them.
>
> (Field notes, February 10, grade 6)

The concern that popular girls would become stuck-up was so widespread that some girls were warned in advance. For example, in the yearbook of a new cheerleader, someone wrote, "Have fun in high school. Just don't get stuck-up."

Cheerleaders were considered by many to be the most snobbish, but this label was also applied to other girls who sat on the "popular" side of the cafeteria. Many thought that these girls had become less friendly since coming to Woodview Middle School:

> Nancy said how she talked to her at Parkside, and in fact, when they were in seventh grade, they had talked to each other alot, but now this girl never talks to her. It has only been since she came to Woodview that she had turned into such a snob.
>
> (Field notes, February 10, grade 8)

Schofield (1981) found similar patterns in her study of a racially integrated middle school. Girls in the top group, which was mainly white and middle class, often ignored the black girls in the school. The black girls, in turn, felt that the girls in the top group were stuck-up and conceited.

Popular girls were generally considered stuck-up, but some were considered friendly when they were not with other members of their group. This was reported to be true of Susan, who was not in the top group but who did sit on the popular side of the cafeteria:

> She said that Susan was nice if she got her away from Karla. This was another idea that she talked about several times—that some girls would be snotty and not talk to you if they were with one group, but if they were away from one or two of the most popular girls, then they would talk to you.
>
> (Field notes, February 10, grade 6)

Thus, popular girls do not necessarily dislike less popular girls. Rather, they may be concerned about their friends' reactions to their associations with less popular girls. This is probably due to the close relationship between status and friendship among girls. Just as girls become more popular if they have popular friends, they may become less popular if they associate with less popular people. But popular girls may also ignore less popular girls because they simply do not have the time or energy to maintain friendships with all the girls who would like to be their friends.

POPULARITY AND DISLIKE

These dynamics gave rise to the perception that popular girls were unfriendly and led to an increase in negative sentiment. Some of the students who talked about disliking popular girls were their former close friends. It is not surprising to find that former friends no longer like each other, but the negative feelings toward popular girls were often stronger than those toward other students and frequently took the form of active dislike. As we have seen, friendships with popular girls are an important source of peer status. Consequently, the loss of one of these friendships is salient; the student not only loses a good friend, she loses an opportunity to be more popular. At the same time, the former friend's preference for a new peer group makes the relatively lower status of her old group more salient. This was evident in the reaction to Penny's change in friendships after she made the freshman pom-pom team:

> Bonnie told me that ever since Penny made the pom-pom team she goes over and sits

with the popular girls. She told me that she was going to tell Penny something today but that she had chickened out. I asked her what it was and she said, "I was going to tell her if she comes and sits with us, 'Why don't you go over and sit with your new friends if your old friends aren't good enough for you?' "

(Field notes, April 9, grade 8)

Penny's change in group membership was the topic of conversation on several days and led many of her old friends to actively dislike her. Because peer status was so important to these girls, a former friend's transfer to a higher-status group was more painful and led to stronger feelings of resentment than her transfer to another lower-status group.

Popular people were disliked not only by former friends but by many of the students in the school. As discussed earlier, some students felt that members of the top group and other students who sat on the popular side of the cafeteria ignored them. Even though being ignored by other students was extremely common in the school, we mainly heard complaints about being ignored by popular students. Again, it is likely that interaction with popular students was so salient that being ignored by them was also particularly salient. Many students took the snobbery of popular people very seriously, as if it automatically implied they were not as good.

Also, because some students had negative experiences with members of the top group, the whole group was branded with certain labels. We found that some top-group members were less group-oriented than others and initiated interactions with a wider range of girls. Though some girls mentioned these differences, most girls felt that all of the top-group members were stuck-up. They were quick to interpret a lack of response from popular girls as snobbish and tended to apply this interpretation to all group members. This stereotype led many girls to avoid further contact with top-group members, thereby minimizing the possibility of further painful rejection.

This process was most evident in regard to the top group, but a similar process occurred in regard to the students who sat on the popular side of the cafeteria. Some students viewed all the students who sat on the popular side as stuck-up and attempted to avoid any contact with them. This presented problems when less popular girls were assigned to that side of the cafeteria for clean-up duty.

As the lunch went on, she said that she would really hate to work over there and that if she couldn't get out of it she was going to pretend to be sick and throw up so she could get out of it, because she was just not going to work over there. She said she didn't like anybody over there and that nobody who sat over there liked her. After I asked why, she said, "I don't know. They're just stuck-up."

(Field notes, April 4, grade 7)

This girl applied the label *stuck-up* to a much larger group of students and tried to avoid contact with half of her classmates. Other eighth graders also mentioned this basic division between popular and unpopular students.

R—That's what confused Donna and me. We'd hear about the popular people, but then it seems not a lot of people like them really.

D—I know.

R—You wonder, well isn't being popular being someone that everybody likes and it doesn't really seem that way a lot of times.

K—No, only the popular kids like the popular kids and the unpopular kids only like unpopular kids.

R—Uh huh.

K—It's like that.

D—It depends.

K—It's like segregation of unpopular people and popular people.

(Interview, May 20, grade 8)

Many of the girls formed stereotypes about other girls, but the nature and type of the stereotypes varied depending on their position in the overall social hierarchy. For example, girls who sat on the popular side of the cafeteria but who were not in the top group saw the top-group members as stuck-up but did not view themselves that way. They, however, tended to classify all of the students on the other side of the cafeteria as "grits."[11] The students who sat on the less popular side identified one particular lower-status group as "grits." In general, there was a tendency to apply broader stereotypes to students who were further away in the overall hierarchy and with whom one had less contact. The stereotypes in turn often served to prevent contact and therefore limited the amount of information that students received—information that might have challenged the stereotypes.

In some cases, students were aware of the stereotypes regarding their own group but did not agree with them. This was true of some of the top-group members who knew that they were perceived as being stuck-up but did not agree with this perception.

---

[11] *Grits* is a term associated with lower-class people in this region of the country and refers to an inexpensive type of food.

R—You say that a lot of girls envy cheerleaders.
D—Yeah. A lot of 'em get close friends. But then others, they think that they're stuck-up and they get to hate us [nervous giggle] and say all this stuff.
C—And like they start rumors and stuff. And say they don't like us and stuff.
D—And in slambooks,[12] "Who are your enemies? Cheerleaders, Number 21" or somethin'. [laughs]
R—Is that really hard on you all when that happens?
D—Well it makes us feel bad because, well, we don't really think we're stuck-up. But like we have one big group, you know, that like we're all good friends with. And then the others, I guess they just feel that the cheerleaders and basketball and football players all just kind of hang around together. And then if you're not in something like that or you don't make it, then you just think that, you know, well, that we're *stuck-ups* [embarrassed emphasis on last word, then laughs] or something.
(Interview, March 31, grade 7)

According to the cheerleaders, the people who were not in the top group saw the cheerleaders as stuck-up and therefore disliked them and started rumors about them. They did not perceive themselves as being stuck-up, nor did they think that their close friends saw them that way. Interestingly, these girls also reported that they never sat on the other side of the cafeteria because "that's where all the grits sit." This suggests that the "grit" stereotype was so accepted by the group that they did not view it as a reflection of either their own or their friends' superior attitude toward others, an attitude that probably contributed to others' negative perception of them.

CONSEQUENCES FOR GROUP INTERACTION

One consequence of the negative stereotype of popular girls was a growing tendency to avoid interaction with them. Since the entire popular group was often viewed as snobbish, many girls stopped approaching any of the popular girls for fear of being rejected, even though there were clear differences in the degrees of friendliness among the popular girls. One of the more outgoing popular girls considered this to be one of the main disadvantages of being popular:

M—Then, a lot of times, people don't talk to the popular kids because they're kind of scared of them and they don't know their real personality. So that's kind of a bummer when you're considered to be popular because you don't usually meet a lot of other people because they just kind of go, "Oh."
(Interview, April 29, grade 8)

As long as interaction between groups was avoided, stereotypes remained unchallenged. Consequently, all the popular girls continued to be viewed by many as stuck-up, despite individual differences in their actual interactional styles.

The negative label was so salient for girls that it also affected interaction within groups. If one group member failed to acknowledge or was not especially friendly to another group member, she was frequently accused of being stuck-up. The considerable anxiety surrounding the use of this label was evident when one girl would tease another and jokingly accuse her of being stuck-up. In most cases, these accusations were taken seriously and denied rather than treated in a light or humorous manner.

Girls who were thought to be better than other group members were also accused of being stuck-up, even when they had little control over this perception. For example, in several groups, girls from higher-status families were the least liked members of their group, while in other groups, girls from lower-status families were the least liked. In general, it appears that girls strongly uphold an egalitarian norm and view members who are better or worse than other group members as less desirable friends. Consequently, girls are concerned about being more successful than their friends and about being less successful.

The negative labelling also made it more difficult for shy girls to make friends. Some girls ignored others and failed to respond to friendly initiations because they were shy. In many cases these girls were also perceived as being stuck-up. One girl said that before she got to know and like her friend, she thought her friend was a snob. Several girls told us that it was hard for them to make friends because they were shy and other girls assumed they were stuck-up.

The underlying problem for peer interaction is that ignoring others can be easily misinterpreted. Any behavior can have several potential meanings and can thus be misunderstood, but the act of ignoring someone provides even fewer cues and is therefore even more likely to

[12] Slambooks are notebooks with questions to which students respond and then sign a number instead of their name. These informal "questionnaires" are very popular with middle school girls and typically include a number of questions regarding interpersonal relationships.

be misinterpreted. For example, Schofield (1981) found that white girls avoided interacting with black girls because they were intimidated by the black girls' more aggressive style of talk. However, the black girls assumed that they were being avoided because the whites thought they were too good to play or work with blacks. Because these social images hindered interaction between the groups, these misunderstandings were never cleared up. In general, the tendency to misinterpret all acts of being ignored as indications of snobbishness is likely to hinder the development of positive peer relations among girls.

THE CYCLE OF POPULARITY

These findings indicate that popularity has a fairly predictable cycle among adolescent girls. First, a few girls become identified through cheerleading elections as an elite group. Immediately after, many students make offers of affiliation, and these girls experience a marked increase in popularity. In part, this reflects a general tendency for high-status people to be liked (Newcomb, 1961). This tendency is further strengthened by the fact that friendships with popular girls are important avenues for girls' status.

However, there are limits to the number of friendships that any one person can maintain. Because popular girls get a high number of affiliative offers, they have to reject more offers of friendship than other girls. Also, to maintain their higher status, girls who form the elite group must avoid associations with lower-status girls. For both of these reasons, these girls are likely to ignore the affiliative attempts of many girls, leading to the impression that they are stuck-up. Thus, shortly after these girls reach their peak of popularity, they become increasingly disliked.

This process is a general one, but there are some aspects of it that are unique to adolescents. Among adults, there is also a strong relationship between affiliation and status. In general, adults maintain more distance from people they dislike and from people with higher status (Goffman, 1967; Brown, 1965). This may occur because lower-status people are more likely to be rejected, and thus are likely to feel antagonism toward higher-status people. This interactional norm, then, is an important means of minimizing antagonism between status levels (Brown, 1965).

The adolescents in this study did not follow this norm. The status hierarchy was still developing, so many of the students, not expecting rejection, initiated friendly interactions with higher-status girls. However, the rejection of these initiations did cause anger and resentment. This suggests that adolescents are still in the process of learning certain basic interactional norms regarding the relationship between status and affiliation.

This also helps to explain why the resentment toward popular girls is so strong among adolescents. Rejection by higher-status people is always likely to be somewhat painful due to the loss of potential rewards, but it is likely to be more painful when it is unexpected. In other words, when adults are rejected by higher-status people, it is often expected and may even be part of the anticipated risk when an initiation is undertaken. Adolescents who are not aware of this high risk of rejection are likely to be more resentful when it occurs.

One final point concerns whether or not the cycle of popularity leads to loss of status as well as loss of affiliation. In this study, even though the popular girls became increasingly disliked, they maintained membership in an elite group and therefore maintained their visibility. In earlier grades, when elite groups are less likely to exist, this cycle could lead to loss of status as well as loss of affiliation.

DISCUSSION

Given the importance of social avenues for status among girls, it is not surprising that they become increasingly concerned with popularity during early adolescence. Furthermore, the salience of being labelled a snob may also contribute to girls' concern with being viewed as friendly and nice. To avoid this label, they are likely to be friendly to people they do not like. Rosenberg and Simmons (1975) found that girls are more likely to act nice to people they dislike and to smile when they are unhappy during middle adolescence than during childhood or early adolescence. This could very well be a response to a greater concern with being viewed as snobbish or stuck-up.

The negative feelings toward high-status girls might also explain why girls become less concerned with achievement during early adolescence. To surpass one's friends appears to have more costs for girls than for boys, because achievement is not a main avenue for peer status for girls and because the avenues that do exist for girls are more arbitrary and therefore less widely accepted. In addition, or perhaps as a consequence, girls appear to value equality more than boys and seek to minimize individual differences.

There is some evidence that this concern with being too successful affects females' academic behavior. Coleman (1966) found that although high school girls tried to get good grades, few sought to be outstanding academically. This avoidance of academic success has previously been attributed to concerns about relationships with boys, but it is possible that it may also be related to concerns about relationships with other girls, specifically to the desire not to be viewed as superior to one's friends. More research investigating the extent to which females adhere to an egalitarian norm and how this norm influences their academic achievements is needed.

It is also important to consider the role school activities play in promoting different avenues for peer status for females and males. Many schools now provide equal sports opportunities for females and males, but males' sports still have greater visibility in the school and in the community. This greater visibility promotes the importance of male athletics and cheerleading as avenues for peer status.

More research examining the effect of extracurricular activities on peer status is needed. As girls' sports activities become more established, it is important to determine their influence on girls' status. Also it is important to compare status processes in schools in which academic achievement is an important avenue for peer status with status processes in schools in which it is not. This area needs further investigation before clear policy implications can be drawn, but in the meantime, promoting girls' sports or giving more visibility to other achievement activities in which girls participate may provide girls with alternative avenues for peer status.

More research on the nature and implications of peer relations among adolescents is also needed. We need to examine more closely the relationship between status and friendship for boys as well as girls. We also need to look at the implications of these processes of social stratification within schools. Since peers are important agents of socialization (Corsaro, 1979; Kandel, 1978; Alwin and Otto, 1977), it is important to examine the different types of norms, values, and styles of communication that develop in different peer groups as a result of these stratifying processes.

We should also consider other environments that promote similar social stratification processes. One particular topic that needs further investigation is how these social processes affect adult females in work settings. We need to study how women respond to the availability of new avenues for status, such as work-related achievements. Those women who seek these new avenues may need to learn a new set of norms, which are likely to be more familiar to men. Other women may continue to pursue social avenues by being particularly nice toward other workers or by actively participating in social activities related to work. In most work settings, where achievement is the main avenue for recognition and rewards, focusing on social avenues for success could prove detrimental to female workers. At the same time, high-status women may continue to be perceived more negatively than high-status men, which may lead some women to avoid competing for higher-status positions. We also need to determine whether adult females adhere to an egalitarian norm and, if so, how this norm influences their occupational achievements.

Finally, we need to examine other long-term consequences of this process. For example, females who are concerned with being perceived as snobbish may develop strategies to avoid this label. They may be friendly to people they dislike or they may mask anger and dislike with a smile (Hochschild, 1979; Eckman, 1972). These possible long-term outcomes deserve more attention in future studies.

In summary, we found that a system of social stratification developed among students during their middle school years. This system was formed and maintained by a number of interactional processes, including the avoidance of certain individuals and the establishment of group boundaries. More research is needed to examine these important processes of social stratification in other educational and work settings. Also, the implications of these processes for peer relations, female socialization, and status processes in work settings need further investigation.

REFERENCES

Alwin, D. F. and L. B. Otto
1977 "High school context effects on aspirations." Sociology of Education 50:259–73.

Brown, R.
1965 Social Psychology. New York: Free Press.

Coleman, J. S.
1966 The Adolescent Society. New York: Free Press.

Corsaro, W.
1979 "We're friends, right?: Children's use of access rituals in a nursery school." Language in Society 8:315–36.

Cusick, P.
1973 Inside High School. New York: Holt, Rinehart and Winston.

Douvan, E. and J. Adelson
1966 The Adolescent Experience. New York: Wiley.

Eder, D. and S. Sanford
Forthcoming "The development and maintenance of interactional norms among early adolescents." In P. Adler and P. Adler (eds.), Sociological Studies of Child Development. Greenwich, CT: JAI Press.

Eckman, P.
1972 "Universals and cultural differences in fa-

cial expressions of emotion." Pp. 207–83 in J. K. Cole (ed.), Nebraska Symposium on Motivation 1971. Lincoln: University of Nebraska Press.

Fine, G. A.
1981 "Friends, impression management, and preadolescent behavior." Pp. 257–72 in G. Stone and H. Farberman (eds.), Social Psychology Through Symbolic Interaction. New York: Wiley.

Goffman, E.
1963 Behavior in Public Places. New York: Free Press.
1967 Interaction Ritual. New York: Doubleday.

Hallinan, M. T.
1979 "Structural effects on children's friendships and cliques." Social Psychology Quarterly 42:43–54.

Hochschild, A.
1979 "Emotion work, feeling rules, and social structure." American Journal of Sociology 85:551–75.

Kandel, D. B.
1978 "Similarity in real-life adolescent friendship pairs." Journal of Personality and Social Psychology 36:306–12.

Labov, W.
1972 Language in the Inner City: Studies in the Black English Vernacular. Philadelphia: University of Pennsylvania Press.

Lofland, L.
1973 A World of Strangers. New York: Basic Books.

Newcomb, T. M.
1961 The Acquaintance Process. New York: Holt, Rinehart and Winston.

Rosenberg, F. R. and R. G. Simmons
1975 "Sex differences in the self-concept in adolescence." Sex Roles 1:147–59.

Rosenberg, M.
1965 Society and the Adolescent Self-Image. Princeton: Princeton University Press.

Sanford, S. and D. Eder
1984 "Adolescent humor during peer interaction." Social Psychology Quarterly 47:235–43.

Schofield, J.
1981 "Complementary and conflicting identities: Images and interaction in an interracial school." Pp. 53–90 in S. Asher and J. Gottman (eds.), The Development of Children's Friendships. Cambridge: Cambridge University Press.

Sherif, M., O. J. Harvey, B. J. White, W. R. Hood, and C. W. Sherif
1961 Intergroup Conflict and Cooperation: The Robbers Cave Experiment. Norman, OK: University of Oklahoma Press.

Simmons, R. G., D. Blyth, E. Van Cleave, and D. Bush
1979 "Entry into early adolescence: The impact of school structure, puberty, and early dating on self-esteem." American Sociological Review 44:948–67.

Simmons, R. G., F. R. Rosenberg, and M. Rosenberg
1973 "Disturbance in the self-image at adolescence." American Sociological Review 38:553–68.

Thrasher, F. M.
1927 The Gang. Chicago: University of Chicago Press.

DETERMINANTS OF ELEMENTARY SCHOOL GRADING

JEFFREY LEITER JAMES S. BROWN
North Carolina State University

Sociology of Education 1985, Vol. 58 (July):166–180

This article examines the determinants of the grades teachers give to students. It distinguishes such meritocratic sources of grades as the student's widely valued and classroom-specific achievements (the former measured by standardized test scores) from such nonmeritocratic sources as race, sex, and track level. The data trace one cohort in a single school district as it passes through the first, second, and third grades. We use three-stage least-squares analysis to estimate separate nonrecursive models for reading and mathematics. We find that grades reflect classroom-specific achievement more than widely valued achievement but that the strongest effect derives from the generalization of grading across subjects. This reflects an interactive process between student and teacher rather than a simple pattern of general student achievement or generalized teacher assessment of noncognitive student traits.

We evaluate how teachers grade their students by distinguishing between two sets of determinants: student achievement and other factors that are unrelated to achievement. These other factors, which include the student's reputation, track placement, deportment in class, race, social class, and sex, move grades away from a pure evaluation of achievement. We also investigate the impact of grades on achievement by analyzing the causal processes that relate reading and mathematics grades and achievement among second and third graders.

Grades are important because they convey signals to the student they describe. As such, grades may encourage the underconfident student, discourage the overconfident student, spur the underachieving student to extra effort, or lull the successful student into complacency (Davidson and Lang, 1960; Evans, 1976; Kirschenbaum, Napier, and Simon, 1971). Also, grades may be used by others to evaluate an individual's ability. Among these consumers of grades are other students, other teachers (including those who will instruct the student in the future), school administrators (including those charged with admitting the student to selective schools and programs), and employers. Jencks et al. (1979) found that grades mediate a substantial part of the impact of academic ability on the number of years of schooling attained. This is likely due to a combination of the signalling and evaluative effects of grades.

DETERMINANTS OF GRADING

We conceive of grading as a teacher behavior. Possible determinants of this teacher behavior are the student's achievement and the teacher's expectations of the student.

Teachers sometimes claim that they take student effort or progress into account when assigning grades, especially in elementary school (Terwilliger, 1966). Most often, however, grades are meant to measure a student's performance relative to other students or to some ideal (Dreeben, 1968; Terwilliger, 1966; Waller, 1932). To the extent that the grades teachers assign reflect student achievement, they can be seen as meritocratic evaluations. Clifton (1981), Pedulla, Airasian, and Madaus (1980), and Williams (1976) found that grading is substantially meritocratic.

Achievement in school has two components: widely valued achievement and classroom-specific achievement. Most schools try to teach a body of basic cognitive skills that includes "the ability to manipulate words and numbers, assimilate information, [and] make logical inferences" (Jencks et al., 1972:53). These are the skills generally measured by standardized tests. Teachers may differ in the extent to which they value the development of such skills in their students, but they are compelled by the school system, directly via curriculum guides and indirectly via standardized testing, to instruct their students in these skills. Even teachers with their own classroom agendas feel obligated to prepare their students for standardized tests (Kohl, 1967). Thus, the grades teachers give may reflect student acquisition of skills that the school system or educational circles define as valuable.

A teacher may also award grades on the

We appreciate the suggestions of Gary Hill, Carrie Knowles, Peter Marsden, Mary Haywood Metz, Joel Rosch, Teresa Scheid-Cook, Mary Scheuer Senter, Robert Serow, Matthew Zingraff, and anonymous reviewers for *Sociology of Education*. The data were gathered with funds from a Faculty Research and Professional Development Grant at North Carolina State University. Address all correspondence to the authors at the Department of Sociology and Anthropology, North Carolina State University, Raleigh, NC 27695.

basis of achievements that s/he considers particularly important: for example, creativity in writing, ingenuity in problem solving, clear organization, fluid verbal delivery, or witty expression. These skills and accomplishments are not measured by standardized tests, but they represent achievements nonetheless, and as such, their assessment by grades can be considered meritocratic. (Of course, the student may be hard put at first to figure out "what the teacher wants.")

But grades may also reflect factors that are unrelated to achievement. The deviation of grades from an accurate assessment of achievement amounts to biased or nonmeritocratic evaluation. Factors that influence grades after taking account of the effect of achievement constitute determinants of such bias. Williams (1976:233) found that grades are "affected markedly by the . . . expectations that teachers have for students" (see also Clifton [1981]). These expectations may concern either cognitive (i.e., academic) achievement or compliance with behavioral norms (i.e., deportment). Because of these expectations, teachers may make distorted evaluations of homework and examinations (Finn, 1972) or enter on report cards grades that are not justified by classroom performance. There are a number of possible sources of such expectations and, hence, of nonmeritocratic evaluation: the student's reputation, the student's track placement, the teacher's prejudice, and the student's conformity to the teacher's preferred behavior patterns.

Student's reputations are frequently spread by informal conversation among teachers (Boocock, 1980). Also, students' grades and scores on aptitude and achievement tests from previous years are usually available for teachers to scrutinize. Teachers who take advantage of these opportunities and remember these previous grades and scores form expectations of students, which may distort their evaluations of the students' achievements (Brophy and Good, 1974). Moreover, teachers may assign grades similar to previous grades for fear of having to justify different evaluations (Schlechty, 1976). Similarly, teachers responsible for awarding several grades to the same student may try to avoid marked differences among the grades, because such differences may call for special justification to parents or to the principal, who expect essentially constant performance across subjects and from year to year.

A class whose composition is determined by alleged measures of previous achievement—including test scores, grades, or recommendations—may have a group reputation that becomes attached to each of its students (Cooper and Good, 1983). Also, teachers may use grades to justify track placement *post hoc*. In a study of one high school, Rosenbaum (1978) found that high grades were harder to obtain in the lower tracks. But in a study of eight high schools, Alexander, Cook, and McDill (1978) found that track placement had little effect on grades.

Teachers may have prejudices that influence how they grade students. They may believe that ability varies with race, ethnicity, social class, or sex, either generally or for particular subjects. In studies of high school students, Williams (1976) and Clifton (1981) found that race and ethnicity had no effect on teacher expectations. They point out, however, that demographic variables may have greater direct effects on teacher expectations in earlier grades (see also Doyle, Hancock, and Kifer [1972] and Harvey and Slatin [1975]). In later grades, race, ethnicity, social class, and sex may indirectly affect teacher expectations via their effects on earlier student performance and attitudes.

Teachers may give lower grades to students who challenge discipline standards, who question commonly held viewpoints, who appear to be uninterested or uninvolved in activities the teacher organizes, who through frequent absence seem to betray a lack of commitment to school, or who show little interest in high-status cultural activities, such as art and classical music (Bowles and Gintis, 1976; Brophy and Good, 1974; DiMaggio, 1982; Gravenburg and Collins, 1976). That is, teachers may award grades on the basis of student attitudes or behaviors that do not bear on learning. Teachers' grading may also indicate their preference for other student attitudes and behaviors that may influence learning: for example, promptness or neatness with homework. The teacher, especially, may see the relevance of such matters for achievement. We therefore expect student compliance to be more related to classroom-specific achievement than to widely-valued achievement. Each teacher probably has the same behavior preferences in all subjects, but these preferences are likely to vary from teacher to teacher. (We will investigate, however, the alternative possibility that teachers' preferences are the same, that they reflect a schoolwide culture.) Overall, therefore, we are speaking of the impact on grading of student compliance with classroom-specific, non-subject-specific attitudes and behaviors.

Determinants of Grading via Achievement

So far, we have specified the determinants of the grades teachers give to students. These grades have consequences, chiefly for subsequent achievement, that may shape later grades through meritocratic evaluation. Therefore, a complete understanding of the determination of grading requires some consideration of the determination of achievement, both widely valued and classroom-specific.

Achievement in a subject may theoretically be traced back to ability, but the two can rarely be measured separately (Jencks et al., 1972). Previous achievement is a determinant of current achievement because it subsumes ability in the subject (and, thus, any alleged determinants of ability, such as social class) and because most cognitive learning is cumulative.

A student's achievement in a particular subject is influenced not only by abilities and past achievements in the subject but also by skills and resources that are not specific to the subject. These include skills that are generally useful for the kind of learning valued in school; parents' support of school work, a resource that may vary from year to year; and the student's commitment to academic work, which may also vary over time. In addition to these resources, the student may have skills—for example, test-taking skills—that enhance his or her measured achievement, although perhaps not the achievement itself. The learning environment also contributes to student achievement. These environmental resources include physical facilities, support personnel, and any teacher attributes that are constant across subjects. The impact such resources have on academic achievement probably varies among students, but it is constant across subjects.

As suggested earlier, grades give students signals that may motivate or discourage effort and achievement (Bloom, 1976; Dreeben, 1968; Maehr, 1976; Salili et al., 1976). Moreover, previous grades can create teacher expectations, which may result in differential treatment of students. That is, the quantity of interaction, quality of reinforcements, difficulty of questions, and time allowed for answers to questions may vary according to a teacher's expectations of a student (Brophy and Good, 1974); Cooper and Good, 1983; Rist, 1970). Through these and other process variables, teacher expectations are realized as student performances.

Assignment to a particular class on the basis of some measurement of ability or previous achievement may influence current achievement in two ways. First, such assignments, like grades, signal the expectations held by others. Second, learning opportunities may vary by track if effective teachers, classmates with special qualities, and instructional resources are unevenly allocated among tracks or if instructional organization or content varies among tracks (Sørensen, 1970). Several studies, after controlling for previous achievement, found higher achievement in higher tracks (e.g., Alexander et al., 1978; Heyns, 1974; Leiter, 1983).

Wiley (1976) and Stallings (1980) found that "time on task" was an important determinant of achievement. To the extent that misbehavior, lack of concentration and involvement, and absenteeism diminish time on task, achievement suffers.

We do not expect race and sex to have large direct effects on achievement. Any differences in ability due to race, social class, and sex (see, for example, Hunt, 1961; Jencks, 1980; Jensen, 1973; Maccoby and Jacklin, 1974) are subsumed in the earliest measure of achievement. However, race, class, and sex may affect subsequent achievement indirectly by injecting nonmeritocratic expectations and bias into grades. The grades, in turn, may shape teacher expectations, and, hence, learning opportunities for students, and may signal teacher expectations to students, influencing their motivation to achieve. Any remaining direct effect of race, class, or sex on achievement likely reflects differential allocations of resources for learning by administrators rather than by teachers.

DATA AND VARIABLES

The data for this article describe one cohort of students in a rural consolidated district in North Carolina. This cohort consisted of students who passed from first grade in 1977–78 through second grade in 1978–79 into third grade in 1979–80. Only those students with complete data on the variables to be analyzed were considered, leaving 213 students in the six elementary schools of the district.[1] The

[1] In 1979–80, the district had 364 third graders. Twenty-eight of these were special-education students, who were excluded from the analysis because they were graded differently than the rest of the students. Fifty-five of the students were excluded because they were retained in grade at some point in their elementary school careers before the 1979–80 school year. Retention introduces possible influences that deserve careful attention, which is beyond the range of this article. In particular, the complex interaction of achievement, ability, age, motivation, reputation, deportment, and social development requires special conceptualization and analysis (see the review in Jackson [1975]). Retention presents particular analysis problems in this district because of its concentration in one of the six schools: Forty-eight percent of the retained students in our data set began in one school. Inclusion of retained students here would have contaminated the analysis with numerous unanalyzed but correlated school-level variables. Sixty-eight other students were excluded

district strictly adhered to the practice of grouping its elementary school students by achievement into self-contained classrooms. Within school and grade, classroom assignments were based on reading achievement test scores from the previous May.

All the data were taken from students' individual records, which were kept in the district office. At the end of the school year, before the achievement test results were available, the student's teacher (each class had one teacher for all its academic subjects) recorded one grade for reading and one for mathematics. These grades, which summarized report-card grades from the entire school year, ranged along a fourteen-point scale from F to A+.

The widely valued portion of student achievement in reading and mathematics is measured by raw scores, grade equivalents, or mastery levels on nationally utilized achievement tests administered each May throughout the district.[2] General resources for learning, not specific to either subject, are measured by the effect of the test score in one subject on the test score in the other subject. For example, in the regression analysis, a significant effect of the reading test score on the mathematics test score, net of the previous mathematics test score and other predictors, suggests that abilities, skills, and resources not specific to mathematics contribute to widely valued mathematics achievement. As laid out in the earlier discussion of the general resources concept, a significant effect for this variable may derive from diverse causes, but the statistical controls that such an effect would have to survive limit the interpretation.

The track level in reading and in mathematics is the class mean for the achievement test scores in reading and mathematics, respectively, from the previous May's testing. Student's race, sex, and days absent were available from district records. Days absent serves as a partial indicator of time on task (time off task but in school is unmeasured). Unfortunately, in these data we cannot distinguish between time-on-task effects on grading due to quantity of learning opportunity and effects due to teacher judgments of student commitment to learning. No measure of social class was available, but in this rural North Carolina county, race can serve as a partial indicator.[3] Social-class effects on student ability or motivation not correlated with race should largely be subsumed in the earliest measure of achievement.

A direct measure of the teacher's perceptions of student conformity to preferred attitudinal and behavioral patterns is unavailable. The teachers recorded no grade for deportment, nor any indication of behavior problems, on the district office records. A proxy measure is available, however. The relationship between the grade given in one subject and the grade given by the same teacher in the other subject may cautiously be used for this purpose when it is estimated net of the effects of current and previous widely valued achievement, the previous grade, race, sex, track level, and absenteeism. So estimated, the

---

from the analysis because of incomplete data. Data were missing for many students who entered the district after the first grade. Data on their pretransfer schooling was often unavailable or incomparable. Exclusion of special-education and retained students, while justifiable, does limit the relevance of our findings. We have no reason, however, to think that exclusions due to missing data have altered the results. In fact, on the average, students included in this analysis and those excluded due to missing data do not have significantly different ($p = .05$) third-grade mathematics and reading grades and test scores.

[2] The analysis was constrained to use achievement test scores from the batteries chosen by the district and the following scoring form recorded in cumulative records that year:

The language of the reading subtests of the norm-referenced California Achievement Test does not give special advantages to students of a particular race (Marwit and Neumann, 1974). Its strength is in comparing students' achievements, rather than in measuring performance relative to learning objectives (Smith, 1978). The strength of the criterion-referenced Diagnostic Mathematics Inventory is its utility for individualizing instruction. It suffers from overemphasis on computation and fact, rather than on mathematical reasoning (O'Brien, 1978).

[3] In the county where these students live, family incomes differ greatly by race. Families with a white head of household had an average annual income of $18,742 in 1979, but those with a black head of household had an average annual income of only $11,402 (U.S. Bureau of the Census, 1980).

Grade	Testing Date	Subject	Test[a]	Form of Score
First	May 1978	Reading	CAT reading	Raw score
First	May 1978	Mathematics	DMI	Objectives achieved
Second	May 1979	Reading	CAT reading	Raw score
Second	May 1979	Mathematics	DMI	Objectives achieved
Third	May 1980	Reading	CAT reading	Grade equivalent
Third	May 1980	Mathematics	CAT mathematics	Grade equivalent

[a] CAT = California Achievement Test; DMI = Diagnostic Mathematics Inventory.

grade given in the other subject may stand for the teacher's assessment of the student's classroom-specific achievement in that subject or the teacher's generalized (i.e., not subject-specific) assessment of the student's conformity to attitudes and behaviors that are either unrelated to academic achievement (e.g., style of dress, choice of friends) or related to achievement but not subject-specific (e.g., neatness or regularity of homework). Thus, a positive net effect of one grade on the other grade could mean that the student's classroom-specific achievements in both subjects were parallel and that the teacher gave correlated grades to reflect such correlated classroom-specific achievements. Alternatively, a positive net effect could point to the teacher's use of grades to assess general (i.e., not subject-specific) characteristics of the student.

The operationalization of achievement is particularly crucial to the analysis and subsequent interpretation. Widely valued achievement is measured by scores on tests administered throughout the district. Our use of standardized achievement tests is narrower than most. In common practice, these tests are used as measures of achievement per se; residual gains on such tests are used as measures of teacher and school effectiveness (Veldman and Brophy, 1974). The district in question uses the tests in just this way, as the sole measure of achievement and the basis for grouping students into classes.

Classroom-specific achievement is captured by the grades teachers award. However, we can assume that when awarding grades, teachers consider widely valued achievement and nonmeritocratic evaluations as well. Therefore, to isolate the impact of classroom-specific achievement on grades, we must partial out these other effects. The effect of widely valued achievement can easily be partialled out by controlling for test score. Nonmeritocratic effects are harder to control. Race, sex, and track level are specified in the data, and their distinct effects on grading can be identified and removed. But the effect of student conformity to preferred behavior patterns can only be indirectly measured. As discussed above, the effect of the grade given in one subject on the grade given in the other subject can be used as a proxy for student conformity. However, an effect of one grade on the other grade may indicate parallel achievements in the two subjects. Moreover, some of the attitudes and behaviors the teacher prefers may promote achievement. Therefore, some part of any effect of one grade on the other grade may well be meritocratic. With the present measures, we can only establish the upper bound to nonmeritocratic grading (beyond race, sex, and track-level effects). Thus, after all predictors have done what they can, residual variation in grade received is probably due to classroom-specific, subject-specific achievement.

ANALYSIS PLAN

Figure 1 illustrates the causal relations to be estimated. The causal expectations already explained need not be repeated, but the reciprocal causal paths between grade and test score in the same year require further comment. The effect of test score on grade is simply the extent to which the teacher includes widely valued achievements, measured by the standardized test, in the grade. The effect of grade on test score is more complex, actually twofold. First, the test score measures achievements, some of which the teacher has included in the grade. Beyond this, however, the grades a student receives all year, which are then summarized in the office file, may have a signalling or motivating effect on the acquisition of widely valued skills measured at the end of the year on the standardized test. Thus, the reciprocal paths between grade and test score imply that the grade can influence itself via its effect on the test score. First, grades may have a positive or negative effect on a student's acquisition of widely valued skills, which are measured at the end of the year by the standardized tests. The teacher may then include widely valued achievement in the grade.

Figure 1 indicates the need for both longitudinal and multiple-regression analyses. The causal process to be analyzed requires the measurement of grades and test scores at several intervals. In the longitudinal analysis, we can assume that many unmeasured variables are subsumed in earlier measures of an outcome. Thus, social class and other family background effects on grading and test scores (beyond those correlated with race) are largely subsumed in earlier grade and test score measures (see Hanushek [1977] for a defense of this approach in school effects research).

Figure 1 also indicates that most outcomes are multiply determined. The multiple determination of outcomes means that possible interpretations of regression coefficients can be narrowed to net effects. For example, a positive net effect of the reading test score on the mathematics test score does not mean that performance on the mathematics test depends upon reading ability, because this ability has already been controlled by the earlier mathematics test score, on which it had an effect. Likewise, the direct effect of race or sex on grades or test scores does not include race or

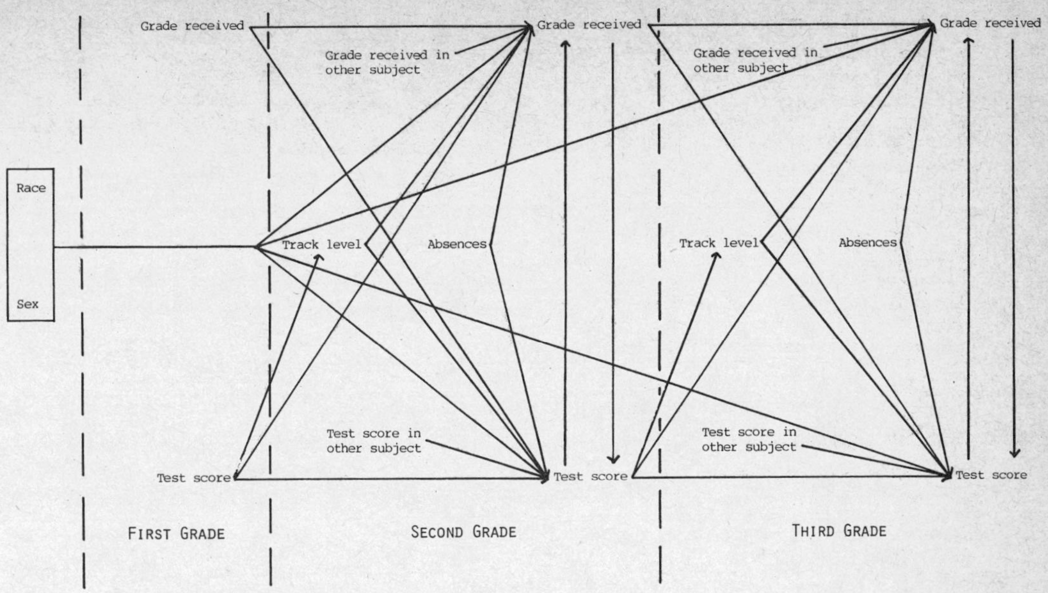

Figure 1. Causal model. (Block presentation of race and sex is for simplicity only. The effect of each variable is designated by an arrow from the block.)

sex differences in ability or motivation, because these are controlled by the effects of earlier grades or test scores, themselves determined partly by race and sex. Thus, the net effects of race and sex should be interpreted as differential rewards, resource allocations, and reinforcements by race and sex.

The longitudinal analysis suggested by Figure 1 is a decomposition of associations between variables into direct causal effects, indirect causal effects, and noncausal (i.e., unanalyzed or spurious) components. The sum of these three is the total relationship (i.e., zero-order slope) implied by the model as specified. The model-implied zero-order relationship should approximate the observed zero-order relationship. Small differences may arise from rounding error (the six decimal places used in the matrix computations were rounded to two). For the overidentified portion of the model (i.e., the determination of test scores and grades in the third grade and track level in the second and third grades), larger differences signal model misspecification (Pedhazur, 1982). For the just-identified portion (i.e., the determination of test scores and grades in the second grade), however, the model-implied and observed zero-order relationships are constrained to equal one another regardless of the adequacy of the specification. The matrix approach outlined by Fox (1980) provides a convenient method for this decomposition.

Because reciprocal causation is assumed in the model, ordinary-least-squares estimation is inappropriate. Therefore, we used three-stage least-squares estimation.[4] The grades and test scores in the other subject were used as instrumental variables to overcome identification problems and to obtain predicted values for the reciprocally related endogenous variables. Fox's (1980) method includes provisions for decomposing relationships in nonrecursive models such as ours.

If variable X is to be an instrument for variable Y in the reciprocal relationship between variables Y and Z, then X must meet two key provisions. First, it must have a strong net relationship with Y. As the tables will show, this requirement is well fulfilled here. Second, X must have no direct effect on Z (Heise, 1975). Since model estimation depends on the second assumption, this requirement can only be justified through theory and logic (Asher, 1976). In the present study, we must argue that grades in one subject do not affect test scores in the other, net of other causes, and that test scores in one subject do not affect grades in the other, net of other causes.

The meaning of the first half of the statement depends on the interpretation given to the grade in the other subject. It may mean that the teacher's perception of student conformity to

[4] Three-stage least-squares analysis is theoretically preferable to two-stage least-squares analysis (Johnston, 1972:395), should yield the same results as two-stage least-squares analysis for the just-identified equations, and is the medium in SAS for obtaining the covariance matrix of the error terms, which is needed for the effect decomposition.

preferred attitude and behavior patterns does not have a net effect on the acquisition of widely valued skills. A zero-order relationship is undeniable: The extent to which the teacher communicates approval of the student's general behavior and personality almost certainly affects learning in most subjects. The student, however, can infer the teacher's generalized evaluation directly from the grade given in the subject in question. The student need not look to other grades to make this inference. Hence, the generalized evaluation (grade in other subject) has its effect on widely valued learning in a given subject (test score) through the grade given in the same subject. This fits the requirement for an instrumental variable precisely. Alternatively, the first half of the statement may mean that the general (i.e., not subject-specific) level of achievement graded by the teacher does not have a direct net effect on subject-specific widely valued achievement. Despite the clear zero-order impact of the general achievement level on test scores in a given subject, the requirement for the instrumental variable is met, because this impact is again transmitted via the grade given in the same subject, which, like the grade in the other subject, is affected by any general pattern of achievement.

The second half of the statement means that general (i.e., not subject-specific) abilities and resources for learning have no direct effect on the grade received in a particular subject. Again, the zero-order relationship is clear, because the subject-specific, widely valued achievement that teachers likely include in grades is influenced by general abilities and resources. The teacher, however, need not *directly* consider these general factors in giving a grade for a specific subject, because the student's widely valued achievement in that subject already captures the student's general abilities and learning resources. Thus, the effect of general abilities and resources on the grade in a given subject passes exclusively through the test score for that subject: General abilities and resources influence subject-specific, widely valued achievement, which in turn influences grading. This again fits the requirement for instrumental variables.

The decompositions were computed separately for the second and third grades. Since the estimation yielded standardized coefficients to input into Fox's algorithm, we can interpret and compare the effects as one would path coefficients. Indirect effects sum all indirect paths from cause to outcome variable, but only those indirect paths whose separate components are all substantively significant contribute notably to the overall indirect effect. This makes it much easier to interpret indirect effects. Among the indirect effects are seemingly endless "reverberations" between reciprocally related variables. Even when the structural coefficients on these paths are fairly large, however, the reverberation quickly dies away after a single cycle.

ANALYSIS

Reading

Table 1 presents the decomposition of effects on students' reading grades and test scores. (The parallel analysis for mathematics follows in Table 2.) As the table shows, widely valued achievement, measured by end-of-the-year standardized test scores, was not an important determinant of the grades teachers gave in second or third grade. Reading grades, thus, did not reflect this important element of merit net of other causes.

The grade received in first grade shaped the grade assigned in the second grade. This may reflect (1) a meritocratic continuity of classroom-specific achievements, (2) a nonmeritocratic contamination of grading by student reputations transmitted from the earlier grades, or (3) the shaping of teacher expectations, which in turn shape student achievement. However, since first-grade grades had no effect on second-grade test scores, we must disregard the third possibility; widely valued achievement ought to be influenced by teacher expectations if classroom-specific achievement is.

The first-grade test score had a fairly strong effect on the grade assigned in the second grade. Since this effect was net of the second-grade test score, it can be explained with some confidence as a reputation or expectation effect. We cannot say to what extent the effect simply shows that teachers bring grades in line with earlier test scores and to what extent it shows that teachers fit their expectations and the learning opportunities they offer students to these earlier test scores. In either case, the effect was much reduced the next year.

By far the strongest force shaping grading in both years was represented by the coefficients for mathematics grades. This effect may be interpreted either as the teacher's perception of student conformity to preferred attitude and behavior patterns or as a strong tendency toward parallel achievement in various subjects. The strength of this effect is particularly noteworthy given that the effects of many other variables on grades assigned had already been considered before computing these coefficients.

Race, sex, track level, and time on task (absences) had no effect on the grades students were assigned.

Table 1. Decomposition of Standardized Effects on Second- and Third-Grade Reading Grades and Test Scores ($N = 213$)

	Second Grade										Third Grade									
	Grade Received[a]					Test Score[a]					Grade Received[a]					Test Score[a]				
Variable	1	2	3	4	5	1	2	3	4	5	1	2	3	4	5	1	2	3	4	5
Ascriptive																				
Race (1 = nonwhite, 2 = white)	.09	−.01	.32	.40	.39	.03	.01	.33	.38	.38	.00	.04	.25	.29	.29	.14*	.01	.29	.44	.45
Sex (1 = male, 2 = female)	.01	−.01	.17	.18	.17	.05	.00	.13	.18	.18	.04	.01	.13	.19	.19	.03	.03	.12	.17	.17
First grade																				
Reading grade	.26*	−.02	.42	.66	.66	.08	.03	.50	.61	.61		.04	.52	.56	.59		.01	.52	.53	.58
Reading test score	.35*	−.10	.43	.67	.67	.36*	.08	.33	.77	.76		.09	.51	.61	.60		.15	.50	.65	.71
Second grade																				
Reading grade		−.02	1.02	1.00	1.00	.12	.00	.61	.73	.74	.10	−.01	.55	.64	.68	−.16*	.07	.68	.59	.61
Mathematics grade	.51*	−.01	.26	.77	.77		.06	.56	.62	.64		.05	.59	.64	.60		−.05	.66	.61	.54
Reading test score	−.16	.00	.89	.73	.74		−.02	1.01	.99	1.00	.09	.06	.48	.63	.65	.39*	.05	.25	.70	.73
Mathematics test score		−.06	.64	.58	.58	35*	−.01	.38	.72	.73		.05	.52	.57	.57		.15	.51	.66	.66
Track level	−.04	−.01	.53	.48	.50	.07	−.01	.53	.59	.64		.01	.41	.42	.40		.03	.47	.50	.55
Absences	.03	−.01	−.07	−.05	−.06	.04	.00	−.05	−.01	.01		.01	−.09	−.08	−.02		.02	−.01	.01	−.03
Third grade																				
Reading grade			.64	.64	.68			.63	.63	.65		.03	.96	.99	1.00	.19*	.01	.46	.65	.67
Mathematics grade			.60	.60	.65			.57	.57	.59	.59*	.02	.20	.81	.81		.12	.50	.61	.61
Reading test score			.59	.59	.61			.70	.70	.73	.16	.01	.49	.65	.67		.03	.95	.98	1.00
Mathematics test score			.65	.65	.69			.67	.67	.75		.07	.60	.67	.69	.44*	.01	.33	.78	.78
Track level			.60	.60	.62			.85	.85	.88	.01	.00	.54	.55	.56	.00	.00	.61	.62	.67
Absences			.04	.04	−.03			.03	.03	−.05	.02	.00	−.08	−.06	−.07	.02	.01	.00	.03	.01
Variance explained	.68*					.74*					.72*					.70*				

[a] 1 = direct effect; 2 = indirect effect; 3 = noncausal component; 4 = model-implied zero-order standardized slope; 5 = observed zero-order standardized slope (i.e., zero-order correlation).

* Significant at the .05 level.

The determinants of widely valued achievement would be more important for grading if test scores had a larger effect on grade assignment. We should note these determinants, however, for what they show us about the test results. Notable among them are the test score from the previous year, the grade received the same year, race, and general abilities and learning resources. The effect of the previous year's test score indicates the stability and cumulation of widely valued achievement. The grade received the same year affected widely valued achievement only in the third grade, and only weakly even then, indicating that grades and standardized tests do not measure the same skills. The weak effect may also indicate that report-card grades given during the year did little to motivate or demotivate student acquisition of widely valued skills. Moreover, the motivational effect of grades one year on test scores the next were not any larger, though in one case the direction was reversed. Race, but not sex or track level, affected widely valued achievement only weakly in the third grade. General abilities and learning resources, measured by mathematics test scores, had effects on the widely valued part of reading achievement at least as strong as any other determinant. These effects persisted despite numerous controls.

Interpretation of these results for reading (the same is true for mathematics) has been facilitated by the absence of important indirect effects. We have been able to concentrate on the direct effects. Note also that the model appears to be well specified, judging by the match between model-implied and observed zero-order slopes for the overidentified third-grade equations. This, too, is largely true for the mathematics results.

Mathematics

Table 2 presents the parallel analysis for the mathematics grades. In many important aspects, the findings are quite similar to those for reading grades. Again, previous grades had a significant net effect on grades assigned, indicating some combination of continuity of classroom-specific skill attainment, reputation effects, and expectation effects. The effect of previous grades on mathematics grades, unlike their effect on reading grades, persisted through the third grade. Moreover, mathematics grades closely paralleled reading grades, as indicated by the large coefficients for same-year reading grades. This indicates either generalized classroom-specific achievement across the two subjects or grading based on student traits other than subject-specific achievement. As in reading, race, sex, and time on task (absences) had no effect on grading.

We should note three differences from the analysis of reading grades. First, mathematics grades more consistently reflected the widely valued achievement measured by standardized tests (i.e., both mathematics coefficients are in the same direction, and the third-grade coefficient reaches statistical significance), an important meritocratic element of mathematics grading. The determinants of widely valued achievement, therefore, were more important for mathematics grades than for reading grades because of their indirect effects. These determinants include (1) general abilities and learning resources (reading test scores) in both grades; (2) motivational or signalling effects of the previous year's grade on the third-grade test score; (3) a weak continuity of widely valued mathematics achievement, but only from second to third grade; (4) the third-grade grade, for the third-grade test score, probably marking an overlap in the content of these two evaluations; and (5) race, but only weakly in the second grade.

Second, the previous year's test score had a smaller impact on mathematics grades, especially in the second grade. This means that either teachers responded less in mathematics than in reading to the reputation carried by test scores or differences in expectations or learning opportunities arising from such reputations had less impact on classroom-specific mathematics achievement.

Finally, track level had a greater impact on mathematics grades. The student's track assignment had no net effect on his or her reading grade, but students in higher tracks received slightly lower mathematics grades, at least in the third grade, net of other determinants. This finding corresponds to other results from these data, in which track effects were stronger for mathematics than for reading (Leiter, 1983). The direction of this effect, however, is contrary to Rosenbaum's (1978) finding that the grades of students in higher tracks are boosted.

Note the greater difference between model-implied and observed zero-order relationships for track level than for other predictors of mathematics grades. In fact, this difference exceeds that for any predictors of reading grades, including track level (see Table 1). This suggests misspecification involving track level in the mathematics case. We had assumed that the effects of track level on grading and test scores would best be modelled by using as a measure of track level the mean test score from the previous year in the subject in question. Students were assigned to these classes, however, purely on the basis of reading test scores. Therefore, any grouping effect

Table 2. Decomposition of Standardized Effects on Second- and Third-Grade Mathematics Grades and Test Scores ($N = 213$)

	Second Grade										Third Grade									
	Grade Received[a]					Test Score[a]					Grade Received[a]					Test Score[a]				
Variable	1	2	3	4	5	1	2	3	4	5	1	2	3	4	5	1	2	3	4	5
Ascriptive																				
Race (1 = nonwhite, 2 = white)	.09	.02	.28	.40	.40	.15*	−.01	.27	.41	.40	−.07	.02	.29	.23	.23	−.05	.05	.38	.37	.37
Sex (1 = male, 2 = female)	.04	−.01	.14	.17	.16	−.05	.00	.13	.08	.06	−.03	.01	.18	.16	.15	.01	−.01	.17	.18	.16
First grade																				
Mathematics grade	.14*	.02	.43	.58	.58	.13	−.01	.38	.50	.50		.04	.45	.49	.51		.07	.47	.54	.55
Mathematics test score	.08	.00	.45	.53	.53	.06	.00	.45	.51	.52		.02	.48	.50	.62		.04	.52	.55	.58
Second grade																				
Mathematics grade		−.02	1.05	1.03	1.00	−.09	.00	.81	.72	.68	.24*	.07	.35	.66	.66	.23*	.04	.45	.73	.70
Reading grade	.51*	−.01	.28	.78	.77		−.05	.64	.60	.58		.16	.51	.67	.65		.14	.55	.69	.69
Mathematics test score	.18	.00	.54	.72	.68		−.02	1.04	1.02	1.00	.02	.00	.52	.54	.57	.17*	.07	.45	.71	.71
Reading test score		.12	.55	.67	.64	.67*	−.01	.11	.77	.73		.01	.61	.63	.59		.17	.58	.75	.75
Track level	−.02	.00	.28	.26	.29	.02	.00	.26	.28	.41		−.01	.28	.27	.41		.00	.18	.18	.29
Absences	−.07	−.01	−.02	−.10	−.10	−.06	.01	.02	−.03	−.04		−.02	−.10	−.12	−.15		−.03	−.04	−.07	−.06
Third grade																				
Mathematics grade			.66	.66	.66			.54	.54	.57		.05	.97	1.02	1.00	.20*	.01	.51	.71	.69
Reading grade			.58	.58	.60			.52	.52	.57	.58*	.03	.22	.82	.81		.12	.57	.69	.69
Mathematics test score			.73	.73	.70			.71	.71	.71	.25*	.01	.45	.71	.69		.05	.98	1.03	1.00
Reading test score			.57	.57	.54			.60	.60	.66		.12	.52	.64	.61	.44*	.02	.34	.81	.78
Track level			.54	.54	.54			.74	.74	.75	−.13*	.00	.51	.39	.44	.04	−.02	.55	.56	.64
Absences			−.03	−.03	.00			−.03	−.03	−.03	−.09	.00	−.07	−.16	−.15	.00	−.02	−.03	−.05	−.04
Variance explained	.67*					.58*					.73*					.74*				

[a] 1 = direct effect; 2 = indirect effect; 3 = noncausal components; 4 = model-implied zero-order standardized slope; 5 = observed zero-order standardized slope (i.e., zero-order correlation).

* Significant at the .05 level.

may be better captured by the class mean for reading than by the mean for mathematics, even in the case of mathematics achievement and grading. On the one hand, the class is likely to be more homogeneous in reading scores than in mathematics scores. On the other hand, the teacher's expectations for the class may be formed more by the class's reading than by its mathematics composition.

DISCUSSION

The findings are complex. A summary and commentary can be organized, however, around the question, Do teachers assign grades on the basis of meritocratic or nonmeritocratic criteria? The discussion also needs to note the key differences between reading and mathematics and the limits on certainty in answering.

Meritocratic grading measures one or both of the two types of academic achievement: widely valued and classroom-specific. Widely valued achievement is measured by standardized test scores. Mathematics grades include a weak to moderate current test score component, but reading grades do not show any influence of current widely valued reading achievement. These results do not strongly support a meritocratic interpretation of grading.

A weakness of this study is the lack of a measure of classroom-specific achievement independent of grades assigned—for example, results on teacher-designed examinations. We are left with two ways to estimate the effects of classroom-specific achievement on grading, each of which has shortcomings. First, we looked at the effects of the previous year's grades and interpreted these effects as the result, in part, of continuity in classroom-specific achievement. We found such effects in both subjects. This approach has some merit but also some problems. On the one hand, what is classroom-specific about achievement if it continues across years? This type of achievement needs to be redefined as school- or district-specific achievement (but not valued widely enough to be measured on standardized tests). This redefinition would make previous grades a less likely determinant of a specific teacher's grading. On the other hand, an effect of the previous year's grade may indicate more than continuity in achievement. It may indicate stable student traits, such as willingness to complete assignments, that enhance actual achievement in all classrooms but not on standardized tests. Alternatively, it may indicate nonmeritocratic grading via reputational contamination or differential expectations and learning opportunities. Given these alternative interpretations, effects of the previous year's grade do not help determine whether grading is meritocratic or nonmeritocratic.

A second approach to assessing the impact of classroom-specific achievement on grading in the absence of an independent measure is to interpret residual variation in the grade as a result of this factor. Substantive interpretation of residuals has a history among very well-regarded social science analyses (e.g., Duncan, 1968; Jencks et al., 1972), but this does not make it any less risky. The tightest logic that defends a particular interpretation of a residual can be shredded by a good argument for an uncorrelated omitted variable. With hesitation, then, we conclude that the residual variation in grades, which ranges here from 33 to 27 percent, is due to the impact of classroom-specific achievement on grading. This impact is essentially equal in the two subjects, but it decreases somewhat from second to third grade. Since a residual variation of 30 percent corresponds to a standardized effect of .55, the meritocratic effect of classroom-specific achievement on grading may be quite strong.

We see that meritocratic effects are weak for widely valued achievement, for which we have a good measure, but strong for classroom-specific achievement, for which we do not. What can be said of nonmeritocratic effects on grading? First, the effects of race, sex, and track level are either weak and scattered or absent. Teachers do not regularly discriminate on the basis of demographic or class-assignment factors. One qualification to this blanket statement may be that race or sex could well affect grades received in the first grade. In this article, we have not analyzed these possible causal relations, because we lack the data we need, for first grade or earlier, to make the modelling of first-grade grades comparable to second- and third-grade grades. If the effect of race or sex on grades is felt in the first grade, it may be passed on to second- and third-grade grades indirectly. Indeed, we have argued that most social-class effects uncorrelated with race are subsumed in first-grade grades and test scores in just this way.

The strongest determinant of grading in this analysis is consistently the grade in the other subject. We have offered two possible interpretations: parallel achievement across subjects and student conformity across subjects to teacher preferences[5] for certain atti-

[5] Grades could reflect student conformity to attitudes and behaviors that are preferred throughout the school, not just by one teacher. To investigate this possibility, we used as a regressor the grade in the other subject given by the previous year's teacher instead of the grade in the other subject given in the same year. We found the effect absent or

tudes and behaviors either related or unrelated to learning. Student conformity refers to student characteristics that are not reflected in past grades or past or present test scores. These could be noncognitive characteristics related to personality or deportment, but confidence in this interpretation would be improved by the use of a measure whose manifest meaning is unambiguous—for example, grades for deportment.

The parallel achievement and student conformity interpretations seem altogether different: Only the first is consistent with the idea that grades are meritocratic, subject-specific evaluations of achievement; the second suggests that grades are nonmeritocratic assessments of personality characteristics (see Bowles and Gintis [1976:134–139] on personality assessments in high school grading). These seemingly contradictory interpretations, however, may suggest two aspects of the same process. The basic process involves the shaping of teacher expectations of the student on the basis of limited information, communication of these expectations to the student, and the student's reaction to these expectations. For example, consider how a student who loves competitive sports interacts with a teacher who so emphasizes academics as to become suspicious of the academic motivation of jocks. The teacher can communicate disapproval to the student in many ways, including grading. The student may become discouraged about the possibilities of academic success in that teacher's classroom and redouble his/her emphasis on sports, now truly deemphasizing academics. The teacher, in turn, may believe that his/her initial judgment is confirmed. Variations on this example play to the same conclusion. The interactive cycle begins simply with the student's poor class performance or with the teacher's discouragement of the student for reasons other than the student's motivation or commitment—for example, the student's style of dress or the teacher's experience with the student's sibling. In all cases, the cycle leads to both poor achievement and the award of poor grades in all subjects.

Seeing such an interactive process as an important possible source of correlated grades moves us past questions of blame: for example, Did the student deserve bad grades? Did the teacher give the nonconforming student a chance? We come to view student and teacher as partners in the social construction of student academic performance and teacher evaluation of that performance. This moves us away from attempts to determine whether grades are meritocratic assessments of student achievement or nonmeritocratic signals of teacher power to extract student compliance. Rather, interpretation of grading from the interactionist perspective (Blumer, 1969; Hewitt, 1979) emphasizes the indeterminacy of what students and teachers can know about one another's intentions and their consequent interpretation of one another's actions on the basis of limited, but generalized and hard to dislodge, past experience of the other. The imperviousness of expectations to contradictory evidence in large measure sets up a self-fulfilling prophecy (Darley and Fazio, 1980; Merton, 1968), by which the student who expects poor support from the teacher comes to fail and the teacher who expects poor performance from a student finds he or she can give bad grades regretfully but in good conscience.

What should we make, then, of the strong positive effect of the grade in one subject on the grade in the other? Certainly, one explanation is that the student had a good year or a bad year in all the subjects. Another explanation is that the teacher discriminated in grading between students who conformed and students who did not conform to preferred behavior patterns. However parsimonious these interpretations, the interactionist explanation, linking student and teacher in a self-justifying web of expectation and action, is a worthy alternative.

How strong, then, are the nonmeritocratic effects on grading? On the one hand, the effects of race, sex, and track level were weak. On the other hand, the grade in the other subject had a strong effect, which may be interpreted as meritocratic or nonmeritocratic. How is this incompatibility in the findings to be explained? First, the effect of the grade in the other subject may be due to parallel achievement across subjects, indicating meritocratic grading. Alternatively, according to the interactionist argument, one may rule out any overtly nonmeritocratic grading but accept the possibility that deviation from subject-specific meritocratic assessment takes place through subtle processes largely invisible to student and teacher.

Overall, then, the results are not definitive. They point, however, to enough evidence of nonmeritocratic inputs into grading to raise serious questions and suggest further steps in research on the meritocratic pretensions of elementary school grading.

---

much reduced when the grade in the other subject from the previous year was substituted. This indicates that the effect was peculiar to the teacher, not characteristic of the school's faculty. Of course, this additional finding is also consistent with our original interpretation that the effect was due to parallel achievement across subjects in the same year.

Appendix. Zero-Order Correlations and Descriptive Statistics for Variables Used in Analyses (N = 213)

Variable	2	3	4	5	6	11	12	13	18	19	20	Mean	SD
Ascriptive													
1. Race (1 = nonwhite, 2 = white)	−.02*	.25	.31	.25	.27	.29	.16	.21	.37	.37	.20	1.48	.50
2. Sex (1 = male, 2 = female)		.22	.18	.16	.11*	.16	.13*	.03*	.17	.13*	−.02*	1.54	.50
First grade													
3. Reading grade			.62	.76	.53	.45	.36	−.09*	.52	.46	.01*	10.10	2.74
4. Reading test score				.51	.70	.74	.58	−.06*	.67	.58	.01*	41.70	11.18
5. Mathematics grade					.47	.38	.26	−.03*	.48	.41	.90*	10.69	2.59
6. Mathematics test score						.39	.49	−.13*	.43	.37	−.02*	28.79	5.55
Second grade													
7. Reading grade	.17	.66	.67	.58	.52	.50	.29	−.06*	.62	.55	−.03*	9.77	2.61
8. Reading test score	.18	.61	.76	.52	.57	.64	.48	.01*	.88	.79	−.05*	53.81	13.90
9. Mathematics grade	.16	.54	.57	.58	.53	.47	.29	−.10*	.57	.54	.00*	10.70	2.45
10. Mathematics test score	.06*	.50	.59	.50	.52	.54	.41	−.04*	.69	.75	−.03*	39.42	9.20
11. Reading track level	.16	.45	.74	.38	.39		.77	.06*	.69	.61	−.02*	41.62	8.22
12. Mathematics track level	.13*	.36	.58	.26	.49			.04*	.52	.47	.00*	28.65	2.66
13. Absences	−.03*	−.09*	−.06*	−.03*	−.13*				.04*	.01*	.63	5.73	5.70
Third grade													
14. Reading grade	.19	.59	.60	.51	.52	.40	.37	−.02*	.56	.51	−.07*	9.64	2.74
15. Reading test score	.17	.58	.71	.48	.54	.55	.42	−.03*	.67	.68	.01*	39.92	13.89
16. Mathematics grade	.15	.57	.59	.51	.62	.41	.41	−.15	.49	.44	−.15	9.78	3.01
17. Mathematics test score	.16	.58	.68	.55	.58	.48	.29	−.06*	.68	.64	−.04*	40.86	8.87
18. Reading track level	.17	.52	.67	.48	.43	.69	.52	.04*		.90	.01*	53.62	12.12
19. Mathematics track level	.13*	.46	.58	.41	.37	.61	.47	.01*			.00*	39.07	7.21
20. Absences	−.02*	.01*	.01*	.09*	−.02*	−.02*	.00*	.63				6.29	6.39

NOTE: Correlations reported in Tables 1 and 2 are excluded.
* Not significant at the .05 level.

REFERENCES

Alexander, K. L., M. Cook, and E. L. McDill
1978 "Curriculum tracking and educational stratification: Some further evidence." American Sociological Review 43:47–66.

Asher, H. B.
1976 Causal Modeling. Beverly Hills, CA: Sage.

Bloom, B. S.
1976 Human Characteristics and School Learning. New York: McGraw-Hill.

Blumer, H.
1969 Symbolic Interactionism: Perspective and Method. Englewood Cliffs, NJ: Prentice-Hall.

Boocock, S. S.
1980 Sociology of Education: An Introduction. 2nd ed. Boston: Houghton Mifflin.

Bowles, S. and H. Gintis
1976 Schooling in Capitalist America: Educational Reform and the Contradictions of Economic Life. New York: Basic Books.

Brophy, J. E. and T. L. Good
1974 Teacher-Student Relationships: Causes and Consequences. New York: Holt, Rinehart and Winston.

Clifton, R.
1981 "Ethnicity, teachers' expectations, and the academic achievement process in Canada." Sociology of Education 54:291–301.

Cooper, H. M. and T. L. Good
1983 Pygmalion Grows Up: Studies in the Expectation Communication Process. New York: Longman.

Darley, J. M. and R. H. Fazio
1980 "Expectancy confirmation processes arising in social interaction sequences." American Psychologist 35:867–81.

Davidson, H. H. and G. Lang
1960 "Children's perceptions of their teachers' feelings toward them related to self-perception, school achievement and behavior." Journal of Experimental Education 29:107–18.

DiMaggio, P.
1982 "Cultural capital and school success: The impact of status culture participation on the grades of U.S. high school students." American Sociological Review 47:189–201.

Doyle, W., G. Hancock, and E. Kifer
1972 "Teachers' perceptions: Do they make a difference?" Journal of the Association for the Study of Perception 7:21–30.

Dreeben, R.
1968 On What is Learned in School. Reading, MA: Addison-Wesley.

Duncan, O. D.
1968 "Inheritance of poverty or inheritance of race." Pp. 85–110 in D. P. Moynihan (ed.), On Understanding Poverty: Perspectives from the Social Sciences. New York: Basic Books.

Evans, F. B.
1976 "What research says about grading." Pp. 30–50 in S. B. Simon and J. A. Bellanca (eds.), Degrading the Grading Myths: Primer of Alternatives to Grades and Marks. Washington, D.C.: Association for Supervision and Curriculum Development.

Finn, J.
1972 "Expectations and the educational environment." Review of Educational Research 42:387–410.

Fox, J.
1980 "Effect analysis in structural equation models: Extensions and simplified methods of computation." Sociological Methods and Research 9:3–28.

Gravenburg, O. and G. Collins
1976 "Grades: Just a measure of conformity." Humboldt Journal of Social Relations 3:58–62.

Hanushek, E. A.
1977 "A reader's guide to educational production functions." Paper presented at the National Institute of Education Conference on School Organization and Effects, San Diego.

Harvey, D. G. and G. T. Slatin
1975 "The relationship between child's SES and teacher expectations: A test of the middle-class bias hypothesis." Social Forces 54:140–59.

Heise, D. R.
1975 Causal Analysis. New York: Wiley.

Hewitt, J. P.
1979 Self and Society: A Symbolic Interactionist Social Psychology. Boston: Allyn and Bacon.

Heyns, B.
1974 "Social selection and stratification within schools." American Journal of Sociology 79:1434–51.

Hunt, J. M.
1961 Intelligence and Experience. New York: Ronald Press.

Jackson, A. B.
1975 "The research evidence on the effects of grade retention." Review of Educational Research 45:613–35.

Jencks, C.
1980 "Heredity, environment, and public policy reconsidered." American Sociological Review 45:723–36.

Jencks, C., S. Bartlett, M. Corcoran, J. Crouse, D. Eaglesfield, G. Jackson, K. McClelland, P. Mueser, M. Olneck, J. Schwartz, S. Ward, and J. Williams
1979 Who Gets Ahead? The Determinants of Economic Success in America. New York: Basic Books.

Jencks, C., M. Smith, H. Acland, M. J. Bane, D. Cohen, H. Gintis, B. Heyns, and S. Michelson
1972 Inequality: A Reassessment of the Effect of Family and Schooling in America. New York: Basic Books.

Jensen, A. R.
1973 Educability and Group Differences. New York: Harper and Row.

Johnston, J.
1972 Econometric Methods. 2nd ed. New York: McGraw-Hill.

Kirschenbaum, H., R. Napier, and S. B. Simon
1971 Wad-ja-get? The Grading Game in American Education. New York: Hart.

Kohl, H.
1967 36 Children. New York: New American Library.

Leiter, J.
1983 "Classroom composition and achievement gains." Sociology of Education 56:126–32.

Maccoby, E. and C. N. Jacklin
1974 The Psychology of Sex Differences. Stanford, CA: Stanford University Press.

Maehr, M. L.
1976 "Continuing motivation: An analysis of a seldom considered educational outcome." Review of Educational Research 46:443–62.

Marwit, S. J. and G. Neumann
1974 "Black and white children's comprehension of standard and nonstandard English passages." Journal of Educational Psychology 66:329–32.

Merton, R. K.
1968 Social Theory and Social Structure. Enlarged ed. New York: Free Press.

O'Brien, T. C.
1978 "Diagnostic mathematics inventory." Pp. 401–5 in O. K. Buros (ed.), The Eighth Mental Measurements Yearbook. Vol. 1. Highland Park, NJ: Gryphon.

Pedhazur, E. J.
1982 Multiple Regression in Behavioral Research: Explanation and Prediction. 2nd ed. New York: Holt, Rinehart and Winston.

Pedulla, J. J., P. W. Airasian, and G. F. Madaus
1980 "Do teacher ratings and standardized test results of students yield the same information." American Educational Research Journal 17:303–7.

Rist, R. C.
1970 "Student social class and teacher expectations: The self-fulfilling prophecy in ghetto education." Harvard Educational Review 40:411–51.

Rosenbaum, J. E.
1978 "The structure of opportunity in school." Social Forces 57:236–56.

Salili, F., M. L. Maehr, R. L. Sorensen, and L. J. Tyans, Jr.
1976 "A further consideration of the effects of evaluation on motivation." American Educational Research Journal 13:85–102.

Schlechty, P. C.
1976 Teaching and Social Behavior: Toward an Organizational Theory of Instruction. Boston: Allyn and Bacon.

Smith, K.
1978 "California achievement test: Reading, 1970 edition." Pp. 1160–63 in O. K. Buros (ed.), The Eighth Mental Measurements Yearbook. Vol. 2. Highland Park, NJ: Gryphon.

Sørensen, A. B.
1970 "Organizational differentiation of students and educational opportunity." Sociology of Education 43:355–76.

Stallings, J.
1980 "Allocated academic learning time revisited, or beyond time on task." Educational Researcher 9:11–16.

Terwilliger, J. S.
1966 "Self-reported marking practices and policies in public secondary schools." Bulletin of the National Association of Secondary School Principals 50:5–37.

U.S. Bureau of the Census
1980 Census of Population and Housing, 1980. Summary Tape File 3A. Machine-readable data file. Washington, D.C.: U.S. Bureau of the Census (producer).

Veldman, D. J. and J. E. Brophy
1974 "Measuring teacher effects on pupil achievement." Journal of Educational Psychology 66:319–24.

Waller, W.
1932 The Sociology of Teaching. New York: Wiley.

Wiley, D. E.
1976 "Another hour, another day: Quantity of schooling, a potent path for policy." Pp. 225–65 in W. H. Sewell, R. M. Hauser, and D. L. Featherman (eds.), Schooling and Achievement in American Society. New York: Academic Press.

Williams, T.
1976 "Teacher prophecies and the inheritance of inequality." Sociology of Education 49:223–36.

THE REVEALED INFLUENCE OF CLASS, RACE, AND ETHNICITY ON LOCAL PUBLIC-SCHOOL EXPENDITURES

BYRON W. BROWN
Michigan State University

DANIEL H. SAKS
Vanderbilt University

Sociology of Education 1985, Vol. 58 (July):181–190

Over the past decades, there has been considerable interest in how the ethnic, racial, and class composition of a community affects its behavior. There have been numerous discussions of how the ethnic background of immigrants interacted with conditions they faced in urban or rural America to produce group behavior and community choices that contributed to the relative performance of those groups (e.g., see Sowell, 1981; Glazer and Moynihan, 1963; Glazer, 1983; Lieberson, 1980). One choice has received particular emphasis: a group's commitment to increased education for its own members and others. Most of this scholarly work has relied on historical and survey methods to analyze differences in various groups' commitments to educational improvement. In this article, we use a new technique and Michigan school-district data from 1970 to identify how the ethnic, racial, and class composition of heterogeneous communities systematically affects levels of local public educational expenditures.

The literature on school spending contains three types of hypotheses that need to be distinguished. The first hypothesis is that the demand for school spending varies with income and that the relationship is probably not monotonic but instead U-shaped—i.e., the rich and the poor favor larger expenditures. While that sounds straightforward, it is in fact one of the most confusing areas of debate. One favored explanation is that the poor want large school budgets because they do not pay very much of the cost and the rich want large budgets because they are "public-regarding" persons who are glad to pay for the betterment of the community (Wilson and Banfield, 1964). This explanation, however, illustrates a possible confusion between a price effect and an income effect. According to this logic, if the poor pay a smaller share of a publicly provided good, they will demand more because they face a lower price. But we also expect that if prices are held constant while income is varied, expenditures on any commodity will begin at some subsistence or threshold level, rise as income increases, and eventually level off as demand for the commodity is sated.[1] Therefore, the rich may demand more despite having to pay a higher share of the cost (or price). It is also possible that the very poor, seeing education as a path to a better life for their children, are willing to pay a disproportionate share of their income for schooling (again, holding price constant).

If this hypothesis about spending is correct, a typical family's demand function for schooling will have a nonmonotonic relation to income. As Figure 1 shows, demand as a function of family income (Y_f) (other things, including price, held constant) falls to point A then rises to a peak at B. If public-regardingness is extremely important, it will push the point where that curve reaches a maximum out to extremely high income levels.

A second set of hypotheses concerns the effects of race and ethnicity on public expenditures. In the early versions of their theory, Wilson and Banfield (1964) suggested that Northern and Southern Europeans brought quite different values with them to America and that these imported tastes determined the political choices such groups made. In later versions (Wilson and Banfield, 1971) they retreated from identifying a particular ethos with a particular country of origin. But they still maintained that members of an ethnic or racial group fit predominantly into one of two opposing world views about the role of government: a public-regarding, or unitary, ethos and a private-regarding, or individualistic, ethos. These views could manifest themselves either directly in attitudinal survey data or indirectly through ethnic variations in voting patterns or (with long and variable lags) through variations in political institutions. The local school system is an especially good place

The authors contributed equally to this article. They wish to thank several anonymous referees for *Sociology of Education* for helpful comments on an earlier draft. Address all correspondence to Professor Daniel H. Saks, Peabody College, Vanderbilt University, Nashville, TN 37203.

[1] There have been many studies of these relationships, called Engel curves. For a discussion, see Ramsey (1974).

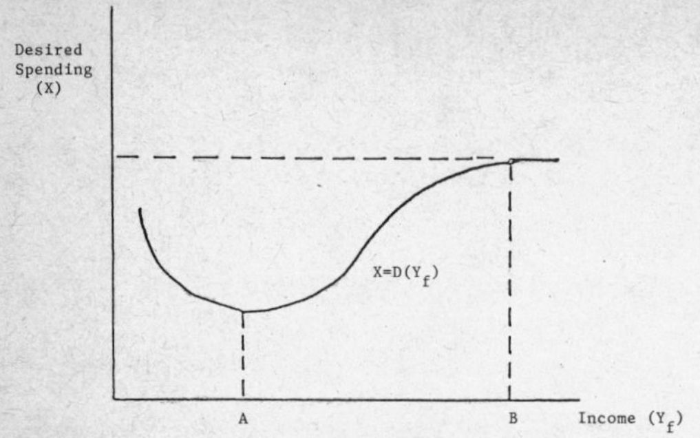

Figure 1. Demand for spending may be a non-monotonic function of income.

to examine these issues. As Hamilton and Cohen (1974:206) have suggested, "The American public school system is the greatest monument to the Unitary Ethos, and school district government is the epitome of its structural prescriptions." Those who subscribe to that ethos, therefore, will want to spend more on an activity such as education.

One need not attach such grand labels to the differing attitudes and behaviors of groups. Sowell (1981) takes a much narrower and more historically grounded approach to group differences in decision making. He relates group attitudes to past and present conditions to which groups adapted, and he emphasizes the effect of costly information on decision making. He also stresses that there can be considerable variation within groups because of members' different experiences. This puts the question of the differing educational choices of groups into an empirical framework. Groups may or may not differ *on average*. Detailed historical understanding is required to predict such differences. The first step is to observe whether groups, on average, have different demand curves. This article is directed toward an empirical test of such differences.

The final set of hypotheses we will discuss concerns the assimilation of an ethos. For example, in Wilson and Banfield's (1971) terms, do "individualistic" Southern and Eastern European ethnics eventually mimic the dominant "unitary" Northern European WASPs? Thus, we might test the hypothesis that Northern European ethnics want higher school expenditures than Southern/Eastern European ethnics (other things being equal) and that the children of the latter are more like their Northern European counterparts. More generally, the question is whether those identified as ethnic minorities tend to have different educational demands than those who are at least third-generation Americans. At issue, then, is the pace of assimilation in such matters.[2]

We turn now to a more detailed discussion of the theory that will lead to estimation of a model to test these various hypotheses.

FAMILY DEMANDS FOR SCHOOL EXPENDITURES

Understanding the family's demand for school expenditures is an essential building block in any empirical model of how school-district expenditure levels are set. Our strategy is to model a family's demand for school expenditures and then ask how that model is affected by systematic differences in tastes.

We expect the demand for a commodity marketed in the *private* sector to be a function of that commodity's price, the prices of all other commodities, and the consumer's income and tastes. *Publicly* provided goods, however, are peculiar, because the amount actually consumed by any family is not necessarily equal to either the amount demanded or the taxes paid per family. In this section we present a model of a family's demand for schooling, and in the next section, we show how to deduce the family's demand when observed consumption is not necessarily equal to the amount demanded.

We can express a family's demand for schooling as a constrained utility maximization problem. Thus,

$$X = D(Y_f, SEV, AID, Z, T),$$

where X is the demand for local school expenditures per family;[3] SEV is the state-equalized valuation (tax base) per family in the community; AID is revenues or grants per family given by the state to the local school district; Y_f is the family's normal or permanent income;[4] Z is a vector of variables measuring school-district characteristics, such as how schooling services are distributed across members of the community; and T is a vector of taste variables, which might vary across race and ethnic groups. Since SEV, AID, and other community characteristics are fixed at the time a family makes its judgment about desired expenditures, in practice, X is the only decision variable.[5]

[2] The question of assimilation is particularly complicated for American blacks not only because of racial prejudice and historical and institutional prevention of assimilation but also because so many current northern urban blacks are first- or second-generation migrants from the rural South.

[3] Schooling is measured in dollar units rather than in quantity units because no natural units of measurement seem to suggest themselves.

[4] We regard school taxes as if they were a proportion of permanent (expected) income, even though in practice the tax is levied on property. Given the unresolved dispute over the regressive versus progressive nature of the property tax (Aaron, 1975), it is not an unrealistic assumption.

[5] Of course, families either influence what a com-

Let us examine the arguments of the demand function in more detail. First, if schooling is like other commodities,[6] the relation between desired expenditures per family (X) and permanent family income (Y_f) is likely to be that shown in Figure 1. Notice that if most people are in the income range to the left of point B, the relationship will be approximately U-shaped. The price of schooling to a family is Y_f/SEV,[7] since a dollar of a family's tax contribution will be matched by more resources from others in the community the larger the average wealth (tax base) of the community.

Second, the distribution of schooling services has two important dimensions: (1) the division between those who use the public schools and those who (either for lack of children or through choice of nonpublic schools for their children) do not use the public schools and (2) the distribution of schooling services or quality among those children in the schools. The question of how the distribution of benefits affects demand is made more complex by the related question of whether families derive utility from consumption by other families. For example, families without children may still support expensive public schools because they want to help their neighbors' children or because they think that good schools will pay off in added capital values for their houses if and when they sell them (because housing sales are tied to public schooling services in the United States). In general, however, we expect families without school children to demand lower school budgets than families who are currently receiving schooling services. Also, if local schools spend more (or fewer) resources on the better students at the expense of (in aid of) the lower-achieving students, demands for school expenditures may be affected.

munity provides or move into communities that have the appropriate mix of community characteristics. Since this is not an article about the process of political decision making but rather about outcomes and tastes, we can ignore the relative roles of exit and voice in establishing the conjunction of those two variables. We assume that whatever the process, it occurs over a short period of time, so that most members of a community are satisfied (given their constraints) with the outcomes. For two interesting statistical approaches to the process problem, see Shlay and Rossi (1981) and Smith (1979).

[6] The per-family tax base in the community (SEV) is fixed or constant for the family's decision.

[7] In our data set, intergovernmental grants (AID) are all lump-sum payments that are not affected by school-district behavior. Matching grants, if available, are additional price variables. Also, SEV includes all the nonresidential wealth in the community that goes into the property tax base and reduces the cost to community residents of an additional educational expenditure.

Finally, it is through the taste component of demand, T, that we hope to capture the effects of ethnicity. Ethnic groups may vary in their preferences (goals). There are two relevant distinctions to be considered. First, different ethnic groups facing the same prices, income, and tax system may, on average, differ in their valuations of some personally consumed good or service. Second, ethnic groups may differ in the utility they derive from knowing that others are receiving a particular good or service. For a privately provided good, we could perhaps distinguish the two effects by observing how much potential income individuals of different ethnic groups are on average willing to forfeit so that others may have a particular commodity or service. But when a good or service is, for technological or political reasons, provided by a community and is in principle available to all members of a community, expenditures are no longer an indication of differences in this respect, since individuals must spend more to get more for either themselves or others.[8] The only way one could ever measure differences in the two kinds of preference for true public goods is through some kind of extremely sophisticated attitudinal survey that is beyond the current state of that art. So, to the extent that Wilson and Banfield's (1971) hypotheses concern the distinction between own and neighbor's consumption, they cannot be tested by either ecological techniques, voting studies, or even survey methods. Basically, we cannot know whether members of an ethnic group desire a particular public good or service for themselves or others or both. That kind of distinction is best observed in private markets. What we can do here is determine whether different ethnic groups, faced with the same opportunities, tend to demand different amounts of publicly provided goods (i.e., school expenditures).

Why might ethnic groups faced with the same opportunities differ in their desires for

[8] The problem is intensified when public goods are unequally provided. For example, improving sidewalks "confers trivial benefits on those voters who are not likely to walk on them" (Wilson and Banfield, 1964:876). Where there is a highly unequal distribution of the publicly provided good, it may be possible to test for differences in tastes by looking at the voting patterns and market behavior of the affected and unaffected groups. However, there could be subtle indirect interdependencies between the two groups due to either logrolling (i.e., their opportunity sets are such that one group cannot get sidewalks, for example, without other groups getting sidewalks) or explicit utility (i.e., one many benefit from living in a community in which more residents have sidewalks). In any case, we consider the distribution of school services in the work reported below.

school expenditures? One reason is variation in the sets of values among the countries of origin. Presumably, the values of the old country were functional in that society, and because of habit-persistence, these values adjust slowly to American norms. Thus, one expects differences among ethnic groups in their desires for local school expenditures. Wilson and Banfield (1963) focus on the taxonomy of this variation (i.e., on Protestant-Catholic, Northern European-Southern European differences) rather than on its causes, but they conclude that this variation among ethnic groups can be expected to change (perhaps very slowly) after migration.

An alternative reason for ethnic differences in preferences concerns immigrants' desires for vertical mobility and the supposedly facilitating role of good schooling in achieving such an objective. In this case, one would not expect much difference among ethnic groups in their desires to spend money on local schooling, but one would expect immigrant groups in general to favor higher levels of school spending. If we can devise a statistical method for holding opportunities constant across ethnic groups, then perhaps we can determine which of the ethnic preference patterns is most consistent with the data on school expenditures. In the next section, we outline a technique for estimating family demands for schooling from data on community decisions.

FAMILY DEMANDS FOR SCHOOLING AND COMMUNITY DECISIONS

It is difficult to estimate the family demand curves for commodities that are provided only by communities. We could ask people how they feel about large school budgets, but their answers would not necessarily reflect their responses to a real situation. We can observe their voting behavior, but here we are faced with the problem of relating votes in specific elections to the general problem of the shape of the demand curve. We choose to tackle the problem through what might be called a revealed influence model of community political decisions. Our assumption is that in a polity in which there is a simple majority vote rule, no policy can in the long run deviate very far from that which would command a majority vote. We thus invoke a median voter rule[9] so that we can relate the school expenditure levels in communities to the families in such communities. The special trick in this case is to use such a rule when family demands for the particular spending level are U-shaped with respect to income. We believe we have a simple method for applying median voter theorems to such empirical situations.

Consider a community with an income distribution like the one shown in the lower panel of Figure 2. In such a community, we can conceive the political process to be such that the desired spending of a family with the median income is equal to the actual spending in the community. The demand curve is monotonic in the income range of families in that community, and in such situations, the median voter is the median-income family, because half the families want to spend more and half want to spend less (Black, 1948; Brown and Saks, 1983). If all the voters in a community lay along a monotonic portion of the demand curve, then we could assume that observations on communities were also observations on families, and we could then see how desired family spending varied with family income by observing how chosen community spending varied with community median income (prices and all other relevant variables, of course, held constant).

Now consider the U-shaped demand curve in Figure 3. Most communities will not meet the monotonicity condition because of the presence of voters in both the falling and rising parts of the curve. Thus, we could not regard the community's decision as the decision of the

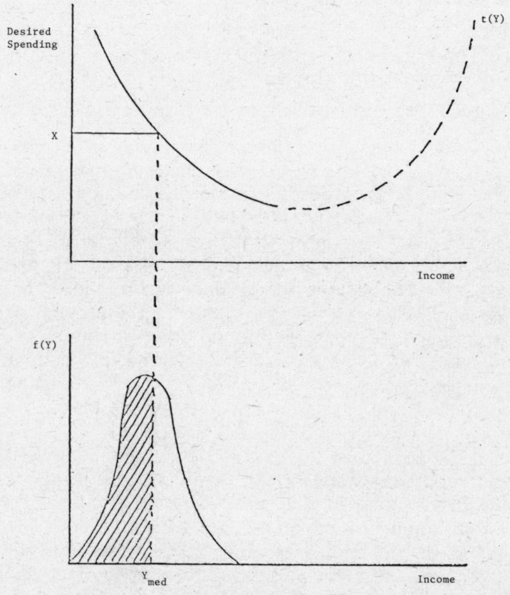

Figure 2. When the demand curve is monotonic, the individual demand can be found from community data.

[9] For further references in the economics literature on the applications of median voter rules, see Brown and Saks (1983).

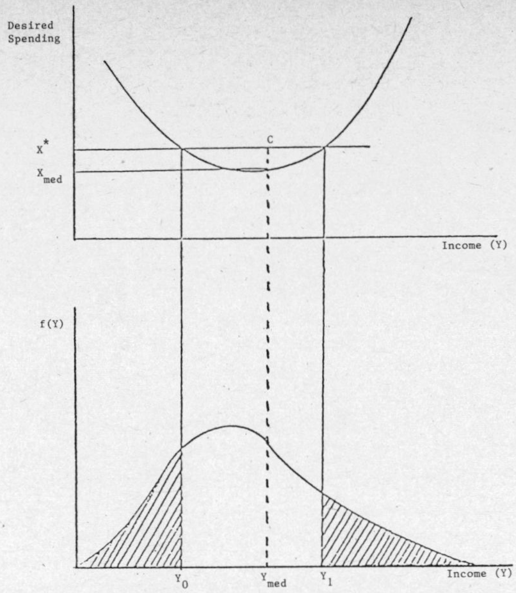

Figure 3. When the demand curve is U-shaped, the equilibrium spending (X^*) is favored by a coalition of voters from different parts of the income distribution.

median-income family. Figure 3 shows why. In the community shown, richer and poorer voters form an implicit coalition against the middle. Thus, the median-income family's desired spending (call it X_{med}) lies below the community's desired spending (X^*).[10] Knowledge about the size of the difference between actual and desired spending for the median income family is necessary if we are to use information on the community's income distribution to sort out the true relation between X and Y_f. It turns out that the difference is a function of two things: (1) the variance of the community's income distribution (the wider the tails, the larger the opportunity for coalitions from opposite ends of the income distribution) and (2) the location of the income distribution along the demand curve (e.g., if the distribution lies far to the right or left, it will lie within a monotonic portion of the curve, as in Figure 3, and there will be no difference between the actual and desired X of the median-income family).

We can express the difference between the median-income family's actual consumption and desired spending (hereafter called the *bias*) as follows:

$$\text{bias} = g(G, Y_{\text{med}}), \tag{1}$$

where G is the Gini coefficient (our measure of the variance of income) and Y_{med} is median income in the community (our measure of the location of the income distribution). In our empirical work, we tried a variety of measures for the spread of the income distribution, including the coefficient of variation and the variance of the logarithm of income, but we found no significant difference in the results. Our model suggests that the bias will be nonnegative (nonpositive) if the demand curve is U-shaped (inverted U-shaped) in income. The bias should approach zero as G, the spread of the income distribution, goes to zero and should become smaller the further the community's income distribution lies from the minimum (maximum) of the demand curve.

We can put all this together to derive an estimation equation for the relation between spending per family (X) and income, based on school-district data. Our dependent variable is local revenues per family for support of the schools. A quadratic equation in Y_{med} will permit estimation of a U-shaped function:

$$X = A + BY_{\text{med}} + CY^2_{\text{med}}. \tag{2}$$

For the bias, the following functional form approximates our desired relation:

$$\text{bias} = [\beta - \alpha(Y_{\text{med}} - \delta)^2]G, \tag{3}$$

where the parameters α, β, and δ are to be estimated. By including terms for this bias in our estimating equation, we can determine the relation between X and Y_{med} even when such a relationship is U-shaped.[11] Had we neglected such terms, we would have implicitly imposed monotonicity on such a relation. Thus, the full relation between local school revenue (X) and income, observed from data on the community income distribution, is

$$X = A + BY_{\text{med}} + CY^2_{\text{med}} + [\beta - \alpha(Y_{\text{med}} - \delta)^2]G. \tag{4}$$

Of course, to estimate such an equation from observed data, it must be augmented by a stochastic term and by variables for prices, the

[10] When the relation between X and Y_f is an inverted U, X_{med} lies above X^*, and the community choice underestimates the family demand at that income.

[11] We experimented with a wide variety of functional forms for our relation, including higher- and lower-order polynomials, cross-product terms, and transcendental functions, but none of these provided a significantly better fit for the data. It was important for our purposes not to force a nonlinearity if a linear relationship would do as well. Indeed, the whole problem of estimating the bias would not exist if the demand function was monotonic. The functional form for the bias is not the only one or even necessarily the best we could have tried, but it has the advantage of allowing us to test, rather than force, hypotheses about the size, direction, and significance of the bias.

distribution of schooling benefits, and tastes, since these and other unobserved variables change across observations. In particular, we want to see how the relation between spending (X) and income (Y_{med}) shifts when a community has more or fewer of particular ethnic or racial groups.[12] This will allow us statistically to sort out the hypotheses enumerated at the beginning of this article.

DATA

Our dependent variable is local revenue per family and is intended to approximate X in the model. Thus, the analysis focuses on the residents' actual demands, as opposed to total school revenues or expenditures, which would include measures of state aid. State aid is treated here as an independent variable.

The explanatory variables fall into four groups: (1) measures of the racial and ethnic composition of the population; (2) measures of the income distribution and level of wealth; (3) factors related to the distribution of educational benefits; and (4) other relevant community characteristics.

The data are for 500 Michigan school districts and were obtained from two sources: the 1970 Census Fourth Count Population School District Tapes, prepared by the National Center for Education Statistics (n.d.), and the Michigan Educational Assessment Program, 1970–71, reported by the Michigan Department of Education (1971). Table 1 gives a summary of the variable names, units of measurement, and their means and standard deviations.

The measure of racial composition is the proportion of white students, reported by the Michigan Department of Education. Two measures of ethnic composition are used: (1) the proportion of the school district's population that is of Northern European stock and (2) the proportion that is of Southern/Eastern European stock (defined by the Census Bureau as including both native and foreign-born individuals).[13] In addition to these two broad aggregates, we include the proportions of the population from the four largest ethnic groups in Michigan: British, German, Polish, and Italian. To test the assimilation hypothesis, we also include the proportions of these groups who were born abroad.

Our measure of median income and the Gini coefficient were derived from census data on each school district.[14] The Gini coefficient and an index of skewness in the income distribution were computed using a method suggested by Kakwani and Poddar (1976).[15] A detailed discussion of the derivation appears in Brown and Saks (1983). Other income and wealth data included in the analysis are the state-equalized valuation of property per family (*SEV*) and the state aid per family (*AID*).

Distributional factors that might affect voters' demands for school expenditures include the fraction of families with children, the average number of children per family in families with children, and the fraction of students in private schools. Also included are the mean and standard deviation of student test scores, which measure the intraschool distribution of benefits. (See Brown and Saks [1983] for an explanation of these variables and a rationale for including them.)

We have also included a variable to measure the relative cost of schooling in a district. Teachers' salaries, though commonly used as a measure of these costs, are not satisfactory, because teacher qualifications (i.e., years of experience, master's degree) vary across districts. We therefore used salaries adjusted for these differences in qualifications.[16] Salaries may also vary across districts because teachers may insist on greater compensation for working with the children of certain ethnic groups. Without an appropriate teacher-cost measure, we would conclude that those groups have

[12] In our specification, the entire demand function makes a parallel shift up or down, on average, for a particular group. One can certainly imagine more complex adjustments that depend, for example, on income or price and make the function rotate. We did not feel that our data and method could identify such subtle specifications; therefore, we focus on the simple shift in the demand curve.

[13] Northern European here includes British, Irish, Norwegian, Swedish, Danish, Dutch, Swiss, French, and German. Southern/Eastern European includes Polish, Czechoslovakian, Austrian, Hungarian, Yugoslavian, Russian, Lithuanian, Rumanian, Greek, and Italian.

[14] Because of data limitations, we include the incomes of renters as well as owners in the calculation of the income distribution. This is tantamount to an assumption that property taxes are ultimately borne by the renters who are eligible to vote.

[15] See Brown and Saks (1983) for a discussion of why skewness is important in isolating the bias discussed above and in identifying the price effects of changes in community income. The skewness index takes a value of 1 if the distribution is symmetric, less (greater) than 1 if it is skewed to the right (left).

[16] This was done by regressing the natural logarithm of observed average teacher salaries on average years experience and proportion of teachers with master's degrees and then by computing the residuals in the equation for each school district. The resulting difference, the residual average teacher salary, is our measure of the cost difference between districts for similar-quality teachers. See Brown and Saks (1983) for further explanation.

Table 1. Weighted Means and Standard Deviations of School-District Variables

Variable		Mean	Standard Deviation
Local revenue per family ($1,000)		.405	.160
Median family income ($10,000)		1.08	.249
State aid per family ($1,000)		.346	.121
State equalized valuation per family ($1,000)		15.6	6.93
Proportion of white students		.926	.150
Proportion of population from Northern European stock[a]		.057	.026
Proportion of population from Southern/Eastern European stock[b]		.058	.059
Proportion of population from British stock		.015	.009
Proportion of population from German stock		.021	.011
Proportion of population from Polish stock		.017	.025
Proportion of population from Italian stock		.010	.015
Mean achievement score (fourth graders)		50.08	2.65
Standard deviation of achievement scores		8.42	.714
Number of families in district (10,000)		15.0	55.8
Fraction of families with children		.610	.0608
Average children per family in families with children		1.79	.159
Fraction of students in private schools		.0948	.0776
Teacher cost measure		.0	.0852
Gini coefficient		.322	.0338
Index of income distribution's skewness (α/β)		.903	.0403
Sample information			
Number of metropolitan core districts:	15		
Number of city districts:	23		
Number of town districts:	103		
Number of urban fringe districts:	114		
Number of rural districts:	245		

NOTE: Estimates are weighted in proportion to the square root of the number of families in the school district.

[a] Includes British, Irish, Norwegian, Danish, Dutch, Swiss, French, and German.

[b] Includes Polish, Czechoslovakian, Austrian, Hungarian, Yogoslavian, Russian, Lithuanian, Greek, and Italian.

different demand curves when in fact they face different prices.

Finally, we include several variables to control for the size and urbanization of our districts, since these characteristics should also have important effects on demand for schooling. In addition to the number of families in each district, we incorporate a set of dichotomous variables representing five community types: (1) metropolitan core—a city with a population of 50,000 or more (1970); (2) city—a community with a population of 10,000 to 50,000; (3) town—a community with a population of 2,500 to 10,000; (4) rural community—a community with a population of less than 2,500; and (5) suburb—a community of any size whose economic focal point is a metropolitan core or city. Each community-type variable was coded 1 for a district of corresponding type, 0 otherwise. In the regressions reported below, the variable for rural communities was the omitted base.

EMPIRICAL RESULTS

We estimated the relationship between local revenue per family and our independent variables using weighted[17] ordinary-least-squares regression. The results are presented in Table 2. As the table shows, the relationship between income and desired spending on schools is not monotonic. Figure 4 shows the demand curve when the Gini coefficient is equal to zero and when all variables except income are at their weighted means. Therefore, if we have specified the functional forms correctly, this represents the true individual family demand curve. The curve has been plotted over the range of observed median incomes: approximately $4,000 to $24,000. The demand curve is U-shaped and reaches a minimum at about $8,200. Piele and Hall (1973) cite survey studies in the political science literature that show a U-shaped curve. Vanecko and Kroenfeld (1977) find a similar result.

The coefficients for race and the ethnic-background variables in Table 3 show a uniformly positive relationship between community spending and large black and foreign-stock

[17] Because we used grouped data from school districts, we weighted by the square root of the number of families in the district to eliminate heteroskedasticity in the error term.

Table 2. Weighted Regression Estimates of Local Revenue per Family (Standard Errors in Parentheses)

Variable	Regression Coefficient
Intercept	.396
Median family income	−1.07
	(.666)
(Median family income)^2	.649**
	(.288)
Gini coefficient	−1.604
	(1.098)
Gini × median family income	3.407*
	(1.976)
Gini × (median family income)^2	−1.822**
	(.865)
State aid per family	.0738*
	(.0421)
State equalized value	.0178**
per family	(.00053)
Proportion of white students	−.0542
	(.0370)
Proportion of population from	.258*
Northern European stock[a]	(.141)
Proportion of population from	.241**
Southern/Eastern European stock[b]	(.063)
Mean achievement score	.0060**
	(.0020)
Standard deviation of	.0137**
achievement score	(.0054)
Fraction of families with	.0825
school-age children	(.0930)
Fraction of students in	−.2465**
private schools	(.0533)
School-age children per family in	−.335
families with children	(.217)
(School-age children per family	.0790
in families with children)^2	(.0584)
Teacher cost measure	−.0494
	(.0375)
Total number of families	−.000234**
	(.000072)
Index of income distribution's	.0256
skewness (α/β)	(.0683)
Dummy variables	
Metropolitan core	.111**
	(.017)
City	.0313**
	(.0134)
Town	−.00267
	(.00895)
Urban fringe	.0243**
	(.0113)
R^2	.85

NOTE: Estimates are weighted in proportion to the square root of the number of families in the school district.

[a] Includes British, Irish, Norwegian, Swedish, Danish, Dutch, Swiss, French, and German.

[b] Includes Polish, Czechoslovakian, Austrian, Hungarian, Yugoslavian, Russian, Lithuanian, Greek, and Italian.

* Significant at the .10 level.
** Significant at the .05 level.

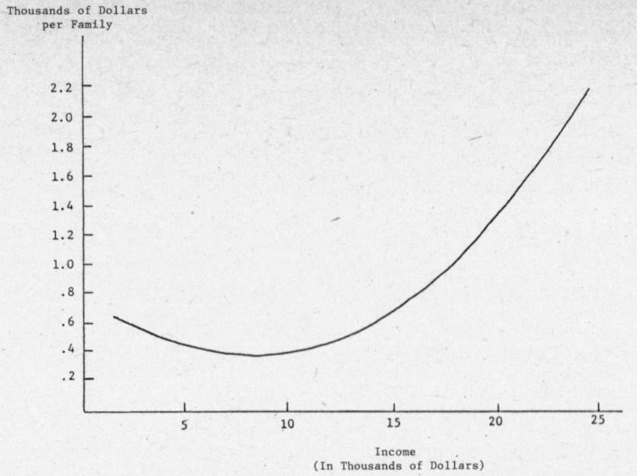

Figure 4. Estimated Demand for Local Public Education as a Function of Income when the Gini Coefficient is Set to Zero.

populations. This relationship holds even after the effects of variations in income are held constant. We have separated the correlational effects of being black or of foreign stock from the effect of being poor because an effect independent of income exists. An all-black school district spends about $54 (13 percent) more per family than a similar all-white district. That a larger black population is associated with more spending on education is consistent with other studies (cf. Piele and Hall, 1973; also see Lieberson, 1980:364).

Both Northern and Southern/Eastern European ethnic groups have significant and large positive relationships to school spending. The observed relationship for Southern/Eastern Europeans is contrary to Wilson and Banfield's (1971) hypothesis that those groups are more private-regarding and therefore favor lower

Table 3. Regression Coefficients for Race and Ethnicity Variables (Standard Errors in Parentheses)

Variable	Regression Coefficient
Proportion of white students	−.061
	(.037)***
Proportion of population from	.642
British stock	(.428)**
Proportion of population from	−.398
German stock	(.289)*
Proportion of population from	.097
Polish stock	(.145)
Proportion of population from	.391
Italian stock	(.265)**

NOTE: Other included independent variables are the same as in Table 2.

* Significant at the .20 level.
** Significant at the .15 level.
*** Significant at the .10 level.

spending. More interesting, perhaps, is the observation that the regression coefficients for the two groups are very nearly identical, suggesting that simply being of foreign stock is more important than being from a particular region.

If immigrants come to the U.S. with a particular public-spending ethos that differs from the ethos of the native population, we might expect the foreign ethos to decay with succeeding generations. Because the Census Bureau's classification distinguishes between native-born and foreign-born persons of foreign stock, a rough test of this "rate of decay" is possible. We reestimated the equation in Table 2, adding as variables the proportions of the Northern and Southern/Eastern European groups that were foreign-*born*. The coefficients for the added variables were small (−.0005 and −.012) and insignificant ($t = -.009$ and −.29), and the coefficients for the foreign-stock variables did not change appreciably, becoming .261 and .245 for the Northern and Southern/Eastern European groups, respectively. Thus, the hypothesis that the effects of being of foreign stock diminish over just one generation is not supported by the data, at least as far as the broad aggregates are concerned.[18]

Our price variable, state-equalized value per family (*SEV*), has effects consistent with a negatively sloped demand curve. The elasticity of demand for locally raised school expenditures with respect to *SEV* is approximately .7 when the variables are at their weighted means.

Achievement scores seem particularly to be associated with levels of spending. Spending is higher in schools with high mean achievement scores and in schools with a higher standard deviation of scores. These latter schools are more "elitist" (see Brown and Saks, 1975).

The fraction of families with school-age children and the number of children per family seem to have little effect on spending. As hypothesized, the proportion of students in private school does seem to be strongly correlated with spending. Urbanization also seems to be associated with more spending. The largest cities spend the most, followed by smaller cities and the suburbs. Towns and rural districts spend the least. Note that the sheer size of districts, measured by the number of families, is significant and negative; therefore, the community-type effect is not one of mere size. Still, we cannot be sure whether the effect of community type is due to tastes or to some other unmeasured factor reflecting differences in costs. Our teacher salary cost variable seemed to have no effect on spending.

[18] We estimated the equation again using the proportions of the Michigan population from the state's four largest ethnic groups. The coefficients for the other variables changed only slightly. For the ethnic groups, we see a drop in the significance levels, compared to the aggregates, and a wide variability in effects among groups. The rank order of the four ethnic groups by the size of the regression coefficients is as follows: British (most spending), Italians, Poles, and Germans. Unfortunately, the standard errors of these coefficients are too high to permit confidence about such conclusions.

CONCLUSION

The empirical work on the effects of race, class, and ethnicity on local government activity has relied almost completely on survey and voting data. We have shown how a simple model of the political process enables us to use data on actual community decisions to test hypotheses about underlying family demands. It goes without saying that at best, such a technique tells us how real-world behavior statistically corresponds to the hypotheses we are considering. Conclusions about causality must depend on the weight of evidence from a variety of sources.

Our findings are consistent with, though do not prove, the following behavioral relationships:

1. Holding price fixed, desired spending for schools in Michigan appears to be a U-shaped function of income. The poor and upper middle classes apparently want to spend more on schools than the middle classes.
2. Blacks and ethnics of European stock appear to want to spend more on schooling than other Americans, after controlling for income and price. The differences are especially large and significant for the ethnics.
3. There appears to be no difference in demands for school expenditures between Northern and Southern/Eastern European ethnics.
4. We cannot observe effects of assimilation in our model. The expected difference in tastes for school expenditures between those born abroad and those whose parents were born abroad was not visible.

REFERENCES

Aaron, H. J.
1975 Who Pays the Property Tax? Washington, D.C.: Brookings Institution.

Black, D.
1948 "On the rationale of group decision-making." Journal of Political Economy 56:23–34.

Brown, B. W. and D. H. Saks
1975 "The production and distribution of cognitive skills within schools." Journal of Political Economy 83:571–94.
1983 "Spending for local public education: Income distribution and the aggregation of private demands." Public Finance Quarterly 11:21–45.

Glazer, N.
1983 Ethnic Dilemmas 1964–1982. Cambridge, MA: Harvard University Press.

Glazer, N. and D. P. Moynihan
1963 Beyond the Melting Pot: The Negroes, Puerto Ricans, Jews, Italians, and Irish of New York City. Cambridge, MA: MIT Press.

Hamilton, H. D. and S. H. Cohen
1974 Policy-Making by Plebiscite: School Referenda. Lexington, MA: Lexington Books.

Kakwani, N. C. and N. Poddar
1976 "Efficient estimation of the Lorenz curve and associated inequality measures from grouped observations." Econometrica 44:137–48.

Lieberson, S.
1980 A Piece of the Pie: Black and White Immigrants Since 1880. Berkeley, CA: University of California Press.

Michigan Department of Education
1971 Local District Results, Michigan Educational Assessment Program, 1970–71. Machine-readable data file. Lansing: Michigan Department of Education (producer).

National Center for Education Statistics
n.d. 1970 Census Fourth Count Population School District Tapes, Michigan. Machine-readable data file. Washington, D.C.: National Center for Education Statistics (producer).

Piele, P. K. and J. S. Hall
1973 Budgets, Bonds, and Ballots: Voting Behavior in School Financial Elections. Lexington, MA: Lexington Books.

Ramsey, J. B.
1974 "Limiting forms for demand functions: Tests of some specific hypotheses." Review of Economics and Statistics 56:468–77.

Shlay, A. B. and P. H. Rossi
1981 "Keeping up the neighborhood: Estimating net effects of zoning." American Sociological Review 46:703–19.

Smith, R. A.
1979 "Decision making and non-decision making in cities: Some implications for community structural research." American Sociological Review 44:147–61.

Sowell, T.
1981 Ethnic America: A History. New York: Basic Books.

Vanecko, J. J. and J. Kroenfeld
1977 "Preferences for public expenditures and ethno-racial group membership: A test of the theory of political ethos." Ethnicity 4:311–36.

Wilson, J. Q. and E. C. Banfield
1963 City Politics. New York: Vintage.
1964 "Public regardingness as a value premise in voting behavior." The American Political Science Review 58:876–87.
1971 "Political ethos revisited." The American Political Science Review 65:1048–62.

FINISHING COLLEGE: THE EFFECTS OF COLLEGE TYPE

WILLIAM VELEZ
University of Wisconsin—Milwaukee

Sociology of Education 1985, Vol. 58 (July):191–200

This study uses multivariate analysis to determine the odds that a sample of high school seniors will earn a bachelor's degree. The study compares the effects of attending two-year and four-year colleges and finds that where one starts college drastically affects the chances of completing the baccalaureate. Students who start in two-year colleges are less likely to finish than students who start in four-year colleges. However, other variables, such as religious background (i.e., being Jewish), educational aspirations, academic performance in college, participation in a work-study program, and living on campus, exert substantial positive effects on finishing. The study finds that nonwhite students with low educational aspirations are more likely to finish college than similar white students, but white students with high aspirations are more likely to finish than comparable nonwhite students.

INTRODUCTION

More than twenty years have passed since the publication of Burton Clark's article "The 'Cooling Out' Function in Higher Education" (1960), in which he argued that two-year colleges teach some of their students to lower their aspirations and reconcile themselves to obtaining a two-year degree. Since the publication of Clark's article, the role of two-year colleges in American higher education has grown tremendously (Thomas et al., 1981). Higher education plays an important role in promoting economic mobility in American society, and social scientists have found that a college degree has considerable positive impact on occupational attainments and earnings (Jencks et al., 1979:Ch. 6). Since one of the goals of two-year colleges is to prepare students for transfer to four-year institutions, it is important to assess the potential effects of two-year colleges on the educational achievements of their students.

Alba and Lavin (1981) suggest that two-year colleges have a discouraging effect on educational attainment, and indeed, dropout rates in two-year colleges are known to be high (Astin, 1977). Anderson (1981) found that a two-year college entrant has a higher probability of dropping out during the first two years of college. However, until recently, there had been no serious research effort to determine whether these effects were attributable to characteristics of the institutions or to the background characteristics of the students who entered them.

Alba and Lavin (1981), in a study of CUNY students, concluded that two-year colleges function as a separate track within higher education. While controlling for differences in academic background, they compared students who started in community colleges with those who started in senior colleges and found that "students placed in the two-year schools did not stay as long in school, earned fewer credits and were less likely to earn the baccalaureate than academically similar students placed in the senior colleges." Furthermore, "senior college placement apparently doubled a student's chances of earning the degree within five years" (Alba and Lavin, 1981:235). Although very revealing of the role of the two-year college, Alba and Lavin's study is not very conclusive for a number of reasons. First, they could not control for curriculum in their sample, so community-college students in vocational curricula were compared to senior-college students. Second, they did not use multivariate analyses to determine the effects of a number of variables, in addition to college type, on finishing college. Therefore, they have no way of ascertaining the relative effects of college type on the probabilities of getting a bachelor's degree. Finally, their findings may be applicable or relevant to New York City but may not be representative of the nation as a whole.

Of course, it is generally assumed that students starting in a two-year college are less likely to finish a four-year degree than students starting in a four-year college. There may be

---

I want to thank Wendell Bell, Henry A. Walker, and Susan Olzak for a number of insightful comments. I am also indebted to Rajshekhar G. Javalgi for his research assistance. In addition, two anonymous reviewers for this journal provided useful criticism, enabling me to move my analysis toward greater clarity. Address all correspondence to the author at the Center for Demography and Ecology, University of Wisconsin, 4412 Social Science Building, 1180 Observatory Drive, Madison, WI 53706.

"articulation" problems in some state systems—i.e., two-year college students may lose credits when transferring to four-year colleges. Also, there may be more stigma attached to dropping out after two years in a four-year college than in a two-year college. Finally some students choose a two-year college because all they really want is an associate's degree. *Finishing* to them may mean two years in one setting and four years in the other.

But there are other possible reasons for the negative effects of two-year colleges. First, students enrolled in two-year colleges are more likely to be exposed to peer influences that encourage them to leave an academic track for vocational schooling or employment. Second, they are more likely to have off-campus jobs. Third, they are more likely to be dissatisfied with certain features of the college environment and, therefore, are likely to be less integrated into college. Finally, two-year students are more likely to have lowered their achievement goals. In studying persistence up to the third year of college, Anderson (1981) found that the effects of college type are mediated by all the above processes.

The factors affecting college completion can be grouped into five categories: (1) personal background, (2) academic processes, (3) psychosocial processes, (4) institutional factors, and (5) institutional integration. Personal-background variables include parents' socioeconomic status (SES) and the student's sex, race, and religion (or whether or not the student is Jewish). Academic processes include high school curriculum enrollment (track), number of math courses taken in high school, and high school and college grades. Psychosocial processes include the student's educational aspirations (the highest level of education s/he plans to attain) and the student's perception of mother's educational aspirations for her/him. Institutional factors include type of control (indicating whether the student attended a public or private college) and college type (indicating whether the student first attended a two-year or a four-year college). Institutional integration is measured by two variables: living quarters in the fall of 1974 (indicating whether or not the student was living in a dormitory, fraternity house, or sorority house) and participation in a work-study program in the fall of 1974.

In studying the effects of these variables, I am assuming that the college attainment process is complex and that the student brings in characteristics, aspirations, and experiences that can be mediated and only partially transformed by the specific college type. That is, I expect these variables to have similar effects on college attainment among two-year and four-year entrants, but I also expect college type to have an independent effect on college completion.

THE COLLEGE ATTAINMENT PROCESS

Traditional societal values, socialization practices, and situational constraints have generally worked to the advantage of males, enabling them to achieve many desired goals more successfully than females. A longitudinal study of a large southwestern university found that male community-college transfer students were more likely to graduate than female transfer students (Hollahan, Green, and Kelley, 1983). I hypothesize that in this sample, males have a higher finishing rate than females.

Anderson's (1981) study of college attrition shows that a student's race has a small effect on college persistence up to the second year and that blacks have slightly higher odds of persisting than whites. The returns of education to young blacks are now, for the first time, similar to the returns to comparable whites (Wilson, 1978). Furthermore, Velez (1983) found that nonwhite students transfer from two-year to four-year colleges at higher rates than comparable white students. Assuming that this advantage holds throughout college, I expect nonwhite students to have higher odds of completion than white students.

Historically, Jews, on average, have attained higher levels of education than white gentiles (Lieberson, 1980). Their greater educational achievement is attributed to their higher socioeconomic status and to their higher rates of literacy upon immigration to the United States, compared to other immigrant groups (Steinberg, 1981). In addition, Jewish culture emphasizes respect for learning, which also has a positive effect on educational attainment (Olneck and Lazerson, 1974). Thus, I hypothesize that being Jewish, other things being equal, is positively and causally related to finishing college (Featherman, 1971; Anderson, 1981).

Previous research has shown that academic performance has a significant effect on college completion (Pantages and Creedon, 1978; Astin, 1977). This effect can be direct: i.e., a student's grades can be so low that s/he is dismissed from college. Also, as Anderson (1981:5) suggests, low grades can "indicate a lack of fit between the student and the academic standards of the college" and may lead to lowered goals. Therefore, I expect that a student's high school and college grades significantly and positively affect the student's chances of finishing college.

Thomas (1978) has shown that having high educational aspirations is causally related to finishing college. Students in this study were asked to indicate the highest level of education they planned to attain: (1) less than four years of high school; (2) four years of high school but no college; (3) vocational, technical, business, or trade school; (4) junior college; (5) four years of college; (6) graduate or professional school. In preliminary analyses of the data, I noted that a significant proportion of the respondents (26 percent) did not answer this question. I used further tests to determine whether this group of students was distinctive in any way. Simple cross-tabulation of race and educational plans showed that minorities (Hispanics, blacks, and Native Americans) were twice as likely as whites to leave the question unanswered. I also discovered that a majority of these nonrespondents (75 percent), in response to another question, indicated that they had no immediate plans to attend college (within the first year after high school graduation). Moreover, all the nonrespondents indicated that they had not formed college plans in previous years of high school.

One could speculate that nonrespondents were alienated from school and from the questionnaire process and probably had no desire to attend college. Alternatively, one could speculate that these students wanted to go to college, but for some reason (e.g., lack of funds, perceived personal deficiencies, personal problems) were uncertain about their immediate plans. This uncertainty could have caused them to disregard the question on educational aspirations. Normally, nonrespondents are considered missing cases and are eliminated from the sample. However, in consideration of the latter hypothesis, I include them in the analysis.

There remains the question of whether the finishing rate of this subsample differs substantially from the finishing rate of the subsamples of students who answered the question. I hypothesize that students who were uncertain about their college plans have higher finishing rates than students who had not planned to attend college, but lower finishing rates than students who had planned to attend, *ceteris paribus*.

Recent studies have found that significant others have an important influence on college access, performance, and attrition (Reitzes and Mutran, 1980; Velez, 1982; Anderson, 1981). I hope to extend these findings by showing that a student's perception of parents' high educational expectations reinforces the student's commitment to obtain a four-year degree.

Institutional integration may have an important intermediary effect on the relevance and effectiveness of the college experience. Residence and employment are used as relevant predictors because of "their implications for conflict with the student role, peer influence, integration into the college versus the social systems, and achievement goals" (Anderson, 1981:4). For example, working off campus while in school presents a potential role conflict because it decreases a student's chances for interaction with faculty and other students. Having a work-study job, on the other hand, increases a student's opportunities for interaction with faculty and students outside of class, thus augmenting integration.

Residential factors are also likely to affect college completion. Feldman and Newcomb (1969) found that students who joined sororities were more gregarious, more self-confident, and more assertive than other students. They also found that students who lived in dormitories participated in more extracurricular campus activities and obtained higher grades than students who lived elsewhere (also see Griffeth, 1958). Students who live on campus, in a dormitory, fraternity house, or sorority house, interact primarily with other college students, are structurally integrated into the college, and are insulated from external influences (Astin, 1977). In contrast, students living either at home with parents or in other off-campus living arrangements are exposed to fewer integrating influences and are more likely to be influenced by nonstudents whose attitudes toward college are not favorable (Chickering, 1975).

METHOD

Sample

This study follows the educational careers of a sample of students who were high school seniors in 1972. The data are taken from the *National Longitudinal Survey of the High School Class of 1972* (National Center for Education Statistics, 1980). The NLS is a two-stage probability sample: Schools were sampled first, then students were sampled within schools. In the spring of 1972, the Educational Testing Service administered the test battery and base-year questionnaire to 16,683 seniors enrolled in 1,070 public, private, and parochial secondary schools in the fifty states and the District of Columbia. Schools in low-income areas and schools with high proportions of minority students were sampled at about twice the normal rate. The first follow-up survey was done in the fall and spring of 1973–74, the second follow-up in the fall of 1974, the third follow-up in the fall of 1976, and the fourth follow-up in the fall of 1979.

Included in the nonwhite category were blacks, American Indians, and Hispanics. Students of Asian ethnicity were excluded from the sample. Although the term *Hispanic* is associated with national or ethnic origins, and although most Hispanics could be classified as white on strictly racial grounds, for the purpose of this study they are classified as nonwhite.

It is important to note that the NLS only sampled seniors. Therefore, because minorities have higher dropout rates than whites, the minority students included in the sample are a very special group.

Initially, a 50 percent random sample of all students enrolled in an academic program in any college in the fall of 1972 or 1973 was obtained, yielding 6,029 cases. Then, only those students enrolled in 1972 with no missing values were selected, yielding a sample of 3,169 students. Approximately 84 percent of the students in the sample were white, and 16 percent were nonwhite. Male and female students were equally represented in the sample.

Variable Measurement

Following is a description of the variables included in the analysis.

SES is "a composite of five components: father's education, mother's education, parents' income, father's occupation, and household items. Each component variable was standardized and given equal weight in calculating the composite index" (Fetters, 1976:2). *Sex* was coded 1 if the respondent was male, 0 if the respondent was female. *Race* was coded 1 if the respondent was white, 0 if the respondent was nonwhite. *Religion* is a dichotomous variable distinguishing Jewish respondents from non-Jewish respondents: Jewish = 1, non-Jewish = 0.

High school curriculum is an original seven-category variable obtained from school records. This variable was recoded as a dichotomous dummy variable indicating enrollment in academic or other curricula: academic curriculum = 1, other curricula = 0. *Math* is the number of math courses the student took in high school. *High school grades* indicates a student's grade-point average, which was obtained from school records. This variable was coded into 14 categories, from A+ to F. *College grades* represents the student's response to a question on the first follow-up, which asked students to indicate how they had done in all their education since high school. Responses ranged from "mostly A" to "mostly below D." This variable was coded into eight categories. In most cases, these grades represent freshman year academic performance. *Aptitude* is "the composite value of test scores in four areas: vocabulary, reading, letter groups, and mathematics. The mean of the four standardized scores serves as an ability index" (Fetters, 1976:2).

Plans indicates the highest level of education the student plans to attain. The variable was coded as follows: if the respondent plans to complete high school, vocational/technical school, or less (or if the respondent did not answer), college plans = 0; if the respondent plans to obtain a two-year college degree, college plans = 1; if the respondent plans to complete four years of college, graduate school, or professional school, college plans = 2.[1] *Race*plans* is an interaction term, coded 1 if the respondent is white and aspires to a four-year degree or greater. *Uncertainty* is a dichotomous dummy variable indicating whether or not the student responded to the question on college plans: if the student did not respond, uncertainty = 1; if the student did respond, uncertainty = 0. *Mother's educational aspirations* is a student's perception of mother's aspirations for her/him. The variable was coded as follows: high school, vocational/technical school, or less = 0; two-year college = 1; four-year college, graduate school, or professional school = 2.[2]

Control indicates whether the student was enrolled in a public or private college in October 1972: private = 1, public = 0. *College type* indicates whether the student was enrolled in a two-year or four-year college in October 1972. Only those students in academic curricula are included: four-year college = 1, two-year college = 0.

Living quarters indicates the type of residence in which the student lived in October 1974. This variable was recoded as a dummy variable: dormitory, fraternity house, sorority house = 1; parents' home or other off-campus housing = 0. *Work-study program* is a dummy variable indicating whether or not the student

[1] Use of the categorical measures, however, resulted in only a marginal improvement in fit (chi square = 1,274.7); and the resulting coefficients for the other variables were negligibly different from those reported in Table 2. The only noticeable change was in the coefficient for race, which shifted from −0.665 to −0.573. Consequently, I retained the more parsimonious specification reported here.

[2] I also experimented with categorical codings permitting nonlinear effects for college plans and mother's aspirations. The effects were distinctly nonlinear. For college plans, the coefficient contrasting two-year college with high school, vocational/technical school, or less was a statistically insignificant 0.025, and the coefficient contrasting four-year college or more with the same omitted category was 0.542. The analogous coefficients for mother's aspirations were 0.046 (insignificant) and 0.343.

had a work-study job in the fall of 1974: work-study job = 1, no work-study job = 0.

Finishing college was created from "three Fourth Follow-up Questionnaire items: (a) years of education at vocational, trade or business school as of October 1979 (Item 66); (b) highest level of college education as of October 1979 (Item 67); and (c) kind of degree earned (Item 76)" (Riccobono et al., 1981:App. L.2). This variable was recoded as a dummy variable: bachelor's or graduate degree = 1, less = 0.

RESULTS

Effects of Background Variables

In the NLS sample, students from high-SES families had larger predicted probabilities of finishing than students from low-SES families, although the magnitude of the effect was only moderate.

Males and females had the same finishing rate—about 60 percent. The zero-order correlation between sex and finishing (0.001) suggests an absence of sex effects (see Table 1). In the full equation, however, I found that males had a significantly (6 percent) higher probability of finishing than females (see the last column of Table 2).

White students in the sample had substantially higher rates of college completion than nonwhite students: 62 percent of the white students graduated from college, compared to only 49 percent of the nonwhite students. The zero-order correlation between race and finishing (0.103) also suggests an advantage for white students. But when all other independent variables are included in the logit equation, a completely different picture emerges: White students who planned to obtain at least a four-year degree had slightly higher probabilities of finishing than comparable nonwhite students, but nonwhite students with low educational aspirations had substantially higher probabilities of finishing than similar white students (by 16 percent). White students who had no plans to attend college might simply be killing time. But similar nonwhite students may have a stronger commitment to finishing, because the economic/occupational payoff is relatively larger for them (Jencks et al., 1979). Since the multivariate analysis yields different results than the zero-order correlation, the apparent advantage of whites over nonwhites must be due to other variables, rather than to race per se.

The effects of religion are very large: Being Jewish increased a student's probability of finishing by 25 percent. The coefficient for religion is the second strongest predictor in the

Table 1. Correlation Matrix for College Attainment Equation

	1	2	3	4	5	6	7	8	9	10	11	12	13	14	15	16	17
1. SES	1.00																
2. Sex	.018	1.00															
3. Race	.401	.053	1.00														
4. Religion	.127	−.002	.095	1.00													
5. High school curriculum	.228	.019	.134	.100	1.00												
6. Math	.120	.209	.081	.086	.302	1.00											
7. High school grades	.126	−.183	.174	.047	.243	.199	1.00										
8. College grades	.128	−.149	.147	.052	.152	.057	.413	1.00									
9. Aptitude	.353	.005	.413	.100	.328	.299	.488	.309	1.00								
10. Plans	.232	.019	.201	.081	.282	.213	.300	.104	.355	1.00							
11. Uncertainty	−.166	.027	−.217	−.062	−.157	−.127	−.277	−.092	−.333	−.814	1.00						
12. Mother's aspirations	.159	.058	.014	.033	.210	.135	.146	.041	.100	.337	−.094	1.00					
13. Control	.122	−.008	.055	.020	.122	.081	.092	.060	.112	.093	−.059	.060	1.00				
14. College type	.169	−.006	.044	.068	.264	.185	.277	.005	.277	.227	−.164	.320	.196	1.00			
15. Living quarters	.136	−.043	.028	.069	.164	.154	.191	.121	.173	.185	−.109	.144	.242	.228	1.00		
16. Work-study program	−.002	−.081	−.047	−.025	.047	.035	.132	.090	.080	.079	−.032	.060	.114	.140	.247	1.00	
17. Finishing college	.217	.001	.103	.124	.262	.208	.327	.251	.268	.296	−.140	.248	.153	.366	.416	.225	1.00

Table 2. Logit Coefficients for Significant Predictors of College Attainment

Variable	Coefficient[a]	SE	T-ratio	First Derivative[b]
SES	.293****	.072	4.06	.070
Sex	.255***	.096	2.66	.061
Race	−.665***	.222	3.00	−.160
Religion	1.050***	2.730	3.83	.252
High school curriculum	.188*	.104	1.80	.045
Math	.052**	.027	1.97	.012
High school grades	.096****	.020	4.80	.023
College grades	.353***	.039	9.14	.085
Plans	.173	.195	0.89	.042
Race*plans	.927****	.245	3.75	.222
Uncertainty	1.001****	.285	3.51	.240
Mother's aspirations	.314****	.084	3.75	.075
College type	.780****	.114	6.83	.187
Living quarters	1.790****	.121	14.80	.430
Work-study program	.943****	.165	5.71	.226
Constant	−5.135****	.430	12.00	

χ^2 = 1,269.94
Percent of predictions correct = 77
N = 3,169

NOTE: Preliminary analyses failed to show any significant effects for the aptitude and control variables. They are not included in the logit equation, since they do not alter, in a random or systematic way, the values of the significant predictors.

[a] The coefficient expresses the incremental effect of the independent variable on the log of the probability of finishing college. The criterion variable is the log of finishing rather than not finishing in any of the six academic years following college entrance in the fall of 1972.

[b] Derivatives are calculated using the equation $b = P^*(1\text{-}P^*)$, where b is the relevant coefficient and P^* is the estimated probability (Hanushek and Jackson, 1977:188–189). The sample proportion is assumed to be a reasonable estimate of P^*. Under this assumption, partial derivatives are interpretable as the net change in the probability of finishing college associated with a unit change in the exogenous variables.

* Significant at the .10 level.
** Significant at the .05 level.
*** Significant at the .01 level.
**** Significant at the .001 level.

equation, which indicates that Jews have an educational orientation that is not captured by the college plans variable (Steinberg, 1981).

Effects of Academic Processes

Table 2 shows that students who were enrolled in a college preparatory track in high school had slightly better chances of finishing college. The number of math courses a student took in high school also had a very small positive effect on finishing.

Students who got good grades in high school and college had a higher predicted probability of finishing. The effects of high school grades are cumulative; i.e., they determine whether or not a student is selected into the next level of schooling. The effects of college grades are larger: A student with an A average had a 34 percent higher probability of finishing than a student with a C average. A good academic performance may increase a student's integration into college life and raise the student's achievement goals. On some campuses, it may even help a student get into a college dorm.

Effects of Psychosocial Processes

Students who had formed college plans in their senior year of high school and students who were uncertain of their plans had larger predicted probabilities of finishing than students with no college plans. Surprisingly, among nonwhite students, those who were uncertain were more likely to finish college than those who had college plans. Also, Table 2 shows that the interaction term (*race*plans*) had a stronger positive effect on finishing than college plans alone. Among white students, however, those who had college plans and those who were uncertain had about the same advantage over those who had no plans. In any case, the results indicate that students who were uncertain about college in their senior year of high school had a high desire to obtain a higher education and, once enrolled in college, were much more committed to finishing than those with no college plans.

A student who perceived his/her mother to have high educational aspirations for him/her had a larger probability of finishing than one who perceived such expectations to be lower.

Effects of Institutional Factors

The control-type variable had no effects on college completion. Students enrolled in private colleges enjoyed no special advantage over those enrolled in public colleges.

Where one began college (i.e., in a two-year or a four-year school) did, however, have an important effect on college attainment. A student who started in a four-year college had a 19 percent higher probability of finishing than a student who started in a two-year college. By the fall of 1976, 42 percent of the four-year college entrants had already finished the baccalaureate, compared to only 12 percent of the two-year entrants. By the fall of 1979, 79 percent of the four-year college entrants had finished, compared to only 31 percent of the two-year entrants.[3] In the logit equation, the large and positive coefficient for college type indicates that the greater finishing rates among four-year college entrants cannot be explained by selection factors.

Effects of Institutional Integration Processes

Living quarters had the largest significant effect on the probability of finishing college. Students who lived on campus were 43 percent more likely to finish college than students who lived off campus. There are a number of possible reasons for this large positive effect. First, employed students who live on campus work fewer hours than employed students who live off campus. Second, students who live on campus have more academically oriented friends. Finally, these students are more integrated into college life (see Anderson, 1981). This pattern, however, may be due to the forces of self-selection and group membership, rather than to the independent effects of living quarters. A student may choose to live in a particular residential arrangement that "fits" his/her characteristics and orientations to campus life (Feldman and Newcomb, 1969). Also, fraternities and sororities are known to be selective in their recruitment of new members, admitting only those students who have values and orientations similar to those held by active members (Bohrnstedt, 1966).

Students who had work-study jobs had a 23 percent higher probability of finishing college. It is very plausible that participating in a work-study program has a positive effect on recent educational goals (the college plans variable in this study reflects high school goals). Also, being able to work on campus prevents a student from holding a regular job, in which s/he is more likely to find encouragement for vocational education and work (Anderson, 1981). Some students hold work-study jobs simply for extra money. But many students work to pay off the cost of tuition, housing, or meals. It is probable that for these students, a work-study job is a proxy for financial need. However, the zero-order correlation between SES and work-study program is about zero, suggesting that these jobs are not given solely on the basis of financial need.

The combined effect of the institutional integration variables is larger than the effects of the other variable clusters. However, there is a question whether these variables are simply endogenous to college type. The zero-order correlations between college type and living quarters (0.228) and between college type and work-study program (0.140) suggest that the opportunities to live on campus and participate in a work-study program are more available in four-year colleges. To test whether these two variables added predictive power beyond that of college type, I tested two models for finishing college, using the root-sum-squared-error test (RSSE) (see Table 3). Living quarters and work-study program are included in Model 2, but not in Model 1. As Table 3 shows, the RSSE is 377.60 for Model 1, and 69.30 for Model 2, indicating that Model 2 offers greater predictive power than Model 1. The proportion of correct predictions for each model (73 percent for Model 1, 77 percent for Model 2) also proves that living quarters and work-study program have significant and independent effects on finishing college.

DISCUSSION

This study has shown that where students start college drastically affects their chances of finishing the baccalaureate. Students who start in two-year colleges have lower odds of finishing than students who start in four-year colleges. However, other variables, such as religious background, academic performance in college, college plans, living quarters, and participation in a work-study program, also exert substantial effects on finishing.

The large positive effect of being Jewish on finishing college indicates the continuing im-

---

[3] These figures, of course, are for those students who were in an academic program for at least one semester in college and for which complete information was available. Of all the original respondents in the NLS class of 1972 for which information was available as of the fourth follow-up, 26 percent obtained at least a bachelor's degree. Of those who attended college, 42 percent graduated by the fall of 1979. However, some of the students included in the pool from which the graduation rate is calculated may have been enrolled in vocational programs. (See Riccobono [1981:App. L.2] for the criteria used to construct the educational attainment variable.)

Table 3. Comparison of Predictive Power of Two Models of Finishing College

	Actual	Predicted	Root Sum Squared Error (RSSE)[a]	Percent of Correct Predictions	χ^2	*N*
Model 1	1,856	2,123	377.60	73	916.59	3,169
Model 2	1,856	1,905	69.30	77	1,269.94	3,169

NOTE: Model 1 includes 13 explanatory variables: SES, sex, race, religion, high school curriculum, math, high school grades, college grades, plans, race*plans, uncertainty, mother's aspirations, and college type. Model 2 includes two additional variables: living quarters and work-study program.

[a] The root sum squared error is defined as follows:

$$RSSE = \left[\sum_{i=1}^{2} (\hat{q}_i - q_i)^2 \right]^{1/2}$$

where q_i = actual share for i = 1, 2; and $\hat{q}_i$ = predicted share for i = 1, 2.

portance of religio-ethnic group membership. It is possible, for some historical reasons, that growing up Jewish gives one a different orientation toward educational achievement—an orientation that is not reflected in the college plans variable. Since this effect is independent of SES and mother's aspirations, a cultural explanation is more appropriate. Olneck and Lazerson (1974:473), who studied the educational achievements of German and Russian Jews, suggest that a Jewish upbringing may stimulate high levels of educational attainment by encouraging "mental agility, close attention to the meaning of words, and lively criticism." They also suggest that Jewish families are more willing than other ethnic/religious groups to tolerate economic burdens in order to keep their children in school for extended periods. In sum, Judaism fosters respect for learning, trust in educational institutions, and a belief that educational attainment will translate into occupational attainment.

There is no evidence that the college experience eliminates many of the achievement differences between the sexes (Astin, 1977). Therefore, the effects of college attendance on women's achievement must be interpreted cautiously. Women may attend college for other than academic or professional reasons, or they may place more emphasis than men on certain aspects of college life. For example, supportive personal interactions with faculty members are important to female students (Hearn and Olzak, 1981), but these interactions are less available to women in higher education. In any case, a female student's lower odds of finishing college may result from a general cooling-out process that specifically affects women.

The effects of academic performance may indicate that students use grades as feedback, to modify or reaffirm their achievement goals. Grades are used as a measure of academic competence, thus students base their educational decisions on them. Some theorists view grades as teachers' judgements, in many cases unrelated to the actual intellectual accomplishment of a student: "Any grade is a communication about past performance; but it also sets the stage for future performance. Future performance will be affected by the grade, and especially by the interpretation put on the grade" (Goldsmid and Wilson, 1980:313). Aptitude may partially determine college grades, but the effect of grades on college completion probably reflects the importance of motivation, how hard one works, and actual performance, rather than aptitude.[4]

The positive effects of high educational aspirations on educational achievement point to the importance of psychosocial variables and images of the future (Bell and Mau, 1971). Students who had planned to attend college, graduate school, or professional school generally had higher rates of college completion than students who had not planned to attend. However, students who were uncertain about their college plans in their senior year of high school were at least as likely to finish as students who had planned to attend college.

The large effects of the institutional integration variables indicate that success in college depends in part on active involvement in all aspects of the college environment. Living and working on campus exposes the student to peer influences that encourage studying and increase achievement goals. It also increases the likelihood of interaction with faculty and other college functionaries, which socializes the student to academic life and its goals. The im-

[4] The correlation coefficient between aptitude and college grades was 0.309, a moderately large relationship. Preliminary analyses failed to show any significant effects of academic aptitude on finishing.

portance of living on campus and having a work-study job suggests the usefulness of the concept of "total institutions," first suggested by Goffman (1961), to account for the college attainment process. Living and working on campus approximates membership in a total institution, which enforces upon the student the formal rules, activities, and goals of higher education. Although a student's attendance at college may indicate that s/he has already accepted the goals of the institution, active involvement in campus activities may strengthen such goals or socialize low-aspiring students into accepting them. Students who are actively involved in campus life follow a tight schedule of school activities (either academic or social), and they are constantly in the company of other students, which makes their academic performance more public. Thus, the most prestigious and selective colleges and universities have higher graduation rates because of the superior academic performance of their students and because they are more able, due to greater financial resources, to provide campus housing and work-study jobs.

The effects of living and working on campus can offset the negative effects of starting in a two-year college. Two-year college entrants who lived and worked on campus had greatly increased odds of finishing. However, while 34 percent of the four-year college students were living on campus in 1974, only 13 percent of the two-year college students were able to do so (see Table 4); and four-year college students were three times more likely to hold work-study jobs than two-year college students.

This study has shown that two-year and four-year colleges constitute different tracks within higher education and that these tracks are associated with very different educational life chances (Karabel, 1972). The results suggest that policies aimed at increasing the amount of campus housing and the number of work-study jobs will increase the rates of college completion for all students, but especially for those who start in two-year colleges.

Table 4. Means and Standard Deviations by College Type

Variable	Two-Year College Students	Four-Year College Students	All College Students
SES	.11	.36	.28
	(.68)	(.72)	(.72)
Sex	.50	.49	.49
	(.50)	(.50)	(.50)
Race	.81	.86	.84
	(.39)	(.36)	(.37)
Religion	.03	.05	.04
	(.17)	(.22)	(.21)
High school curriculum	.48	.74	.66
	(.50)	(.44)	(.47)
Math	4.06	4.79	4.56
	(1.82)	(1.83)	(1.87)
High school grades	7.78[a]	9.47[b]	8.95[b]
	(2.84)	(2.75)	(2.78)
College grades	5.50[c]	5.57[c]	5.53[c]
	(1.34)	(1.35)	(1.35)
Aptitude	2.06	2.44	2.33
	(.17)	(.65)	(.68)
Plans	1.09	1.74	1.53
	(.84)	(.66)	(.78)
Uncertainty	.24	.11	.15
	(.43)	(.32)	(.35)
Mother's aspirations	1.41	1.85	1.71
	(.76)	(.51)	(.63)
Control	.08	.25	.20
	(.26)	(.43)	(.40)
Living quarters	.13	.34	.28
	(.34)	(.48)	(.45)
Work-study program	.05	.15	.12
	(.22)	(.36)	(.32)
Finishing college	.31	.79	.60
	(.45)	(.52)	(.50)
N	1,398	1,771	3,169

[a] C+ (letter grade).
[b] B− (letter grade).
[c] B (letter grade).

REFERENCES

Alba, R. D. and D. E. Lavin
1981 "Community colleges and tracking in higher education." Sociology of Education 54:223–47.

Anderson, K. L.
1981 "Post-high school experiences and college attrition." Sociology of Education 54:1–15.

Astin, A. W.
1977 Four Critical Years. San Francisco: Jossey-Bass.

Bell, W. and J. A. Mau
1971 The Sociology of the Future. New York: Russell Sage.

Bohrnstedt, G. W.
1966 "Processes of seeking membership in and recruitment by voluntary social organizations." Ph.D. dissertation, Department of Sociology, University of Wisconsin, Madison.

Chickering, A. W.
1975 Commuting Versus Resident Students. San Francisco: Jossey-Bass.

Clark, B. R.
1960 "The 'cooling out' function in higher education." American Journal of Sociology 65:659–76.

Featherman, D. L.
1971 "The socioeconomic achievement of white religio-ethnic subgroups: Social and psychological explanations." American Sociological Review 36:207–22.

Feldman, K. A. and T. M. Newcomb
1969 The Impact of College on Students. San Francisco: Jossey-Bass.

Fetters, W. B.
1976 "Student questionnaire and test results by academic ability, socioeconomic status, and religion." National Center for Education Statistics Report No. 76–235. Washington, D.C.: U.S. Government Printing Office.

Goffman, E.
1961 Asylums: Essays on the Social Situation of Mental Patients and Other Inmates. Garden City, NY: Doubleday.

Goldsmid, C. A. and E. K. Wilson
1980 Passing on Sociology: The Teaching of a Discipline. Belmont, CA: Wadsworth.

Griffeth, P. L.
1958 "Type of residence as a factor in academic achievement at the State University of Iowa." Ph.D. dissertation, State University of Iowa.

Hanushek, E. and J. E. Jackson
1977 Statistical Methods for Social Scientists. New York: Academic Press.

Hearn, J. C. and S. Olzak
1981 "The role of college major departments in the reproduction of sexual inequality." Sociology of Education 54:195–205.

Hollahan, C. K., J. L. Green, and H. P. Kelley
1983 "A six-year longitudinal analysis of transfer student performance and retention." Journal of College Student Personnel 24:305–10.

Jencks, C. et al.
1979 Who Gets Ahead? The Determinants of Economic Success in America. New York: Basic Books.

Karabel, J.
1972 "Community colleges and social stratification: Submerged class conflict in American higher education." Harvard Educational Review 42:521–62.

Lieberson, S.
1980 A Piece of the Pie: Black and White Immigrants Since 1880. Berkeley, CA: University of California Press.

National Center for Education Statistics
1980 National Longitudinal Survey of the High School Class of 1972. Machine-readable data file. Washington, D.C.: National Center for Education Statistics (producer).

Olneck, M. R. and M. Lazerson
1974 "The school achievement of immigrant children: 1900–1930." History of Education Quarterly 14:453–82.

Pantages, T. J. and C. F. Creedon
1978 "Studies of college attrition: 1950–1975." Review of Educational Research 48:49–101.

Reitzes, D. C. and E. Mutran
1980 "Significant others and self-conceptions: Factors influencing educational expectations and academic performance." Sociology of Education 53:21–32.

Riccobono, J., L. B. Henderson, G. J. Burkheimer, C. Place, and J. R. Levinsohn
1981 National Longitudinal Study: Base Year (1972) through Fourth Follow-up (1979): Data File User's Manual. Report No. 0884/73–18S. Research Triangle Park, NC: Research Triangle Institute.

Steinberg, S.
1981 The Ethnic Myth: Race, Ethnicity, and Class in America. Boston: Beacon Press.

Thomas, G. E.
1978 "The influence of ascription, achievement, and educational expectations on the post-secondary enrollment of blacks and whites." Report No. 257. Baltimore: Center for the Social Organization of Schools, Johns Hopkins University.

Thomas, G. E. (ed.)
1981 Black Students in Higher Education. Westport, CT: Greenwood Press.

Velez, W.
1982 "Access to college in the U.S. during the seventies: Disaggregating a status attainment model." Paper presented at the Annual Meeting of the Midwest Sociological Society, Des Moines, IA.
1983 "The college attainment process in the U.S. during the seventies." Ph.D. dissertation, Department of Sociology, Yale University.

Wilson, W. J.
1978 The Declining Significance of Race: Blacks and Changing American Institutions. Chicago: University of Chicago Press.

Volume 58 Number 4 October 1985

SOCIOLOGY OF EDUCATION

A Journal of the American Sociological Association

GUEST AND TOLNAY
Agricultural Organization and Educational Consumption in the U.S. in 1900

BAKER, ESMER, LENHARDT, AND MEYER
Effects of Immigrant Workers on Educational Stratification in Germany

SAHA
The Legitimacy of Early School Leaving: Occupational Orientations, Vocational Training Plans, and Educational Attainment Among Urban Australian Youth

ADLER AND ADLER
From Idealism to Pragmatic Detachment: The Academic Performance of College Athletes

EVERHART
On Feeling Good About Oneself: Practical Ideology in Schools of Choice

SOCIOLOGY OF EDUCATION (ISSN 0038–0407) is published quarterly in January, April, July and October by the American Sociological Association, 1722 N Street, N.W., Washington, D.C. 20036 and is printed by Boyd Printing Company, Albany, New York. Second class postage paid at Washington, D.C. and additional mailing offices. *POSTMASTER:* Send address changes to *Sociology of Education*, 1722 N Street, N.W., Washington, D.C. 20036.

MANUSCRIPTS and communications for the Editors should be addressed to the Editor, SOCIOLOGY OF EDUCATION, Department of Sociology, University of Notre Dame, Notre Dame, IN 46556.

Concerning advertising, changes of address and subscriptions, address the Executive Office, American Sociological Association, 1722 N Street, N.W., Washington, D.C. 20036. Annual membership dues of the ASA, $40–$125 ($12 of this amount may cover a subscription to *Sociology of Education*); Associate, $40; Student Associate, $25. Subscription rate for members, $12; nonmembers, $21 U.S., $24 elsewhere; institutions, $28 U.S., $31 elsewhere; single issues, $5. New subscriptions and renewals will be entered on a calendar year basis only. *Changes of Address:* Six weeks advance notice to the Executive Office, and old address as well as new, are necessary for change of subscriber's address. Claims for undelivered copies must be made within the month following the regular month of publication. The publishers will supply missing copies when losses have been sustained in transit and when the reserve stock will permit.

SOCIOLOGY OF EDUCATION

A JOURNAL OF RESEARCH IN SOCIALIZATION AND SOCIAL STRUCTURE

PUBLISHED BY
THE AMERICAN SOCIOLOGICAL ASSOCIATION

OCTOBER 1985 VOLUME 58, NUMBER 4

CONTENTS

Agricultural Organization and Educational Consumption in the U.S. in 1900 . . . . *Avery M. Guest and Stewart E. Tolnay* 201

Effects of Immigrant Workers on Educational Stratification in Germany . . . . *David P. Baker, Yilmaz Esmer, Gero Lenhardt, and John Meyer* 213

The Legitimacy of Early School Leaving: Occupational Orientations, Vocational Training Plans, and Educational Attainment Among Urban Australian Youth . . . . *Lawrence J. Saha* 228

From Idealism to Pragmatic Detachment: The Academic Performance of College Athletes . . . . *Peter Adler and Patricia A. Adler* 241

On Feeling Good About Oneself: Practical Ideology in Schools of Choice . . . . *Robert B. Everhart* 251

EDITORIAL POLICY

This journal exists to provide a forum for studies of the sociology of education and human social development. The aim is to publish research on how social institutions and/or individuals' experience within them impinge upon educational processes and social development. Such research could span various levels of analysis, ranging from the individual to the structure of relations among social and educational institutions. In an increasingly complex society, important educational issues arise throughout the life cycle. The content of this journal is meant to reflect this diversity by presenting a balance of papers which deal with education at the institutional and organizational levels as well as at the individual level, at all stages of schooling and with respect to all types of education. Contributions are invited from persons of any discipline whose objectives are consonant with those of this journal.

Contributors' papers are evaluated, through a peer-review process, entirely in terms of quality. *All* methodologies are welcome. The journal appears quarterly, January, April, July, and October.

A processing fee of $10 is required for each paper submitted. Such fees are waived for student members of the ASA. This reflects a policy of the ASA Council and Committee on Publications and affects all ASA journals. It is a reluctant response to the rapidly accelerating costs of manuscript processing. A check or money order, made payable to the American Sociological Association, should accompany each submission. The fee must be paid in order to initiate manuscript processing.

SOCIOLOGY OF EDUCATION

CONTRIBUTORS

■ Avery M. Guest is professor of sociology at the University of Washington. His research interests are the community, demography, and human ecology. Stewart E. Tolnay is assistant professor of sociology at the University of Georgia, where he studies historical and modern fertility transitions. This article is part of a larger study of American fertility in the late 1800s, which has shown that the changing economic role of children was an important factor in the fertility transition in the late nineteenth century.

■ David P. Baker is assistant professor of sociology at the Catholic University of America, where he also has joint appointments in the National Center for Family Studies and the Center for the Study of Youth Development. His research interests include the sociology of education and human development. He is currently studying the relationship between U.S. immigration and the expansion of Catholic schools and child welfare institutions between 1850 and 1920. Yilmaz Esmer received his Ph.D. in sociology from Stanford University and is currently associate professor of sociology at Bogazici University in Istanbul. His interests are social change and development, migration, and research methods. Gero Lenhardt is senior researcher at the Max Planck Institute for Human Development and Education, where he studies the sociology of formal education, industrial sociology, and the theory of western rationalization. John Meyer is professor of sociology at Stanford University. His research interests are the sociology of education, organizations, and comparative sociology. He is currently involved in several projects on the comparative study of educational expansion. This article is part of an ongoing project, conducted at the Max Planck Institute, on immigrant labor, work, and education.

■ Lawrence J. Saha is reader and head of the Department of Sociology at the Australian National University. His research interests are the sociology of education, urban sociology, and social change and development. He is currently analyzing the relationship between social structure, schooling, and life plans in eighteen countries and has recently co-authored a book (with I. Fagerlind), *Education and National Development: A Comparative Perspective* (Oxford: Pergamon, 1983).

■ Peter Adler is assistant professor of sociology at the University of Tulsa. His interests are qualitative methodology, socialization, the sociology of sport, deviance, and the family. Patricia A. Adler is assistant professor of sociology at Oklahoma State University, where she studies qualitative methodology, contemporary sociological theory, the sociology of children, deviance, and the family. Professors Adler and Adler are co-authors of a forthcoming book, *Joining the Crowd: Membership Roles in Field Research* (Beverly Hills: Sage), which discusses the methodology used in this article. They are also co-editors of an annual series, *Sociological Studies of Child Development,* published by JAI Press.

■ Robert B. Everhart is associate professor of education and sociology at the University of California at Santa Barbara. He is currently writing a book on adolescent cultures in nontraditional schools.

Notice to Contributors

(Revised September 1981)

STATEMENT OF ASA POLICY ON MULTIPLE SUBMISSION

Submission of manuscripts to a professional journal clearly implies commitment to publish in that journal. The competition for journal space requires a great deal of time and effort on the part of editorial readers whose main compensation for this service is the opportunity to read papers prior to publication and the gratification associated with discharge of professional obligations. For these reasons the ASA regards submission of a manuscript to a professional journal while that paper is under review by another journal as unacceptable.

AUTHOR'S RESPONSIBILITY: *Manuscripts which do not adhere exactly to these suggestions will be immediately returned for revision. Only articles in the form specified below will be sent out for refereeing.*

The 1974 edition of the *Publication Manual* of the American Psychological Association (available from A.P.A., 1200 17th St., N.W., Washington, D.C. 20036) is very helpful in clarifying headings, abbreviations, table preparation and the like.

Since manuscripts are evaluated as anonymous submissions, please keep identifying material out of the manuscript. Attach a cover page giving authorship, institutional affiliation, acknowledgments, and the date the article is submitted. Provide only the title as identification on the manuscript and abstract. Every effort should be made by the author to see that the manuscript itself contains no clues as to the author's identity.

Submission and Preparation of Manuscripts

1. Submit four (4) copies and retain the original for your files. Copies may be Xerox, mimeograph or multilith, but not carbons.
2. Enclose a stamped self-addressed postcard for acknowledgment of manuscript receipt. Since manuscripts will not be returned by reviewers to the editorial office, the editorial office will not return them to authors.
3. All copy must be *typed, doublespaced* (including indented material, footnotes and references) on 8½ by 11 inch white opaque paper. Line must not exceed six (6) inches. Margins must be a minimum of one inch.
4. Include four (4) copies of an abstract of no more than 150 words.
5. Type each table on a separate page. Insert a location note at the appropriate place in the text, e.g., "Table 2 about here." Send copies, retain originals.
6. Figures must be professionally prepared. Send copies, retain originals.
7. Clarify all symbols with notes in the margins of the manuscript. Circle these and all other explanatory notes not intended for printing.
8. Three kinds of footnotes are possible each serving a different purpose:

   a. Content footnotes. Content footnotes are explanations or amplifications of the text. Because they are distracting to readers and *expensive* to include in printed material, an author should include important information in the text and omit irrelevant information. *Content Footnotes Will Not Be Allowed Generally.*

   Rather than footnoting long or complicated material, such as proofs or derivations unnecessary to the text, consider (i) indicating in a *short* footnote that the material is available from the author, (ii) depositing the material in a national retrieval center and including an appropriate footnote, or (iii) adding an appendix. If an appendix is used, the reference in text should read: "(see Appendix A for complete derivation)."

   Text footnotes should be numbered consecutively throughout the article with superscript arabic numerals. If, after a footnote occurs it is later mentioned, use a parenthetical note "(see Footnote 3)," rather than the superscript number.

   b. Reference footnotes. Footnotes are used for reference purposes only to cite material of limited availability. Acceptable reference footnotes include (i) legal citations, which should follow the footnote style of *A Uniform System of Citation* (1967) published by the Harvard Law Review Association, (ii) copyright permission footnotes, (iii) unpublished works; works in progress.

   c. Table footnotes. Table footnotes are appended *only* to a specific table. Footnotes to a table should be *lettered* consecutively *within* each table with superscript lowercase letters.
9. Acknowledgments, credits and grant numbers are placed on the title page with an asterisk.

Reference Format

A. *In the Text:* All source references are to be identified at the appropriate point in the text by the last name of the author, year of publication, and pagination where needed. Identify subsequent citations of the same source in the same way as the first, *not* using "*Ibid.*," "*op. cit.*," or "*loc. cit.*" Examples follow:

1. If author's name is in the text, follow it with year in parentheses. [". . . Duncan (1959) . . ."]

2. If author's name is not in the text, insert, in parentheses, the last name and year, separated by a comma [". . . (cf. Gouldner, 1963 . . ."]

3. Pagination (without "p." or "pp.") follows year of publication after a colon. [". . . Kuhn (1970:71)."]
4. Give both last names for dual authors. Give all last names on first citation in text for more than two authors; thereafter use "et al." in the text. When two authors have the same last name, use identifying initials in the text. For institutional authorship, supply minimum identification from the beginning of the complete citation. [". . . U.S. Bureau of the Census, 1963:117) . . ."]
5. Separate a series of references with semicolons and enclose them within a single pair of parentheses. [". . . (Burgess, 1968; Marwell et al., 1971; Cohen, 1962) . . ."]

B. *In the appendix:* List all items alphabetically by author and, within author, by year of publication, in an appendix, titled "REFERENCES". The reference appendix must be complete and include all references in the text. The use of "et al." is not acceptable in the appendix; list the names of all authors. (See A.4. for text format.)

If there is more than one reference to the same author and year, distinguish them by the letters a, b, etc. added to the year. [". . . Levy (1965a:331) . . ."]

Give the publisher's name in as brief a form as is fully intelligible. For example, John A. Wiley and Sons should be "Wiley."

If the cited material is unpublished, use "forthcoming" with name of journal or publisher; otherwise use "unpublished."

Use no underlining or italics.

Examples follow:

1. *Books:*

Jud, G. J., E. W. Mills, Jr. and G. W. Burch.
1970 Ex-Pastors. Philadelphia: Pilgrim Press.

U.S. Bureau of the Census
1960 Characteristics of Population, Volume I. Washington, D.C.: U.S. Government Printing Office.

Bernard, C.
[1865] An Introduction to the Study of Experimental Medicine. Dr.
1957 Henry Copley Greene. New York: Dover.

2. *Periodicals:*

Conger, R.
Forthcoming "The effects of positive feedback on direction and amount of verbalization in a social setting." Pacific Sociological Review.

Kerckhoff, A. C. and R. T. Campbell
1977a "Black-white differences in the educational attainment process." Sociology of Education 50:15–27.
1977b "Race and social status differences in the explanation of educational ambition." Social Forces 55:701–14.

3. *Collections:*

Davie, M.
1938 "The pattern of urban growth." Pp. 133–61 in G. Murdock (ed.), Studies in the Science of Society. New Haven: Yale University Press.

See recent issues for further examples.

MANUSCRIPTS FOR THE *ASA ROSE SOCIOLOGY SERIES*

Manuscripts (100 to 300 typed pages) are solicited for publication in the *ASA Arnold and Caroline Rose Monograph Series*. The Series welcomes a variety of types of sociological work—qualitative or quantitative empirical studies, and theoretical or methodological treatises. An author should submit three copies of a manuscript for consideration to the Series Editor, Professor Ernest Q. Campbell, Department of Sociology, Vanderbilt University, Nashville, TN 37235.

AGRICULTURAL ORGANIZATION AND EDUCATIONAL CONSUMPTION IN THE U.S. IN 1900

AVERY M. GUEST
University of Washington

STEWART E. TOLNAY
University of Georgia

Sociology of Education 1985, Vol. 58 (October):201–212

Most previous studies of the development of national educational systems have focused on the role of changes in the urban-industrial social structure. In contrast, this article investigates the importance of the organization of agriculture—the degree of mechanization, the availability of farmland, and the extent of farm ownership. The analysis focuses on variations in educational consumption across states and counties in the United States in 1900, when the school system was in mid-transition to its contemporary pattern. The data suggest that variations across geographic units in the total amount of education consumed per school-age child were primarily due to differences in the length of the school year, not to the propensity of children to be enrolled in or to attend school on a regular basis. Agricultural features of rural areas, especially the degree of farm mechanization and the availability of farmland, emerge as stronger predictors of overall educational consumption than urban-industrial factors.

In recent years, an extensive literature has focused on the relationship of social and economic development, sometimes known as modernization, to the expansion of educational systems in contemporary and historical societies (see, for instance, Meyer et al., 1979). Many historical studies have analyzed the extensive growth of the American educational system between the Civil War and World War I (Ayres, 1920). This growth created probably the most educated population in world history, at least in terms of formal schooling.

Much of the literature (e.g. Field, 1976) views educational expansion as a necessary consequence of urban-industrial development. In particular, it is believed that the occupational skill demands of urban-industrial societies inevitably stimulate a need for more educated workers. However, other scholars (Bowles and Gintis, 1976; Collins, 1979) have downplayed the necessary relationship between urban-industrialism and educational development. Rather, they have attributed expansion to the action of political-economic elites, particularly to attempts to socialize the working class to values of docility and obedience.

According to Rubinson and Ralph (1984), a combination of these processes was operating in the U.S. They suggest that early educational expansion was largely due to status competition and that later expansion was due to requirements for a more technically skilled workforce. Regardless of the perspective employed, most researchers assume that the primary impetus for educational expansion came from urban areas in the U.S. Consistent with this assumption, many studies have focused on educational development within individual urban areas (Katz and Davey, 1978; Troer, 1975).

These previous approaches have failed to recognize that educational expansion in the U.S. occurred while the nation was largely rural and agricultural. In this respect, the U.S. differed from a country such as England, which experienced sustained, rapid urban-industrial development in the late nineteenth and early twentieth centuries. For example, by 1900 only 39.7 percent of the U.S. population was living in urban places with 2,500 or more inhabitants (Eldridge and Thomas, 1964:198), and 37.7 percent of the labor force was still employed in agriculture (U.S. Bureau of the Census, 1949:64). Therefore, it is reasonable to suspect that the major social impetus for educational development in the U.S. came from the very sector that has often been perceived as lagging or retarded in social and economic development (Vinovskis, 1983). Unfortunately, only limited information is available on urban-rural variations in educational development in the U.S. during the late nineteenth century (Jensen and Friedberger, 1976; Kaestle and Vinovskis, 1980; Soltow and Stevens, 1977).

This article analyzes the influences of the rural-agricultural environment on educational consumption patterns in a cross-section of the

---

This research has been supported by a grant from NICHD, "U.S. Fertility in 1900." We are grateful to S. Ryan Johansson and James C. McCann for comments on an earlier version and to Stephen N. Graham for substantial assistance in computer programming. A previous version of this article was presented at the Annual Meeting of the Pacific Sociological Association, Portland, Oregon, March 1984. Address all correspondence to Avery M. Guest, Center for Studies in Demography and Ecology, Department of Sociology, University of Washington, Seattle, WA 98195.

U.S. in 1900. It investigates the causal importance of three characteristics of agricultural communities—the degree of farm mechanization, the availability of farmland for expansion, and the extent of ownership of the agricultural means of production. Although the study is cross-sectional, we believe the results suggest longitudinal processes of change.

Of the two data sets used in the analysis, one permits research on aggregate variations in educational consumption across 46 state-level units of analysis in 1900. Previous research has analyzed interstate variation in educational consumption, but our study is innovative because it attempts to determine how much of this variation is due to interstate variation in agricultural characteristics. The second analysis builds upon the first. Using a representative 1/750 sample of households from the 1900 U.S. manuscript census (Graham, 1980), we link children, aged 10 to 14, and their families with characteristics of the county in which they reside. Within separate farm and nonfarm samples, county agricultural and nonagricultural characteristics are related to individual-level variations in months of school attended per year.

PREVIOUS RESEARCH

Educational consumption in a population is difficult to measure with a single indicator. The development of an educational system can be measured by the highest grade the average individual completes or by the number of days per year the average individual attends school. Contemporary studies of education tend to use the first measure, but this is generally difficult to obtain for historical populations. As a result, researchers have relied more on the average number of school days attended per school-age child during any year (total school days attended by all children/total school-age children). This measure may be considered a product of three probabilities: (1) the proportion of school-age children who actually enroll at some time during the school year (total school-age children enrolled/total school-age children); (2) the proportion of open school days that are actually attended by enrolled students [total school days attended by all children/(total days community kept schools open × total school-age children enrolled)]; (3) the number of days that schools are open for attendance (total days community kept schools open). Thus, the number of school days attended by the average student is (1)×(2)×(3). The social organization of a society's urban-industrial and agricultural sectors may influence the average number of school days attended by children in the community through any or all of the three components.

The importance of distinguishing among these components was emphasized by Meyer et al. (1979) in their analysis of cross-sectional variations in school attendance patterns in the U.S. between 1870 and 1930. Consistent with other research (Landes and Solmon, 1972), they found that the average length of the public school year in the community had a strong positive association with the degree of urbanization and industrialization. However, when other variables were controlled, they found that the propensity to be enrolled in school was negatively related to urbanization. Meyer et al. also found that enrollment propensity was strongly and positively related to a Republican voting orientation and to the evangelical Protestant religious affiliation of the population. They suggested that schools were created in response to a rural-based, entrepreneurial commitment to do God's will in the world. The extension of the school year apparently depended more on factors such as urbanization and industrialization, which are more closely linked to what is loosely described as modernization.

Other researchers (Kaestle and Vinovskis, 1980; Soltow and Stevens, 1977), investigating enrollments in both public and private schools, found that the propensity to enroll in school was at least as great among rural children as it was among urban children at various time points in the late 1800s. However, these analyses show that very high proportions of both urban and rural children enrolled in school at some time during the year, suggesting that enrollment was an accepted pattern for most U.S. children by the late 1800s. In their study of Massachusetts, Kaestle and Vinovskis also found that educational formalization and bureaucratization, which are highly correlated with the length of the school term in the community, were more developed in urban areas.

THE AGRICULTURAL SECTOR

There have been great historical and regional differences in the organization of rural life in the U.S. American farming in areas outside the South underwent an extensive process of mechanization and growth in productivity in the period after the Civil War (Higgs, 1971). Urbanization, industrialization, and an increase in educational consumption occurred at roughly the same time. North (1959) suggested that the agricultural sector was especially important in transforming American society into a high per capita modern economy. Nowhere was the process of agricultural change more evident than in the Midwest and West. The development of railroads opened the interior for trade with other parts of the country and the world. Furthermore, because of economic development in many parts of Europe, the demand for food grew, stimulating American farmers to increase their productivity.

The mechanization of agriculture, or the replacement of relatively unskilled labor by machine production, may influence educational systems in two major ways. First, mechanized agricultural systems require more advanced educational skills, both to operate the machinery and to handle the accompanying complex managerial tasks. Second, and perhaps more importantly, mechanized systems reduce the need for relatively unskilled labor. Since children are especially useful for performing routine, simple tasks, one may hypothesize that farm mechanization reduces the demand for child labor and thus frees increasing numbers of children to attend school on a regular basis.

Some research supports this hypothesis. In his study of the American West in the late nineteenth century, North (1959) found that the mechanization of agriculture was accompanied by an increase in educational expenditures. Medoff and Buchele (cited in Bowles and Gintis, 1976:177) found that interstate variations in agricultural mechanization in the West in the late 1800s were significantly and positively related to variations in public education expenditures. Guest's (1981) analysis of interstate variations in fertility in 1900 indicates that states with mechanized farming systems had relatively low fertility. Much of this relationship was due to the mediating effects of child labor. Agriculturally mechanized states had a reduced need for child labor, which led to a decreased demand for high fertility.

The amount of land available for agricultural expansion is another factor that may encourage consumption of schooling. Economists have been especially interested in the social consequences of the intensive agricultural development that occurred in some parts of the U.S., particularly the Northeast, during its early history (see, for instance, Easterlin, Alter, and Condran, 1978; Forster and Tucker, 1972; Leet, 1975, 1976; Yasuba, 1961). As the nineteenth century progressed, the amount of land available in the older regions for new cultivation declined, thus constraining productivity for individual farm households. A shortage of farmland may influence educational consumption in two ways. First, areas with small plots and little land for expansion have relatively low labor demands; thus, a surplus population is available to attend school. Second, when land is limited, farm parents may recognize the difficulties in buying or controlling currently uncultivated land and, therefore, may have an incentive to send their children to school to develop skills for nonagricultural employment.

Evidence on the relationship between the availability of farmland and educational consumption is mixed. In an investigation of U.S. farm families in 1860, Easterlin et al. (1978) argued that the importance of child labor differed little between old and new settled areas. However, Guest and Tolnay (1983) found that the amount of available farmland was significantly and negatively correlated with the development of the educational system in the late 1800s.

Another important factor to consider is the extent of farm ownership. The United States has stood out among European-settled countries in its high rates of farm ownership, although historical trends in this agricultural characteristic are less evident than those reported for mechanization and land availability. High rates of tenancy are typically associated with little individual social or economic mobility and strong ties to a communal social system (Paige, 1975:36). But in countries with high rates of farm ownership, most farmers believe that social and economic improvement is possible, and education is seen as an important means to that end. Furthermore, farm owners are heavily individualized, dependent on their own initiative and innovative behavior. To the extent that education imparts job skills, it may be perceived as an important means of enhancing farm productivity and the social standing of the farmer.

INTERSTATE VARIATIONS

The analysis in this section focuses on educational consumption in 46 state-level units in 1900. Oklahoma is not included, primarily because so little data from the late 1800s are available (it was not a state in 1900). North and South Dakota are combined into one state unit, because much of the available data from the late 1800s are combined, although they were separate states by 1900.

Data on the consumption of public education for children aged 5 to 18 are drawn from the report of the U.S. Commissioner of Education (1901). The Commissioner's annual reports in the late 1800s and early 1900s provide an invaluable compendium of information about the development of the U.S. educational system. Data on social structural characteristics of states are primarily drawn from the 1900 decennial census. Thus, in this investigation, we are able to utilize closely linked educational and census data.

As noted above, the total number of school days consumed per school-age child is a product of three components: the proportion of children enrolled in school, the proportion of days attended, and the length of the school term. Thus, it is possible to assess exactly the role of each in explaining variations in the total (Duncan, 1967). Using regression analysis with logarithmic transformation, we find that the standardized regression coefficients for the three components are, respectively, 0.251, 0.427, and 0.675. Thus, total consumption of schooling is most strongly influenced by the length of the school term in the community. In contrast, the attendance propensity has very little impact, indicating that interstate variations in the educational consumption of enrolled children were due to variations in the length of the school year. The effect of enrollment propensity is more mixed; i.e., it has an intermediate influence on total consumption.

Using the standard rules of path analysis (Duncan, 1967), we find that the effects of the social structural variables on total educational consumption are completely mediated by the three components. That is, the relationship can be completely decomposed into the contribution of each social structural variable through each component. The contribution of a social structural variable to total consumption through each component is dependent on the strengths of two associations: the relationship of the social structural variable to the component and the relationship of the component to total educational consumption. Social structure has its greatest impact on total consumption through a specific component when each of these two relationships is strong.

STATE SOCIAL STRUCTURE

The relationship of social structural variables to educational consumption is shown in Table 1. The table presents the zero-order Pearsonian correlations between total educational consumption, its components, and various aspects of the social structure. The social structural variables are divided into three sets of indicators: agricultural structure, urban-industrialism, and wage levels. The possible influences of agricultural structure and urban-industrialism require little further discussion.

We have included variables for wage levels in manufacturing as indicators of the relative economic advantages of schooling. Unfortunately, information on general wage levels by state is not available for 1900. We hypothesize that high child wages caused communities to

Table 1. Pearsonian Correlations Between Social Structural Variables and Educational Consumption Measures, in Forty-Six States in 1900

	Component[a]				Mean
	1	2	3	4	(SD)
Agricultural variables					
Mechanization: average value, farm implements, and machinery per farm	.50*	.22	.71*	.75*	158.7 (84.9)
Improved: proportion of arable land that is improved	.14	.13	.41*	.37*	.474 (.203)
Owned: proportion of farmers owning their land	.39*	.11	.25	.36*	.739 (.111)
Urban-industrial variables					
Urban: proportion of population that is urban	.14	.42*	.79*	.70*	.331 (.205)
Nonagricultural: proportion of labor force employed outside agriculture	.27	.35*	.80*	.74*	.617 (.184)
Manufacturing: proportion of labor force employed in manufacturing	.20	.36*	.73*	.66*	.232 (.115)
Wage variables					
Male: average wages in manufacturing for male employees over age 16	.46*	.05	.45*	.52*	483.8 (141.8)
Female: average wages in manufacturing for female employees over age 16	.40*	.17	.43*	.51*	253.2 (53.5)
Child: average wages in manufacturing for child employees aged 10 to 15	.16	−.02	−.06	.02	166.9 (79.9)

Sources: Eldridge and Thomas (1964:Table 1.53), U.S. Bureau of the Census (1902:Table 1, 1904a:Tables 147–149, 1904b:Table 41), U.S. Commissioner of Education (1901:Tables 1, 2, 4, 6, 7).

[a] 1 = enrollment propensity, 2 = attendance propensity, 3 = length of school year in the community, 4 = total days of school consumed per school-age child.

* Significant at the .05 level.

increase their children's involvement in the labor force at the expense of their education. In contrast, relatively high wages for adults probably stimulated support for education. To some degree, high adult wages reflected high skill requirements for jobs. Thus, the community had an incentive to support education as a means of preparing children for a relatively skilled occupational structure. Male adult wages may have served as a particularly strong incentive for educational development. The vast majority of married women did not work; thus, females would have gained economic benefits from attending school for only short periods of their lives.

The correlation coefficients in Table 1 vary greatly in absolute size with the measure of educational consumption and its components. In general, total consumption and the length of the school year are strongly related to the social structural variables, and the patterns of relationships are quite similar. Thus, it seems that the length of the school year is clearly dominant in mediating the effects of social structure on total consumption of schooling: The length of the school term is the strongest component of total consumption and is also a strong correlate of social structure.

In contrast, the enrollment and attendance propensities have much weaker relationships with social structure; therefore, they must have much less effect than length of school term on the relationship between social structure and total educational consumption. Furthermore, attendance propensity is weakly related to total consumption, indicating that it has very little mediating effect between social structure and educational consumption. Enrollment propensity has intermediate effects on total consumption but relatively weak relationships with the social structural variables. Thus, although more important than attendance propensity, enrollment propensity still has a relatively small role in producing the relationship between social structure and educational consumption.

Consistent with previous research, we find that total consumption of schooling and especially the length of the school year are strongly related to the urban-industrial variables. Wage levels for adult men and women also have strong positive associations with these educational variables. However, contrary to predictions, child wages show little relationship with these schooling indicators.

Since we are primarily concerned with the influence of the agricultural variables, it is gratifying to find that they also have the anticipated effects. Total consumption of schooling and length of the school year are especially related to farm mechanization and, to a lesser extent, to measures of farm ownership and the availability of land. In fact, total consumption of schooling is more strongly associated with farm mechanization than any other variable in the table.

The propensity to attend school is strongly and positively related to the urban-industrial variables. This may partly indicate that social control agencies were more effective in urban than in rural areas in enforcing the school attendance legislation that existed in most states outside the South in 1900. However, attendance propensity is only weakly related to the agricultural and wage variables.

As previous research has shown (Meyer et al., 1979), the propensity to enroll in school is weakly related to urban-industrial influences. As this study shows, it has a strong positive association with the degree of farm mechanization and a weaker association with farm ownership. Enrollment propensity is also significantly and positively related to adult male and female wage levels.

To summarize, it appears that the relationship between educational consumption and social structure primarily reflects variations in the length of the school term in the community. Not surprisingly, urban-industrial influences and wage levels appear to be important in understanding variations in educational consumption, but the correlations suggest that the agricultural organization of communities may also be important.[1]

Some of the social structural variables are quite highly correlated. This multicollinearity creates serious problems in assessing their partial effects (Gordon, 1968). In particular, the three urban-industrial variables are so highly intercorrelated (Pearsonian r's > 0.75) that they appear redundant. The wage levels have strong correlations with several other

[1] Religious compositional variables were not included in the analysis, even though Meyer et al. (1979) suggest that they are important. Protestant states probably have more developed educational systems than non-Protestant states, but whether this occurs because Protestant ideology particularly encourages private education or because non-Protestants are more likely to operate private schools is difficult to determine. Meyer et al. have tried to define a Protestant evangelical orientation of states, but their index of orientation apparently includes high weightings for groups such as Congregationalists and Unitarians (Thomas, 1978), who were either evangelical only in some areas or seemed hardly evangelical at all. Others (Ralph and Rubinson, 1980) have argued that native white and foreign-born children in 1900 had equivalent rates of school attendance. On the whole, our measures of agricultural organization seem to do as well or better than the ethnoreligious variables.

variables, but all the correlations (except that between male and female wages [0.84] are less than 0.70; thus, in our opinion, they are within acceptable levels. The three measures of agricultural organization are mildly related to each other (r's < 0.40). They have stronger correlations with some of the urban-industrial and wage variables, but problems of collinearity are not as great as with the urban-industrial and wage-level variables.

To assess the partial effects of the variables, we ran three sets of multiple regression equations (see Table 2). The first set included only the three agricultural variables. The second set included the wage levels of adult males and children and percentage urban, which we used to indicate urban-industrialism. The third set included both the agricultural and nonagricultural variables. Thus, it is possible to assess the overall influence of these groups of variables in relationship to each other.

Both agricultural and nonagricultural variables by themselves explain large amounts of variance in total consumption and length of

Table 2. Standardized Regression Effects of Social Structural Variables on Educational Consumption Measures, in Forty-Six States in 1900 (Standard Errors are in Parentheses)

	Component[a]			
	1	2	3	4
Agricultural variables				
Mechanization: average value, farm implements, and machinery per farm	.29 (.19)	.14 (.23)	.29* (.10)	.35* (.11)
Improved: proportion of arable land that is improved	.40* (.15)	−.02 (.18)	.32* (.08)	.38* (.09)
Owned: proportion of farmers owning their land	.35* (.14)	.09 (.17)	.12 (.08)	.25* (.08)
Nonagricultural variables				
Urban: proportion of population that is urban	−.25 (.14)	.40* (.17)	.50* (.08)	.33* (.08)
Male: average wages in manufacturing for male employees over age 16	.25 (.19)	−.21 (.23)	.16 (.10)	.17 (.11)
Child: average wages in manufacturing for child employees aged 10 to 15	.14 (.12)	−.02 (.15)	−.10 (.07)	−.02 (.07)
R^2 for all variables	.439	.199	.838	.816
R^2 for agricultural variables only	.353	.070	.655	.728
R^2 for nonagricultural variables only	.220	.184	.701	.605

[a] 1 = enrollment propensity, 2 = attendance propensity, 3 = length of school year in the community, 4 = total days of school consumed per school-age child.

* Significant at the .05 level.

the school term. The sets of variables share extensive overlap in explained variance; i.e., the variance explained in the third regression is much less than the sum of the variances explained in the first two regressions. It is particularly important to note that the agricultural variables add sizable amounts of variance to that explained by the nonagricultural variables in predicting enrollment, length of school term, and total consumption.

When we examine specific structural variables, we find that two of the three agricultural variables and the percentage urban have statistically significant partial effects on total consumption and the length of the school year. Farm ownership has a statistically significant partial effect on total consumption, but an insignificant effect on the length of the school year. The hypothesized causal relationship between the agricultural variables and these important measures of educational consumption is therefore supported.

Even though farm mechanization has the strongest zero-order correlation with enrollment propensity, only the farm ownership and improved land variables are statistically significant predictors. Consistent with previous research, none of the nonagricultural variables have statistically significant partial effects. Urbanization is the only statistically significant partial predictor of school attendance.

Given problems of data availability, we are able to focus only on public education. Comparable data on private education were not collected by the Commissioner of Education at the turn of the century. Fortunately, only a small proportion of school-age children attended private schools in 1900. In 36 of the 46 state units, an average of 5.7 percent of all school-age children were enrolled in private school (U.S. Commissioner of Education, 1901:Table 11).

It is possible, nevertheless, that the consumption of schooling varied across states according to differences in the importance of private education. However, when we included various indicators of state differences in private education, we found that they had only minimal effects on the relationship of the components to total consumption and on the relationship of social structure to total consumption and each of the components.

It is also possible that educational consumption varied according to differences in age structure. We expect states with a high proportion of children in their late teens to consume less education, primarily through nonenrollment and nonattendance, than states with a high proportion of young children. Unfortunately, the available published data did not systematically report the consumption of education by specific ages. However, statistical control for the proportion of children aged 15 to 18 had little influence on our previous conclusions.

SCHOOL ATTENDANCE PATTERNS IN RURAL SETTINGS

The state-level data suffer from an important limitation: They do not permit examination *within* rural settings. Given the major focus of our investigation—the linkage between agricultural organization and educational consumption—it is important to focus specifically on rural children. An alternate set of data allows such a restriction in scope. In the following analysis, the 1/750 public use sample of the 1900 census manuscripts is used to examine the schooling patterns of rural, native white children of native parentage. We appended the aggregate contextual characteristics of the county of residence to individual and household records. For each child, months in school are reported; therefore, it is possible to relate aggregate characteristics of the county to individual propensities to attend public or private school.

The sample consists of all children of the appropriate parentage and nationality who were between the ages of 10 and 14 and who were living with their mothers at the time of census enumeration. This particular age interval was chosen partly because it falls between the younger primary school ages, when schooling was extremely widespread, and the older secondary school ages, when attendance declined sharply. Rubinson and Ralph (1984:142) have suggested that technical change in the social environment had its strongest effect on attendance in the higher primary grades. We restricted the sample to children living with their mothers for three reasons. First, we originally developed the sample to investigate the relationship between the economic value of children and mothers' fertility behavior. Second, by restricting the sample to children living with their mothers, we could easily link the children to household characteristics. Finally, children not living with their mothers are likely to be quite geographically mobile; thus, their educational consumption patterns might not reflect the normal environment in which they had grown up.

The control for ethnicity (native whites of native parentage) permits us to investigate a relatively homogeneous group that should not be seriously affected by racial or ethnic discrimination and should be heavily influenced by residential environment. Nevertheless, in other analyses, we found that many of the contextual variables worked similarly for blacks and foreign-born individuals.

We estimate that the sample includes over 90 percent of all the native white children in the public use file who were aged 10 to 14 and who had native parents.

Enumerators in the 1900 census were asked to report months of school attended during the previous 12 months for all school-age children. A zero was to be entered for all children who had not attended school. As the census officials of the time discovered, significant percentages of school-age children had missing data for school attendance. They could not determine the degree to which the nonreports were due to reporting failure or to the enumerators' assumptions that nonattenders should not be reported. Obviously, our estimates of school consumption depend on our treatment of these missing data. Our analysis of the missing cases in the public use file showed that they were similar to those who attended zero months of school in their rates of employment. The Census Bureau itself tended to treat the missing cases as nonenrolled. Given these patterns, we decided to treat children with missing data and children who had not attended as nonenrolled, although this may have produced an artificially low estimate of school consumption.

In Table 3, we report the distribution of months enrolled for rural farm and nonfarm children; we include information on urban children for comparison. The categories are based on the modern definition of a rural place—a community with fewer than 2,500 inhabitants. The average months of school attendance was clearly greatest in urban areas and lowest in the farm sector. This pattern is less evident for any enrollment at all (less than one month as opposed to more).

The individual-level data on months of school attended during the preceding year allow us to distinguish between the propensity to enroll or not enroll, but they do not let us distinguish between the amount of school consumption that was due to restrictions on the length of the school year and the amount that was due to the propensity to attend while school was open. Unfortunately, it was not possible to determine the length of the school year in individual counties. Official state educational reports frequently indicated the average length of the school year by county, but the data were sometimes reported in noncomparable form. Furthermore, we did not have the resources to retrieve county reports for all or most states in 1900.

We do not believe this limitation is as great as it appears. As our state-level analysis demonstrated, most of the relationship between total educational consumption and social

Table 3. Percentage Distribution of Months in School, for Native White Children Aged 10 to 14 with Native Parents, in 1909

Months in School	Urban ($N = 1{,}330$)	Rural: Nonfarm ($N = 1{,}173$)	Rural: Farm ($N = 2{,}677$)	Total ($N = 5{,}180$)
Missing, no report	12.4	15.4	14.3	14.1
0	1.3	3.0	4.3	3.2
1	0.0	0.5	1.5	0.9
2	0.4	1.9	6.4	3.8
3	0.2	3.2	8.4	5.1
4	0.5	4.2	10.5	6.5
5	1.2	5.5	12.5	8.0
6	1.5	7.5	12.0	8.3
7	1.7	10.7	9.9	8.0
8	9.8	18.2	11.3	12.5
9	51.8	25.7	7.5	23.0
10 or more	19.2	4.2	1.3	6.5
Total	100.0	100.0	99.9	99.9
Percent attending	86.3	81.6	81.3	82.6
Mean duration (months)	7.7	6.0	4.6	5.7

Source: Graham (1980).

structure, especially among those enrolled, was due to variations in the length of the school year. School attendance propensity had weak relationships with both social structure and total educational consumption. We have little reason to believe that the patterns would be noticeably different if the focus were shifted to a lower level of aggregation.

Given our findings about the importance of the length of the school year in understanding variations in educational consumption, it seems reasonable to focus on aggregate county characteristics in explaining individual variations. The educational consumption of individual children must have been heavily influenced by community decisions on the length of the school term. Indeed, in analyses not reported in this article, we found that individual child and household attributes such as the employment status of mother and father and the age and number of siblings were relatively weak predictors of individual variations in educational consumption. Moreover, there was little evidence of statistical interactions between individual and contextual-level characteristics in predicting educational consumption for individual children.

We should acknowledge, nevertheless, that characteristics of *individual* farms have not been included in the analysis because the public use sample did not link the population and farm census schedules. Farm characteristics of individual children may have influenced their educational consumption in different ways than county-level farm characteristics.

In Table 4, we present for individual children the zero-order Pearsonian correlations between their aggregated county characteristics (drawn from published census reports) and their individual months in school. The sample is smaller than the sample in Table 3 because respondents with missing data for the independent variables were eliminated. Separate analyses were conducted for farm and nonfarm residents to allow for unique effects of the county characteristics on schooling within types of residence. This is desirable given the potential for farm and nonfarm families to respond differently to the agricultural conditions prevailing in their areas. In other analyses, we found (not surprisingly) that the urban children responded very little to the agricultural characteristics of their counties.

We again divided the variables into three different sets, but we had to make slight changes in variable definitions because of data availability problems. We analyzed only total educational consumption (individual months of school), partly to keep the study manageable, but also because total educational consumption is probably the best measure of educational development. As suggested earlier, it is probably influenced most strongly by the length of the school term in the community.[2]

The correlations between social structure and educational consumption are strongest among farm children. The correlation for nonfarm children exceeds that for farm children in only one variable (female wages). This may partially reflect the somewhat wider range of

[2] Analysis of the relationship between county-level characteristics and enrollment propensity for individual children was not particularly revealing. Urbanization and industrialization had small effects within the various samples; the major explanatory variables were agricultural characteristics and male wage levels.

Table 4. Pearsonian Correlations Between County Social Structural Variables and Total Educational Consumption in 1900

	Type of Residence	
	Rural Nonfarm ($N = 1{,}028$)	Rural Farm ($N = 2{,}009$)
Agricultural variables		
Mechanization: average value, farm implements, and machinery per farm	.31*	.46*
Improved: proportion of arable land that is improved	.25*	.36*
Owned: proportion of farmers owning their land	.01	.06*
Urban-industrial variables		
Centadj: respondent's county or adjacent county has city with a population greater than 50,000	.10*	.25*
Manupcp: number of manufacturing establishments per capita	.27*	.39*
Wage variables		
Male: average wages in manufacturing for male employees over age 16	.32*	.42*
Female: average wages in manufacturing for female employees over age 16	.17*	.11*
Child: average wages in manufacturing for child employees aged 10 to 15	.15*	.15*

Source: Inter-University Consortium for Political and Social Research (1980).
* Significant at the .05 level.

variation in schooling for the farm children, as was shown in Table 3. The social structural variables operate over a wider range of variation in the farm sample. At the same time, the stronger associations in the farm sample suggest that the social forces considered here were more germane to the schooling patterns of farmers' children.

All the agricultural variables have the expected relationships with educational consumption. For both groups, greater mechanization, a larger proportion of improved land, and more extensive farm ownership were accompanied by greater school attendance. Though statistically significant, the correlation for farm ownership is extremely modest. The urban-industrial characteristics are also positively correlated with schooling: Greater urban influence and a larger concentration of manufacturing establishments are associated with longer school terms. Finally, manufacturing wages for adult males and females are positively correlated with schooling, but remuneration of child workers apparently does not foster shorter school years, as was originally hypothesized.

Some readers may be troubled because the relationships at the county level are much lower than those at the state level. However, one should remember that the state-level data were aggregate, and the county-level data involve relationships between aggregate county-level variables and *individual* school consumption.

Table 5 shows the partial effects of the county characteristics when all are regressed on educational consumption for both of the rural samples. Since the intercorrelations among the social structural variables are somewhat lower across counties than they are across states, we decided to include all of them in both equations.

Following a strategy similar to that used in the first part of the article, we ran three sets of regressions for each population. The first included only the agricultural variables, the second included only the nonagricultural variables, and the third included both agricultural and nonagricultural variables. The explained variances for each set are reported in Table 5, and the partial regression coefficients (in standardized form) are shown for the final, most inclusive equation. The unstandardized regression coefficients showed similar results.

Some feel for the relative importance of sets of variables may be gained by comparing the explained variances from the three regressions. As might be expected, the agricultural variables are considerably more important for the farm sample; they explain about twice as much variance than in the nonfarm sample. It is clear that the agricultural and nonagricultural variables share substantial overlap in predictive power for both groups. This is especially true for the farm children: The addition of the nonagricultural characteristics increases the amount of explained variance by only 9.2 percent. For the nonfarm sample the corresponding increment to R^2 is 31.4 percent.

Turning to the partial effects of individual

Table 5. Standardized Regression Effects of County Social Structural Variables on Total Educational Consumption in 1900 (Standard Errors are in Parentheses)

	Type of Residence	
	Rural Nonfarm ($N = 1{,}028$)	Rural Farm ($N = 2{,}009$)
Agricultural variables		
Mechanization: average value, farm implements, and machinery per farm	.12*	.21*
	(.04)	(.03)
Improved: proportion of arable land that is improved	.14*	.17*
	(.04)	(.03)
Owned: proportion of farmers owning their land	.02	.06*
	(.04)	(.02)
Urban-industrial variables		
Centadj: respondent's county or adjacent county has city with a population greater than 50,000	−.10*	.07*
	(.03)	(.02)
Manupcp: number of manufacturing establishments per capita	.15*	.12*
	(.04)	(.03)
Wage variables		
Male: average wages in manufacturing for male employees over age 16	.16*	.12*
	(.04)	(.03)
Female: average wages in manufacturing for female employees over age 16	.01	.01
	(.04)	(.02)
Child: average wages in manufacturing for child employees aged 10 to 15	.02	−.02
	(.03)	(.02)
R^2 for all variables	.163	.272
R^2 for agricultural variables only	.124	.249
R^2 for nonagricultural variables only	.133	.227

* Significant at the .05 level.

social structural variables, we find general consistency with the patterns for zero-order correlations shown in Table 4. However, in this case, the partial effects are somewhat weaker because of the intercorrelations among the variables. The agricultural variables, especially farm mechanization and proportion of improved land, have rather impressive effects on the length of the school year for both groups. The effect of farm ownership on the schooling of farm children is significant, but it is considerably weaker than the effects of the other agricultural variables. As suggested by the comparison of R^2 above, the prevailing agricultural characteristics of the county of residence played a greater role in shaping the schooling patterns of farm children.

In contrast, specific nonagricultural variables are more effective in predicting the schooling of nonfarm residents. Among the statistically significant effects shown in Table 5, the concentration of manufacturing establishments and adult male wages in manufacturing both have slightly greater influence in the nonfarm equation. Urban influence is also stronger among nonfarm residents, but we cannot explain why it is negative. Finally, neither adult female wages in manufacturing nor child wages has a statistically significant effect for either group of children.

These findings lend further support to the general inferences drawn from the state-level analysis described above. It appears that the conditions of agricultural organization, specifically the degree of farm mechanization and the availability of additional arable land, were important in shaping the demand for schooling in rural America. Nonagricultural conditions were also relevant in this regard, but they were more important for nonfarm residents, and only secondarily important for farm residents.

SUMMARY AND CONCLUSION

Although our results are entirely cross-sectional, we believe that they may have important implications for understanding the development of American public education. As we have pointed out, the modernization of the U.S. involved both the heavy mechanization of agriculture and the gradual expansion of agricultural settlement, especially in the nineteenth century. Each of these changes reduced the economic role of children in the society and thereby altered the need and demand for education.

We have not attempted to resolve the controversy generated by the clash between conflict and functionalist theorists over the true explanation for increased U.S. schooling during the past few decades. As Rubinson and Ralph (1984) have suggested, there is merit in both perspectives. Nevertheless, our analysis has perhaps reinforced the functionalist interpretation of educational expansion in nineteenth century America by showing that the agricultural characteristics of the society were related in predictable ways to variations in the consumption of schooling.

When the state- and individual-level analyses are considered together, our results strongly suggest that the technical, albeit agricultural, aspects of the environment required or permitted the growth of modern schooling. The primary effect appears to have been exerted through collective decisions about the appropriate length of the school term, decisions that were made to suit the prevailing social organization of the community. For individual children, such decisions may have imposed constraints on schooling opportunities, which were independent of the needs or desires of specific families.

A considerably weaker community technical effect operated through children's propensity to enroll in school. Our analyses stress the importance of environmental influences on the value and necessity of schooling within certain settings, but it is also possible that the propensity to enroll was influenced by the circumstances faced by individual families. If so, then individual decision making would also have been a component shaping total consumption of schooling. As we have pointed out, however, because of data limitations, we cannot determine how characteristics of the individual child's farm influenced individual variations in levels of schooling. In any case, since much of the variation in children's schooling was due to the length of the school year in the community, it seems unlikely that the inclusion of controls for these characteristics would change our major conclusions about the importance of community social organization.

Although our analysis of the mechanisms through which agricultural organization affected schooling is clearly functionalist, it is possible that alternative (or complementary) arguments concerning status competition or elite activities could be used to explain additional aspects of educational expansion among the rural population. For example, processes such as those posited by conflict theorists may have operated in community-level decisions to define the maximum length of the school year. Given space limitations, we leave to other researchers an elaboration of such status competition theories.

Generalizations from one society must be made cautiously. Yet we believe these results may have important implications for our understanding of the dramatic expansion of educational systems throughout the world during the past three decades. Theories of school system development have been based on the view that change must emanate from the urban-industrial sector. Our results suggest that the agricultural community is itself sharply differentiated and that some sectors of the agricultural community are leading advocates of educational change. Obviously, agricultural systems in other parts of the world cannot be analyzed with exactly the same variables used here. But we need to focus more attention on how the functions of children change as agricultural economies modernize.

REFERENCES

Ayres, L. P.
1920 An Index Number for State School Systems. New York: Russell Sage.

Bowles, S. and H. Gintis
1976 Schooling in Capitalist America. New York: Basic Books.

Collins, R.
1979 The Credential Society: An Historical Sociology of Education and Stratification. New York: Academic Press.

Duncan, O. D.
1967 "Path analysis: Sociological examples." American Journal of Sociology 72:1–16.

Easterlin, R., G. Alter, and G. A. Condran
1978 "Farms and farm families in old and new areas: The northern states in 1860." Pp. 22–84 in T. K. Hareven and M. A. Vinovskis (eds.), Family and Population in Nineteenth Century America. Princeton: Princeton University Press.

Eldridge, H. T. and D. S. Thomas
1964 Population Redistribution and Economic Growth: United States, 1870–1950. Part III. Demographic Analyses and Interrelations. Philadelphia: American Philosophical Society.

Field, A. J.
1976 "Educational expansion in mid-nineteenth century Massachusetts: Human capital formation or structural transformation?" Harvard Educational Review 46:521–52.

Forster, C. and G. S. L. Tucker
1972 Economic Opportunity and White American Fertility Ratios, 1800–1860. New Haven: Yale University Press.

Gordon, R. A.
1968 "Issues in multiple regression." American Journal of Sociology 73:592–616.

Graham, S. N.
1980 1900 Public Use Sample Users' Handbook. Seattle: Center for Studies in Demography and Ecology, University of Washington.

Guest, A. M.
1981 "Social structure and U.S. inter-state fertility differentials in 1900." Demography 18:465–86.

Guest, A. M. and S. Tolnay
1983 "Children's roles and fertility: Late nineteenth-century evidence." Social Science History 7:355–80.

Higgs, R.
1971 The Transformation of the American Economy: 1865–1914. New York: Wiley.

Inter-University Consortium for Political and Social Research
1980 Guide to Resources and Services: 1979–1980. Ann Arbor: Institute for Social Research, University of Michigan.

Jensen, R. J. and M. Friedberger
1976 Education and Social Structure: An Historical Study of Iowa, 1870–1930. Chicago: Newberry Library.

Kaestle, C. F. and M. A. Vinovskis
1980 Education and Social Change in Nineteenth-Century Massachusetts. New York: Cambridge University Press.

Katz, M. B. and I. E. Davey
1978 "School attendance and early industrialization in a Canadian city: A multivariate analysis." History of Education Quarterly 18:271–93.

Landes, W. and L. Solmon
1972 "Compulsory schooling legislation: An economic analysis of law and social change in the nineteenth century." Journal of Economic History 32:54–97.

Leet, D. R.
1975 "Human fertility and agricultural opportunities in Ohio counties: From frontier to maturity, 1810–1860." Pp. 138–58 in D. C. Klingaman and R. K. Vedder (eds.), Essays in Nineteenth-Century Economic History: The Old Northwest. Athens, OH: Ohio University Press.
1976 "The determinants of the fertility transition in antebellum Ohio." The Journal of Economic History 36:359–78.

Meyer, J. W., D. Tyack, J. Nagal, and A. Gordon
1979 "Public education as nation-building in America: Enrollments and bureaucratization in the American states, 1870–1930." American Journal of Sociology 85:591–613.

North, D. C.
1959 "Agriculture in regional economic growth." Journal of Farm Economics 41:943–58.

Paige, J. M.
1975 Agrarian Revolution. New York: Free Press.

Ralph, J. H. and R. Rubinson
1980 "Immigration and the expansion of schooling in the United States, 1850–1970." American Sociological Review 45:943–54.

Rubinson, R. and J. H. Ralph
1984 "Technical change and the expansion of schooling in the United States, 1890–1970." Sociology of Education 57:134–52.

Soltow, L. and E. Stevens
1977 "Economic aspects of school participation in mid-nineteenth century United States." Journal of Interdisciplinary History 8:221–43.

Thomas, G. M.
1978 "Institutional knowledge and social movements: Rational exchange, revival religion and nation-building in the United States, 1870–1896." Ph.D. dissertation, Stanford University.

Troer, S. K.
1975 The Public and the Schools: Shaping the St. Louis System, 1838–1920. Columbia, MO: University of Missouri Press.

U. S. Bureau of the Census
1902 Manufacturers, Part II. States and Territories. Washington, DC: U.S. Government Printing Office.
1904a Abstract of the Twelfth Census of the United States: 1900. Washington, DC: U.S. Government Printing Office.
1904b Special Reports. Occupations at the Twelfth Census. Washington, DC: U.S. Government Printing Office.
1949 Historical Statistics of the United States, 1789–1945. Washington, DC: U.S. Government Printing Office.

U.S. Commissioner of Education
1901 Report for the Year 1899–1900. Vol. 1. Washington, DC: U.S. Government Printing Office.

Vinovskis, M. A.
1983 "Quantification and the analysis of American antebellum education." The Journal of Interdisciplinary History 12:761–86.

Yasuba, Y.
1961 Birth Rates of the White Population in the United States, 1800–1860: An Economic Study. Studies in Historical and Political Science, Series 79, No. 2. Baltimore: Johns Hopkins University.

EFFECTS OF IMMIGRANT WORKERS ON EDUCATIONAL STRATIFICATION IN GERMANY

DAVID P. BAKER
Catholic University of America

YILMAZ ESMER
Bogazici University

GERO LENHARDT
Max Planck Institute for Education and Human Development

JOHN MEYER
Stanford University

Sociology of Education 1985, Vol. 58 (October):213–227

When guestworkers arrived in West Germany in the late 1950s, they were considered a temporary labor force. However, despite government policy and public attitudes, they have become a permanent part of German society. We examine how the large-scale immigration of foreign workers into West Germany has affected the educational stratification of the native population. Two models of host society adaptation are considered: (1) an incorporation model, in which the immigrants enter at the bottom of the domestic stratification system and cause massive upward mobility of the native population, and (2) an external model, in which immigrants remain outside most aspects of the domestic order and cause little status change in the native population. Aggregate longitudinal analyses have uncovered two trends: (1) at the national level, the influx of foreigners has caused German students to move out of the lowest stream of secondary school into the higher streams; and (2) at the local level, the presence of foreigners in some areas has caused horizontal outmigration of German families with school-aged children. These different trends may be a function of different patterns of regional economic development. The findings suggest that Germany's adjustment to the mass immigration of guestworkers fits the incorporation model.

The impact of immigration on domestic stratification is a traditional and important sociological theme. One aspect of this theme is the effect of immigration on the structure of schooling in modern societies (Ralph and Rubinson, 1980; Collins, 1971, 1976). In this article, we consider how the recent large-scale immigration of foreign workers into West Germany has affected the educational stratification of the native population. Specifically, we consider how the presence of foreign children in the secondary school system has affected the track placement of German students. We examine this relationship at the national, state, and county levels. Our central question is simple: Does the foreign population remain external to the educational stratification system, relegated to an expanded track, or does it become incorporated, thereby pushing the native population upward in the educational structure?

BACKGROUND

In present society, economic production and exchange are organized on a world scale, but populations are organized within nation-states by citizenship rules. Dialectically linked, the world economy and the nation-state have gained in strength and importance over a long period. This relationship has produced many inconsistencies, some of which arise from the problem of relating a labor force that is increasingly based in the nation-state to an economy that is increasingly shifting and international. One way to resolve this inconsistency is to fix labor forces in place and move capital investment around to fit the fixed labor system. But a number of institutional forces within the nation-state resist the maximal use of this strategy. For example, rich states do not always encourage the flight of capital (and thus

The research reported here was conducted at and supported by funds from the Education, Work, and Societal Development Division of the Max Planck Institute for Education and Human Development. The authors want to thank the director of this division, Karl Ulrich Mayer, for his support of the Guestworker Research Project. They are also grateful to Lou Trommer and Helmut Köhler for their assistance in collecting data, Julie Baker for her help in the data analysis, and Peter Roeder, Richard Rubinson, and Thor Thorlindsson for comments on earlier drafts. Address all correspondence to David P. Baker, Department of Sociology, Catholic University of America, Washington, DC 20064.

jobs), and poor states try to constrain the influx of capital for fear of domination. To avoid capital movement, states have encouraged the flow of labor through immigration policies. In this article, we examine the ramifications of a labor immigration strategy within one nation-state.

A number of models of immigration and its political regulation have been implemented in various states at various times. Considered together, these models form a continuum. At one extreme is the incorporation model—common in some periods of American history (Gordon, 1964)—in which labor moves easily to more successful countries and becomes integrated into the bottom of the domestic stratification system, driving the native population upward. Such a system might limit international inequalities but increase domestic inequalities, since new, lower strata are added to the system. Such models of free immigration may be especially common under conditions of rapid economic expansion and in political and cultural systems open to penetration and the incorporation of new populations.

At the other extreme are exclusionist systems, which attempt to maintain strong economic and cultural boundaries. The recent historical period, in which themes such as national unity and cultural integration have been emphasized, has celebrated exclusionary models and has deplored large-scale labor flows. Unlike incorporation models, exclusionary models create greater domestic equality and greater international inequality. International inequalities among formally autonomous and bounded national societies are astounding, and domestic inequalities are considerably smaller than most of the classic theories anticipated: We live in a world in which one's most important capital or status asset is one's citizenship (Meyer, 1980).

Between these two extremes lie a series of models that promote immigration for economic purposes while they exclude immigrants from political and cultural domains. In these systems, immigrants remain outside most aspects of the domestic order and constitute a kind of external colony (Portes, 1979; Olzak, 1983). The native population may gain economically, but the political and cultural order is retained. This is not what occurred in the cities of the American North in the late nineteenth century. Rather, it is similar to what happened in the American South in an earlier period: The importation of large numbers of slaves permitted the domestic economy to expand, but it did not directly create major upward shifts in the status structure of the citizenry. Such systems of partial exclusion have been quite common in modern history. Wallerstein (1974) believes they are characteristic of economic expansion in peripheral areas of Western society.

It is interesting to consider the contemporary immigration of foreign workers into Northern Europe in this light. Since World War II, rapid economic expansion has created a contradiction between labor and capital supply. One solution has been the rapid increase in the exportation of economic capital. Another has been the massive importation of foreign workers, primarily from Southern Europe and the Mediterranean countries. In 1981, 9.5 percent of West Germany's labor force was foreign—about 4.5 million people (Castles, 1984). Most of these foreign workers held low-status jobs. Other Northern European countries have also had high percentages of foreign workers: France, 6.4 percent; The Netherlands, 4.9 percent; Belgium, 8.7 percent; Sweden, 5.4 percent; Great Britain, 7.2 percent; and Switzerland, 22.9 percent. Almost all these figures represent large increases over earlier decades. For example, in 1960 only 1.7 percent of the West German labor force was foreign (Castles, 1984).

An ideology of internal or external nationalist expansion—a line of thinking in disrepute after World War II—did not play a role in conceptions of the immigration process in any of these countries. Instead, the notion that immediate labor force demands could be met by importing temporary workers prevailed (Rist, 1978). The underlying assumption was that the migrants would eventually return to their native countries—an assumption shared by the migrant populations themselves (Heckmann, 1981). The whole process was made easier by the rules of the European Economic Community (EEC), which permitted easy labor migration and blocked restrictive applications based on citizenship. But workers from outside the EEC were granted the same access, and after the first waves of migration, most foreign workers came from outside of this community. In 1980, Turks made up the largest fraction of West Germany's foreign population, followed by Yugoslavs and Greeks. Of the 4.5 million foreign workers, 1.5 million were Turks, 632 thousand were Yugoslavs, and 300 thousand were Greeks (Köhler and Trommer, 1981).

Gastarbeiter (guestworker) originally implied a politically controlled program in which foreign workers were expected to migrate into and out of Germany according to labor market requirements. Young, healthy, single, male foreigners would come to Germany for a few years and would be replaced by others (or nobody) as the business cycle demanded. But the state management of immigration took on more political functions and affected the implementation of the program. The state served interests of its own, well beyond passive economic management (Dohse, 1981). Economically, the state gained a broader tax base with low overhead costs for social services. Politically, the reliance on immigrant labor with weak political rights made it possible to tightly control labor and provided sufficient labor competition to fight inflation. It also helped backward areas by providing inexpensive labor for farm and small business work. Internationally, the program provided Germany with close links to Mediterranean states, keeping markets open.

Thus, immigration policy has been an important instrument in the state's political arsenal. Its importance has increased as the international division of labor has become more differentiated and as the modern state has taken on more responsibility for structural problems in civil society.

But because of the state's self-interested involvement, the program has never been based solely on simple labor force requirements. In practice, despite the original expectations, the foreign worker communities have remained while unemployment has increased; and the mostly male workers have been joined by their wives and children. (Governmental interference in such processes was hard to contemplate in postwar Europe.) Some individual workers and families do return to their countries of origin, but others find their way in (sometimes illegally) despite recession-fueled attempts to block them (Rist, 1978; Castles, 1984). Indeed, the birth rate is considerably higher in the guestworker population than in the native population (Max Planck Institute, 1983). Thus, since the oil crises in 1973, when the German government began vain efforts to block the growth of the foreign population, the guestworker population has increased from about 4 million to 4.5 million.

Immigration has not provoked major social conflicts, even though unemployment has risen throughout Western Europe. But ideologically and organizationally, Northern European countries, in which notions of national ethnic and cultural unity are typically more developed than they are in the U.S., have had much difficulty accepting the situation. The current, center-right government in Germany believes that most of the foreign labor force should be motivated to go back home and that the remaining labor should be integrated as soon as possible. But by *integration* they mean cultural assimilation, not the real expansion of political rights for members of foreign communities. Only the radical (Green) opposition party advocates equal rights for foreigners.

Thus, the relationship between the immigrant population and the domestic nation-state is unclear. The German state, like most other Northern European countries, advocates an exclusionary policy. Their pronouncements read as if the strong turn-of-the-century nation-state were still in place and the compromises of the twentieth century had never happened. The official position is that foreign workers are temporary, that they can be sent home when unemployment rises. They are not considered part of the national culture, society, or educational system (there are even some segregated schools). In this exclusionary model, the immigrants keep the domestic economy moving then go home; they make everyone richer without altering society and its status order. But political efforts to exclude immigrants run counter to practical programs promoted by the same state for the integration of the foreign populations. These programs reflect the German state's inability to implement the stated exclusionary policies even when unemployment calls for it.

The obstacles to an exclusionary strategy are many. Germans, still reminded of the horrors of coercive nationalism, find this strategy very offensive. The churches, welfare organizations, and liberal public object strongly. The business community resists state intervention in personnel policies (and a reduction in the labor force). But most important are the obstacles at the international level: Germany is linked politically and economically to the EEC, to NATO, to numerous other states (through bilateral treaties), and to international agencies (e.g., the United Nations Charter of Human Rights). This network of interdependencies prevents Germany from capriciously expelling its foreign population. For example, Turkey has direct market and treaty relations with Germany and a myriad of indirect relations through the EEC, NATO, and the United Nations. Thus, Turkey (which for economic reasons cannot absorb millions of its emigrated citizens) has the means to prevent Germany from expelling Turks.

In Europe, the multiplicity of citizenships within a single society has become a permanent phenomenon. In Germany in the last one hundred years, periods without large-scale foreign employment have been rare. This trend has created a society much different from the classical Western nation-state, which was based upon equality in terms of uniform citizenship and civil rights. Relative equality prevails in the labor market, but it exists between groups with quite different political and welfare relations to the several involved states. International agreements between

Germany and other countries have far-reaching effects on even the private lives of individuals: Education, cultural and religious practices, family relations, political activities, and displays of ethnic sentiments are subject to international agreements that have different effects on different ethnic groups. In short, a puzzling combination of economic and political structures characterizes the formerly uniform national societies.

We examine the social order in West Germany to determine whether it is as exclusive as formal German immigration policy suggests or whether there is more complete interdependence and incorporation.

How much has the social organization of West Germany been altered by the presence of guestworkers? This central question could be investigated in many areas of the social order. Most obviously, it is important to consider how guestworkers have affected the distribution of the native West German population across occupational groups. The literature on American stratification during the great period of industrialization and immigration between the Civil War and the 1920s suggests that the low-status immigrant population increased domestic opportunity structures and created upward mobility.

In this article, we can consider only one aspect of the question—the impact of foreign immigration on the distribution of West German students within the educational hierarchy. In other words, we investigate whether the guestworkers' children are simply added on, as a temporary appendage, with no effect on the stratification of the West German educational system, or whether they are incorporated into the bottom and create upward mobility and increased educational opportunity for the native population. Our investigation is made possible by the degree to which the West German educational system continues to be organized around formalized, nationwide tracks, which are considerably important in terms of status and opportunity.

CATEGORIES OF GERMAN SECONDARY EDUCATION

Like almost all developed countries, West Germany has a relatively homogeneous elementary school system. Elementary school lasts from four to six years. There is some tracking, but not much, and in principle all students are exposed to the same curriculum and the same standards.

But West Germany's secondary school system diverges sharply from the homogeneous and comprehensive systems in most developed countries (Benavot, 1983). After much controversy, West Germany, almost alone among Western countries, rejected proposals for comprehensive secondary schooling (Max Planck Institute, 1983). The West German states, which have primary constitutional authority over education, have hardly touched on the traditional distinction between the three main types of secondary schools—the *Gymnasium,* the *Realschule,* and the *Hauptschule.* The Gymnasium is a nine-year program leading to the degree required for university entrance. It has traditionally been a selective and demanding institution. The Realschule leads to a certificate intended to permit entry into white-collar, business, or skilled trade occupations. The program is three years shorter than the Gymnasium program, but it is also relatively demanding. The Realschule certificate is not sufficient for admission to the university, but it can provide formal (albeit rare) access to programs that are. The Hauptschule has the lowest status and provides the least career opportunities. The program is shorter (including primary school, about nine to ten years), and the schools are not selective. Traditionally, the great majority of Germans were enrolled in the Hauptschule, but since the expansion of higher education in the last twenty years, the Hauptschule has enrolled students who are quite low in status, ability, previous performance, and aspirations (Max Planck Institute, 1983). (See Figure 1 for a diagram of the German school system.)

The secondary school system is divided into two levels. The first level, Secondary I, includes the fifth through tenth years of schooling—all of the Hauptschule and Realschule curricula and two thirds of the Gymnasium curriculum. The second level, Secondary II, includes the last three years of the Gymnasium, full-time vocational school, part-time vocational school, and apprenticeship. Though the system is not completely fixed, the track chosen in Secondary I largely determines further steps. Attendance in the Hauptschule, Realschule, or Gymnasium in Secondary I limits the range of options in the higher levels of the system. The options in Secondary II reflect the qualitative differences between the types of schooling in Secondary I. Clearly, educational stratification begins in Secondary I, which greatly affects further schooling and access to occupational categories. Unlike Americans, who use much higher levels in the school system as definitional criteria, Germans can, and do, use the relative differences occurring at Secondary I to define themselves vis-à-vis the entire educational system. Political attempts to introduce comprehensive schools, or at least some organizational structures of them, had only limited success.

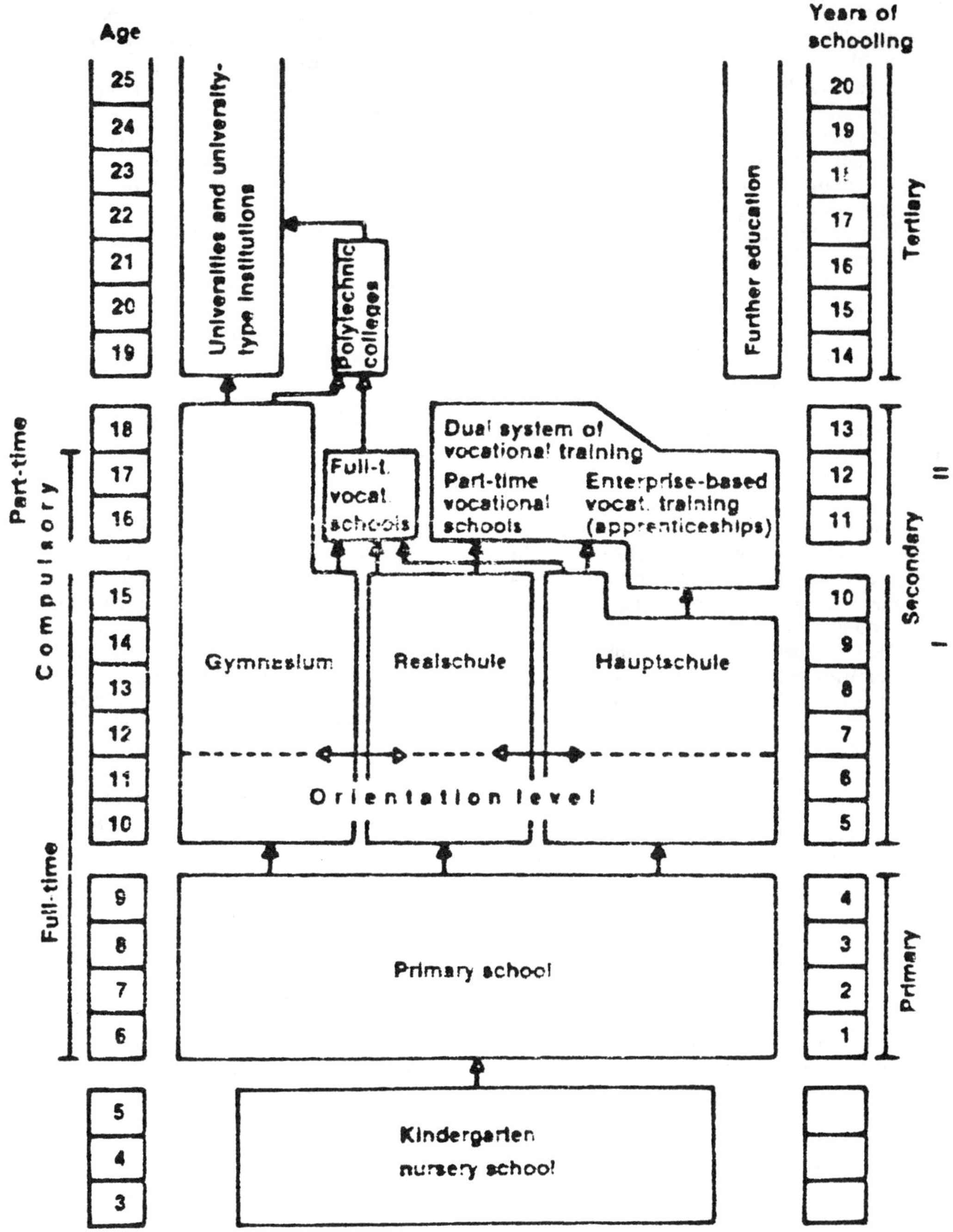

Figure 1. Diagram of the structure of the German school system. (Adapted, by permission, from Max Planck Institute, 1983:Figure 2.1.)

The three main types of schools in Secondary I are closely associated with substantive status rights. There is a great deal of mismatching, of course, but in German thinking, each type of school is linked to a particular social status. The Gymnasium is linked to the university-prepared official, intellectual, and professional roles. The Realschule is linked to the middle and bourgeois classes. The Hauptschule is linked to the working and lower classes. Class imagery is highly developed in German society, as are the meanings of the basic educational categories (Müller, 1978).

Our investigation approaches the stratification topic directly. Our central question is whether the presence of foreign children decreases the probability that German children will attend the Hauptschule. We suppose that the reallocation of students to the Realschule or Gymnasium affects their future social status, their class-related behavior (including their occupational choices), and thus the rates of expansion of various occupations in Germany. The formal distinctions between the three types of school have remained clear and strong because of the relative centralization of the German system, which keeps schools in each category homogeneous in resource materials, curricula, and teacher status. Also, residential segregation is lower in Germany than in the United States; therefore, the schools in a given category are likely to be more homogeneous in the types of students they recruit.

We should note some trends toward the equalization of the three basic tracks, despite the retention of strong distinctions. The curricula of all three types of schools now claim scientific bases for their authority and appropriateness for students, replacing some vague ideas about the importance of folkways, which prevailed in the Hauptschule until recently. Teacher training is now more homogeneous. Also, more career paths have opened up possibilities for transition from the Hauptschule to other levels, even if the proportions of students able to make these transitions are very small (Leschinsky, 1983).

IMMIGRATION AND REASONS FOR EDUCATIONAL STRATIFICATION

An incorporation model provides many mechanisms by which German children might be moved upward in the educational stratification system in response to the presence of foreigners. These mechanisms differ in the level of social structure at which they might operate, yet they are mostly played out through individual student, parent, and teacher choices. We note some of these to illustrate the different ways in which the German secondary school allocation decision is made.

At the national level, there is much public debate about the integration of foreign students into the German educational system. Some are demanding complete segregation, while others are demanding complete and rapid assimilation. The media, intellectuals, educational officials, and teachers' unions have all publicly discussed such matters. As a result of this public attention, German children and parents, already quite aware of the less rewarding educational streams, may feel even more encouraged to strive for a higher stream. In addition, since they are aware that foreigners perform many unskilled jobs, they may feel that merely being German in this stratified labor system entitles them to upward mobility. Also, at the organizational level, the general German population decline may stimulate an incorporation of foreigners into the system, which would directly affect educational stratification. A refined multilevel statistical analysis, of a kind we cannot now perform, might show that the increase in the foreign worker population has a distinct national-level time-series effect on the decrease in German enrollment in the Hauptschule.

At the state and county levels, all the processes above might operate. But at these levels, there are officials with direct political and bureaucratic authority over education. These officials decide how many schools of various types to build or close. Even the simplest decision they might make—the decision to do little—has implications for our analysis. If the proportion of available positions in the three streams is held constant over time, and if many foreign children are introduced at the bottom, German children will move up. At the local level, factors such as ethnic fear, competition, and hostility may also enter into the school placement decision. All these mechanisms generate upward mobility of German children in the educational system.

Of course, another response to the influx of foreign children is the relative expansion of the Hauptschule. This could occur through general social planning or through the accumulation of individual choices. Conflict could be minimized by segregating the foreign children within districts or schools.

A METHODOLOGICAL PROBLEM

An examination of the data on the changes in German Hauptschule enrollments in counties and states is a test of our hypothesis of individual upward mobility only if we examine the same groups of Germans over time. But inasmuch as foreign immigration into a state or community causes outmigration (and especially selective outmigration) of the German population, the data permit a less precise test of our hypothesis. The remaining German population is different from the population present before the foreign immigration. As we note below, this creates a problem in our analysis: The movement of Germans out of communities with foreigners makes it impossible for us to ascertain whether their children move up in the educational system. This problem is not serious when we consider data at the national level, but here we must rely on changes over time, which might be due to many factors. The problem is also minor in our analyses of the states, but the cases are obviously restricted. The problem is greatest at the community level, particularly in certain states, but we can at least provide analyses revealing the extent of the problem.

Our solution is to present analyses at all three levels. National data are subject to multiple interpretations but are not affected by outmigration. At the other extreme, county data permit detailed analyses; but because of outmigration, they lead to ambiguous conclusions. At this level of analysis we expect to find some regional differences in selective outmigration of Germans, which may in turn create differences in educational stratification.

THE DISTRIBUTION OF FOREIGN CHILDREN WITHIN THE EDUCATIONAL SYSTEM

The organization of schooling for foreigners varies among states, communities, and schools. Bavaria advocates a policy of segregation, the purpose of which is to educate foreigners in their culture of origin and facilitate their return home when economic conditions dictate. At the other extreme, the city-state of West Berlin advocates a policy of rapid integration and redistribution of children so that the Germans are in the majority. But practice (on which there is limited information) varies from policy. In Bavaria, along with the Greek national schools created under an agreement between Bavaria and Greece, one can find many mixed classes in areas with few foreign children. In Berlin, the concentration of foreigners in the Kreuzberg section (60 percent of the primary school students are foreign) creates schools that are de facto Turkish. In the Zehlendorf section, the schools are German to a much higher degree. Overall, segregation may be decreasing: There are fewer new foreigners who do not speak German; and as school staffs and others try to keep schools open against demographic trends, foreigners become a useful resource.

Whatever the degree of segregation, most foreign children enter the secondary school system at the lowest level—the Hauptschule—and remain there, usually in mixed classes and schools. This is generally true in Germany, and it is widely discussed (Max Planck Institute, 1983). In 1979, 38 percent of all 13 year olds and 78 percent of all foreign 13 year olds (including those outside the migrant category) were enrolled in the Hauptschule. Well over 90 percent of the Turkish students—the largest and most recent ethnic group—were enrolled in the Hauptschule. Foreign workers have low status and are alien to an educational culture that some see as relatively closed. It is not surprising that they do not do well in the system.

DATA

School enrollment and other data were collected on the national level (1960–1982), on the state level (1978–1982), and on the local level (1976–1982). The local data came from 110 counties (*Kreise*) in 3 of the 11 states. Twelve of the counties are in Berlin, a single metropolitan area; 54 are in Nordrhein-Westfalen, a large, old, industrial area with many interlinked cities and a few rural areas; and 44 are in Baden-Württemberg, a recently developed area of medium-sized towns and cities, including Stuttgart, the large state capital.

In 1980, 7.5 percent of West Germany's population was foreign. One third of this population lived in Nordrhein-Westfalen (1.4 million), but all three states we studied had above average percentages of foreigners: Baden-Württemberg, 8 percent; Nordrhein-Westfalen, 10.1 percent; Berlin, 11 percent. The proportion of foreigners varied considerably across counties in these three states, ranging from 31 percent in the Kreuzberg section of Berlin to 1.8 percent in Coesfeld in Nordrhein-Westfalen.

For the reasons outlined above, we focus our analysis on the Secondary I level of the school system. We collected data on Secondary I enrollment, the population size, and occupational categories from published (Köhler and Trommer, 1981) and unpublished sources. Most of the data were supplied by the Ministries of Education in the states under study. Each of these offices produces yearly reports of school enrollments and other relevant educational data. Unfortunately, they do not completely coordinate their efforts; therefore, in some cases we had to construct comparable indices for analyses at the county level. The variables are briefly defined below, and the means and standard deviations of the variables used in the analysis are presented in Table 1.

For the national-level analysis, we used an annual series of data (from 1960–1982) on the sizes of the foreign population and the foreign student population. We also used a series on German student enrollments in the Hauptschule, Realschule, and Gymnasium. For the state-level analysis, we used the percentage of German Secondary I students enrolled in the Hauptschule and the percentage of Secondary I students who were foreign. The number of years between 1970 and 1980 that the state was under a Social Democratic administration was

Table 1. Means and Standard Deviations of Variables

Variable	1976	1977	1978	1981	1982
State level ($N=11$)					
Percent of German Secondary I students enrolled in the Hauptschule			38.0 (9.2)		32.6 (9.7)
Percent of Secondary I students who are foreign			3.0 (1.7)		
Number of years between 1970 and 1980 that the Social Democratic Party was in power			5.9 (4.7)		
Ratio of the percent of German Secondary I students enrolled in the Hauptschule in 1982 to the percent enrolled in 1978			0.9 (0.1)		
County level (total $N=110$: Baden-Württemberg $N=44$, Nordrhein-Westfalen $N=54$, Berlin $N=12$)					
Percent of German Secondary I students enrolled in the Hauptschule					
Total	42.6 (9.1)				35.0 (10.0)
Baden-Württemberg	41.6 (7.2)				33.5 (7.8)
Nordrhein-Westfalen	45.8 (6.5)				40.5 (6.3)
Berlin	26.9 (9.9)				16.4 (5.9)
Percent of Secondary I students who are foreign					
Total	4.1 (3.2)				7.8 (3.2)
Baden-Württemberg	4.1 (1.3)				7.9 (1.5)
Nordrhein-Westfalen	3.2 (1.5)				8.1 (4.2)
Berlin	7.8 (8.2)				17.3 (14.3)
Percent of Germans in the working class					
Baden-Württemberg	61.2 (7.4)				58.3 (7.2)
Nordrhein-Westfalen	55.5 (9.5)				53.6 (9.6)
Berlin	—				—
German population					
Baden-Württemberg		188,612 (99,850)		189,589 (99,756)	
Nordrhein-Westfalen		292,949 (145,866)		289,089 (139,969)	
Berlin		144,745 (57,672)		136,892 (56,102)	
Foreign population					
Baden-Württemberg		18,676 (17,371)		21,206 (19,601)	
Nordrhein-Westfalen		22,427 (18,821)		26,576 (23,233)	
Berlin		15,823 (8,784)		20,496 (11,115)	
Percent of German population of secondary school age					
Baden-Württemberg		9.4 (1.3)		8.4 (1.3)	
Nordrhein-Westfalen		9.2 (1.3)		6.6 (1.5)	
Berlin		4.0 (1.0)		3.8 (1.0)	
Percent of total Secondary I students enrolled in the Hauptschule					
Baden-Württemberg	43.7 (7.0)				36.5 (7.2)
Nordrhein-Westfalen	47.7 (6.5)				43.7 (6.4)
Berlin	29.1 (12.4)				24.2 (11.8)

also coded, since some researchers consider this a force in changing the relative size of the Hauptschule. For the local-level analysis, we used the German and foreign Secondary I enrollments and age cohort sizes (for 1976 [or 1977] and 1982 [or 1981]), enrollments in the Hauptschule, and German and foreign population-size statistics. We also coded the proportion of all employed Germans in working-class occupations, since this variable is a substantial factor in Hauptschule enrollment.

EVIDENCE

National Level

Figure 2 reports the relevant educational trends in Germany since 1960. It shows the steep rise in the foreign population of West Germany in the last twenty years. It also shows the more recent expansion of foreign children into the school system. This relative expansion is more significant in light of the overall decline (for demographic reasons) in German secondary school enrollment.

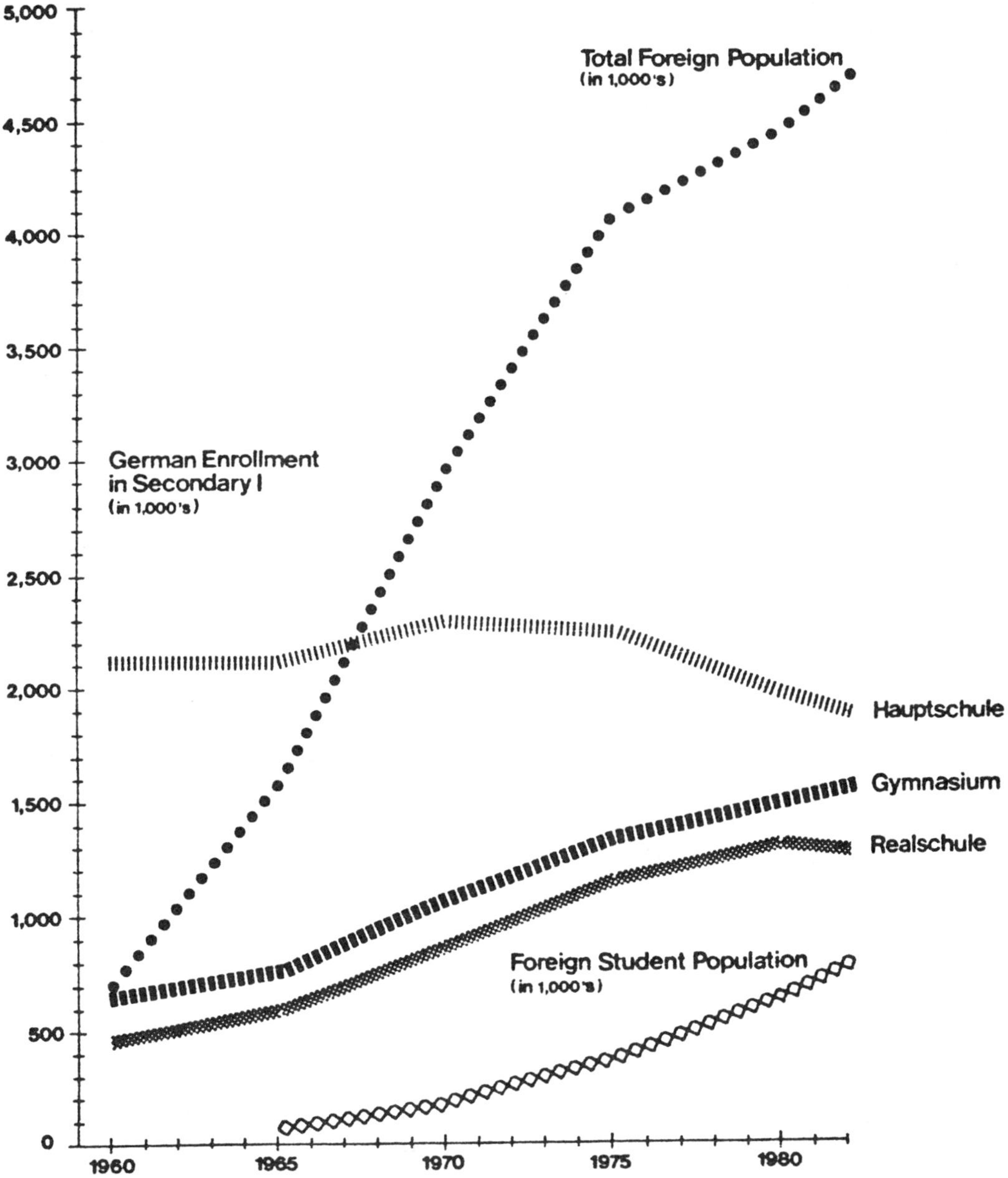

Figure 2. Foreign population in Germany and German enrollment in types of Secondary I schools since 1960.

Figure 2 also shows the decline in the rates of Hauptschule enrollment among the German students and the corresponding expansion of Gymnasium, or pre-university, enrollments.

Are these general trends related? Certainly, the status mobility arising from the influx of foreign workers is not the only cause of long-term Gymnasium and university expansion in Germany. Nearly all Western countries have experienced increases in university enrollments in the same period, though the increase in Germany was exceptionally large (Max Planck Institute, 1983). The rapid jump after about 1965 could easily be due to other processes: a multifaceted university reform movement to catch up with other Western countries, to provide more educational equality for females, and so on. Likewise, a combination of a general upward movement and an overall decline in the German school-aged population over the last two decades is certainly one cause for the sharp decline in Hauptschule enrollment.

The national-level data describe two striking trends, and though it is difficult to be confident in a causal interpretation, the data certainly suggest it. It is difficult to proceed with a time-series analysis on the national level because of the simultaneous operation of too many related factors concerning the guestworker population and the decrease in German enrollment in the Hauptschule at the state and community levels.

State Level

Using the 11 states of the German Federal Republic as units of analysis, we tested whether the presence of foreign children in a state's school system decreased the number of German children in the Hauptschule over time. There are only 11 states in West Germany, so it was not possible to include many variables in the analysis, nor was it reasonable to expect statistically significant effects. But we can show the direction of the effects of foreign enrollment in 1978 on the percent of Germans enrolled in the Hauptschule in 1982. We held constant an earlier measure of the dependent variable in order to control historical differences among the states.

The analysis is presented in Equations 1 through 4 of Table 2. To Equations 2 and 4 we added the state's political composition, since it is often argued that the decline in Hauptschule enrollment results in part from Social Democratic (liberal) efforts to increase educational equality and access to the universities and the middle classes. In Equations 3 and 4, we changed the dependent variable to the ratio of the percent of German Secondary I students enrolled in the Hauptschule in 1982 to the percent enrolled in 1978. This variable reflects the change in the proportion of Germans who entered the lowest level of secondary school and allows us to show the influence of foreign students on this trend. All the analyses show the expected negative effects. The states with more foreign students had greater declines in the proportion of German students in the bottom track. These effects are statistically significant in only one equation, but they suggest that German students are moving up to the Realschule or the Gymnasium partly because of foreign enrollment. A state's political composition had a negligible influence on subsequent German enrollment in the Hauptschule.

Community Level

Using data from the 110 counties in Baden-Württemberg, Nordrhein-Westfalen, and Berlin, we tested whether the presence of foreign students in a county's school system decreased the number of German Secondary I students in the Hauptschule. We controlled for the fraction of all German Secondary I students in the Hauptschule in 1976. This variable holds constant the historical factors contributing to variations in German enrollment in the Hauptschule. We also controlled for the size of the German working class, a factor of some importance, since the working class has historically been the source of Hauptschule enrollment. Before reforms in the German school system, most secondary school students enrolled in the Hauptschule. This has changed since the development of the Realschule and the expansion of the Gymnasium, but the Hauptschule is still the educational track in which children from working-class families are overrepresented (Max Planck Institute, 1983).

The cross-sectional analysis of German Hauptschule enrollment for the counties of Baden-Württemberg and Nordrhein-Westfalen (we have no data on county class composition for Berlin) is presented in Equation 5 of Table 2. The equation shows, as we expect, that German Hauptschule enrollment was greater in counties with larger working-class populations. But, as hypothesized, the equation also shows that German Hauptschule enrollment was lower in counties with more foreign students.

The longitudinal analysis of the same variable is presented in Equations 6 and 7. This analysis provides more support for a causal interpretation. The equations show, as we expect, that German Hauptschule enrollment in 1982 was greatly affected by German Hauptschule enrollment in 1976. There is obviously a great deal of continuity. But more important, both equations show that the presence

Table 2. Effect of the Percent of Secondary I Students Who are Foreign on the Percent of German Secondary I Students Enrolled in the Hauptschule, in States and Counties (Standard Errors are in Parentheses)

					Independent Variables								
					Percent of Secondary I Students who are Foreign			Percent of German Secondary I Students Enrolled in the Hauptschule		Number of Years Social Democratic Party was in Power	Percent of Germans in the Working Class		
Dependent Variable	Equation	State	N	Constant	1976	1978	1982	1976	1978	(1970–1980)	1977	1981	R^2
State level													
Percent of German Secondary I students enrolled in the Hauptschule	1		11	.68		−.90 (.54)			.91 (.10)*				.97
	2		11	.68		−.88 (.63)			.91 (.11)*	−.004 (.200)			.97
Ratio of the percent of German Secondary I students enrolled in the Hauptschule in 1982 to the percent enrolled in 1978	3		11	.86		−.03 (.01)*			.87 (.14)*				.72
	4		11	.87		−.04 (.02)			.87 (.15)*	.004 (.004)			.73
County level													
Percent of German Secondary I students enrolled in the Hauptschule	5		98[a]	2.60			−.62 (.29)*					.61 (.12)*	.53
	6		110	−.61	−.50 (.07)*			1.02 (.03)*					.94
	7		98[a]	−4.10	−.14 (.05)*			1.10 (.04)*			−.11 (.02)*		.96
	8	Baden-Württemberg	44	−.89			−.57 (.27)*					.67* (.12)	.54
	9	Nordrhein-Westfalen	54	21.90			−.05 (.17)					.35 (.07)*	.30
	10	Berlin	12	10.80			.32 (.08)*						.59
	11	Baden-Württemberg	44	−6.50	−.41 (.29)			1.00 (.06)*			−.00 (.06)		.92
	12	Nordrhein-Westfalen	54	−2.80	.24 (.15)			.97 (.04)*			−.04 (.03)		.94
	13	Berlin	12	1.60	.00 (3.10)			.55 (.15)*					.83

[a] The percent of the population in the working class was not available for districts in Berlin.
* Significant at the .05 level.

of foreign students in 1976 had an additional negative effect.

We thus find statistically significant and convincing evidence supporting our hypothesis. In counties with large foreign enrollments, Germans were less likely to enroll in the Hauptschule. After controlling for past historical trends and the size of the German working class, we found that for every 1 percent increase in foreign enrollment in the secondary school system, German Hauptschule enrollment decreased by one fourteenth of a percentage point. Since foreign enrollments are high in many counties, this finding suggests that substantial numbers of Germans avoid the lowest secondary school track and enroll in the Realschule and the Gymnasium, which offer more links to higher education and better occupational prospects than the Hauptschule. The evidence suggests, then, that guestworkers are incorporated into the system and that this affects the educational stratification and perhaps occupational stratification of the host population.

Because of possible outmigration effects, we expect different patterns of results in the different states. Separate analyses of German Hauptschule enrollment for the counties in each of the three states are presented in Equations 8 through 13. The cross-sectional analyses of Hauptschule enrollment within each state are presented in Equations 8 through 10, and the longitudinal analyses are presented in Equations 11 through 13.

The overall pattern is quite clear and holds up through analyses performed state by state. In Baden-Württemberg, we found clear evidence that the expansion of the foreign student population raised the educational status of the native German students. We found no such pattern in the other two states; indeed, the presence of the foreign population had no effect at all.

These differing results led us to reconsider the range of possible educational and social responses to an influx of low-status foreign workers. Clearly, one possible response, both official and unofficial, is the assignment of foreign students to the lowest track and the reassignment of German students to higher tracks, thereby creating a boundary between foreign students and German students. But another obvious response is horizontal outmigration. In the U.S., where educational tracks are less strongly segregated and institutionalized than in Germany, outmigration—e.g. white flight—is a common reaction to an influx of ethnic minorities. The desire for educational insulation is generally considered an important cause of the very high degree of residential segregation between class and ethnic groups in the U.S.

Migration to escape close residential and educational proximity to foreigners is a possible reaction in Germany too, even though the educational tracks offer more effective insulation. But the prevalence of migration varies considerably among the three German states in our study in a way that is consistent with our empirical results. Berlin is a single large city. In describing its population composition, it is common to use the standard sociological concept of replacement: Foreigners move in and the local Germans move out to other districts. If this is a common process, it might explain why Equations 10 and 13 show positive effects of foreign enrollment. The German population may or may not move up the educational ladder as foreigners move in at the bottom; but if they do, they move elsewhere first. When horizontal outmigration occurs, only the very low-status Germans remain in the foreign districts. Therefore, the vertical mobility we expect occurs in districts other than those with high concentrations of foreigners. It seems reasonable to suppose that Germans interested in upward mobility for their children (like Americans fleeing from contact with low-status groups) would be especially inclined to move, despite the technical competitive advantages of remaining in areas with many foreigners.

Exactly the same process is occurring in Nordrhein-Westfalen. The Ruhr region, composed of many highly linked urban areas, is in a period of economic decline. By reputation, there is much horizontal mobility, and commuting is easy and common. Thus, it is probable that in this region too, an increase in the foreign population is associated with a decrease in the German population, not with an increase in the educational status of the native German population.

Baden-Württemberg, on the other hand, is undergoing an economic boom, attracting guestworkers and Germans alike. The counties in this state are relatively independent, and their population centers are geographically separate. Outmigration among the Germans is less common. Germans faced with integrated institutions may choose solutions other than migration. In this state, particularly, we found (as hypothesized) that an increase in foreign enrollment was associated with a decrease in German enrollment in the Hauptschule.

This leads us to the analyses of German population movements among counties, shown in Table 3. Equations 1 through 3 show that the size of the foreign population affects the size of the German population. We held constant the size of the previous German population, which

Table 3. Effect of the Size of a County's Foreign Population on the Size of the County's German Population, for Each State (Standard Errors are in Parentheses)

					Independent Variables			
Dependent Variable	Equation	State	N	Constant	Foreign Population in 1977	German Population in 1977	Percent of Germans in the Working Class in 1977	R^2
German population in 1981	1	Baden-Württemberg	44	−14,423.00	−.14 (.08)	1.02 (.01)**	229.8 (105.0)	.99
	2	Nordrhein-Westfalen	54	2,332.00	−.36 (.10)**	1.00 (.01)**	48.2 (117.0)	.99
	3	Berlin	12	247.00	−.24 (.09)*	.97 (.01)**	na	.99
Percent of German population that was of secondary school age in 1981	4	Baden-Württemberg	44	−.01	.0002 (.0002)	.99 (.04)**	.002 (.01)	.95
	5	Nordrhein-Westfalen	54	−.002	−.001 (.0009)**	.91 (.03)**	.009 (.003)**	.97
	6	Berlin	12	.03	−.0005 (.0001)**	.42 (.08)**	na	.94

* Significant at the .05 level.
** Significant at the .01 level.

naturally has a strong inertial effect. We also held constant the proportion of the previous German population that was working class.

The results are clear: In both Nordrhein-Westfalen and Berlin, the size of the foreign population had a large negative effect on the size of the German population. In these states, as a county's foreign population increased, its German population decreased. This is understandable considering the regional development and physical structure of Berlin and Nordrhein-Westfalen. Germans in these states can easily change their residence (even move from one county, or Berlin district, to another) and keep their jobs. For these Germans, horizontal outmigration is perhaps the most expedient response to an influx of foreigners. However, we cannot determine from our data whether or not the children of these individuals experience an increase in educational status in their new residences.

In Baden-Württemberg, the size of the foreign population had a negative but insignificant effect on the size of the German population. The foreign population was simply integrated into the stable, native population. In this state, commuting is less practicable. Therefore, upward mobility within the community is the most expedient response to the presence of foreigners. This is one plausible explanation for the significant upward mobility of German students in the counties of Baden-Württemberg.

In Equations 4 through 6 of Table 3, we investigate a more subtle aspect of the same question: Does the presence of a large foreign population suppress not only the total German population but especially the portion of that population that is in secondary school? In Nordrhein-Westfalen and Berlin, the answer is clearly yes; and as expected, in Baden-Württemberg, the answer is no. Thus, in the former two states, the counties with large foreign populations are especially likely to lose German secondary school students. Three explanations for this tendency come to mind. First, employed persons with school-aged children may move out of foreign-inhabited districts for economic reasons. Second, such families may move out of these districts for familial and educational reasons (i.e., to avoid schools with high concentrations of foreigners). Third, these families may send their children to schools outside the district—certainly a feasible alternative to migration in Berlin. We cannot, however, determine which of these explanations is appropriate.

In both the total population analysis and the school-aged population analysis, we found regional differences in the response of Germans to the presence of foreign children and their families. If we had more complex data, we could trace the separate effects and determine how each institution was changed by the influx of a socially defined low-status ethnic group.

TOTAL DISTRIBUTIONAL IMPACT OF FOREIGNERS

We now consider how the influx of foreigners affects the distribution of all types of students, both German and foreign, in a community's secondary school system, specifically among the Secondary I tracks. The question addressed in Table 2 is refined: Do the foreign students in a county lead Hauptschule enrollments to increase? Or do they produce massive upward mobility among German students and thus, despite their placement in this lowest track, cause Hauptschule enrollments to decrease? The dependent variable, then, is the percent of Secondary I students (German and foreign) who enroll in the Hauptschule. We know that the proportion of foreign students in the Hauptschule is increasing, so if we find a negative or zero slope we have further proof that foreign enrollment creates an upward shift in the school system.

In Equations 4 through 6 in Table 4, we present the longitudinal effects of the presence of foreign students on the proportion of all students enrolled in the Hauptschule. Our measure of class is held constant, as is our measure of the previous student distribution. (The simple cross-sectional analysis is presented in Equations 1 through 3 of Table 4.)

The findings for Baden-Württemberg, where horizontal migration is rare, are the most striking: The addition of foreigners to the bottom of the system led the size of the bottom track to decrease (though the finding is not statistically significant). The German student population was redistributed upward, offsetting the influx of foreign students into the Hauptschule. In Baden-Württemberg, Germans left the Hauptschule at about the same rate as foreign students entered.

In Nordrhein-Westfalen and West Berlin, we found the opposite trend: The presence of foreign students led Hauptschule enrollments to increase. We assume that some Germans were lost because of horizontal outmigration, but the Germans that remained were working-class individuals with strong orientations to the Hauptschule tradition.

MECHANISMS

In some areas, the presence of foreigners seemed to increase the educational status of German children. In other areas, it led to outmigration of Germans, the status consequences of which are unknown. The mechanisms through which status can increase obviously include the reactions of children and their parents to schooling experiences: For example, German children may gain academic self-confidence by competing with foreigners of low status and limited linguistic competence. In Germany, this process is supported by official practice: When a student finishes the primary grades, the school makes an explicit recommendation regarding the student's placement in the secondary school system. The recommendation is not binding but it is influential.

Data from Berlin show that despite the great influx of foreign children, the schools continue to send students to the Hauptschule at about the same frequency as in the past—about 35 percent (Baumert, forthcoming; see also Schümer, 1985). The analyses also show that the Germans who enroll in the Hauptschule are increasingly likely to complete the program, even though they represent the end product of more and more negative educational selection.

It is obvious that the educational system produces evaluations that are highly relative to the population being assessed (a phenomenon more surprising in Germany than in the normatively decentralized United States) (Lenhardt, 1984). Primary school recommendations are determined by the available secondary school slots. Secondary school success rates are kept relatively constant despite a changing pool of competitors.

These arguments imply that the system works the way it does less through ethnocentrism than through its absence. The Germans move up because they assess themselves (and are organizationally assessed) in the same pool with foreigners. As a result, foreigners also benefit from foreign expansion. In Berlin, for-

Table 4. Effect of the Percent of Secondary I Students Who are Foreign on the Percent of Secondary I Students Who Enroll in the Hauptschule (Standard Errors are in Parentheses)

					Independent Variables				
					Percent of Secondary I Students Who are Foreign		Percent of Secondary I Students Enrolled in the Hauptschule	Percent of Germans in the Working Class	
Dependent Variable	Equation	State	N	Constant	1976	1982	in 1976	in 1981	R^2
Percent of Secondary I students enrolled in the Hauptschule	1	Baden-Württemberg	44	−3.9		−.07 (.27)		.70 (.12)**	.49
	2	Nordrhein-Westfalen	54	21.1		.40 (.17)*		.36 (.08)**	.34
	3	Berlin	12	10.5		.78 (.08)**		na	.90
	4	Baden-Württemberg	44	−7.1	.14 (.32)		.99 (.08)**	−.01 (.08)	.89
	5	Nordrhein-Westfalen	54	−4.4	.98** (.16)		1.01 (.04)**	−.07 (.03)*	.93
	6	Berlin	12	1.6	.46 (.24)		.65 (.16)**	na	.95

* Significant at the .05 level.
** Significant at the .01 level.

eigners are decreasingly enrolling in the Hauptschule and are increasingly entering the higher tracks (Baumert, forthcoming). In Berlin, the proportion of foreign students is large, and the birth rate among Germans is low; therefore, foreigners are needed to fill educational slots above the bottom track.

CONCLUSION

We have some evidence that foreign children are incorporated at the bottom of the German educational system, creating some upward mobility among German students. We found this trend at the national, state, and county levels. However, in two of the states we studied, this trend was offset by the horizontal outmigration of Germans—especially German students—in the face of high foreign enrollments.

The evidence suggests that an incorporation-upward mobility model is the most accurate description of the effect of immigration on educational stratification in West Germany. Instead of remaining external to the stratification system, guestworkers occupy the bottom rung and cause the native population to be redistributed upward.

The incorporation of foreign workers into domestic society occurs even as the official debate over the fate of these individuals continues in Northern Europe. Perhaps this official debate, in which the older nation-states pretend they have controlled the problem, can no longer be taken very seriously. The economic, military, and political realities of Northern Europe can no longer accommodate the nation-state style, which is characterized by absolute control over internal populations. European states are so highly constrained by a web of international rules and interests that something analogous to the multinational states of pre-nineteenth century Europe may be returning as a basic political model.

REFERENCES

Baumert, J.
Forthcoming "Trends and perspectives of secondary education in West Berlin." European Journal of Education.

Benevot, A.
1983 "The rise and decline of vocational education." Sociology of Education 56:63–67.

Castles, S.
1984 Here for Good: Western Europe's New Ethnic Minorities. London: Pluto Press.

Collins, R.
1971 "Functional and conflict theories of educational stratification." American Sociological Review 36:1002–18.
1976 "Review of schooling in capitalist America: Educational reform and the contradictions of economic life." Harvard Educational Review 46:246–51.

Dohse, K.
1981 Ausländische Arbeiter und Bürgerlicher Staat [Foreign Workers and Capitalist State]. Koenigstein: Hain.

Gordon, M.
1964 "Assimilation in American life." Daedalus 92:263–85.

Heckmann, F.
1981 Die Bundesrepublik: Ein Einwanderungsland [The Federal Republic of Germany: A Country Open to Mass Immigration]. Stuttgart: Klett-Cotta.

Köhler, H. and L. Trommer
1981 Auslander in der Bundesrepublik Deutschland [Foreigners in the Federal Republic of Germany]. Munich: Deutsches Jugendinstitut.

Lenhardt, G.
1984 Schule und Bürokratische Rationalität [Formal Education and Bureaucratic Rationality]. Frankfurt: Suhrkamp.

Leschinsky, A.
1983 "Geschichte des Schulwesens im Sekundarbereich I" [History of the lower cycle of secondary education]. Pp. 163–97 in Enzyklopadie Erziehungswissenschaft. Vol. 8. Stuttgart: Klett.

Max Planck Institute for Human Development and Education
1983 Between Elite and Mass Education in the Federal Republic of Germany. Albany: SUNY Press.

Meyer, J.
1980 "The world polity and the authority of the nation-state." Pp. 109–37 in A. Bergesen (ed.), Studies in the Modern World-System. New York: Academic Press.

Müller, W.
1978 "Klassenlage und lebenslauf" [Social class and life course]. Habilitationsschrift. Mannheim: Universität Fakultät für Sozialwissenschaften.

Olzak, S.
1983 "Contemporary ethnic mobilization." Annual Review of Sociology 9:355–74.

Portes, A.
1979 "Illegal immigration and the international system: Lessons from recent legal Mexican immigration to the U.S." Social Problems 26:425–38.

Ralph, J. and R. Rubinson
1980 "Immigration and the expansion of schooling in the United States, 1890–1970." American Sociological Review 45:943–54.

Rist, R.
1978 Guestworkers in Germany: The Prospect for Pluralism. New York: Praeger.

Schümer, G.
1985 "Daten zur Entwicklung der Sekundarstufe I" [Data on the development of secondary education]. In Materialien aus der Bildungsforschung. Berlin: Max Planck Institute for Human Development and Education.

Wallerstein, I.
1974 The Modern World-System. New York: Academic Press.

THE LEGITIMACY OF EARLY SCHOOL LEAVING: OCCUPATIONAL ORIENTATIONS, VOCATIONAL TRAINING PLANS, AND EDUCATIONAL ATTAINMENT AMONG URBAN AUSTRALIAN YOUTH

LAWRENCE J. SAHA
Australian National University

Sociology of Education 1985, Vol. 58 (October):228–240

In Australia, students can leave high school after Year 10, the approximate end of compulsory schooling, or continue through Year 12. Some early high school leavers enter into apprenticeships or enroll in vocational training programs, the impact of which has not been extensively examined. The availability of vocational training programs to early school leavers provides an alternative path to occupational attainment and thus may serve to legitimate early school leaving. This article reports findings from a study of urban Australian students who were about to leave high school after Years 10, 11, and 12 and who either had plans to enroll in college or in vocational training programs or had no plans to pursue further education or training. Linear regression (path) models are replicated for males and females and for those whose fathers were born in Australia, the United Kingdom, or Europe. The intention to pursue vocational training is negatively related to school attainment for all six groups, and with few exceptions, it is unrelated to socioeconomic background, type of school attended, and career orientations. Possible interpretations and implications of the findings are discussed.

It is generally accepted that young people's expectations about their future occupations are related to their actual educational and occupational attainment. Sewell and his colleagues, in studies of Wisconsin youth, have shown that expectations and related variables, such as need achievement, self-image, and aspirations, intervene between prior variables (family socioeconomic status, mental ability, the influence of significant others, and academic performance) and measures of educational and occupational attainment (Gasson, Haller, and Sewell, 1972; Sewell, Haller, and Portes, 1969). The findings concerning the effects of social-psychological variables on attainment are inconsistent, but it has been demonstrated that some motivational factors are relatively important determinants of eventual attainments and earnings (Duncan, Featherman, and Duncan, 1972).[1]

The most consistent findings in studies of career ambitions concern the effects of socioeconomic background (Sewell and Hauser, 1975), sex (Marini and Greenberger, 1978), and race and ethnicity (Howell and Frese, 1982). Studies have shown that socioeconomic status is directly related to educational and occupational plans, but the relationship appears to be stronger for females and weaker for blacks (Spenner and Featherman, 1978) and some ethnic groups (Portes, McLeod, and Parker, 1978). However, despite empirical evidence of the determinants of these social-psychological variables, well-developed theoretical interpretations of the relationships have been lacking. Indeed, Spenner and Featherman (1978) have argued that there still does not exist among researchers a generally accepted ordering of the variables determining ambitions. There is even less agreement about the definitions of these variables. However, there is general agreement about their intervenient position in the educational and occupational attainment models (Howell and Frese, 1982).

I want to thank Shirley Halton and Julie Myers for technical assistance and Owen Dent and anonymous reviewers for comments on an earlier draft. Address all correspondence to the author at the Department of Sociology, Faculty of Arts, Australian National University, G.P.O. Box 4, Canberra, A.C.T. 2601, AUSTRALIA.

[1] Duncan et al. (1972) found that the regression coefficient for expected occupation and father's occupation (0.31) closely corresponded with the coefficient for actual status attainment and father's occupation (0.33). They argue that "the aggregate of students implicitly understands fairly accurately the prevailing degree of relationship between origin and achievement" (p. 110). Likewise, Sewell et al. (1969) found that occupational aspirations were the second most important determinants of occupational attainment ($\beta = 0.19$), surpassed only by educational attainment ($\beta = 0.38$). Thus, "each aspiration variable appears to have the predicted substantial effects on its respective attainment variable" (Sewell et al., 1969:88). More specifically, Sewell and Hauser (1975:107–109) found that a 10-point increase in occupational aspirations on the Duncan SEI was worth 1.5 points in attained occupational status and $95 in earnings.

Most researchers have adopted a socialization and stratification model to locate ambitions in the larger context of status attainment. Thus, ambition is believed to indicate acceptance of society's occupational hierarchy and the criteria for achievement within that hierarchy (Turner, 1960). However, while it is unlikely that an individual could attain high status within this hierarchy without high ambitions, these alone are not sufficient. High ambitions must be provided with a suitable context or set of facilitator variables, "which might reasonably influence the expression of aspirations in attainments" (Gasson et al., 1972:3). Thus, it is necessary to conceptually divide ambition into aspirations and expectations. The former reflect an acceptance of the positive values society places on high levels of educational and occupational attainment; the latter indicate a recognition of the contextual or structural limitations to this attainment (Han, 1969).

This article follows the above argument and focuses on the determinants of educational attainment among a sample of urban Australian youth. The model used here differs from other attainment models because it includes measures of occupational aspirations and expectations and postschool vocational training plans. This latter variable is particularly relevant, since it takes into account the perceived impact of postschool vocational training on career prospects. The sociological literature relating schooling to occupational attainment has ignored the possibility that vocational training programs provide an alternative avenue for the relative improvement of job possibilities. Students often choose vocational programs after their options for further education have been closed off due to poor grades, financial difficulties, or family opposition. Thus, these programs represent an alternative to formal schooling (Williams et al., 1981; Poole, 1983). However, Wilms and Hansell (1982), in a study of American youth, found that vocational training enhances job placement and later earnings only for low-SES students in low-status jobs.

THE AUSTRALIAN CONTEXT

The Legitimation of Early School Leaving

Compulsory schooling in Australia is defined in terms of age, and in most states it extends from ages 6 to 15. Only Tasmania requires schooling to age 16. Because of this age-grade pattern, it is generally possible for young people to leave school after Year 10, even though formal secondary schooling continues through Year 12. In most states, individuals leaving school before Year 12 can obtain a certificate based on school assessment, such as the School Certificate in New South Wales or the Junior Certificate in Queensland (Commonwealth Department of Education, 1977). These students are not considered dropouts, as in the American system, but simply early school leavers. The relatively low retention rates beyond Year 10, combined with the institutionalization of early leaving by the granting of intermediate certificates, affords a unique opportunity to examine the effects of additional years of schooling and vocational-school plans on the career orientations of Australian youth.[2]

The existence of an institutionalized and legitimate alternative route to occupational attainment makes more explicit the workings of a societal reward structure, particularly in the relation of schooling to work. Unlike the American educational system, which retains its students as long as possible before selection and allocation take place, the Australian system legitimates early leaving and thereby provides a system of early selection, a system with its own rewards. The pay-off of vocational training for occupational attainment in Australia was measured by Broom et al. (1982:74–75). Using the ANU 2 scale (Broom et al., 1977), they found that each year of informal education added about 19 status points to a male's first occupation, each year of apprenticeship added 10 status points, and each year of technical education added 17 status points. These effects are small compared to the effects of college: Each year of college added 29 status points to a male's first occupation, and a college degree added 83 status points. If the effects of socioeconomic background on vocational training plans are consistently high, we can infer that vocational training serves a "cooling-out" function in Australia, as it does in the United States (Pincus, 1980).

Ambition and Attainment

There has been less attention directed to the effects of aspirations and expectations on educational and occupational attainment in Australia than in North America. But there is evidence suggesting that aspirations and expectations are important factors in the attainment

[2] In 1976, at about the time of this study, the rate of full-time participation in schooling for Australian youth aged 16 to 18 years (the approximate ages for students in Years 10 to 12) was 40.2 percent and was declining for males. At this time, Australia ranked 14th in school participation among 19 OECD countries (Karmel, 1981). School retention rates differed between the states and territories: An average of 75 to 98 percent continued to Year 10, and 23 to 63 percent continued to Year 12 (Commonwealth Department of Education, 1977).

process. In a small follow-up study of student educational and occupational aspirations, Poole (1983) found that 36 percent of those interviewed held the jobs they had expected to have when they were 14 years old. Furthermore, Carpenter, Western, and Foster (1980) found that the effect of Year 12 educational aspirations on eventual college enrollment was 0.48 for males and 0.42 for females. Their findings were consistent with the findings of comparable American and Swedish studies and showed that "aspirations not only affect attainments but also act as key mediating variables in transmitting anterior factors into subsequent behaviours" (Carpenter et al., 1981:269). Indeed, all the Australian evidence suggests that ambitions (i.e. aspirations, expectations, or both) are important in the attainment process.

Sex and Ethnicity Effects

Consistent with studies in North America and elsewhere, Australian studies have found considerable variation between males and females in educational and occupational attainments. Until 1978, males had higher levels of educational attainment than females; but in 1978, females surpassed males in educational attainment (Karmel, 1981). Nevertheless, Australian males, irrespective of school-leaving plans, tend to have higher and wider-ranging occupational aspirations and expectations than females, who tend to aspire to relatively fewer, sex-typed occupations. Furthermore, the career orientations of males are more predictable, in terms of the known causal factors (Saha, 1982). Finally, males are more successful than females in the attainment of their postschool goals, particularly with respect to entry into college (Carpenter and Western, 1983).

Australia has a large immigrant population, so ethnicity is particularly important in analyses of schooling and the labor force. In 1971, for example, 26.5 percent of the labor force was foreign-born, and as is typical in most high-receiving countries, most of these immigrants were concentrated at the lower end of the occupational structure (Richmond and Zubrzycki, 1981).

Consistent with assimilation theory, the distribution of immigrant groups in the Australian workforce is directly related to the similarity of their cultures to Anglo-Australian culture. For example, in 1971, 10.6 percent of English-speaking immigrant males, most of whom were from the United Kingdom and Ireland, were professionals, compared to 7.2 percent of non-English-speaking males. Conversely, 61.6 percent of the English-speaking males were craftsmen or foremen or lower, compared to 69 percent of the non-English-speaking males. The comparable figures for the Australian-born were 14.7 and 41.8 percent (Richmond and Zubrzycki, 1981). Thus, the occupational distribution of English-speaking immigrants falls between the distributions of the Australian-born and the non-English-speaking immigrants.

Ethnicity is also related to school outcomes. Students with non-English-speaking immigrant parents tend to have higher educational and occupational aspirations and tend to stay in school longer than students with Australian-born parents (Martin and Meade, 1979). At the same time, however, they do not perform as well academically as students with Australian or English-speaking parents (Marjoribanks, 1979). Nevertheless, there is considerable similarity in perceived life chances among all students in Australia. Students with immigrant parents are as optimistic about "making it" in the world of work as students with Australian parents (Poole, 1981). However, we have less understanding about the importance of ambitions and postschool vocational plans for these students' educational and occupational attainments.

In general, then, the structure of Australian schooling, particularly the institutionalization of early school leaving and the legitimacy of differentiated postschool plans, provides an alternative career path for some school students. Variations by sex and ethnicity in the use of this alternative strategy have not been adequately explored and represent a central focus of this investigation.

THE DATA AND CAUSAL MODEL

The data used in this analysis are taken from a study conducted by the Australian Sales Research Bureau (ASRB, n.d.) in the mid-1970s during a period of relative economic stability and low unemployment in Australia.[3] The study was based on a stratified random sample of 125 schools in the six state capital cities and Launceston, Tasmania. The stratified-random procedure ensured representativeness for sex, city, year of leaving, and type of school attended (government, Roman Catholic, or non-Catholic independent).[4] When the study

[3] At the time of the study, the unemployment rate was less than 2 percent. By the late 1970s, it had increased to well over 6 percent (Blakers, 1978). Thus, students' responses to questions on occupational aspirations and expectations were probably not influenced by perceived crises in the economy or workforce, as they might have been in more recent times.

[4] The six cities were Sydney, Melbourne, Bris-

began, 2,525 school students in Years 10, 11, and 12 were identified as imminent leavers—i.e., they planned to leave school at the end of the academic year. Only the definite leavers were included in the study.[5] The response rate for those students identified as imminent leavers was 86 percent, resulting in a sample of 2,153 students.

The survey was designed to investigate school leavers' knowledge and opinions about careers in private industry and business. It included questions on father's birthplace, father's occupation, and student's preferred and expected occupations. Descriptions and codes for these and other variables in the model follow.

Father's occupation (*FOCC*) is a surrogate measure of family socioeconomic status and was derived from responses to the following item: "[Give the] type of work your father does. (Describe as fully as you can the type of work.)" The original ASRB codes were recoded using the ANU 2 occupational scale. Values range from a high of 915 for independent medical practitioners to a low of 331 for unskilled laborers in food, beverage, and tobacco industries (Broom et al., 1977).

Type of school attended (*PSCH*) is a dichotomous variable: private schools (Roman Catholic or non-Catholic independent) were coded 1, government schools were coded 0.

Student's preferred occupation (*POCC*) was determined by responses to the open-ended question, "If you had a completely free choice, what occupation would you most like to have?" Responses were recoded using the ANU 2 scale.

Student's expected occupation (*EOCC*) was determined by responses to the following item: "Describe fully the occupation you expect to have during most of your working life." Responses were recoded using the ANU 2 scale.

Vocational training plans (*VOCAT*) were determined by responses to the question, "What work (or full-time studies) do you expect to be doing this time next year?" Responses were recoded into a dichotomous variable: plans to pursue further technical education, apprenticeships, or vocational training programs were coded 1; all other responses were coded 0.[6]

Educational attainment (*EDATT*) is measured by the student's year in school, since all students interviewed intended to leave school at the end of that year. Year 12 was coded 3, Year 11 was coded 2, and Year 10 was coded 1. Year 12 students who intended to enroll in a university or college of advanced education the following year were coded 4.[7]

---

bane, Adelaide, Perth, and Hobart. Launceston, the second largest city in Tasmania, was added to compensate for Hobart's much smaller size, relative to the other capital cities. The random sample of schools was obtained from lists provided by the Australian Council of Educational Research. Random replacement procedures were used for schools that could not participate in the study. Sixty-seven government schools, 38 Roman Catholic schools, and 20 non-Catholic independent schools participated in the study. The questionnaires were administered by classroom teachers, who were instructed to follow procedures that would minimize the possibility of student response bias.

[5] For most Australian students, Year 10 marks the end of compulsory schooling. Since schools, regions, and states vary considerably in retention rates beyond Year 10, it is difficult to estimate how many students will stay or leave after completing any given grade. Furthermore, students are not required to declare their intentions to terminate schooling at the end of Year 10, 11, or 12. Therefore, the present study included only those students who had declared, in the final month of the academic year, that they would not be returning the following year. Thus, their grade level at the time of the study represents their level of educational attainment.

[6] Vocational training programs include a wide variety of postsecondary school options, many of which are offered in the technical and further education institutions. Examples of such programs include apprenticeships; certificate and subdiploma courses for technicians in manufacturing, commerce, community service, farming, mining, and other industries; and preparatory programs for trade and skilled occupations. These programs are available to students who leave school before Year 12 and who cannot pursue studies at universities or colleges of advanced education.

[7] This procedure was followed in order to rule out possible contamination of the *VOCAT* variable and thus underestimation in the regression estimates. Because the *VOCAT* variable was dichotomized, many responses, including plans to attend college or university, were included in the "other" category. An inspection of the cross-tabs showed that 28.7 percent of the 726 Year 12 students hoped to enroll in college the following year. Since the data were collected in the final month of the academic year, nearly all these students would have had the necessary grades and courses to pursue those aspirations. This assumption is consistent with the Canadian findings of Porter, Porter, and Blishen (1982), who found that educational goals are more likely to be achieved the later they are made. In fact, the regression estimates using both procedures did not differ much, but the effects of vocational training on educational attainment were slightly greater when all four codes were used. For example, the unadjusted and adjusted coefficients for Australian males were −0.328 (three codes) and −0.355 (four codes); the corresponding coefficients for females were −0.326 and −0.348. In addition, the amount of variance explained increased in three equations and remained about the same for the other three. Thus, the procedure used here is empirically and conceptually the most preferable.

The ethnic background of the students was determined by father's birthplace. Many ethnic groups were represented in the original sample, but this analysis focuses on three groups: Australians, British and Irish, and Europeans. The latter category includes approximately equal numbers of Mediterraneans (Greek, Italian, and Yugoslav) and Northern Europeans (German, French, and Dutch). The European category includes culturally diverse groups, but it provides a contrast with the other two Anglo categories. To avoid possible interaction effects, the analysis was replicated for males and females in each ethnic category. The maximum group sizes for each replication are as follows: Australian males, 708; Australian females, 650; British and Irish males, 130; British and Irish females, 106; European males, 167; European females, 137. Because pairwise deletion procedures were used, the *N*s for the actual regression estimates vary slightly.

The causal model, which is similar to the social-psychological model of status attainment (Sewell, Haller, and Ohlendorf, 1970), is based on the assumption that aspirations, expectations, and vocational plans intervene between socioeconomic background, type of school attended, and educational attainment. The dependent variable is educational attainment, and the single exogenous variable is father's occupation, a proxy for socioeconomic background. The endogenous variables are school type, occupational aspirations, occupational expectations, and vocational training plans, in that order.

Using a causal ordering based on temporal and conceptual proximity (Haller, 1982), the model assumes that (1) father's occupation affects the type of school a person attends; (2) the type of school influences occupational aspirations, which represent general cognitive orientations toward the occupational structure; and (3) occupational aspirations affect occupational expectations, which are conceptually more specific and temporally more proximate to educational attainment. These expectations in turn influence vocational training plans, which are postulated as the most specific and proximate determinants of educational attainment. The model assumes that the social-psychological variables—aspirations, expectations, and plans—represent variations in cognitive structures, which intervene between socioeconomic background and educational attainment (Haller, 1982). The model also assumes that vocational training plans, which represent an alternative career path, serve to legitimate early school leaving. Thus, it might be hypothesized that while background, school, and ambition variables have little effect on vocational training plans, the latter exercise

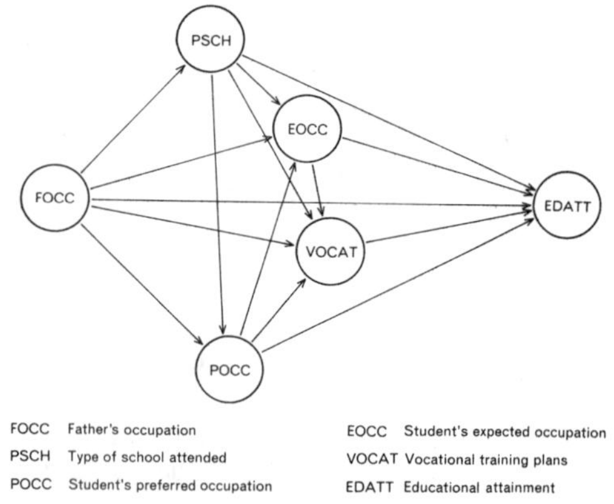

Figure 1. The Causal Model of Educational Attainment

a significant negative effect on educational attainment. In other words, a student does not choose to enroll in a vocational training program, and thus leave school early, because s/he is from a lower socioeconomic background, attended a government school, or has lower ambitions. The inclusion of the vocational plans variable in the model is therefore both theoretically and empirically relevant in further explicating the educational attainment process, particularly in Australia.

The relationships in the causal model are shown in Figure 1. The model does not include an ability or performance variable, and to this extent it might be considered misspecified or spurious (Pedhazur, 1982).[8] However, this omission is not problematic in this particular model because a surrogate measure, educational attainment, which is affected by ability and performance, is included (Shea, 1976). Research on school attainment in Australia has shown that school leaving is strongly related to academic achievement (Poole, 1983). Also, Meade (1982), in his study of Sydney adolescents, found that both high ability and high aspirations were necessary for the completion of secondary school and the attainment of the Higher School Certificate.

However, Sewell and Hauser (1980) have argued that ability in particular exercises strong direct effects on academic performance, perceived encouragement from significant others, and educational and occupational aspi-

[8] There are differing views about the causal location of ability and achievement variables with respect to ambitions and motivations. For example, Turner (1964) suggests that students who have high aspirations are motivated to learn the tasks that lead to high intelligence-test performance. In this line of reasoning, ability and performance are regarded as outcomes of aspirations rather than as causal factors.

rations. But they note that these latter variables mediate between ability and educational and occupational attainment. It can be argued, therefore, that the alleged bias that results from the omission of ability and performance is minimized when aspiration and expectation variables are included in the model.

The correlation coefficients, means, and standard deviations for the variables are shown in Table 1. The means for father's occupation (*FOCC*) are higher for the Australian students than for the European students. On the other hand, the means for preferred and expected occupations (*POCC* and *EOCC*) are highest for European males. For all sex and ethnic categories, the means for preferred and expected occupations are higher than the means for father's occupation, an indication, perhaps, of the mobility ideology among most young people. In general, males had higher mean preferred and expected occupations than females. (British/Irish females had higher mean expected occupations than their male counterparts.) The mean educational attainment of

Table 1. Zero-Order Correlations, Means, and Standard Deviations for Each Sex and Ethnic Group

	FOCC	*PSCH*	*POCC*	*EOCC*	*VOCAT*	*EDATT*	Mean (Males)	SD
Australian								
FOCC	—	.195*	.184*	.274*	.000	.221*	564.7	127.2
		(708)	(619)	(614)	(659)	(627)		
PSCH	.234*	—	.069*	.143*	−.028	.103*	.4258	.4948
	(650)		(653)	(650)	(700)	(671)		
POCC	.176*	.036	—	.531*	.097*	.293*	613.3	129.7
	(580)	(602)		(595)	(615)	(583)		
EOCC	.211*	.071*	.445*	—	.198*	.411*	596.0	128.2
	(591)	(617)	(558)		(629)	(591)		
VOCAT	−.112*	.004	−.032	−.013	—	−.266*	1.223	.4165
	(623)	(654)	(582)	(601)		(644)		
EDATT	.255*	−.035	.280*	.358*	−.374*	—	2.119	1.135
	(584)	(612)	(545)	(562)	(596)			
Mean (females)	561.4	.3582	597.8	564.8	1.352	2.134		
SD	127.2	.4798	111.4	100.2	.4779	1.074		
British/Irish								
FOCC	—	.036	.257*	.317*	−.112	.269*	545.8	123.2
		(130)	(106)	(111)	(107)	(107)		
PSCH	.232*	—	−.031	.084	−.028	−.039	.2000	.4015
	(106)		(110)	(115)	(110)	(112)		
POCC	.101	.178*	—	.619*	−.081	.249*	613.6	130.3
	(90)	(91)		(101)	(95)	(93)		
EOCC	.394*	.132	.635*	—	−.011	.433*	558.8	107.9
	(91)	(92)	(80)		(99)	(96)		
VOCAT	.068	−.059	.017	.139	—	−.302*	1.264	.4426
	(100)	(103)	(85)	(89)		(98)		
EDATT	.123	−.064	.293*	.298*	−.409*	—	1.821	1.067
	(87)	(90)	(77)	(79)	(85)			
Mean (females)	556.0	.248	601.8	573.1	1.456	1.867		
SD	126.9	.434	116.7	94.2	.501	1.041		
European								
FOCC	—	−.030	−.037	.189*	−.066	.196*	501.9	108.8
		(167)	(149)	(139)	(148)	(130)		
PSCH	−.017	—	−.069	.019	−.077	−.109	.324	.469
	(137)		(159)	(148)	(158)	(141)		
POCC	.085	−.138	—	.543*	.131	.153*	667.4	146.1
	(121)	(129)		(138)	(147)	(128)		
EOCC	.226*	−.183*	.279*	—	.093	.317*	638.8	143.9
	(114)	(122)	(113)		(139)	(123)		
VOCAT	−.092	.026	−.080	−.052	—	.497*	1.361	.482
	(125)	(134)	(122)	(118)		(131)		
EDATT	.187*	−.121	.446*	.608*	−.436*	—	2.099	1.110
	(97)	(104)	(93)	(95)	(102)			
Mean (females)	514.9	.288	601.5	568.1	1.381	2.173		
SD	126.3	.454	114.0	93.6	.487	1.136		

NOTE: Males are above the diagonal, females are below. Pairwise-present numbers of cases are in parentheses.

* Significant at .05 or less.

Australian and European males and females was slightly more than 11 years. The British/Irish males and females had the lowest mean attainment—less than 11 years.

The regression estimates for each ethnic and sex category are shown in standardized and metric form in Tables 2 and 3 respectively. Equation estimates across groups are compared using the metric coefficients, and variable estimates within groups are compared using the standardized coefficients (Pedhazur, 1982).

OCCUPATIONAL AMBITIONS, VOCATIONAL TRAINING PLANS, AND SCHOOL ATTAINMENT

The most consistent patterns in Table 2 are the strong positive and negative effects of occupational expectations and vocational training plans (*VOCAT*) on educational attainment. These patterns are more interesting when one considers that occupational aspirations and expectations had inconsistent effects on vocational training plans. Indeed, except for the significant positive effects of occupational expectations on vocational training plans for Australian males and British/Irish females, the ambition variables had no significant effects on plans. The intention to pursue vocational training was not determined by low ambitions, even though vocational plans necessitate early school leaving. Thus, the decision to leave school early was related, in part, to the pursuit of an alternative career path, which was independent of occupational ambitions and the other variables in the model. What is surprising is that for Australian males and European females, occupational expectations were directly related to vocational training plans, further suggesting that vocational training is not a cooling-out strategy for eventual occupational destination but a legitimate strategy for attaining preferred and expected occupations.

The relationship between preferred and expected occupations was almost as consistent: For all but one category (namely, European females) preferred occupation had a significant positive effect on expected occupation. Clearly, the acceptance of society's dominant

Table 2. Path Coefficients and R^2 by Sex and Ethnicity

			Independent Variables					
	Ethnicity	*N*	*FOCC*	*PSCH*	*POCC*	*EOCC*	*VOCAT*	R^2
Males								
PSCH	Australian	708	.195*					.038
	British/Irish	130	.036					.001
	European	167	−.030					.001
POCC	Australian	619	.177*	.035				.035
	British/Irish	106	.258*	−.040				.067
	European	149	−.039	−.070				.006
EOCC	Australian	595	.168*	.076*	.494*			.319
	British/Irish	101	.165*	.096	.579*			.419
	European	138	.211*	.064	.555*			.343
VOCAT	Australian	595	−.050	−.049	−.009	.223*		.045
	British/Irish	95	−.113	−.036	−.114	.098		.022
	European	138	−.076	−.075	.090	.060		.028
EDATT	Australian	583	.090*	.011	.096*	.403*	−.355*	.310
	British/Irish	93	.118*	−.093	−.090	.455*	−.294*	.299
	European	123	.095	−.152*	.036	.333*	−.538*	.414
Females								
PSCH	Australian	650	.234*					.055
	British/Irish	106	.232*					.054
	European	137	−.017					.000
POCC	Australian	580	.177*	−.005				.031
	British/Irish	90	.063	.163				.035
	European	121	.083	−.137				.026
EOCC	Australian	558	.131*	.025	.421*			.217
	British/Irish	80	.346*	−.057	.610*			.516
	European	113	.203*	−.147	.241*			.140
VOCAT	Australian	558	−.120*	.032	−.021	.020		.014
	British/Irish	80	.012	−.076	−.106	.211*		.033
	European	113	−.083	.013	−.067	−.013		.014
EDATT	Australian	545	.159*	−.095*	.124*	.271*	−.348*	.306
	British/Irish	77	.080	−.172	.165	.249	−.461*	.332
	European	93	.013	.021	.274*	.512*	−.386*	.602

* Coefficient is twice its standard error.

Table 3. Path Regressions and Intercepts by Sex and Ethnicity

	Ethnicity	Independent Variables *FOCC*	*PSCH*	*POCC*	*EOCC*	*VOCAT*	Intercept (Constant)
Males							
PSCH	Australian	.0008*					−.0016
	British/Irish	.0001					.1356
	European	−.0001					.3893
POCC	Australian	.1806*	9.0965				507.4233
	British/Irish	.2727*	−13.0173				467.3898
	European	−.0527	−21.7882				700.9328
EOCC	Australian	.1697*	19.6388*	.4888*			192.0331
	British/Irish	.1448*	25.7463	.4802*			180.0105
	European	.2794*	19.6179	.5469*			127.1994
VOCAT	Australian	−.0002	−.0413	.0000	.0007*		.0822
	British/Irish	−.0004	−.0395	.0004	.0004		.5046
	European	−.0003	−.0766	.0003	.0002		.2282
EDATT	Australian	.0008*	.0259	.0008*	.0036*	−.9677*	−.7752
	British/Irish	.0010*	−.2469	.0007	.0045*	−.7081*	−.5648
	European	.0010	−.3601*	.0003	.0026*	−1.2409*	.3548
Females							
PSCH	Australian	.0009*					−.1370
	British/Irish	.0008*					−.1939
	European	−.0001					.3182
POCC	Australian	.1549*	−1.1808				511.2970
	British/Irish	.0580	43.8181				558.6657
	European	.0749	−34.3677				572.8295
EOCC	Australian	.1032*	5.2244	.3783*			278.8116
	British/Irish	.2568*	−12.4327	.4931*			136.5908
	European	.1501*	−30.1963	.1981*			380.3532
VOCAT	Australian	−.0005*	.0316	.0001	.0001		.5939
	British/Irish	.0001	−.0811	−.0005	.0011*		.0808
	European	.0003	.0140	−.0003	.0001		.7521
EDATT	Australian	.0013*	−.2118*	.0012*	.0029*	−.7829*	−.6262
	British/Irish	.0007	−.4116	.0015	.0027	−.9596*	−.4180
	European	.0001	.0540	.0027*	.0062*	−.9001*	−2.7370

* Coefficient is twice its standard error.

occupational values, indicated by high occupational preferences, raised the level of expected occupational destinations. It is not clear why the effect was lower (albeit significant) for European females. The means for occupational preferences and expectations for European females (601.5 and 568.1) do not differ appreciably from the means for other females (see Table 1). Poole (1983) argues that female students tend to be more conforming and more influenced by teachers. Thus, they usually achieve higher grades (academic conformity) but have lower realistic expectations about career attainment (societal conformity). European females have high occupational preferences, indicating their acceptance of societal values, but because they are female *and* of European origin, they are much less optimistic and less consistent in their occupational expectations. Research has shown that young European females experience considerable pressure toward traditional sex role behavior, particularly with respect to educational and occupational choices (Isaacs, 1981). In addition, they may be less knowledgeable about the occupational world, or they may be confused about their own ability to attain their preferred occupations. For whatever reason, compared to the other groups, the European females exhibited a less consistent pattern in their articulation of occupational preferences and expectations.

In general, the causal model performs reasonably well: At least 30 percent of the variance is explained for all ethnic and sex categories. The model explains more variance for European students than for Australian and British/Irish students, and with the exception of Australian students, it explains more variance for females than for males. The metric coefficients in Table 3, which indicate actual points on the ANU 2 occupational status scale, permit a closer analysis of these ethnic and sex differences.

Consistent with research in the United States and elsewhere, this study found that socioeconomic status (*FOCC*) exercised notable direct effects on the career orientations of some school leavers, although this effect varied considerably by ethnicity and sex. Socioeconomic background had a significant positive effect on preferred occupation for all Australians and for British/Irish males. Thus, a 100-point increase in father's occupation was worth increases in occupational preferences of 18.1 and 27.3 points for Australian and British/Irish males and 15.5 points for Australian females. There was no significant effect for the other groups. If our interpretation of preferred occupation is correct, then for these students, higher socioeconomic background directly affected the status level of the jobs they wanted, all other things being equal. However, for all Europeans and for British/Irish females, socioeconomic background had no effect on occupational preferences.

Socioeconomic background directly affected the expected occupations of all sex and ethnic groups. It had the strongest direct effects on the expected occupations of European males and British/Irish females: Every 100-point increase in father's occupational status was associated with increases of 28 and 26 points in expected occupations. Thus, irrespective of sex and ethnicity, these students perceived their occupational destinations to be consistent with their own social origins. For all groups except Australian females, father's occupation had no significant effect on vocational training plans. For Australian females, father's occupation had a negative effect on plans: The higher the status of father's occupation, the lower the likelihood that a student planned to pursue vocational training after leaving school. While this effect is expected, the absence of any effect for the other groups is surprising. We will discuss this absence later. Finally, it is important to note that for Australian males and females and British/Irish males, socioeconomic background was directly related to educational attainment (*EDATT*).

Private-school attendance (*PSCH*) had no significant effect in the model, perhaps because the "private" category, as in the United States, includes schools of varying socioeconomic compositions, ranging from the elite independent schools to the mixed-status parochial schools. Nevertheless, it is useful to note that private-school attendance had a direct positive effect on occupational expectations (20 status points) for Australian males and a negative effect on educational attainment (one-third and one-fifth year of school) for European males and Australian females. These latter effects reflect either the lower retention levels of these two sex and ethnic groups in private schools or the concentration of these groups in private schools with low retention rates.[9]

Preferred occupation, a generalized social-psychological disposition, had considerable positive effects on expected occupation for all ethnic and sex groups. As already noted, the effect was considerably less for European females, particularly when compared with European males. A 100-point increase in preferred occupation status resulted in a 20-point increase in expected occupation status for European females and a 55-point increase for European males. The direct effects of preferred occupation on educational attainment were mixed: They were significant only for Australian males and females and European females. But the effects for the latter were small, amounting at most to one-fifth year of schooling for every 100-point increase in preferred occupation status.

The pattern of the effects of occupational expectations is considerably different. Occupational expectations had little effect on vocational training plans, but they had significant positive effects on educational attainment for all groups except British/Irish females. The effect was largest for European females: For every 100-point increase in the status of expected occupation, they completed almost two thirds of a year of schooling. This strong effect contrasts sharply with the smaller effects for Australian and British/Irish females. One explanation for the difference lies in the traditional sex role argument made earlier. A European female who aspires to a high-status occupation is not conforming to traditional sex role norms and is probably exceptional among her cultural peers. Such a person, having set her goals high, strives much harder to realize her ambitions. Schooling, insofar as it is a means to a high-status career, is a more important objective for this student than for a student whose career ambitions are conventional and less exceptional.

Vocational training plans, while virtually unaffected by the prior variables in the model, had consistent and significant negative effects on educational attainment. Irrespective of socioeconomic background, type of school attended, and occupational aspirations and expectations, students who intended to pursue

[9] These findings are consistent with those reported by Coleman, Hoffer, and Kilgore (1982). They found that Catholic-school and other private-school students had higher cognitive achievement and higher educational expectations than public-school students. They also found that among students planning to work after leaving high school, those from the public schools were more likely to have "lined up" a job, a tendency attributed to the greater number of vocational programs in public schools. The Coleman study did not, however, examine sex differences in these patterns.

vocational training left school earlier. For European males the intention to pursue some form of vocational training resulted in a reduction in educational attainment of 1.2 years, the largest for all sex and ethnic categories.

The general pattern suggests that the intention to pursue vocational training was largely independent of socioeconomic background, type of school attended, and ambition. There was a slight but significant negative effect of father's occupation on vocational training plans for Australian females, indicating a tendency for some lower-SES students to choose this career preparation strategy. Nevertheless, the choice of vocational training is largely undetermined in the model, as indicated by the low proportion of variance explained. It is not a career strategy for a particular socioeconomic class, ethnic group, or sex. Thus, vocational training programs, which necessitate early school leaving, represent a legitimate alternative to formal academic schooling. This observation is further supported by the fact that an intermediate school certificate, which can be obtained after Year 10, is the minimum requirement for entry into apprenticeships and other vocational programs.

THE DISAGGREGATION OF CAUSAL EFFECTS ON EDUCATIONAL ATTAINMENT

To examine the complexity of the processes reflected in sex and ethnic differences more closely, the original relationships in the model were decomposed into direct, indirect, and total effects (see Table 4). The coefficient for total effects takes into account the direct and indirect causal effects on the dependent variable, net of spuriousness due to unanalyzed effects of the exogenous variables and analyzed and unanalyzed prior effects of the endogenous variables. Thus, the coefficient for total effects can be interpreted, like any regression coefficient, as "change in *Y* per (controlled) unit change in *X*" (Lewis-Beck and Mohr, 1976: 43).

In general, the pattern that emerges from the disaggregation procedure shows that the social-psychological variables had strong total effects on educational attainment for all sex and ethnic categories. In contrast, father's occupational status had moderate total effects, and type of school attended had small effects. Thus, the overall pattern is consistent with findings from American research and confirms

Table 4. Coefficients for Direct, Indirect, and Total Effects of Independent Variables on Educational Attainment (*EDATT*)

	Ethnicity	Direct Effects	Indirect Effects	Total Effects
Males				
FOCC	Australian	.090	.105	.195
	British/Irish	.118	.015	.133
	European	.095	.116	.211
PSCH	Australian	.011	.051	.062
	British/Irish	−.093	.058	.035
	European	−.152	.059	−.093
POCC	Australian	.096	.202	.298
	British/Irish	−.090	.297	.207
	European	.036	.136	.172
EOCC	Australian	.403	−.079	.324
	British/Irish	.455	−.029	.426
	European	.333	−.032	.301
VOCAT	Australian	−.355	—	−.355
	British/Irish	−.294	—	−.294
	European	−.538	—	−.538
Females				
FOCC	Australian	.159	.077	.236
	British/Irish	.080	.051	.131
	European	.013	.158	.171
PSCH	Australian	−.095	−.005	−.100
	British/Irish	−.172	.048	−.124
	European	.021	−.118	−.097
POCC	Australian	.124	.121	.245
	British/Irish	.165	.201	.366
	European	.274	.149	.423
EOCC	Australian	.271	−.007	.264
	British/Irish	.249	−.097	.152
	European	.512	.005	.517
VOCAT	Australian	−.348	—	−.348
	British/Irish	−.461	—	−.461
	European	−.386	—	−.386

the salience of the social-psychological model of status attainment (Sewell and Hauser, 1980).

A closer inspection of the effects of the social-psychological variables on attainment uncovers some important variations. First, for males, the impact of preferred occupation on educational attainment was mostly mediated, but for females, the direct effects were consistently large, and for European females, they constituted 65 percent of the total effects. In other words, for females, simply wanting to attain a high-level occupation exerted a direct effect on school attainment, but for males, these preferences were mediated through specific knowledge of attainment possibilities (*EOCC*) and the strategies to pursue them (*VOCAT*). Second, the effects of expected occupational attainment were direct for all categories; there was no mediation through vocational training plans.

The disaggregation of effects further explains the process whereby leaving early or completing secondary school is accomplished, but there appear to be no systematic variations in this process by ethnicity.

DISCUSSION AND CONCLUSION

Young people formulate career plans early in their schooling. To the extent that these anticipated destinations affect attainments, there is an ordered process in which students prepare for their future stations in the workforce. However, as these Australian data indicate, the impact of occupational aspirations and expectations varies by ethnicity and sex, suggesting that the ordered progression through school and ultimately to work is not perceived in the same way by all students. To some extent, variations in occupational expectations indicate a recognition of opportunities and limitations in the occupational structure and differences in the underlying cultural and social values that influence a young person's ultimate educational and occupational attainments.

There is little evidence in these data to suggest that any one of the ethnic or sex groups is directly favored through ascription: Compared to the other variables in the model, father's occupation was only moderately important in explaining early or late school leaving in this sample of urban school leavers. The only variable that had less impact was the type of school attended. Indeed, socioeconomic background had little direct effect even on the intention to pursue vocational training, which suggests that this option was chosen not only by students from lower socioeconomic backgrounds. However, as was noted earlier, this does not mean that educational attainment is meritocratic; students from higher socioeconomic backgrounds do tend to stay in school longer. It appears that the effects of socioeconomic background operate mainly through occupational expectations, and this social-psychological disposition does differentiate between early and late school leavers. Furthermore, one can argue that the relative indeterminacy of the intention to pursue vocational training highlights its role as an alternative career path, and because of the negative effects of vocational training on school attainment, early leaving is legitimated. Thus, while some Australian students leave school early because of low occupational aspirations and expectations, others leave early because they choose a particular career. The latter students do not necessarily have low aspirations and expectations.

As the imminent school leavers perceived, there are two paths to occupational attainment: Students can leave school early and pursue vocational training, or they can stay in school longer to complete secondary school or pursue tertiary studies. The legitimacy of the two paths does not imply that their respective occupational destinations have the same status. But compared to the path chosen by those who leave school early with no plans for further training, vocational training represents a legitimate alternative.

The differentiation between formal schooling and alternative career paths has received little attention in the status-attainment literature in Australia and in the United States. Previous research into the process of occupational attainment has assumed that formal schooling is the single most effective way to raise one's ultimate occupational destination. These data, although specific to the Australian school system, suggest that the decision to leave school early and enroll in a vocational program is a rational choice, parallel to the decision to stay in school longer and pursue tertiary studies. Furthermore, for the student who is forced to leave school early because of financial, academic, or other reasons, the decision to pursue vocational training outside formal school may salvage otherwise blocked aspirations.[10]

[10] Recent evidence from Australia suggests that this pattern may be changing. During the economic recession and growing unemployment of the early 1980s, there has been an apparent (possibly short-term) decline in the proportion of males completing Year 12 and a decline in the proportion of high-ability students entering higher education (Commonwealth Tertiary Education Commission, 1982). Many of these students are entering the workforce earlier through vocational training programs rather than making the longer-term investment in higher education. Thus, the pattern described here, which prevailed through the 1970s and which represented an option for early school leavers, is threatened by students from higher socioeconomic backgrounds, who are presumably more talented and more competitive.

It cannot be inferred from these findings that legitimate alternative career paths exist in the U.S. However, the study of the determinants of lower educational attainment in the U.S. in the context of alternative career paths might offer an insightful challenge to the assumption that formal schooling is the only salient strategy for the attainment of occupational ambitions.

REFERENCES

Australian Sales Research Bureau
n.d. Survey of School Leavers' Attitudes Towards the Business Community. Melbourne: Australian Sales Research Bureau.

Blakers, C.
1978 School and Work. Canberra: Australian National University Press.

Broom, L., P. Duncan-Jones, F. L. Jones, and P. McDonnell
1977 Investigating Social Mobility. Departmental Monograph No. 1. Canberra: Department of Sociology, Research School of Social Sciences, Australian National University.

Broom, L., F. L. Jones, P. McDonnell, and T. Williams
1982 The Inheritance of Inequality. London: Routledge and Kegan Paul.

Carpenter, P. G. and J. S. Western
1983 "The facilitation of attainment aspirations." Australian and New Zealand Journal of Sociology 19:305–18.

Carpenter, P. G., J. S. Western, and W. G. Foster
1980 "Social background, aspirations and educational achievement among Queensland youth." Pp. 30–41 in I. D. Smith (ed.), Youth, Schooling and Employment. Melbourne: Australian Association for Research in Education.
1981 "Origins, aspirations and attainments." Pp. 262–69 in M. J. Lawson and R. Linke (eds.), Inquiry and Action in Education. Melbourne: Australian Association for Research in Education.

Coleman, J. S., T. Hoffer, and S. Kilgore
1982 High School Achievement: Public, Catholic and Private Schools Compared. New York: Basic Books.

Commonwealth Department of Education
1977 Primary and Secondary Schooling in Australia. Canberra: Australian Government Publishing Service.

Commonwealth Tertiary Education Commission
1982 Learning and Earning: A Study of Education and Employment Opportunities for Young People. Canberra: Australian Government Publishing Service.

Duncan, O. D., D. L. Featherman, and B. Duncan
1972 Socioeconomic Background and Achievement. New York: Seminar Press.

Gasson, R. M., A. O. Haller, and W. H. Sewell
1972 Attitudes and Facilitation in the Attainment of Status. Rose Monograph Series in Sociology. Washington, DC: American Sociological Association.

Haller, A. O.
1982 "Reflections on the social psychology of status attainment." Pp. 3–28 in R. M. Hauser, D. Mechanic, A. O. Haller, and T. S. Hauser (eds.), Social Structure and Behavior. New York: Academic Press.

Han, W. S.
1969 "Two conflicting themes: Common values versus class differential values." American Sociological Review 34:679–90.

Howell, F. M. and W. Frese
1982 Making Life Plans: Race, Gender and Career Decisions. Washington, DC: University Press of America.

Isaacs, E.
1981 Greek Children at School and After. ERDC Report No. 29. Canberra: Australian Government Publishing Service.

Karmel, P.
1981 Education in the Eighties. Australian Education Review No. 15. Melbourne: Australian Council for Educational Research.

Lewis-Beck, M. S. and L. B. Mohr
1976 "Evaluating effects of independent variables." Political Methodology 3:27–47.

Marini, M. M. and E. Greenberger
1978 "Sex differences in occupational aspirations and expectations." Sociology of Work and Occupations 5:147–78.

Marjoribanks, K.
1979 "Ethnicity, family environment, school attitudes and academic achievement." Pp. 189–201 in P. R. de Lacey and M. E. Poole (eds.), Mosaic or Melting Pot: Cultural Evolution in Australia. Sydney: Harcourt, Brace, Jovanovich.

Martin, J. I. and P. Meade
1979 The Educational Experience of Sydney High School Students. Commonwealth Department of Education Report 1. Canberra: Australian Government Publishing Service.

Meade, P.
1982 "Equality of educational opportunity of students of non-English-speaking migrant origin and students with Australian-born parents." Pp. 541–46 in Educational Research in the 1980s: Collected Papers. Melbourne: Australian Association for Research in Education.

Pedhazur, E. J.
1982 Multiple Regression in Behavioral Research. 2nd ed. New York: Holt, Rinehart and Winston.

Pincus, F. L.
1980 "The false promises of community colleges: Class conflict and vocational education." Harvard Educational Review 50:332–61.

Poole, M. E.
1981 "Life chances: Some comparisons of migrant and non-migrant Melbourne adolescents." Education Research and Perspectives 8:3–12.
1983 Youth: Expectations and Transitions. Melbourne: Routledge and Kegan Paul.

Porter, J., M. Porter, and B. R. Blishen
1982 Stations and Callings: Making it Through the School System. Toronto: Methuen.

Portes, A., S. A. McLeod, and R. N. Parker
1978 "Immigrant aspirations." Sociology of Education 51:241–60.
Richmond, A. H. and J. Zubrzycki
1981 "Occupational status in Australia and Canada: A comparative study of the native and the foreign born." Comparative Social Research 4:91–110.
Saha, L. J.
1982 "Gender, school attainment and occupational plans: Determinants of aspirations and expectations among Australian urban school leavers." Australian Journal of Education 26:247–65.
Sewell, W. H., A. O. Haller, and G. W. Ohlendorf
1970 "The educational and early occupational status attainment process: Replication and revision." American Sociological Review 35:1014–27.
Sewell, W. H., A. O. Haller, and A. Portes
1969 "The educational and early occupational attainment process." American Sociological Review 34:82–92.
Sewell, W. H. and R. M. Hauser
1975 Education, Occupation and Earnings: Achievement in the Early Career. New York: Academic Press.
1980 "The Wisconsin longitudinal study of social and psychological factors in aspirations and achievements." Research in Sociology of Education and Socialization 1:59–99.
Shea, B. M.
1976 "Schooling and its antecedents: Substantive and methodological issues in the status attainment process." Review of Education Research 46:463–526.
Spenner, K. T. and D. L. Featherman
1978 "Achievement ambitions." Annual Review of Sociology 4:373–420.
Turner, R.
1960 "Sponsored and contest mobility and the school systems." American Sociological Review 25:855–67.
1964 The Social Context of Ambition. San Francisco: Chandler.
Williams, T., M. Batten, S. Girling-Butcher, and J. Clancy
1981 School and Work in Prospect: 14-year-olds in Australia. Melbourne: Australian Council of Educational Research.
Wilms, W. W. and S. Hansell
1982 "The dubious promise of post-secondary vocational education: Its payoff to dropouts and graduates in the USA." International Journal of Educational Development 2:43–60.

FROM IDEALISM TO PRAGMATIC DETACHMENT: THE ACADEMIC PERFORMANCE OF COLLEGE ATHLETES

PETER ADLER
University of Tulsa

PATRICIA A. ADLER
Oklahoma State University

Sociology of Education 1985, Vol. 58 (October):241–250

This study examines the relationship between athletic participation and academic performance among athletes involved in big-time college sports. Drawing on four years of participant observation of a major college basketball program, we trace athletes' involvement in academics throughout their college careers. We show that, contrary to popular belief, most athletes enter college with optimistic and idealistic goals and attitudes about their impending academic careers. However, their athletic, social, and classroom experiences lead them to become progressively detached from academics. As a result, they make pragmatic adjustments, abandoning their earlier aspirations and expectations and gradually resigning themselves to inferior academic performance. We conclude that the structure of universities with big-time athletic programs and the athletes' patterned experiences within these universities undermine their attainment of the professed goals of the educational system. We discuss several policy implications of this research.

In recent years, the relationship between the athletic participation and academic performance of college athletes has become a topic of scholarly concern. The sociological literature in this area, however, has been inconsistent in its findings. Some studies have cited a weak positive relationship, claiming that although most college athletes had poor academic records in high school, they have higher GPAs, lower attrition rates, and a greater likelihood of graduating than nonathletes because they receive extra tutoring, more attention, and special "breaks" (Hanks and Eckland, 1976; Henschen and Fry, 1984; Michener, 1976; Shapiro, 1984). But most studies of college athletes have found a negative relationship between athletic participation and academic performance. These studies conclude that athletes are unprepared for and uninterested in academics, that they come to college to advance their athletic careers rather than their academic careers; therefore, they have lower GPAs, higher attrition rates, and lower chances of graduating than other students (Cross, 1973; Edwards, 1984; Harrison, 1976; Nyquist, 1979; Purdy, Eitzen, and Hufnagel, 1982; Sack and Thiel, 1979; Spivey and Jones, 1975; Webb, 1968).

We are indebted to Jean Blocker for providing collegial support throughout the research portion of this project. We want to thank David Altheide, Gary Alan Fine, John Johnson, Peter Manning, Carol Warren, Louis Zurcher, and anonymous reviewers for comments on an earlier draft. This is a modified version of a paper presented at the Annual Meeting of the American Sociological Association, San Antonio, August 1984. Address all correspondence to the authors at the Department of Sociology, University of Tulsa, 600 S. College, Tulsa, OK 74104.

Our research, which also finds a negative relationship, extends previous studies in several ways. First, we show that although most college athletes ultimately become disillusioned with and detached from academics, many begin their college careers idealistically, caring about academics and intending to graduate. Second, we show that the structure of college athletics fosters the academic deindividuation of athletes. We trace the stages through which athletes progress as they become socialized to their position in the university environment and learn its structural characteristics. We describe how their academic goals and behavior become increasingly influenced by their athletic involvement. The initial academic aspirations of freshman athletes are considerably varied, but these various individual ideals gradually give way under the force of the structural conditions athletes encounter. Thus, by the time athletes complete their eligibility requirements, their academic attitudes and goals closely resemble each other's. This process, which reduces individual differences between athletes, is accompanied by collective academic detachment and diminished academic performance. Third, using a longitudinal analysis of process and change, made possible by our method of data collection, we show the influence of interconnecting factors on athletes' progression through college. This is the first systematic participant-observation study of college athletes. Such an in-depth, ethnographic investigation of this area (suggested by Coakley, 1982; Fine, 1979; Loy, McPherson, and Kenyon, 1978; Purdy et al., 1982) is useful for two reasons: (1) it enables us to determine whether athletic participation hinders or enhances academic performance, and (2) it reveals the factors and processes that produce this relationship.

We begin by discussing the setting in which this study was conducted and our involvement with members of the scene. We then examine the athletes' academic attitudes, goals, and involvement in their first months on campus. Next, we analyze their involvement in three spheres of university life—athletic, social, and classroom—and the impact of this involvement on their academic attitudes and performance. Last, we discuss the series of pragmatic adjustments they forge, which reflect the gradual erosion of their earlier academic goals and idealism. We conclude by offering a structural analysis of athletes' experiences within the university, which shows how and why they become progressively alienated and detached from academics. We suggest several educational and athletic policies that might help to ameliorate this situation.

METHODS AND SETTING

The Research

Over a four-year period (1980–1984), we conducted a participant-observation study of a major college basketball program. We used team field research strategies (Douglas, 1976) and differentiated, multiperspectival roles to enhance our data gathering and analysis. I (first author) was initially granted access to the team because the coaches became interested in our earlier works on the sociology of sport (Adler and Adler, 1978; Adler, 1981). After reading these and talking with me, they perceived me as an expert who could provide valuable counsel on interpersonal, organizational, and academic matters. Although college and professional sport settings are generally characterized by secrecy and an extreme sensitivity to the insider-outsider distinction (see Jonassohn, Turowetz, and Gruneau, 1981), I gradually gained the trust of significant gatekeepers, particularly the head coach, and was granted the status and privileges of an assistant coach. As the "team sociologist," my primary duty was to informally counsel players on social, academic, and personal matters and help them make the adjustment to college life and athletics. This role allowed me to become especially close to the athletes, who came to me with their problems, worries, or disgruntlements. Becoming an active member (Adler and Adler, forthcoming) and interacting with other members on a daily basis was also the only way I could penetrate the inner sanctum and achieve the type of rapport and trust necessary for the study.[1]

The second author assumed the outsider role, "debriefing" me when I returned from the setting, looking for sociological patterns in the data, and ensuring that I retained a sociological perspective on my involvement. She helped me conduct a series of intensive, taped interviews with 7 of the coaches and with the 38 basketball players who passed through the program during the four years.[2] She also helped construct the final analysis and written reports.

The Setting

The research was conducted at a medium-size (6,000 students) private university (hereafter referred to as "the University") in the mid-south-central portion of the United States. Most of the students were white, suburban, and middle class. The University, which was striving to become one of the finer private universities in the region, had fairly rigorous academic standards. The athletic department, as a whole, had a very successful recent history: The women's golf team was ranked in the top three nationally, the football team had won their conference in each of the previous four seasons, and the basketball team was ranked in the top forty of Division I NCAA schools and in the top twenty for most of two seasons. They had played in postseason tournaments every year, and in four complete seasons they had won approximately four times as many games as they had lost. Players were generally recruited from the surrounding region. Most of them came from the lower and middle classes, and 70 percent of them were black. In general, the basketball program represented what Coakley (1982) and Frey (1982) have termed big-time college athletics. Although it could not compare to the upper echelon of established basketball dynasties or to the really large athletic programs that wield enormous recruiting and operating budgets, its recent success has compensated for its small size and lack of historical tradition. The University's basketball program could best be described as up-and-coming. Because the basketball team (along with other teams in the athletic department) was ranked nationally and sent graduating members into the professional leagues, the entire athletic milieu was imbued with a sense of seriousness and purpose.

ACADEMIC EXPECTATIONS

Contrary to the recent negative thought, noted earlier, most of the athletes we observed

[1] For a more detailed discussion of the methodological issues involved in this research, see Adler (1984).

[2] Some individuals were interviewed several times, at various stages of their socialization process.

entered the University feeling idealistic about their impending academic experience and optimistic about their likelihood of graduating. Their idealistic orientation and aspirations derived from several sources. First, they had received numerous cultural messages that a college education would enhance their ability to be successful in our society (cf. Semyonov and Yuchtman-Yaar, 1981). These messages were reinforced by their families, their most outspoken significant others. One sophomore described his family's involvement in his academic career:

> When my mom call she always ask me, first, "How you feelin'," second, "How you doin' in school?" She won't even let me talk 'bout basketball 'til she hear I'm doin' okay in school. She always be thinkin' 'bout my future and wantin' me to get that degree.

College coaches also reinforced these messages. During recruitment, the coaches stressed the positive aspects of a college education and the importance of graduating (cf. Cross, 1973). The athletes accepted the rhetoric of these sports personnel (what Tannenbaum and Noah [1959] called "sportuguese"), but they never really considered what a college education entailed. Thus, a third factor fostering their optimism about academics was their naïve assumption that after attending college for four years they would automatically get a degree. They never anticipated the amount or kind of academic work they would have to do to earn that degree. Many of them had not taken a sequence of college preparatory courses in high school.[3] Thus, their optimism was based largely on their "successful" academic careers in high school ("I graduated high school, didn't I?") and on their belief that as college athletes they would be academically pampered ("I heard you can get breaks on grades because you're an athlete"). Arriving freshmen commonly held the following set of prior expectations about their future academic performance: (1) they would go to classes and do the work (more broadly conceived as "putting the time in"); (2) they would graduate and get a degree; and (3) there would be no problem.

Of the entering athletes we observed, 47 percent (n = 18) requested placement in preprofessional majors in the colleges of business, engineering, or arts and sciences, indicating their initially high academic aspirations and expectations. One sophomore gave the rationale behind his choice of a major:

> You come in, you want to make money. How do you make money? You go into business. How do you go into business? You major in business, and you end up having to take these business courses, and you really don't think about it. It sounds okay.

Despite warnings from coaches and older teammates that it would be difficult to complete this coursework and play ball, they felt they could easily handle the demands.

Another group of freshmen, who had no specific career aspirations beyond playing professional basketball (45 percent, n = 17), were enrolled by coaches in more "manageable," athletic-related majors such as physical education or recreation.[4] However, most of these individuals believed that they too would get a degree. Though they had no clear academic goals, they figured that they would somehow make it through satisfactorily. Only a small number of individuals in our sample (8 percent, n = 3) entered college with no aspirations of getting a degree. Either these individuals were such highly touted high school players that they entered college expecting to turn professional before their athletic eligibility expired, or they were uninterested in academics but had no other plans. Their main concern, then, was to remain eligible to play ball. But they never seriously considered the possibility that they would be barred from competition because of low grades.

In their first few months on campus, athletes' early idealism was strengthened. During these summer months, the coaches repeatedly stressed the importance of "getting that piece of paper." Once the school year began, freshman athletes attended required study halls nightly, were told how to get tutors, and were constantly reminded by the coach to go to class. One freshman, interviewed during the preseason, indicated his acceptance of the coaches' rhetoric:

> If I can use my basketball ability to open up the door to get an education, hopefully I can use my degree to open up the door to get a good job. . . . I think that's really important to Coach, too, 'cause in practice he always be mentioning how important the degree is an' everything.

Although these athletes unquestionably cared more about their athletic and social lives

---

[3] Several sociological studies have noted that the admission standards for athletes are lower than those for the general student body, leading to the admission of academically marginal, ill-prepared students (Edwards, 1984; Purdy et al., 1982; Sack, 1977; Shapiro, 1984; Spady, 1970).

[4] This figure includes a small number of athletes who decided, usually during their sophomore or junior years, not to play professionally but to go into an athletically related occupation such as coaching.

than their academic performance, getting through school, at least in the abstract, was still important to them. For most, this period of early idealism lasted until the end of their freshman year. After this time, their naïve, early idealism gradually became replaced by disappointment and growing cynicism as they realized how difficult it was to keep up with their schoolwork. They encountered unexpected problems in the articulation of the athletic, social, and academic spheres of the University.

ATHLETIC EXPERIENCES

A major difference athletes encountered in moving from high school to college lay in the size of the athletic sphere. In high school, athletics was primary to their self-identities; but in college, it played an even more central role in their lives. It dominated all facets of their existence, including their academic involvement and performance.

A primary change in their athletic involvement was rooted in the *professionalization* of the sport. Upon entering college, freshman athletes immediately noticed its commercialization (cf. Coakley, 1982; Eitzen, 1979; Hoch, 1972; Sack, 1977; Underwood, 1980). They were no longer playing for enjoyment. This was big business ("there's a lotta money ridin' on us"). As a result, basketball changed from a recreation to an occupation (cf. Ingham, 1975). The occupational dimensions of the sport and their desire to perform well intensified the pressure to win (cf. Odenkirk, 1981; Underwood, 1980). A senior described this emphasis on winning:

> In college the coaches be a lot more concerned on winning and the money comin' in. If they don't win, they may get the boot, and so they pass that pressure onto us athletes. I go to bed every night and I be thinkin' 'bout basketball. That's what college athletics do to you. It take over you mind.

Professionalization also brought with it the fame and glamour of media attention. During the season, athletes were regularly in the newspaper and on television and were greeted as celebrities whenever they ventured off campus. Overall, then, the professionalization of college athletics drew athletes' focus to this arena and riveted it there.

Playing on the basketball team also demanded a larger share of athletes' *time* in college than it had in high school. In addition to the three hours of practice daily ("two-a-days" on weekends during the preseason), players were expected to watch films of other teams, to be available for team meetings, to return to their dorm rooms by curfew, and to leave the campus for two to five days at a time for road trips.[5] They also had to spend a certain amount of their time with athletically related others: the media, fans, and boosters (rich businesspersons who contributed money and wanted to feel close to the program). This involvement often conflicted with potential academic time: Afternoon practice conflicted with the required courses or labs in certain majors, games and road trips conflicted with the time athletes needed for exams and term papers, and booster functions cut into their discretionary time. By the end of their first year, most athletes acknowledged that their athletic-related activities affected their academic performance. As one senior explained:

> We got to go two-a-days, get up as early as the average student, go to school, then go to practice for three hours like nothing you have ever strained. . . . It's brutal 'cause you be so tired. Fatigue is what makes a lot of those guys say "Chuck it, I'm goin' to sleep." You don't feel like sittin' there an' readin' a book, an' you not goin' comprehend that much anyway 'cause you so tired.

Fatigue (cf. Edwards, 1984) and restricted time for studying caused many athletes to give up and cease caring about their academic work. Thus, rather than use the little free time they had to catch up on their studies, they usually chose to spend it socializing or just sleeping.

Athletes' academic performance was also affected by *coaches' intervention* in their academic lives. Assistant coaches handled academic matters for the athletes, declaring their majors, registering them for courses, adjusting their schedules, and periodically contacting their professors (to monitor their progress). Athletes, therefore, were largely uninvolved in academic decision-making and did not interact directly with professors, academic counselors, or academic administrators. As a result, they failed to develop the knowledge, initiative, or, in many cases, the interest to handle these academic matters themselves. As one sophomore stated,

> The day before class you go up to the office and they hand you a card that got your schedule all filled out on it. You don't say nothin' or think nothin' 'bout it, you just go. And it kinda make you feel like you not involved in it, 'cause you don't have nothin' to do with it. Like it's they's job, not yours.

[5] Edwards (1984:7) has estimated that during the season, basketball players spend fifty hours a week preparing for, participating in, recovering from, and traveling to games.

Because the coaches managed these administrative matters, the athletes developed a false sense of security, a feeling that someone was looking out for them academically and would make sure that they were given another chance, a feeling that they could foul up and not have to pay the consequences. They believed that their coaches dominated their professors and the administrators, that they would be "taken care of" academically, and that they need not involve themselves in this arena. This also led them to distance themselves from their academics and to diminish their effort.

Having formed this belief, many athletes were surprised to discover, usually sometime during their sophomore or junior year, that this overseeing and management extended to administrative areas only. Coaches placed them in their courses, but they could not guarantee them special breaks. Athletes then realized, often too late, that they were responsible for attending classes and completing their assignments on their own and that they had to do the same work that other students did to pass their courses. Many athletes were shepherded through high school; therefore, they were ill-equipped to assume responsibilities in college and often failed to fulfill them.

Finally, the athletes received greater *reinforcement* for athletic performance than for academic performance. No one closely monitored their academic behavior, but they were carefully watched at games, practices, booster functions, and on road trips. The celebrity and social status they derived from the media, boosters, and fans brought them immediate gratification, which the academic realm, with its emphasis on future rewards, could not offer.

With a few exceptions, athletes' experiences within the academic realm brought neither close contact nor positive reinforcement. Like many other college students, athletes generally found their professors aloof and uninterested. One freshman gave his impressions of college professors:

> At my high school back home, the teachers would make sure everyone done the reading before we went on to the next subject. The teachers really cared if the students got behind, so sometimes they would teach individually. But here, by the next time the class meets, they ask if anyone has any questions, and if no one says anything, then most of them would give a pop quiz. I cannot really say the teachers care here, because if you get behind it's your problem, not theirs.

Given the paucity of contact with the faculty, the lack of reinforcement within the academic realm, and the omnipresence of the coaches, media, fans, and boosters, who provided both positive and negative feedback on daily athletic performance, it became easier for athletes to turn away from academics and concentrate their efforts on sport.

SOCIAL EXPERIENCES

The athletes' social experiences also affected their academic performance. Their social lives at the University were dominated by their relationships with other athletes. They had initially expected to derive both friendship and status recognition from a wide variety of students, both athletes and nonathletes, as they had in high school (cf. Coleman, 1961; Cusick, 1973; Eitzen, 1975; Rehberg and Schafer, 1968; Spady, 1970). But instead of being socially integrated, they found themselves isolated (cf. Antonelli, 1970). They were isolated geographically because they were housed in the athletes' dorm in a remote part of campus. They were cut off temporally by the demands of their practices, games, study halls, and booster functions. They were isolated culturally by their racial and socioeconomic differences from the rest of the student body. They were isolated physically by their size and build, which many students, especially women, found intimidating. A freshman described his feelings of social alienation:

> This school is nothing like I thought it would be when I left home. The social life is very different and I have to adjust to it. A main problem for me are the white people. Where I grew up, all my friends were black, so I really don't know how to act toward whites. Here, when I speak to some of them, they just give me a fake smile. I really can't understand the people here because this is college and everyone should have a good time socially.

Since they had few opportunities to interact with nonathletes, they formed extremely strong social bonds among themselves. Housed together in a dorm reserved almost exclusively for male athletes (primarily football and basketball players), they were bonded together into a reference group and peer subculture. Relations within this group were especially cohesive because they lived, played, and travelled together.

Within the dorm, athletes exchanged information about various individuals and how to handle certain situations. This helped them form common attitudes and beliefs about their athletic, social, and academic experiences. The peer subculture thus provided them with a set of norms and values that guided their interpretations and behavior within these three realms.

One of the most predominant influences of

the peer subculture was its anti-intellectual and anti-academic character (cf. Coleman, 1960; Sack, 1977). Typically, dorm conversation centered on the athletic or social dimensions of the athletes' lives; little reference was made to academic, cultural, or intellectual pursuits (cf. Meggysey, 1971; Shaw, 1972). As one junior remarked,

> If a athlete was living in the dorm with just ordinary people, what do you think they'll be talkin' about? Ordinary things. But you got all athletes here. What are they goin' be talkin' about? It won't be Reaganomics, believe me. It'll definitely by *Sports Illustrated*.

Separating athletes from other students thus made their athletic reality dominant and distanced them from any academic inclinations they may have had. The same athlete continued:

> The two images are set apart because one side of us is, "My momma send me to school to be a engineer, and in order to be a engineer I gots to go to class every day and study hard," and the other side is "I come to school to play basketball. I didn't come to school to study that hard." So to keep those two images apart, to keep you thinking basketball night and day, they puts you in with all these other jocks dreamin' in they dream worlds.

The athletes' peer subculture also subverted academic orientations by discouraging them from exerting effort in academics. In fact, individuals who displayed too much interest, effort, or success in academics were often ridiculed, as one player described:

> When most of the other guys are making D's and F's, if I work hard and get a B on a test, if I go back to the dorm and they all see I got a B, then they goin' snap on [make fun of] me. So mosts of the guys, they don't try. They all act like it's a big joke.

Like the Chicano subculture Horowitz (1983) observed, the athletes' peer subculture valued education in the abstract, yet the commitments valued by the athletes' subculture conflicted with the commitments necessary to make that value carry over into practical reality. Their peers thus provided them with excuses and justifications that legitimated their poor academic performance and neutralized the importance of this realm in their self-identities.

CLASSROOM EXPERIENCES

Athletes' attitudes toward academics and their effort and performance were also affected by the difficulties and disillusionments they encountered in the classroom. Athletes believed that many professors labeled them as jocks because they looked different from most of the other students, they were surrounded in their classes by other athletes, and they were identified by coaches early in the semester to the professors as athletes. They perceived, then, that professors treated them differently from the general student body. On the one hand, because of the widely held subcultural lore that as college athletes they would have special privileges and because of the important and visible role they played at the University, they commonly thought that professors would accord them greater tolerance—i.e., extra tutoring sessions, relaxed deadlines, relaxed academic standards (cf. Raney, Knapp, and Small, 1983). This perception was fostered by their placement, especially in their freshman year, in courses taught by sympathetic faculty members who tried to give them extra attention or assistance. Because of these placements, athletes often began college thinking that academics would not be a major concern. On the other hand, athletes also encountered a number of less sympathetic professors who they thought stereotyped them as dumb jocks or cocky athletes. In these cases they "rejected the rejectors" (Sykes and Matza, 1957), using persecution as a rationale for disengaging from academics. One player discussed his experiences with professors:

> Some are goin' help you, if they can, and you can always tell who they are 'cause you got a bunch o' athletes in you class. Some try to make it harder on you. They're out to get you 'cause they feel like you living like a king and it shouldn't be that way. With those jerks, it don't matter how hard you try. They gonna flunk you just 'cause you a athlete.

This differential treatment served to reinforce their perceptions that they were athletes more than students. Therefore, when they returned to their dorm rooms at night, exhausted and sore from practicing, it became easier for them to rationalize, procrastinate, and "fritter" (Bernstein, 1978) their time away instead of studying.

Athletes also became uninterested in academics because of the *content* of their classes. Many individuals placed in physical education or recreation courses, even those who were fairly uninterested in academics from the beginning, felt that their courses lacked academic or practical merit and were either comical, demeaning, or both. One sophomore articulated the commonly held view:

> How could I get into this stuff? They got me takin' nutrition, mental retardation, square

> dancing, and camp counseling. I thought I was goin' learn something here. It's a bunch o' b.s.

When athletes enrolled in more advanced or demanding courses to fulfill their requirements, they often found themselves unequipped for the type of work expected. Because of their inadequate academic backgrounds, poor study habits, tight schedules, peer distractions, and waning motivation, the athletes often became frustrated and bored. Their anticipated positive feedback from academics was replaced by a series of disappointments from low grades and failed classes. One player described how his failures made him feel inadequate and uncertain:

> When I first came here I thought I'd be goin' to class all the time and I'd study and that be it. But I sure didn't think it meant studyin' all the time. Back in high school you just be memorizin' things, but that's not what they want here. Back in high school I thought I be a pretty good student, but now I don't know.

Athletes' experiences in the classroom were thus very different from their preconceptions. The work was harder and they were not taken care of to the extent they had imagined. Because of the intense competition in the athletic arena, they became obsessed with success (Harris and Eitzen, 1978). Their frequent academic failures (or, at best, mediocre grades) led to their embarrassment and despair, which caused them to engage in role-distancing (Ball, 1976) and to abandon some of the self-investment they had made in their academic performance. To be safe, it was better not to try than to try and not succeed. As we noted earlier, this posture was reinforced by their peer subculture.

ACADEMIC ADJUSTMENTS

As college athletes progressed through school, they changed their perspectives and priorities, re-evaluating the feasibility of their originally optimistic, albeit casually formed, academic goals. This caused them to effect a series of *pragmatic adjustments* in their academic attitudes, efforts, and goals.

First, whenever possible, athletes externalized the blame for their academic failures. Failures, for instance, were not caused by their own inadequacies or lack of effort but by boring professors, stupid courses, exhaustion, the coaches' demands, or injury. This allowed them to accept the frequent signs of failure more easily and served as an important neutralizing mechanism for their competitiveness.

More importantly, athletes re-examined their academic goals. Because of their initially optimistic expectations, some athletes had declared majors based on career choices that sounded good to them or their parents (e.g., doctor, teacher, engineer, or businessman). About one fourth of the individuals who began in preprofessional majors stayed in these majors all the way through college and graduated.[6] Nevertheless, these individuals generally expended less effort and had less success than they had initially anticipated. Though they graduated in their original major, their academic performance was largely characterized by an attitude of getting by; in most cases, they achieved only the minimum GPA and took the minimum number of hours required for eligibility. One junior discussed how his attitude toward academics had changed during his years at college:

> If I was a student like most other students I could do well, but when you play the calibre of ball we do, you just can't be an above-average student. What I strive for now is just to be an average student. My best GPA was 2.75. You just don't find the time to do all the reading.

More commonly, athletes in preprofessional majors found that a more concrete adjustment was necessary. The remaining three quarters of this group dropped out of preprofessional programs and enrolled in more manageable majors. This shift indicated that they had abandoned both their academic idealism and their earlier career goals. Nevertheless, they still maintained the goal of graduating, regardless of the major. As one player commented,

> Look at George [a former player]. He was a rec major, but now he's got a great job in sales, working for some booster. It don't matter what you major in as long as you keep your nose clean and get that piece of paper.

Athletes who began their college careers with lower academic aspirations, majoring in physical education or recreation, made corresponding adjustments. Approximately one fifth of these athletes held on to their initial goal and graduated in one of these fields. But like the preprofessional majors, they did not perform as well as they had planned. The other four fifths realized, usually relatively late, that their chances of graduating from college were slight. This genuinely distressed them, because getting a degree had become both a hope and an expectation. They shifted their orientation,

---

[6] These figures represent rough estimates based on the number of individuals who graduated, the number of individuals who used up their eligibility, and projections for individuals still in the program. They are intended to be suggestive rather than exact.

then, toward maintaining their athletic eligibility. A junior's remarks illustrate how this shift affected his attitude toward academics:

> I used to done thought I was goin' to school, but now I know it's not for real. . . . I don't have no academic goals no more. A player a coach is counting on, that's all he think about is ball. That's what he signed to do. So what you gotta do is show up, show your smilin' face, try as hard as you can. Don't just lay over in the room. That's all the coach can ask. Or else you may not find yourself playing next year.

By their senior year, when they had completed their final eligibility requirements, many members of this last group entirely abandoned their concern with their academic performance.[7] As one senior put it,

> I just be waitin', man. I be waitin' for my shot at the NBA. I be thinking about that all the time. Once the season is over, I be splittin'. I don't see no reason to go to classes no more.

As a result of their experiences at the University, athletes grew increasingly cynical about and uninterested in academics. They accepted their marginal status and lowered their academic interest, effort, and goals. They progressively detached themselves from caring about or identifying themselves with this sphere.

DISCUSSION

We have just described how college athletes progress from an early phase of idealism about their impending academic experiences to an eventual state of pragmatic detachment. The initial differences among the athletes in academic aptitudes, skills, and expectations eventually erode, causing even motivated freshmen to slip into a pattern of diminished interest and effort. The universality of this transformation (albeit with variations) suggests that there is something endemic to universities with big-time athletic programs that significantly affects athletes' orientations and behavior. An overview of the structural characteristics and embedded processes athletes encounter can help explain how and why their behavior changes.

First, athletes are overwhelmed by the demands and intensity of the athletic realm, which absorbs their concentration and commitment. They react by willingly entering the vortex of media celebrity and fantasies about future professional athletic careers. Second, athletes find themselves socially isolated from other students because of their geographic and temporal separation and their physical and cultural differences. In this way, athletes resemble Simmel's strangers—i.e., individuals who are full-fledged members of the group yet at the same time are outside of the group (cited in Wolff, 1950:402–408). By being part of, but not like, the larger student body, athletes experience the tension between nearness and distance. This heightens their sensitivity to their strangeness and focuses their attention on those elements they do not share with other students. As a result, the internal cohesion of their peer subculture becomes strengthened and their self-identities become more firmly anchored within it. Finally, for many athletes, the gap between their academic abilities and the university's expectations brings failure, frustration, and alienation. The peer subculture exacerbates the situation by devaluing academic involvement and neutralizing academic failure. Athletes respond by gradually withdrawing from their commitment to academics.

These structural factors are ultimately much stronger predictors of athletes' academic success than any of their initial individual characteristics. Their early academic involvement varies according to their goals, intelligence, talent, parents' attitudes, and other individual attributes, but the common structure of their experiences erodes many of these distinctions. Some athletes excel in all areas of college, and their success is well-publicized (cf. Looney, 1984). But most college athletes become disillusioned with academics by the time their athletic eligibility expires. This combination of structural factors influencing athletes' behavior, admittedly an extreme example, could also explain the academic careers of other students. Students who are distracted by an outside interest (i.e., a job or an avocation), who belong to a peer group that de-emphasizes the value of academics (i.e., a fraternity), and who become frustrated in the academic realm are likely to be academically unsuccessful in college.

The transformation athletes undergo corresponds to Goffman's (1959) conception of occupational role progression, in which the attitudes of persons socialized to a new social status (here, college athlete) evolve from belief to disbelief. This process begins with the learning and internalization of charter values. For college athletes, this occurs during the final year of high school and the freshman year of college, when they form moderately high aspirations and expectations about their aca-

[7] Ironically, however, even the marginal players never abandoned their dreams of making it in the NBA.

demic futures. A period of desocialization then ensues, in which athletes progressively realize the structural constraints framing their situation. They become unable to accommodate the myriad, often conflicting, expectations and demands confronting them. As a result, they make choices and establish priorities that compromise their early idealism. Expediency thus supplants a concern for academics (Ingham and Smith, 1974), leading them to engage in role-distancing and to forge pragmatic adaptations that undermine their academic performance.

This in-depth investigation confirms the findings and interpretations of those studies positing a negative relationship between athletic participation and academic performance at universities with big-time athletic programs. We extend these analyses by showing that college athletes' academic performance is multifaceted and is determined less by demographic characteristics and high school experiences than by the structure of their college experiences. Athletes progress through a pattern of experiences, which first raises their hopes and then diminishes their opportunities for attaining the professed goals of the educational system.

Given the revenue that athletic programs generate, it may be unrealistic to expect this structure to change dramatically. However, there are several policy implications that can be derived from this research. First, athletes should be sheltered, as much as possible, from the enticing whirlwind of celebrity. This can best be accomplished by reinstituting the ban on freshman eligibility. Second, athletic dorms should be abolished and athletes should be better integrated into the larger university culture. In these ways we can begin to transform college athletes from strangers into neighbors. Third, athletes should be provided with more academic role models and advisors. The current arrangement, in which athletic personnel masquerade as academic advisors, functions counterproductively to the academic goals of the university. Only after these changes are made can college athletes begin to meet the goals of the educational system.

REFERENCES

Adler, P.
1981 Momentum: A Theory of Social Action. Beverly Hills, CA: Sage.
1984 "The sociologist as celebrity: The role of the media in field research." Qualitative Sociology 7:310–26.

Adler, P. and P. A. Adler
1978 "The role of momentum in sport." Urban Life 7:153–76.

Adler, P. A. and P. Adler
Forthcoming Joining the Crowd: Membership Roles in Field Research. Beverly Hills, CA: Sage.

Antonelli, F.
1970 "Psychological problems of top-level athletes." International Journal of Sport Psychology 1:34–39.

Ball, D.
1976 "Failure in sport." American Sociological Review 41:726–39.

Bernstein, S.
1978 "Getting it done: Notes on student fritters." Pp. 17–23 in J. Lofland (ed.), Interaction in Everyday Life. Beverly Hills, CA: Sage.

Coakley, J. J.
1982 Sport in Society. 2nd ed. St. Louis: Mosby.

Coleman, J. S.
1960 "Adolescent subculture and academic achievement." American Journal of Sociology 65:337–47.
1961 The Adolescent Society. New York: Free Press.

Cross, H. M.
1973 "The college athlete and the institution." Law and Contemporary Problems 38:151–71.

Cusick, P. A.
1973 Inside High School. New York: Holt, Rinehart and Winston.

Douglas, J. D.
1976 Investigative Social Research. Beverly Hills, CA: Sage.

Edwards, H.
1984 "The collegiate arms race: Origins and implications of the 'Rule 48' controversy." Journal of Sport and Social Issues 8:4–22.

Eitzen, D. S.
1975 "Athletics in the status system of male adolescents: A replication of Coleman's 'The Adolescent Society'." Adolescence 10:268–76.
1979 "Sport and deviance." Pp. 73–89 in D. S. Eitzen (ed.), Sport in Contemporary Society. New York: St. Martin's.

Fine, G. A.
1979 "Preadolescent socialization through organized athletics: The construction of moral meanings in little league baseball." Pp. 79–105 in M. Krotee (ed.), Dimensions of Sport Sociology. Corning, NY: Leisure Press.

Frey, J. H.
1982 "Boosterism, scarce resources and institutional control: The future of American intercollegiate athletics." International Review of Sport Sociology 17:53–70.

Goffman, E.
1959 The Presentation of Self in Everyday Life. Garden City, NY: Anchor Doubleday.

Hanks, M. P. and B. K. Eckland
1976 "Athletics and social participation in the educational attainment process." Sociology of Education 49:271–94.

Harris, D. S. and D. S. Eitzen
1978 "The consequences of failure in sport." Urban Life 7:177–188.

Harrison, J. H.
1976 "Intercollegiate football participation and academic achievement." Paper presented at the Annual Meeting of the Southwestern Sociological Association, Dallas.

Henschen, K. P. and D. Fry
1984 "An archival study of the relationship of intercollegiate athletic participation and graduation." Sociology of Sport Journal 1:52–56.

Hoch, P.
1972 Rip Off the Big Game. New York: Doubleday.

Horowitz, R.
1983 Honor and the American Dream. New Brunswick, NJ: Rutgers University Press.

Ingham, A. G.
1975 "Occupational subcultures in the work world of sport." Pp. 337–89 in D. W. Ball and J. W. Loy (eds.), Sport and Social Order: Contributions to the Sociology of Sport. Reading, MA: Addison-Wesley.

Ingham, A. G. and M. D. Smith
1974 "The social implications of the interaction between spectators and athletes." Pp. 189–224 in J. Wilmore (ed.), Exercise and Sport Science Reviews. Vol. 2. New York: Academic Press.

Jonassohn, K., A. Turowetz, and R. Gruneau
1981 "Research methods in the sociology of sport." Qualitative Sociology 4:179–97.

Looney, D. S.
1984 "He came out picture perfect." Sports Illustrated 60, 22:44–50.

Loy, J. W., B. D. McPherson, and G. Kenyon
1978 Sport and Social Systems. Reading, MA: Addison-Wesley.

Meggysey, D.
1971 Out of Their League. Berkeley, CA: Ramparts.

Michener, J. A.
1976 Sports in America. New York: Random House.

Nyquist, E. B.
1979 "Wine, women, and money: College athletics today and tomorrow." Educational Review 60:376–93.

Odenkirk, J. E.
1981 "Intercollegiate athletics: Big business or sport?" Academe 67:62–66.

Purdy, D. A., D. S. Eitzen, and R. Hufnagel
1982 "Are athletes also students? The educational attainment of college athletes." Social Problems 29:439–48.

Raney, J., T. Knapp, and M. Small
1983 "Pass one for the gipper: Student athletes and university coursework." Arena Review 7:53–59.

Rehberg, R. A. and W. E. Schafer
1968 "Participation in interscholastic athletics and college expectations." American Journal of Sociology 73:732–40.

Sack, A. L.
1977 "Big time college football: Whose free ride?" Quest 27:87–97.

Sack, A. L. and R. Thiel
1979 "College football and social mobility: A case study of Notre Dame football players." Sociology of Education 52:60–66.

Semyonov, M. and E. Yuchtman-Yaar
1981 "Professional sports as an alternative channel of social mobility." Sociological Inquiry 1:47–53.

Shapiro, B.
1984 "Intercollegiate athletic participation and academic achievement: A case study of Michigan State University student-athletes." Sociology of Sport Journal 1:46–51.

Shaw, G.
1972 Meat on the Hoof. New York: St. Martin's.

Spady, W. G.
1970 "Lament for the letterman: Effects of peer status and extra-curricular activities on goals and achievement." American Journal of Sociology 75:680–702.

Spivey, D. and T. A. Jones
1975 "Intercollegiate athletic servitude: A case study of the black Illinois student-athletes, 1931–1967." Social Science Quarterly 55:939–47.

Sykes, G. M. and D. Matza
1957 "Techniques of neutralization." American Sociological Review 22:664–70.

Tannenbaum, P. M. and J. E. Noah
1959 "Sportuguese: A study of sports page communication." Journalism Quarterly 36:163–70.

Underwood, J.
1980 "The writing is on the wall." Sports Illustrated 52, 21:36–71.

Webb, H.
1968 "Social backgrounds of college athletes." Paper presented at the Annual Meeting of the American Alliance for Health, Physical Education, and Recreation, St. Louis.

Wolff, K. H. (ed. and trans.)
1950 The Sociology of Georg Simmel. New York: Free Press.

ON FEELING GOOD ABOUT ONESELF: PRACTICAL IDEOLOGY IN SCHOOLS OF CHOICE

Robert B. Everhart
University of California, Santa Barbara

Sociology of Education 1985, Vol. 58 (October):251–260

There is probably no single concept currently generating more discussion in the field of sociology of education than *ideology* (Apple, 1979; Giroux, 1981; Karabel and Halsey, 1979; Sharp, 1980). Despite the currency of the concept, few terms are as inconsistently used, ill-defined, and often-times vacuous as *ideology*. Indeed, the term has been given various definitions: (1) "maps of problematic social reality and matrices for the creation of collective conscience" (Geertz, 1964:64); (2) a "system of belief; a set of values serving mainly as a keyhole through which the outside world is observed" (Flakser, 1971: 11); (3) a complex of ideas serving to legitimate the existing social order (Mannheim, 1936); and (4) the ideas of the ruling class, "which are the ideal expression of dominant material relations" (Marx and Engels, 1964:59–60). These various definitions have led to a spate of critical studies (Flakser, 1971; Seliger, 1977; Carlsnaes, 1981), which call into question the utility of the concept as it is typically defined.

Studies of such macrosocial phenomena as the schooling process use the concept of ideology in a number of ways. Most often, ideology is defined as a system of beliefs and practices passed on by educational organizations, which perpetuate a class-based society. For example, Bowles and Gintis (1976) integrate a wealth of data to support the proposition that the function of schooling is to reproduce the class structure that precedes schooling. Because they used a structuralist approach, however, they did not adequately consider the dynamics operating within schools, which preserve, modify, or transform ideological formations (Hogan, 1982). Countering the structuralist model is a more dynamic paradigm that focuses on individuals' acquisition of ideas (Giroux, 1981). Instead of defining the school as the promulgator of objective truths, instead of viewing teachers and students as receptors of values and truths, this paradigm focuses on the manner in which ideological patterns are created and re-created through ongoing social processes. In this sense then, ideology is not just a set of beliefs passed on; rather, it is phenomenological in nature, growing out of intentionality and human activity. This dynamic, more interactive paradigm, which focuses on the formation of ideas as well as their structure, captures the fundamental essence of ideology—a dialectical process that produces images and behaviors related to those images.

We can thus define ideologies as

> systems of representations which signify a set of relationships which are real but which hide another set of relations between people which are no less real (Sharp, 1980:92).

Sharp focuses upon a central aspect of ideology—its mystifying element—but her definition does not fully acknowledge the active role of individuals in producing ideologies. It is important to conceive of ideologies as lived, as sets of practices that support certain meanings, which, in turn, reverse themselves to create the illusion that they are objective. These are what Althusser (quoted in Heath, 1972:23) calls practical ideologies, or

> complex formations of montages of notions-representations-images on the one hand, and of montages of behaviors-conducts-attitudes-gestures on the other.

Althusser's conception of practical ideology permits us to go beyond the notion that ideology is a cloud of ideas and to focus upon individual and group practices that produce orientations to social structural regularities.

To study ideology and its practical accomplishments in education is to study education in process. This investigation, which belongs to the critical ethnography genre, attempts to untangle the complex relationship between educational practice and sociocultural production and reproduction. The article focuses upon the generation of ideology in three alternative schools, or "schools of choice." These schools, which usually have progressive philosophies, are explicitly designed to provide choices for students, teachers, and parents. Other seminal studies of public and private schools of choice have focused on the tensions

Appreciation is due the anonymous reviewers whose invaluable suggestions improved this article. Address all correspondence to the author at the Department of Education, University of California, Santa Barbara, CA 93106.

between social control and individual freedom (Metz, 1978; Swidler, 1979) and the manner in which progressive practices may be dysfunctional for working-class students (Sharp and Green, 1975). The current study moves the theme of these studies a stage further by examining how the practices prevailing within these schools may produce both explicit and implicit ideologies that mystify basic routines and undermine the progressive intents of those schools.

After a brief review of methodology and a description of the three schools in which the study took place, I will discuss the schools' focus on the psychological development of their students. I use the concept of *possessive individualism* to place this focus in context. This concept will be examined within a set of beliefs and in daily practice. In both instances, I will focus upon how the students' positive feelings about themselves developed under a progressive rubric. I will conclude by discussing how practical ideology, rooted within a specific class culture,[1] militated against the intended generalized purposes of the schools and deterred a more critical educational process. I will also discuss some general implications and possible remedies.

METHODOLOGY

This study was conducted as part of a yearlong study (1979–80) of the development of adolescent cultures in schools of choice. The study reported here examined how the promotion of choice in these schools affected the structure of early adolescent peer culture. I investigated the role of student opportunity structures in an earlier study of a traditional junior high school (Everhart, 1983). The three schools studied here were selected because they ostensibly had different opportunity structures and because their location permitted daily field work.

Because of the focus on practical ideologies and adolescent cultures, I adopted the role of fieldworker. I worked in two of the schools, and a graduate student worked in the third. Both of us were participant observers two or three days a week from October through June. We observed all classes, analyzed documents, and conducted interviews with about one third of the parents, all the teachers, and all students who were at least 11 years old. In addition, we participated in the daily life of the school by tutoring, assisting on field trips, and serving as discussion leaders in numerous school activities.

SETTING

This study was conducted in three schools of choice located in a medium-size community on the West Coast. The schools, one public and two private, shared many characteristics but also differed along certain dimensions. They shared a commitment to the development of student self-esteem through the promotion of choice and involvement in school activities. But they differed in the specific manner in which that goal was achieved in the school's daily routine.

The first school, which we will call Garden,[2] was a private junior high school (grades 7 through 9) that was three years old when this study began. Garden enrolled 50 students and employed five full-time teachers. The school was founded by a woman who had taught at a local private college preparatory school. Her motivation for founding Garden grew, in part, out of her dissatisfaction with the traditional curriculum at her former school.

A local newspaper reporter characterized Garden as a school that steered a middle course. Teachers at the school emphatically stated that Garden was *not* an alternative school, in the traditional sense of the term, meaning that it was not a structureless school with divergent academic expectations. In the year I spent at the school, I found that the pedagogy in most classes was similar to that in other secondary schools in the area. But Garden differed from these other schools in its blend of informality and tradition. It was informal in its interpersonal relations and in its focus on a multitude of schoolwide activities meant to integrate the curriculum with real-life experiences, but it was traditional in the scope and sequence of its academic classes and the usual top-down manner in which they were conducted. The teachers emphasized the importance of developing a lasting rapport with students, which they believed was central to the distinctiveness of the school. Students were encouraged to express their feelings toward each other and towards teachers. One teacher, speaking for many, noted that at Garden, "there is a lot of sharing, a lot of honesty, a lot of intimacy."

The second school we studied, Freeway, was a public alternative elementary and junior high school with about one hundred students and four teachers. Formed about five years earlier, during the crest of the alternative-school movement, this school was designed to

[1] *Class culture* refers to a particular way of life and to the ideologies associated with that way of life (Johnson, 1979).

[2] All school and person names are fictitious.

provide an "open" environment for learning. According to the Freeway literature, "children receive plenty of instruction in academic subjects, [but] the emphasis is on personal responsibility and self-direction." Instead of classes, Freeway provided "learning experiences." Teachers used the child as a point of departure in arranging the school curriculum. In other words, students were given considerable latitude in choosing the activities in which they would engage.

The rationale for such a learning environment lay not so much in its alleged advantages for the development of academic skills as in its advantages for the development of social and personal skills. Providing students with choices helped them to learn responsible decision making, to take the initiative, and to feel good about themselves. The most senior teacher at Freeway was fond of noting that students could learn to read at any age, but the development of self-esteem preceded all else.

Campus, a private school founded the year the study began, was the smallest and youngest of the three schools in this study. It enrolled 15 to 20 students, most of whom came from an area near a major state university. Four "leaders" (only one of whom worked full time) managed the school. The parents of Campus students were not as affluent as the parents of Garden students (tuition at Garden was $2,100 per year) nor as well educated as the parents of Freeway students. Campus parents tended to be drawn from the local counterculture, comprised mostly of disaffected and transient college dropouts. Founded in part by a Comprehensive Education Training Act (CETA) grant, the school was preoccupied with economic survival during much of its existence, and by the end of the study it closed.

The objective of Campus, according to the head teacher, was "to make school a real-life situation." Technical or academic knowledge was taught, but it was not the focus of learning. Campus's teachers and parents, like those at Freeway, believed that personal growth and self-esteem were fundamental to and preceded academic achievement. At Campus school, such a commitment to the development of self-esteem arose from the belief that the school was an extended family in which school and personal issues were inseparable. "We all help each other here," said Campus's founder, "and it doesn't matter who it is or what the problem is."

Thus, the curriculum at Campus "evolve[d] from the student's needs." Lessons or activities were not usually arranged in advance, because teachers believed such predetermination was unnecessary to the child's mental preparation. Instead, as at Freeway, learning experiences were provided for students, and students decided what they wanted to learn and when activities were most appropriate. According to one campus teacher, "all knowledge is within the person; it's just a matter of it coming out."

Related to this belief that knowledge was inherent within the individual was the belief that schools should prepare children for survival in an uncertain future. Teachers and parents believed that nuclear destruction, economic collapse, and the ineffectiveness of political systems were very real possibilities in their children's lifetime. Parents, especially, believed that the problems of society were beyond the control of the average citizen and that their children's preparation for survival in an imperfect society was the best that could be expected. Thus, the premium all three schools placed on the development of self-confidence and self-esteem was a form of anticipatory socialization.

In sum, the three schools in this study were founded to provide a range of choices for parents and students. Parents assumed that traditional schools, because they did not provide choices, were unduly constraining and retarded the development of self-esteem and self-actualization. The mission of the schools in this study was to foster the development of academic skills and nurture personal and social growth. All three schools emphasized the latter more than the former; Garden was the lowest on this scale and Campus the highest. All three schools, which were attended largely by students from the middle class, espoused the liberal belief that students must be educated humanely and must develop personal strengths if they are to adapt to the world of tomorrow.

We turn now to a more detailed description of the development of practical ideology and its relationship to the dominant class culture of the school. For the sake of brevity, our analysis will center on some basic parent and teacher beliefs and the manner in which these beliefs were played out in educational practice.

ON FEELING GOOD ABOUT ONESELF: IDEOLOGY AS BELIEF

Parents

Parents had various reasons for choosing one of the three schools in this study rather than a more convenient local school, but they all believed that the development of strong psychological and interpersonal skills was an essential part of the schooling experience. Parents believed that self-confidence was imperative for growth, and they expected the schools to foster this self-confidence in their children.

Parents and staff in all three schools wanted the children "to feel good about themselves."

Imbedded in this phrase (and all that surrounded it) was the belief that through the development of confidence and positive affect, through positive reinforcement in the school and in the home, as students grew in maturity and became increasingly self-satisfied with their role, virtually anything was possible. Resting at the heart of this logic was the ideology of individualism—the belief that the individual could be equipped with the necessary personal characteristics to successfully compete, now and in the future, within the marketplace of other individuals.

This process is very similar to MacPherson's (1962) and Apple's (1982) description of possessive individualism, a concept derived from seventeenth- and eighteenth-century political theory. *Possessive individualism* refers to the notion that the individual is the proprietor of his or her own person or capacities and owes or derives from society little or none of those capacities. To be human is to be free from dependence on others; thus, freedom grows out of possession of self. Based on Hobbesian and Lockean political theory, possessive individualism advocates the orderly exchange of free relations in a free market.

Parents who emphasized the importance of the possessive individual were confident of the results of their children's self-esteem. One parent of a Garden ninth-grade student, when asked what she thought her daughter should learn, replied,

> She should come away from her schooling experience feeling good about herself, having a sense of self-worth. By that I mean she should be able to accomplish things and have success in what she accomplishes. I have always believed that if there is self-worth, if the person feels good about himself, they can do anything which they want. *There is no obstacle which they cannot overcome*. (emphasis added)

This theme was reiterated by other parents at all three schools. They believed that feeling good about oneself was important because it provided the basis of individual initiative and the self-education that was crucial to child development. Parents believed that schooling should be more self-regulative—i.e., based on student initiative—and that the school environment should be more natural and open, not like the more traditional schools, where students were typically "led" into areas the teacher deemed important. Parents believed that only through the development of such a strong personal base could students maximize their opportunities in a self-regulative educational environment.

"Feeling good about yourself is crucial," explained one mother of a 14-year-old Freeway student. "Why is this true?" I asked. "What makes it so important?" She continued:

> It leads to personal creativity, and personal creativity is what education is all about. It means learning to read because of an interest in rocks, for example, and not because reading is on the schedule for the day. Personal creativity means going to the beach, finding that you're interested in rocks, and learning to read because of the interest. In that way, learning to read is not a task in itself.

A parent of a Campus child echoed this refrain when she stated that academics were secondary to the purposes of schooling. For her, academic knowledge did not come from external sources; rather, it was generated within and by the individual's sense of self-worth and the responsibility that "naturally follows that self-worth." She believed that children, given the freedom to learn, would learn because *they* wanted to, not because someone else wanted them to. She noted that her own son, who was two to three years below normative levels in math and reading when he began at Campus last year, was catching up and was having his best year in school because he saw the importance and value of reading and mathematics.

Teachers

Teachers, like parents, believed that the purpose of schools of choice was to help build in children the self-esteem and confidence necessary to survive in a marketplace of uncertainty. At Freeway, for example, teachers tried to play down formalized status differences between students and teachers, because they believed that such differences hindered productive student/teacher interactions. Less restrictive interactions were viewed as essential because of the perceived direct linear relationship between strong self-concept and school success. According to a female teacher at Freeway, keeping role relationships fluid and negotiable was important:

> I think it is important that they have a right to say when they are not comfortable doing something. It's important that they learn to get validation from each other. The teacher doesn't become the total source of validation in the school.

Teachers believed that other desirable outcomes emerged from the attempt to minimize role distance between adults and students. For example, students were encouraged to develop problem-solving procedures among themselves, thereby building their own interpersonal networks and more cohesive peer groups. Leanna, the senior teacher at Freeway, stressed the desire to

> build self-confidence, so all people can share. We feel this is important as they share, for we want them to bring family concerns as well. This can't be done if they aren't strong, if the group isn't strong.

Another Freeway teacher believed that teachers were unnecessary for learning and that it was important for students to use each other as resources rather than use the teacher as an intermediary. He believed that students could solve problems with minimal adult intervention and thus could teach each other if given sufficient time and opportunity.

> If I intervene to make corrections, the group will side with the violator and will gang up against me. This will accomplish nothing. I really believe that it's necessary for groups to decide for themselves what's important and then carry out those decisions with only the minimal guidance of the teacher.

Teachers tried to develop in their students such characteristics as responsibility, self-confidence, and a predisposition toward self-learning. They believed that students at traditional public schools were apathetic toward school because they lacked these characteristics. Garden teachers believed that individuals had the power to overcome adversity and make themselves into what they wished. With few exceptions, the Garden staff believed that the overall program was designed to build the self-confidence and responsibility so necessary to the development of the possessive individual.

Campus, like Garden and Freeway, was unabashedly devoted to the development of a self in control of its own destiny. Thus, the push to help children develop and express their feelings was constant and strong. Joe, a young teacher, characterized the program at Campus as child-centered. He explained by drawing a triangle and writing at the apexes of the triangle, "child-centered," "subject-centered," and "teacher-centered." Next, he drew a dot near the "child-centered" apex and said, "This is where I am. I think it's important for children to receive a consistent approach, to know what to expect. What I do is to permit children total freedom. I see my presence as a resource only." I asked, "What if they choose to do nothing?" He replied, "That's fine. My belief is that when they're ready to learn, they will."

Jane and Mike, two other Campus teachers, echoed this philosophy and believed that the program at Campus promoted it. "Self-esteem is the most important thing we teach in this school," Jane said. "All else follows from that." Mark also felt that the development of self-esteem was important, and he hoped to develop it through a greater sense of "humanistic spirituality." I asked him what he meant by this term.

> Thoughts, minds, bodies, hearts, and spirit are all part of everything. They are all of oneness with the world. We teach that only your mind separates you from a oneness with the world, makes you feel separate from the rest of the world.

Thus far, we have focused on the belief, shared by parents and teachers in this study, that the primary determinants of a student's success in school are self-esteem and self-confidence. But possessive individualism focuses not only on the present; it also has implications for an individual's future. Thus, another important goal was adaptability. Most parents were pessimistic about what the general state of affairs would be a decade later. Economic constriction, environmental pollution, and nuclear destruction were among the projections made. Given this bleak scenario, parents could not predict with much accuracy what specific academic skills their children might need to survive the future. Faced with this uncertainty, parents considered adaptability to be the natural and necessary outcome of both independence and self-confidence. Most parents believed that adaptability would be important in their children's livelihood and noted that their children must be independent and confident enough to make choices.

Adaptability was also important in the social model most adults used to guide their thinking. The future world was envisioned as a free market in which needed skills and psychological dispositions would be exchanged. But since the specific attributes of the world of the future were so problematic, it was difficult for parents and teachers to determine the specific cognitive and interpersonal skills that would be needed. The best parents and teachers could do was instill in the children the psychological strength necessary to persevere, to adapt, and to be confident in an unsure world. They believed that the most critical characteristic for success in the future was the ability to make decisions. The practice of making choices, from which an individual developed a sense of self-esteem, was considered fundamental to adaptability and success in the future.

The consistency of these beliefs among parents and teachers reveals the pervasiveness of possessive individualism—the belief that the individual has the power to be self-determining. Individuality, personal efficacy, and self-worth were considered extremely important for students in both the present and the future. *Adaptability* became synonymous for *freedom,* and freedom was considered a function of possession in a society in which "free, equal individuals related to each other as proprietors of their own capacities and of what they have acquired by their exercise" (MacPherson, 1962:3).

Let us examine how this mosaic of belief was played out in practice.

ON FEELING GOOD ABOUT ONESELF: IDEOLOGY AT WORK

As we have seen, the development of the self-esteem and self-confidence necessary for students to feel good about themselves was a primary agenda in all three schools. This was accomplished in relatively open educational environments that minimized authority relations between teachers and students.

At Campus and Freeway, the daily ritual of the "circle" or "core" groups provided students the best opportunity to develop self-esteem and self-confidence. These groups, which included the whole school or the whole class, met every day for 15 to 45 minutes to discuss a variety of issues and concerns. By examining some of the patterns of behavior in these core groups, we are able to understand how a practical ideology of individualism and choice was constructed by school participants.

At Freeway, after morning recess, each class proceeded to its room. Students typically sat on the floor or on old sofas in one corner of the room. Three general topics for discussion (news, problems, and sharing) were permanently written on a blackboard, and students were allowed to sign their name under one of the topics and to discuss an issue related to that topic during core time. The group leader, a student selected on a rotating basis, served as moderator of the discussion. Thus, issues discussed during core time were student-initiated, although teachers also signed their name on the board and raised issues of concern.

Many students agreed that core time gave them a chance to discuss issues and problems. One student at Freeway described the process:

> We all get together and sit down on pillows and stuff and then we share things or talk about news like what's going on, or even some problems. This is a chance for people to get out their feelings, to sort of talk about what's on their minds. It kind of helps us to get things out of our systems a bit.

However, despite the staff's encouragement of student participation in core group, and despite the students' belief that core group gave them an opportunity to get things out of their systems, it was not valued by most students, partly because they considered it too unstructured, too flexible, and too nonpurposive. One eighth-grade student thought it was a waste of time. Two other eighth-grade girls believed that the essential problem was the students' lack of interest in the content of core and their disruption of the discussion. Much of the time, the teacher had to intervene to restore order:

> People start talking in there and it takes [the teacher] five hours to get people to shut up. People are always telling other people to shut up in there, and they're always having little private conversations. There's not much else that goes on in there.

Even when core group proceeded fairly smoothly, the subject matter discussed was often uninteresting to most students. For example, Don, a somewhat marginal member of a class of early adolescents, thought core was "boring as hell." I asked him why:

> Oh, it's just that everybody else always talks and whenever I try to say something I'm told that my ideas aren't any good. You have to remember that I'm not a favored person in this school, either by the kids or even some of the teachers. But if I have to go outside of core 'cause [the teacher] makes me go, I just go outside and pretend I am listening.

Part of what Don said was true. He was not afforded opportunities to express his views, because many regarded his comments, which reflected his unorthodox interest in fantasy, as "off the wall." When he did comment or initiate discussion, his inputs tended to be dismissed as stupid.

Other students confirmed Don's evaluation of core group, although from a somewhat different perspective. They believed that core group was too open, that because it had no definable purpose, it drifted into a somewhat purposeless period when anything goes but nothing happens. Sally, one of the more highly respected eighth graders, commented:

> I listen a lot to what people say, but don't say much myself. . . . I would like to see people leave that are not interested in participating. Teachers should be more strict in core group because the only time it is interesting is when there are just a few of us there and we sit around talking. Lots of people there make it uninteresting because there's lots of bickering and fighting and bullying kind of stuff going on.

There were times when core-group discussion was focused and student involvement was high and intense, but this was rare and tended to occur only when the teacher actively moderated the discussion. Most of the time, core-group discussion was dominated by student-initiated agendas that moved in directions only minimally influenced by the teacher. Issues such as the capture of American diplomats in Iran during the Iranian revolution, energy shortages and the underlying reasons for such, and drug abuse were frequently discussed at Freeway, but students did not demonstrate (nor did teachers encourage) the analytical and critical skills needed to address such topics. Thus, the discussion meandered; topics were introduced without much concern for their relevance and were perfunctorily resolved. In the absence of direction from the teacher, the students devised their own agenda, and the teacher, consistent with the school's emphasis on the development of the students' self-esteem and self-confidence, acquiesced. For example, during a discussion of alternative transportation forms, the teacher asked the students to reflect on the advantages of electric busses. After a few students responded, John, another student, changed the topic:

> "Eleven people were killed in a concert when the Who was playing. They just totally got wiped out. Wow! Pow!" The teacher asked, "Why do you think that happened?" John replied, "Because the Who is cool." "Get down!" another student exclaimed, clapping his hands. "That's what happened with Jimi Hendrix. He died of an overdose," added another student.

The teacher, wanting the students to stay with a subject they would explore in detail, abandoned the discussion of transportation and took up the discussion of the Who concert:

> "I want to ask what Don and Rick would do in a situation like this." Don responded, "I'd camp out five days ahead of time." "I'd cruise," Scott added, "get up on the back seat with a pair of binoculars. Then I'd tell all of those dudes to move out of my way."

After about thirty minutes of discussion, core group was over and it was time for another class. A variety of issues had been introduced, but few of them were explored. Students changed agendas as rapidly as topics were introduced, and the teacher, who valued student-generated meaning systems, gave the students free rein.

Core was not the only instructional form in which the development of self-esteem was emphasized. All the schools offered classes designed to help students develop specialized individual interests. For example, Freeway offered courses such as "Auto Mechanics for Girls," "Computers," and "Dungeons and Dragons"; and Garden offered "Bicycle Maintenance," "French Cooking," and "Environmental Studies." A brief examination of classroom dynamics in one class at Garden illustrates how a practical ideology focusing on self-esteem was developed and reinforced by an emphasis on student enjoyment of school.

Garden offered an environmental studies course that provided students with hands-on experience of the application of biological principles to the natural world. Students in this class regularly took field trips to various natural habitats, marine science exhibits, and local museums. Though substantive course content was emphasized, the teacher believed it was equally important that students discuss their feelings about issues related directly and indirectly to the class. It was considered extremely important that the students value and enjoy environmental studies. Thus, the environmental studies teacher permitted students' agendas to dominate much of the classroom routine. But instead of viewing this informality as an intrusion on her role, the teacher accepted it as one of the factors creating an atmosphere in which students could "feel good about their education."

The prevalence of student agendas indicates the importance placed on the enjoyment of school and the development of self-esteem through such enjoyment. Parents at all three schools frequently told me how much their children enjoyed school and how rare this was among children aged 12 to 15.

The teachers' promotion of student agendas in the classroom signified their belief that self-esteem was best fostered by allowing students to grapple with issues on their own, without much structure or direction. As noted earlier, teachers believed that learning should take place in a "natural environment," that children (like crops) would develop best if simply nurtured. Too much direction, most believed, was not only unnecessary but counterproductive. A regulated curriculum, one teacher said, "is too much like regular school. It makes children dependent on teachers." The largely middle-class adults connected with these schools believed that traditional schools had failed because "they turn students off." Because students at Campus, Freeway, and Garden enjoyed school, the schools were considered successful.

But some parents, teachers, and students questioned the success of the three schools. A parent of a Garden student thought that the school was too protective, that it was "an unreal world in which feeling good is the primary goal." One of the teachers at Garden believed that the school had sold out to the "me generation" and had lost sight of its goal to "help students confront the realities of war, racism, and a society with the wrong priorities." At Freeway and Campus, some students preparing for graduation expressed the fear that they hadn't learned anything. While they enjoyed school, they questioned their ability to make it in a traditional school environment.

Thus, the practical ideology of possessive individualism was contradictory, generating both hope and discontent. Explicit in this ideology was the belief that providing individuals with the opportunity to take charge of their lives would help them become stronger and more self-assured. This outcome was realized to some extent among the students in this study. At the same time, however, minimum consideration was given to the social context in which individuals live—the competing beliefs, actions, and ideologies individuals must confront. This created various degrees of doubt and insecurity among the students. To a considerable extent, then, students possessed restricted choices within an organizational context that defined the parameters of those choices. Thus, the practical ideology implicitly limited the individualism it promoted. The very structure of the roles and incentive systems in these schools, by failing to address the social context of individualism, fostered an ethos of possessive individualism.

FEELING GOOD AS PRACTICAL IDEOLOGY

The movement toward private and public schools of choice is one indication of concern by well-intentioned parents and educators that children develop the psychological attributes necessary for proaction in an increasingly problematical world. Thus, the movement toward self-fulfillment through schooling continues. As Duke (1978:126) noted, "the search for community is a theme present throughout much of contemporary American society." Rather than viewing the trend toward choice as only a vestige of the alternative-school movement of the 1960s, this article argues that the forces driving educational choice persist into the present, although under different auspices.

I have shown that the movement toward student self-fulfillment in these schools existed within the context of possessive individualism. Yet this context spawned a practical ideology that fostered self-confidence and independence on the one hand but undermined the desired self-assurance on the other. The contradictory nature of this process raises the question, How is it possible to foster both individualism and a sense of social and moral understanding? Individualism presupposes a free market of equal individuals with equal power and resources. But because of the nature of a class-based society, and because of the choices made in schools through organizational arrangements and agendas, such equality does not exist. Thus, the beliefs that rotate around the emphasis on feeling good about oneself serve little more than an explicit ideology that helps generate a practical ideology played out in everyday life. There seems, then, to be a fundamental dilemma inherent in the concept of possessive individualism: Without some complementary belief about social cohesion and the place of the individual in society, a focus on individual attributes is necessarily incomplete.

A clearer understanding of the nature of the possessive individual is difficult to achieve and has demanded the attention of scholars in the sociology of education for some time. Much of this research has centered on the role of teachers and students within the social system of the classroom. Waller (1965), for example, studied the effect the teacher had on student life in schools. Noting the distinction between the "friendly role" and the "authority role" that teachers play, Waller concluded that some tension was natural and necessary if schooling was to be productive for both students and teachers.

More recent studies have been done by Cusick (1973), Metz (1978), and Swidler (1979). In her study of alternative schools, Swidler noted that some of the teachers were so uncertain of their role that they "downplayed their own skills while emphasizing student virtues" (1979:125). Because a clear understanding of the optimal relationship between student and teacher roles was absent, students were often able to persuade teachers not to assign homework. Similarly, Metz concludes that in the absence of sufficient authority, teachers must use personal influence to promote learning—a phenomenon readily evident at Garden, Freeway, and Campus.

Strategies to resolve these dilemmas focus upon a clearer conception of the role of the teacher. For example, Cusick maintains that secondary-school teachers should realize that their primary role is that of a teacher—an imparter of knowledge—and should not take too seriously the friendly role discussed by Waller and advocated in most alternative schools. Kozol (1972) goes even further, arguing that teachers who advocate minimal intervention in the learning process are irresponsible.

Of course, Kozol refers primarily to inner-city black children, not to middle-class children who attend schools such as the three studied here. But the same principles seem to apply, for as we have seen in this study, the failure to go beyond general affective states generates a practical ideology that reinforces those aspects of school choice that regenerate the middle-class culture from which they emanate (Graubard, 1972; Kozol, 1972). In the schools in this study, feeling good about oneself became a surrogate for the hard intellectual work of understanding the context within which we have to worry about whether there will be a world to inhabit a generation hence, the political and social nature of third world revolutions, and the politics of water resources. In the absence of a more critical educational process (Shor, 1980; Giroux, 1983), which helps build an understanding of the political nature of knowledge, schools of choice may build cocoons around students, fostering individual agency but not an awareness of the social context in which it rests.

The creation of schools of choice in which the practical ideology is not as contradictory as it is in these schools is no easy matter. One concern is organizational. Schools such as Garden, Freeway, and Campus were intended, in part, to be participative, but there are obvious degrees beyond which such openness is not productive. In his analysis of the alternative-school movement, Deal (1975) concludes that the most successful schools were those that developed an organizational structure with a division of labor, clear roles, specified goals, and teacher responsibility, all within a framework of student autonomy. Thus, some consideration must be given to the creation of an organizational structure that generates a modicum of predictability and routine.

A second necessity for schools of choice is a critical focus on ideology itself—its nature and the dynamics by which it is created through *practice*. Greater teacher awareness of the manner in which educational practice is both purposeful and ideological can help modify practice. The data from this study reveal that few teachers had such awareness. Shor (1980) has documented teaching and learning strategies that move us toward critical understanding of ideology. These and other strategies can be profitably examined by teachers, trainers of teachers, and those of us in the research community interested in putting sociological theory into practice. To ignore such practices is to invite "reform as stability" (Popkewitz, 1982)—a pattern in education to which we are all too well accustomed.

REFERENCES

Apple, M. W.
1979 Ideology and Curriculum. London: Routledge and Kegan Paul.
1982 "Curricular form and the logic of technical control: Building the possessive individual." Pp. 247–74 in M. W. Apple (ed.), Cultural and Economic Reproduction in Education. Boston: Routledge and Kegan Paul.

Bowles, S. and H. Gintis
1976 Schooling in Capitalist America. New York: Basic Books.

Carlsnaes, W.
1981 The Concept of Ideology and Political Analysis. Westport, CT: Greenwood Press.

Cusick, P.
1973 Inside High School. New York: Holt, Rinehart and Winston.

Deal, T. E.
1975 "Alternative schools: An alternative postmortem." Pp. 482–99 in J. V. Baldridge and T. E. Deal (eds.), Managing Change in Educational Organizations. Berkeley, CA: McCutchan.

Duke, D. L.
1978 The Re-transformation of the School. Chicago: Nelson Hall.

Everhart, R. B.
1983 Reading, Writing, and Resistance: Adolescence and Labor in a Junior High School. London: Routledge and Kegan Paul.

Flakser, D.
1971 Marxism, Ideology and Myths. New York: Philosophical Library.

Geertz, C.
1964 "Ideology as a cultural system." Pp. 47–76 in D. E. Apter (ed.), Ideology and Discontent. New York: Free Press.

Giroux, H. A.
1981 Ideology, Culture, and the Process of Schooling. Philadelphia: Temple University Press.
1983 Theory and Resistance in Education. South Hadley, England: Bergin.

Graubard, A.
1972 Free the Children. New York: Vintage.

Heath, S.
1972 The Nouveau Roman. London: Elek.

Hogan, D.
1982 "Education and class formation: The peculiarities of the Americans." Pp. 32–78 in M. W. Apple (ed.), Cultural and Economic Reproduction in Education. Boston: Routledge and Kegan Paul.

Johnson, R.
1979 "Three problematics: Elements of a theory of working-class culture." Pp. 201–37 in J. Clarke, C. Critcher, and R. Johnson (eds.), Working Class Culture. London: Hutchinson.

Karabel, J. and A. H. Halsey (eds.)
1979 Power and Ideology in Education. New York: Oxford University Press.

Kozol, J.
1972 Free Schools. New York: Bantam.

MacPherson, C. B.
1962 The Political Theory of Possessive Individualism. Oxford: Oxford University Press.

Mannheim, K.
1936 Ideology and Utopia. New York: Harcourt, Brace, and World.

Marx, K. and F. Engels
1964 The German Ideology. Translated by S. Ryazanskaya. Moscow: Foreign Languages Publishing House.

Metz, M. H.
1978 Classrooms and Corridors. Berkeley, CA: University of California Press.

Popkewitz, T.
1982 "Educational reform as the organization of ritual: Stability as change." Journal of Education 164:5–28.

Seliger, M.
1977 The Marxist Conception of Ideology. Cambridge: Cambridge University Press.

Sharp, R.
1980 Knowledge, Ideology and the Politics of Schooling. London: Routledge and Kegan Paul.

Sharp, R. and A. Green
1975 Education and Social Control. London: Routledge and Kegan Paul.

Shor, I.
1980 Critical Teaching and Everyday Life. Boston: South End Press.

Swidler, A.
1979 Organization Without Authority. Cambridge, MA: Harvard University Press.

Waller, W.
1965 The Sociology of Teaching. New York: Wiley.